A Conceptual-Analytic Study of Classical Indian Philosophy of Morals

Publications in PHISPC-CONSSAVY Series

HISTORY OF SCIENCE, PHILOSOPHY AND CULTURE IN INDIAN CIVILIZATION

General Editor & Project Director: **D.P. Chattopadhyaya**

Conceptual Volumes

* Part 1	Science, Philosophy and Culture: Multi-disciplinary Explorations	D.P. Chattopadhyaya & Ravinder Kumar (eds.)
* Part 2	Science, Philosophy and Culture: Multi-disciplinary Explorations	D.P. Chattopadhyaya & Ravinder Kumar (eds.)

VOLUME I The Dawn and Development of Indian Civilization

* Part 1	The Dawn of Indian Civilization (up to *c.* 600 BC)	G.C. Pande (ed.)
* Part 2	Life, Thought and Culture in India (from *c.* 600 BC to *c.* AD 300)	G.C. Pande (ed.)
* Part 3	India's Interaction with Southeast Asia	G.C. Pande (ed.)
* Part 4	A Golden Chain of Civilizations: Indic, Iranic, Semitic and Hellenic upto c. 600 BC	G.C. Pande (ed.)
➢ Part 5	A Golden Chain of Civilizations: Indic, Iranic, Semitic and Hellenic from c. 600 BC to c. AD 600	G.C. Pande (ed.)
➢ Part 6	Purāṇas, History and Itihāsa	Vidya Niwas Misra (ed.)

VOLUME II Life, Thought and Culture in India (AD 300–1100)

* Part 1	Life, Thought and Culture in India (AD 300–1000)	K. Satchidananda Murty (ed.)
* Part 2	Advaita Vedānta	R. Balasubramanian (ed.)
* Part 3	Theistic Vedānta	R. Balasubramanian (ed.)
* Part 4	Origin and Development of the Vaiśeṣika System	Anantalal Thakur
➢ Part 5	A Social History of Early India	B.D. Chattopadhyaya (ed.)
➢ Part 6	Pūrvamīmāṁsā from an Interdisciplinary Point of View	K.T. Pandurangi (ed.)

VOLUME III Development of Philosophy, Science and Technology in India and Neighbouring Civilizations

* Part 1	History of Indian Science, Technology and Culture (AD 1000–1800)	A. Rahman (ed.)
* Part 2	India's Interaction with China, Central and West Asia	A. Rahman (ed.)
* Part 3	Development of Nyāya Philosophy and its Social Context	Sibajiban Bhattacharyya (ed.)
* Part 4	Philosophical Concepts Relevant to Science in Indian Tradition	Pranab Kumar Sen (ed.)
➢ Part 5	Philosophical Concepts Relevent to Science in Indian Tradivion	Pranab Kumar Sen (ed.)
* Part 6	India and China: Twenty Centuries of Civilizational Interaction and Vibrations	Tan Chung & Geng Yinzeng
➢ Part 7	The Trading World of the Indian Ocean, AD 1500–1800	Om Prakash (ed.)

VOLUME IV Fundamental Indian Ideas of Physics, Chemistry, Life Sciences and Medicine

* Part 1	Chemistry and Chemical Techniques in India	B.V. Subbarayappa (ed.)
* Part 2	Medicine and Life Sciences in India	B.V. Subbarayappa (ed.)
* Part 3	Indian Perspectives on the Physical World	B.V. Subbarayappa
➢ Part 4	The Tradition of Astronomy in India: Jyotiḥśāstra	B.V. Subbarayappa

VOLUME V Agriculture in India

➢ Parts 1 & 2	A History of Agriculture in India	Lallanji Gopal & V.C. Srivastava (eds.)

VOLUME VI Culture, Language, Literature and Arts

➢ Part 1	Aesthetic Theories and Forms in Indian Tradition	S.S. Barlingay, Kapila Vatsyayan and D.P. Chattopadhyaya (eds.)
➢ Part 2	Architecture in India	M.A. Dhaky (ed.)
* Part 3	Indian Art: Forms, Concerns and Development in Historical Perspective	B.N. Goswamy (ed.)
➢ Part 4	Language, Grammar and Linguistics in Indian Tradition	V.N. Jha
• Parts 5–10	PHISPC in Regional Languages and Literatures	(Under Plan)

VOLUME VII The Rise of New Polity and Life in Villages and Towns

* Part 1	The State and Society in Medieval India	J.S. Grewal (ed.)
* Part 2	Religious Movements and Institutions in Medieval India	J.S. Grewal (ed.)
➢ Parts 3,4&5	Religious Systems of India	S.R. Saha, N.S.S. Raman, M. Rafique and others (eds.)

VOLUME VIII Economic History of India

➢ Part 1	Economic History of India from Thirteenth to Seventeenth Century	Irfan Habib (ed.)
➢ Part 2	Peasant History of Late Pre-Colonial and Colonial India	B.B. Chaudhuri
* Part 3	Economic History of India from Eighteenth to Twentieth Century	B.B. Chaudhuri (ed.)

VOLUME IX Colonial Period

* Part 1	Medicine in India: Modern Period	O.P. Jaggi
➢ Part 2	Women in India: Ancient and Medieval Period	Bhuvan Chandel (ed.)
* Part 3	Women of India: Colonial and Post-colonial Periods	Bharati Ray (ed.)

VOLUME X Towards Independence

* Part 1	Development of Indian Philosophy from Eighteenth Century Onwards	Daya Krishna
➢ Part 2	Colonial Development, Education and Social Awareness up to 2000	S. Gopal, Ravinder Kumar & S. Bhattacharya (eds.)
* Part 3	Historical Perspectives of Warfare in India: Some *Morale* and *Material* Determinants	S.N. Prasad (ed.)
* Part 4	Cultural Foundations of Mathematics: The Nature of Mathematical Proof and the Transmission of the Calculus from India to Europe in the 16th c. CE	C.K. Raju

---

* Already Published

➢ In the Process of Publication

• Under Plan

History of Science, Philosophy and
Culture in Indian Civilization

General Editor: D.P. Chattopadhyaya

Volume XII Part 1

A Conceptual-Analytic Study of Classical Indian Philosophy of Morals

RAJENDRA PRASAD

An imprint of **Concept Publishing Company**

Project of History of Indian Science, Philosophy and Culture [PHISPC]

Sub Project: Consciousness, Science, Society, Value and Yoga [CONSSAVY]

CENTRE FOR STUDIES IN CIVILIZATIONS

Cataloging in Publication Data—DK
Courtesy: D.K. Agencies (P) Ltd. <docinfo@dkagencies.com>

Prasad, Rajendra
A conceptual-analytic study of classical Indian philosophy of morals / Rajendra Prasad
p. cm. — (History of science, philosophy, and culture in Indian civilization ; v. 12, pt. 1)
Includes bibliographical references (p.)
Includes index.
ISBN 13: 9788180695445
ISBN 10: 8180695441

1. Ethics—India—History. 2. Social ethics—India—History. 3. Philosophy, Indic. I. Title. II. Series: History of science, philosophy, and culture in Indian civilization ; v. 12, pt. 1.

DDC 170.954 22

Publication of this Volume and much of the research it represents have been made possible by continuing grants with full financial assistance from the Department of Secondary and Higher Education, Ministry of Human Resource Development, Government of India, which has supported multidisciplinary exploration of the Project of History of Indian Science, Philosophy and Culture.

Jointly published by Professor Bhuvan Chandel, Member Secretary, DD-24, Kalkaji, New Delhi 110019 and Concept Publishing Company, A/15-16, Commercial Block, Mohan Garden, New Delhi-110059 (INDIA), *Phones*: 25351460, 25351794, *Fax*: 091-11-25357103, *Email*: publishing@conceptpub.com
for the Project of History of Indian Science, Philosophy and Culture

ISBN -13: 978-81-8069-544-5
ISBN -10: 81-8069-544-1

First Published 2008

Printed at
Concept Publishing Company, New Delhi

Typeset in Nalandabas, 11.5/14 pts.
Typeset by Print Services

In obeisance to
My Mother
Late Bela Devi
whom I lost at such an early age of mine
that I could not have
a memory of her motherly touch
but whom I will never forget

Centre for Studies in Civilizations

Governing Board

Contents

Preface

यस्य नास्ति निजा प्रज्ञा केवलं तु बहुश्रुतः
न स जानाति शास्त्रार्थं दर्वी सूपरसानिव

Yasya nāsti nijā prajñā kevalam tu bahuśrutah
Na sa jānāti śāstrārtham darvī sūparsāniva.

(*Mahābhārata, Dyūtaparva*, 55.1)

'He, who has no creative intellect of his own, who has only listened to (collected) the views of many others (about them), does not know what those authoritative works really mean, just as a spoon does not know the taste of the soup (it so many times moves in).'

This book is a component of the Project of History of Indian Science, Philosophy and Culture, being the first part of the parent volume *Consciousness and Value*. The second part, partly written and edited by me, is *A Historical-Developmental Study of Indian Philosophy of Morals*. In both the parts, the terms 'philosophy of morals', 'ethics', 'ethical theory', 'moral philosophy', etc., are used synonymously. 'Ethics' is sometimes in philosophical, or social-scientific, literature, also used to denote moral codes, practices, etc., of a people. In this work too sometimes it is used in that sense. But when it is, the context of its use makes it definitively clear that it is so used.

The project, as its name suggests, aims at presenting, through historical studies, India's contribution to the world. In the case of the achievements of classical India in the realm of value-studies, a strong thought has been lingering, and continues to linger, in my mind, that the career of its general theory of value and, more particularly, of its moral philosophy, is of such a type that neither its conceptual, nor its normative, structure is likely to be made clear by a purely historical study alone. I have always felt that a separate, book-length, systematic and theoretical discussion of it was required to do that and to provide a support to the proposed, or any, historical volume on Indian ethics. Such a work is also needed because almost all existing writings on Indian ethics offer only something like a bag of mixed Indological and loosely historical, or semi-historical, studies, in a non-conceptual-analytical manner, generally shying away from subjecting any basic view to a philosophical criticism. My feeling has been shared by Professor D.P. Chattopadhyaya. Knowing very well my philosophical leaning, he himself suggested, before I had actually begun working on the Project as an Editorial Fellow, that, whatever else I did, I should write a conceptual-analytic account of the Indian philosophy of morals. His suggestion encouraged me, almost like a trusted friend's advice to a habitual drinker to drink another bottle of his favourite wine.

I have been studying and writing on some of the basic concepts of classical Indian moral philosophy for the last three or four decades, in a pick-and-choose manner. All along in my journey in this territory I have found that the Indian ethical corpus is like a drum, rich in its musical potentialities, but by itself not producing any sound, let alone a musical sound. To make it yield a musical sound, one has to beat it in a particular style and with sophistication and grace. The philosophical beating of a corpus, ethical or otherwise, can be done only with the tool of logical or conceptual analysis. The philosopher can, then, get out of it the theories or views its progenitors intended it to yield, or even better ones, or even some which are not worth having and therefore are indicative of the fact that the corpus needs to be modified, remodelled, or interpreted in a different manner. Such eventualities are to be welcomed because they contribute to *philosophical progress.*

The Indian ethical corpus, like any classical one, does not always speak in the same voice, and therefore, it can be taken by different thinkers to mean different things. That is why no claim is made here that the kind of moral philosophy it has been taken to yield is the only one which it can yield. If another writer brings out another kind of yield, let him do that. Such exercises also contribute to progress, of course, provided they are done without any doctrinal or *ancestral bias* and all the steps which are taken in them to reach their destination are logically sound.

The homeland of Indian ethics is generally taken to be Indian philosophy. This practice is in order, even though ethical ideas are found even in some non-philosophical works, for example, in anecdotes, myths and mythologies, epics, etc. I have taken into account some such works as well but still consider Indian ethics as housed in Indian philosophy. Therefore, I have first characterized, or rethought, the Indian style of philosophizing, ascertained its distinctive status as a cognitive inquiry and then located the place of ethics in it. In course of doing that I have found that Indian philosophy's admitting the possibility of ethics has entailed that the world and the individual have to be accepted as real because it is the individual who has to lead a moral life and to lead it in the world he lives in, the only world we are acquainted with. I have shown that it is the realization of this fact which has motivated the *Advaitin* Śankara to tone down his abstract metaphysical monism.

All along in this work, as I have done in my others, I have taken all classical writings as human documents, as works written, or words uttered, by human beings. I do not mind calling them *ṛṣis*, saintly knowers or seers of truths as the truths appeared to them. But I am against having, what I have called elsewhere, the *ṛṣi bias,* the bias that what (a thinker called) a *ṛṣi* has said is too sacrosanct to be criticized or critically evaluated. I am also against having any *ancestral bias* to the effect that our classical corpus, which is our ancestral heritage, is never to be criticized. It is obvious that the two biases would block philosophical or *intellectual progress* because having them would not let us make new uses of classical ideas, i.e. not allow us to build new conceptual structures on any part of the classical corpus. Resistance to taking such steps springs from the wrong notion that critically evaluating the view of a *ṛṣi* is to show him disrespect and so is to put a classical idea to a new use. This is a retrogressive understanding of a classical achievement. Classical ideas are our capital. They will survive and grow only by our investing them in new philosophical enterprises and not by our putting them on a pedestal and worshipping them with flowers and sandal-paste and songs in their praise. Therefore, I have criticized classical ethical views if demanded by logic and addressed all classical thinkers, even Rāma, Kṛṣṇa, Śiva, etc., by their names without prefixing the names with any honorific word, though my respect for them is in no way less than anyone else's.

Critical evaluation of a theory and exhibiting a possibility of a reconstruction's removing some weak point in it add to the theory's survival-value. Therefore, I have done both, wherever necessary, in an objective, open-minded, fashion. I have also tried to present Indian ethics as ethics, as the term 'ethics' or its equivalent, 'moral philosophy', etc., is used in philosophical literature, and neither as 'Indian' in a regional sense, nor as an appendix to Indian metaphysics or theology, without denying that it has links with almost all sectors of Indian philosophy, or philosophy in general.

My appraisal, or even statement, of Indian ethical theory, has been given from the point of view of a man who has to live it, i.e. to live his life in accordance with it, and not from that of one who discusses it only as a piece in the history of classical Indian philosophy, i.e. as a record of how some Indian thinkers ethicized, no matter whether or not it has any relevance today. This seems to me the most reasonable way to ascertain the strengths or weaknesses of any ethical theory.

In my characterization of the theory I have depended almost exclusively on original sources. I have very sparingly referred to modern interpretations. Where I have done so, it is either to show their untenability, or to convince the reader that the way I have understood a certain issue is in no way strange or bizarre because some orthodox scholars have also understood it the same way. The motivation for doing the latter is to show that the implications which this understanding of the issue yields, as I have drawn them from it and the orthodox scholars have not, are not from my distorted viewpoint, but from a current or prevalent understanding of the issues.

Since the parent volume of the present work is *Consciousness and Value*, the reader may think that this work should also have discussed the classical Indian philosophy of aesthetics. I have not done that because an independent book on Indian aesthetics is in preparation in the Project as a separate venture.

When I started writing this book, I did not expect it to be of its present size, and to take as much time as it has done, nor did I expect it to be in any way arduous. But my expectations were belied as soon as I began doing the drill. And, it became so engrossing and time-consuming that I could not check what I have said in it with what I have written on some related themes in my other works. But in spite of all this I have enjoyed working on the book largely because of the constant encouragement, sympathy and appreciation I have received from Professor D.P. Chattopadhyaya, the Chairman of the Project and of the Centre for Studies in Civilizations. He is one of the rare and fast vanishing class of people who do not believe that he who pays the piper must call the tune. I am greatly indebted to him for having given to me an unfettered right to write the book even in a 'wrong' way if my logic convinces me that that is the right way.

I am also very thankful to Professor Bhuvan Chandel, Project Coordinator of the Project and the Centre, for giving me whatever help I needed from her and her office.

The second half of Chapter 13 and the major portion of Chapter 14 were written at Kanpur at my eldest son-in-law, Dr Ajay K. Srivastava's residence when my wife was undergoing radiation therapy in a hospital there. Ajay and my daughter Asha provided me with all the facilities and emotional support in what was a difficult time for all of us in the family, which enabled me to continue my writing work even under those circumstances. The support I have received from my wife, even when she was ill, and from all my children and grandchildren is exemplary. My blessings to all of them.

The book has been written with an international readership in mind. Care has been taken to make its language, as far as practicable, non-technical, or the least technical, so that even he who has no training in moral philosophy or philosophy, Indian or Western, may not find it unintelligible. Its chapters are interconnected, but a reader can read selectively some chapter or chapters without any undue strain on his understanding. Whenever a Sanskrit word occurs, generally its English equivalent has been given. If that has not been done in some cases, the context of its use has been made clear so that a reader who ignores the Sanskrit word would have no difficulty in understanding what is said therein. However, how successful I have been in achieving all this can be judged only by the discriminating reader.

Patna
17 January 2006

Rajendra Prasad

General Editor and Author

D.P. Chattopadhyaya has studied, researched on law, philosophy and history, and has taught at various universities in India, Asia, Europe and the USA from 1954 to 1994. Founder-Chairman of the ICPR (1981–90) and President-cum-Chairman of the IIAC (1984–91), Chattopadhyaya is currently the Project Director of the multidisciplinary 96-volume PHISPC and Chairman of the CSC. Among his 35 books, of which he has authored 18 and edited 17, are *Individuals and Societies; Individuals and Words; Sri Aurobindo and Karl Marx; Anthropology and Historiography of Science; Induction, Probability and Skepticism; Sociology, Ideology and Utopia; Cultures and Ideologies; Interdisciplinary Studies in Science; Society, Science, Value and Civilizational Dialogue* and *Philosophy to Science, Phenomenology and Other Essays.* He is a Life Member of the Russian Academy of Sciences and a Member of the International Institute of Philosophy, Paris. Besides, he has also held high public offices, namely, of Union Cabinet Minister and State Governor.

Rajendra Prasad, formerly senior professor of philosophy and head of the department of humanities and social sciences of Indian Institute of Technology (I.I.T.), Kanpur, has studied and researched on modern logic, moral philosophy and analytic philosophy in Indian and U.S. Universities. He has been awarded several fellowships and honours in India and abroad. He has published seven books, the most recent being *A Conceptual-Analytic Study of Classical Indian Philosophy of Morals*, a predecessor of the present volume, in the same series of PHISPC. He has edited another book published by Indian Institute of Advanced Study, Shimla. In addition, he has to his credit more than a hundred research papers published in periodicals in India and abroad.

General Introduction

I

It is understandable that man, shaped by Nature, would like to know Nature. The human ways of knowing Nature are evidently diverse, theoretical and practical, scientific and technological, artistic and spiritual. This diversity has, on scrutiny, been found to be neither exhaustive nor exclusive. The complexity of physical nature, life-world and, particularly, human mind is so enormous that it is futile to follow a single method for comprehending all the aspects of the world in which we are situated.

One need not feel bewildered by the variety and complexity of the worldly phenomena. After all, both from traditional wisdom and our daily experience, we know that our own nature is not quite alien to the structure of the world. Positively speaking, the elements and forces that are out there in the world are also present in our body-mind complex, enabling us to adjust ourselves to our environment. Not only the natural conditions but also the social conditions of life have instructive similarities between them. This is not to underrate in any way the difference between the human ways of life all over the world. It is partly due to the variation in climatic conditions and partly due to the distinctness of production-related tradition, history and culture.

Three broad approaches are discernible in the works on historiography of civilization, comprising science and technology, art and architecture, social sciences and institutions. Firstly, some writers are primarily interested in discovering the general laws which govern all civilizations spread over different continents. They tend to underplay what they call the noisy local events of the external world and peculiarities of different languages, literatures and histories. Their accent is on the unity of Nature, the unity of science and the unity of mankind. The second group of writers, unlike the generalist or transcendentalist ones, attach primary importance to the distinctiveness of every culture. To these writers, human freedom and creativity are extremely important and basic in character. Social institutions and the cultural articulations of human consciousness, they argue, are bound to be expressive of the concerned people's consciousness. By implication they tend to reject concepts like archetypal consciousness, universal mind and providential history. There is a third group of writers who offer a composite picture of civilizations, drawing elements both from their local and common characteristics. Every culture has its local roots and peculiarities. At the same time, it is pointed out that due to demographic migration and immigration over the centuries an element of compositeness emerges almost in every culture. When, due to a natural calamity or political exigencies people move from one part of the world to another, they carry with them, among other things, their language, cultural inheritance and their ways of living.

In the light of the above facts, it is not at all surprising that comparative anthropologists and philologists are intrigued by the striking similarity between different language families and the rites, rituals and myths of different peoples. Speculative philosophers of history, heavily relying on the findings of epigraphy, ethnography, archaeology and theology, try to show in very general terms that the particulars and universals of culture are 'essentially' or 'secretly' interrelated. The spiritual aspects of culture like dance and music, beliefs pertaining to life, death and duties, on analysis, are found to be mediated by the material forms of life like weather forecasting, food production, urbanization and invention of script. The transition from the oral culture to the written one was made possible because of the mastery of symbols and rules of measurement. Speech precedes grammar, poetry prosody. All these show how the 'matters' and 'forms' of life are so subtly interwoven.

II

The PHISPC publications on History of Science, Philosophy and Culture in Indian Civilization, in spite of their unitary look, do recognize the differences between the areas of material civilization and those of ideational culture. It is not a work of a single author. Nor is it being executed by a group of thinkers and writers who are methodologically uniform or ideologically identical in their commitments. In conceiving the Project we have interacted with, and been influenced by, the writings and views of many Indian and non-Indian thinkers.

The attempted unity of this Project lies in its aim and inspiration. We have in India many scholarly works written by Indians on different aspects of our civilization and culture. Right from the pre-Christian era to our own time, India has drawn the attention of various countries of Asia, Europe and Africa. Some of these writings are objective and informative and many others are based on insufficient information and hearsay, and therefore not quite reliable, but they have their own value. Quality and viewpoints keep on changing not only because of the adequacy and inadequacy of evidence but also, and perhaps more so; because of the bias and prejudice, religious and political conviction, of the writers.

Besides, it is to be remembered that history, like Nature, is not an open book to be read alike by all. The past is mainly enclosed and only partially disclosed. History is, therefore, partly objective or 'real' and largely a matter of construction. This is one of the reasons why some historians themselves think that it is a form of literature or art. However, it does not mean that historical construction is 'anarchic' and arbitrary. Certainly, imagination plays an important role in it.

But its character is basically dependent upon the *questions* which the historian raises and wants to understand or answer in terms of the ideas and actions of human beings in the past ages. In a way, history, somewhat like the natural sciences, is engaged in answering questions and in exploring relationships of cause and effect between events and developments across time. While in the natural sciences, the scientist poses questions about nature in the form of hypotheses, expecting to elicit authoritative answers to such questions, the historian studies the past, partly for the sake of understanding it for its own sake and partly also for the light which the past throws upon the present, and the possibilities which it opens up for moulding the future. But the difference between the two approaches must not be lost sight of. The scientist is primarily interested in discovering laws and framing theories, in terms of which, different events and processes can be connected and anticipated. His interest in the conditions or circumstances attending the concerned events is secondary. Therefore, scientific laws turn out to be basically abstract and easily expressible in terms of mathematical language. In contrast, the historian's main interest centres round the *specific* events, human ideas and actions, not *general* laws. So, the historian, unlike the scientist, is obliged to pay primary attention to the circumstances of the events he wants to study. Consequently, history, like most other humanistic disciplines, is concrete and particularist. This is not to deny the obvious truth that historical events and processes consisting of human ideas and actions show some trend or other and weave some pattern or other. If these trends and patterns were not there at all in history, the study of history as a branch of knowledge would not have been profitable or instructive. But one must recognize that historical trends and patterns, unlike scientific laws and theories, are not general or purported to be universal in their scope.

III

The aim of this Project is to discover the main aspects of Indian culture and present them in an interrelated way. Since our culture has influenced, and has been influenced by, the neighbouring cultures of West Asia, Central Asia, East Asia and Southeast Asia, attempts have been made here to trace and study these influences in their mutuality. It is well known that during the last three centuries, European presence in India, both political and cultural, has been very widespread. In many volumes of the Project considerable attention has been paid to Europe and through Europe to other parts of the world. For the purpose of a comprehensive cultural study of India, the existing political boundaries of the South Asia of today are more of a hindrance than help. Cultures, like languages, often transcend the bounds of changing political territories.

If the inconstant political geography is not a reliable help to the understanding of the layered structure and spread of culture, a somewhat comparable problem is encountered in the area of historical periodization. Periodization or segmenting time is a very tricky affair. When exactly one period ends and another begins is not precisely ascertainable. The periods of history designated as ancient, medieval and modern are purely conventional and merely heuristic in character. The varying scopes of history, local, national and continental or universal, somewhat like the periods of history, are unavoidably fuzzy and shifting. Amidst all these difficulties, the volume-wise details have been planned and worked out by the editors in consultation with the Project Director and the General Editor. I believe that the editors of different volumes have also profited from the reactions and suggestions of the contributors of individual chapters in planning the volumes.

Another aspect of Indian history which the volume-editors and contributors of the Project have carefully dealt with is the distinction and relation between civilization and culture. The material conditions which substantially shaped Indian civilization have been discussed in detail. From agriculture and industry to metallurgy and technology, from physics and chemical practices to the life sciences and different systems of medicines—

all the branches of knowledge and skill which directly affect human life—form the heart of this Project. Since the periods covered by the PHISPC are extensive—prehistory, proto-history, early history, medieval history and modern history of India—we do not claim to have gone into all the relevant material conditions of human life. We had to be selective. Therefore, one should not be surprised if one finds that only some material aspects of Indian civilization have received our pointed attention, while the rest have been dealt with in principle or only alluded to.

One of the main aims of the Project has been to spell out the first principles of the philosophy of different schools, both pro-Vedic and anti-Vedic. The basic ideas of Buddhism, Jainism and Islam have been given their due importance. The special position accorded to philosophy is to be understood partly in terms of its proclaimed unifying character and partly to be explained in terms of the fact that different philosophical systems represent alternative world-views, cultural perspectives, their conflict and mutual assimilation.

Most of the volume-editors and at their instance the concerned contributors have followed a middle path between the extremes of narrativism and theoreticism. The underlying idea has been this: If in the process of working out a comprehensive Project like this every contributor attempts to narrate all those interesting things that he has in the back of his mind, the enterprise is likely to prove unmanageable. If, on the other hand, particular details are consciously forced into a fixed mould or pre-supposed theoretical structure, the details lose their particularity and interesting character. Therefore, depending on the nature of the problem of discourse, most of the writers have tried to reconcile in their presentation, the specificity of narrativism and the generality of theoretical orientation. This is a conscious editorial decision. Because, in the absence of a theory, however inarticulate it may be, the factual details tend to fall apart. Spiritual network or theoretical orientation makes historical details not only meaningful but also interesting and enjoyable.

Another editorial decision which deserves spelling out is the necessity or avoidability of duplication of the same theme in different volumes or even in the same volume. Certainly, this Project is not an assortment of several volumes. Nor is any volume intended to be a miscellany. This Project has been designed with a definite end in view and has a structure of its own. The character of the structure has admittedly been influenced by the variety of the themes accommodated within it. Again it must be understood that the complexity of structure is rooted in the aimed integrality of the Project itself.

IV

Long and in-depth editorial discussion has led us to several unanimous conclusions. Firstly, our Project is going to be *unique,* unrivalled and discursive in its attempt to integrate different forms of science, technology, philosophy and culture. Its comprehensive scope, continuous character and accent on culture distinguish it from the works of such Indian authors as P.C. Ray, B.N. Seal, Binoy Kumar Sarkar and S.N. Sen and also from such Euro-American writers as Lynn Thorndike, George Sarton and Joseph Needham. Indeed, it would be no exaggeration to suggest that it is for the first time that an endeavour of so comprehensive a character, in its exploration of the social, philosophical and cultural characteristics of a distinctive world civilization—that of India—has been attempted in the domain of scholarship.

Secondly, we try to show the linkages between different branches of learning as different modes of experience in an *organic* manner and without resorting to a kind of reductionism, materialistic or spiritualistic. The internal dialectics of organicism without reductionism allows fuzziness, discontinuity and discreteness within limits.

Thirdly, positively speaking, different modes of human experience—scientific, artistic, etc., have their own individuality, not necessarily autonomy. Since all these modes are modification and articulation of *human* experience, these are bound to have between them some finely graded commonness. At the same time, it has been recognized that reflection on different areas of experience and investigation brings to light new insights and findings. Growth of knowledge requires humans, in general, and scholars, in particular, to identify the distinctness of different branches of learning.

Fourthly, to follow simultaneously the twin principles of: (a) individuality of human experience as a whole, and (b) individuality of diverse disciplines, are not at all an easy task. Overlap of themes and duplication of the terms of discourse become unavoidable at times. For example, in the context of *Dharmaśāstra*, the writer is bound to discuss the concept of value. The same concept also figures in economic discourse and also occurs in a discussion on fine arts. The conscious editorial decision has been that, while duplication should be kept to its minimum, for the sake of intended clarity of the themes under discussion, their reiteration must not be avoided at high intellectual cost.

Fifthly, the scholars working on the Project are drawn from widely different disciplines. They have brought to our notice an important fact that has clear relevance to our work. Many of our contemporary disciplines like economics and sociology did not exist, at least not in their present form, just two centuries ago or so. For example, before the middle of nineteenth century, sociology as a distinct branch of knowledge was unknown. The term is said to have been coined first by the French philosopher Auguste Comte in 1838. Obviously, this does not mean that the issues discussed in sociology were not there. Similarly, Adam Smith's (1723–90) famous work *The Wealth of Nations* is often referred to as the first authoritative statement of the principles of (what we now call) economics. Interestingly enough, the author was equally interested in ethics and jurisprudence. It is clear from history that the nature and scope of different disciplines undergo change, at times very radically, over time. For example, in India by '*Arthaśāstra*' does not mean the science of economics as understood today. Besides the principles of economics, the *Arthaśāstra* of ancient India discusses at length those of governance, diplomacy and military science.

Sixthly, this brings us to the next editorial policy followed in the Project. We have tried to remain very conscious of what may be called indeterminacy or inexactness of translation. When a word or expression of one language is translated into another, some loss of meaning or exactitude seems to be unavoidable. This is true not only in the bilingual relations like Sanskrit-English and Sanskrit-Arabic, but also in those of Hindi-Tamil and Hindi-Bengali. In recognition of the importance of language-bound and context-relative character of meaning we have solicited from many learned scholars, contributions, written in vernacular languages. In order to minimize the miseffect of semantic inexactitude we have solicited translational help of that type of bilingual scholars who know both English and the concerned vernacular language, Hindi, Tamil, Telugu, Bengali or Marathi.

Seventhly and finally, perhaps the place of technology as a branch of knowledge in the composite universe of science and art merits some elucidation. Technology has been conceived in very many ways, e.g., as autonomous, as 'standing reserve', as liberating or enlargemental, and alienative or estrangemental force. The studies undertaken by the Project show that, in spite of its much emphasized mechanical and alienative characteristics, technology embodies a very useful mode of knowledge that is peculiar to man. The Greek root words of technology are *techne* (art) and *logos* (science). This is the basic justification of recognizing technology as closely related to both epistemology, the discipline of valid knowledge, and axiology, the discipline of freedom and values. It is in this context that we are reminded of the definition of man as *homo technikos.* In Sanskrit, the word closest to *techne* is *kalā* which means any practical art, any mechanical or fine art. In the Indian tradition, in *Śaivatantra,* for example, among the arts (*kalā*) are counted dance, drama, music, architecture, metallurgy, knowledge of dictionary, encyclopaedia and prosody. The closeness of the relation between arts and sciences, technology and other forms of knowledge are evident from these examples and was known to the ancient people. The human quest for knowledge involves the use of both head and hand. Without mind, the body is a corpse and the disembodied mind is a bare abstraction. Even for our appreciation of what is beautiful and the creation of what is valuable, we are required to exercise both our intellectual competence and physical capacity. In a manner of speaking, one might rightly affirm that our psychosomatic structure is a functional connector between what we are and what we could be, between the physical and the beyond. To suppose that there is a clear-cut distinction between the physical world and the psychosomatic one amounts to denial of the possible emergence of higher logico-mathematical, musical and other capacities. The very availability of aesthetic experience and creation proves that the supposed distinction is somehow overcome by what may be called the bodily self or embodied mind.

V

The ways of classification of arts and sciences are neither universal nor permanent. In the Indian tradition, in the *Ṛgveda,* for example, *vidyās* (or sciences) are said to be four in number: (i) *Trayī,* the triple Veda; (ii) *Ānvīkṣikī,* logic and metaphysics; (iii) *Daṇḍa-nīti,* science of governance; (iv) *Vārttā,* practical arts such as agriculture, commerce, medicine, etc. Manu speaks of a fifth *vidyā,* viz., *Ātma-vidyā,* knowledge of self or of spiritual truth. According to many others, *vidyā* has fourteen divisions, viz., the four Vedas, the six *Vedāṅgas,* the *Purāṇas,* the *Mīmāṁsā, Nyāya,* and *Dharma* or law. At times, the four *Upavedas* are also recognized by some as *vidyā. Kalās* are said to be 33 or even 64.

In the classical tradition of India, the word *śāstra* has at times been used as synonym of *vidyā. Vidyā* denotes instrument of teaching, manual or compendium of rules, religious or scientific treatise. The word *śāstra* is usually found after the word referring to the subject of the book, e.g., *Dharma-śāstra, Artha-śāstra, Alaṁkāra-śāstra* and *Mokṣa-śāstra.* Two other words which have been frequently used to denote different branches of knowledge are *jñāna* and *vijñāna.* While *jñāna* means knowing, knowledge, especially the higher form of it; *vijñāna* stands for the act of distinguishing or discerning, understanding, comprehending and recognizing. It means worldly or profane knowledge as distinguished from *jñāna,* knowledge of the divine.

It must be said here that the division of knowledge is partly conventional and partly administrative or practical. It keeps on changing from culture to culture, from age to age. It is difficult to claim that the distinction between *jñāna* and *vijñāna* or that between science and art is universal. It is true that even before the advent of modern age, both in the East and the West, two basic aspects of sciences started gaining recognition. One is the *specialized character* of what we call scientific knowledge. The other is the concept of *trained skill* which was brought close to scientific knowledge. In the medieval Europe, the expression 'the seven liberal sciences' has so often been used simultaneously with 'the seven liberal arts', meaning thereby, the group of studies by the *Trivium* (Grammar, Logic and Rhetoric) and *Quadrivium* (Arithmetic, Music, Geometry and Astronomy).

It may be observed here, as has already been alluded to earlier, that the division between different branches of knowledge, between theory and practice, was not pushed to an extreme extent in the early ages. *Praxis,* for example, was recognized as the prime *techne.* The Greek word, *technologia* stood for systematic treatment, for example, of Grammar. *Praxis* is not the mere application of *theoria,* unified vision or integral outlook, but it also stands for the active impetus and base of knowledge. In India, one often uses the terms *Prayukti-vidyā* and *Prayodyogika-vidyā* to emphasize the practical or applicative character of knowledge. *Prayoga* or application is both the test and base of knowledge. Doing is the best way of knowing and learning.

That one and the same word may mean different 'things' or concepts in different cultures and thus create confusion has already been stated before. Two such words which in the context of this Project under discussion deserve special mention are *dharma* and *itihāsa.* Ordinarily, *dharma* in Sanskrit-rooted languages is taken to be conceptual equivalent of the English word *religion.* But, while the meaning of religion is primarily theological, that of *dharma* seems to be manifold. Literally, *dharma* stands for that which is established or that which holds people steadfastly together. Its other meanings are law, rule, usage, practice, custom, ordinance and statute. Spiritual or moral merit, virtue, righteousness and good works are also denoted by it. Further, *dharma* stands for natural qualities like burning (of fire), liquidity (of water) and fragility (of glass). Thus one finds that meanings of *dharma* are of many types—legal, social, moral, religious or spiritual, and even ontological or physical. All these meanings of *dharma* have received due attention of the writers in the relevant contexts of different volumes.

This Project, being primarily historical as it is, has naturally paid serious attention to the different concepts of history—epic-mythic, artistic-narrative, scientific-causal, theoretical and ideological. Perhaps the point that must be mentioned first about history is that it is not a correct translation of the Sanskrit word *itihāsa.* Etymologically, it means what really happened (*iti-ha-āsa*). But, as we know, in the Indian tradition *purāṇa* (legend, myth, tale, etc.), *gāthā* (ballad), *itivṛtta* (description of past occurrence, event, etc.), *ākhyāyikā* (short narrative) and *vaṃśa-carita* (genealogy) have been consciously accorded a very important place. Things started changing with the passage of time and particularly after the effective presence of Islamic culture in India. Islamic historians, because of their own cultural moorings and the influence of the Semitic and Graeco-Roman cultures on them, were more particular about their facts, figures and dates than their Indian predecessors. Their aim to bring history close to statecraft, social conditions and the lives and teachings of the religious leaders imparted a mundane character to this branch of learning. The Europeans whose political appearance on the Indian scene became quite perceptible only towards the end of the eighteenth century brought in with them their own view of historiography in their cultural baggage. The impact of the Newtonian Revolution in the field of history was very faithfully worked out, among others, by David Hume (1711–76) in *History of Great Britain from the Invasion of Julius Caesar to the Revolution of 1688* (6 Vol., 1754–62) and Edward Gibbon (1737–94) in *The History of the Decline and Fall of the Roman Empire* (6 Vol., 1776–88). Their emphasis on the principles of causality, datability and continuity/linearity of historical events introduced the spirit of scientific revolution in European historiography. The introduction of English education in India and the exposure of the elites of the country to it largely account for the decline of the traditional concept of *itihāsa* and the rise of the post-Newtonian scientific historiography. Gradually, Indian writers of our own history and cultural heritage started using more and more European concepts and categories. This is not to suggest that the impact of the European historiography on Indian historians was entirely negative. On the contrary, it imparted an analytical and critical temper which motivated many Indian historians of the nineteenth century to try to discover and represent our heritage in a new way.

VI

The principles which have been followed for organizing the subjects of different volumes under this Project may be stated in this way. We have kept in view the main structures which are discernible in the decomposible composition of the world. The first structure may be described as physical and chemical. The second structure consists, broadly speaking, of biology, psychology and epistemology. The highest and the most abstract structure nests many substructures within it, for example, logic, mathematics and musical notes. It is well known that the substructures within each structure are interactive, i.e., not isolable. The more important point to be noted in this connection is that the basic three structures of the world, viz., (a) physico-chemical, (b) bio-psychological, and (c) logico-mathematical are all simultaneously open to upward and downward causation. In other words, while the physico-chemical structure can causally influence the bio-psychological one and the latter can causally influence the most abstract logico-mathematical, the reverse process of causation is also operative in the world. In spite of its relative abstractness and durability, the logico-mathematical world has its downward causal impact on our bio-psychological and epistemological processes and products. And the latter can also bring about change in the structures of the physical world and its chemical composition. Applied physics and bio-technology make the last point abundantly clear.

Many philosophers, life-scientists, and social scientists highlight the point that nature loves hierarchies. Herbert Simon, the economist and the management scientist, speaks of four steps of partial ordering of our world, namely; (i) chemical substances, (ii) living organisms, tissues and organs, (iii) genes, chromosomes and DNA, and (iv) human beings, the social organizations, programmes and information process. All these views are in accord with the anti-reductionist character of our Project. Many biologists defend this approach by pointing out that certain characteristics of biological phenomena and process like unpredictability, randomness, uniqueness, magnitude of stochastic perturbations, complexity and emergence cannot be reduced without recourse to physical laws.

The main subjects dealt with in different volumes of the Project are connected not only conceptually and synchronically but also historically or diachronically. For pressing practical reasons, however, we did not aim at presenting the prehistorical, proto-historical and historical past of India in a continuous or chronological manner. Besides, it has been shown in the presentation of the PHISPC that the process of history is non-linear. And this process is to be understood in terms of human praxis and an absence of general laws in history. Another point which deserves special mention is that the editorial advisors have taken a conscious decision not to make this historical Project primarily political. We felt that this area of history has always been receiving extensive attention. Therefore, the customary discussion of dynastic rule and succession will not be found in a prominent way in this series. Instead, as said before, most of the available space has been given to social, scientific, philosophical and other cultural aspects of Indian civilization.

Having stated this, it must be admitted that our departure from conventional style of writing Indian history is not total. We have followed an inarticulate framework of time in organizing and presenting the results of our studies. The first volume, together with its parts, deals with the prehistorical period to AD 300. The next two volumes, together with their parts, deal with, among other things, the development of social and political institutions and philosophical and scientific ideas from AD 300 to the beginning of the eleventh century AD. The next period with which this Project is concerned spans from the twelfth century to the early part of the eighteenth century. The last three centuries constitute the fourth period covered by this Project. But, as said before, the definition of all these periods by their very nature are inexact and merely indicative.

Two other points must be mentioned before I conclude this General Introduction to the series. The history of some of the subjects like religion, language and literature, philosophy, science and technology cannot for obvious reason be squeezed within the cramped space of the periodic moulds. Attempts to do so result in thematic distortion. Therefore, the reader will often see the overflow of some ideas from one period to another. I have already drawn attention to this tricky and fuzzy and also the misleading aspects of the periodization of history, if pressed beyond a point.

Secondly, strictly speaking, history knows no end. Every age rewrites its history. Every generation, beset with new issues, problems and questions, looks back to its history and reinterprets and renews its past. This shows why history is not only contemporaneous but also futural. Human life actually knows no separative wall between its past, present and future. Its cognitive enterprises, moral endeavours and practical activities are informed of the past, oriented by the present and addressed to the future. This process persists, consciously or unconsciously, wittingly or unwittingly. In the narrative of this Project, we have tried to represent this complex and fascinating story of Indian civilization.

Centre for Studies in Civilizations
New Delhi and Kolkata

D.P. Chattopadhyaya

CHAPTER 1

Introduction: On Studying Classical Indian Ethics Philosophically: Some Problems and Prejudices

1.1 ETHICS, MORALITY AND MORAL PHILOSOPHY

Ethics, as generally conceived in philosophical circles, is a *normative* inquiry into the nature of what a man ought to aim at, what sort of character traits he should cultivate, what sort of obligations he should fulfil, what sort of rights he is entitled to have, etc. Putting all this in a synoptic form, we can say that it is a *normative* inquiry into man's goals or *values, virtues* or desirable qualities of character, *obligations* or duties, and *rights* or justified (or justifiable) claims. It is said to be a normative inquiry or study because it is a study into what he ought to do or be, and not just one into what he actually does or wants to be. That is why we say that it is not a (purely) descriptive or empirical, but an evaluative, inquiry. It does not, however, mean that it pays no attention to what he actually does or wants to do and to be, to what he is disposed to do or to prefer to be. Without knowing what sort of a creature man is, what sort of dispositions or propensities he has, i.e. what he may, or can, do and may, or can, be, it is not possible to arrive at a realistic, practicable or implementable theory about what he ought (or ought not) to do, or what he ought (or ought not) to be. All this is a logical consequence of the conceptual truth that it can meaningfully be said that he ought to do something, or be an individual of a certain sort, only if he can do that thing or can be the individual of that sort.

When we say that it is a study about what a man ought to do, etc., normally we take him to be an individual living in a *society*. This is so because ethical problems arise generally, or more visibly, in his social transactions, i.e. in the network of very many different types of relations which exist (or may exist) between him and other members of his society.

In fact, every society, small or large, is also a moral *community*. A society may be as small as a nuclear family of a husband and his wife, or as large as the totality of all humans, or even larger than that when moral relations are extended to animals and plants as well, making human beings responsible even for their well-being in virtue of the benefits they receive from them, or the services they render to them.

The idea of the society as the community of all humans, or of all humans and non-humans, is clearly visible in a classical Indian saying that a man of morally sensitive character (*udāracarit*) treats the entire world (*vasudhā*) as his family (*kuṭumba*). This saying is really a *normative* principle to the effect that, to be an ideal moral person, one ought to treat the whole world as dear to oneself as if it were one's own family. It is not a statement of fact that everyone, or even anyone, actually does that. It is, thus, to aver that the *ideally moral person* is only he who has as much care and concern for the well-being of everyone in the world as he has for any member of his own family.

An *ideal* is an ideal, and, therefore, one does not fail to lead a moral life if one is not the ideally moral person. But one has to respect a certain minimum of the moral relations existing between oneself and other members of the society; the larger the society, the more generous one's morality, or moral character, is. Observance of moral relations among themselves by the members of a society is necessary because it is this observance which sustains the society, or converts a collectivity into *community*. Not only an individual has, therefore, a moral code to observe; even a group of individuals has to have a moral code and observe it. It has to do that in order to survive, in a viable manner as a group and to avoid conflicts with any one of its members as well as with any other group. For example, a young man has to observe the moral relations relevant to his social status in his family; for instance, the relation of respecting the elders of his own family as well as those of his neighbourhood. The same young man, when he becomes a student in a teacher's school, becomes a member of a new group, or small society, i.e., of the group of students studying in the same school. He then has to observe the *moral code*, or the *moral rules*, applicable to a student, the code which constitutes the morality of the group of students. We may call it students' morality.

It is this moral code, or morality, which classical Indians call the *āśrama dharma* of a *brahmacārī*; it simply means the observance of the moral norms relevant to an individual when he is in that stage of his life in which he is receiving instruction, along with some other such individuals, from a teacher while residing on the campus of the teacher's school. An individual may, thus, pass through several stages in his lifetime: for example, the stage of student, the stage of seeker of some job, the stage of job-performance which may be that of practising some *profession* etc. He may practise professions of different types during different periods of his professional career, each profession requiring a more or less different moral code. But in whichever stage he is, he would have to observe the moral code relevant to that stage, otherwise he would not be able to function successfully as a member of the group he belongs to. Classical Indian thinkers chart out the lifetime of an individual into, as we shall see later, only four stages. They think that all possible stages he may pass through can be comprehended, or accommodated, in these four stages. They may or may not be, and we may even say that the classical four-fold division cannot fully or correctly represent the very many things which a modern individual does in his lifetime. Still it remains true, and will remain always true that an individual will always have to observe some sort of morality, or some set of moral rules, through whichever stage of his life he passes. This has to be the case because it is the observance of moral rules and norms by the members of a group, or even the society at large, which sustains or keeps the group or the society at large in order, i.e. functioning in a healthy manner.

In this way there emerges the morality of various groups, i.e. teachers' morality, parents' morality, householders' morality, kings' morality, priests' morality, servants' morality, warriors' morality, etc. Thus, in a natural, very smooth way, we not only come to have the notion of an *individual's morality*, but also that of a group morality which includes, as hinted at above, the notion of *professional morality*. A group of individuals practising a profession form a group, a professional group. Being a group of a specific type, every professional group has to observe the moral code appropriate to it, i.e. the relevant moral relations among the members of the same profession. A member of such a group has also to observe appropriate moral relations between him and a beneficiary of his professional service. In addition, he has also to observe the relevant moral relations between a member of his profession and one of another profession if the two professions have links which have to be honoured to allow or help each one of them to flourish.

Morality, thus, functions as a sustaining agent of social life. It is this ethical or societal truth which some modern Indian grammarians and etymologists as well as some modern Indian philosophers are never tired of emphasizing by saying that dharma, in the sense of morality, is that which sustains the human world, or the social world. There is no objection even to saying that it sustains the world. For a human being the human world, his social world, is the world he lives in. He knows by acquaintance only this world, and therefore, we can say that this world is for him, for any human being, the world. That is why it may be said that *dharma* sustains the world. All this is natural because of the world's being what it is and morality's or *dharma*'s being what it is.

But the ilk of linguists and philosophers mentioned above sometimes seem to be averring that *because* the word *dharma*, being derived from the root *dhṛ*, the equivalent of 'to sustain', means that which sustains, *dharma* sustains the world. This claim seems to be, on its first blush completely innocent, an axiomatic truth. But it contains a thick fog inside itself which when cleared makes it either a mere *syntactic* or *verbal* statement, or an untenable inference of a substantive statement from a linguistic statement, of an empirical truth from a grammatical truth. Since *dhṛ* means to sustain, *dharma* a derived form from it, means that which sustains. Therefore, if these linguists and philosophers only mean to state that the word *dharma* (because of its being derived from *dhṛ*) means that which sustains, their statement is only a statement *about* the *etymological* meaning of the word *dharma*; that is, it is only a *grammatical statement*, one about the word, *dharma*, and not a substantive statement, not one about *dharma*, about the thing or institution which *dharma* is and what it in fact does.

It is not logically right to infer a substantive statement about anything from what the word or phrase denoting it grammatically means. This is so because there may not exist anything which it denotes, or the thing which it denotes may exist but may not function the way the grammatical statement of its meaning claims it to function. For example, the phrase 'completely frictionless pully' grammatically means a pully which functions in a completely frictionless manner. Mathematicians use the concept of such a pully and perform mathematical operations which are valid and involve the use of this concept in a positive way. But they admit the physical truth that there cannot exist a pully which is completely frictionless. On a much simplier level, the Sanskrit word *vidhura* etymologically means, when applied to a man, one who is sad or grief-stricken having lost his wife. But from this we cannot infer of every man who has become a *vidhura* by losing his wife that he is grief-stricken because it is possible and sometimes a truth that an individual becomes happy when his wife dies. It is possible that in a society there is no *vidhura* because both a husband and his wife die at the same time. Even in that society the grammatical statement about the word *vidhura* would be true. But the substantive statement about a *vidhura's* being grief-stricken would be false. The upshot of this detour into elementary syntactics is that no substantive statement about what *dharma*, the classical Indian equivalent (or even near equivalent) of morality, is or does, can be inferred from the grammatical meaning of the word *dharma* or 'morality'.

To say that *dharma* sustains the world *because* the word *dharma*, its linguistic name (in Sanskrit), means that which sustains, also amounts to making a social reality, or *dharma*, depend on a grammatical feature of the word *dharma*. Whether or not the observance of *dharma* sustains the world, or society, can be ascertained by finding out what its observance does, and not by consulting a Sanskrit dictionary. Whether or not it did that in ancient India too can be determined by looking into a book on the history of ancient India and not by looking into a dictionary of ancient Sanskrit. If we could do that by looking into the dictionary, writing a book on the history of ancient Indian ethics would be child's play. By looking into the dictionary we can find, of course, the meaning of the word *dharma* but only the meaning of the word. It is the failure to realize this which seems responsible for many scholars, of the type mentioned above, thinking that it is very easy to say what *dharma* or ancient Indian conception of morality, is. But it is far from the truth.

What is true of the word *dharma* is also true of the English words 'morality' and 'ethics'. 'Morality', English etymologists say, is derived from 'mores' which means custom, convention, etc. 'Ethics', they say, is derived from 'ethos' which means character, not necessarily moral character but character in the sense of a dramatic character, i.e., a person's performing a role in a drama. It is clear that by knowing any set of customs or conventions we cannot understand what morality is, not even what the morality of the people, the knowledge of whose customs or conventions we have acquired, is. Nor can we understand, rather more obviously, what ethics is by having an understanding of dramatic character-acting or role-playing, howsoever knowledgeable our understanding of this may be. This is why modern moral philosophers pay no attention to the *etymology* of 'morality' or of 'ethics' in their moral philosophizing, not even in writing a history of ethics, not even in writing the history of the ethics prevalent in a particular region of the world in a particular period of its history.

It seems more sensible to say that classical Indian linguists or ethicists need a word to name the agency which sustains the human society, the human world, or the world. As a name for this agency, we may say, they coin from *dhṛ* the word *dharma* in the manner an expert coins a word when he needs one for performing a certain function or a set of functions. We may also say, and equally sensibly, that the classical usage in its natural source evolves, as it generally does, the word *dharma* as a name for the agency and in due course it gets its many-faceted connotations and denotations which it has in the classical Indian corpus. And, thereupon, etymologists find that this word can be derived from the root *dhṛ*.

In fact, this is generally true of the growth of any language. First words come into ordinary usage because of the demands of life. In course of time their usage gets established, and then linguists or etymologists research their etymology. It is important to point out here that there are some conceptual, or even normative, problems in calling *dharma* a sustainer of the world. But this introduction is not the right place to discuss them. Here we are concerned with only opening the door through which we can enter the big sprawling building which Indian ethics is. The conceptual problems hinted at above can be properly discussed only after we become well acquainted with the inner apartments of the building. Therefore, they will be taken up in the chapter on *dharma*.

It is felt by many thinkers that an individual is not exhausted by his social relations, by his moral performances, howsoever wide his society and the network of his social relations and his morality may be. After doing all that he ought to do as a member of the society, i.e. all that he ought to do to fulfil his moral obligations and responsibilities, some residue is left in him which is still unfulfilled and needs to be fulfilled. This residue could be anything. e.g. aesthetic, intellectual, spiritual, etc. For a Kālidāsa it is, some would say, the satisfaction of his poetic creativity, for a Dharmakīrti the formulation of a theory of logic, for a Śankara not only the establishment, on logical, intellectual, grounds, of the theory of the identity between the Self and *Brahman* but also the realization of that identity in his life, etc., etc. How this residue's satisfaction is related to an individual's functioning as a morally impeccable person will be discussed much later in the work. This way to proceed is in the fitness of things for a work of this type which is primarily a philosophical, conceptual, study of classical Indian ethics. It is so because only after forming a knowledgeable idea of what ethics and what classical Indian ethics is, shall we be in a position to correctly understand and evaluate any view about the relation between ethical or moral life and the fulfilment of the non-ethical or extra-ethical residue in human aspiration, of course, if there is such a residue.

'Ethics' has been used in the discussion so far, and will be used all along in this work, to mean the same thing as moral philosophy or philosophy of morals, including normative ethics, metaethics, applied ethics, etc. This is the way it is also currently used in philosophical, ethical, literature, Therefore, 'ethical' and 'moral' are also used synonymously. Mostly in earlier works, sometimes, or in some contexts, even today, 'ethics' is also used to mean the actual, prevailing, ethical practices or beliefs of a group, or of a country, during a certain period of its history. This is done, for example, in someone's saying that classical Indian ethics is different from modern Indian ethics, or that some sector of classical Indian ethics is still prevalent, or that the ethics of a secular political party is different from that of a religious political party, etc. In this work, 'ethics' is used sometimes in the first and sometimes in the second sense; however, the context of each use will make it clear in which sense it has been used. That is why this practice does not cause any problem. Using 'ethics' in the two senses becomes sometimes necessary because there is no word other than it to denote, in a descriptive sense, the ethical practices and beliefs actually in vogue in the life-history of a people at a certain time, as neatly as it does. And, since common usage also uses 'ethical' synonymously with 'moral' and 'ethics' synonymously with moral thinking, moral theorizing, moral philosophy or philosophy of morals, there is nothing wrong in doing the same thing in philosophical usage; of course, with caution that no confusion is caused. When there is a high probability, however, of the use of 'ethics' or 'ethical' causing some blockade in understanding, we shall use 'ethical theory' or 'ethical philosophy' instead of 'ethics' to refer to ethical or moral inquiry. Similarly, to avoid confusion, the term 'ethical code' or 'moral code' will be used to refer to ethics or morality in vogue, i.e. to refer to a set of ethical or moral practices or beliefs of a people.

The above account of ethics or moral philosophy has been given in a general way without keeping in mind the peculiarities or distinctive features of ethics done in any particular country or culture. This account is as much true of Indian ethics as it is of Western ethics. There need be no surprise in this being the case because in *generalities* the two are not different from each other. But we must also discuss how ethics has been done in classical India to understand its distinctive character, while realizing that for it to have a distinctive character does not amount to its not being ethics in a sense in which Western, or non-Indian, ethics is ethics. Because of their failure to understand this simple truth, some Western writers claim that there is no ethics in classical Indian philosophy, or corpus. On the other hand, some Indian writers, on account of the same failure on their part, go to the other extreme of saying that Indian philosophy goes beyond, or transcends, ethics. This view too amounts to admitting that there is no ethics in Indian philosophy. For any discipline to go beyond or transcend an inquiry is to overfly it, to leave it behind, and therefore not to include it within itself. Both of these positions will be discussed in some detail in chapter 5. But we must first say something more about ethics as conceived in classical Indian philosophy. This the next section will do.

1.2 ETHICS AS *NĪTIŚĀSTRA* IN INDIAN NOMENCLATURE

The generally used Indian name for ethics is *nītiśāstra.* It is also very much in current circulation in almost all modern Indian languages. Even in Sanskrit there does not seem to exist another word which may be called an equivalent of 'ethics' or 'moral philosophy' better than it. Therefore, we shall also follow the beaten track and use it as the Indian name for ethics, or use 'ethics' as well as 'moral philosophy' or 'philosophy of morals' as the English term for *nītiśāstra.*

Nītiśāstra means a study of or an inquiry into, the nature of *nīti.* The word *nīti,* as per Sanskrit etymology, is derived from the root *nī,* meaning to take one, or enable one, to attain, or to reach to. *Nīti,* so formed, is an abstract noun meaning that which takes one to, or enables one to attain. It can thus be said to denote or stand for any technique, plan, policy, direction, strategy, management, conduct, behaviour, expertise, etc. which takes one to. This is what Sanskrit dictionaries do in listing its equivalents. But as to what is that to which it takes one is not indicated by the root meaning of the term. Therefore, etymological analysis or meaning of the term cannot be of much help in understanding the nature of *nītiśāstra.* To know what is that it leads one to we have to look into the usage of the term 'nīti'. In general classical usage the object to which it leads one, or is capable of leading one, is said to be one's objective, goal, the object one aims at, or intends to attain. Even this sense is too broad, as the general usage of a term is likely to yield, to make *nītiśāstra* an equivalent of ethics or moral philosophy. This is so because one may aim at attaining something which is non-moral, or unethical or immoral. In fact, the term *nīti* is used sometimes in this broad sense in such classical terms as *rajanīti* (political strategy) *kūtanīti* (diplomacy, any clever strategy), *bhedanīti* (divisive policy, a policy to create division between groups), and in such modern Indian terms as *videśa nīti* (foreign policy), *yuddhanīti* (war policy or strategy), *arthanīti* (economic policy), etc. Any one of these policies or strategies may aim at something moral, non-moral (i.e. neither moral nor immoral) or even immoral.

Because of the usability of *nīti,* in the broad sense in which an immoral strategy will also be *nīti,* even the term *nītiśāstra* can be used to denote an inquiry or system which tells us what is the best policy to adopt to achieve something which is immoral. This is the sense in which Vidura[1] uses it when he tells Yudhiṣṭhira that he should know Duryodhana's *nītiśāstra* to protect his family from Duryodhana's antagonistic actions. He says it on the occasion when Yudhiṣṭhira and other members of his family are leaving

Hastinapūra for Vāraṇāvata. Vidura knows that Duryodhana will try to keep causing trouble for Yudhiṣṭhira and his family even after their shifting to Vāraṇāvata. That is why he advises him, in a secret language, that he should know Duryodhana's *nītiśāstra,* meaning by it his scheme of evil designs, immoral moves, which he may adopt to *eliminate* his family. He offers his advice in the form of a general principle to the effect that he who knows his enemy's *nītiśāstra,* he should adopt appropriate measures to protect himself from the evil designs, immoral actions, of the enemy. The use of *nītiśāstra* here definitely means adoption of evil, immoral, designs by Duryodhana and not that of any moral means. Vidura knows that Duryodhana has no respect for ethics, i.e. *nītiśāstra,* meaning a system of morality. Still, he speaks of his *nītiśāstra,* obviously meaning by it his immoral policy of always troubling Yudhiṣṭhira's family.

But *nītiśāstra* is also used in the sense of 'ethics' in classical Indian axiological contexts, and in modern India it has become the most commonly used Indian equivalent of 'ethics' to denote ethics in its classical Indian as well as modern Indian form. This is done in contexts in which 'nīti' is used only to denote a moral policy or a morally commendable move. When this is done, the morally positive sense of *nīti* becomes more clearly visible in its adjective form 'naitika' which means unambiguously moral or ethical in a normatively positive sense. Its antonym, 'anaitika' therefore means immoral. For the same reason, *naitikatā,* the abstract known form of *naitika,* means morality and 'anaitikatā' the abstract noun form of *anaitika,* means immorality.

To make the word *nīti* directly connote something positively normative, i.e. something which is essentially moral, or ethical, some writers elucidate its meaning, i.e., interpret it to mean, only that sort of policy, or methodology, etc., which enables its user to attain his desirable ends in a desirable manner, and some even interpret it as that which leads to the attainment of the four puruṣārthas, *artha, kāma, dharma* and *mokṣa.* There is no conceptual difficulty in interpreting it in these ways which restrict the use of *nīti* to denote only a positively normative, desirable, policy. In fact, this is what has happened and in modern usage 'nīti' has acquired this normative sense. That is why to denote a policy or strategy which is immoral or undesirable the word 'kunīti' or 'durnīti' is used. Each one of the two means bad, undesirable, policy or strategy. Contrariwise, for a policy of a high moral rating the word *sunīti* is used. The upshot of all this is that *nītiśāstra* has indubitably become the Indian equivalent of ethics, an inquiry into the nature of morality. But this is not because of its etymological meaning but because of the usage it has acquired in philosophical and non-philosophical literature.

As an example of the positively normative use *nīti,* we can mention Kṛṣṇa saying to Arjuna that he, i.e. God himself, is the *nīti,* the righteous policy, of those who want to be victorious in a righteous war.[2] That by *nīti* he means righteous, or ethical, policy is clear from the context of its use. In the Pancatantra[3] of Viṣṇu Śarmā too it is used in a positively evaluative sense when he says that anyone who reads this book of *nītiśāstra,* or listens to a narration of its contents by someone else, will not be defeated even by Indra, the king of gods. On the same line of thinking, Bhīṣma tells Yudhiṣṭhira[4] that when there was complete lawlessness in the world, on the request of the gods, *Brahmā* for the first time created or presented a *nītiśāstra* consisting of a hundred thousand chapters. This work was reduced to ten thousand chapters by *Śiva,* Śiva's reduced to five thousand chapters by Indra, Indra's reduced to three thousand chapters by *ṛṣi Bṛhaspati,* and Bṛhaspati's reduced to one thousand chapters by *ṛṣi Śukra.* The details of this *nītiśāstra* which Bhīṣma narrates to Yudhiṣthira contains a miscellany of do's and don't's meant for human beings in different positions and professions. All the do's in the narration are not ethical, nor are all the don't's unethical in a restricted sense of 'ethical' and 'unethical'. But all of them are of practical significance, ensuring healthy governance by a king and a peaceful social life for an individual, and therefore normatively positive.

The use of *nīti,* and therefore of *nītiśāstra,* in the works mentioned above, can be quite sensibly taken to be fictional or mythological. But it is clear from them that classical Indian thinkers consider ethics to be essential for a meaningful and purposeful private as well as public life. It may be that the classical way of putting ethical things may not clearly reveal the ethical theory or theories from which they ensue. But there must have been some such theory or theories, constituting classical Indian ethics, otherwise the do's and don't's, ethical or normative in a broad sense, would not have been presented with the kind of force and vivacity with which they have been presented in some works of the above type. It is such works which constitute the ethical folklore of classical India.

1.3 PROBLEMS AND PREJUDICES

Any modern writer, in trying to present classical Indian philosophy of morals as a philosophical inquiry in an objective, a rational or conceptual, manner, faces some problems because of some built-in features of the classical Indian style of doing ethics, i.e. because of classical philosophers' way of ethicizing. Classical philosophers do not present clear-cut, neat, ethical theories in treatises which may be called works on nītiśāstra. Ethical ideas occur in multifarious types of contexts and in discussions of different types of problems. There are theories which they presuppose or suggest. But very often these theories are not apparent. Rather, they have to be extracted and reconstructed out of materials available. Another complicating factor is that a good number of ethical ideas occur mixed up with metaphysical and theological ideas in the contexts of discussions about the puruṣārthas, and almost always in those of the nature of mokṣa, as well as those of discussing the relation between man and god or heaven. The latter is largely the case with philosophers or poets of Bhakti schools. The result is that it is very tempting for a man of a speculative or theological bent of mind to conclude that Indian ethics is spiritual ethics or religious ethics. To hold such a view would mean that Indian ethics always presupposes some sort of spiritualist metaphysics or some sort of theology.

A fallout of all this would be that it is not meant for him who does not accept any spiritualist metaphysics or does not believe in the existence of any god or heaven. But the worst fallout would be that then Indian ethics would not remain tenable at all if the spiritualist metaphysics itself, or the theology itself, which it presupposes, is found to be untenable.

And, it cannot be ruled out ab initio that one cannot lead an ethical life if one does not believe in the doctrine of mokṣa, or that *mokṣa* may not be called an ethical value. Similarly it cannot be taken as an a priori truth that belief in god, having a theology, is a necessary condition for being moral. Rather, as will be shown in the chapter on *mokṣa,* it is not logically safe to define the concept of the moral rightness of an action either in terms of any concept of *mokṣa,* or in terms of any concept of god.

Because of the occurrence of ethical ideas in *mokṣa*-related or theological contexts, the spiritualist or theologist may think, of course mistakenly, that the non-spiritualist or atheist cannot have an ethics, or has no ethics, meaning by ethics a philosophy of morals. This is what has happened in a number of writings on the views of Cārvākas about the spiritualist-theological interpretation of Indian ethics. They are accused of having no ethics. But the fact of the matter is that they deny the spiritualist-theological interpretation of ethics, i.e. a way of understanding ethics, and not ethics as such. Rather they present a *reductio ad absurdum* refutation of the interpretation which grounds ethics on a spiritualist or theological platform. What they intend to say is that if ethics is so grounded, then since there is no convincing reason for accepting any spiritualist metaphysics or any theology which believes in the existence of god or heaven, there cannot be any reason for there being any ethics, and consequently for anybody's being ethical. But there is an ethics, a hedonist ethics, and there are individuals who follow it. Therefore, the spiritualist-theological interpretation or grounding of ethics, they conclude, is not tenable. Their argument may be invalid but its invalidity has to be demonstrated.

Secondly, hedonism is an ethical theory and one who holds it cannot be said to be a denier of ethics. It may be an invalid theory but that too is to be demonstrated, and not to be brushed aside for not being an ethical theory. It is dismaying to see modern Indian writers on Indian ethics accusing *Cārvāka*s of denying ethics and not doing that when they write on Western hedonism; rather, they unhesitatingly accept the latter as a bonafide ethical theory. They do that because they fail to notice the distinction between denying a *theory about* the foundation of ethics, i.e. one *about* ethics, which is a metaethical theory, and an ethical theory which hedonism is. *Cārvāka*s deny the spiritualist-theological metaethics and not ethics.

This interpretative, philosophical injustice done to *Cārvāka*s is very similar to the injustice done to them by accusing them of denying inference. Here too they deny a theory of inference, a metalogical theory, and not inference itself. There is a distinction between denying a *theory about* inference and denying inference. They deny the Nyāya theory about inference, which may even be called the Indian theory because in its essentials it is accepted even by the other systems. According to this theory the *hetu vākya*, the premise stating the relationship between the reason and the object inferred must be an *empirical*, universal, generalization and also *necessarily* true, and therefore the conclusion must also be *certainly* true and net just probably, or contingently, true. *Cārvāka*s deny it on the ground that an empirical universalization or generalization can have, at best, only a high degree of probability and cannot be claimed to be *necessarily* true. Therefore, the conclusion of an inference in which it occurs as a premise can also claim, at best, to have a high degree of probability and not to have certainty, or to be necessarily true.[5]

Some metaphysical presuppositions, postulates, or dogmas, in a non-pejorative sense, of Indian ethics also need careful handling. Some of these postulates are the beliefs in the karmic worldview, *rebirth*, and life in the world as essentially unhappy or full of suffering. To mention just one problem, the *karmic* worldview seems to deny human freedom of will, or human agency. In spite of this, when classical thinkers do moral philosophy they do it, nonchalantly, without questioning human agency. This means that the *karmic* view does not hinder them from ethicizing and that, according to them, the *karmic* view does not question the possibility of ethics or ethical action, though it *appears* to do that. Here too a philosophical interpretation of Indian ethics has to probe into the nature of the *karmic* theory to explore how its apparent denial of human agency is reconcilable with the possibility of ethicizing and of ethical living, or requiring human beings to lead an ethical life.

On account of the mixture of ethical ideas with theological ideas, in discussions of ethical issues quite often discussions or prescriptions of certain ritualistic performances also occur. This fact may lead one to confuse an ethical prescription with a prescription of performing a ritual. But doing that would water down the dignity of the ethical and on some occasions it elevates an unethical performance to the status of the ethical, or even to a higher status than that of the ethical. Such a thing happens when the ritual of sacrificing an animal to propitiate a deity is prescribed, and the prescription occurs in the context of discussing an ethical issue, for example, in the context of an individual's propitiating a deity for the speedy recovery of his son from a serious ailment, or for causing rainfall to protect crops yielding foodgrains when drought is likely to cause several people die of starvation. The objective, speedy recovery of his son, as well as saving many people from death because of starvation, is ethically commendable. But still, sacrificing the animal for this purpose remains unethical.

Indian ethics has been largely presented, as we shall see, in the social context of the four stages (*āśramas*) in an individual's life in a society consisting of four *castes* or varṇas, the prevailing societal situation in those times. But it is not a regional ethics, not an ethics meant to be valid only for the then Indian society, just as classical Indian logic is not presented as a logic valid for classical Indians only. Indian ethics is ethics per se, claimed to be valid for every society because members of every society form some groups or classes and every member of it passes through several stages in his life. Therefore, its interpretation has to be given in terms which make its universalist character clearly visible. It is a problem to extricate it from its social setting but it has to be done, the problem has to be solved.

A philosophical, conceptual, account of Indian ethics, therefore, has to be reconstructive. It has to put together little bits, the ethical things, said in very many different contexts, all of which not being overtly ethical. That they have been said in this way need not surprise us because there is no sphere of life, private, social, political, even intellectual or academic, etc., in which an ethical thing may not occur. The reconstruction has to be done here, as anywhere else, by putting relatable bits together by exploring the possible ways in which they can be conceptually related without doing any logical offence to what they are intended to connote or denote. In such a situation, more than one mode of reconstruction may be possible. This possibility is often a real possibility, and so it may be even in our dealing with classical Indian ethics. And, the more the ways in which it is done, the merrier it would be, considering the creative value of a reconstructive exercise. Such exercises or excursions, in any field of any classical philosophy, are very likely to contribute to making *philosophical progress.* There is no reason to think that they would not do that in the field of classical Indian philosophy of morals.

There are, however, some intellectual, interpretative, *prejudices* which, if not overcome, dissuade an interpreter from undertaking the task of a reconstructive interpretation not only of classical Indian ethics but of any area of classical Indian philosophy. Therefore, the account of some of the prejudices given here may be applied even to a reconstructive work in another area of classical Indian philosophy, of course with some suitable modifications or adjustments.

An important, or rather the most potent prejudice, against a reconstructive interpretation of Indian ethics in a modern idiom is the belief held by many about the nature of Indian ethics. It is to the effect that Indian ethics has a distinctive character on account of which it is to be presented in typically Indian colours. Any reconstructive interpretation by conceptually relating classical Indian ideas in ways not already so related in classical works, would go against the spirit of Indian ethics. Therefore, these ideas have to be presented verbatim as they occur in classical Indian works. Those who hold this belief do not realize that a viable ethical idea or principle is not a regional idea or principle with a regional shape. Its linguistic formulation certainly will be different in different languages. But if it is, say, a tenable principle applicable to Indians of a certain class, say, to *brāhmaṇas*, i.e. the individuals whose profession is to acquire knowledge and to impart it to others considered fit to receive instruction, even then it must be applicable to all such people though they are not called *brāhmaṇa* and the four-fold caste system does not exist in their society. This sort of generalizability or *universalizability* is a built-in feature of every ethical norm, principle, or practice.

Secondly, presenting relatable Indian ideas in a conceptually related fashion, even though they have not been so presented in any classical work, is not necessarily, or always, to distort their contours. Rather, it may enable them to shine better and reveal more clearly their real strengths or weaknesses. Even to reveal their weaknesses is to do them a genuine service because, then, some creative modern mind may reformulate them sans those weaknesses. This kind of reconstruction will definitely be in terms of modern conceptual terminology. Some of those who are prejudiced against such an attempt have the false fear or suspicion that it is bound to emit a foul smell of some Western methodology. In fact, this is typically an Indian methodology. The classical Indian commentarial methodology is a methodology of this very type as will be shown in chapters 2 and 3.

A reconstructive method is likely to be critical. But being critical is a philosophical virtue rather than a vice. Reconstruction and revaluation work like the motors in automobiles in the sense that they promote movement or *progress* in philosophical theorizing, and therefore in ethical thinking. There is a view held by some responsible and well-meaning scholars, Indian as well as non-Indian, that ethical theorizing in classical India gets stagnated after some time. Perhaps it does. And, if it does, it does because classical Indian technical philosophers do not pay as much attention to it as it deserves. They do pay a lot of attention to metaphysics and epistemology including formal logic and philosophical logic as well as philosophy of language. That is why they are even today available in a much more developed form than the form in which classical Indian ethics is available. But the most regrettable thing is that even modern Indian philosophers have not looked at it in a reconstructive and critical manner. Most of them, when they talk about it, they parrot an account handed down to them by some earlier uncritical, reportive, scholars. The result is that it is where it was, say, a hundred years ago, and what it was then is not an elegant philosophical, conceptual and systematic, account of what it was in the form left by classical thinkers.

The prejudices mentioned above make it difficult to solve the problems which we have noted in the beginning of this section. Such prejudices very often become as gripping as are some deep-rooted superstitions. They can be gotten rid of, as can be the latter, not by logical refutation because they are not based on any consciously formulated argument. Only an argument can be refuted, not a prejudice or superstition. The best way for a philosopher to show that they are only prejudices against giving a reconstructive account and therefore should not or need not matter, in giving such an account of classical Indian ethics in a philosophical manner, is to actually try to do it, to go ahead and give such an account in a way best suited to the temper of classical Indian ethics. Assuming that the philosopher's logical luck is favourable to him, the result of his attempt, when rightly seen as what it in fact is, is very likely to be found to be a genuinely philosophical, not a theological or purely reportive, account of Indian ethics; i.e. an account in general conceptual terms and not one in regional, or localized, terms. There would then be a good probability of the dying out of the prejudice or prejudices against interpreting Indian ethics reconstructively, offering the much-needed impetus to presenting it as ethics per se, not just as an ethics of some ancient people of some particular region. Even if they do not completely die out, they would surely be greatly weakened.

1.4 A WAY OUT

India has definitely a very rich classical, ancient, intellectual corpus a good part of which is constituted by philosophical–ethical–cultural–theological ideas. It is natural for different types of modern Indian intellectuals to turn to what the classical Indian intellectuals have done in the areas of their specialization. In doing that their motivations may not be the same, or the same all the time. For example, one may turn to the past corpus only out of curiosity to know what it is, another to get some inspiration or insight to solve an intellectual or practical problem he is presently facing, another to find solace in it because he is dissatisfied with his present, another to explore if he can find in it some materials he can use to construct a new theory, another to locate some 'jewels' of creativity which he may present to the world and satisfy his nationalist, patriotic pride, etc.

Ethical ideas are generally mixed up with cultural ideas. Almost every individual is or is expected to be, proud of his ancient culture. Many Indians turn to it more frequently and more enthusiastically or wistfully when they find their present conditions frustrating.

In being proud of one's ancient culture, one is also very likely to be proud of one's ancient ethics. But in the case of India an average Indian, who is not well-educated, or not even creditably literate, is not likely to have an authentic knowledge of what classical Indian ethics (or culture) is. In fact, such a knowledge cannot be had even by every Indian intellectual because every intellectual does not know Sanskrit, the classical language of the country in which the classical philosophy and ethics have been adumbrated. Therefore, those few who have the expertise to reach to the classical Indian ethical ideas directly because they know the language and have the conceptual ability to rightly assess their role, have a great responsibility to fulfil. It is their intellectual as well as social responsibility to ascertain what role they actually fulfilled in classical Indian life, what role they are *capable* of performing, and to what extent the role they then performed, or are capable of performing, can be said to be unquestionably a moral role on viable objective grounds. Therefore, a doctrinaire individual, committed to a social-ethical point of view, may present a classical Indian ethical idea or practice in a laudatory manner and convince an average Indian of its sacrosanctity and inviolability, even though putting this idea into practice does some gross injustice to him. The average individual does not have the ability to check the authenticity of his presentation, nor has he the logical, conceptual maturity to examine the viability, or tenability of that idea as a moral idea. Therefore, he may be exploited by the intellectual and continue honouring the practice though it is an untenable moral idea or practice as well as detrimental to his legitimate interests.

To take one classical example: Ekalavya chops off his right thumb and presents it to Droṇa as his *gurudakṣiṇā* (sacramental fee to the teacher) when Droṇa asks him to do that. He does that because he has *mentally* accepted Droṇa as his teacher though Droṇa has refused to admit him in his school and has taught him nothing. Droṇa's motive too in asking for the thumb is morally discreditable because it is to ensure that Ekalavya does not become an archer better than, or even equal to, the prince Arjuna, his favourite pupil, and Aśvathāma, his son. This demand of Droṇa, thus, is not only against Ekalavya's interests but also not morally tenable. But still Ekalavya fulfils it because he has been fed on the one-sided ethical principle that, if a teacher asks a pupil to give to him something as his *gurudakṣiṇā*, he ought to give it to him whatever it may be, moral or immoral, and whatever may be the teacher's motivation, moral or immoral, in asking for it. This is a case of an intellectual's exploiting an innocent young man's ethical credulity by invoking a one-sided, unfair, moral principle. Such cases of exploitative use, particularly of a deep-rooted, ethical idea or principle are always possible. Therefore, it is not only academically but also morally required that a classical moral idea is presented in a manner which makes it clear whether or not it is morally tenable on rational grounds and how it is conceptually related to other relevant moral ideas. A conceptual mapping of its location and relationships with other moral ideas on the map of moral categories is thus a requirement which a philosophical account of it cannot afford to ignore without itself becoming an untenable account.

One possible way of a conceptual mapping of Ekalavya's example, or of the moral idea of *gurudakṣiṇā*, has been given above. But this example has been used very well to show that in almost every case there is more than one possible way of doing the mapping. For instance, an orthodox philosopher convinced of the sacrosanctity of the varṇa and *āśrama* system of classical India may interpret Ekalavya's giving his right thumb to Droṇa as an ideal case of a student's devotion to his teacher, of his readiness to obey any order of the teacher, implying the absolute inviolability of the moral principle of a student's obedience to his teacher. This is the way for several decades in the last century the story of Ekalavya was taught to school children, and is still held to be a tenable way of interpreting it by many orthodox scholars of indology, particularly by those who belong to any of the upper castes among Hindus. But if an open-minded conceptualist philosopher looks at this interpretation, he would not need to do any serious probing to realize that treating the principle of devotion to a teacher (*gurubhakti*) as an *absolute* obligation, i.e. as an obligation which *must not* be infringed in any situation, amounts to calling absolute the principle statable as

> Any student ought to obey any order (or fulfil *any* demand) of anyone whom he considers to be his teacher (or one who is his teacher).

The moment this principle, involved in the orthodox grading of the principle of obedience to one's teacher, as an absolute principle, is clearly formulated as above, its untenability becomes obvious. This can briefly be shown as follows: it requires the student to fulfil *any* order of any teacher of his, i.e. even one which is immoral. But no principle requiring the fulfilment of an immoral order can be a valid moral principle. Secondly, it requires him to fulfil any order of *any* teacher of his which means that he ought to fulfil an order even of a teacher who has done a grave injustice to the student, or whose motivation in asking him to do something is in itself immoral. No principle making such a requirement too can be a moral principle. Thirdly, it requires him to obey any order even of one whom he *considers* to be his teacher though he has given no instruction to him, or has blatantly refused to do that. Even on this interpretation, it is not a valid moral principle. Here no right has accrued to the alleged teacher to ask the student to do anything for him; on the other hand, a right has accrued to the student to receive the teacher's thankfulness to him, or his admiration and appreciation for his treating him as his teacher even though he is not *his* teacher. Now we notice that the concept of obligation (on the part of the student to fulfil his teacher's any demand) has been found to be related to, or a bridge to, the notion of *right.*

In the classical Indian tradition a teacher has the right to receive from his student, when offered by him, his *gurudakṣiṇā* and also the right to ask the student to give to him a particular thing as his *gurudakṣiṇā.* In consequence, it is the duty of the student to give it to him. This right is a *moral right* earned by the teacher because of his having imparted instruction to the student and it is a moral duty or moral obligation of the student to give it to him. Ekalavya's fulfilment of the painful duty of offering his right thumb to Droṇa by chopping it off heightens the virtuousness of his moral character. On the other hand, Droṇa's asking him to give it to him with the immoral motivation mentioned above, lowers the virtuousness or moral dignity of his character. This means that the notions of moral duty or obligation, right, and virtue all are conceptually interrelated.

But there is another notion which is larking behind all that happens in this episode. Ekalavya does not request the *guru* (teacher) to tell him what is the reason for his asking him to give a *gurudakṣiṇā* which is going to ruin his career as an archer. A neutral, unbiased person would say that he has the *right* to ask for a reason. His giving him his right thumb is not apparently, going to do to Droṇa any good and is going to ruin his career as an archer. Therefore, he has the right to ask for its reason. This right is a *logical right* because of the unobviousness of the rationality of Droṇa's asking for his right thumb. The *guru*'s moral right to ask his pupil to gave him his *gurudakṣinā* is a resultant of the teacher–student relationship which is a relationship between two rational persons. It is not an accident that the ethics involved here, as elsewhere, is a concern of rational agents and persons. Droṇa is conscious of his moral right to receiving his *gurudakṣiṇā* and Ekalavya is conscious of his moral duty to offer it to him. But Ekalavya is either not conscious of his *logical right* to ask for a reason for the teacher's choosing such a cruel *gurudakṣiṇā,* or he lets it be superseded by his sense of duty. Thus a very important philosophical problem comes out on the surface, namely, the relationship between a logical right and a moral duty, as well as one between a logical right and a moral right.

One possibility must also haunt a philosopher here. This is the possibility of Droṇa, instead of asking for Ekalavya's right thumb, blessing him and expressing his sense of sorrow or grief for not admitting him in his school for whatever reason it might have been. If he does that, it would surely add a great shine to his moral character and water down the injustice that has been done to Ekalavya by him, or by the social system in which he has to work. It may be said it is not morally required of, or obligatory for, him to do that. This may or may not be true, but it also is true that by expressing his sense of sorrow, etc., he would show a very high level of moral integrity. This is so because his doing that, if not obligatory, is certainly supererogatory, i.e. something which is not obligatory but is still capable of heightening the morality, or the virtuousness, of the person who does it.

The high ranking of a supererogatory action is very well recognized in classical Indian ethics. A cautious ethical analyst cannot fail to see that it is suggested, may be in a subdued manner, even in the Ekalavya-Droṇa example. It is suggested because, as we have seen, we can, while reflecting on it, very vividly picture the possibility of Droṇa's directly or indirectly expiating for his not having admitted Ekalavya to his school and thereby raising his moral status. A very clear instance of a supererogatory action and its adding a great moral lustre to the character of its doer is found in the story of *Rāma.* After his return from his exile for fourteen years, he goes first to meet and touch the feet of his step-mother Kaikeyī and not to his own mother Kauśalyā, though it is Kaikeyī who is responsible for his having been required to go into exile. It is not his obligation to go to her first, nor has she any right to expect that he should. Rather, even if he had ignored her, he would have, many may say, deserved no moral blame. But he does not ignore her; rather, he adores her. And, this act of his, along with many others, makes him, as the tradition says, much higher than an ordinary, moral person, a puruṣottama (highest among moral persons) and not just a *puruṣa* (an ordinary moral person).

When looked at in a comprehensive manner, the exercise of analysing the ethical overtones of the Ekalavya–Droṇa episode throws up another, a more fundamental question. It is a question about the very *point,* the purpose or *goal,* of the social framework in which it takes place, the *point* which makes an unfolding of it reveal that the notions of moral obligation, moral right, logical right, virtuousness, etc., are interrelated. More precisely, it is a question about the goal or value which the social framework of the institution or system of education ought to seek in order to safeguard its integrity as a morally viable, well-conducted, institution. The question's thrust is that it must be this goal or value which makes several relevant moral concepts constitute a moral as well as a conceptual network of which they function as interrelated components. The interrelation of these moral or normative concepts indicates that this goal must be some such thing as imparting education by a teacher to his student in the best possible manner, in a selfless and fair manner. We shall see that the classical Indian ethical tradition accepts that this is the *value* or goal which the educational system is intended to seek. When it fails to do that, or gets derailed somewhere in the process, it would say, the reason is to be found, not in the educational system but in the social system, the varṇa vyavasthā then prevalent.

Classical Indian ethics is an important component of classical Indian philosophy. This is not to undervalue its role in classical Indian culture and religion without being isomorphic with either one of them. Therefore, to present it in a proper light it is essential to see the place it occupies in classical Indian philosophy which, like any other philosophy, is a cognitive inquiry. Even the cognitive (and conceptual) character of classical Indian philosophy has to be brought into clear focus. Doing that requires a good deal of rethinking about Indian philosophy because its cognitive character has been underplayed in a good number of interpretative writings on it. Many have overshadowed its cognitivity by declaring it to be basically a spiritual discipline. Those who take this interpretation as a correct or realistic account of it but hold that philosophy per se is a cognitive inquiry, therefore, declare that classical Indian philosophy is not philosophy proper, or not bonafide philosophy. It may be called, they say, at the most, only theology, or religious philosophy if it is to be called philosophy of some kind.

To make its cognitivity clear it is necessary, therefore, that we say first something about the nature and broad types of a cognitive inquiry. Thereupon it would be easier to assess what type of cognitive inquiry it can justifiably be said to be. Therefore, the chapter that follows will discuss two basic concepts of a cognitive inquiry. This will provide a smooth passage to the third and the fourth chapters which will characterize the Indian style of philosophizing as that of a cognitive inquiry. It is obvious that in all these chapters, rather all along even in those which follow, up to the end of the work, a good amount of rethinking and reconstructive organization of a number of relevant philosophical and ethical concepts will have to be done.

NOTES AND REFERENCES

1. *Yo jānāti paraprajñām nītiśāstrānusāriṇīm.*
   Vijñāyeha tathā kuryādāpadam nistared yathā.
   He who understands the mind of his enemy, proceeds according to his (the enemy's) *nītiśāstra*, after knowing that he should adopt such a measure which may save him from the troubles caused by his enemy. *Mahābhārata* (Gita Press, Gorakhpur), Vol. 1, p. 438.21.
2. *Nītirasmi jigiṣatām. Gita*, 10.38. I am the policy of those who want to be victorious.
3. *Pancatantra* (Choukhamba, Varanasi), p. 6.
4. *Mahābhārata*, Vol. V, pp. 4569–78.
5. For a detailed discussion of this issue, see my *Dharmakīrti's Theory of Inference: Revaluation and Reconstruction* (OUP, New Delhi, 2002), pp. 154–6.

CHAPTER 2

Two Concepts of Cognitive Inquiry

2.1 TWO WAYS OF CONCEIVING THE MOTIVATION OF INQUIRY

There may not be a general agreement about the identity of a cognitive inquiry. But one thing is clear. An inquiry is cognitive only if the human faculty or mental agency, which is predominantly operative in conducting the exercise this kind of inquiring consists in, is reason, intellect, or ratiocinative deliberation. I am using these terms in a broad sense, commensurate with the way they are used in common sense or ordinary language. It is important to emphasize their concordance with common sense or ordinary language because, if that is not done, they may be taken by a reader in this or that restrictive sense, depending on his philosophical or theoretical affiliation, or on his familiarity with the restrictive sense or senses in which they have been used in the literature he is acquainted or conversant with. Each one of these terms has been used in more than one restrictive sense in both philosophical and non-philosophical literature. This has been done by thinkers who have used any one of them to denote an agency which they consider competent to successfully conduct a worthwhile inquiry, as well as by those who have used it to denote an agency about the power or ability of which to successfully conduct any worthwhile inquiry they are extremely critical or even pessimistic. On the other hand, if these terms are used in their ordinary, commonsense, sense or senses, there is no better way to characterize a cognitive inquiry than by using any one of these terms, or their equivalents, to denote its conducting, or operative, agency. To say all this does not imply at all that this agency operates single-handed. The possibility of its taking the assistance, or collaboration, of other human powers or abilities is always open. In fact, no human power works in isolation, or in an exclusivist manner.

Every inquiry is purposive in the sense that it is conducted either to satisfy the inquirer's curiosity, i.e. his desire to understand or know the nature of a thing, or to satisfy his desire to find a solution to a problem, practical or theoretical, he is faced with. Therefore, sometimes a distinction is made between a curiosity-satisfying and a problem-solving inquiry. But the distinction is not very substantive. In every curiosity-motivated inquiry there is a problem needing a solution, a hurdle to be overcome. Śaunaka's request to Angirā to tell him what is that by knowing which everything becomes known seems to initiate him into conducting a curiosity-satisfying inquiry, i.e. an inquiry which, if conducted satisfactorily with the help provided by Angirā, will enable him to satisfy his desire to know the basis or foundation of all kinds of knowledge (*sarvavidyā pratiṣṭhā*). In a sense it is. But it is also, if we look deeper into his epistemic motivation which his curiosity really is, a problem-solving inquiry. The number of things which can be known, or which one may need or like to know, is infinite, or at least unmanageable for any individual, like

Śaunaka, because his cognitive abilities are very limited and his life-span is a limited or finite duration of time. Therefore, his problem is how to handle, or manage, this, a general human, predicament. One way to solve this problem is to find out if there is anything knowing which will make everything known and what that thing is if there is any such thing. To get this problem solved he approaches Angirā and participates with him in the inquiry that follows. This inquiry has been presented in the *Muṇḍaka Upaniṣad.* Something similar is the case with Naciketā's request to Yama, as recorded in the *Kathopaniṣad,* to explain to him the nature of the Self (*ātmatatva*) which, on the first look, appears to be a pure and simple ontological quest for the knowledge of the entity 'Self' denotes. But after Yama's telling him what it is and how important it is and revealing that it can be realized only by desireless action, the result of the inquiry is not only the satisfaction of his curiosity but also the solution of his problem of what he should aim at as his final end and what steps he should take to attain this end.

Kṛṣṇa's problem in the *Gītā* is to make Arjuna willing to fight what is called the *Mahābhārata* war because, at the last moment, when Arjuna is expected to be sharpening his arrow to shoot at the enemy, he shows his unwillingness to fight, his strong inclination to leave the battlefield on familial, consequential, and moral grounds which are not at all flimsy. This surprises Kṛṣṇa because Arjuna is a brave, invincible, fighter as well as a well-educated man fully conversant with his contemporary ethical and social norms. The inquiry which ensues through the dialogue between Arjuna and Kṛṣṇa, rather through Arjuna's arguments and Kṛṣṇa's counter-arguments and elaborations of the points which arise therefrom, does aim at motivating Arjuna to fight with full vigour. But it also results in the presentation of a full-blooded theory to the effect that every individual should conduct his life in such a way that he does, in a desireless (*niṣkāma*) manner, all that his *varṇadharma,* the set of duties assigned to the members of the class or caste he belongs to, requires him to do. This means that he should have no desire to produce any sort of consequence by whatever he does in the performance of his duties. This he should do because he will thereby not only not commit any sin but will also attain his summum bonum, *nihśreyas,* his freedom from the chain of birth–death–rebirth. In presenting this account a number of ethical, metaphysical, psychological, sociological, issues come up and are clarified by Kṛṣṇa with the result that the *Gītā* presents a complete theory about how any individual should conduct his life, and not only what a combatant should do. This it does in spite of the fact that its primary motivation is to convince Arjuna that fighting the battle, in spite of the bloodshed and killings and destruction it is expected to cause, is not only not wrong but obligatory for him. This is Kṛṣṇa's problem. Correspondingly, Arjuna's problem is to resolve his doubts about the desirability of fighting the battle in view of what it is likely to cause. But what comes out of the inquiry not only solves his problem but also satisfies his curiosity to know many things he does not know and is very keen to know. Whether or not the solution which Kṛṣṇa offers and Arjuna accepts is a faultless solution, or whether or not the philosophy of life which the dialogue presents is logically tenable, morally sound, or implementable in actual practice, is another matter, and certainly needs to be discussed. But this is not the place to do that.[1] Here it has been mentioned only to show that an inquiry undertaken with the primary motivation to satisfy a curiosity can also be, or invariably is, problem-solving.

The fusion of the two, curiosity-satisfying and problem-solving, functions of a cognitive inquiry, into each other, is an indicator of the fact that a clear demarcation between a theoretical and a practical inquiry cannot be drawn. The classical Indian inquiry which delineates the rights and obligations of the four classes or castes of people then composing the Indian society, formulated in its theory of the *puruṣārthas*, is practical because, one would say, it tells what an individual belonging to a certain caste ought to do and expect others to do for him, and what it requires to be done is intended to make, or is pointful only if it makes, the individual's private and public life better. But this inquiry is also theoretical because it can be viable from the practical point of view only if it is fortified with a cogent, logically sound, conceptual or theoretical, analysis of the concepts of rights, obligation, and some other related concepts, and can back its delineation of the rights and obligations of each class with sound justifying or supporting reasons. Similarly, an inquiry conducted with a view to ascertain whether or not it is necessary to mention the conclusion in the structure of inferential reasoning intended to be presented to someone else, is, by and large, a theoretical venture. Therefore, it may appear that it is of no practical relevance whether the inquiry concludes this way or that way. For example, it does not matter whether we accept Gautama's theory according to which the conclusion is to be stated twice: first, in the beginning of the process, as the proposition to be proven (*pratijñā*) and second, at the end of it as the proposition *proven* (*nigamana*), or we accept Dharmakīrti's theory according to which it is not at all necessary to mention the conclusion even once. But this is not really the case. A logical process, the process of reasoning in which one person presents an argument to another, is a social process in which at least two persons participate. If it is not necessary to mention the conclusion, if the mention of the premises, as suggested by Dharmakīrti, is all that is needed to enable the addressee to draw the conclusion, then the acceptance of Dharmakīrti's model will not only be time-saving, but will also make more elegant the social process of logically convincing the addressee of the truth of a proposition, which a process of inferential reasoning, or arguing, really does or aims to do. The fewer the steps in a reasoning exercise, the less will be the chances of committing a mistake or of the occurrence of confusion. This is another advantage which logical economy can yield.[2]

The practical relevance of a theory of inference, mentioned above, is of course limited to the use of inference in inter-personal communication between persons possessing a certain amount of logical or conceptual sophistication, persons who value or care for economy, elegance, or directness, in their discourse. This is also true of the problem of the search for economy, etc. in the structure of inference, which a theory of inference aims at solving. One of the problems a theory of inference has to solve is how to minimize the number of the constituents of an inference without reducing or curtailing its logical force or effectiveness. It is to solve this problem that Dharmakīrti offers his theory according to which a three-membered conjunction of a certain form is all that is required to be given to yield the conclusion. This problem too is a problem for those who are interested in the formulation of a theory of inference, persons for whom a logical problem is a problem. Such inquiries whose problem-solving performance is of a limited range, or whose practical utility is only for a limited group of people possessing a certain level of cognitive competence, are generally considered to be purely theoretical. On the other hand, many people think that only those inquiries, or the theories which they offer, are practical or problem-solving which are relevant to solving a problem arising in day-to-day affairs of the common man. There are some such inquiries or theories. But most foundational inquiries or theories are judged or found to be problem-solving, or imbued with practical relevance or value, only by people who possess a certain level of competence or a certain kind of aptitude. For example, the ritualistic side of a religion is easily felt by many to be of great practical value, or a great solver of a number of problems, but the practical or problem-solving value of the conception of god as a formless, featureless, absolute is not so easy to understand or appreciate. An individual may consider it of great value simply because his religious preceptor (*dikṣāguru*), or a certain religious book he adores, says that it is. But that is not to really understand or appreciate the value, theoretical or practical, which can justifiably be assigned to it. Very few people really understand the significance of, or all that is stored in, the concept of *Brahman* as *Satchidānanda* and the multi-faceted theory or theories which use it as their root-concept. Many, including some well-educated persons, accept the concept as their guiding star thinking it stands for a supreme reality which is eternally existent, all-knowing, and purely blissful. It will be shown in a later chapter of this volume how difficult it is to comprehend the denotatum of this concept and how different its intended denotatum is from an eternally existent, all-knowing, and totally or purely blissful being.

To take another example, the theory of liberation (*mokṣa siddhānta*) is highly theoretical as well as practical, curiosity-satisfying as well as problem-solving. But for him who is not interested in attaining liberation (*mokṣa*) i.e. does not have the desire to attain liberation (*mumukṣā*), it may not have any practical relevance, or it may solve no problem of his. He may even consider it too theoretical, or too rarified a metaphysical theory with no, or very thin, empirical or logical support. On the other hand, for him who has the desire to attain liberation, believes in its attainability, and in the tenability of any one of the theories about its nature and the method of its attainment, the theory of *mokṣa* he accepts would not only satisfy his curiosity about what ultimate reality is but would also solve his problem about what he ought to do and ought to be.

2.2 TWO WAYS OF CONCEIVING THE END OF INQUIRY

Even after accepting what has been said above as a starting-point, the end or consummation of a cognitive inquiry can be conceived in more than one way, and it has been in fact so conceived. Of the various ways in which it has been, two seem to be the most prominent or significant because each one of them plays a crucial role in determining its conduct in a definitive manner. Moreover, both of them are particularly relevant for a work like the present one which is concerned, in its conceptual as well as in its historical-developmental part, with understanding and examining the classical Indian perspective on the place of such fundamental concepts as those of value, virtue, obligation, etc., in man's personal and public life.

By the end or consummation of an inquiry I mean here the terminus, or the final end, or completion, and not the objective, aim or goal, of an inquiry into the nature of a problem theme, or object, whatsoever it may be.

'End' is used sometimes to mean the terminus, and sometimes to mean the aim or goal of an inquiry. Therefore, stating the sense in which it is used in this section is very important. The difference in the two senses is particularly relevant here because the end, meaning the aim or goal of an inquiry, may be very definite and neatly characterizable. But the search for the goal, the inquiring process, may not have a final end in the sense of a terminus because it may not be possible to achieve the goal once and for all. It may just be possible only to achieve it to an extent which is satisfactory at the time of its achievement, keeping in view the then available resources of the inquirer or the then development of the broad area of thought to which the inquiry concerned belongs. It would be possible, therefore, that it is superseded in future by a better, more comprehensive, or less vulnerable one when some new, or better, resources become available, or that area of thought reaches a higher stage of development.

About any inquiry into the nature of a fundamental concept like that of truth, value, virtue, etc., it may be asked whether or not it is possible for the inquiry to arrive at a conclusion, or a set of conclusions, which are final in the sense that there is no need for the inquiry to go on after having reached or arrived at them. Two views have been held in response to this query which amount to conceiving the end or terminus of inquiry in two different ways. I shall call them the 'No-terminus view' and the 'Final-terminus view'.

2.2.1 No-terminus View of Inquiry

According to the no-terminus view of inquiry there is no end to inquiring into the nature of fundamental concepts like those mentioned above. The inquiring process has to keep going on. What we can do, for example, about ascertaining what is our goal in life, about what we ought to do in order to be what we ought to be, is to arrive at a certain time at some conclusion, or set of conclusions, supported with the best of reasons we can procure, depending on our intellectual equipment, and act in accordance with the conclusions. But we should continue the inquiring process further because our intellectual equipment may change and develop, and further inquiry may confirm, disconfirm, or require us to modify, some conclusion or conclusions reached earlier. Even if it confirms them, it is worth the exercise because it would then strengthen our motivation to follow them. Moreover, there is no guarantee that it would *always* confirm them. The world we live in changes, the demands of life change, our needs and aspirations and capabilities change. Therefore, it is possible that our goals change and the ways to achieve them change. This means that inquiring into what we ought to aim at and what we ought to do to achieve it should be a never-ending process. To think that it has a final terminus, or that the terminus has been reached by some gifted individuals at a certain point of time and therefore there is no need to continue it further, would be inimical to our own growth, apart from being unfaithful to the facts of life we have to live. The obvious implication of this view is that we cannot accept anything as the final, absolute, truth, value, reality, virtue, etc., which we may call the last terminus of our inquiry, after reaching which the inquiry should come to an end for all time to come.

It should be clear that the no-terminus view only denies the possibility of there being a final terminus to inquiring into the nature of some fundamental concepts or problems. It does not deny the possibility of there being *temporary*, occasional, or situational, endings of the search, nor does it deny the possibility of reaching a final terminus in *each and every* inquiry. It does not deny it in such matters as making mathematical, or logical, demonstrations within an accepted or assumed mathematical, or logical formal framework, for example, within a formal deductive system or any other framework programmed on its basis. It is obvious that it does not have to deny it in constructing a formal deductive system. It has only to concede that there may be more than one formal deductive system, each one having its own terminus. But that each one has a final terminus cannot be questioned. The Whitehead–Russell system of deduction, for example, has a different terminus from that of Rosser's, but each one of them has its own final terminus because each one has its own set of primitive terms and axioms.

2.2.2 Final-terminus View of Inquiry

This view of inquiry maintains that there is, in principle, a final end or terminus to inquiring into the nature of such fundamental themes as ultimate reality, truth, obligation, highest value or goal, etc. We can arrive at a final conclusion about what we ought to believe in, do, or aim at; a conclusion which cannot be superseded by another substantially different from it. After reaching a conclusion, say, about the highest value or goal of man (*parama pada* or *puruṣārtha*) we do not need to continue inquiring into what it is any further.

A good number of classical Indian works seem to hold or imply the above view of inquiry. Most modern interpreters of classical Indian philosophy aver that this view is the view of classical Indian thinkers and also consider it the right view of inquiry. Classical thinkers and their modern interpreters, both seem to claim that the classical Indian inquiry into the nature of ultimate reality, value etc., has reached its terminus and has given a set of truths about it which are valid forever. The cognition of these truths, which marks the terminus or end of the inquiry, is said to be supra-sensuous, supra-rational, some sort of spiritual insight or intuition. This view does not close the possibility or legitimacy of an individual's starting the inquiry afresh. But a clear fallout of it is that doing that is not necessary.

Since the inquiry has already reached its consummation in the body of truths it has arrived at, according to this view, an individual can justifiably accept them without any further scrutiny done by himself. He may do that even if he has an alert, probing mind. He would not be doing anything wrong if he moulds his general life-style as suggested or required by those truths in case they pertain to his general, total well-being, i.e. to what his ultimate goal is and what the means to its achievement are. His only obligation is to properly understand what the truths mean. This he can do by studying the works in which they have been stated and adumbrated. A person who does not have the competence to study the works or understand them may also be helped by someone else, say, a teacher (*guru*), to understand them and to follow what they prescribe. In brief, in the final-terminus view, it is not necessary to pursue or push the inquiry any further after the inquiry has reached the terminus. If the classical Indian inquiry into the nature of, say, the ultimate goal or value which man should seek, has reached the terminus, then the goal, as stated by it, may very well be made every man's goal without any further examination of its achievement-worthiness or of its attainability.

It must be clear by now that the final-terminus view of inquiry assumes that it is possible that at a particular point of time some individuals achieve the highest kind of cognitive excellence any man can and that because of being equipped with it they are capable of discovering or arriving at truths which are valid for ever. When it is asserted that some classical Indian thinkers have reached some valid-for-ever truths, the assumption is certainly there that those thinkers have attained the highest kind of cognitive excellence. It is this assumption which is behind the common practice, in classical and contemporary India, of calling some classical thinkers *ṛṣis*, seers of unquestionable truths. The seeing of which the *ṛṣis* are said to be capable is not ordinary, sensuous seeing, but some sort of non-sensuous cognition. It is called seeing because it is comparable to normal, sensuous, seeing in being direct, or immediate, a kind of non-mediated non-sensuous cognition, which may also be called mystical or spiritual perception or intuition. It is comparable to seeing in another respect as well. Normal seeing, non-vitiated, non-obstructed, non-defective seeing, is unerring. If I see a crow sitting on the top of the house across the road, then there is a crow there. If it is not there, I cannot see it to be there. Therefore, what a *ṛṣi* sees to be a truth, must be a truth. Therefore, classical thinkers are called *ṛṣis* to emphasize that what they say to be true is a verdict of their direct non-sensuous experience and cannot be ever untrue, i.e. it must be true for all time to come. Herein we find an irreconcilable difference between the two views about the nature of inquiry, the no-terminus view and the final-terminus view. For the no-terminus view, no result of inquiry can, in principle, be said to be true for ever. This view may be conducive to making intellectual progress but it generates a kind of restlessness because, of course, in principle, at no point an can inquiry be assumed to rest for ever. The final-terminus view seems to get rid of this feeling of restlessness because it offers the hope that a final resting place can actually be found. Classical Indian philosophers have been claimed by modern interpreters to have maintained that such a resting place is already there; we have only to search for it. Some of them have been claimed to have actually reached it. Perhaps they have, perhaps they have not. But certainly they have very earnestly and assiduously tried to search for it. Whatever fate their search has met with, there is no doubt that the search itself is very interesting and worth understanding, irrespective of our preference for the no–final-terminus, or the final-terminus, view of inquiry. This will become clearer in the next chapter which discusses the classical Indian conception of philosophical inquiry.

NOTES AND REFERENCES

1. This topic has been discussed in *A Historical-Developmental Study of Classical Indian Philosophy of Morals* (PHISPC), edited by me. The reader may also refer to chapters 1 and 2 of my *Varnadharma, Niskama Karma and Practical Morality: A Critical Essay on Applied Ethics* (D.K. Printworld, New Delhi, 1999).
2. For a detailed discussion of this issue see chapters 12 and 13 of my *Dharmakīrti's Theory of Inference: Revaluation and Reconstruction* (OUP, New Delhi, 2002).

CHAPTER 3

Philosophizing the Classical Indian Way: A Rethinking

3.1 TALKING ABOUT AND DOING PHILOSOPHY

That classical Indian thinkers did a lot of philosophizing is a historical truth which nobody has questioned and in all likelihood nobody would ever question. But this truth is sometimes so greatly emphasized that, in the minds of many, a proneness is created to conclude that classical Indian thinkers did nothing except philosophizing, or that what they achieved in their philosophizing is higher than all that they achieved in their other inquiries. Neither of these conclusions would be a correct characterization or evaluation of classical Indian philosophizing, or indeed of classical Indian thought in general.

There is another point which is not generally recognized or given due importance. Classical thinkers did philosophize a great deal, but they did not care very much about characterizing or describing what their philosophizing, or philosophizing as such, as per their own understanding of it, consisted in. That is, they did not talk much *about* what they themselves thought of the style, or nature, of their philosophizing. This is not a strange, typically Indian, phenomenon. Early philosophers almost everywhere enjoyed more the first-order activity of doing philosophy than the second-order, metaphilosophical, activity of talking about the first-order activity of doing philosophy. Perhaps because of this, or to compensate for what their forefathers did not find time to do, modern writers on classical Indian philosophy have copiously written on what they think the Indian way of philosophizing consists in. Most of them have overdone it because they seem to have completely satisfied themselves by *describing* it and to have felt no need of doing or *practising* it, i.e. of *philosophizing* in the way they think the classical thinkers philosophized.

There is no specimen of philosophizing available in a writing by a modern Indian philosopher, done in the mode which he himself has claimed to be the mode of classical Indian philosophizing and, directly or by implication, the best mode, or at least a very viable mode, of philosophizing per se. And, this is the case when at least some of the scholars who have made this claim are considered to be highly competent philosophers. This situation is very much like that of a woman's claiming that her mother cooked dinner in such and such a manner, averring further that her mother's manner of cooking is the best manner, but never cooking her own dinner in her mother's way, even though she is, or is considered to be, a good cook. The puzzle in the woman's cooking practice would vanish if it is the case, or we simply assume, that she herself is not a good cook, that she is not capable of cooking the way her mother did, or that she is interested only in talking about the style of her mother's cooking and not at all in practising that style. But it would be uncharitable to think of the woman in this way, and so would it definitely be in the case of quite a few of the modern philosophers who have written about what they consider to be the style of classical Indian philosophizing. It would be so because, as already noted, they are taken to be very knowledgeable or respectable scholars by others in the field.

One reason, in the case of the philosophers' not themselves practising, or being able to practise, what they consider to be the classical Indian style, and also the right style, of philosophizing, may have to do, as it seems to me, with the very way they have characterized or identified the classical Indian style. They seem to have characterized it the way they have, by and large, in order to extol it, to give to it a distinctive status, higher and more elevated than the status they are willing to give to most non-Indian philosophies, particularly to the richly flourishing modern Western, more specifically, modern Anglo-American, philosophies. And, in this characterization of theirs of the classical Indian way, they seem to be totally, or almost totally, in agreement with each other.

The prevalent interpretation of the classical Indian way of philosophizing, the one which is currently in active circulation among academic circles, is a natural product of their agreement. It is quite clear and definitive. Therefore, it can very well be called the received interpretation. This interpretation makes philosophizing the classical Indian way, as will be shown in this chapter, extremely difficult, rather unpractisable or unreachable for the common run of intellectuals. Therefore, there need be no surprise when there is no practitioner of the great art which the classical Indian way of philosophizing, in its received interpretation, has been said to consist in. It is for this reason that when we call a modern Indian philosopher, say, an *Advaitin*, or even a neo-*Advaitin*, we mean either that he accepts the theories of the classical *Advaita* philosophy, or is an erudite exegete of *Advaita* theories, and not that he is a practitioner of the Advaitic method of philosophizing, i.e. one who does his own philosophizing in the way the classical Advaitins did theirs, maybe with some variation. On the other hand, when we call a modern Indian philosopher a conceptual analyst, or even 'accuse' him of being one, it would mean that he practises in his *own* philosophizing the method of conceptual analysis, though his method may be different from the method or methods of others in the field. A philosopher who is *merely* a scholar, a narrator, of what some conceptual analysts have done, would not himself be a conceptual analyst, though it is possible that an individual is both, a good narrator of what conceptual analysts have done and a good practitioner of the craft. One may very well be a good describer or historian of the development of logic as well as a good logician, just as one may be a good commentator as well as a good player of the game of cricket. But normally one would not be called a cricketer, a cricket-player, if one is only a good narrator of what has happened or is happening in a cricket game. We would not, as the *Mahābhārata* does not, call Sanjaya a combatant or fighter of the *Mahābhārata* war, though he is a perfect watcher and narrator of which combatant does what and when on the battlefield, of course by virtue of his having been gifted with a divine power of perception by Vyāsa. We would not even call Vyāsa a combatant even though he had, as the legend goes, acquired a divine power of watching and describing the war without actually being present on the battlefield, or even near the battlefield. In fact, the entire account of the war, or rather of everything which we find in the *Mahābhārata* is Vyāsa's narration.

3.2 RECEIVED INTERPRETATION OF THE CLASSICAL INDIAN WAY

The received, or prevalent, characterization of classical Indian philosophizing, which has been referred to above, is almost invariably expressed by saying that Indian philosophy is *darśana* and not mere ratiocination, or love or search for knowledge, which Western philosophy, by and large, is claimed to be. This statement is taken to be a general truth about the Indian practice of philosophizing, too obviously true to be argued for. But to me it seems equally obvious that it is neither true of the *whole* of Indian philosophy nor the *whole truth* about any sector of it. It is surprising, as the discussion which follows will show, that it has not been questioned, or that it has been given the status of a truth too clear and distinct to be given a critical look.

3.3 CLASSICAL INDIAN PHILOSOPHY AS *DARŚANA:* AN INACCURATE CHARACTERIZATION

The Sanskrit word 'darśana', from the root '*dṛs*', etymologically means visual perception or cognition. In this sense of it, or even in its extended sense to mean perceptual cognition as such, i.e. any knowledge obtainable by the use of an external sense organ as well as by that of introspection, it is obviously inadequate to be used as the designatum of classical Indian philosophy, or of any philosophy, or even of any science. Neither philosophy nor science consists in being a collection of perceptions, howsoever minutely obtained or rigorously organized. And, those who call Indian philosophy *darśana* are too sophisticated to call it *darśana* in this sense. Normally, they use *darśana* to mean non-sensuous, mystical, or spiritual cognition, as direct, immediate, clear and self-certifying as seeing something present before the seer's eyes is. Secondly, it is said to be the mystical perception or spiritual intuition, of the ultimate reality which is claimed to be not cognizable by any sense or reason. To quote Radhakrishnan, 'A *Darśana* is a spiritual perception, a whole view revealed to the soul.'[1] This view is echoed and re-echoed by many others. For example, according to Malkani, Indian philosophy is 'science of the spirit, if we may so call it. It is *ādhyātmika vidyā*. This *vidyā* has nothing hypothetical or speculative about it. It is more properly a way of direct seeing or *darśana*.'[2]

But even in this sense of *darśana* it is inaccurate to characterize Indian philosophy as *darśana*. Classical Indian philosophers do not simply state or report their spiritual intuitions. They also reflect or deliberate on them, even give reasons or considerations to convince or persuade others to accept them as authentic or veridical and suggest steps an inquisitive individual may take in order to acquire the ability to have the kind of experience which having a spiritual intuition is. It is important to realize that merely having the spiritual experience, or giving a report of what it is, is not all that is necessary to make a person a philosopher. Classical thinkers seem to have realized this truth very well.

May it, then, be said to be a correct characterization of classical Indian philosophy to aver that it is a reflective, reasoned account given by classical thinkers of their spiritual intuitions of what the ultimate, most basic reality is? Many seem to think that it is a correct characterization. But definitely it is not. The reason is that it limits too narrowly and inaccurately the scope of classical Indian philosophy to metaphysics or ontology. It leaves out a large area of Indian philosophy: for example, its extremely rich contributions to logic, epistemology, aesthetics, philosophy of language, ethics, conceptual and normative, as ordinarily understood, etc. Ordinarily ethics, conceptual as well as normative, theoretical as well as practical or applied, is considered to be an inquiry which is needed to guide an individual or a group in managing their private and public, i.e., personal, social, political, professional, etc. affairs, to help them in their wordly, day-to-day and also long-range, transactions with other individuals or groups, as well as in their dealings with their environment, both living and non-living.

In his contributions to the above as well as to some other areas of thought, a classical thinker has to use his conceptual, ratiocinative, logical ability to analyse and organize data, as well as his normal empirical ability to feel and to sensuously perceive external things and introspect internal mental states, feelings, moods, etc. In all these areas classical Indian philosophy has a lot to say, and in some of them if it does not offer well-formulated theories, it does provide a lot of raw data for theory-construction. In none of them does *darśana,* spiritual or mystical intuition, play a conspicuously significant role. Therefore, it is not intellectually or logically fair to call classical Indian studies in these areas *darśana* even if *darśana* is used to denote a reflective, intellectual study of *darśanas* or mystical experiences. Therefore, it is not fair to call classical Indian philosophy as such *darśana,* or to use *darśana* as a blanket term to cover anything and everything which classical Indian philosophers have done. A certain part of what some of them have done may be called *darśana,* but a certain part of even Western philosophy may be called *darśana* in this sense of *darśana.* Of course, saying this would depend on the assumption that there are *darśanas*, mystical or spiritual, non-sensuous, non-rational experiences or intuitions. It should also be noted that a philosophical investigation which examines the concept of mystical intuition and concludes that this concept cannot or does not have an instantiation, i.e. there cannot or does not exist an experience which the concept is used to denote, cannot itself be called a *darśana.* But for the sole reason of its being this kind of investigation it would not cease to remain philosophical. What is emphasized here is that it is not justified to call, as many writers do, the entire corpus of classical Indian philosophy *darśana,* and therefore not justified to claim that the use of, or appeal to, mystical or spiritual experience is its most basic, distinctive, and all-pervasive characteristic, i.e. a characteristic which pervades its contribution to each and every area of thought to which it has contributed.

The upshot of what has been shown in this section is that, even as per the practice of classical Indian philosophers, one's having a spiritual experience is neither a sufficient, nor a necessary, condition for one's being entitled to be called a philosopher in the Indian, or even general, sense of the term 'philosopher' or 'philosophy'. It is not a sufficient condition because the fact of *merely having* a spiritual intuition does not make the possessor of this experience a philosopher. In fact, the mere possession of no experience would make the possessor a philosopher. This is true of every cognitive discipline, philosophy, science, or any of the arts.

Having a spiritual experience cannot be called a necessary condition because, if it is, then it would disentitle a large number of eminent non-Indian philosophers to be called philosophers and most of the areas of modern philosophy to be called philosophy. Not only this, it would disentitle a good number of the areas of classical Indian philosophy to be called philosophy, and the philosophers who have done laudable work in those areas to be called (classical Indian) philosophers. This is why I have said that it is not correct to call the entire gamut of classical Indian philosophy *darśana*, or even darśanaśāstra, as is done by many many modern Indian philosophers.

3.3.1 Multiple Motivation behind the Characterization

The basic idea behind the motivation to call Indian philosophy *darśana* is a complex one. It is to highlight that the nature of ultimate reality, according to the majority of classical Indian thinkers, if not according to all, is such (i) that it can be known neither by sense, nor by reason, nor by the combined efforts of both sense and reason, but only by means of some sort of mystical or spiritual intuition and (ii) that the ultimate reality is also the *ultimate value* in the sense that to cognize something as the ultimate reality in a *darśana* (spiritual intuition) is also to cognize, or rather to realize, it as the ultimate value. A cognizer's realizing it may result in his moulding his life-style in a certain manner, or, according to some classical thinkers, to have a direct cognition that he is non-different from the ultimate reality. The second point is to emphasize that the cognition of the ultimate reality is not a neutral, purely theoretical, or conceptual, knowledge. Rather, it is life-transforming, practical experience, some sort of a re-awakening. This means that after knowing the ultimate reality an individual does not become merely more well-informed than what he earlier was. To all intents and purposes, he becomes a different, a changed, person, more elevated than what he was before the change.

It is clear that the above is an amalgam of epistemological–ontological–axiological–logical claims. The first claim can be cogently held only if it can be held that there exists in human equipment an ability to have what is meant by spiritual intuition and that there is something which can be called the ultimate reality having such a nature that it can be cognized only by spiritual intuition. This is a mixed, epistemological–ontological, claim. The second, makes a mixed, an epistemological–ontological–axiological claim to the effect that to cognize the ultimate reality is to transform one's life-style because the ultimate reality is also the highest, the ultimate, value.

The admission of both of the components of (i) is alone necessary for the entitlement of classical Indian philosophy to being called *darśana* or *darśana-śāstra*. Even if (ii) is not admitted by it, i.e. even if it is not the case that the ultimate reality is also the ultimate value, its characterization as *darśana* or *darśana-śāstra* would hold good, if it is true that it admits of both of the components of (i). Its holding (ii) is necessary for its entitlement to being called practical or axiologically motivated. It will be made clear in what follows that to characterize it as *darśana* and as *practical* is to ascribe to it two different, independent, sorts of predicates. It is logically possible that an inquiry is *darśana* but not practical, and practical but not *darśana*.

To assert (ii) is to make a more complex claim than (i). It is, in effect, to make an ontological claim because it is to claim something about the nature of ultimate *reality*, an axiological one because it is to claim something about the nature of ultimate value and its relation to reality, and an epistemological one because it is to claim something about the character of *cognizing* ultimate reality as well as cognizing ultimate value. It is also to make a logical claim because it is to assert that there is something in the very logic of the concept of ultimate reality and in that of the concept of ultimate value that to be the ultimate reality is also to be the ultimate value. It thus involves a denial of the nowadays emphasized logical claim that an evaluative sentence cannot be deduced from a purely factual, or ontological, sentence, or from a set consisting of only factual sentences.

According to it, on the other hand, to say or experience that something is the ultimate reality is also to say or experience, i.e. to entail, that it is also the ultimate value.

3.3.2 Darśana *not Necessarily Identical with Realization*
Mystics generally hold that mystical intuition, which *darśana* is claimed to be, is some sort of a non-sensuous perception, a kind of becoming or realization. But unless it is made definitional that mystical perception is a kind of becoming or realization, there is nothing logically odd in saying that mystical perception, like sensuous perception, or *Yogic* perception, may, in principle, be bare cognition of ultimate reality. *Yogic* perception, as held by the *Nyāya*, is an extraordinary, non-sensuous, kind of perception of things which are not sensuously perceivable. For example, atoms which are too minute, or certain things too distantly located in space, to be sensuously perceived, are perceived in *Yogic* perception by a *yogī*. There is no implication at all that the *yogī*, the perceiver of such a thing, obtains, or becomes, the thing he perceives. No *yogī*, or mystic *yogī*, would like to hold that in, or as a result of, having a *Yogic* perception of a thing, for example, an atom, he would become that thing (atom). Nor would he, or any sensible person, consider this becoming, if it were bound to happen, or possible, even minimally desirable. Certainly, therefore, he would not consider it, his becoming a material atom, a realization of the supreme value. If it were really bound to happen, he would prefer not to use his power of *Yogic* perception, or even not to acquire it. This would be a natural reaction of his because becoming identical with a material atom would mean his dehumanization, i.e. his transformation into a material thing which would be a being of much lower status than the kind of being he, as a human being, in his present status, is.

Any cognition, and therefore mystical cognition, of a reality can be conceived on the above pattern. Cognition, in itself, can obviously be said only to be an epistemic cause, (*jñāpaka kāraṇa*), a cause of making its object cognized or known. It need not be and generally is not, a procuring cause (*prāpaka kāraṇa*), a cause leading to its attainment or realization. This means that it needs to be proven that spiritual perception or intuition, which *darśana* is said to be, is a mystical *realization* of, or *becoming identical with*, the reality it is a mystical perception or *darśana* of.

The cognition of the ultimate reality can be said to a realization only when the ultimate reality is held to be the ultimate, or some sort of non-ultimate, value. This is so because only a value can be said to be realized or realizable. Anything real, as a blank, bare, reality, may only be known or cognized as what it in fact is, and it may be known in a direct or non-direct, in a sensuous or non-sensuous, cognition. The cognition of a bare reality may, therefore, be a neutral, a purely theoretical or information-yielding, observation that it is a reality, or that it is a reality having such and such a feature or set of features.

Classical thinkers are conscious of the above truth and therefore they imbue or identify the notion of ultimate reality with that of ultimate value. For any individual, to cognize a value as a value is, at least, to be moved, or oriented, towards attaining it, and to cognize it in a full-blooded sense is to feel its impact on his life, to realize it in his being. Therefore, what could really make the cognition of ultimate reality a realization would not be this cognition's being a *darśana*, a spiritual intuition. Rather, it would be the ultimate reality's being the ultimate value, or even just a value. The notion of ultimate reality as the ultimate value (or simply a value) is quite distinct from the notion of ultimate reality as simply an existent. Anyone who admits that the ultimate reality is also the ultimate value should have no logical hesitation in admitting that the intuition of ultimate reality is the realization of ultimate value. But many writers on Indian philosophy seem to aver that the intuition's being a realization, a becoming, is an independent, self-sustaining, truth about the character of Indian philosophy. They seem to have missed the truth that an intuition is only a mode of cognition. The claim to its being a realization is consequential to a particular notion of the object it is said to be a cognition of. This object here is said to be the ultimate reality, and the notion of ultimate reality which makes it a realization is the notion of ultimate reality as the ultimate value, or even value. Therefore, what is most basic in the characterization of Indian philosophy is not that it is *darśana*, or based on *darśana*, but that the root concept of its metaphysics is the concept of reality as value and not simply reality as existent.

A cognition of a reality may just be a cognition or revelation of what it is, and nothing more or less than that. Therefore, there would be nothing odd if anyone says that even the spiritual intuition of the ultimate reality is nothing more or less than the cognition of its being such and such. But if the ultimate reality is also the ultimate value, then it may be said that knowing that it is, in a spiritual intuition, is not simply a cognition, but a kind of becoming, a transformation, or realization. However, this also can be claimed only if it is held that the cognition of value is different from the cognition of a fact, empirical or logical. It is different in the sense that it not only yields information about what the cognized object is, but also has an impact on the being or character of the cognizer, insofar as it produces in him a change in his attitudes towards, or ways of looking at, the thing cognized. Therefore, it may guide his thought-patterns and action-patterns which may even amount to basically, drastically, changing his personality. Therefore, ultimate reality being, according to classical Indian views, also the ultimate value, the knowledge of ultimate reality is also the knowledge of ultimate value. To hold further, as this kind of ontology or axiology does, that this knowledge of ultimate reality or value is a kind of realization of the ultimate value, is thus a variety of what in modern analytical philosophy of values is called the non-descriptivist or non-cognitivist theory of the knowledge of values. According to the latter theory, knowledge of a value has built into it the potentiality of being attitude-changing and action-guiding[3], whereas knowledge of any fact does not have such a built-in potentiality.

If there is smoke on that hill, then it is an empirical fact that there is smoke on that hill. The cognition of this fact by a cognizer of it may not produce any effect on any of his attitudes or actions, i.e. it may not incline him to act this way or that way. Similarly, it is a logical fact that if there is smoke on that hill, and wherever there is smoke, there is fire, then there is fire on that hill. Even knowing this fact may not incline the knower to act this or that way. But, one may say, knowing that it is a good thing to sit near a place which has fire when it is cold, would incline the knower who feels cold to reach that place. The thrust of this view is that the cognition of a fact may leave the cognizer cold, indifferent, or unmoved, but the cognition of a value would not, the intensity or extent of impact of the cognition being determined by the strength of the cognizer's conviction about the veracity of his cognition and his estimation of the value cognized. Therefore, as the claim goes, spiritual intuition being fully convincing and the value cognized by it being of the highest status, the impact of spiritual intuition is sure to be extremely deep and extensive.

If a case were made that reality as value could be cognized in a non-mystical way, then Indian metaphysics would not be *darśana* or *darśana-śāstra.* But it would still retain its claim to being a realization of value, to its being practical or axiologically motivated, provided that its claim to reality's also being a value were sustainable. Similarly, if it were shown that all, or the majority of, Indian metaphysical theories held that reality is a pure existent and not at all a value, but they also held that reality was cognizable only in mystical intuition, Indian metaphysics would retain its right to being called *darśana* or *darśana-śāstra,* though it would cease to be axiologically motivated. To conclude, to hold that Indian metaphysics is *darśana* and to hold that it conceives of reality as value, not merely as a neat existent, is to make two logically independent claims about Indian metaphysics. It may be that both are valid claims. But that the conjunction of *both* of them is true of it is a contingent matter. It is not the case that if one of the two is true, the other must also be true, and if one is false, the other also must be false. And, on top of all this, there is the other important truth that the entire corpus of Indian philosophy is not *darśana,* or even *darśana-śāstra,* in the specific sense in which *darśana* is used in calling Indian philosophy or Indian metaphysics *darśana* or *darśana-śāstra.* Therefore, there is not much point in declaring that Indian philosophy is philosophy in a sense very different from the sense in which Western philosophy is philosophy simply because it is *darśana* and the latter is not. But if we agree to use *darśana* or *darśana-śāstra* as the Sanskrit or Indian equivalent of the English 'philosophy', as we normally do, there is nothing wrong in calling a sector of Indian philosophy, or of any philosophy for that matter, *darśana.* But then it would be as accurate to call that sector philosophy, as it would be to call it *darśana.* It is high time to stop fussing about such matters of nomenclature. Therefore, in this work we shall continue calling Indian philosophy philosophy without any fear of being inaccurate. This would not be against the existing academic practice of the use of the term 'philosophy' or 'Indian philosophy' by philosophers as well as non-philosophers, except in some of their orchestrated performances on some ceremonial occasions.

3.4 CLASSICAL INDIAN PHILOSOPHY AS ESSENTIALLY RELIGIOUS: AN UNFAIR FALLOUT OF 2.2

The way of looking at classical Indian philosophy suggested above does not mean, or even imply, that classical Indian philosophy assigns no role, or that it assigns an insignificant role, to spiritual intuition. Even after adopting this way of looking at it, a scholar may call it *darśana* if he pleases. But he must not forget that, in point of accuracy, it is only Indian metaphysics which can be called *darśana,* or better, *darśana-śāstra.* We can thus still make good sense of the basic idea behind the motivation to call Indian philosophy *darśana,* even if we do not consider it to be an inquiry conceptually different from what we mean by the English word 'philosophy'. This is so because we must not forget that only some raw data of a metaphysical theory, or any theory, can, at the most, be said to have been supplied by *darśana.* The further task of constructing a theory, i.e. a philosophy of any sort, out of them can be performed only by reason. That is why the word *śāstra* has to be added to the word *darśana* to yield *darśana-śāstra* if we are enamoured of this term as a label for a classical Indian metaphysical theory, for example, for the metaphysical theory which can be read in some of the *Upaniṣads.*

But too much hammering at a point is quite often counter-productive in any discipline, and therefore in philosophy as well. This seems to have happened in the characterization of Indian philosophy. Many eminent Indian writers have overemphasized the mystical-spiritual-*darśana* aspect of Indian philosophy, and claimed it to be its distinctive and most prominent feature. This overemphasis surely amounts to being unfair to other important aspects of it. In addition, it also seems to be responsible for some Western scholars' thinking that Indian philosophy is not philosophy in the current sense of the term 'philosophy'; at the most it can be called theology, or religious philosophy. Heinrich Zimmer, a widely read author in India and abroad, notes with dismay that when he was a student 'the term "Indian philosophy" was usually considered to be self-contradictory, a *contradictio in adjecto*, comparable to such an absurdity as wooden steel'[4] and that only one of the then professors of philosophy in Germany, Paul Deussen, lectured on Indian philosophy in philosophy classes. Even Zimmer himself, in spite of his saying all this and his great sympathy for Indian philosophies, considers such eminent Indian philosophers as Śankara and Rāmānuja comparable to religious thinkers like St. Augustine, St. Thomas Aquinas, Pascal, et al. He calls Śankara and Rāmānuja 'the great Hindu divines'[5] not even the great Hindu philosophers, let alone calling them just great philosophers. Even Th. Stcherbatsky called Dharmakīrti a great Buddhist logician, and not a great logician, in his *Buddhist Logic*, Vol. 1[6], a work in two volumes which has been given, for several decades, much more importance than it really deserves. It is heartening to see that in the last two or three decades of the twentieth century, Zimmer's cause of dismay had been dispelled, or begun to be dispelled. Western scholars have now begun to realize that Indian philosophy is not theology or religious philosophy, but philosophy, having as hard a cognitive or ratiocinative core as any worthwhile philosophy may have.

Zimmer's dismay, which only incongruously goes with his condescendingly calling Śankara and Rāmānuja great divines, and not great philosophers, provides a good occasion for rethinking why Western scholars have been inclined to call Indian philosophy theology or religious philosophy. The main reason, it seems to me, is, as already hinted at, the importance given by some Indian writers to its metaphysics and their overemphasizing the latter's mystical character, going to the extent of considering its mystical character the unique and distinctive feature of the entire body of thought called Indian philosophy. In the Western tradition generally mysticism and any discourse about moulding an individual's life-style in the light of his own, or anyone else's, mystical, or even non-mystical, experience of any sort, are considered to belong to religion, or theology. They are not considered to belong to philosophy proper, including even philosophy of religion.

It is not even remotely intended here to say, or suggest, that Indian philosophy does exactly what Western philosophy does, or that it would be worthwhile philosophy only if it does what the latter does. But if Indian philosophy is philosophy, then it cannot be absolutely different from Western, or any other, philosophy, as is, for example, cheese different from chalk. Moreover, any attempt to prove that it is would not be worth its salt because, if they really are absolutely different from each other, then at least one of the two would not be philosophy. In fact, there would be a point in proving that *Indian* philosophy is different from *Western* philosophy only if both are philosophies, and that is why the difference has to be only in this or that respect. And, this may be the case even with two specimens of Indian or of Western philosophy.

Zimmer refers, as already quoted, to some German philosophers' considering the term 'Indian philosophy' self-contradictory. This obviously means that what Indian philosophy denotes, or is said to denote, cannot be called philosophy and therefore calling 'Indian philosophy' philosophy is self-contradictory. And, the reason for their thinking this is provided by Zimmer himself in his calling Śankara and Rāmānuja 'the great Hindu divines'.[7] What his saying this amounts to is that two of, or most of, the classical Indian philosophers, are primarily religious thinkers, and that if any philosophy is present in their thinking it is there to meet some demands of, or to render some service to, their religious goals. To be brief, this way of understanding Indian philosophy amounts to saying that Indian philosophy is religion, or, nearer to religion than to what, in the West, or nowadays, is called philosophy.

If is true that in modern academic circles, not only in the West but also in India, philosophy and religion, in general acceptation, have become different kinds of disciplines. Any one of the two may sometimes have some impact on the other, as it may have on science, literature, art, or even political practice. But they would do that while retaining their separate, independent individualities or identities. In any classical discipline, several things are mixed up or discussed together. But it does not mean that all of the things discussed together are conceptually or categorially of the same type. Philosophical and religious things, in the modern sense of the terms 'philosophical' and 'religious', have been discussed together in many classical Indian works. But that would not prove that the two types of things are non-different from each other, let alone prove that Indian philosophy is non-different from religion. Even some classical Indian philosophers' discussing something religious, thinking that it is philosophical, or discussing something philosophical, thinking that it is religious, would not make Indian philosophy non-different from religion. Similarly, some classical Indian philosophers' presenting a scientific theory, thinking that it is a philosophical theory, or presenting a philosophical theory, thinking that it is a scientific one, would not entitle us to say that classical Indian philosophy is non-different from science, or that classical Indian science is non-different from philosophy.

It is not at all the case that by characterizing Indian philosophy as religious, or as inexorably linked with religion, we gain some conceptual advantage in assigning to classical Indian philosophy the high status which we think it deserves. Nor it is the case that we loose that advantage if we do not characterize it that way, i.e. if we characterize it as non-religious or as areligious. To claim of any philosophy that it is a great philosophy because it is religiously inspiring is as childish or futile as it is to claim of a singer that she is a great singer because she is tastefully ornamented.

To think that the spirit or individuality of classical Indian philosophy resides in its possession of a distinctive religious flavour may do injustice to its purely philosophical merits. It may do that in a direct way by encouraging the adopter of this point of view to ignore the real philosophical strengths of classical Indian philosophy. Or, it may simply stand in the way of his correctly seeing and assessing them. It may also work in an indirect but quite drastic manner. Suppose that a philosopher is convinced of the validity of the religious mode of characterizing the character of Indian philosophy. Also suppose that he, as a philosopher, considers philosophy and religion to be conceptually different kinds of disciplines, and philosophical creativity as conceptually different from religious inspiration, as any philosopher worth mentioning nowadays does. It is obvious that he can do all this without denying the importance of either philosophy or religion in human life. Such a philosopher is very likely to be led (or misled) to conclude that Indian philosophy is really religion and not philosophy. He may still accord to it a high status but only as a religion, and not as a philosophy. Therefore, since, according to him, philosophy is not religion, or does not have to radiate religious fervour, he may even say that the term 'Indian philosophy' is self-contradictory, as the philosophers referred to by Zimmer did, considering it comparable to 'wooden steel'. His argument would be, if expanded, to the effect that the term refers to a discipline as philosophy which is not philosophy (because of its being religion). Therefore, it is self-contradictory, he may be construed as saying in defence of his claim, just as the term 'wooden steel' is, because it refers to an object as steel which is not steel (because of its being wooden).

The kind of misunderstanding of the character of Indian philosophy stated above, is generally committed by writers who consider classical Indian metaphysics to be the whole, or the heart, of Indian philosophy and the religious contents of its classical metaphysics as its sole, or most important, contribution to the thought of the world. It is to this class to which the professors referred to by Zimmer, Zimmer himself, and a host of other scholars belong. If a scholar of this class considers philosophy to be basically different from religion, for him it would be a very smooth passage to make the more comprehensive accusation that not only the term 'Indian metaphysics' but even the comprehensive term 'Indian philosophy' is self-contradictory.

On the other hand, another scholar, who does not sharply distinguish between philosophy and religion, and finds the religious, or religious-metaphysical-mixed, content of some classical Indian philosophical works ennobling or inspiring, may become overenthusiastic in his admiration for them as marvels of Indian philosophical achievement. This seems to be true of some of the oft-quoted observations of Paul Deussen and Arthur Schopenhauer on the philosophy of the *Upaniṣads*.

3.4.1 Roots of the Fallout

It is worth exploring if there exists any reason in the writings of some modern Indian philosophers on the character of classical Indian philosophy which has prompted Zimmer's professors and their ilk to think that classical Indian philosophy is primarily religion or theology, and not the kind of cognitive discipline which philosophy, in their sense, or in the modern sense, of the term, is. I am very much inclined to think that there is, and not on flimsy grounds. Many Indian writers even today locate in the alleged religious effulgence of classical Indian philosophy the feature which, they think, not only distinguishes it from Western philosophy but also makes it in some sense superior to the latter. That a good number of modern Western scholars consider classical Indian, or rather Indian, philosophy not very different from religion, is testified from the fact that many Western, particularly American and Canadian universities, employ Indians with a master's, or doctoral, degree in philosophy to teach Indian religions in their departments of religious studies. Most of Indian 'philosophers' teaching abroad teach Indian religions with no compunction that they are philosophers and not scholars of religion. In all likelihood they lack the awareness of the fact that cultivating expertise in any sector of classical Indian philosophy is different from doing so in any Indian religion, in spite of the fact that some of the scholars of classical Indian philosophy have supplied to some Indian religions some of their basic metaphysical and axiological ideas. This practice has hindered both the study of Indian philosophies as philosophies and the study of Indian religions as religions. The result of all this is that many scholars do not make the distinction between Hindu philosophy and Hindu religion, Jaina philosophy and Jaina religion, Buddhist philosophy and Buddhist religion, etc.

Even most Western scholars who have written on any area of Indian philosophy, ethics, or Indian logic, are theologians, teachers in departments of religion, Indologists, or Sanskritists. To the best of my knowledge no eminent Western moral philosopher, or philosopher, with the lone exception of Arthur Danto[8], has written on Indian value theory, or ethics. But surprisingly, Danto's book has not received from Indian readers even a fraction of the attention which, to mention only a few examples, the Indologist-theologian Th. Stcherbatsky's *Buddhist Logic* (Dover) and the Sanskritist D.H.H. Ingalls' translation, *Materials for the Study of Navya Nyāya Logic* (Harward Oriental Series, Vol. 40, Cambridge, Mass., 1951) have, though neither of the two authors is a logician. Even Zimmer, from whose book I have quoted, is an Indologist. So are most of the early and modern Western writers on Indian philosophy. This is true even of the majority of Indian writers on Indian philosophy teaching abroad, except a few like J.N. Mohanthy, since they belong to the department of religious studies and teach courses in Indian religions. It is a common belief among Western scholars that an 'Indian' philosopher, who holds an Indian degree in philosophy or a degree in Indian philosophy, is competent to teach Indian religions, i.e. religions of Indian origin, like Hinduism, Buddhism, Jainism, Śaivism, Vaiṣṇavism, Śaktism, etc. But the same group of Western scholars do not hold a similar view about the competence of the common run of philosophy graduates from a Western university, say, American or British, to teach a course in any religion, whether of indigenous or non-indigenous origin.

Among Indian writers who emphasize, or rather overemphasize the religious temper of classical Indian philosophy, Radnakrishnan is the foremost. His writings have been very influential in the West as well as in India. In fact, he seems to have set the stage for characterizing Indian philosophy as essentially spiritualist and religious. Many scholars still think that his characterization is cent per cent accurate as well as successful in establishing the superiority of Indian over Western philosophy. Referring to the philosophical thought of classical Indian masters, he says: 'Thought, when it thinks itself out to the end, becomes religion by being lived and tested by the supreme test of life. The discipline of philosophy is at the same time the fulfilment of a religious vocation.'[9] This he says in the last chapter, entitled 'Conclusion', of his two-volume work on Indian philosophy. The obvious implication of it, therefore, is that Indian philosophy is essentially or inextricably religious. Any such assertion definitely amounts to theologizing the character of philosophy done by classical Indian thinkers. This view has been repeatedly held by many others.

One of the reasons for Radhakrishnan's and many others holding the above, or a similar, interpretation of the character of classical Indian philosophy, is the fact that in a good number of classical Indian works some philosophical and some religious views have been mixed up with one another, discussed without marking out their differences, or discussed in the same context. This also is the case with some other views or ideas, which we would now call scientific. This is true of ancient works of some other countries as well. It is possible that what a classical thinker presents is really a philosophical theory or idea but he thinks it to be a scientific one, or vice versa. It is also possible that in classical times the distinction between philosophy and science was not clearly marked. I think this was really the case. Be that as it may, if such a thing has happened in classical

Indian thought, it does not entitle an interpreter to say that classical Indian philosophy includes or is non-different from science, or vice-versa. Even if some classical works do not make the distinction between them, since nowadays it is considered worthwhile to do that, it is incumbent on a modern interpreter to distinguish the philosophical from the scientific ideas discussed in classical Indian works. In the case of Indian science this fact seems to have been adequately recognized. By tracing out scientific ideas in some classical works which are considered to be rich in their philosophical-religious content, say, the *Vedas*, historians of Indian science claim that some classical works do contain a good amount of what is nowadays called science.

What has been said above about classical Indian philosophy and science can, *mutatis mutandis*, be said about classical Indian philosophy and religion or theology. Instead of saying that classical Indian philosophy is religious, an interpreter should say that classical Indian thought is rich in both, in what nowadays we call philosophy and in what we call religion. He would, of course, have to support his assertion on the basis of objective, unbiased study of relevant classical Indian works. There is nothing unusual in adding this as a precondition because it is a precondition for making a cognitive claim about any corpus of thought, classical or non-classical, Indian or non-Indian.

A prime reason for calling Indian philosophy religious philosophy or theology seems to be its concern with *mokṣa* or liberation. The attainment of *mokṣa* is considered by the majority of Indian philosophies as well as by Indian religions to be the highest end which an individual ought to realize and can realize. Excepting the *Cārvākas*, all the other systems of Indian philosophy admit the reality and attainability of *mokṣa*. Some of them use different names for it. For example, Buddhists call it *nirvāṇa* and *Sānkhya* thinkers *kaivalya*. They do this to convey differing connotations of the concept of *mokṣa* resulting out of their differing metaphysics, their differing conceptions of the nature of the ultimate reality, more specifically, their differing theories of the nature of the Self. But there is one feature of the concept of *mokṣa* which may be called central, and with regard to this feature, all of them agree. This they do notwithstanding the fact that according to some of them *mokṣa* is a state of the Self which can be attained by an individual only after his physical death, the termination of his bodily existence (*videhamukti*), while according to the rest of them it can be attained by a seeker during the very life in which he seeks its attainment (*jīvanmukti*).

The central, common, feature of the concept referred to above, is that with the attainment of *mokṣa*, the attainer would never be reborn after the termination of his present life. In brief, it is the absolute cessation of its attainer's liability to be reborn. In fact, under all the different names for it used by different Indian systems and in spite of differences in the content of the concept admitted by them in their detailed characterizations of it, the concept of liberation (*mokṣa*) denotes, for all the systems, the complete termination of the liberated individual's liability to be reborn once and for all. That is why it is commonly summarily said to be the state of absolute freedom from the beginningless chain of birth–death–rebirth. The latter is, quite naturally, said to be the condition of bondage, and therefore *mokṣa* is said to be freedom or emancipation from this bondage. Therefore, in this work the term *mokṣa* will generally be used to denote the state of liberation and the other terms used by some systems will be used if and when their specific characterization of the state will need to be discussed or referred to. These are not discussed here because a detailed discussion of the role of the concept of *mokṣa* in Indian value theory will be given later in a separate chapter.

Mokṣa is also said to be a goal of religious aspiration, a prime objective of leading a religious life. Different Indian religions prescribe some religious disciplines, rituals, and ethical codes of conduct which an individual has to follow to attain this goal. But it is also an ontological state, a reality, because it is a state of the Self, rather the original state of the Self, and in attaining, or rather realizing, it, it is necessary to have an authentic knowledge of its nature. It is this knowledge which constitutes, according to some wholly and according to others largely, the content of classical Indian metaphysics. If an individual's knowing what the Self is, is also to realize it, to be or to come back to, the state of his original being, to what he originally is, then knowing the self is also attaining *mokṣa*. Therefore, an interpreter can say that the goal of Indian metaphysics and that of religion is the same and therefore Indian metaphysics is religious metaphysics. If he identifies Indian philosophy with Indian metaphysics, he can then very smoothly slide down to the more comprehensive conclusion that the whole of Indian philosophy is religious. This is what Radhakrishnan and following him many others seem to have done. It is clear, however, that this line of thinking, in all fairness, can at the most show that Indian metaphysics, and not that the whole of Indian philosophy, including its logic, epistemology, etc., is religious.

In the case of Indian metaphysics too it can show that only that sector of metaphysics is religious which aims at ascertaining the nature of the Self. It would not, for example, show that the sector of it which explores the nature of the ultimate constituents of matter, say, the atoms, is a specimen of religious metaphysics. Nor would it show that the sector which ascertains the basic types, or categories, under which all that there is, all that can be said to be real, may be arranged or organized, for example, the categoriology of the *Vaiśeṣika* metaphysics, is a metaphysics of the religious variety. Therefore, if the Indian metaphysician's concern with *mokṣa* is made a ground for calling Indian metaphysics religious, it would justify calling a very tiny segment of Indian philosophy religious, and certainly not calling the whole of it religious. And it would justify calling religious only some, and not all, metaphysical systems religious.

Like some other themes, metaphysical and religious or theological themes have not been always discussed in well-marked separate sections in classical Indian works, nor have they been always sharply differentiated therein from each other. But when we closely examine some of the contextual frameworks in which a topic like that of *mokṣa* has been discussed, with a little bit of analysis, we clearly notice two different modes of talking about it. Some discussions of *mokṣa*, as a state both real and ideal, are theoretical, ratiocinative and analytical. Not only do they present arguments in support of a particular characterization of it, they also attempt to refute, by giving counter-arguments, some arguments which have actually been given as well as some which may be given against that characterization. On the other hand, in some other contexts and sometimes in the same contexts that characterization has been talked about at some places in a neat, cut and dried, practical and persuasive manner, and is accompanied by an account of the steps a *mumukṣu*, a person desirous of attaining *mokṣa*, should take in order to attain it. Such portions of the discussion give the impression that the characterization of *mokṣa* talked about in them is undebatable and therefore the *mumukṣu* should go ahead in patterning his life-style in the manner suggested in order to realize his *mokṣa* as characterized therein. Śankara's *Vivekacuḍāmaṇi* and Vidyāraṇya's *Jīvanmuktiviveka*, among many others, are good examples of both of the two modes.

The abstract, ratiocinative, mode of talking about something can very well be called metaphysical, and the straightforward, action-guiding, mode religious or theological. Such classical ventures may be described in more than one way. We may, to be fair to their spirit, call the ratiocinative parts metaphysical and the practical ones religious. We may as well say that they present a metaphysics with a religion as an adjunct of it, or a religion well-grounded in a metaphysics. Depending on which one of the two we consider more prominently talked about in some relevant contexts, we may even say that in some of them theology has been metaphysicized, and in some others metaphysics has been theologized. All this is being said here to bring out that, as said earlier, it is not correct to say that Indian metaphysics (or philosophy) is not metaphysics (or philosophy) but theology (or religious philosophy). Rather it is possible to present Indian metaphysics (or philosophy), at least a large part of it, in non-theological, non-religious, terms. That it is also a better, or fairer, way to do that will be shown in the next, the concluding section of this chapter.

3.5 REASONS FAVOURING NON-THEOLOGICAL CHARACTERIZATION OF INDIAN METAPHYSICS

Classical Indian metaphysics is broader than what nowadays 'metaphysics' is generally taken to denote. It is broader because, in a sense, it also includes axiology, or at least a good part of axiology. It does that because in all, or almost all, Indian metaphysical systems, the ultimate reality is also the highest value, or closely linked with the highest value. Therefore, we can say that it includes what may becalled a metaphysics of value, or that a good part of it is what may be called axiological metaphysics. Therefore, what will be said of Indian metaphysics below will also apply, *mutatis mutandis*, to axiological metaphysics.

Many writers have presented classical Indian metaphysics in deep religious colours. But, as has been said at the end of the last section, there are some good philosophical reasons for presenting it in a religiously neutral, or non-theological, way without doing any injury to it. Formulating a criterion of reality, determining what can and what cannot be called real, ascertaining whether or not there is something which can be called the absolute, ultimate, or supreme, reality, which sorts of relations may hold among supreme realities if there are many such realities, distinguishing what may be called secondary or phenomenal reality from the supreme reality and ascertaining the relation between the two, determining the relation between reality and value, etc., are bona fide jobs which Indian metaphysics does as seriously and meticulously as any metaphysics may be expected to do. Therefore, an Indian metaphysician is well within the bounds of metaphysics when, on the basis of his explorations, whatsoever they may be, he concludes, for example, that the Self is really such, and such, that it is the supreme reality, that the Self is also the supreme value or very close to the supreme value if we draw a scale of values, that to know it is also to realize it, etc. To hold the claim that to know it is to realize it he would obviously need a theory of knowledge which gives an account of the nature of knowing which knowing the Self is and shows that this kind of knowing is a kind of realizing the object, i.e., the Self, it is the knowing of. He may even say that this kind of cognition cannot be had merely by the use of sense or reason, singly or jointly; the use of intuition or spiritual experience is necessary for it. The tenability of any one of his conclusions, of course, depends on the soundness of his logic, of his reasoning, i.e. of the evidences, he gives in support of them. Classical Indian philosophers realize the importance of giving reasons in discussing the issues mentioned above and other metaphysical issues they deal with. And, their discussions can very well be presented, elaborated, or examined in a non-theological way.

It is true, no doubt, that they also outline, in some works of theirs, the steps an individual should take to realize the Self, the supreme value, i.e. to attain his *mokṣa*, his liberation. This, the practical, job of advising, or guiding, an individual about what he should do to attain his highest spiritual end, may justifiably be said to be the job of religion. Every religion provides help to an adherent to attain what it offers to him as his highest value. Therefore, what we can reasonably say is that many classical Indian philosophers give not only a metaphysics of reality and value but also a religion outlining the steps anyone desirous of attaining the highest value, as characterized by it, should take in order to attain that value. This would mean that they not only have given a metaphysics, but also a religion. This would be fairer, or truer, than saying that they have not given a neat metaphysics, a philosophy of reality and value per se, but a theological or religious metaphysics or philosophy.

The fact of the matter is that Indian metaphysics, like any other metaphysics, gives a theory of ultimate reality. But the ultimate reality, according to it, is also the ultimate value. Therefore, anyone who accepts it and is desirous of attaining the ultimate value, needs to be shown the way to do that. Some of the metaphysicians have tried to do this work as well. Since this kind of work is what a religion is expected to do, in having done it they may be said to have given rise to a religious discipline too. It is worth recollecting here that some of the leaders of what is called the Bhakti school, the school of devotional thinkers, have accepted a metaphysical theory given by another thinker, a metaphysician, and in the light of it presented an account of a religious discipline, a religion, which their disciples are required to follow. They do not have a metaphysics of their own. But they do have a religion, or a sect of a religion, as per their own conception of a religion, capable of enabling their disciples to realize the ultimate reality or value as conceived in the metaphysics they have accepted. All this shows that an Indian metaphysics may suggest a certain religious outlook, or may or may not even be congruent with another. But it is not the same as a particular religious outlook or religion; that is, it is not essentially religious or theological.

The above way of looking at Indian metaphysics keeps intact its philosophical, i.e. metaphysical-axiological, character, without making it essentially religious. It does not have to leave the seeker of liberation in the dark about what to do in order to attain his liberation. At the same time it keeps open the possibility of an individual's being a pure metaphysician interested in formulating, understanding or evaluating a theory of reality, as well as the possibility of his being both a metaphysician and a religious seeker or preacher, with the awareness that being a metaphysician is not the same as being a religious seeker or preacher and vice-versa.

For a modern philosopher writing on, or philosophizing in, the classical Indian style of philosophizing, there would accrue so many advantages from interpreting Indian metaphysics as not being essentially theological, or theologically committed. It would throw open to him many valuable philosophical alternatives. For example, he may just do a minute, neutral, logical analysis of the concept of reality or of value. He may even analyse the concept of *mokṣa* in order to assess the role it can, or cannot, legitimately play in the general theory of human values (*puruṣārthas*) in which it is given by the tradition the highest place. He may do this exercise from a purely non-theological point of view, following dispassionately the lead of his logic in arriving at his conclusion or conclusions. He may, in this venture, locate no deficiency in it, or discover a serious logical problem in accepting the concept as denoting a viable goal of aspiration for an individual of the kind any one of us is, for a real, empirical, person we are acquainted with, for one with the kind of nature and nurture any one of us is circumstanced to have in the world we have to willy-nilly live in. He may or may not locate any conceptual hurdle in accepting the tenability of some of the theories, like those of rebirth (*punarjanma*) and Karmic retributivism, which are the necessary associates, not only of the theory of *mokṣa*, but also of the classical Indian worldview.

Critiques of the type mentioned above and some similar ones would be legitimate philosophical excursions in classical Indian metaphysics. We may call them conceptual or analytical, but brush them aside we cannot. We cannot call them non-metaphysical, non-philosophical, or non-Indian. We cannot do that on the bare ground that they are non-traditional or incongruent with any prevalent interpretation of the tradition. We also should not.

Such open-minded, free, or freelance, if you like, enterprises may indicate some possibility or need of revising, rethinking, Indian metaphysics, of constructing a fresh metaphysics or metaphysical theory, or rather a fresh metaphysical-axiological theory, using some of the ideas from a classical Indian metaphysics as some of its building-blocks. Anyone's doing this kind of creative philosophizing, if luck favours his venture, would neither be impermissible philosophy, nor impermissible by the spirit of classical Indian philosophy. Looking for some bricks and stones, or locating some bricks and stones, in a classical theory to construct a new one was a respectable philosophical practice in classical India. In fact, this is what Śankara has done in his commentaries; he has used some of the ideas of the *Upaniṣads*, the *Brahmasūtras* and the *Gītā* as bricks and stones in constructing his theory of *Advaita.*

Another philosopher may succeed, by following a similar course, in constructing a metaphysical theory different from Śankara's theory as, for example Rāmānuja did, or even a theory different from all classical Indian theories. Raising an objection against the latter, or calling it hurtful to the spirit of Indian philosophy for the simple reason that it is opposed to classical theories would not be a fair philosophical move by any standard of philosophizing, Indian or non-Indian.

Some interpreters think that the *parā-aparā vidyā* distinction, made in some classical works, provides a good ground for treating Indian metaphysics as religious metaphysics and also for rating religious metaphysics higher in merit or status than a religiously neutral one. But the point of the distinction is something different. The arrow in the distinction is intended, as will be shown in the chapter which follows, to draw our attention towards the superiority of an axiological inquiry over a non-axiological inquiry, and not to that of a religious over a non-religious one, nor to that of every philosophical inquiry over a scientific one.

NOTES AND REFERENCES

1. S. Radhakrishnan, *Indian Philosophy* Vol. I (Allen & Unwin, London, 1923), p. 44.
2. G.R. Malkani, 'Philosophical Truth', *Philosophical Quarterly*, Vol. 22, No. 4 (1950), p. 208.
3. See my *Karma, Causation and Retributive Morality* (ICPR, 1989), chapters 3, 4 and 6.
4. Heinrich Zimmer, *Philosophies of India* (Motilal Banarsidass, New Delhi, 1990), p. 27.
5. Ibid., p. 28.
6. See the Preface of my *Dharmakirti's Theory of Inference: Revaluation and Reconstruction* (OUP, New Delhi, 2002).
7. Zimmer, op. cit., p. 28.
8. See Arthur C. Danto, *Mysticism and Morality* (Penguin, UK, 1976).
9. S. Radhakrishnan, *Indian Philosophy*, Vol. 2 (1941), p. 771.

CHAPTER 4

Parā and *Aparā Vidyā*: Superiority of Inquiry as Realizing Highest Value over Other Inquiries

4.1 *PARĀ* AND *APARĀ VIDYĀ*: CONTEXTUAL SETTING OF THE DISTINCTION

The Sanskrit adjective *para* means *parama, sarvoccha*, the supreme, highest. *Vidyā* means wisdom, knowledge, inquiry. It is a noun and feminine in gender. *Parā* is the feminine form of *para*. Therefore, *parā* is used to quality *vidyā*, giving the compound form *parāvidyā*. *Apara* is the apposite of *para*, and its feminine *aparā* the opposite of *parā*. Therefore, the opposite or contrary of *parāvidyā* is *aparāvidyā*. *Aparāvidyā* is a compound formed in the same way as is formed *parāvidyā*. *Apara* or *aparā* therefore, means that which is not *para* or *parā*, i.e., that which is not the highest, the supreme, the most basic or foundational, kind of inquiry, and aparāvidyā any inquiry which is not the highest, supreme, or foundational. It is thus an inquiry of a lower order or rank. To call any inquiry parāvidyā is to accord to it the highest status and to call another *aparāvidyā* is to accord to it a lower status.

It is obvious that only one inquiry can be given the highest rank. We cannot even say that a certain *type* of inquiry is of the highest rank. The very concept of a type implies the possibility of there being more than one token or specimen of it. If we say that an inquiry of type P is of the highest rank and there are two inquiries of this type, Q and R, then we shall be forced by our own logic to say that both Q and R are of the highest rank. This would mean that Q is of the highest rank and R is also of the highest rank. But we can say this neither of Q nor of R. To have the highest rank is to have a rank higher than the rank which any other comparable object has. This is true neither of Q nor or R. Q cannot be said to have a rank higher than the rank which all other inquiries of its type have because there is R, an inquiry of its type, having a rank than which its rank is not higher. For a similar reason, R also cannot be said to have the highest rank, i.e. a rank higher than the rank which all other inquiries of its type have, because its rank is not higher than the rank of Q, another inquiry of the same type as its own, i.e. of the type P.

The *parāvidyā–aparāvidyā* distinction occurs at several places but its account in the *Mundaka Upaniṣad* is very significant for its conceptual discussion which is the objective of this section. The reason for my saying this is that it also gives a concrete context in which the account occurs. Even if the historicity of the persons participating in the dialogue is not convincingly ascertainable, the importance of the context it mentions cannot be doubted. It cannot be doubted because it is a good specimen of a possible situation in which a question of the type, which the distinction aims at answering, can arise, or be raised by an inquisitive individual.

The context, as recorded in the *Mundaka,* is as follows:

Śaunaka, a householder desirous to attain the highest kind of knowledge, requests, with due respect, the saint-philosopher (*ṛṣi*) Angiras to impart to him the knowledge of that by knowing which everything that there is becomes known.[1] Śaunaka's request or question seems to imply that he assumes that there is some such thing knowing which would yield the knowledge of all that there is, or of all other things which are worth knowing. But it first needs to be proven that there is such a thing because it is possible that there is no such thing. If there is no such thing, a quest for the knowledge of such a thing would not be different from a wild-goose chase. Śankara's explanation of this implication, real or apparent, is that Śaunaka's request, if made fully explicit, is to impart to him the knowledge of that, if there really is any such thing, which would make all other things known. He has not used the 'if-clause' in the expression of his request only to protect its brevity.

It is obvious that unless there is such a thing, its knowledge cannot be had and therefore cannot be communicated to anyone. Śankara's explication is that it is an open question in response to which Angiras is free to say that there is no such thing and therefore there is no point in seeking its knowledge, if he is convinced that there is no such thing. Since he is convinced that there is such a thing, he proceeds to answer the question the way he does; that is, by explaining to him the nature of the inquiry which yields the knowledge of it and also the nature of some other inquiries which do not. The *Muṇḍaka Upaniṣad* in which this discussion has been recorded also tells us what this thing is and therefore what sort of knowledge its knowledge is. According to Śankara's interpretation of the *Mundaka* position, this thing is the *Brahman* or the Self, and to know it is to know that the Self, which is the same as the *Brahman,* is alone real and nothing else is. In this section the nature of this reality will not be discussed because here we are concerned with ascertaining the *nature of the inquiry* whose subject of study this reality is. We are not concerned here with the nature of this reality itself, nor with the justification of giving to it the ontological status that is given by Angiras, Śankara and others, nor with the question whether or not such a status can justifiably be given to anything whatsoever.

There is another ambiguity, or unclarity, in Śaunaka's question which has not been noticed in the tradition but which should not be ignored by anyone who discusses the nature of his query today, in the year 2007. The question is likely to suggest that he wants Angiras to tell him what is that by knowing which every detail about everything which exists would become known. Knowing any actual feature of anything existent is an empirical matter. All such empirical details about everything, or even about a particular thing like the colour of the body of the pen with which I am at the moment writing, can obviously not be known once and for all by knowing the nature of anything howsoever basic or foundational it may be. Nor is it worthwhile to know every detail about everything even if it were possible to do so. Obviously, then, Śaunaka, who is a serious and judicious seeker of knowledge, is not likely to ask Angiras to impart to him the knowledge of a reality which is either not possible or not worth imparting and seeking. Therefore, his intention or motivation has to be interpreted in some other way.

Śankara[2] thinks that his motivation may be interpreted in either of the following two ways: It is possible that he has heard some learned people saying that there is such a thing knowing which by an individual makes everything known to him i.e. makes him omniscient. Or, Śaunaka knows that anyone, who knows what the substance, or metal, called 'gold' is, also knows what the different varieties of gold are. Therefore, using his common sense, he thinks that if there is any basic substance from which everything else has come out, then by knowing that substance he would know everything that there is.

Either one, or even both, of the two possibilities may, à la Śankara, be true of Śaunaka. He may be interested in ascertaining from Angiras what that thing is, if there is such a thing, whose knowledge makes its knower omniscient. He may equally sensibly be motivated to ascertain whether there is a substance or reality the knowledge of which enables its knower to know all things that there are, just as knowing the nature of the particular substance gold enables him to know what the different varieties of golden things are.

It seems to me, however, that even the above, quite liberal-looking, interpretation of Śaunaka's question, given by Śankara, does not bring out to the surface, in clear vision, the philosophical point of Śaunaka's query. To be omniscient means to know every detail about all that there is, or that there may be, i.e. everything about everything which is empirically real or possible. The knowledge of the basic substance, from which everything empirically real has come out, and from which everything empirically possible may come out if it every becomes empirically real, however, can make its possessor cognizant only of the fact that such and such is the substance from which a particular thing, say, my pen, has come out, or out of which it has been made. It would not make him cognizant of every real feature which it presently has or may have in future, unless we assume that it neither has, nor can ever have, any new feature, formal or substantival, which the basic substance does not have.

To make the above assumption would virtually amount to denying, without proving, the possibility of the occurrence of any change in the nature or structure of anything which exists, or may at any time exist, in the empirical world. It would also amount to denying, again without proving, the possibility of the occurrence of any change in the relationship which one empirical thing may have with any other thing of its own type, or with anything of a different type. All this would mean that there cannot be anything in an empirical thing, in a collocation of empirical things, or in the totality or collocation of all things which the empirical world is, if it does not exist in the basic substance. This would be a clear affirmation of the unreality of change in the world, that is, of the non-difference of everything of the world, as well as of the world itself, from the basic substance. If this is done, then certainly knowing what the basic substance is, would be knowing everything which is there. Therefore, one may say, by knowing the basic substance the knower would become omniscient (since he would then know everything which is there).

The unpleasant implication of the view stated above would be that the assertion of a knower's acquiring omniscience, knowledge of everything that there is, by acquiring knowledge of the basic substance, would be only the assertion of his acquiring knowledge of the basic stuff by acquiring knowledge of the basic stuff. That is, it would be the assertion of a clear truism. It would have to be a truism because everything which is there has been claimed to be non-different from the basic stuff. That is why knowing the basic stuff is knowing the basic stuff and not knowing the different varieties of empirical things actually found in the empirical world, in the world we live in, or are acquainted with, or in the world Śaunaka lives in or is acquainted with. This would obviously mean that to know the basic substance is not to know everything that there actually is and therefore not to be really omniscient. The knower of the basic substance can be said to be omniscient only if we define omniscience to mean knowledge of the basic substance and nothing more or less than it. But this would amount to making a verbal point and therefore to transforming Śaunaka's genuine question into a verbal one. It would, because it would be answerable by adopting the verbal device of defining omniscience as meaning nothing other than knowledge of the basic substance if, of course, there is such a substance.

Śankara's use of the common-sense example of gold as an instance of a basic substance is relevant only to the verbal point the truism stated above makes, rather than to the point it is intended by him to make. An individual who knows that there is a substance called 'gold', or what gold is, would not know, solely as a result of this knowledge, what the very many different kinds of things made out of gold are, things which are as different from each other as, say, as a (gold) nib is from a (gold) nosepin. As a result of knowing what gold is, the knower would certainly know what is the substance of things of a certain class, of the things made out of gold. To know this is, in a sense, to know what they are. But certainly it is not to know everything or every important thing about what they in fact are. A lady may know that both a gold nib and a gold nosepin are made out of the same substance, gold, yet she may not know that a gold nib is a part of a writing instrument and a gold nosepin a decorative ornament to be worn by a woman on only one side of the end of her nose.

Śaunaka's question is important but certainly the motivation in asking it is not that he be informed of what is that knowing which would make him omniscient in the sense of knowing everything about everything that there is or may be. The verbal expression of his question does, however, suggest that it is. That is why Śankara interprets it is the way he does, specifying that he wants to be informed of the basic stuff out of which everything that is has come, assuming that knowing what this stuff is, is to become omniscient, to become informed of everything about everything. But to become omniscient in this sense is neither possible nor desirable, as has been shown above. Therefore, we have to interpret his use of the phrase 'all, or everything becomes known' (*sarvam vijñātam bhavati*) in another way which would also amount to interpreting the concept of being omniscient in a sense different from the sense in which it means being cognizant of everything about everything that is there, or that may be there. We have to do some such thing if we take his quest as really serious and well-intentioned, and not as a misoriented quest, which it in fact is not. That we should do it and even the direction in which we should go in this journey have clearly been suggested in the very beginning of the *Muṇḍaka*.

The *Mundaka* begins with asserting that the knowledge of *Brahman*, which Brahmā imparts first to his eldest son, is the basis of all other kinds of knowledge (*sarvavidyā-pratiṣthā*).[3] It is this knowledge which is later in the dialogue said by Angiras to be the *parāvidyā*, the highest kind of knowledge. It is this, the basis of all other kinds of knowledge, which, we shall see, Śaunaka seeks from Angiras. By requesting Angiras to tell him what is that by knowing which he would know everything that is there, Śaunaka seeks to be imparted the knowledge of that thing whose knowledge is the *basis* or justifying ground (*pratiṣthā*) of all other kinds of knowledge (*sarvavidyā*), i.e. of the knowledge of all other things that there are, or there may be. Therefore, his motivation in asking the question he asks Angiras to answer is not to become omniscient, in the sense of becoming the knower of everything about everything, but to have that sort of knowledge which is the *justifier* or *certifier* of, which contains the reason for, every other kind of knowledge's being (veridical) knowledge. That is why Angiras begins his answer by explaining to him the nature of this kind of knowledge, the highest kind of knowledge, which he calls *parāvidyā*. He also mentions the inquiries which are of the lower kind, *apara*, so that Śaunaka may not call an *aparāvidyā* a *parāvidyā*. He does not begin forthwith by proceeding to tell him in a cut and dried manner what that thing is whose knowledge is the highest kind of knowledge. The mention of that thing comes a little later.

Let us make a little more clear the *justificatory* character of Śaunaka's intention in asking the question he requests Angiras to answer. The adoption of procedure by Angiras to answer it may appear to be inappropriate if we limit our gaze only to Śaunaka's verbal presentation of his query. We may think that it would have been more appropriate if Angiras had proceeded straight on to telling him the identity of that basic stuff whose knowledge would have made Śaunaka omniscient, if there was such a stuff and Angiras knew what it was, rather than his taking the detour of first explaining what constituted *parā* and what constituted *aparā vidyā*. But if we are cognizant of the breathing spirit of the classical Indian pursuit of knowledge, the general motivation behind its propensity to inquire into the nature of reality, or, rather, into the nature of anything whatsoever, we would soon realize that it is always guided by the normative belief that any inquiry is to be conducted only if it ought to be conducted, only if conducting it is pointful or worthwhile. We may even say that its spirit is pragmatic. In a sense it is, but not in William James's or John Dewey's sense, but in Charles Pierce's or C.I. Lewis's sense, the sense in which the pursuit of any inquiry is worthwhile only if it has the potentiality to help its pursuer to lead an all-round satisfying and well-informed life, not necessarily limited to the fulfilment of the needs of his mundane, earthly, existence. It is the knowledge of this kind of stuff or truth, which Śaunaka begs Angiras to pass on to him so that he knows what is that the knowledge of which makes any inquiry worthwhile. The knowledge of such a stuff is, therefore, found to be foundational or basic. It is also found to be infused with *normative force* or justifying power. It is by virtue of this force or power that some inquiries are worthwhile and some others unworthy to be conducted, and among worthwhile inquiries some higher or more elevated than some others. Therefore, it is quite appropriate for Angiras to proceed, in answering Śaunaka's question, by giving a characterization of the nature of the highest, the most basic, kind of inquiry, which is what the Sanskrit term *parāvidyā* means.

4.2 *PARĀ* AND *APARĀ VIDYĀ*: THE DISTINCTION CHARACTERIZED

As already said at the end of the last section, Angiras begins his response to Śaunaka's question by saying that, as per the tradition, the knowers of *Brahman* (*Brahmavidyā*) have unhesitatingly been saying that that there are two kinds of knowledge (*vidyā*) to be acquired, or inquiries worth conducting (*veditavya*). Of these two, one is of the highest kind or status (*parā*), and the other of not the highest, but of a lower kind (*aparā*). It is important to note here that both of the two kinds of inquiries are worth conducting, or both of the two kinds of knowledge are worth acquiring (*veditavya*).

This means that the lower, *aparā*, kind of inquiries are not to be shunned or looked down upon. Ranking them as *aparā*, lower, and thereby contradistinguishing them from what is ranked as *parā*, the highest, is, therefore, to highlight some other point and not to forbid or discourage their cultivation. This point, as we shall see, is that the *parā* inquiry, that which is given the highest rank, is basically concerned with the acquisition of the highest value (*parama puruṣārtha*), with the consummation or fulfilment of the final, most comprehensive, goal of human life. An *aparā* inquiry is also not uncalled for, or of no use, since it serves some important needs of human life, but it is not *primarily* or *directly* concerned with the acquisition of the highest value.

This is the clear implication of calling both the kinds of knowledge *veditavya*,[4] which means worth pursuing or acquiring, implying thereby that the subject-matter of both are worthy of being known. This is a fair reading of the intention of the distinction in the *Muṇḍaka*. It may be interpreted differently, i.e. given a different colour, by a philosopher to fit in with his own philosophical orientation or predilection. It will soon be shown that such a thing has happened with Śankara's characterization of the distinction. But what has been said above clearly shows that the intention of the original statement of the distinction in the *Muṇḍaka* is not to declare that the inquiries which come under the *aparā* category do not constitute worthwhile knowledge, or are of no value at all.

The *aparā* category consists, according to the *Muṇḍaka*, of all the four *Vedas, Ṛgveda, Yajurveda, Sāmaveda* and *Atharvaveda*, science of pronunciation (*śikṣā*), code of rituals (*kalpa*), grammar (*vyākaraṇa*), etymology (*nirukta*), metre (*chanda*), and astrology (*jyotiṣa*). The *parā* category, on the other hand, consists of the inquiry by which the Imperishable (*akṣara*), the ultimate reality, is known (*jñāta*), or attained or realized (*prāpta, adhigamyate*).[5] This is so because the word *adhigamyate*, used to state what is achieved by the cultivation of *parāvidyā*, means 'is known' (*jñāta*') as well as 'is attained, or, realized' (*prāpta*). That is, by its cultivation the ultimate reality is known or realized. Therefore, it would be in order if an interpreter claims that *parāvidyā*, the higher of the two kinds of inquiries, enables its successful pursuer to know, or to attain or realize, the ultimate reality. The pursuer cannot attain it without first knowing what it is. Therefore, an interpreter may explicitly only say that it enables the pursuer, to attain it, because he would then, *ipso facto*, be also saying, by implication, that it enables him to know it. He may, therefore, even use the two terms, 'know' and 'realize' (or 'attain'), in talking about ultimate reality, synonymously, since knowing it is realizing it in his usage.

The general consensus of classical as well as modern interpreters of classical Indian philosophy is that, according to the *Upaniṣadic*, or rather the entire classical Indian philosophical, corpus, excepting the *Cārvākas*, the nature of ultimate reality as well as of knowing it is such that knowing it is the same as attaining or realizing it. It would obviously follow then that an interpreter of the *Mundaka* conception of *parāvidyā* would be free to say that *parāvidyā* results in the knowledge of ultimate reality, or in the realization of ultimate reality, or in both the knowledge and realization of ultimate reality, as it suits his temperament or the context of his discussion.

It is this identity or isomorphism of knowing and realizing which is claimed to be the main cause or reason of Indian philosophy's being a practical, and of its not being a purely intellectual or theoretical, pursuit. Maybe that is really the case. But it seems to me that there is also present in at least some classical Indian philosophies a conception of a purely intellectual understanding, or knowledge, of the nature of ultimate reality which, only when supplemented with some practical measures, they would say, turns or results into a realization of it. They, however, would also add that only after turning into realization the intellectual cognition of ultimate reality deserves to be called proper or right knowledge of ultimate reality.

While commenting on the *Muṇḍaka*'s 1.i.5, referred to in note 4, what Śankara says about *parāvidyā* amounts to averring that *vidyā* in *parāvidyā* means 'the realization of the thing to be known' i.e. the realization of the ultimate reality, the Imperishable, which is for him the *Brahman* or the Self. It does not, according to him, mean merely the knowledge derived from understanding the 'assemblage of words found in the (books called) *Upaniṣads*'. This *vidyā*, or realization, he goes on, 'is called the higher knowledge since, even after the mastery of the assemblage of words, the realization of the Imperishable is not possible without some other efforts consisting in approaching a teacher and so on, as well as cultivating detachment.'[6]

From the lines quoted above, it is clear that *some sort of knowledge* of ultimate reality is attainable by an individual by reading an authentic book, or a set of authentic books, about what it is, hearing oral accounts of what it is presented by learned men in their discourses, from informal, cultural–religious–social talks and tales, etc. In fact, many people form their metaphysical–religious–axiological opinions, even their opinions about god or what they consider to be the ultimate reality, by these means. Certainly such opinions will not constitute *parāvidyā*. But what Śankara intends to emphasize is that even a knowledge of ultimate reality arrived at as a result of a well-conducted, meticulously pursued, course of intellectually understanding the contents of standard works on the nature of ultimate reality, say, the *Upaniṣads* and some other books like Śankara's commentaries on them, would not be *pāravidyā*. It is possible, though, that an individual possessing an astute intellect and sincere motivation reads the above-mentioned books, does not find any defect in their presentation, is convinced by what they say, and, therefore, accepts the view about the nature of ultimate reality adumbrated in them. He would have, Śankara or many a modern interpreter would say, only an *intellectual* knowledge of ultimate reality and not a realization of it. Therefore, his knowledge of ultimate reality would not be a specimen of *parāvidyā*. To convert it into a specimen of *parāvidyā* he would need to go to a competent spiritual teacher (*guru*), cultivate detachment or desirelessness (*niṣkāmatā*), etc. That is, he would have to follow a practical, spiritual discipline (*sādhanā*).

All this is what an individual ought to do to realize the ultimate reality. He ought to realize the ultimate reality because the ultimate reality is also, according to the majority of classical Indian thinkers, the ultimate value. It is by realizing it that he attains what is his highest end or objective (*parama puruṣārtha*). The achievement of this objective can be attained, thus, only by cultivating *parāvidyā*. We can even say that *parāvidyā* consists in realizing the ultimate reality, and not in a mere intellectual knowledge of it. The acquisition of none of the inquiries listed under the head *aparā* can do that. For this very reason all of them are considered lower than or inferior to *parāvidyā*, though this does not mean that all of them are useless. This being the real purport of the distinction between *parāvidyā* and *aparāvidyā*, it was said earlier that the point of the distinction was not to downgrade a certain set of inquiries or studies but to give the highest place to that inquiry which enables or helps man to attain his highest end, his sumum bonum. Suppose it is shown by someone sometime in the near or distant future, in a conclusive manner, that it is not the realization of the ultimate reality, but something else, which is the highest value. Or, it is shown that nothing can be called the ultimate reality, and therefore the realization of ultimate reality must yield the position of the highest value to something else. In all such cases, too, it would be in keeping with the classical Indian distinction to call that inquiry *parāvidyā* which would then enable or help man to attain his highest end. If someone shows convincingly that there is nothing which is eternally, for ever, the highest end, but different things in different times deserve to be called the highest end, even then the distinction would remain valid. In that case, different inquiries in different times would be nameable as *parā* if different inquiries are needed to help man to attain his highest end in different times. All of these alternatives are hypothetical possibilities. But to rule them out *ab initio*, to hold it as an a priori truth that none of these and similar alternative positions can or will ever be held, that no *other* conception of ultimate reality, of knowledge of ultimate reality and of ultimate value, better in merit than, or equivalent in merit to, the *Upaniṣadic* or the classical Indian conception of these things, encapsulated in the *Upaniṣadic* theory of *parāvidyā*, can or will ever be put forth by the human mind, would amount to holding a too closed view of the capabilities of the human mind. It would mean that the human mind even today is not, and would never be, even as creative as it was in *Upaniṣadic* times, what to speak of having developed, or of developing anytime, into a more creative agent. It would also smack of some sort of ancestral pride or prejudice because it would amount to holding that our forefathers have done such great philosophical things that nothing different from them but of equivalent merit or better than them can be done or needs to be done. What a reputed philosopher, the late Professor Kali Das Bhattacharya once told this writer about another reputed philosopher, his elder brother, the late Professor Gopinath Bhattacharya, in response to a query about the writings of his elder brother illustrates that such a pride or prejudice is not just imaginary. He told the present writer that Professor Gopinath Bhattacharya held that there was no need for writing anything in philosophy because everything worth writing had been written by our forefathers (i.e. classical Indian philosophers).

What I want to emphasize is that we do not have to deny the possibility of alternative conceptions of ultimate reality, knowledge of ultimate reality, or ultimate value, or the possibility of anyone's today or tomorrow holding a view about these things better in theoretical or practical merit. We do not, because as long we accept that there is something which is the highest value, whatever may be its nature, no matter whether it is eternal or non-eternal, absolute or relative, there would be an inquiry into what it is and how it can be achieved. That inquiry would then be *parāvidyā*, and all inquiries not concerned with the highest value would be *aparāvidyā*, as per the *Upaniṣadic* mode of distinguishing between *parāvidyā* and *aparāvidyā*. This mode would not work only when a nihilist position is held, a position according to which there is nothing which can be called a value. But even then there would be inquiries dealing with non-values. A different criterion may still be provided to classify those inquiries into *parā* and *aparā vidyā*, though this criterion would have nothing to do with the pursuit of any value.

The *Mundaka* statement of the distinction, on a common sense, philosophically non-committal, reading of it, does not mean or imply, as already pointed out, that any one of the inquiries under the *aparā* category is not a genuine inquiry, or that it does not yield any worthwhile knowledge. And, in fact, none of them is unworthy of being cultivated. For example, the *Vedas* are deservedly claimed by many, Indian as well as non-Indian, scholars of repute, to be the earliest records of human thought. They constitute the bedrock of a large sector of classical Indian thought. The *Cāraka*, Jaina and Buddhist thinkers do question their authoritativeness. But they do that largely because they are claimed by some of the then thinkers to be revealed texts, or texts possessing sanctity of such a type that the validity or truth of any one of the views expressed in them cannot be questioned. If they were treated by the then thinkers as *human* documents, of whatever importance they preferred to attach to them, and the views expressed in them were considered open to rejection, refutation, or modification, in the manner in which views expressed in any human document are, howsoever important they may be, they would not have rejected them, or would not have rejected them outright.

The utility of other *aparā* inquiries, likewise, cannot be denied. *Śikṣā* the science of pronunciation, what is nowadays called phonetics, even if it is meant to be the science explaining how *Vedic* words are to be pronounced, is useful because it helps the hearer to understand their meaning. The performance of *kalpa*, the code of rituals, too, serves some purpose. The performance of a ritual may not yield the result it is claimed to yield. But still the performance may give some satisfaction to the performer that he has done at least a part of what he should have done to attain his objective. This satisfaction may be only psychological, or a consolation. But even then it would be useful because it would help him to keep his mental balance at least to some extent intact. *Vyākaraṇa*, grammar, is similarly an important science for understanding the structure and function of language, *Vedic* or non-*Vedic*, as well as a necessary tool for successful linguistic communication. The importance of *nirukta*, etymology, the science of derivation of a word from its root, frequently used in explaining the meaning of certain words in Sanskrit writings, too, cannot be denied. Similarly, the importance of *chanda*, metre, in poetry, is too obvious to be emphasized.

It is true, however, that none of the disciplines included in the *aparā* category is concerned, or directly concerned, with the knowledge of ultimate reality and acquisition or realization of the highest value, the two being, as has been shown earlier, identical. Even the study of the *Vedas* is not. The concept of *mokṣa*, the highest end of man according to classical Indian philosophies, is not present, or not clearly present, in the *Vedas*. Therefore, the primary reason for calling the above inquiries *aparā* is their not being concerned with the knowledge of ultimate reality or the attainment of the highest value, and not their being of no use at all in human life.

Parāvidyā is really the name of the inquiry concerned with the knowledge of ultimate reality, or to say the same thing, the attainment of ultimate value. Śankara says very straightforwardly: 'That, after knowing which all becomes known, is the subject-matter of the higher knowledge of Brahman.'[7] The *Mundaka* too says in unambiguous terms that the Immutable, i.e. *Brahman*, is the highest end (*mahatpadam*), the most desirable for all (*vareṇyam*) and the highest among all desirable things (*varistham*).[8] Śaunaka's request to Angiras, in effect, is to be informed of the nature or identity of this very thing. Angiras's response to him is that it is *Brahman* and *Brahman* is known, not by studying the *Vedas*, etc., but by the higher kind of inquiry which is very different from studying the *Vedas*, etc. Since it is the highest reality or value, the inquiry which leads to its knowledge or realization is naturally higher than or superior to all other inquiries dealing with things other than *Brahman*, the highest reality and value, or rather the reality as the highest value. The subject-matter of the inferior (*aparā*) inquiries is therefore bound to be of a lower status than the subject-matter of the higher, the *parā*, inquiry because the *parāvidyā*'s subject-matter is the highest reality which is also the highest value.

Anyone who cultivates *parāvidyā*, 'who knows that supreme *Brahman* becomes *Brahman* indeed (*Brahma eva bhavati*). In his line is not born anyone who does not know *Brahman*. He overcomes grief, and rises above aberrations, and becoming freed from the knots of the heart, he attains immortality.'[9] All this means that the knower of *parāvidyā* is freed from bondage i.e., the chain of birth-death-rebirth, from all kinds of suffering which any embodied being, i.e., any individual, is bound to experience as long as he has not realized *Brahman*. That is, knowing *Brahman* is to attain the highest end of man, i.e., *mokṣa*. None of the *aparā* inquiries, howsoever meticulously cultivated, can enable him to attain this end.

The upshot of what has been said above is that *parāvidyā* is the inquiry which enables its cultivator to attain his highest end. Any other inquiry whose cultivation does not have the capability to do that is *aparā*. The latter may also be useful because its cultivation may be of some instrumental value in helping the cultivator to attain some of his cherished goals in his day-to-day, mundane life as long as he is not liberated. Therefore, to call an inquiry *aparā* is not to condemn it outright.

An impression may be created by a remark of Śankara in his commentary on 1.i.4 of the *Mundaka*. He says therein that *aparāvidyā*, 'the lower knowledge, is, instead, ignorance'[10] (*avidya*). Again, in his commentary on 11.ii.1 he says that its subject-matter being unreal, it is 'the domain of ignorance'.[11] He reminds us again and again that the subject matter of *parāvidyā*, on the contrary, is the truth which can never be sublated. But what any *aparāvidyā* offers as a truth is not of that type. This is the case because its subject-matter is not the ultimate, eternal reality, that is, reality in the true sense of the term. Its subject-matter is unreality and that is why knowing it is not different from remaining ignorant of reality.

The position of Śankara, stated above, is more a terminological than a contentual characterization of *aparāvidyā* (and also of *parāvidyā*). Śankara's notion of reality and truth is a very restrictive one. In his sense only that is real which is eternal and only that is true which is unsublatable. Therefore, it becomes a terminological matter to say that only that sort of inquiry whose subject-matter is eternal and which yields unsublatable truths would yield genuine knowledge and constitute a genuine inquiry. Consequently, only such an inquiry would be entitled to be called *parāvidyā*. No other inquiry would. Therefore, the result of cultivating any inquiry of the latter sort would not be different from cultivating ignorance. This means that such an inquiry would be at the most an *aparāvidyā*, if we want to call it a *vidyā*. When Śankara calls an *aparāvidyā* 'a domain of ignorance', he does so keeping in his mind his restrictive notion of reality and truth mentioned above, and not their ordinary, normal meaning. His concept of ignorance or *avidyā* is also, therefore, a restrictive, and not the ordinary, one. Thus the utility of *aparāvidyā* in the day-to-day life of an individual is not really denied by him by calling it a domain of ignorance in his technical sense of ignorance.

That he himself does not consider every *aparāvidyā* completely useless is clear from what he says in his commentary on 1.i.4. He says therein that the lower, *aparāvidyā*, is 'the knowledge of virtue and vice and their means and ends'.[12] This knowledge constitutes the subject-matter, or at least a large part of the subject-matter, of ethics, or ethical concerns. Therefore, if we take his views about ethics, quoted above, seriously, ethical concerns would fall under the category of man's lower concerns. To say this, or to think on this line, would very greatly downgrade the importance of our ethical concerns which are necessary, indispensable, conditions for leading not only a social but also a religious, spiritual, value-seeking life. Śankara would not like to undervalue the importance of ethics in human life. Therefore, calling an inquiry an *aparāvidyā* is *not to be taken in the sense of declaring it to be of no value at all.*

In the case of ethics, there is a good reason even for calling it *parāvidyā*, or a necessary adjunct of *parāvidyā*. In any scheme of grading inquiries in the light of their role in the pursuit of values, the case of ethics for a higher position than many is much stronger than the case of any other inquiry. This is so because the pursuit of no value would be worth its salt if it is not conducted in an ethically impeccable manner. A case may even be made for including the concern with spiritual values in the domain of ethical concerns because ethics too is said to be concerned with the highest value or values. This matter will be taken up for elaboration in Chapter 5.

4.3 *PARĀVIDYĀ* AS AN INQUIRY WITH A FINAL TERMINUS

Parāvidyā, the knowledge of *Brahman*, the ultimate reality as well as the highest value, was first imparted, the *Muṇḍaka* says, by Brahma, the creator of the world, to his eldest son Atharvā. Atharvā imparted it to Angir who passed it on to Satyavaha and Satyavaha passed it on to Angiras. It is to Angiras, as we have seen in the previous sections, that Śaunaka makes his request to be enlightened about the nature of that by knowing which everything will become known. To him Angiras responds by saying that thing is *Brahman* and the inquiry which enables anyone to know *Brahman* is *parāvidyā*.[13] Angiras and several others also say that *parāvidyā* is known or acquired neither by sense nor by reason, but by spiritual intuition which is unfaultable. The *Muṇḍaka* account of the origin of *parāvidyā* stated above, if taken literally, means that *parāvidyā* is a god-given knowledge, a knowledge of divine origin, which a human being can acquire only by spiritual perception or intuition. Each one of its two properties, the property of its divine origination and the property of its acquisition only by intuition, would singly make *parāvidyā* an inquiry having a final terminus. It would do that because each one of them is, as per general acceptance, a property which would make any *vidyā*, whose property it is, absolutely unfaultable and irreplaceable by a better or higher *vidyā*.

Let us first take the property of its divine origination, the theory that the history of *parāvidyā* begins with its first presentation by the god Brahmā to his eldest son. This theory has two noteworthy implications. One implication is that even for Brahmā it is extremely important. This is obvious from his choice of its first recipient. The eldest son in the Indian social system occupies a very high status in his family and is treated with great affection and trust. Brahmā's choosing none other than his eldest son, Atharvā, to be the first recipient, shows that he considers *parāvidyā*, which is the same as *Brahmavidyā*, to be so important that it is to be passed on, or taught, only to him who is dear and deserving.

That it has been given a very elevated, or the most elevated, status in classical Indian thought is evident from the way it has been treated in Angiras's initiation of Śaunaka into it and also from its discussion or respectful references at almost all other places it has been talked about in classical Indian philosophical writings. Modern writers on classical

Indian philosophical themes, too, do not seem to have differed from classical masters in their admiration for it.

The second implication of taking the account of its divine origin literally is that *parāvidyā* is a *vidyā* or inquiry which, in knowing or realizing *Brahman*, reaches the final terminus of inquiry into the nature of ultimate reality and value. That is, after knowing *Brahman*, after reaching the final goal, no further search for the identification of ultimate reality or value is needed. And, since this final terminus has already been reached and its nature explained in some classical Indian works, we need only follow the discipline prescribed by classical thinkers for realizing this end. A believer in the theory of its divine origin may argue in the following way:

Śaunaka wants to know from *Angiras* what is that after knowing which everything which is there becomes known. Angiras has told him, and through him all human beings, what that thing is. There is no reason to consider Śaunaka's query illegitimate and Angiras's answer to it invalid. After our knowing the answer, nothing remains unknown about the ultimate reality and value. Therefore, no further effort for knowing it needs to be made. Since the ultimate ground for anything which is there has been made known and the ultimate ground is also the ultimate value, no further inquiry needs to be made to ascertain what is our final end or goal. The quest for knowledge of what we ought to know and what we ought to do and be, the journey of inquiring into the nature of ultimate reality and value, must come to an end because the end of the road has been reached. The quest for knowledge, the inquiry for ascertaining why what is there is there, why anything worth valuing is worth valuing, must come to a complete halt. There is no need for any one of us to be another Śaunaka. The classical Śaunaka has already elicited from the classical Angiras the *parāvidyā* answering these queries. And, this *vidyā* is not the latter's brain-child, a human product. It is a *vidyā* of divine origin, handed down to him by another unfaultable *ṛṣi* in a line of *ṛṣis*, each one receiving it from his predecessor, the line starting from the god Brahmā's imparting it to Atharvā for the first time.

The above is not an imaginary piece of reasoning. It its, rather, an elaboration of what some modern interpreters have said about *parāvidyā*, though not as explicitly as done above. This line of thinking can very well be a natural child of taking the *Mundaka* account literally.

It may be said that it would be more appropriate or rational to take the account of the divine origin of *parāvidyā* as mythical or allegorical, as a device or strategy to highlight its most elevated status among the inquiries which human beings undertake or are likely to undertake. Whether we take it as a myth, or as a report of what at some point of time actually happened, it is clear that the account intends to ascribe an extremely respectable beginning to the history of *parāvidyā*. Every inquiry has a beginning. How it began very often is a good indicator of how important or unimportant an event its beginning was.

That the divine-origin-account is mythical and not historical is not difficult to understand. In many a case in classical Indian works a certain view is claimed to have been propounded by, or received from, a god only to emphasize its being an unquestionable truth, or its being fundamental to an inquiry or a set of inquiries. For example, Bhattojidikṣita, in his *Siddhāntakaumudī*, a famous work on Sanskrit grammar, when he states the basic set of fourteen principles (*sūtras*) of Sanskrit grammar, says that the set was given to man by the god Śiva (or Maheśvara). The set is also generally referred to as *Maheśvarasūtrani* (Maheśvara principles).

It is obvious that Bhattojidikṣita adopts this procedure only to emphasize the importance, or foundational character, of these principles or rules of Sanskrit grammar, or rather, for understanding the structure of Sanskrit language. Every natural language is a human phenomenon, and so is Sanskrit. The basic, or even secondary, rules according to which any natural language functions, or is structured, are discovered by watching the various ways in which it works, the multifarious kinds of speech-acts it performs. They are not invented, prescribed, or legislated by any individual or group, human or divine. That is why linguistics is an empirical science, and not a deductive or axiomatic system like geometry or a propositional calculus.

It does not even do honour to Śiva to think of him as having done the unnecessary work of formulating the basic rules of Sanskrit grammar, a work unwanted because the rules are not, as already said, to be formulated but to be found out. Śiva does not need this 'honour' to be done to him, if it is an honour at all, by a Bhattojidikṣita. Among the three, Viṣṇu, Brahmā, and Śiva, Śiva already occupies an extremely high and prestigious position in Hindu mythology. This is clear from the mythological assertions that it is he who performed the most difficult and important jobs like the job of drinking the venom taken out of occans after their churning by gods and demons, the venom which if not drunk by him would have destroyed the entire world; the miraculous job of bearing the 'unbearable' force with which the river Gangā descended from the world of gods to the world of mortals; the most unpleasant work of effecting the destruction of the world (pralaya) at the expiry of every term of its existence, etc. etc.

Attributing the formulation of its grammar's basic rules to Śiva does not do an honour even to the Sanskrit language. Because of its being a *natural language*, the rules of its grammar, of its syntax, semantics, or pragmatics, etc., cannot be a set of one-time formulated rules, even a set of one-time Śiva-formulated rules, waiting to be discovered and recorded by a grammarian. Neither does saying that its rules are to be empirically discovered from the many ways in which it operates do any dishonour to it. It does not, because this fact about it is a fact about all *natural languages*, about all members of the family of which it is a member. Only the rules of an *artificial language*, which Sanskrit is not, like those of a logistic system, are prescribed or formulated rules.

Therefore, it is quite reasonable or even rational, to take the alleged Brahmā-given character of *paravidyā* as mythical or allegorical as is the case with the above account of the basic set of grammatical principles. If this is done, one motivation or reason for the concept of *parāvidyā* leading to the final-terminus view of inquiry into the nature of ultimate reality or value will no longer hold good.

It seems to me that even classical commentators do not believe in the divine origin of the basic principles, or, of any principle, of any discipline. A divinity, a god, by definition, cannot give any principle whose meaning is vague, unclear, ambiguous, or which needs to be given a justification or reasoning to establish its validity. If it suffers from any one of these defects, it would *ipso facto* imply that its propounder suffers from some deficiency. This would not then be a divinity because a divinity cannot, again by definition, suffer from any deficiency. To attribute some deficiency to, for example, Brahmā, the creator of the world, would militate against the very concept of Brahmā as presented or held in Indian thought. But the fact that several classical thinkers have felt the need to comment on some allegedly divinely given ideas or principles and to explain and to make them more and more intelligible, shows that they do not consider them well-stated and their propounder perfect. Further, different commentators have given different interpretations of these ideas or principles all of which are not commensurate with one another, though every commentator or interpreter considers his interpretation all correct. This fact certainly shows the liability of the ideas or principles to be interpreted differently. This liability or potentiality is nothing but another name for ambiguity or imprecision in presentation, and therefore cannot go with the theory of, or belief in, the divine formulation of the ideas liable to be multifariously interpreted. If not all, many of such problems will vanish if we drop the theory of the divine origin of these views, and take the account of their divine formulation as merely allegorical, or strategic, offered as divine in order to emphasize their importance. We can, therefore, take the works in which they have been stated and adumbrated as human documents. This procedure will do no injustice to the views concerned, and will also nullify one cause of the concept of *parāvidyā*'s leading to, or suggesting, a final terminus-view of inquiry into reality or value.

Let us now take up the other feature of *parāvidyā*, the epistemic claim that it is attainable only by intuition which is an unfaultable giver of knowledge. This feature may be said to be another reason, a human but a good reason, for making *parāvidyā* an inquiry with a final terminus. This reason is human because it derives or emanates from the nature of human agency, i.e. intuition, by which alone ultimate reality or value is said to be cognized or realized. As has already been said, *Brahman*, the ultimate reality and value, or the ultimate reality as value, is said to be known, not by sense, nor by reason, but by spiritual intuition which gives irrefutable, unfaultable, knowledge. And, knowing it is the same as realizing it. This point has been made by many classical thinkers. Modern writers on classical Indian philosophy or religion have not only not questioned this but seem to have corroborated it. It can be said to represent, therefore, the general consensus about how ultimate reality or value is known. We can also call it the received interpretation of classical Indian conception of the knowledge of ultimate reality and value, as well as of classical Indian ontology, axiology, or axiological ontology. The important thing to note is that this interpretation is not only claimed to be the correct interpretation of the classical Indian point of view. It is also, by many, claimed to be *the* correct approach to understanding the nature of reality and value, or *the* correct way of doing ontology or axiology.

Parāvidyā, as conceived in the *Muṇḍaka*, or rather in the entire *Upaniṣadic* literature, is *Brahmavidyā* or *Ātmavidyā*, i.e. the *vidyā* which enables its possessor to realize *Brahman* (or *Ātman*, as both '*Brahman*' and '*Ātman*' denote the same entity) as the highest reality and value. It is possible that a philosopher accepts the concept of *parāvidyā* as a valid, a denoting, concept, but may not accept *Brahmavidya* as its denotatum. That is, he may agree with Angiras that there is an inquiry which when conducted properly enables the inquirer to know or realize the highest reality and thereby make everything that is there known and the highest value realized. But this inquiry is not *Brahmavidyā*. For example, a Buddhist may say that this inquiry consists in inculcating a thorough understanding of the four noble truths and following the eightfold noble path outlined in the fourth noble truth. Or, a *Sānkhya* philosopher may say that *parāvidyā* is knowing the nature of *puruṣa* and *prakriti* with the full realization that *puruṣa* is completely unrelated (*asanga*) to *prakriti*. All the three, Angiras, the Buddhist, and the *Sānkhya* philosopher, would then agree with each other that there is a *vidyā* which is *parāvidyā*, that the concept of *parāvidyā* is a non-empty, instantiable, denoting concept. They would disagree with each other about the identity of its denotatum, about *what* it actually denotes (without questioning that there *is* a *vidya* which it denotes).

Anyone who accepts that the concept of *parāvidyā* is a denoting concept, no matter what its denotatum is, and that it can be acquired only by intuition which is unfaultable, would have to admit that *parāvidyā* is an inquiry with a final terminus. This has to be the case because of conceiving intuition as the giver of unfaultable knowledge of ultimate reality and value, and conceiving ultimate reality and value as knowable only by intuition. The final terminus of *parāvidyā*, therefore, would be reached when the intuition of any individual, say, Angiras's, has conveyed to him what is the nature of ultimate reality or value. Since its verdict cannot, by definition, be wrong, in any way questionable, or sublatable by a superior truth, after knowing what its verdict is, the inquiry, i.e. *parāvidyā*, must come to its final end. There would be no point in continuing it further. All this may not happen in the life of a particular individual, but in principle it can happen.

Now, suppose classical Indian philosophy, or that particular sector of it which is called ontology (admitting the possibility of its being axiological), is *parāvidyā*. Then it would, in principle, be possible that it could some day reach its final terminus, or termination, when someone's inquiry succeeds in knowing the highest reality and in telling the world what it is. It would also then be the duty of any sensible, sincere, inquirer to reach that terminus by reading his presentation of *parāvidyā* and leading a life in accordance with his directives. All this would mean that he should work towards reaching a stage at which all further ontological–axiological search would become unnecessary. This is not different from saying that to work for attaining *parāvidyā* is to work for the end or termination of ontology–axiology. It is obvious that, if philosophy in its entirety is considered to be *parāvidyā*, attaining *parāvidyā* would, for the attainer, amount to causing all philosophizing come to a dead end as far as his cognitive, evaluative, concerns are concerned.

4.4 SOME THEORETICAL CONSEQUENCES OF *PARĀVIDYĀ* AS THE END OF INQUIRY

To acquire *parāvidyā* is, as the discussion so far has shown, to reach the end of inquiry into the nature of the most foundational reality and value, to reach that which is the basis of all that there is and ought to be, the basis of the knowledge of everything that is to be known (*sarvavidyāpatiṣthām*). Therefore, it is the culmination of ontological–axiological inquiry. Acquiring it may not affect further search in other areas of philosophy, or of inquiry in general, which falls under the category of *aparāvidyā*. But it would be a very good reason for not doing any further work in ontology and axiology. Rather, there would not be any point in pursuing further any inquiry which is ontological or axiological. Therefore, the possibility of making any genuine progress in this sector of philosophy would be ruled out. Rather, the desire to know anything more, the curiosity (*jñīpsā* or *jijñāsā*) about reality or value, would, or should, die out for ever.

An Angiras, or a staunch believer in his point of view, would say that it must die out, after acquiring *parāvidyā*, because there would remain nothing left unknown about the ultimate reality and value. This would really be, or should be, the logical consequence of acquiring *parāvidyā* as it has been conceived in the classical Indian tradition and approvingly dilated upon in the writings of several modern interpreters of classical Indian philosophy.

The above fallout of the acquisition of *parāvidyā*, makes the curiosity which may survive its acquisition unjustified or unreasonable. Curiosity is a great intellectual virtue. Sometimes its propelling force, even when its existence looks apparently unjustified, leads to some of man's greatest philosophical or theoretical achievements. After being taught that when $x - 2 = 0$, $x = 2$ and that when $x^2 = 4$ then $x = \pm 2$, if a child asks why in the former x is not equal to ± 2 when in the latter it is, we may dub his curiosity uncalled for and brush it aside as being childish (in a pejorative sense). But it is curiosity of this kind which led Bertrand Russell to work for the systematization of arithmetic (or rather mathematics) and to reduce it to logic.

Denigration of, or downgrading, curiosity at any stage as unjustified is very likely to adversely affect intellectual progress. Śaunaka goes to Angiras and prays to be instructed about *parāvidyā* because he is curious to know what is the ultimate reality and value. It is because he ceases to be curious after Angiras's telling him that it is *Brahman* that he does not ask him why *Brahman* is considered to be so. Curiosity involves a propensity to question the tenability of a view offered, of course not ad infinitum, but certainly with perseverance and tenacity. Śaunaka does not even question the Brahmā-given character of *parāvidyā*, nor does he ask a question of the type which Euthyphro asks in Plato's *Euthyphro.* If he had, his question would have had some such form: Is it the case that the knowledge that *Brahman* is the most basic reality and value is *parāvidyā because* it has been imparted by Brahmā, or is it the case that Brahmā has imparted it *because* it is *parāvidyā*? Whatsoever answer Angiras would have given, his answer would have certainly contributed to some further progress in philosophical thinking.

In religious matters, sometimes, the curiosity, the propensity, to know more, to probe further and further, is considered undesirable. In most religions, or religious practices, there are stages at which a disciple is advised or required to raise no question or doubt. In the *Gītā*, for example, Kṛṣṇa tells Arjuna, in an authoritative voice, that a doubting, questioning individual destroys himself and therefore Arjuna need not question or doubt what he (Kṛṣṇa) advises him to do.[14] This practice of making questioning or doubting certain ideas, principles, or even theories impermissible is not strange or bizarre for a religion because ultimately every religion is based on, or requires, unquestioning faith in certain ideas, principles, persons, or theories. But this is not the case in philosophy, or science.

It is clear from what has been said in the preceding section that it is not the mere assignment to intuition the role of being the organ for acquiring *parāvidyā* which makes *parāvidyā* an inquiry with a final terminus, or, rather, makes *parāvidyā* itself the final terminus of ontology and axiology. It is, in fact, the conception of intuition according to which what intuition yields is true for ever, and therefore is not questionable or faultable. It is this conception, or conviction, which is the main reason for many philosophers' holding that intuition is epistemically superior to sense and reason. What sense, or reason, they say, yields, may not be always veridical. But what intuition yields is. Moreover, the nature of reality is such that neither sense nor reason can reach it. This view that intuition alone can reach reality and what it reveals about it is unfaultable or unsublatable, naturally leads to the conclusion that a theory based on the findings of intuition cannot, in principle, be replaced by a better theory. Therefore, an individual like Angiras, or like

Śaunaka who accepts what his preceptor offers, would have nowhere to look for after having known by intuition what reality and value, or reality as value, is.

Since acquiring *parāvidyā* is to reach the final terminus in ontological–axiological thinking, further philosophical progress in this sector would be not possible. It would not be, no matter whether the terminus is reached in *parāvidya* because (a) of its allegedly divine origin, or (b) of its being the result of intuition, or (c) jointly of both (a) and (b). The theory of the divine origin, as has been shown, may be ignored as being allegorical, or heuristic, offered mainly to emphasize the paramount importance of *parāvidyā*. Therefore, it seems that the only sensible thing to do in order to explore if there can be found any way to save the possibility of philosophical progress, is to re-look into the conception of intuition responsible for this fate of the theory of *parāvidyā*. But before doing that it is methodologically necessary to say, in brief, something about what philosophical progress consists in.

4.5 PHILOSOPHICAL PROGRESS

Philosophical progress is a variety of cognitive progress. An individual can contribute to it only if he makes a creative use of his intellect, using the term 'intellect', in a broad sense. He can be creative in more than one way. But whenever he is, he is because, or only if, he adds something to the existing fund of philosophical knowledge, or achievement, in the area he works. He must show some innovativeness in methodology, content, appraisal of work done by any contemporary or predecessor of his, etc. He would be equally innovative if he raises some new questions but does not answer them, gives some new meaning to an old question, offers a new argument for an old theory, draws a new conclusion from an old argument, etc.

A mere survey, or report, howsoever accurate or faithful it may be, of what some others have done, even though they have become greatly respected in the tradition or in the eyes of several philosophers, would not be an instance of *creative* philosophy and therefore would not make any substantial contribution to philosophical progress. But it would have some utility if it makes available the ideas propounded by some great masters to a reader who wants to be acquainted with them but has no time to read the latters' works, or has no training or talent to understand them without the kind of assistance which it provides. However, its contribution to philosophical *progress* would be nil or almost nil.

It is a conceptual or logical, and not merely a contingent, truth that survey-type works, which include all types of exegetical, expository, reportive, synoptic, even interpretative, ones, can have only a secondary, tertiary, or putting it metaphorically, piggyback, status or value. There must *pre-exist* some ideas, views, theories, arguments, etc., given by some earlier creative philosophers in order that a surveyor, summarizer, interpreter, or exegete, gives an account of what they are, or what they, really, in their pristine purity, are, as all such scholars claim to do. When such works are done for a pretty long period of time in the history of a country's philosophy, the stock of ideas to be recounted is bound to become scantier, and succeeding exegeses bound to be repetitive or uninformative. This is natural because the existing stock of ideas, in any discipline, worth recounting, howsoever rich, being a man-made stock, cannot be infinite. Thus, it is no wonder that reading some descriptive accounts of the views propounded in even such classics as the

Upaniṣads is like listening to the same music played on different copies of the same musical cassette on different cassette-players.

Critical, even creative, reconstructive, or innovative, works depend on some other works. There must be available to the critic a work worth examining or appraising. But worthwhile criticism is always creative. A good critic uses his critical, creative abilities to explore where the work examined faults, where in it are components which can be used to build newer or better theoretical structures in the area it belongs to, or in some other area, what sort of leads it offers for further research in the present-day state of the craft it is relevant to, etc. In fact, some creative critics pick up a work, classical or contemporary, not with the primary objective of determining its strengths and weaknesses, but to present their own creative thinking via giving apparently a commentary on the latter. In effect, they use the ideas they comment on as pegs to hang their own thoughts on Śankara's commentaries (*bhāṣyas*) are good specimens of this kind. Except for some very early classical Indian philosophers, most others who have contributed to philosophical progress have used this method.

Sometimes, rather quite often, a creative philosopher adopts a *direct* method. That is, he begins with discussing some of the views of some other thinker and via his comments on them evolves his own position on some theme or themes, a position sustainable in its own right, or on the strength of its own arguments related to but independent of the arguments offered by the philosopher commented on. Sometimes he adopts an *indirect* method of procedure. He does not expressly begin with a view of another philosopher but proceeds in, what I would like to call in the absence of a more graceful terminology, a *hypothesizing or 'if-then' manner*. He proceeds in some such way as the following:

If a philosopher offers an objection to the position I have maintained, it can be replied to in such and such a way; if he offers another position claiming to be better than mine, it can be shown to be defective in such and such a way, or shown to be already comprehended in my position, etc.

To conclude, a philosopher's work will not contribute to philosophical progress if it only describes what someone else has said. Therefore, if a conception of philosophy, or of inquiry in general, makes it impossible, unnecessary, or unrespectable, for an individual to develop, in any area of philosophy, a view of his own which may be critical, reconstructive, innovative, or incongruent with a traditionally respectable or prevalent view though well stated and supported with good reasons, then that conception would in all likelihood block philosophical progress. It would surely make it difficult, or unfashionable. Such a situation may be brought about by adhering too seriously or committedly to the concept of *parāvidyā* as the ideal of philosophy *and* taking it as an accomplished fact that this ideal has been realized, i.e. *pāravidyā* has already been provided by thinkers like Angiras. Then the only thing left for an individual to do would be to write or present an exegesis of it and not to contribute anything of his own, i.e. not contribute to philosophical progress.

All this would be true, a believer in the theory of *parāvidyā* may point out, only in a particular sector of philosophy which consists of ontology and axiology, or mystical speculative axiological ontology, because only this sector is *parāvidyā*. In other sectors, rather in all other areas of human inquiry, which come under the category of *aparāvidyā*, the concept of *parāvidyā* would not bar an individual from making a contribution of his own, critical or creative, i.e. from contributing to philosophical or intellectual progress. But even barring a creative mind from presenting a view of his own in the sector of ontology–axiology, by making philosophical progress in this sector impossible or uncalled for, is a great philosophical or intellectual loss. It is worthwhile, therefore, to rethink the concept of *parāvidyā* with a view to exploring if anything can be done to it to save the possibility of contributing to philosophical progress, the possibility of creative philosophizing, even in the sector of ontology–axiology which, strictly speaking, the concept covers.

4.6 RETHINKING THE CONCEPT OF *PARĀVIDYĀ* IN THE CONTEXT OF PHILOSOPHICAL PROGRESS

The concept of inquiry as having no final terminus is promotive of, or cogenial for, keeping the process of inquiring continued. It may be said to have halts, to have achieved important ends. But howsoever great a goal reached by it at a point of time may be, it would not, in principle, be its final goal, or terminus, beyond which it cannot or need not go. This advantage which the no-final-terminus-view of inquiry has, the final-terminus-view cannot have. The *Muṇḍaka* concept of *parāvidyā*, which is, by and large, the generally accepted, or current, concept of it even in modern interpretations of *parāvidyā*, makes it an inquiry which reaches its final terminus in knowing or realizing *Brahman* as the highest reality and value. Being an inquiry which has already reached its final terminus, as per the tradition, by thinkers like Angiras and others, it annuls the possibility, as we have seen, of making any further progress in the ontology–axiology sector of philosophy, in the sector whose heart it constitutes.

The above feature of the concept of *parāvidyā* seems to have been extended or generalized in an assumption made by many modern interpreters about classical Indian philosophy in its entirety. The assumption is to the effect that classical Indian philosophers are *ṛṣis* or *munis*, seers of eternal truths. In a sense every great thinker can be called a seer, whether he is classical or modern, Indian or non-Indian. But many interpreters believe, or claim, that classical Indian philosophers are *ṛṣis* in the sense that what they have said is eternally true and therefore cannot be ever modified, replaced by a more inclusive truth, superseded, or falsified, etc. Then the practice of giving to them the status of *ṛṣis* becomes something like a bias which may, because of the unavailability of a more elegant terminology, be called *ṛṣi bias*, as I have done in some of my earlier writings. An interpreter who holds this general view would naturally hold or think that there is a final terminus of philosophical inquiry which has been reached by classical Indian thinkers. Perhaps this view is responsible for the fact that there has not been made in modern times any noticeable progress, or even any move to make progress, by philosophizing in the style of philosophizing characteristic of classical Indian philosophers. This is glaring in the area of value-theory when most of classical Indian thinkers considered the ultimate reality to be also the ultimate value, or rather, conceived of the ultimate reality as the ultimate value. It is surprising that this state of affairs has come into being, even though a large number of modern Indian scholars consider the classical Indian style of philosophizing and its value-orientedness highly desirable and a pride-worthy contribution of classical India to the axiological heritage of the world.

The result of all this is that the classical philosophical corpus of India is at the same spot where it was left by the ancient *ṛṣis*. In contrast to the Indian situation, Platonic thought, for example, on the other hand, has been carried further and further in diverse directions by later Western thinkers, and more extensively and intensively in modern times. If Plato were reborn today as the same Plato that he was, he would be amazed at the exuberance of philosophizing his philosophizing has given rise to. Surely, he would find it extremely hard to trace the ancestory of a large number of these philosophizings to his own. It is not very difficult to imagine, in contrast, what even a later classical Indian philosopher, say, Śankara, on whose works a lot has been written, would feel if he were reborn and looked at the volumes written on his thought and impressively arranged on the shelves of a modern Indian library.

It seems to me that one way to get out of this crippling situation in Indian philosophy would be to loosen a little the tight hold of the final-terminus-conception of classical Indian philosophy, particularly of its ontology–axiology sector, i.e. of *parāvidyā*. This is so because other sectors come under *aparāvidyā*. Each one of them can be taken as a no–final-terminus-inquiry simply by getting rid of, or reducing the grip of, the *ṛṣi bias*. To do this we have only to stop treating the views of classical Indian philosophers as absolutely uncriticizable, unmodifiable, or irreplaceable, partly, or wholly, by better ones. We can still continue regarding them as *ṛṣis*, as highly respectable, creative, thinkers. There is nothing odd in it because to criticize a thinker's views, to take some pieces from them and use them as raw materials to construct new theoretical or normative structures, etc., is to respect what they have done, what their views have achieved. On the other hand, to simply adore them, to parrot them in written or oral performance, is very similar to treating them as curios only worth keeping in a museum but not as objects fit to be used in any new construction or reconstruction. This would be only thinly different from ignoring them. Subjecting them to critical, revaluative reflection, on the other hand, is to bring them back to life, to make them re-live in current thinking.

We have, therefore, to see if we can and if we can, how we can, loosen the grip of the final-terminus-conception of *parāvidyā*. We have to do this because it is this sector of classical Indian philosophy which is considered, almost by definition, to have reached its final terminus in the works of some classical thinkers. One way of doing it is, as already hinted at, to probe a little searchingly into the concept of intuition which is the alleged means of acquiring this kind of knowledge or *vidyā*. We have seen that its elevated status may be attributed to its divine origin, its Brahmā-giveness, and/or to its having been yielded by intuition (or spiritual intuition). We have also seen that the claim to its being Brahmā-given may be taken as mythical or allegorical, an instance of the classical Indian convention of attributing divine origination to views, theories, principles, etc. in order to give them respectability. Therefore, in a theoretical discussion, the alleged divine origination of *parāvidyā* may be ignored. The only other remaining ground of its elevated status then is its intuitive character. Therefore, let us look into it a little critically and open-mindedly to see if there can be located in it any window through which the fresh air of the no-final-terminus-view may be let in.

Parāvidyā, to put it in common-sense language, is an inquiry into what we ought to believe in as the highest, or most basic, reality and what we ought to do in order to be what we ought to be. The knowledge of these things, which constitutes *parāvidyā*, is said to be attained only by intuition, and not by sense or reason. This intuition, as has been already said, is not what is common-sensically meant by the term. It is claimed to be of a special kind and therefore is called spiritual intuition, non-sensual, non-rational.

Empirical studies of the world, the kind of studies which natural sciences do, on one view, are the only kind of studies which offer authentic knowledge, true propositions, about what things are, how they can be related to one another, etc. This kind of knowledge is important in its own way, and helps us to understand the nature of the world we live in. To deny its importance would amount to flying in the face of facts. But it also is true, a scholar of classical Indian philosophy would say, that the acquisition of this kind of knowledge is not sufficient to make our life worthwhile; it is not, because it does not tell us what we ought to do and be. *Parāvidyā*, the intuitive knowledge of *Brahman*, or of something else, as the ultimate reality and value, on the other hand, he would say, not only tells us what is the ground of all that there is, but also what we ought to aspire after in order to be what we ought to be. It therefore does what no science can do.

It must be admitted that the intuitive character of *parāvidyā* does not rule out the possibility of anyone's trying to ascertain afresh what is the ultimate reality or ultimate value. It simply makes it unnecessary. For example, since Angiras already has it and is willing to impart it to Śaunaka, there is no need for Śaunaka to conduct the inquiry afresh. He can very well open his mind to receive it from Angiras and mould his life in accordance with it, just as Angiras received it from Satyavaha and patterned his life-style accordingly. He too did not try to do the inquiry afresh.

When we probe into the concept of intuition, the organ of its acquisition, we have to admit that even the intuition which is said to be spiritual, is a human gift or power. Brahmā, or *Brahman* does not intuit. Nor does the Self intuit, or need to intuit. Self, in the context of *parāvidyā*, is consciousness. Consciousness cannot be said to intuit or to need to intuit, or to know or to need to know, the ultimate reality because it itself is the ultimate reality. Nor can we say that it ought to be this or that because it already is what it ought to be, or what anything ought to be. That is why the Self is said to be a non-doer (*akartā*), non-experiencer (*abhokta*), etc. It is the individual, the *Jīva*, a being like any one of us, who is an embodied self, who needs to know the ultimate reality because he is or may be ignorant of it, and who needs to try to be what he ought to be because he is not what he ought to be. And, this individual is a finite being. Intuition, or the ability to intuit, is a power or ability of his, and therefore it must be a finite power or ability.

Perhaps it is the realization by classical thinkers that intuitiveness is a finite human power which prompts them to admit that intuitions by different thinkers may sometimes differ. There do exist wide differences among the views of classical Indian philosophers who are considered to have been equipped with intuitive power. Some of these thinkers have also tried to prove that their results are truer than those of some others. This is why there has come into being a vast classical corpus of views about truth, reality, value, etc., arrived at by thinkers who are allegedly gifted with supra-sensuous, supra-rational, intuitive, abilities, Speaking philosophically, this is not a misfortune. Rather, it is good fortune because it provides a good field for an open-minded, critical, creative, philosopher to exercise his logical acumen to determine which one of these views is more sustainable or retainable than another on logical, rational grounds.

The thinkers who are considered to have arrived at a body of finality-claiming-truths, do not simply say that they have intuited them and stop there; they also give some grounds or reasons for their support, maybe sometimes emerging out of an interpretation of some earlier writing. Whenever two views, for which some grounds have been offered, conflict with, or differ from, each other, the most appropriate or the only method to decide which one of the two is mare tenable than the other, is to examine their supporting grounds and the logical bond between the grounds and the views claimed to be grounded on them. The net result of such an examination may go in favour of one, or may even show that none of them is tenable, or that each one of them is not wholly, but only partly, tenable, that is, tenable only in some respects.

When two sense-empirical claims conflict with each other, the dispute between the two can be settled by sensuously ascertaining what really is the case. For example, when sitting in their drawing room, a man says that the cow in his backyard is black and his wife says that it is white, assuming that the same cow cannot be wholly black *and* wholly white at the same time, the best way for anyone to settle the dispute between the two is to go to the backyard and see the cow there. But such a method of direct confirmation, or verification, or even an indirect one, is not available, even to a very able philosopher of the common-garden variety, in the case of disagreements about non-sense empirical matters: for example, about a disagreement concerning the nature of *mokṣa,* salvation, the spiritual end, which is said to be the highest end a human being can attain. An *Advaitin* holds that the state of *mokṣa* is a state of consciousness which is a state of pure, unmixed, bliss, and is attainable by an individual even when he is alive. A *Naiyayika,* on the other hand, claims that *mokṣa* is a state completely bereft of consciousness, and therefore is neither a state of bliss nor of painlessness, because only a state of consciousness can be a state of bliss, or painlessness, or even of pain. Consequently, *mokṣa* can be attained by an individual only after his death because as long as he is alive he cannot be completely bereft of consciousness. For a philosopher who is neither a committed *Advaitin,* nor a committed *Naiyāyika,* when he is confronted with the task of assessing these conflicting theories, the most sensible way to proceed would be to examine the tenability of the grounds on which each on of the two theories is based. This would be the case with whatsoever motivation he intends to make the assessment. There could be more than one kind of motivation; but it has to be kept in mind that the act of assessment is performed in a logically fair-minded fashion. A philosophical game is not philosophical if it is not played in a logically fair manner.

If the ultimate ground, or an important component of the ground, for holding either one, or both, of the two theories turns out to be an appeal to some sacred text (*śruti*), the philosopher would have no alternative except to rationally examine the (a) the tenability of the *śruti* and (b) the *śruti*'s probative power to prove or support the tenability of the theory which is claimed to be grounded on it.

In this venture of assessing the tenability of the *Advaitic* and *Naiyāyika* theories of *mokṣa,* the philosopher's motivation could be practical, or theoretical, or both practical and theoretical. It would be practical if he intends to determine whether *mokṣa* as characterized by the *Advaitic* theory, or as characterized by the *Naiyāyika* theory, is, in an absolute sense, or in a relative sense, i.e. in comparison to the latter, the best thing whose attainment he should make his own highest end (*parama puruṣārtha*), and would like to recommend to others that they too should do the same thing. It would be theoretical if his intention is primarily to examine the logic or reasoning given in support of each of them in order to ascertain its strength as well as weakness. He may end up even with the conclusion that the reasoning given to back neither of them is faultless. In doing all this with an open mind, quite obviously, the philosopher has to use his probing intellect, his reasoning, his logic, and not any mystical, supra-rational, power of cognition or adjudication. It is also possible that his is a mixed motivation in being both practical and theoretical. Such a motivation is generally had by a thinker who believes in the maxim that he can justifiably engage himself, or advise someone else to engage himself, in the pursuit of a goal so elevated as to be called the highest goal for any individual, or even in the pursuit of a goal of a lower rank, only after being convinced, on good rational grounds, of its overall desirability or achievement-worthiness.

Any attempt to reconcile, or adjudicate between two different views intuitively arrived at by any human being, even a *ṛṣi*, in bound to involve the use of discussive reasoning. This is likely to provide a good reason to the rationalist or intellectualist for saying that intuitive revelations cannot be accepted as final truths, or that intuition cannot be accepted as a giver of all-time true, or wholly true, views or propositions. But to me there seems to be a silver lining in the finitude of man's intuitive power responsible for this situation. We can make a logical use of the notion of intuition's finitude to liberalize, at least a little bit, the notion of *parāvidyā* in such a way that it ceases to be an inquiry which once completed is completed for ever, an inquiry with no possibility of growth. This would obviously mean that then it would not remain an inquiry with a final terminus. The reasoning for liberalization may proceed as follows:

In spite of its authoritativeness, or fittingness, for being the proper organ for the cognition or realization of the ultimate reality and value (or ultimate reality as value), being a human power or equipment, intuition suffers from finitude. Therefore, its results are at the most *prima facie* final, i.e. final, all other considerations remaining the same. We may take them as final in the sense that we may mould our life-style, our cognitive, conative and affective aptitudes, in accordance with them as long as they are not superseded by, modified in the light of, better intuitions. Like our other abilities, even the intuitive ability may become weaker or stronger. This means that we may reach a stage in our ontological–axiological inquiry at which we feel we have got an intuitive realization of ultimate reality and value, that we have attained *parāvidyā*. But we must not completely stop our search. We must not think that we have reached the absolutely final terminus. We must not, because it is possible that we have the good luck to have, at some later time in our further search, better, stronger, intuitions which may require us to modify our present ontological–axiological understanding, our present *parāvidyā*. No *parāvidyā* would then mean the dead end of our ontological–axiological inquiry. It would be a *parāvidyā* as far as it goes, as long as it is not replaced by another. It would still remain a *parāvidyā* because it would tell us what we ought to know and ought to be. It is *parā* (supreme) *vidyā* (knowledge) because it is concerned with ultimate *reality as value*, as that which ought to be realized. It would not be concerned with ultimate reality as merely existent, as that which is simply there or which must be there. Speaking in terms of the present condition of the inquirer, the seeker, it would be *parāvidyā* because of its being concerned with ascertaining what he ought to be and how he can be what he ought to be.

Classical philosophers who have adumbrated or talked about the concept of *parāvidyā* do not really intend to present a concept very different from the one which has been outlined above. It is perhaps their mode of presentation which makes it appear that it is a *vidyā* which once attained makes all further inquiry into the nature of ultimate reality and value redundant or unjustified. They adopt such a mode perhaps to highlight the importance of the inquiry of *parāvidyā*, man's search for the highest value in his pursuit of the various kinds of inquiries he is likely to engage himself in. Had they really believed that after knowing that *Brahman* is the highest reality and value by any *ṛṣi*, or even a group of *ṛṣis*, all search for knowledge must have come to an end, the stream of philosophy would have, in all likelihood, stopped with the *Upaniṣads*. But it did not. Rather, it really acquired great force in its flow and extensively expanded its area only *after* the adumbration of, or commenting upon, certain views in them. Even if the open-endedness read into the concept of *parāvidyā*, as has been done in this section, is not in consonance with the import of the classical concept of *parāvidyā*, it is philosophically desirable to think of the concept as open-ended. It is desirable because doing that would be more congenial to promoting philosophical progress in the ontological–axiological domain which primarily is the area of *parāvidyā*.

4.7 *PARĀ–APARĀ* AND PHILOSOPHY–SCIENCE DISTINCTION

In modern interpretations, the concept of *parāvidyā* is generally taken to denote an ontological–axiological inquiry which has reached its final terminus. It is also claimed by some scholars that Indian philosophy in its entirety is *pārāvidya* and, therefore, superior to science. The superiority of philosophy over science is said to consist in the fact that the reality which philosophy reaches, or succeeds in characterizing, is of a higher order or status than the reality which sciences have reached or can reach. We have seen that it is wrong to consider the whole of Indian philosophy as *parāvidyā*. Only a particular kind of ontology–axiology is *parāvidyā* as per the classical conception of *parāvidyā*, the kind according to which *Brahman* is the highest reality and value. The emphasis is more, as has been shown, on *parāvidyā*'s being concerned with the highest value, with the highest reality as also the highest value, with what is our ultimate goal, than with telling us what sorts of things are really there in the world. It is obvious that no science is primarily concerned with the highest value and therefore cannot be called *parāvidyā*. But no scientist would feel humiliated, as no logician would, on his area being called *aparā*, because the *parā-aparā* distinction would then be just a conceptual distinction. Both, the scientist and the logician, would agree that an inquiry concerned with the highest value would be of higher merit, of course if it presents a defensible theory, than one which is concerned with something else. This would not mean that no science, or no inquiry under the *aparā* category, has any importance or utility. Even classical Indian thinkers would not call every inquiry they put in the *aparā* category absolutely unimportant.

If, on the other hand, *parāvidyā* is conceived as an inquiry which, after having reached the final terminus, makes redundant all further inquiry into what man's highest value is, a scientist would prefer calling his particular science, or science as such, *aparā* to calling it *parā*. He would rather feel obliged to his philosopher colleague, of course ironically, for putting science in the *aparā* basket and on that account considering it inferior to Indian philosophy put in the *parā* basket. Similar would be the reaction of the logician and of a host of other philosophers working in such areas as theory of knowledge, philosophy of language, metaethics, philosophy of science, etc., to mention a few of them.

Coming back to science, if the concept of *parāvidyā* is used in the restrictive sense as referring to an inquiry with a reachable final terminus, as allegedly illustrated in its having been already reached in some classical Indian philosophy or philosophies, a modern scientist, Indian or non-Indian, would feel extremely happy with science's being given the lower status of *aparāvidyā*. He would feel so because he would very strongly like to keep scientific inquiry not only always alive but even more and more intensified. This he can reasonably do only on science's being categorized as an inquiry with no final terminus, i.e. as an *aparāvidyā*. On the other hand, its being categorized as *parāvidyā*, in the restrictive sense of being an inquiry with a final terminus, would require him to work for the end or termination of scientific inquiry. This it would do because then, being *parāvidyā*, science too would have a reachable final terminus after reaching which scientific inquiry must come to an end. This he would not consider a happy state of affairs. Even a weak belief that there is a final terminus of scientific inquiry is likely to dampen the scientist's searching spirit which enables him to progress from one stage to another. Scientific inquiry is an ongoing process for which every stage of achievement is in principle a temporary halt, and not the final terminus, the end of the road. In fact, it is a scientist's sticking to this ideal of inquiry, which has played an important role in making science progress the way it has done, and imbued him with the confidence that he would not let the process of progress ever come to a grinding halt.

Whatever be their subject-matter and methodology, empirical sciences, including both natural and social sciences, conduct a lot of descriptive, explanatory, systematizing exercises. None of these exercises would make it a *parāvidyā*, an inquiry into the nature of the highest value. The same is the case with some other inquiries which engage themselves largely in such exercises as conceptualizing, analysing, axiomaticising, etc., as mathematics and some philosophies do. Ethics, conceptual, pure, and applied, deals with such things as virtues, values, rights, obligations, etc., which are to be pursued, acquired, inculcated, cultivated, protected, etc. in order to make man's day-to-day, normal, life, personal, social, and political, as cohesive and happy as the relevant conditions in the world he lives in permit. Even this kind of inquiry, though it deals with values, would not be *parāvidyā*. Moreover, no ethical philosopher, cognizant of the complexities of moral life, would agree to calling ethics an inquiry which has a fixed, final, terminus after reaching which he has to cry 'halt' to his inquiring propensity, or after reaching which the moral man must stop caring for ethical things.

All of the inquiries, scientific and ethical, mentioned above, would be *aparāvidyā*, but not for that reason unimportant. They would be *aparāvidyā* even when the concept of *parāvidyā* is liberalized, as suggested, into the form of an inquiry with no all-time final terminus. They would be so because and only because they do not have as their target the highest value in the sense in which it is understood in the context of *parāvidyā*. They, or someone of them, may even hold that there is nothing which may be called the highest value, or that there is no *Brahman*, or that the concept of reality and the concept of value being logically different, even if *Brahman* were accepted to be the ultimate reality, it would not follow that *Brahman* was also the ultimate value, etc., etc. Thus, calling them, or any inquiry, *aparāvidyā* and calling *Brahmavidyā parāvidyā* is basically to make a conceptual classification or categorization, and not to downgrade an inquiry say, any science, by categorizing it as *aparāvidyā*.

That science contributes a lot to the betterment of our moral life is a well-established fact. But still a feeling or belief lurks in minds of many, including some philosophers, that sciences are fundamentally, or largely, descriptive and explanatory inquiries. An empirical scientist, a psychologist, a physiologist, a medical scientist, or a physicist, for example, can easily counter anyone's, even the philosopher's, this understanding of his role by pointing out that he does not merely describe what the world consists of. Rather, by finding out how the world, inanimate and animate, actually functions, he also gives authentic information about what man's needs and wants and aspirations are, what his capabilities and limitations are, and how much he can hope to successfully achieve. That is, he not only tells an individual what he wants and what he does not want to achieve; he also tells him what is *in his interest* to want to have and what to want to not have, and how much he can reasonably hope to have. Therefore indirectly, and sometimes even directly, he tells him what he should and what he should not want to have. In fact, he constantly aims at finding out ways and means to improve the chances of his achieving what is in his interest and thereby making the world more comfortable for him. This claim could have been made even by classical Indian scientists, psychologists, political thinkers, chemists, medical scientists, etc. And, when the claim is made by a modern scientist, Indian or non-Indian, it would be foolish to call it fake or false or mere bragging.

It is a fact that science, to a very large extent, determines not only our understanding of what the world is and of how it functions but also our choices, our wants and aspirations. It *determines* not only the methods, or means, required to fulfil our ends, but also a good number of the ends themselves. A scientist was never and is definitely not today comparable to the cricket commentator whose role is only to accurately describe which player is doing what on the playground when the game is going on. He always played, and is playing today, in a clearly noticeable way, the role of a guide giving clear hints which way we should move our bat if we want to win a game on our life's court.

The classical Indian philosopher, while upholding the doctrine of *parāvidyā* need not deny the scientist's role outlined, though very briefly, above. He may admit that the scientist not only guides our selection of means to our ends but also sometimes guides our choice of ends. But none of the ends, he would say, which science motivates us to choose is an end final in the sense that its fulfilment would give complete and permanent satisfaction, a satisfaction after the attainment of which nothing else would still be there to be attained. Science does not tell us what we ought to do in order that we be what we really or ultimately ought to be.

According to the majority of classical thinkers what we ought to be is non-different from what we *really* are. We are not *in fact* what we really are because we do not see what we really are on account of a veil of ignorance obstructing our vision of what we really are.

Classical thinkers may be even interpreted to have said, or to imply by what they have said, that science does not tell us what we really are, or does not tell us the complete truth about what we really are. Therefore, it needs to be augmented, and not to be supplanted, by another kind of inquiry competent to give knowledge of what we really are and of what we ought to do. It is this knowledge which we need to have in order to be what we really are, i.e. to return to the original state of our being. It is clear from all this that the distinction between *parāvidyā* and *aparāvidyā*, or the classification of inquiries into *parāvidyā* and *aparāvidyā* is the child of a particular classical Indian philosophical, specifically of an ontological–axiological, theory. It is not a theory-neutral distinction. It is not the result of an empirical generalization about, nor a result of a conceptual analysis of, the functions which various sorts of inquiries actually perform.

We can, however, take the characterization of the *parā–aparā* distinction out of its textual moorings and look at it as a general mode of classifying various kinds of inquiries.

If we do this exercise, then it becomes a mode of grading inquiries from the point of view of their concern with values, a mode which gives the highest (*parā*) place to that inquiry which is concerned with the highest value and the method of realizing it. This would imply that all those inquiries which do not do that are of a lower type (*aparā*), i.e. lower than the highest, whatever be their subject-matter, methodology, or objective. To me it seems to be the classical thinkers' intended meaning of the distinction which may not be clearly visible because of their style of presentation. If this is accepted, then we can say that the distinction is intended to highlight that an inquiry, which enables man to *correctly know* what he should aim at as his ultimate, final, all-consummating, value, the supreme goal of his life, and to *successfully attain* that goal, occupies the highest place among the various kind of inquiries he conducts or is capable of conducting. *Vidyā*, in *parāvidyā* and *aparāvidyā*, is a term having a very broad or wide sense, and the nearest word as its English equivalent seems to be 'inquiry', and not 'science' or 'philosophy'. Both of the two latter terms have acquired in current usage a specific denotation and connotation. That is why most scholars would say that philosophy and science denote and connote different kinds of inquiries or enterprises. This does not imply, however, that they cannot interact or collaborate with each other.

In establishing the plausibility or validity of this claim about *parāvidyā*, *Upaniṣadic* and *Vedāntic* thinkers use a good amount of logic in addition to their appeal to the views and experiential reports of their respected predecessors. In examining their logic and interpretation of recorded experiential reports both philosophy and science can cooperate with each other. Philosophers can assess their logic and scientists their experiential claims. For example, as a limited empirical analogue of the mystical state of salvation attained by an individual in his lifetime, a unified, undifferentiated, experience of the identity of *Brahman* and Self in the state of deep, dreamless sleep (*susupti*) has been given in the *Māṇḍukya Upaniṣad* and *Advaitic* literature. It has been said that in dreamless sleep one gets a temporary glimpse of what the mystical experience is like. A philosopher can examine the validity of the reasoning given to show that a dreamless sleep is an evidence or illustration of the nature of the reality revealed in the mystical experience of the nature of *Brahman*, or the Self, or the identity of the two. The scientist can cooperate with him by showing whether or not sleep is possible without dreams. This is not a petty empirical matter. Suppose neuroscientists show that no sleep is dreamless. Then this empirical example which the *Upaniṣadic*, or *Vedāntic*, thinker, has to tell an ordinary individual what the mystical experience is like will become unavailable to him. I am referring to this possibility because a neurosurgeon of great repute, Professor Ram Murty of Chennai, once said in a lecture that no sleep was dreamless. Another very bright young neurosurgeon, Dr A.K. Agrawal of Patna, after consulting a lot of literature on the neurology of sleep and dreams confirms that there is so far no evidence of sleep being at any time dreamless. On the other hand, even if sleep is dreamless sometimes, if the philosopher shows that no valid inference can be drawn from an instance of it about the nature of any kind of reality mystical experience is claimed to reveal, this too would very adversely affect the validity of the *Upaniṣadic* claim about the nature of the highest reality and of the viability of calling an inquiry dealing with it *parāvidyā*.[15]

The characterization of the *parā–aparā vidyā* distinction, as suggested above, is hopefully, fair to the spirit of the classical Indian conception of *parā* and *aparā vidyā* as well as to that of modern science. A modern scientist would readily agree to giving the highest place to the inquiry, if such an inquiry is possible, which tells us, in a conclusively convincing manner, what is that by achieving which we would realize all our genuine aspirations, the consummation of all that we ought to know, seek, and be. He would agree to do that without feeling any insult to his self-respect as a scientist, or to the dignity of his science, because what this, the allegedly *parā* inquiry, claims to do is not what his scientific inquiry claims to do. He would greatly prize its results and welcome anyone's highlighting them because they are of prime importance to every human being and therefore to him as well. He, a scientist, too, is a human being. All this, of course, depends on the alleged *parā* inquiry's being a viable, tenable, inquiry, as tenable as a human inquiry can be.

4.8 THE CONCEPT OF INTUITION: A TERMINOLOGICAL CLARIFICATION

In writings in English on Indian philosophy, theology and even literature, the word 'intuition' is quite often used, primarily in the context of the knowledge of ultimate reality or truth. When ultimate reality is conceived also as ultimate value, the cognition of value is also said to be had by intuition. 'Intuition', in all such discussions, as has been pointed out at the very beginning of this work in Chapter 1 and used in the succeeding chapters, denotes a form or power of cognition which is non-sensuous or supra-sensuous, non-rational or suprarational, a mode of direct, immediate, cognition. It is also called spiritual intuition. All along in this work 'intuition' will generally be used in this sense, even in those occurrences of it in which it is not qualified with such words as 'non-sensuous', 'non-rational', etc. This will be done to keep a good liason with the usage of the term in the existing literature on the themes discussed in it.

The words 'supra-sensuous' and 'supra-rational' appear to be emotively more pleasing, or cognitively more positive, than 'non-sensuous' and 'non-rational' but contentually, or in respect of their knowledge-yielding capability, the former pair and the latter pair are non-different. Therefore, they will be used synonymously, if and when they are used. To avoid unnecessary misunderstanding, I shall generally use the positive-looking pair. This is only a matter of stylistic convenience. The important thing to ascertain is whether or not any philosophical or conceptual advantage accrues from admitting that certain things pertaining to man's pursuit of values, if any things at all, are cognized or confirmed in a supra-sensuous manner. The same thing can be said in another way by saying that it deserves to be examined whether or not it is necessary to appeal to some such power of cognition in order to understand, or make more intelligible, any aspect of our concern with values, ascertainment or acknowledgement of obligations, recognition of rights, inculcation of virtues, emancipation from disvalues, the nature of consciousness or experience we have in all of these and other related phenomena of evaluative relevance, etc.

'Intuition' is also a word of ordinary language, a common-sense word, meaning the ability to have a flash or insight, a direct or immediate mode of cognition which might have matured as a result of varied normal sense-experiences and uses of reasoning or reflection on internal and external things. It is this sense in which we speak of our linguistic intuitions, moral intuitions, a mother's intuition of her son's being hungry, our logical or mathematical intuitions, etc. In this sense, too, intuitions are very important. This is clear from such utterances as the following: The correct use of an expression of ordinary language is finally determined by the (linguistic) intuitions of a native speaker of the language it belongs to; a correct criterion of moral rightness or wrongdoing must not conflict with our moral intuitions about what is morally right or wrong; the test of logical consistency or inconsistency in affirming or denying something about something else must not conflict with our logical intuitions about what is not and what is logically sound, etc. If and when 'intuition' is used to denote what it means in its common-sense, ordinary, usage, it will be made clear that it is so used either by prefixing it with 'common sense', 'normal', 'ordinary', etc., or by the context it occurs in.

4.9 A CONCLUDING DISCLAIMER

It should be obvious by now that giving the most elevated status to *parāvidyā* in the realm of inquiries makes no claim to the effect that an individual should stop pursuing any *aparā* inquiry and devote all his energies to that of *parāvidyā,* nor to the effect that the acquisition of the *aparā* inquiry is of no use to the acquisition of *parāvidyā.* It is a fact that it was possible in classical India and is possible today for an individual to lead a successful, or fairly successful, life without being aware of there being an inquiry of the type *parāvidyā* is said to be, or without caring for it even after having been aware of its exposition by some great *ṛṣis.* In Viṣākhadatta's well-known historical drama *Mudrārākṣasam,* which is generally accepted to be as good a record of what then happened as a book of history may be, Cāṇakya is portrayed as a successful manager of political affairs without having any care or consideration for *parāvidya.* But it is also a fact that whatever he does, the book says, even getting any actual or potential rival of Candragupta killed, he considers it worth doing because of its being required by ethics or political ethics.

He gets Parbataka killed by the venom-carrying woman (*viṣakanyā*) who has been sent by Rākṣasa, the prime minister of Parbataka, to kill Candragupta; he uses false propaganda to make Malayaketu, Parbataka's son, believe that Rākṣasa has got his father killed and therefore have hatred for Rākṣasa even though Rākṣasa is innocent and sincerely devoted to him. Cānakya's justification for these and many other similar actions of his is that they are morally justified. They are morally justified because they are required in order to make secure Candragupta's kingship. He is convinced that Candragupta's being the king of Magadh is not only politically right but also morally right. Therefore, anything done to make his kingship safe and stable is morally right, no matter if it involves the use of fraudulent means, or is even an act of getting a person killed.

Cāṇakya's political practice is a good indicator of the moral truth that any conduct of any individual living in a social order is really justified if and only if it is morally justified. That it is a good indicator is true, no matter whether or not Cāṇakya's own actions, which he considers morally justified, are really morally justified.

Parāvidyā is to be acquired by an individual belonging to a social order. Therefore, whatever that individual does in order to acquire any *vidyā, parā* or *aparā,* has to be morally justified, or at least not morally wrong. This point is recognized by classical thinkers as is evident from their making it a precondition for anyone's acquiring *parāvidyā,* that is, for realizing the ultimate reality as the ultimate value, that he leads a morally impeccable life. Therefore, it is necessary to understand the kind of role which ethics, according to classical Indian philosophers, plays, or is assigned to play, in human life. This topic will be taken up in the next chapter.

NOTES AND REFERENCES

1. *Kasminnu bhagavo vijñāte sarvavidam vijñātam bhavatiti. Mundaka Upaniṣad,* 1.1.3, p. 77 in Swāmī Gambhīrānanda (trans.), *Eight Upaniṣads,* Vol. 2 (Advaita Ashrama, Calcutta, 1990). 'O adorable sir, (which is that thing) which having known, all this becomes known?'
2. Ibid., p. 78.
3. Ibid., 1.i.1., p. 75.
4. Ibid., 1.i.5, p. 80.
5. Ibid.
6. Ibid., p. 81.
7. Ibid., p. 107.
8. Ibid., p. 123.
9. Ibid., 1.i.9, p. 163.
10. Ibid., p. 80.
11. Ibid., p. 108.
12. Ibid., p. 79.
13. Ibid., 1.i.1–3, pp. 75–77.
14. *Gītā,* 4.40.
15. For a detailed critical discussion of the concept of dreamless sleep see my *Varnadharma, Niskama Karma and Practical Morality: A Critical Essay on Applied Ethics,* Chapter 4 (D.K. Printworld, Ltd., New Delhi, 1999).

CHAPTER 5

Ethics, Indian Philosophy and *Parā–Aparā Vidyā* Categoriology

5.1 A CONGENITAL PROBLEM

Classical Indian philosophers do not talk much about what they take ethics or moral philosophy to stand for, just as they do not about philosophy itself. They do not do it inspite of the fact that their philosophizings are, to a large extent, value-centric, as has been shown in Chapters 2 and 3. This is not a strange phenomenon, nor a typically Indian phenomenon. Almost all classical philosophers, or inquirers, concentrate primarily on the first-order activity of engaging themselves in conducting an inquiry in the manner they consider appropriate or suited to the nature of its subject-matter. They do not seem to have considered it worthwhile to turn around and look back on what they have been doing and engage themselves in the second-order activity of reflecting over and talking about the mature of the inquiry they have been conducting. In the case of classical Indian ethics this practice creates a serious problem. It does so because ethical ideas occur in very many different corners of the classical corpus and generally in mixed contexts. The contexts are mixed in the sense that in the same contexts in which ethical ideas occur, there also occur, and in a form closely related to them, some other sorts of ideas. These latter ideas are sometimes ontological, sometimes theological, sometimes epistemological, sometimes logical, sometimes political, sometimes even diplomatic or strategic, and very often of more than one sort.

Such a situation naturally makes it extremely difficult for a modern writer to locate the place which ethics occupies, or to ascertain the place which can be given to ethics in classical Indian philosophy. If in his journey into Indian philosophy, he is looking for well-knit, well-marked, full-fledged, ethical theories presented as theories standing predominantly on their own legs with only minimal support from other disciplines, he may conclude that ethics has no place in it. He would not be totally incorrect, but he would neither be fully fair to the spirit of Indian philosophizing or theorizing about morals. He would not be totally incorrect because classical Indian philosophers have not adopted the method of philosophizing, in their concern with morals, which is congenial to the formulation of a comprehensive ethical theory covering the entire field, or even a particular sector of it. That is why historians of ethics have failed to locate any Indian ethical theory comparable, for example, to the ethical theory of David Hume, or of Immanuel Kant. I would like to add that it would not be possible to locate in Indian moral philosophy an ethical theory comparable even to that of Plato or Aristotle. But still it would not be fully fair to conclude that there is no ethical theory, and therefore no ethics, in Indian philosophy. It would not, because the style of Indian moral philosophizing in very different from that of the great masters in the history of Western ethics. The Indian philosophers' style of ethical theorizing will be briefly stated in section 5.2 of this chapter and will be explained further and illustrated in Chapter 6. It consists in doing piecemeal, topical, analysis of moral issues as rooted in concrete contexts, real or imaginatively pictured, expressed in a description, sometimes of a real situation, sometimes of a mythological one, sometimes of a situation in a life-like fable, sometimes of one in a fable in which plants, animals, rivers, or mountains, etc., play important roles. Theories are there in a bold way but not in a bold colour. The outcome of this procedure is that nothing is neglected. Each one of theoretical, applied, conceptual, normative, environmental, etc., ethics is, to at least some extent, attended to. Therefore, in Indian classical ethics generally no problem arises, or arises seriously, as to how to bridge the gap, if there is one, between theoretical ethics and applied ethical, metaethics and normative ethics, general ethics and professional ethics, human-centric and non-human-centric or environmental ethics, etc.

Another reason for there not being grand or comprehensive ethical theories seems to be that technical philosophers, who have the logical and theoretical expertise to discuss, in a cohesive and precise manner, ethical issues and to present a well-reasoned, systematic, ethical theory, have not discussed them in detail, or in volumes exclusively devoted to ethics, as some ancient Greek philosophers have done. As examples of classical Greek books on ethics we can easily mention some of Plato's dialogues like *Protagoras, The Republic,* etc. and Aristotle's *Nicomachean Ethics.* But there is no such book in the classical Indian philosophical corpus, discussing ethical issues comprehensively and presenting a systematic, full-fledged, ethical theory.

Ethical things have been copiously talked about in the Indian corpus, but mostly in philosophically non-technical works, for example, in the epics, the *Mahābhārata* and the *Rāmāyaṇa,* in some *Purāṇas* like the *Bhāgavata,* in some *smṛtis* like the *Manusmṛti,* in some ethico-socio-political works, like Cāṇakya's *Arthaśāstra, Sūtras* and *Nītisūtras*, in Vātsyāyana's *Kāmasūtra,* in some of the *Dharmaśāstras*, in the *Dhammapada,* etc. This is not to ignore the occurrence of ethical ideas, and some ethical discussions in the *Vedas* and in several of the *Upaniṣads*. Even books of fables like Nārāyaṇa Pandita's compilation *Hitopadeśa* and Viṣṇu Śarmā's *Pañcatantra* contain a lot of ethical ideas, principles, precepts, etc., explained through interesting stories. In fact, the use of stories, even involving animals and plants, has been resorted to even in the epics.

All of these works contain abundantly ethical ideas, views, precepts, principles, rules, norms, etc., operative in, or relevant to, a large variety of situations which may arise in man's personal, social and political transactions, as well as in his relationship with his environment, animate and inanimate. But none of them contains any comprehensive, well-structured, full-fledged, ethical theory. The *Gītā,* notwithstanding the fact that it is only a part of the *Mahābhārata,* has acquired the status of almost an independent ethico-theological work, possessing for many scriptural authority. Some people do claim that it presents a complete ethical theory. But it does not. This I have shown, in some detail and in a critical manner in *A Historical–Developmental Study of Classical Indian Philosophy of Morals*[1] and in my earlier work *Varṇadharma, Niṣkāma Karma, and Practical Morality: A Critical Essay on Applied Ethics.*[2] The same can be said of some Mīmāmsā works which deal with ethical issues.

Not only ethics but even other areas of Indian philosophy, at least in their early career, have a mixed character. Metaphysics, theology, and axiology have in many discussions merged with each other. Even some scientific ideas have occasionally entered into a discussion which is primarily metaphysical, theological, axiological, or of a mixed character.

Even Indian epistemology and logic do not present an exception to this feature of classical Indian philosophy. The two are not only mixed with each other, constituting what is called *pramāṇaśāstra,* but also with certain ideas from other areas. For example, ethics has entered Indian logic in a very substantial, though indirect manner. To give an illustration, according to Dharmakīrti, in any inference (a) the *hetu* must be present in the *pakṣa,* (b) wherever the *hetu* is present, the *sādhya* must be present, and (c) wherever the *sādhya* is not present, the *hetu* must also be not present. The three-membered conjunction of the propositions stating (a), (b) and (c) will constitute, therefore, the complete premise-set of the inference, and none of (a), (b) or (c) is to be false. This means that anyone giving a permissible inference is not, by the very definition of an inference, allowed to use a false proposition as a premise. When all the premises are true and the conclusion is correctly drawn, no untruth can be inferred and therefore asserted on the basis of any inference. This procedure amounts to saying that none should use inference to assert an untruth, or contrariwise, that one should use inference only to assert a truth. Saying this is obviously saying an important ethical thing without doing that in a preceptorial manner. This interpretation of the practice of defining an inference is true of all Indian theories of inference.

However, epistemology-logic got separated quite early from the parent stock, though not completely. It is on account of this separation that we have some full-fledged classical theories of knowledge and of logic. But the separation of logic from epistemology has not proceeded as fast, or as thoroughly, as it should have. This is the reason why the distinction between formal logic, philosophical logic, and philosophy of logic in the corpus of classical Indian logic has not yet been highlighted, not even by modern Indian logicians. Rather, there are scholars galore who still think that epistemology-logic, *pramāṇaśāstra,* is one discipline, and separating one from the other would destroy its Indianness, the distinctive character of classical Indian epistemology-logic.

The mixture of different sorts of philosophical ideas in a classical corpus is not something strange or bizarre. The classical mind is more synthetic-speculative than analytical-discursive, though in the later developments in Indian philosophy there are numerous examples of highly sophisticated works of theory-construction exhibiting a very high degree of excellence in analytical-discursive reasoning, particularly in the field of logic.[3]

That several things were mixed with one another in the classical corpus is no reason for presenting them in that, or in similar, mixed form even today. This is not at all to say that different areas of philosophy are completely disparate, with well-marked boundaries separating one from the other. The fact of the matter is that in the world of philosophy, and so in the world of classical Indian, or Indian, philosophy, almost every area of philosophy touches every other area. But still each one of these areas has its own individuality, its own identity, and each area's identity has to be recognized, respected and properly characterized. In this respect, the world of philosophy is very much like the (geographical) world we live in. It is the majority of modern Indian writers' presenting Indian philosophy in theological terms, or in a manner which does not highlight the individuality of Indian philosophy as distinct from that of religion, which has misled some Western scholars to hold that Indian philosophy is not philosophy but theology. Similarly, the delineation of Indian moral philosophy, or ethics, as done by some modern writers, in a manner which does not characterize its own individuality, and therefore does not properly distinguish it from moral pedagogy or scheme of preparing oneself for achieving some mundane or religious goal, has misled some Western writers to think that there is no ethics in classical Indian philosophy.

Indian ethics did not, unfortunately, get separated from others, as epistemology-logic did, and therefore has not attained till date even that amount of independence which each one of the latter couple has. Even modern writers on Indian ethics have not been able to present Indian ethics as ethics per se, as a discipline in its own right and not as a subsidiary or companion of another, as far as it is possible to do that without disfiguring its original, classical, soul. This job is really a tough one for anyone who wants to do it conscientiously and in a conceptually cohesive manner. The difficult nature of the job, primarily caused by the fact of Indian ethics having been mixed with other areas, is compounded by another fact. This other fact is the emphasis, and not always, or totally, a misplaced one, on the importance of man's spiritual goal, accompanied with a certain understanding or conception of the relation of leading an ethical life with the pursuit of the spiritual goal.

5.2 A METHODOLOGICAL MIST

As it has been shown in the preceding chapter, classical Indian philosophers, at least a few of the prominent ones, have given the place of the highest honour, among man's cognitive inquiries, to his cognition of the *spiritual reality*, or to his *spiritual cognition* of the ultimate reality. The ultimate reality, according to them, is also the ultimate value. Therefore, its cognition has been asserted by them to be the realization of the highest value. It is to make it unambiguously denotative of this, its axiological feature, that they have given to this cognition or inquiry the name *parāvidyā*. But it has also been made clear there, in the discussion of the nature of this inquiry, that the characterization as *parāvidyā* is true only of a small sector of classical Indian philosophy, of its speculative axiological metaphysics, and not of all sectors of it, and that mistaking it to be true of all of them may cause an interpretative mishap. It may cause this by yielding some implications about Indian philosophy which are not true of it and therefore give it a distorted appearance. This mishap in depicting the character of Indian philosophy has happened, of course, in different forms, on account of some Western as well as some Indian scholars (mistakenly) taking the whole of Indian philosophy as a spiritual inquiry.

Their mistaken interpretation has created for them a mist around it on account of which they have not been able to correctly locate in it all that it actually contains, or to correctly ascertain what it does not. For example, some Western scholars, as already discussed in Chapter 4, have claimed that there is nothing philosophical in it. Since in the present chapter we are concerned with the place of ethics, or, moral philosophy, in classical Indian philosophy, we shall be concerned here specifically with the implication of the spiritualist interpretation of (the whole of) Indian philosophy for this particular issue. To anticipate what is going to be explained in what follows, it has led some Western scholars to aver that in Indian philosophy there is no ethics in the sense of ethical or moral theorizing.

Some Indian interpreters, on the other hand, have claimed, with pride, that Indian philosophy may not have what Westerners call ethics. But this is not a defect because it, according to them, has to its credit something which goes beyond, or which supersedes, what Westerners call, or is generally called, ethics. Surprisingly, they think that by proving this, assuming that they have succeeded in proving it, they have rebutted the Western accusation that there is lack of ethics in Indian philosophy. In fact, their adoption of this strategy, as will be made gradually clear, not only does not rebut but virtually concedes the validity of the Western charge. They do not realize that their logic surreptitiously leads to this unfortunate concession. They do not realize that going *beyond* a certain point does not imply having gone *through* it, or having gone beyond it *after reaching* it. A point beyond another point can very well be reached both in logic and in practice, both in a cognitive and a physical journey, by adopting a route which does not touch or pass through that point. Moreover, by having reached the point Q beyond the point P the traveller may not make good the lapse of not having also reached P. This will matter, of course, if and only if the point P, which he has missed, is so important that missing, or passing over, it is a serious lapse. Ethics, quite obviously, occupies such an important place in human life. A philosophical, or any inquiry, into the cognitive, conative, or affective aspects of it cannot afford to bypass it. Its bypassing ethics will surely impoverish it. All this is as true of classical Indian philosophy and classical Indian life, as it is of any philosophy done in any period of human history. Classical Indian philosophers are not oblivious of this fact as is evidenced by the emphasis they have put on the importance of ethics in all walks of life. The way they have done it is not less forceful than the way any philosopher anywhere has. Quite naturally, therefore, it can be said that ethics occupies in Indian philosophy a place at least as respectable as the place which any other component of it does. And, this is true of ethics in the ordinary, normal, sense of the term.

To see all this we have to wait a little. Here I want to point out that some scholars of a certain philosophical orientation, Western as well as Indian, have not been able to properly *identify* and therefore *characterize* the *distinctiveness*, or individuality, of the style of classical Indian theorizing or philosophizing about ethical issues. Therefore, if one group, primarily the Western, has straightforwardly declared that there is no ethics in Indian philosophy, the other, primarily the indigenous, group has equally forcefully maintained that ethics has been assigned in Indian philosophy only a subsidiary role in man's pursuit of values, a view which too fails to see the status which Indian philosophy has actually given to ethics.

The reason, or the primary reason, responsible for the Western writers doing this is their not being able to see ethical theorizing in classical Indian works on account of a methodological or conceptual mist. This mist their logical eyes have not succeeded in piercing through in order to see what it hides. The mist they themselves have created by their obsession with, or sticking too rigidly to, a particular conception of ethics. This conception is modelled on the pattern of such comprehensive ethical theories as those of Plato, Aristotle, David Hume, Immanuel Kant, George W.F. Hegel, John Stuart Mill et al. According to it an individual philosopher's philosophy, or the philosophy of a school or group of like-minded philosophers, can be said to have a philosophy of morals, or ethics, only if it has at the centre of it, or as a well-marked component of it, a comprehensive ethical theory, or a comprehensive set of related theories. This theory, or set, is to be constructed on a grand scale in the sense that it should cover all, or almost all, themes pertaining to man's ethical and metaethical concerns, i.e. the ethical and metaethical issues relevant to his private and public life. Thus, to be credited with having an ethics, or ethical theory, a philosophy must or should have a more or less well-organized, neatly marked out, *system* of morals or of moral and metamoral ideas. The philosophers who have (allegedly) given such a system consider it rich enough to provide solutions, or, at least ingredients by using which a philosopher, or an intelligent layman, can obtain solutions, for all or almost all ethical problems; that is, he can find solutions of ethical problems which arise in his, or anyone else's, life, no matter whether they are problems relating to personal, social, or professional, etc. matters.

With this conception of a philosopher's way of doing ethics at the back of their mind, the Western philosophers try to find out whether or not there is ethics in the works of classical Indian philosophers. When they fail to locate it there, they say, they are justified in saying that there is no ethics or ethical theory in Indian philosophy. What happens here is that their conception of ethics, or that of a philosophical way of doing ethics, has created a mist which does not allow them to see the ethics, or ethical theorizing, done by Indian philosophers in a style different from the grand style of first constructing a comprehensive ethical theory and then trying to solve or clarify particular ethical problems in accordance with that theory. The classical Indian philosopher's style of ethical theorizing is, as it seems to me, to proceed by doing something like what some Western philosophers, particularly since the later part of the twentieth century, have begun doing. It consists in reflecting on moral issues by doing piecemeal analysis of concrete, individual problems which arise, or may be imaginatively reconstructed as arising, in well-marked-out situations. It is liberal enough to acknowledge that significant roles may be played in these situations not only by human beings but also by non-humans which may be animate like a plant or an animal, or even inanimate like a hill or a river. In fact, there does not seem to exist for them any unbridgeable gulf between the animate and the inanimate worlds. And, this method of progressively theorizing by way of piecemeal analysis is applied to clarify personal as well as social problems, to solve moral dilemmas, to draw the boundaries of the application of moral principles, to determine whether a certain character-trait is a conditional or an absolute virtue, whether it is a virtue of a saint, a householder, or a ruler, or of all the three, etc., etc. The result of proceeding in this way is that there does not exist any watertight division between theoretical ethics, applied ethics, conceptual ethics, normative ethics, bioethics, etc. Not that any one of them has been totally ignored. Rather, ethicizing has been done in a composite manner. By analysing it a modern philosopher may come to the conclusion that in this specimen the emphasis is on a conceptual issue, in that on a normative one, in a third one on practical or pragmatic advice, for example, on deciding how to apply a moral concept or principle in a certain situation, etc. All this will be made clearer in the chapter that follows.

The Indian respondents to the no-ethics charge against Indian philosophy, as already said, seem to have overshot their target. They adopt the device of highlighting the *mokṣa*-orientedness, the spiritual goal-orientedness, of Indian philosophy. Their strategy is to claim that Indian philosophy has discovered the highest goal which man ought to seek. This goal is spiritual and is of much higher value than the value which is all that a mere ethical life, however impeccably lived, can enable a man to obtain. Ethical life is just a means, an instrument, a ladder, a footstool, for reaching this spiritual state. The wisest thing to do, therefore, is to transcend, to go beyond, ethics in order to reach the spiritual height.

The obvious implication of this view is to deny the primacy, the intrinsic value, of the ethical. This attitude towards the ethical is sure to belittle its importance in human life as normally lived. It would at least water down its value in social life. It would thus mean that Indian philosophy does not give to ethics the status which it is commonly understood as having. As commonly understood, or, as per the common-sense understanding of the nature of ethics, ethics plays a very noble role in making social life cohesive. This is a role, many would say, which is not to be bartered for any other role assigned to it in its place. But the beyond-ethics view would imply that a man who leads a good ethical life in his private and public dealings but does not transcend or go beyond it, i.e. does not use it as a means to attain the spiritual, would become inferior to him who does the latter.

The upolder of this view too does not recognize that Indian philosophy fully acknowledges the intrinsic dignity of ethics in the life of an individual as well as in that of a society. He does not, because he also is not able to see through the methodological mist his own methodology of characterizing Indian philosophy as going beyond ethics creates around Indian philosophy, or more specifically, around its conception of ethics. He thinks that this methodology exhibits that Indian philosophy accords to ethics a respectable place in its household. But what the adoption of the methodology really yields is the contrary of it. We shall see in the discussion of this methodology of characterization that it is not very different from the no-ethics characterization in being, like the no-ethics characterization, unfair to the delineation of the *place* which ethics has in Indian philosophy and to that of the kind of *inquiry* the ethics that Indian philosophy has is. To show all this, first the no-ethics characterization and then the beyond-ethics characterization will be examined in the coming two sections.

5.3 INDIAN PHILOSOPHY AS LACKING ETHICS

To mention an example from amongst Western philosophers, W.T. Stace arrives at his conclusion that Indian philosophy lacks ethics by first trying to show that Indian philosophy is not really philosophy but religion. It is for this reason that, he thinks, it has not been discussed or included in books on the history of philosophy by Western writers. This view of his he presents in his book on the history of Greek philosophy[4] which is more popular and extensively read by students and teachers of philosophy in India than in Great Britain, the country where it was first published and has been reprinted several times after its first printing. Nor is it popular or widely read in the United States, the country in which Stace spent the major part of his academic career.

Before taking up an academic career as a researcher in and teacher of philosophy, Stace was a member of the Indian Civil Service. In the early part of the last century he was posted as a magistrate in the then Ceylon (present-day Sri Lanka). During that period India, Burma and Ceylon were under the political control of Great Britain, forming together an important part of the famous British Empire. There were Indians in Ceylon and the citizens of India were free to visit Ceylon and those of Ceylon to visit India. It is likely that Stace studied some classical Indian philosophies there. I am not very sure if he ever visited India and came in direct contact with some traditional Indian philosophers. But the serious philosopher and writer that he is, it is not likely that he formed his opinion about Indian philosophy merely on the basis of some hearsay information about its character. Therefore, it is very likely that he did study some classical Indian works and some interpretative ones on them. He is not an Indologist like A.B. Keith or Max Mueller. Apart from making some remarks about the general character of Indian philosophy, he has not given in any work of his an extensive account, critical or exegetical, of any Indian philosophical theme. But since his remarks are pointed, candid, and based on (allegedly) some philosophical or conceptual reasons, I have chosen them for examination here. To the best of my knowledge, no Indian writer on Indian philosophy has done that in spite of the fact that almost everyone who has attained a master's degree in philosophy from an Indian institution is expected to have read his book on the history of Greek philosophy, already referred to, in which he records his reasons for Indian philosophy's being religion and not philosophy.

'Opinions may differ', says Stace, 'as to whether India ever had any philosophy.' One of the main reasons why 'Indian thought is not usually included in histories of philosophy' is, according to him, the fact that 'philosophy in India has never separated itself from religious and practical needs. The ideal of knowledge for its own sake is rarely to be found. Knowledge is desired merely as a means towards salvation. ... This is not the scientific, but practical spirit. It gives birth to religions, but not to philosophies.'[5] Philosophy presents whatever it deals with 'scientifically, in the form of pure thought', but 'religion gives it in the form of sensuous pictures, myths, images, and symbols'.[6] This feature of Indian thought 'gives the second reason why Indian thought is more properly classed as religious than philosophical. It seldom or never rises from sensuous to pure thought. It is poetical rather than scientific. It is content with symbol and metaphors in place of rational explanations, and all this is a mark of the religious, rather than the philosophical, presentation of the truth.'[7]

It is true that many Indian philosophers emphasize the instrumental value of knowledge, that is, its value in enabling its possessor to acquire his objectives which may be earthly or secular, or spiritual or religious. This they do in order to provide an effective motivation to acquire knowledge of whatever there is as well as of whatever deserves to be aspired after, i.e. knowledge of truths and of values. But while emphasizing this feature of the pursuit of knowledge, they do not ignore the intrinsic value of knowledge. The fact that several popular sayings in Sanskrit, coming down from classical times, emphasize the value of knowledge as knowledge is a good sign of the great importance which was given in the classical Indian life-style to the pursuit of knowledge for its own sake as well as for its felicific results. For example, the saying that a gentleman acquires scholarship (*vidyā*) not for the sake of scoring victory in a debate (*vivādāya*) but for acquiring knowledge, does not merely state a fact. It, in effect, proclaims that scholarship, which is a form or kind of knowledge, is to be attained for its own sake, for the sake of making the acquirer a better knower or individual than he was before its acquisition. Even the saying that it is his acquisition of knowledge by means of which an individual attains his freedom (*jñānena mukti*) and not by his becoming a shaven-headed monk (*na tu muṇḍanena*) *appears* to emphasize the instrumental value of knowledge, but it need not, or does not, do that. Freedom also means freedom from ignorance, which may be said to be identical with knowledge, or even the result of knowledge. But even when freedom is said to be the result of knowledge, it, the result, would not be different from knowledge, from that of which it is said to be a result. That is, the intention behind the saying is to assert that knowledge is an intrinsic value as well, i.e. a value to be sought not only for the sake of its utility, but also for its own sake. The most forceful and clearest formulation of the view that knowledge is the only thing which is in itself and for itself a value, rather the highest value and reality, is given in Śankara's *Advaitism.* His *Advaitism* is, according to many the consummation of *Upaniṣadic* views. But Stace takes, or mistakes, even them to be assigning to knowledge only an instrumental or practical value, and therefore to be religious and not philosophical, or to be more religious than philosophical.

But the other reason, which Stace has for calling Indian thought religious and not philosophical, occurs at the end of the quotation given above. And, it seems that he considers it to be his primary or the strongest reason. It is, according to him, the fact that Indian thought does not give or have 'rational explanations'. His main argument seems to be that Indian philosophy does not provide rational foundations for its basic claims, for the basic ideas or propositions which are central to it, or for what it claims to be true, real, or good, in some fundamental sense. The organ of any philosophical inquiry, he would say, is reason or ratiocination, and not non-reason. Since reason is not the organ of the 'so-called' Indian philosophizing, Indian philosophizing is not philosophizing proper.

The above kind of interpretation or characterization of the Indian style of philosophizing has already been shown to be untrue of it in Chapters 3 and 4. It has been shown in Chapter 4 that even that particular sector of Indian philosophy, its speculative-axiological ontology, which may be called *paravidyā,* has to use a good amount of reasoning or ratiocination. This it has to do in spite of the fact that it is, speaking from the religious or theological point of view, the most sensitive zone of Indian philosophy. It is a sensitive zone because it has features which may lead or mislead one to consider to it be religious, and not philosophical, or closer to religion than to philosophy. But taking this lead would not, as has been therein shown, be fully fair. Moreover, it is only one sector of Indian philosophy, and not the whole of it. Since all this has been already discussed in detail, let us limit the discussion here to the examination of Stace's reasoning for his very specific charge that there is no ethics, or moral philosophy, in Indian philosophy.

Ethics, or moral philosophy, is an important sector of philosophy. Therefore, it must and does involve the use of reason, since philosophy itself is a rational inquiry. Since Indian philosophy is not, or is not adequately, rational, Indian or Hindu—Stace quite often uses 'Hindu' to mean 'Indian'—philosophy cannot have, or cannot assign an important place to, ethics. Indian philosophy is the parent body of Indian ethics if there is anything called Indian ethics. The organ of any ethical theorizing, of any moral philosophy, obviously is reason. Since the main organ of Indian philosophy itself, of the parent body, is not reason, Indian philosophy cannot have ethical theorizing, or ethics, as an important component of it. This seems to be Stace's reasoning when he says that 'although Hinduism has its scale of values, and its doctrine of development, it has no rational foundations for these, and though it has the idea of higher and lower, yet, because this is without foundation, it lets it slip, it never *grips* the idea, and so easily slides into the view that all is equally divine.'[8] Obviously such a philosophical corpus cannot have any philosophy of values, and therefore, any moral philosophy or ethics. This conclusion of his he reasserts in another popular book of his which came out only a few years after the one I have been referring to. In the second work he says that 'the Hindu God', meaning by it the *Upaniṣadic-Advaitic Brahman*—'is abstract. It is only the concrete Idea'—meaning by it something like Hegel's spirit—'which produces concrete morality and law out of itself. The One'—meaning by 'One' the Hindu God—'abandons the multiplicity of the world to itself, and the element of unity, reason, order, is therefore not found in this world. And since morality is essentially the product of reason and unity, it is lacking here. No doubt Hindus have their moral codes. But morality and righteousness are no essential part of worship in this sphere.'[9]

By saying that morality is lacking in Hinduism, or Hindu corpus of thought, Stace means that the concept of morality, which comprehends that of righteousness and other allied concepts, is not present or articulated in it. If this is really the case, there cannot be in it any moral or ethical theorizing, i.e. moral philosophy or ethics. There may still be moral practices but not moral conceptualization or reasoning. Thinking on this line, Stace admits that there are moral codes, or mores, i.e. practices or examples of customs, conventions, actions, or even schemes of life, which Hindus consider moral, or immoral, and which may be so considered even by non-Hindus. But in the name of moral philosophy or ethics, they have nothing worthwhile to offer.

Something similar to Stace's denial of any noticeable existence of ethics in Indian philosophy is the view of A.B. Keith presented in an important writing of his.[10] Keith is a famous Indologist very greatly respected even today in India and abroad in circles of Indologists and writers on classical Indian philosophical themes. Farquhar,[11] another Indologist, as quoted by Sarasvati Chennakesavan in her introductory book[12] emphatically says, in an essay of his that 'There is practically no ethical philosophy within the frontiers of Hindu Thinking'. Of Western Indologists, Keith has exercised a great influence on writers on Indian philosophy, perhaps greater than many others, in shaping the interpretation or interpretations of the character of Indian philosophy. Therefore, I shall discuss here in some detail his views and ignore Farquhar's.

Keith is very emphatic in saying that '... the dominating feature in the philosophy of India is that the question of right conduct never attained the dignity of a subject to be propounded for serious consideration'.[13] Very often those, particularly Indian writers, who claim that Indian philosophy contains a very rich moral philosophy, refer to the *Brahmanas* and *Upaniṣads*. These scholars quote lines and lines verbatim in their oral and written performances to make this point. But according to Keith '*Brahmanas* do not develop any theory of morality' and 'the ethical content of *Upaniṣads* must be said to be negligible and valueless ... there is made no attempt to make the theoretical philosophy a ground of morality of any sort. There are, here and there, moral maxims enunciated, but these are of no consequence and rise in no way above popular morality'. The *Upaniṣadic* philosophers, Keith thinks, 'must have felt an exaggerated value to attach to their speculations, and have completely failed to see that morality is the most objective and essential part of philosophy, and is something other than sacrificial activity or intellectual gymnastics'. He admits that in some *Upaniṣads* duties of individuals, in accordance with the position held by them in their society, have been mentioned, for example, the *Taittirīya* offers a list of duties which a student is required to fulfil. But the mere mention of any number of moral maxims, duties, or virtues, etc., would not make, Keith would say, any moral philosophy. Keith also mentions utterances made by some gods, here and there, which amount to debunking morality, and several immoralities committed by some of them, as described in Indian mythological literature.[14]

Keith's conclusion, like Stace's, is that not only in the Vedic-Upaniṣadic literature, but in Indian philosophy as a whole, there is no, or very little, moral philosophy. This is *not*, to be fair to Stace and Keith, equivalent to saying that classical Indians did not care for morality, or had no moral ideas or principles. Rather, what they and others—who hold that in Indian philosophy there is no ethics, or is in a very minimal, marginal, way—mean to bring out is that the content of *moral philosophy*, or of ethics in the sense of ethical theorizing, in Indian philosophy is very little. By moral philosophy they obviously mean a systematic discussion of the nature of man's moral goals or norms in his personal, public, political life, i.e. of his values, virtues, obligations, rights, etc., along with a discussion of the criterion of rightness or moral worth of an individual as well as of an action done or doable by him, of freedom of will, human agency, weakness of will, moral luck, etc.

This conception of moral philosophy or ethics has survived, and is no longer a Western conception in any regional, geographical, or even cultural, sense. What I mean to say is that this conception of moral philosophy can be said to be an objective conception, a conception which any moral philosopher, or philosopher, acquainted with the present-day state of the craft of doing moral philosophy, would consider acceptable. It would not matter whether his own predilection is for conceptual ethics, normative ethics, descriptive ethics (which some social scientists do), or applied ethics, etc.

The reasons for the neglect of moral philosophy by classical Indian philosophers, according to many who think that moral philosophy has been neglected by them, to mention some of the most important ones, are: classical Indian philosophers' excessive preoccupation with the ideal of salvation (*mokṣa*) and their *karmic* worldview which, being deterministic, leaves no room for human agency or freedom of will or of action. Whether or not these two alleged reasons have in them the potentiality to cause the neglect of moral philosophy, if the neglect is a fact, will be discussed in Chapters 14 and 15 which deal with salvation and the *karmic* worldview. Hence I shall be concerned with only ascertaining whether or not there is in Indian philosophy any moral philosophy worth discussing or mentioning, and if it is, in what form it is.

A common-sensical, straightforward, logical way to refute the charge of there being no ethics in Indian philosophy would be, any open-minded philosopher would think, to locate philosophical facts which directly or indirectly illustrate the existence of ethics in Indian philosophy, and of ethics in the same theoretical, conceptual sense in which 'ethics' has been used in the charge. The charge will also get refuted, he may say, even if it is shown in a convincing manner that there exist in Indian philosophy some inklings, clear marks, or arrows indicating directions in which ethical theorizing should go, or in which a moral philosopher should go to evolve an ethical theory or a set of ethical theories. Even indicating the existence of a skeleton or a blue-print of an ethical theory, or of a good hinterland containing raw materials for moral philosophizing, for constructing some moral theory or theories out of those raw materials by using some conceptual cement to make them hold together, in one or more than one way, would also refute the charge, or at least greatly weaken it. Adopting any one of the above strategies would be an attempt to meet the no-ethics charge face to face, and would definitely be a dignified philosophical venture.

But this, the straightforward method has not been used by modern Indian philosophers, or has not been used with the seriousness of purpose it deserves to be used with. On the contrary, some influential interpreters have used another method, a method which consists in trying to nullify the charge by allegedly showing that Indian philosophy goes beyond ethics. For brevity's sake I shall call this method 'beyond-ethics method'. The reason, or a prime reason, behind the motivation to use it is (a) their *axiological conviction* that there exists in Indian philosophy a discipline which goes beyond ethics and is therefore higher than it and (b) their accompanying *methodological* or *logical conviction* that by showing that Indian philosophy goes beyond ethics they can conclusively refute, or make null and void, the no-ethics charge against it.

An attempt will be made in section 5.5 to show that there is ethics in Indian philosophy in the sense in which ethics is used in the no-ethics charge, and thereby to meet the charge face to face. But before doing that the beyond-ethics method of meeting the charge will be discussed and examined. It is necessary to do that because of its strong grip on the minds of many even today. In most of the cases it is a result of the upholder's adherence to some non-philosophical consideration. A non-philosophical consideration is generally more tempting, particularly in respect of ethical-religious matters, than a philosophical or rational-logical consideration. Perhaps this is the main reason, or one of the main reasons, for the beyond-ethics method's remaining till date unexamined, or for not having been thoroughly examined, by modern philosophers who have written on classical Indian ethics. Surprisingly, since the last few years of the twentieth century, the number of philosophers as well as of non-philosophers under its sway has increased, and seems to be increasing further. But this is not the sole reason for my examining it in some detail here. There is also another, a good logical or philosophical, reason for doing that. It is the reason that this method, the beyond-ethics method, does not really, or effectively, refute the no-ethics charge against Indian philosophy. Rather, it may even be seen as implicitly supporting it.

5.4 INDIAN PHILOSOPHY AS GOING BEYOND ETHICS

This view, offered as a device to meet the no-ethics charge against Indian philosophy, consists in the attempt to demonstrate that Indian philosophy does not lack ethics but goes beyond, or transcends, it. It does insofar as its axiology, a proponent of the view would say, goes much further than the point ethics goes to, or can go to. Ethics too, he admits, provides a philosophy of values, i.e. a philosophy about what a human being, or a group of human beings, ought to aim at, seek, or aspire after, in the kind of social world he, or the group, lives in, or has to live in. In their inquiry into the nature of human values, Indian philosophers, he avers, go beyond the frontiers or boundaries of ethical inquiry because they have discovered a value which is higher than any value a life which is merely ethical can reach to, i.e. a value superior to all ethical values. The scheme of values, or the scheme of life, which Indian axiology presents, is such that after realizing it, the individual who has realized it would transcend the scheme of life which may emerge as a result of realizing only ethical values. Therefore, since Indian axiological inquiry transcends ethical inquiry, or the life lived as per the former transcends the life lived merely as per the latter, Indian philosophy has, or offers, something superior to ethics. Consequently, the proponent of this view concludes, it cannot be said to have no ethics. By pointing this out he thinks that he has adequately refuted the no-ethics charge against Indian philosophy, or, speaking in positive terms, that he has proven that it has ethics since he has proven that it has something higher than ethics. Ethics in all this discussion means, or must mean, ethics as ordinarily understood, i.e. it must be taken in the sense in which it has been taken in the no-ethics charge. That sense of it has been already explained in the concluding portion of the last section.

Indian axiological theory presents the concept of *mokṣa* as the highest value (*parama puruṣārtha*). It is said to be a spiritual value which is realized by leading a prescribed style of life. Ethical or moral life, i.e. life in accordance with ethical norms, has to be lived as a means to attaining or realizing *mokṣa*. But when *mokṣa* is realized, the *mokṣa*-realized life transcends the boundaries of ethics. It transcends them in the sense that requirements of ethical life are no longer obligatory for the *mukta*, the individual who has realized *mokṣa*. It is a life more meritorious than a life in which *mokṣa* has not been realized even though all ethical values have been.

This point of view has been very popular among modern interpreters of Indian philosophy and has been considered by many to have adequately met the charge of no-ethics in Indian philosophy. It has been casually expressed in numerous works on Indian philosophy, and generally taken to be unquestionable. In fact, it has assumed the status not only of an axiomatic, but that of a sacred, or from a nationalist point of view, a pride-worthy, truth about Indian philosophy. That is why questioning it, or subjecting it to critical scrutiny, is very likely to be considered by many to be something like an act of sacrilege or blasphemy.

Almost all those—and their number is legion—who uphold this view seem to have ignored, or to have not realized, the implications of championing the cause of transcending ethics. This is surprising because these implications are very clear in some of the statements in some classical works about what a liberated (*mukta, mokṣaprāpta*) individual may or may not do in case he considers himself to have reached a point in the axiological space which is beyond the boundaries of ethics. All this will be clear as we proceed on in the discussions which follow.

It is obvious that this mode of transcending ethics can be said to be true, if it is true, only of the person who has realized *mokṣa* in the very life in which he has tried to realize it, i.e. only of the *jīvanmukta*. The requirements of ethics are applicable only to a living person who has his mental and physical powers in a normal, healthy condition. A dead man can do nothing and therefore neither anything ethical, nor anything unethical. There is the saying that a dead man tells no lie; there could very well be another saying that a dead man tells not even a truth, simply because he can tell nothing. All this means that the theory of transcending ethics can hold good, if it holds good as a philosophical theory, only if the theory of *jivanmukti* holds good on the ground of its own logical merit. Therefore, the theory of transcending ethics may be held, if they consider it worth holding, only by those schools of Indian philosophy which accept the possibility of attaining *mokṣa* by an individual while remaining alive, for example, by *Jaina, Bauddha, Sānkhya, Advaitic* thinkers. It cannot be said to true of thinkers belonging to those schools of Indian philosophy which only admit the possibility of an individual's attaining salvation after his death (*videhamukti*), for example, of *Nyāya* thinkers. Therefore, it cannot be said, as many modern interpreters say, or seem to say, that Indian philosophy, meaning by it the entire body of Indian philosophy, upholds the theory of transcending ethics. Almost all of these scholars believe in the doctrine that an axiology which transcends ethics is philosophically better or sounder than one which does not. Therefore, they think that if they claim it to be true of Indian philosophy as such, they would thereby be also claiming that Indian philosophy's approach to ethics is better than any other philosophy's which does not hold the doctrine of transcending ethics. This may be an additional reason for their claiming that Indian philosophy as such pleads for going beyond ethics.

It is important to note here that it does not seem absolutely unquestionable, to say even of all the schools which accept the possibility of *jīvanmukti*, that, according to them, an enlightened individual, say, a *jīvanmukta*, occupies a position outside the area of ethics. It is not at all easy to locate in a *Jaina* or *Bauddha* philosophical work a remark which even seemingly declares that a *jīvanmukta* is exempt from all moral requirements, positive or negative, i.e., free to do, or not to do, anything which is morally obligatory or forbidden for an ordinary, unliberated, but morally conscientious individual. *Jaina* as well as *Bauddha* literature is very vast. It is not logically safe, therefore, to say that no such remark occurs in any work of either one of the two schools. But it is extremely unlikely, or almost impossible, that it does. This is so because both of the two schools' primary and initial motivation is ethical, and not spiritual or religious. If they also develop into a religion or any kind of spiritual philosophy, as they can be said to have done, they do that because of being *demanded by their ethics.* Therefore, they do not seem to subscribe to the view that the spiritually enlightened individual, the *jīvanmukta*, occupies a position which is outside the zone of ethics.

It is very significant to refer, in this connection, to the Buddhist principle that the *bodhisattva*, the enlightened, should postpone attaining his liberation (*nirvāṇa*) in order that he may help other individuals to attain not only their liberation but also their mundane welfare. This is an ethical, a highly elevated altruistic, principle. It virtually prescribes that one should sacrifice one's own chance of attaining *nirvāṇa*, one's spiritual goal—since *nirvāṇa* or *mokṣa* is taken to be a spiritual goal—in the interest of morality or ethics. Caring for others' welfare of any kind, spiritual or mundane, is clearly ethical because it is altruistic. And, to make this sacrifice is to make the greatest sacrifice because *nirvāṇa* is the highest value. It is to sacrifice, in effect, one's chance of attaining *nirvāṇa* forever because the number of individuals needing to be helped is infinite. Similarly, a Jain philosopher would never consider it permissible for any individual, howsoever enlightened, to go out of the bounds of morality, for example, to infringe the principle of *ahimsā* i.e. of complete abstinence from doing in word, thought, or action, anything which hurts any living creature mentally or physically. As has been shown earlier, the Jain theory of conditional predication (*syādvāda*) is an example of the application of the principle of non-violence to a logical theory which determines in a broad way which mode of predicating one thing of another is, or is not, permissible.

The theory, to put it very briefly, says that in predicating one thing of another we should always prefix the predication with the word *syāt* which means 'perhaps', 'probably', etc. That is, in place of saying 'X is P' or 'X is not P' we should say 'Perhaps X is P', or 'Perhaps X is not P'. If we say 'X is P', it means that it is wrong to say that X is not P. Therefore, if the addressee believed that X is not P, it would hurt his feelings, as he would then feel that he has been accused of saying an untruth, something he should not have said. Thus, it would cause some mental hurt, or injury, to him, and violate the principle of non-violence. All this can be said to be true of all judgements or statements, positive or negative, i.e. of statements which affirm or deny a predicate of another thing. Therefore, a Jain thinker would say, all statements should be prefixed with some such phrase as 'perhaps', 'probably', 'it is possible that', 'it is likely that', etc. This is clearly an example of the entry of ethics into logic, in the theory of predication or judgement-formation concerning everything, mundane or spiritual. It can therefore be said to be an ethical theory or requirement as well, and an ethical requirement applicable to an ordinary, unliberated, as well as to a liberated, individual. This is a good example of the sacrosanctity or primacy of the ethical, and thus a declaration of the stand that ethics is not to be transcended by anyone, howsoever spiritually elevated he may be.

In fact, the validity of the concept or theory of transcending ethics may at the most be said to have been mainly maintained or suggested in some *Upaniṣadic-Advaitic* works. But quite a good number of modern interpreters virtually take it to be a general or common feature of all Indian philosophical schools. This they do when they present it as the *Indian conception* of ethics, or as the *Indian position* about the place of ethics in philosophy. They certainly exclude the *Cārvāka* from this characterization. That does not very much matter because the *Cārvāka* philosophy is generally treated by them more as an aberration than as a bona fide constituent of the body politic of Indian philosophy. But, as has been said in the previous few pages, this characterization of Indian philosophy as such, or of the Indian philosophical attitude towards ethics, is not absolutely correct. It has been generally claimed to be correct by those who consider the *Upaniṣadic-Vedāntic* mode of philosophizing the mode in which Indian philosophizing has achieved its consummation or best expression. It is a short step from this point to proceed to averring that ethics itself gets consummated or sublimated when (axiological) philosophy transcends or goes beyond the boundaries of ethics. This would be tantamount to saying that an individual's life led in accordance with morality gets transformed into a higher, or the highest, kind of life when it goes beyond the realm of moral ends and obligations and devotes itself to realize, and realizes, the spiritual goal, the highest goal any individual can achieve or realize.

One may read some remarks or utterances in some *Upaniṣads* and *Vedāntic* works as suggesting or implying that on attaining enlightenment or *mokṣa* by an individual there is nothing which he is obligated to do because of its being ethical, or obligated to abstain from doing it on account of its being unethical. Such remarks, if they cannot be explained away, may be taken to imply that the enlightened individual is outside the zone of morality. But this implication may not obviously prove that a philosophy which considers such possibilities laudable, or even permissible, is better in philosophical merit, or is fairer in giving to ethics its due, than another which considers the boundaries or limits of ethics transgressable or transcendable under no condition, on any non-ethical ground, even spiritual or religious, without resulting in something undesirable or impermissible. It may also be the case that the implication does the reverse, that it adversely affects the tenability of the philosophy which yields it, i.e. the tenability of the philosophy which permits or requires the transcendence of morality, or even becoming indifferent to or unconcerned with morality. All this has to be carefully ascertained by examining what the claim of Indian philosophy's going beyond ethics really amounts to. It is important to do that because all, or almost all, those who hold that Indian philosophy, or a certain sector of it, goes beyond ethics, seem to do that because of their belief that, since it goes beyond ethics, it is a better philosophy than any other which does not.

It is not difficult or inconvenient to examine the beyond-ethics standpoint as an independent view about the Indian conception of ethics, or even as a general value-theory. But to do justice to it, it would be more befitting to examine it by way of discussing some actual modern adumbration of it which is fairly representative of this point of view and adequately detailed. Unfortunately, there are not many such adumbrations of it. Most of the scholars who consider it a faithful and favourable characterization of the classical Indian position assume it to be obviously true and leave it after stating it in a casual or synoptic fashion. I will select two presentations of it for discussion here, one by H. Bhattacharyya and the other by T.M.P. Mahadevan. While discussing these modern presentations, references to classical ideas will keep coming up at almost every point, and they will do that even when modern presentations are shown to be inadequate, untenable, or lacking in any respect whatsoever.

The main motivation in choosing the modern ones is that classical thinkers do not talk much about the viability or merit of transcending ethics. They do ethics, or axiology, make some remarks or statements concerning man's pursuit of ethical, or spiritual, goals. These remarks do not establish in any systematic, logical manner, but may be taken to suggest, that transcending ethics is a superior kind of search for values, superior to remaining confined within the bounds of ethical search. This suggestion some modern Indian interpreters have taken seriously, or rather too seriously. They have taken those remarks as conclusively confirming the interpretation that man's pursuit of values gets consummated only when he realizes the highest spiritual value of self-realization and that when he does that, he transcends ethics, i.e. occupies a position on the axiological map which is outside the bounds of morality. And, in being transcended, or left behind, ethics does not get, they think, dishonoured or humiliated, i.e. infringed.

Proceeding on the lines mentioned above, Bhattacharyya, after stating that in classical Indian society, individuals belonging to each one of the four castes, while passing through each one of the four stages into which an individual's life was divided, were assigned different sets of duties in accordance with their different castes and stages, along with some duties common for all of them, says:

> The philosophers of India improved upon this conception by linking moral obligation with the stage of spiritual attainment. A man who has succeeded in seeing through the illusory character of the mundane existence feels himself under no further obligation to follow certain moral prescriptions, just as he considers himself free not to observe certain modes of social custom or religious worship.[15]
>
> ... The prevailing attitude of the Upaniṣads is to advise men to desist from all actions right or wrong and to take to the path of meditation and realization, forgetting altogether this distinction of good and bad.[16]
>
> ... It was difficult to decide what actions were ethically indifferent on the human level, but it was agreed that spiritual enlightenment (*Brahmajñāna, bodhi, samyak jñāna*) was included in this category [i.e. in the category of ethically indifferent actions], 'for at this stage the spiritual aspirant was regarded as having transcended all distinctions of good and evil and established an attitude of apathy towards all earthly happenings and as having conquered completely all attachment (*rāga*), aversion (*dveṣa*) and ignorance (*moha*).[17]

Postponing the analysis of Bhattacharyya's interpretation to be taken up together with another instance of the beyond-ethics characterization, to be given very shortly, it is very obvious that, according to classical Indian philosophy as per his characterization, a man who has attained spiritual enlightenment, the highest value, transcends or goes beyond the boundaries of ethics or morality. This is clear from his saying that spiritual enlightenment belongs to the category of the ethically indifferent, that the enlightened individual is apathetic, i.e. indifferent, to the distinctions of good and evil, right and wrong, i.e. indifferent to all morality. Naturally, a man who is indifferent to morality transcends ethics. Since, according to Indian philosophy spiritual enlightenment is the highest goal which every individual can and ought to attain, the target of every individual should be, in effect, to transcend ethics because, as a consequence of his attaining spiritual enlightenment, he would automatically go beyond ethics. Therefore, Bhattacharyya can quite reasonably be said to be interpreting Indian philosophy as holding that ethics is to be transcended. This is virtually the same thing as holding that Indian value-theory goes beyond ethics. This claim of his he seems to hold to be valid not only of the *Upaniṣadic-Vedāntic* but of the whole, or at least of a larger sector, of Indian philosophy. This I say because he takes spiritual enlightenment to denote not only *Brahmajñāna*, the *Upaniṣadic-Vedāntic* term for the highest value, but also *bodhi* and *samyakjñāna*. *Bodhi* is primarily a Buddhist, and *samyakjñāna* for many of the schools, a term for spiritual enlightenment.

The other instance of the beyond-ethics characterization, referred to above, which I am going to discuss is T.M.P. Mahadevan's. Mahadevan has briefly mentioned it at many places in different contexts. But he has exclusively devoted one writing of his[18] to it. Therein he claims very strongly, with something like the zeal of a committed religionist, that it is the correct characterization of the Indian conception of ethics, or of the place of ethics in Indian philosophy. He even seems to go further and claim that, as a characterization per se, it is *the* correct one of the nature of ethics, or of the place of ethics in value-inquiry. This amounts to holding that ethics properly understood is an inquiry which must be transcended. An obvious implication of this view is that the Indian conception of ethics characterized as being transcended in the realization of the spiritual is superior to any other which does not admit the justifiability or necessity of transcending ethics. It is this account of the beyond-ethics characterization, as given by Mahadevan, which I have chosen for analysis and examination in some detail here. In my analysis or examination of it I shall not at all be concerned with discussing whether or not the Indian, i.e. the beyond-ethics, conception is superior to the Western conception of ethics. I shall not, even though Mahadevan has made the claim that it is, and that it is superior because in the Indian conception ethics is to be transcended whereas in the Western conception it is not. This kind of claim is of no philosophical importance. It may foster the claimant's nationalistic pride. But nationalistic pride has no place in academic philosophy.

Mahadevan's account is a representative, typical, example of the method used by some modern Indian philosophers or religionists of a traditionalist, particularly *Advaitic*, orientation, to refute the charge that there is no ethics in Indian philosophy. His strategy consists in trying to show that what Indian philosophy has may not be ethics in the same sense, or in a similar sense, in which ethics is understood by Western philosophers, or by some modern Indian philosophers of a non-traditionalist bent of mind. Taking ethics in that sense, the kind of axiology which Indian philosophy has goes beyond ethics. Therefore, since it has something higher, better, something which transcends ethics, the argument goes, the accusation that it lacks ethics falls flat.

In the very first paragraph of the presentation Mahadevan is forthright in declaring that his attempt to exhibit the beyond-ethics character of Indian philosophy is 'based on a conviction that if one is confined strictly within the frontiers of ethics one runs the danger of getting bogged and missing the life-giving and exhilarating air of the free land of the Spirit.'[19] This is metaphoric but highly laudatory statement about what an individual can get by entering into the land of the Spirit. It clearly implies, or presupposes, that (a) there is a land of the Spirit, (b) what an individual's entry into it can give to him is of a much higher value than what his leading an ethical life can give, (c) his remaining confined within the frontiers of ethics, that is, his caring only for what ethics requires him to do and thereby leading a life, even impeccably, in accordance with ethical requirements, will hinder his entry into the land of the Spirit, and therefore (d) he has to go beyond, or outside, the world of ethical requirements. All of (a), (b), (c) and (d) cumulatively imply that a philosophy of life, or rather philosophy as such, in order to provide to a man proper guidance for leading a life of the highest quality must go beyond ethics. This is what Indian philosophy does as per its characterization by Mahadevan and its other interpreters of his ilk.

The (a), the first implication of Mahadevan's initial statement, mentioned in the last paragraph, the statement that there is a land of the Spirit, is basic or central to his beyond-ethics theory. To an individual who does not believe in it, or considers it false or unprovable, Mahadevan's theory would carry no weight at all. This statement about the reality of the Spirit is one of the most basic statements of the *Upaniṣadic* and *Vedāntic*, particularly *Advaitic*, thought. Its exponents have given their reasons or grounds for affirming it. Mahadevan considers those reasons unquestionable and therefore takes the statement to be incontrovertible. He offers of his own to prove the reality of the Spirit. Any attempt to examine the classical thinkers' reasons will take me far afield into the interior of *Upaniṣadic-Vedāntic* ontology. Therefore, I will not do that. I will content myself here with pointing out that Mahadevan's, or any philosopher's, such a plea for transcending ethics will be contingent on the assumption of the reality of the spirit and will carry no force with an individual who does not accept this assumption. Further discussions in this chapter will also show that it would not be impossible for him to lead an ethical life even after the rejection of the assumption. However, here my main concern is to ascertain whether or not it is a fair characterization of Indian philosophy to hold that it goes beyond ethics and also whether or not the beyond-ethics characterization, if true, can be said to have refuted the no-ethics charge against Indian philosophy. But let us first see what is Mahadevan's reasoning or justification for transcending ethics in order to enter into the land of the Spirit and for calling the mode of life lived as a result of this transcendence a higher kind of life than the life lived in accordance with ethical requirements, i.e. a life remaining within the boundaries of ethics.

Mahadevan has in his mind a particular kind of characterization of Indian philosophy behind his earnestness to exhibit that it goes beyond ethics. This characterization is not a new one, not a result of his own insight into the way or ways in which classical Indian philosophers have done their philosophizings. It is the same, prevalent, one which has been stated umpteen times by several of his and our contemporary Indian scholars, philosophers as well as non-philosophers. It is the characterization that Indian philosophy is *darśana* and not science, or philosophy in the Western sense, our old friend we have met with in Chapter 2 and found it not loyal to every area of classical Indian philosophy. But before trying to establish that its being *darśana* justifies its going beyond ethics or enables it to do that, Mahadevan attempts to show what he calls the fundamental defect of Western philosophy. He seems also to hold that it is this defect which makes its conception of ethics as well defective and that, since Indian philosophy does not suffer from this defect, its conception of ethics is not defective. This, the Indian conception of ethics, according to him, is that ethics can get sublimated only in being transcended, as it really is in Indian philosophy.

As he puts it, 'Philosophy, according to the most generally accepted view in the West does not differ from science as far as its method is concerned. The philosopher is a theorizer even as the scientist is. He cogitates about the world as a whole while the scientist investigates the nature of a particular aspect of it.'[20] On this characterization, even the subject-matter of philosophy becomes qualitatively or categorially the same as that of science. Both cogitate about the world. The only difference is that philosophy cogitates about the world as a whole, taking it in its entirety, while science about an aspect or a part of it, taking it in parts. Since both of them cogitate, whatever 'cogitate' in his usage means, their method, on his own admission, is the same. Therefore, both of them are the same type of inquiry, using a similar method to study the same subject-matter, i.e. the world. But Mahadevan calls Western philosophy similar to science only in its method. And, even this (methodological) sort of philosophy's similarity with science is not tolerable to him; it makes Western philosophy, in his estimation, a lower, an inferior, kind of philosophy. This is clear from the fact that he considers it to be 'the fundamental defect of Western philosophy'.[21]

The characterization of Western philosophy which Mahadevan has given is well-known, rather a textbookish one. It is the characterization with which almost every textbook on general philosophy, written by an Western, or an Indian, scholar from a traditionalist point of view for a long time in the early part of the twentieth century used to begin. But it is surprising that a scholar like Mahadevan sticks to this characterization in 1950. By that time Western philosophy had, by and large, rejected this characterization. It had, because it had broken away from speculative philosophy the exponents of which had held, or seemed to have held, this characterization of philosophy. It had broken away as a result of the three revolutions which had by that time taken place in the history of Western philosophy. These three were Logical Atomism, Logical Positivism, and Linguistic Analysis, each succeeding one displacing, improving upon, and thereby going beyond the preceding one or ones. Each one of the three movements unambiguously and convincingly maintained that both the subject-matter and method of philosophy were different from those of science. The first one of the three movements, Logical Atomism, had been inaugurated as early as 1918 in Bertrand Russell's work. 'The Philosophy of Logical Atomism' published in three consecutive issues of the *Monist*.[22] The second, Logical Positivism, had been inaugurated in 1924 with the founding of the Vienna Circle by Moritz Schlick, and years before 1950, it had been almost forgotten and superseded by the third, Linguistic Analysis, inaugurated by Wittgenstein, and had by then begun to dominate Western philosophizing. It is a matter of dismay that even then Mahadevan goes on harping on the tune that 'European philosophy which broke off from the apron strings of theology has in what is known as the modern era, clung fast to the coat-tails of physical science. Reliance on science has become almost an obsession with the Western philosopher.'[23] In support of this characterization of his, or rather of his understanding of the temper of Western philosophy, he refers only to the way in which, according to him, Descartes and Locke do their philosophizing. It seems that he is either oblivious of, or does not care about, the ways in which later, his own contemporaries, or a little earlier, Western philosophers did their philosophizing, and the ways in which they characterized the nature of philosophical inquiry.

His reference to Descartes and Locke is certainly an out-of-date reference, and, therefore, it may lessen our surprise on his sticking to an outdated, textbookish, characterization of Western philosophy. But it certainly increases our sense of dismay. I am not suggesting that he should have accepted the characterization of philosophy's job which emerged out of the three revolutions. I am only trying to point out that there is no justification in his continuing to give a characterization of Western philosophy which might have been true of it once upon a time but had been rejected by Western philosophers themselves much before the time of his rehearsal of it in 1950.

Indian philosophy does not have to be a science, or to cling fast to the coat-tails of a science, Mahadevan thinks, because it is *darśana*. 'But philosophy as *darśana* is quite different. Though it employs the rational method of inquiry, it is aware of the limits of reason. What it aims to give us is not so much knowledge by description as knowledge by acquaintance. Philosophy, in a word, is self-realization.'[24] This is what philosophy, as Indian philosophy, is for Mahadevan. He calls it *darśana* and not even *darśana-śāstra.*

He seems to think that philosophy can stop clinging 'fast to the coat-tails of physical science', or of any science whatsoever, only by being *darśana,* some sort of spiritual intuition. But, as has been said above, the three twentieth-century movements in Western philosophy have shown that that is not at all necessary. Mahadevan's own phraseology—in saying that Indian philosophy is knowledge by acquaintance and not knowledge by description—is a Western one. As early as 1910–11 Russell distinguishes between two kinds of knowledge in his influential essay 'Knowledge by Acquaintance and Knowledge by Description'.[25]

I am not saying that Mahadevan is wrong in calling Indian philosophy *darśana.* Whether or not he is, or whether or not Indian philosophy is *darśana,* is an independent issue. What I am saying here is only that philosophy does not have to be called *darśana* in order to be prevented from being a science, or from being necessarily related to or dependent upon any science. Rather, admitting that it is really *darśana* may motivate one to say that it is a science. He may claim that it is a spiritual science which uses spiritual intuition to know what spiritual reality is and characterizes it in a language appropriate for giving an account of it as accurately as it is humanly possible to do. It would then be comparable to any empirical science, say, a physical science. The latter, for example, uses sense-perception aided with proper instrumentation and experimentation to know what a physical reality is and gives an account of its findings in a language appropriate for this task, which is ordinary language fortified with some technical phraseology specially designed to make the account as accurate as possible. There would certainly be a difference between the two: to get its facts spiritual science would use spiritual experience, and to get its facts physical science would use sense-experience. But they would remain empirical sciences. Therefore, Mahadevan's, and many others', attributing to Indian philosophy the property of being *darśana* may lead one to conclude that Indian philosophy is a science of a sort because a spiritual science is also a science. This conclusion would not be illogical. But it would certainly be the contrary of what Mahadevan claims to be true of the character of Indian philosophy. It would not merely tie Indian philosophy to the coat-tails of spiritual science but would identify it with, or merge it into, the latter.

Secondly, if this 'spiritual science' is claimed to be not a science but a religion, or closer to a religion than to any science, then Mahadevan's, or anyone's, characterization of Indian philosophy as *darśana* would amount to identifying Indian philosophy with a religion, or at least to tieing it to the coat-tails of a religion. And, in either one of the two cases, the autonomy of Indian philosophy as a cognitive inquiry would be destroyed or endangered. It would then be no less destroyed or endangered than the autonomy of philosophy in the West is alleged to be by Mahadevan by identifying philosophy with, or tying it to the coat-tails of, a natural science.

By 'self' in 'self-realization', when he says that Indian philosophy is self-realization, Mahadevan does not mean the ego, the psychological self of an individual, but that which is present in everything. To be brief, it is the self as understood in the *Advaita Vedānta,* the school to which Mahadevan belongs. 'Morality', he says, 'is one of the modes of self-realization' and therefore it 'cannot become the content of a natural science—even though that science be biology'.[26] This obviously means that ethics which deals with morality, or whose subject-matter is morality, is not a natural science. Mahadevan thinks that he has made a great advance in philosophizing about morality by saying that ethics is not a science. It is amazing for anyone to entertain any such a thought in 1950 when as early as 1903, G.E. Moore[27] conclusively demonstrated in his *Principia Ethica,* chapter 1, by the enunciation of his naturalistic fallacy-method of argumentation, that a moral judgement can neither be reduced to nor inferred from a factual proposition, or from a set of factual propositions, and thereby proved that ethics cannot be called a natural science. This conclusion has since then been further strengthened by many other philosophers, even though most of them disagree with Moore on more than one issue in ethics. The logical inappropriateness of calling ethics a science has been forcefully maintained even by some eighteenth-century philosophers like Francies Hutcheson and David Hume, more than a century before Moore's formulation of the naturalistic fallacy. All this has been very ably shown by Arthur Prior[28] in his *Logic and the Basis of Ethics.*

Mahadevan thinks that ethics cannot be a natural science only if it is held to be a mode of self-realization, as is done, according to him, in the Indian conception of ethics. But the studies mentioned above have conclusively proven that it is not necessary to go that far to achieve this objective. Ethics does not have to be a mode of self-realization in order to retain its autonomy in relation to science. That is, in order to avoid being, or being reducible to, a natural (or even a formal) science, it need not be linked with self-realization, though it may be for some other reason. Here again, as it has been done in the case of Mahadevan's and others' attribution of the property of being *darśana* to Indian philosophy, a similar disclaimer needs to be recorded. It is not being held here that Mahadevan is not right in characterizing the Indian conception of ethics as a mode of self-realization, nor is it held that ethics, as per the Indian conception or understanding of it, is not a mode of self-realization. What is held here is simply that ethics per se, or as conceived in Indian philosophy, does not have to be a mode of, or means to, self-realization in order to avoid being a natural, or any sort of, science. This point about ethics in general has been so forcefully and convincingly made by many that it does not need to be elaborated here.

Mahadevan's motivation too, in calling ethics as conceived in Indian philosophy a mode of self-realization, is not merely to underline the fact of its not being a natural science. Rather, it is to offer a ground or reason for making the further claim that ethics as conceived in Indian philosophy transcends, or goes beyond, the boundaries within which ethics as ordinarily conceived, or as conceived in Western philosophy, is supposed to operate, function, or to be applicable. It is the former kind of ethics, i.e. ethics as conceived in Indian philosophy, which is, for Mahadevan, genuine ethics, or ethics as it ought to be.

This view about ethics, or about Indian ethics, would be tenable if and only if it is the case that in ethics's transcending the boundaries of ordinary morality, or in its being a mode of self-realization, the role of morality in man's private and public life is in no way devalued or undervalued. This is so because the empirical world in which he lives requires him to lead both a private and public life, and in both morality plays a very crucial role. Rather, he cannot play the role of a viable individual, or of a viable member of any society, if he does not care for morality, or does not give to it the importance it deserves to receive from him. Further, to maintain that genuine ethics transcends ordinary ethics it needs to be shown that (a) in being made genuine, i.e. a mode or means of self-realization, ethics *has* to, or *must*, transcend ordinary, normal, morality, (b) self-realization justifies the transcendence, and (c) the dignity of self-realization itself would not get in any way adversely affected if its attainment in any way involves, or is likely to involve, transgression of ordinary ethics or morality concordance with which is needed in the conduct of normal private and public life.

Moreover, it is of prime importance that the concept of transcending or going beyond ethics is properly understood in order to ascertain whether or not it is likely to justify, or to even condone, infringement of a prescription or prohibition which is morally impeccable as per our common-sense moral intuitions, i.e. impeccable according to ethics as ordinarily understood. If, for example, it undervalues a cherished value like that of filial affection, permits non-fulfilment of an obligation like that of a conjugal duty, encourages non-cultivation of a virtue like that of feeling moved on account of someone else's unhappiness, condones violation of anyone's right like the right of another individual to cultivate a virtue, etc., then its own ethical value or rank on the axiological ladder would become highly questionable.

For the sake of brevity, now onwards I shall use the term 'transcendent ethics' for the axiological inquiry which transcends ethics as ordinarily understood. It is this kind of normative inquiry which Mahadevan has in mind when he speaks of ethics as conceived in Indian philosophy and as going beyond ethics as ordinarily understood or conceived in Western philosophy. This is largely true of the already discussed H. Bhattacharyya's interpretation of Indian ethics as well, though he thinks that the need for transcending ordinary ethics is given greater emphasis in the *Upaniṣadic-Vedāntic* literature than it is given in others.

Correspondingly, I shall henceforth use only 'ethics' as short for ethics as ordinarily understood, or as conceived in Western philosophy. Even Mahadevan does the same thing elsewhere when he calls ethics the inquiry concerned with ascertaining the criterion or criteria of what is right and wrong, good and bad, etc., in man's private and public life. And, in support of his notion of ethics, he refers to J.S. Mackenzie's *A Manual of Ethics*, a book[29] used in Indian universities as a textbook for undergraduate students of philosophy.[30]

The point I want to emphasize here is that if transcendent ethics in any way sanctions, or recommends what (ordinary) ethics prohibits or derecommends, or vice versa, then there would be a serious problem. There would be because the kind of social life we lead and *have* to lead, in the kind of world we live and *have* to live in, if we want to live well, is such that the value of ethics or morality in any sphere of it can be ignored at too great a cost. It is morality which, more than anything else, is required to ensure that life in our world does not become, as Thomas Hobbes puts it, 'solitary, poor, nasty, brutish, and short'.[31]

Mahadevan, à la F.H. Bradley, sees in ethics or morality a built-in self-contradiction. I shall not question his understanding of Bradley's position, though I think the point which Bradley is trying to make, or the conclusion he is trying to reach, is very different from what Mahadevan takes either one of them to be. Therefore, I will take his *adoption* of the Bradleyian position about the (alleged) self-contradictory character of morality as his own position. There is nothing wrong in doing that because he makes use of it in reaching his transcendent ethics as freely and authoritatively as a philosopher makes use of a theory of his own formulation to reach a conclusion he intends to reach in his inquiry.

It is very important to remember here that to use a *Bradleyian*, a *Western*, analysis of morality to prove that ethics needs to be transcended, is not to prove that an *Indian* philosophical analysis of morality shows that we must transcend or go beyond ethics. But it is this that Mahadevan seems to be doing. His claim is that as per the Indian theory of what morality is, or can do, ethics has to be be transcended. To substantiate this claim about Indian philosophy he uses Bradley's analysis of morality and takes it to be unfaultable, though it is not, as will be shown a little later. But even if it is and it proves the transcendence of ethics, it would have no bearing on the claim that, as per the Indian conception of ethics, ethics has to be transcended. It would have no bearing, even if the ultimate end or value to be realized as a result of transcending ethics, according to Bradley, is spiritual realization or self-realization, similar to the end which is to be realized, according to Indian philosophy, by going beyond ethics. However, it must not be forgotten that the highest end for Bradley is different from what it is for Indian philosophy.

A Bradleyian theory, or any Western theory, of morals will substantiate a claim about Western philosophy, or about the status of ethics in Western philosophy, and not any claim about Indian philosophy, or about the status of ethics in Indian philosophy. Mahadevan's is a claim about Indian philosophy, more specifically about the status of ethics in Indian philosophy. On this claim Bradley's analysis has no bearing. What Mahadevan should have done is to have given any classical Indian philosopher's analysis of the concept of oughtness, or of some other basic ethical concept, showing that it is self-contradictory, or some other *Indian* argument, to demonstrate that it is necessary, according to Indian philosophy, to go beyond ethics in order to attain the highest value. This Mahadevan does not do, nor does Bhattacharyya. Instead, Mahadevan takes the help of a Western, a Bradleyian, theory. It is puzzling to see his using a Western theory to prove his thesis that, as per Indian axiology, ethics has to be transcended, a thesis he considers uniquely Indian, *Upaniṣadic-Vedāntic,* arrived at by classical Indian *ṛṣis* on the basis of their own analysis and spiritual experience. It becomes more puzzling when we recollect that he resorts to Bradley's theory soon after accusing Western philosophy of suffering from the great defect of being tied to the coat-tails of science.

With this preamble, let us see how Mahadevan exhibits that the self-contradiction present in the very heart of morality justifies or requires that we go to a point located in the axiological space which is beyond ethics. Mahadevan's reasoning may be elaborated as follows:

The concept of 'ought', or obligation, is central to ethics or moral consciousness. To have this consciousness is to feel that something ought to be done, or that something ought not to be done. What ought to be done is that which has neither been done, nor is being done; the ought-to-be-done is different from the already-done as well as from the currently-being-done. Therefore, as soon as the ought-to-be-done is done, the sense, or, awareness of oughtness, i.e. moral consciousness, vanishes. This means that then morality vanishes, or that morality can survive only as long as the duality of ought-to-be-done and already-done survives, i.e. only as long as there is a gap, a tension, or a conflict, between the 'ought' and the 'is'. The moment this gap, tension, or conflict is conquered, there is no feeling of ought and therefore no morality. The self-contradiction of morality is apparent here: Morality to survive requires the awareness that something ought to be done. Its aim is to get the ought, the obligation, acted upon. But the moment the obligation is acted upon, the ought-to-be-done becomes the already-done, the 'ought' becomes the 'is', and therefore ceases to exist. The cessation of ought is the cessation of morality. This means that the notion of morality is self-defeating or self-contradictory because in implementing what it aims at it destroys itself.

The above is, I believe, a fair presentation of Mahadevan's charge that the concept of morality is self-contradictory. Certainly it is more detailed than what he himself has given. He has simply stated in a brief way what Bradley, according to him, has said. Thereupon, he proceeds to use it as his own starting point to reach his conclusion. His conclusion is that the problem born out of the self-contradictory nature of morality is solved, or dissolved, if we transcend or go beyond morality or the zone of ought or obligation. But before examining this conclusion of Mahadevan, let us pause a little, and see whether or not it is fair to say that the notion of morality, or the notion of obligation which he considers central to morality, is self-contradictory.

Reiterating that Bradley's point in calling morality self-contradictory is very different and not dilating on what he means by it because our objective here is not to discuss Bradley's, or any Western philosopher's, position, it is very important to bring out the logical fact that actually doing what ought to be done, or, converting the ought-to-be-done into the done, is not to annul the obligation, not to cause its cessation, but to achieve its fulfilment which is the aim of a morally motivated individual. Even after its fulfilment, an obligation does not cease to be an obligation; it only ceases to be an obligation to be fulfilled. But to say the latter is to say a truism, the truism that a fulfilled obligation is not one which is to be fulfilled. That is why after his fulfilling an obligation, an individual feels a sense of moral pride for having done what he ought to have done. Moral consciousness does not then vanish, but assumes in the fulfilment this person which the person experiences as his feeling of moral pride, his feeling of moral satisfaction. Contrariwise, if he fails to fulfil an obligation, or does what he ought not to have done, even then the obligation does not vanish. Then it survives in his feeling ashamed, guilty, or remorseful, for having done what he ought not to have done (or for having not done what he ought to have). Moral consciousness survives here, and perhaps in a much stronger form, in his torturing sense of repentance, shame, guilt or remorse.

It is possible that sometimes a morally highly elevated individual's fulfilling an obligation costs him his life. But the cessation of his existence would not cause the cessation of obligation or of moral sense. For example, Daśaratha's fulfilling his obligation to Kaikeyī to satisfy any two of her wishes, as per his promise made to her, does cost him his life. But, instead of causing the cessation of any obligation to fulfil a promise, or of the moral sense which is involved therein, it exemplifies the moral grandeur, the intrinsic dignity, of the fulfilment of an obligation. This it does because it presents an *utopian* instance of human greatness demonstrated in the fulfilment of an individual's moral commitment, of the extremely refreshing sunshine with which moral conscientiousness warms man's heart even in the darkest and coldest moments of his private and public life. Daśaratha's is an example of living, becoming immortal, by dying to fulfil his moral obligation.

It is a logical fact or truth that, if X is what ought to be done, after X's having been done, i.e. after the to-be-done, ought-to-be-done X has been converted into the done X, there is no sense in requiring that X ought to be done. This has nothing to do with ethics, or morality, or metaphysics, or spirituality. It is simply a feature of the *concept of ought* or *of obligation.* It is as obvious as is the logical fact or truth that, if an imperative (or order) has been issued to open the door Y, after Y's having been opened, it would be pointless, or logically odd to issue the same imperative. That it cannot be issued has nothing to do with the nature of the thing, the door, which Y names or denotes; rather, it cannot be issued because of the meaning or logical behaviour of the concept of an open door. It is a logical, and not a physical, fact that an open door cannot be asked to be opened.

Mahadevan forgets that a self-contradictory scheme cannot be implemented or acted upon. Had morality been self-contradictory, nothing moral would have ever been done, or would ever be done, just as neither has anybody ever drawn a circular square, nor can anybody ever draw one. Classical Indian philosophers then would certainly not have given so much importance to morality as they have done, and no *ṛṣi* would have said that it is morality, *dharma,* which sustains the world. For the same reason, the etymologist's deriving the word '*dharma*' from the root *dhṛ* and saying on that account that it means that which sustains the world would have been a deceptive device, just as it would have been if an astronomer had said that the axis of the world was a circular square.

The charge that morality is self-contradictory is belied not only by the facts of human life, by man's transactions in his private and public life, but also by the results of philosophical reflection on the conceptual complexities involved in the structure of moral issues. These explorations would not have yielded useful results had morality been self-contradictory. These results, at least a good number of them, are not only theoretically or logically interesting; they are also of great practical importance. For example, a philosopher shows that 'ought' implies 'can', obligation implies ability. He thereby illustrates that, since it is a fact that there are obligations which a man has to fulfil and it is a logical truth that having an obligation implies his having the ability to fulfil it, it follows that he is able, capable, or has the freedom, to fulfil his obligations. Therefore, if he does not fulfil an obligation, there must be something in his psychology or in his surrounding which hinders his fulfilling it. These are very interesting and important facts about the nature of man and his world, and they cannot be denied on the mere ground that a certain theory does not fit in with them.

This conceptual feature of obligation or ought also proves that morality is not self-contradictory. What ought to be done must be, in point of logic, that which can be done, and what can be done, what is doable, implementable, cannot be self-contradictory. It cannot be, because what is self-contradictory cannot be done or implemented. Just as one cannot draw a circular square, one cannot implement a self-contradictory scheme of action, or act according to a principle if the principle is self-contradictory. This means that what is self-contradictory cannot be a moral principle.

We shall have occasion to see that similar reflection on the nature of some moral principles, on the conditions of their implementation in practice, and on their actual implementation in the life of certain important personalities in classical India, reveals very important truths about man's normative concerns, i.e. about his pursuit of values and avoidance of disvalues.

In order that our inquiry may go on, let us accept, for the sake of argument, Mahadevan's interpretation that, as per the classical Indian understanding of the concept of morality (or of ought), morality is self-contradictory. Self-contradiction, wherever it exists, stings the human mind, and thereby motivates it to get rid of it. Classical Indian thinkers too must have felt stung by it, if they found morality infected with it. It is surprising that neither Mahadevan nor anyone else who has interpreted Indian philosophy as having gone beyond ethics, has given an example of any classical Indian thinker's demonstration of morality's, or any moral concept's, being self-contradictory. However, since we have accepted Mahadevan's interpretation, to see what it amounts to, let us not be bothered by his not giving any such example. But this we can justifiably say: if self-contradiction resides in the heart of morality it must have stung our classical thinkers and one would expect them to have done some rethinking of the concept of morality to free it from this evil (or self-contradiction). But instead of doing anything with the concept of morality they, Mahadevan says, advise us to go beyond morality or ethics, to transcend morality, i.e. to leave it behind to its fate, as if it were incurable, and ascend to spiritual realization than which nothing else is better, nor anything else even equal to it in merit.

Let me take up the *remedy* which, according to Mahadevan, classical Indian philosophy advises us to adopt in order to go beyond ethics, in order to place ourselves in a condition in which the self-contradictory character of morality would vanish, or become defunct or dysfunctional. To put it briefly—and it should be noted that Mahadevan too does not present it in an elaborate manner, nor does he fortify it with any well-groomed logical reasoning—it is this:

We can go beyond ethics and thereby free ourselves from all that its self-contradictory nature afflicts us with, classical Indian philosophers tell us, by adopting, as per the *Gītā*, the path of doing whatever we do with no desire, or with no desire for what may result out of what we do, i.e. with no end in view. Rather, we should aim, in whatever we do, at spiritual realization which is the same as self-realization, or realization of the Self present in everything that there is. When we adopt this path, the duality of 'ought' and 'is' is eliminated, nothing is done because it ought to be done and nothing is done to fulfil a particular desire or attain a particular end. Every action is consecrated to attain self-realization. 'Morality is thus', he says 'emptied of its contents' [i.e. oughts and goals] and at the same time filled by attaching it to the supreme end which is the infinite spirit. A reconciliation between form and content [i.e. moral rules and ends] is effected by opening the door that leads us to the region [or the spirit that lies] beyond ethics'[32] (which is the region of actions which have been done, or are to be done, in accordance with this or that principle of moral obligation, or done to achieve this or that moral end).

Since there is no ought here, Mahadevan thinks, there is no self-contradiction. The individual who has achieved spiritual realization, or self-realization, the *mukta*, has no obligation to do anything; rather, he has ceased to be an agent. Mahadevan avers that 'Since there is no agency in him, he is no doer at all. His struggles are all over, the *ought* and the ought-not, the relative good and evil, have no meaning in his case. From the supreme height of spirituality which is his even the so-called good is evil. That metaphysical evil he has transcended by the wisdom that sees the non-dual spirit in all.'[33] He has reached 'the heaven of freedom' and to it 'morality serves as footstool'.[34]

Mahadevan's statement of the remedy is not as innocent as he thinks it is. Firstly, it is not at all clear how getting rid of desires would make morality cease to be self-contradictory if its self-contradictoriness is, as Mahadevan and also classical Indian philosophy, according to him, hold, a congenital feature of it. A desire in itself is neither moral nor immoral, nor is it in itself self-contradictory. What makes it moral or immoral is the object of which it is a desire. The desire to help a man in distress is a moral, or a morally commendable, desire because its object, helping a man in distress, is a morally commendable thing. Similarly, the desire to hurt an innocent man is an immoral, or a morally condemnable, desire because its object, hurting an innocent man, is immoral, or morally condemnable. And, there cannot be a desire with no object, i.e. without being a desire for something, for getting something, for getting rid of something, for avoiding getting something, for retaining the possession of something one has got, etc. Secondly, what makes a desire self-consistent or self-contradictory is also its object. A poor man's desire to eat plum cake may be unrealistic, but it is not self-contradictory. But any man's desire, as the saying goes, to eat his cake and also to keep it intact is self-contradictory. It is self-contradictory because the concept of its object, the concept of eating a cake and keeping it intact, is self-contradictory. Therefore, the *mere* fact of the association of morality with a desire cannot be blamed for making morality self-contradictory, nor can its *mere* disassociation from any desire, or even from all desires if that is possible, can be credited with freeing it from its self-contradictoriness if self-contradictoriness is a natural feature of it.

Secondly, when morality is attached to its supreme end of self-realization, Mahadevan claims it to be emptied of its contents, i.e. of moral oughts, and filled with the supreme end of self-realization. But he does not realize that even then it is not emptied of all oughts. It is then filled with the supreme ought linked with the supreme end of self-realization. It is, because if self-realization is the supreme end, then every action of everyone *ought* to aim at attaining it. If ought is self-contradictory, it is difficult to explain how this ought is not. It cannot be said that it is not self-contradictory on account of its being an ought concerning self-realization. To say it would involve the fallacy of arguing in a circle. Here it is to be proven that the realm of the spiritual, of self-realization, reached after transcending, or going beyond, ethics is, unlike morality, free from all self-contradiction. Therefore, to say that the ought concerning self-realization is not self-contradictory because it is an ought concerning self-realization definitely involves circular reasoning.

But let us assume, for the sake of argument again, that Mahadevan is right in saying that the *Gītā*'s remedy is Indian philosophy's remedy for going beyond ethics and that it is an effective remedy and therefore all desires are to be gotten rid of. Let us also assume that there is a certain individual, who, following this prescription, has actually gotten rid of all desires and imaginatively picture in our mind how he would function or behave in the realm he has landed himself in after transcending morality. Desires are the chief springs of action, of actions which we call voluntary or intentional. It is the potentiality of an individual, i.e. his ability, to do such actions which makes him an agent, or a moral agent, because morality is concerned primarily with voluntary or intentional actions, their motives and objectives, etc. This means that after getting rid of his desires, the individual ceases to be an agent or doer, and Mahadevan admits that he does cease to be one. This means that he would not now be morally assessable or judgeable. This is, Mahadevan would say, because he is outside or beyond the zone of ethics or morality. But now, because of the loss of his agency, he has in effect become an object, a thing, or almost like a thing, and has ceased to be a person. We can definitely then say he is beyond the domain of ethics. But this would not mean that he is beyond ethics because of any defect in ethics. Rather, it is because of his having lost his agency which, one may say, from the normal, day-to-day life, point of view, is a defect in him, or at least is not a virtue.

But Mahadevan would say, as is clear from his words quoted a little earlier, that he has lost his agency not because of any lapse on his part; he has lost it because of his spiritual elevation, because of his having made self-realization his only end, or because of his having attained it.

Let us grant all this and see where it takes us to. There are several things which this position about morality or ethics implies or suggests. One, it clearly implies that in making self-realization his supreme end the enlightened individual has not relinquished *all of his desires,* nor his desires for *all the results* of his actions. This is because he still has *one desire,* namely, the *desire to attain* self-realization (*mumukṣā*) and therefore the *desire for one result* of all of his endeavours, namely, self-realization (*mokṣa*). Therefore, on Mahadevan's own admission, not *all desires* does he have to shun and *not at all the results* of his endeavours does he have to be indifferent to. This admission is inconsistent with his saying, as quoted earlier, that he has to, as required by the *Gītā,* get rid of all desires, or desires for *all the results* of what he does.

Mahadevan, or anyone else who interprets the Indian philosophical approach to ethics on his lines, may say, and some really do, that the aspirant for self-realization has the desire for self-realization but not any desire for any result. This is something untenable. What else is a desire for X if it is not a desire for attaining X (of course, if X has not yet been attained and is worth attaining, as is the case with self-realization in the case of its aspirant's desire for it)?

Two, his admission that the enlightened non-agent has used morality as a footstool to reach his spiritual goal also contains in its bosom features which make his interpretation self-inconsistent in more than one way. (a) Since Mahadevan's spiritual man *makes use* of morality as a footstool, he is still an agent, a doer, and a doer of a complicated set of things. To use morality itself as a footstool to reach the height of spirituality is not a simple affair. (b) Since morality has been used as a footstool, i.e. as a means, morality itself cannot be self-contradictory. Nothing self-contradictory can be used as a means to achieve anything. Nobody can use the figure of a circular square even to draw an onlooker's attention to the figure simply because no such figure can be drawn. Therefore, no such figure can be used in any way and if it can be, it would prove that the figure is not self-contradictory. All this clearly shows that there is more than one self-inconsistency in Mahadevan's interpretation of morality as a footstool to be used in order to go beyond ethics. And, if his method is, as he claims it to be, the method used by the *Gītā*, or by Indian philosophy, or by the *Advaita Vedānta*, to go beyond ethics, then they too are infected with the above self-inconsistencies. Mahadevan and others of his ilk think that by attributing to Indian philosophy the adoption of this method of going beyond ethics they prove that it has gone to greater heights than ethics left to itself can reach, that they have highlighted its glories. But it is a matter of great dismay that their characterization of the method, or their consequential reading of the place of ethics in Indian philosophy, results in the attribution of a number of self-inconsistencies in Indian philosophy's conception of ethics, of course, if their characterization of the latter is right.

There is also another factor which needs to be brought out here from the side of ethics, or morality. Mahadevan has called ethics or morality a footstool, and some others have called it a ladder for climbing to the roof of spirituality.

The analogy of a footstool or of a ladder has been used to underline that morality is a means to be used to attain the spiritual goal. This means that its value consists in, or is totally constituted by, its being instrumental to the attainment of this goal. Mahadevan does not mention anything else which morality may also be used to attain, let alone attributing any intrinsic value to it. Rather, he seems to hold that it has no intrinsic value, and therefore it has only one value, the instrumental value accruing to it from its being instrumental to the attainment of self-realization. This is a highly thinned, or watered down, conception of morality and so of ethics. This view has implications which show that it is not fair to the dignity of morality.

To understand what this instrumental, the footstool, conception of morality makes morality to be, we must remember one important feature of self-realization. Self-realization is, according to Indian philosophy, the highest value or goal which an individual can and should attain, and which once attained is attained for ever. To attain it is to be liberated for all time to come. The liberated, while alive, is not again de-liberated, and obviously he would not need or like to be de-liberated. When his physical death occurs, he is not reborn and therefore there is no question of his becoming de-liberated and needing to be liberated again by using morality as a means. All this will be further explained in Chapter 14.

What has been said above about the nature of self-realization as a one-time attained or attainable goal is, in a sense, an aside, but a relevant one to make visible some of the implications of the footstool conception of morality. Since morality is a means to the attainment of self-realization and after attaining self-realization nothing higher than it is there to attain, after attaining it the attainer may not see any need for morality. Morality may be a means to attaining some lower goals as well, but there would be no point in trying to attain anyone of them after having attained the highest. If morality also had some sort of intrinsic value, i.e. were an end in itself, then there would have been a justification for continuing to cultivate it even after having attained self-realization. But interpreters like Mahadevan have not held that for Indian philosophy morality has both intrinsic and instrumental value. Rather they have maintained that its value consists only in being a means to attaining self-realization. Rather, Mahadevan is candid enough to admit, as already quoted, that to the self-realized individual it loses its importance. 'Since there is no agency in him [the realized individual] he is no doer at all. His struggles are all over. The *ought* and *ought not*, the relative good and evil have no meaning in his case.

From the supreme height of spirituality which is his even the so-called good is evil.'[35] By 'ought', 'ought not', 'relative good and evil', 'the so-called good', etc. he means the values, norms, virtues, etc., i.e. the moral things, which morality requires to be acquired, fulfilled, or cultivated, etc. Moral things can have in Mahadevan's scheme only a relative value or merit because only self-realization has or is absolute value. Therefore, to say of the realized person that 'the *ought* and *ought not,* the relative good and evil, have no meaning in his case' is to say that morality does not matter to him. The 'so-called', i.e. the moral, good for him is evil which he has transcended. That is, he has transcended, left behind, all concern and care for morality. Having become a non-agent, a non-doer, he has become one who cannot do anything. Therefore, he cannot do anything right, or anything wrong, anything obligatory or forbidden. Ethics is obviously not concerned with such a person, since it is concerned with him who has the ability to do the right as well as the ability to do the wrong, and therefore needs guidance as to what is right and what is wrong. Therefore, the *mukta,* the self-realized individual, is outside or beyond the boundary of ethics. We can say that ethics has nothing to do with him, as well as that he has nothing to do with ethics. This is to say that there is no place for ethics in his life.

If Mahadevan's interpretation of Indian philosophy as going beyond ethics is correct, or considered correct—and there are quite a few who think it is correct—the implications drawn above cannot be denied. It also cannot be denied that, then, morality would become a dispensable, disposable commodity, to be disposed off after having been used by an individual to attain self-realization, in the manner of a disposable syringe being thrown away after its having been used to inject a medicine into the body of a patient. Ethics as cognitive inquiry is one into the nature of various theoretical and practical normative problems and themes pertaining to the role played by morality in human life. It would also, therefore, naturally have no place in Indian philosophy, or would be relegated to an unimportant corner of it. It is a pity that a thinker like Mahadevan, who undertakes to exhibit the great axiological achievements of classical Indian *ṛṣis*, is led by his own logic to reach in effect the conclusion that ethics does not occupy an important place, or a place respectable in its own right, in classical Indian philosophy. He may not like to own it, but this is the conclusion his own logic of calling morality self-contradictory and making it at the most a footstool for attaining spiritual realization commits him to accept.

What has been said above shows that the beyond-ethics characterization not only does not meet the no-ethics charge against Indian philosophy, but results in almost affirming or confirming, if not directly then certainly by implication, the stand taken by the proponents of the charge. We have seen that according to Mahadevan's interpretation of Indian approach to ethics, after attaining self-realization, an individual becomes a non-doer, a non-agent. Agency is a constitutive property of individuality, i.e. of being an individual. Therefore, to get rid of it is tantamount to getting rid of one's individuality. This view of Mahadevan, or this implication from his view, is not at all different from John Mckenzie's saying that. 'All down through the history of Hindu thought it has almost been taken for granted that individuality is a limitation, and that as such it is something that must be transcended.'[36]

Mckenzie's point is similar to Mahadevan's. Mckenzie wants to stress that individuality, i.e. agency, being a limitation, according to Hindu philosophies, it has to be transcended, or gotten rid of, and to get rid of it is to lose or destroy one's agency, one's potentiality to do anything moral or immoral. The actualization of this possibility Mckenzie calls the denial of ethics, and Mahadevan calls going beyond ethics. Thus there is a verbal, or a very thin, almost invisible, difference, if any, between the two positions. Therefore, any interpretation of Indian philosophy as going beyond ethics cannot work as an effective philosophical or logical device to meet the charge that there is no ethics in Indian philosophy. And, it definitely cannot meet the charge that, as Mckenzie straightforwardly puts it, 'none of the great [Indian] systems of thought contains anything that can properly be called a system of ethics',[37] meaning by 'a system of ethics' what I have called a grand, comprehensive, ethical theory. It is in this sense of ethics, i.e. in that of systematic ethical theory, that Mckenzie 'bluntly' avers that in Hindu, or Indian, philosophy there is 'no room for ethics'.[38]

Neither Mahadevan, nor any other Indian writer on Indian ethics, tries to meet the no-ethics charge in a straight fashion. Rather, Mahadevan's emphasizing that the individual who has attained self-realization has no obligation is very much like an echo of Mckenzie's conclusion that 'The duties of social life cannot be deduced from the ultimate goal of attainment [i.e. self-realization] as the orthodox [Indian philosophies] understood it, nor can they be shown to stand in any vital relation to it.'[39] If the realized individual has no obligation, because he has transcended morality, then certainly no duty to anyone, and therefore no social duty, can be deduced from his having become a realized soul. And, no social duty can be obligatory for, or binding on, him, i.e. can stand in any 'vital' relation to him.

To interpret Indian philosophy as holding that morality is just a means to attain self-realization, a footstool needed only for climbing to the highest axiological height, is to affirm that Indian philosophy gives the most honourable place to the goal of self-realization, a place higher than the place it has given to morality. And, if it is objectively justified to give this honour to self-realization and to give to morality the status of a footstool then it would also be objectively justified to say that Indian philosophy has given to man a goal or value higher than any goal or value which any theory of morality has given or can give. This supreme goal, being higher than the moral goal, would then be higher than any other (allegedly) supreme goal given by any other philosophy which considers the moral goal itself as the highest goal, or at least not inferior to any other kind of goal. Scholars like Mahadevan think on these lines. It is for this reason that they hold that by transcending morality or ethics Indian philosophy has taken a forward leap in comparison to philosophies which do not go beyond ethics. And, since it is objectively justified to do that, according to them, they claim that Indian philosophy has given the right treatment to morality by giving it the status of a footstool, of a means to self-realization, the supreme goal.

All this they do because they do not realize the adverse consequences of making morality only a means to self-realization. Some of these consequences have been shown above. But there may be quite a few more which would make it almost impossible for a philosopher to justify being moral to an individual who draws these consequences and takes them seriously. That is, it would be impossible, or extremely hard, to give him a satisfactory answer to the question 'Why should I be moral?' if and when asked by him.

To see how answering the above question would become impossible or very hard, let us imagine individuals of the following few types. There is nothing fantastic in making this experiment because it is an experiment in thinking which is a commonly used philosophical tool and the kind of person proposed to be imagined is not a totally fictitious one. In fact, it is not impossible to come across such a person in real life. Let us then proceed to imagine an individual of either one of the following types:

The individual A admits that he knows that self-realization is the highest value but does not feel inclined to attain it. Therefore, he goes on, he does not feel inclined to lead a moral life since morality is to be inculcated as means to attain self-realization. Such an individual is not an impossibility because it is not impossible to consider something highly desirable and still to have no desire, or to have only a weak desire, to attain it. It is commonly believed, as per the Indian tradition, that Duryodhana, a well-educated prince, told Kṛṣṇa that he knew what he ought to do but did not feel inclined to do it, nor disinclined to do what he knew he ought not to do. To help A become inclined to lead a moral life, while sticking to the footstool conception of morality, there would be no other way except making him first inclined to attain self-realization. But doing that is a much harder job than making any individual inclined to lead a moral life on the ordinary, normal, non-transcendentalist, conception of morality, say, the conception of morality as an end in itself, or as the necessary condition of being a dignified person or member of one's society.

Another individual, B, rejects the view that self-realization is the highest value because he considers untenable the metaphysics, the philosophical theory, which has been given to prove that it is. His neighbour C, on the other hand, does the same thing because he holds, as the *Cārvāka* does, a different metaphysics according to which it is not self-realization but something else, say, a happy mundane life, which is the highest value. To give to B or C a reason to be moral the only way available to the holder of the footstool conception would be to prove the tenability of his own metaphysics and the untenability of all types of differing metaphysics, i.e. of all those which tend to prove that something other than self-realization is the supreme goal. This task, again, is an extremely arduous one, and therefore bound to make equally difficult the task of justifying morality, the task of providing a reason for being moral.

There may be another person D who is different from both B and C since he accepts that self-realization is the highest value but holds that morality is not the means to attain it. For example, he may hold, as some devotional poets do, that what enables anyone to attain it is devotion to God and that morality is neither a necessary nor a sufficient condition for its attainment. This is so, he may go on, because God is so kind to a devotee of his that he liberates him if he is sincerely devoted to him, no matter what sort of life he has lived. And, there may be a still different kind of devotee to God, E, who holds that self-realization is not worth attaining because it makes one cease to be liable to be reborn after death. But it is more desirable to continue eternally being born–dead–reborn on this earth because it is here that God incarnated himself in the form of *Kṛṣṇa* and *Rāma.* This is what the Hindi poet Rasakhāna says in an oft-quoted and recited poem of his. The presentation of its content in prose given hereunder does not have the candour and emotional infectiousness which the poem has. But I hope the point which I have mentioned above will be made amply clear by it. What he says runs as follows:

It is better to be reborn than to become liberated and thereby never be reborn again, if one is born as a human being living in the midst of milkmen and milkwomen in any of the villages of Gokula, or even as an animal grazing on the spots where the cows owned by Nanda grazed, or even as a block of stone on the mountain (named 'Govardhana') which Kṛṣṇa lifted up on his little finger to make it function as an umbrella underneath which he provided shelter to all the living beings of Gokula when Indra, the rain-god, started pouring torrential rains on the land of Gokula, or even as a bird which builds her nest on a branch of any of the trees (named 'Kadamba') on the bank of the river Yamunā.[40]

To any individual of either one of the above types, to mention a few, Indian philosophy would not be able to provide a good motivating reason for leading a moral life, if it is interpreted as holding that morality is only, or even primarily, a means to the attainment of liberation. Persons of these types can be easily located in all societies, including Indian society. Indian philosophy's inability to answer the question 'Why should I be moral?' when asked by any one of them would exhibit a serious deficiency in this interpretation of its attitude towards ethics. It would, because it is this interpretation of Indian philosophy which injects this inability into it.

This interpretation is the parent of the other, equally definitive, interpretation of Indian philosophy as a philosophy which pleads for going, and goes, beyond morality or ethics. The beyond-ethics characterization violates the principle of double effect[41] as explained in the foregoing discussion, since it has two effects or features which are not commensurate. Its one effect is to yield a reason for cultivating morality through making morality a means to attaining liberation (assuming, of course, that the concept of liberation is tenable and that it is logically fair to the concept of morality to call morality a means). Its other effect is that, after the attainment of liberation, morality becomes redundant or unnecessary, a commodity to which the liberated may very well, justifiably, be totally indifferent or negligent. The two effects together seem to usher in something like the following directive: Cultivate morality (if you want) to attain liberation, and after attaining liberation treat it as you like. Any such directive would obviously be unfair to the dignity of morality and to the role which it actually plays in human life, or the human world.

Therefore, if Indian philosophy, or any philosophy whatsoever, conceives of ethics as encapsulated in the directive stated above, it would generate doubts about its overall viability as philosophy. More specifically, it would generate doubts about its being fair to ethics and to its ability to properly understand and explain the problems, theoretical and practical, which arise and which may arise, in a man's pursuit of ethical values and fulfilment of ethical obligations in his private and public life.

It is worth mentioning here a very interesting possibility, and quite a sensible one of an individual's offering a valid ethical reason for continuing leading a good moral life and for not attaining self-realization. And, he may do it while accepting the tenability of the concept of self-realization, the instrumentality of morality in attaining it, the Karmic worldview including the theory of rebirth and of freedom from birth–death–rebirth only after attaining self-realization, etc. Such a stand can be cogently taken by a person who believes in what I call the doctrine of the primacy of the moral or ethical, the doctrine that morality needs no justification; it is justified in itself, in just being what it itself is. It may also be instrumental to attaining self-realization, or to preserving social peace, etc. But it is not just a means, and not justified only because it is a means to this or that end; it is an end in itself. For example, a holder of the primacy of the ethical may say that mitigating the suffering of an innocent person is ethically right and it is ethically right simply because it is mitigating the suffering of an innocent person, i.e. because it is what it is; it does not have to be a means to attain something else, not even a means to attain self-realization.

The argument of the holder of the above position may be taken as a counter-attack from the side of the primacy-of-the-ethical thesis on the beyond-ethics thesis. It may run as follows:

There is a lot of suffering in the world, there are people who are poor, starving, uneducated, ignorant, sick, etc. They need to be helped. Helping them to overcome or reduce their suffering is a highly moral work, a work which is in itself morally commendable, worth doing for its own sake. Hence it is intrinsically good or valuable. To wish to be reborn after every death again and again in order to be given an opportunity to help others, to ameliorate their living conditions, is a morally commendable, an intrinsically noble motive. Therefore, it is better to continue getting reborn after each death than to become liberated, since after becoming liberated one goes beyond morality. If a liberated person continues helping others, even then he would be able to do that only in the present life, and not after its termination, since he would not be reborn after his death. He would obviously then not get any more opportunity to do the ethnically noble work of helping others. And, if it is held that he can get liberation only after his physical death (*videhamukti*), as some schools of Indian philosophy hold, then to be liberated would mean being debarred forever from doing this noble service to humanity and other living beings. Hence, for anyone it is a better ideal or goal to do good social service with only the moral desire to help others and to be reborn again and again so that he may be able to do this ethical work again and again. Such a man's own life may not be cent per cent happy. But as an ideal it would definitely be preferable to his getting himself liberated, even if liberation would be a state of bliss or absolute painlessness. He who himself suffers to a great or small extent, but helps others in reducing their sufferings in each life he lives in an endless series of lives, is obviously a better, a morally more elevated, person than another who himself has no suffering, or is blissful, but is not able to help anyone else to reduce his suffering or is at the most able to do that only for a short duration. Therefore, the moralist concludes, it is better to remain unliberated but morally elevated, than to attain liberation and go beyond ethics, i.e. lose all opportunities, or to have only a limited opportunity, for service to others. This kind of reasoning would be a good reasoning for not trying to go beyond ethics even if going beyond ethics would be the state of getting liberated.

But for rejecting the footstool conception of morality, i.e., of morality as a means to attaining liberation, the above reasoning does not conflict with any other basic doctrine of Indian philosophy or of its *karmic* worldview. At the same time it protects the honour of morality which is quite dear to Indian philosophy too. I hope to show in the next chapter that there is a possibility in Indian philosophy of keeping the close link between morality and liberation intact without reducing morality to the status of a means to be left out, or to become unrequired, after becoming liberated. If this possibility is strong enough to support such a characterization of the role of morality according to Indian philosophy, it would prove the otioseness of the beyond-ethics characterization of Indian philosophy. It is therefore worth exploiting, even if its exploitation necessitates some tinkering with some related doctrines of Indian philosophy. That it may lead to a rejection of some components of the received interpretation, or even a revaluation of the character of Indian philosophy, would be no objection to it. The occurrence of such things is natural in any exercise in progressive philosophizing or rethinking, which this kind of exploitative work certainly would be.

It is clear from the preceding discussions that almost all of the problems which have arisen about the Indian conception of ethics have arisen because of the interpreters' claiming that according to Indian philosophy the most important role of morality is to be a means to an individual's attaining his liberation. They emphasize this role of it so much that it appears to have, according to Indian philosophy, no other role, or no other important role. Because of their fascination for, or rather obsession with, its alleged means-to-the-attainment-of-liberation role, they have neglected, and some of them have not cared even to mention, its most obvious, and also important role: the role of working as a social cement, an agent of ensuring the cohesive, cooperative functioning of human society and of preserving a cordial relationship between man and his surroundings, human and non-human, animate and inanimate. Indian philosophy has emphasized these roles of morality much more than they have emphasized its role as a means to the attainment of liberation.

An attempt will be made in the next chapter to highlight this, the neglected, aspect of Indian philosophy's conception of ethics, to show that Indian philosophy has, in a respectable sense, ethics as ordinarily understood; that it does not simply plead for using morality as a means to the attainment of liberation and consequently for leaving it thereafter by going beyond or transcending it. All this will hopefully also exhibit that it does not treat ethics with any indignity, though it appears from the occurrence of the violation of the principle of double effect, mentioned earlier, that it does. The violation itself is the result, we have seen, of its beyond-ethics characterization. We shall see that it grants to ethics all that belongs to it, i.e., gives to it the credit of doing all that it does in the human world. In acknowledging the great role it plays in human life, at places it becomes even tolerant of some incongruities in some of its worldviews or metaphysical constructions or systematizations. And, in doing all this it does not ignore, or ride roughshod over, the sense or senses in which morality or ethics is ordinarily, common-sensically, understood.

5.5 THE BUDDHIST PARABLE OF THE RAFT: ONLY A SEEMING AFFIRMATION OF 5.4

Before concluding this chapter, it is necessary to discuss the real thrust of the Buddhist Parable of the Raft because it is very often mentioned in support of the view that the Buddha compares morality with a raft which is used to cross over a stream to reach the other bank of the stream and then is to be left these because it would be of no further use. This means, several scholars say, that for the Buddha too morality is only a means to attain liberation, which is metaphorically said to be the other bank in the parable, and thereafter it has to be forsaken. That is, thereafter the liberated has to go beyond, or transcend, morality, or ethics, because then it would have no utility for him. The assumption all along in this interpretation is that morality is only a means to liberation, that liberation is the highest value, that a means is always, or by its very nature, inferior in value to the end it is a means to attain, and that there is no loss, normative or axiological, in going beyond or outside the zone of ethics. This assumption is made even by the *Advaitin* Mahadevan, or rather by everyone who claims that Indian philosophy goes beyond ethics and that it is logically or ethically justified to go beyond ethics. I shall examine this assumption a little later in section 5.6.

The Buddha's pleading for going beyond ethics would be quite obviously surprising. It would be because the primary motivation of his, in giving up his comfortable princely life, leaving his devoted charming wife and dear baby son sleeping, uniformed, to adopt the lifestyle of a mendicant in order to search for the truth, is ethical. It is ethical because the truth he seeks to attain or discover is not any highly abstract, foundational, rarefied, metaphysical truth; it is the truth about the nature and causation of human (or animate) suffering and an effective way of its removal. That is why he brushes aside metaphysical questions and their available answers as uncalled for, and is said to have, by modern interpreters, an anti-metaphysical attitude, though some later Buddhist philosophers do enjoy metaphysical discussions and adumbrate their own metaphysical views. His concern with the removal of human suffering is, par excellence, an ethical concern of the highest order as it is not a concern for alleviating the suffering of a particular group or class of individuals, but for that of each and every human being, i.e. for that of all human (or animate) beings located in any part of the universe. Therefore, it is bound to be surprising if such a morally hypersensitive thinker pleads for, or even approves of, going beyond ethics. That is why his Parable of the Raft needs to be closely probed into in order to ascertain whether or not it does what it is generally interpreted as doing, i.e. as averring or recommending that morality is to be left behind or transcended after attaining liberation.

This Parable occurs in the *Majjhima Nikāya*[42] after the Parable of the Water-snake. A misdirected, or misguided, monk Ariṭṭha misunderstands the essence of morality (*dhamma*) and thinks that it allows indulgence in sensual, even sexual, pleasures if done in a detached manner. The Buddha uses the Parable of the Water-snake to explain to him that he is wrongly using the notion of *dhamma*, and therefore he is holding that *dhamma* allows such indulgences and thereby ruining his moral life by indulging in immoralities. *Dhamma* in this parable is compared to a Water-snake. By catching a Water-snake at one end, which is the right end to catch it, an individual can make it lose its poison. But if he catches it at the other end, which is the wrong end to catch it, he cannot make it non-poisonous and therefore is bitten by it and dies. This is what Ariṭṭha does with the notion of *dhamma* and wrongly interprets it to allow him sensual and sexual indulgence if done in a detached manner. And, therefore, he thinks he can do that. The purport of this parable is that *dhamma* is to be understood, to be caught, i.e. grasped, in the right way. If it is understood, or used, in a wrong way, it would lose its liberating or elevating character and may even cause the moral ruin of the wrong user.

It is at this point that the Parable of the Raft occurs. The Buddha imagines a man who has to cross over a stream to reach the other bank of the stream. He makes a raft by collecting grass, sticks, branches and leaves of some trees, etc. and putting them together. Using this raft he crosses to the other bank and no more needs the raft though the raft has been useful to him by enabling him to land on the other bank. Now he has to decide what to do with the raft: to leave it on the dry land or submerge it into the stream, or to carry it on his head or shoulder wherever he goes. He asks the monks assembled there and all the monks agree with him when he says that good sense would require him to leave the raft and not carry it with him. The Buddha concludes:

> Even so, monks, is the Parable of the Raft *dhamma* taught by me for crossing over, not for retaining. You, monks, by understanding the Parable of the Raft, should get rid even of (right) mental objects, all the more of wrong ones.[43]

What the Buddha says is clearly not to get rid of *Dhamma* or morality but to get rid of 'mental objects', i.e. of attachments, propensities, desires to have this or to not have that, the thoughts like this is mine, that is not mine, this is me and that is someone else, etc., etc. All this he makes clear in the later part of the dialogue. He tells the monks that the user of *dhamma,* to attain whatever he uses it to attain, should get rid of his attachments, even his attachment to *dhamma,* his pride resulting out of having used *dhamma* in achieving his goal which may even be his liberation (*nirvana*). The attachment to *dhamma,* or the pride in having followed it rightly, may be called 'right mental object' but such objects are also to be gotten rid of. That is why I say that he does not preach that ethics or morality be left behind, or transcended. He simply preaches that a monk, or any individual, should always follow *dhamma,* or morality but with no attachment to it.

Dhamma in early Buddhism, like its Sanskrit equivalent *dharma* in its later developments and other classical Indian, non-philosophical as well as philosophical works, is a multi-vocal term. In the Buddha's teachings too and in the Buddhist practice it means morality, observance of rituals, cultivation of certain types of character-traits, religious discipline including performance of certain routine duties, etc., etc. Therefore, even if some of the things which following *dhamma* enjoins, according to the Buddha, may have to be given up after attaining liberation, that would not mean that then morality also has to be given up. Further, the Buddha does not say explicitly that the other bank of the stream, in the parable, represents liberation. It may even mean moral perfection. Since the Buddha is a great practical moralist it is quite likely that reaching to the other bank means attaining moral perfection and that *part* or *aspect* of *dhamma,* which has to be used as a means to attain it, is the cultivation of rigorous discipline, living an extremely austere life. Naturally, then, after attaining moral perfection, one would not need to live in the same austere way as one had to live in order to attain the perfection. In the Parable of the Raft the Buddha says that an individual, 'depending on that raft and *striving with his hands and feet,* might cross over safely to the beyond' (i.e. the other bank of the stream).[44] The user of the raft has to strive, to exert, to exercise his hands and feet, to reach his destination; he does not simply sit idly on the raft in a relaxed pose and float on the stream to land on the dry land of the other bank; he has to strain his muscles to let the craft take him to the other side. This kind of strain he no longer would need to do after landing on that side. That is why it is possible that by saying that the raft would be of no use after reaching the other side, the Buddha may be taken to metaphorically mean, by the parable, that after attaining moral perfection by using rigorous *dhāmmic* discipline, the attainer of moral perfection would no longer need to undergo the strain of undergoing a *dhāmmic* discipline as strenuous as the one he had to undergo while he was striving to attain it.

This view is corroborated by Keown and the lines which he quotes from *Anguttara Nikāya* (v. 252) are decisive in showing that the other shore of the stream stands for moral perfection. They run as follows:

> What, Gotama, is the near and what the further shore?
>
> Taking life, Brahman, is the near shore; abstaining therefrom is the further shore. Taking what is not given is the near shore; abstaining therefrom is the further shore. Sexual misconduct is the near shore; abstaining therefrom is the further shore. Falsehood ... spiteful speech ... harsh speech ... idle talk ... coveting ... malevolence ... wrong views ... are the near shore and abstinence therefrom the further shore.[45]

> A little later there occur in the same *Nikāya* the following:
>
> What, Gotama, is the near shore and what the further shore?
>
> Wrong views, Brahman, is the near shore; right views the further shore. Wrong resolve, speech, action, livelihood effort, mindfulness, concentration, wrong knowledge and wrong release are the near shore. Right view and the rest are the further shore.[46]

To conclude, therefore, we can safely say that the Buddha's Parable of the Raft cannot be used to aver that the Buddha recommends that morality or ethics be transcended or left behind at any time, say, after attaining liberation.

Even if there is some inkling in the parable which might be used to support the transcendency thesis, the allegedly going-beyond-ethics character of Buddhist axiology or philosophy, it is totally removed by the later Buddhist theory of the *bodhisattva*. The *bodhisattva* is an individual who has, by his moral training and acquisition of right knowledge, become fit to attain, or is very near attaining, liberation. But, as per the later Buddhism, he is not to proceed to attain it. Rather, he is to postpone attaining it for helping others who have neither acquired the right knowledge nor inculcated the right kind of moral culture. He is to help them to acquire right knowledge and right moral living so that they also become fit to attain liberation. And, the *bodhisattva* is to keep suspended his attainment of liberation as long as there is anyone who needs his help to attain liberation. This amounts to maintaining that he should never try to attain his own liberation because the number of unregenerated people needing his help is infinite, or almost infinite. This is, in effect, to ask him to sacrifice his own chance of getting liberated in order to be able to help others. This is an extremely noble, elevated, kind of ethical altruism, a bold example of the Buddhist affirmation of what I call the primacy of the ethical. Liberation is considered to be the highest value, the highest *spiritual* good. Even then to help anyone to lead a morally cultivated and enlightened life in order that he may become fit to attain his highest (spiritual) good is undoubtedly a highly altruistic work. And, therefore, the Buddhist principle that anyone who becomes a *bodhisattva,* i.e. fit to attain his liberation, should postpone his attaining it to perform the altruistic task of helping others to become fit to attain theirs is certainly to give primacy to the altruistic, the ethical, work primacy over the spiritual task of attaining one's own liberation.

For Buddhism, in determining the moral rightness of an action its doer's motivation or intention (*cetanā*) as well as its consequence or result (*vipāka*) is to be taken into account. In the *bodhisattva*'s postponing his attainment of liberation to help others, both his intention and the result of his action are altruistic. His intention is *altruistic* because it is to *help others,* and the result of his help is altruistic because it is the *fitness of others* to attain their liberation.

Compassion (*karuṇā*) is said to be a natural virtue of the *bodhisattva,* something like his second nature he has cultivated as a result of his moral discipline and acquisition of right knowledge. Compassion itself is a character-trait whose object is, by definition, someone else. Compassion means an attitude of sympathy and kindliness towards others, i.e. an essentially altruistic attitude. When directed by a person towards himself it becomes some sort of self-pity which in no way can be called by Buddhism, or by any other philosophical or religious school, a virtue. Keown quotes from *Bodhisattva-bhūmi* (165.2–9) a paragraph the concluding lines of which, in English translation, are:

'But it is not fitting for a *bodhisattva*, who places the interests of others above all else, to desire little, be free from responsibilities and free from cares as far as the interest of other people is concerned.'[47]

These lines set all doubts at rest about the *bodhisattva*'s being a paradigmatic example of an altruistic person, and the state of *bodhisaṭṭva*hood being a state of moral perfection. This is the highest state an individual can attain before his attainment of liberation, and it is a moral state, a state of moral perfection. In order to preserve his altruism, to keep his altruism unmitigated by his spiritual quest, the *bodhisattva* is free to have desires for the welfare of others, to have responsibilities to promote or safeguard others' interests, and to have a concern for their welfare. He is not to be an absolutely *niṣkāma* (desireless) individual, as the *Gītā*'s ideal individual is required to be. The *Gītā*'s ideal individual (*sthitaprajña*) cannot be altruistic because the desire to contribute to the well-being of others is also a desire and he is not to have any desire. The *Gītā* does say that he is to act for *lokasangraha* but *lokasangraha* does not mean *lokakalyāṇa* (others' welfare). For an individual to act for *lokasangraha* (*lokasangrakārṭha*) simply means to act in order that he be rightly taken, or understood, by the people, by the common man. Being *niṣkāma* he may think he does not have to do anything, even to take care of his own needs, and may therefore vegetate. The common man then may take his example in a wrong manner and think derogatorily of the ideal person as characterized by the *Gītā*. To avoid this possibility he has to continue doing things which a normal person is expected to do but in a detached, desireless manner, thinking it is his duty to do all this. Buddhism does not have to take this detour which the *Gītā* takes and even then does not succeed in bringing in ethical altruism. The *Gītā* cannot recommend that the ideal person should have any altruistic desire because every desireful action, i.e. action motivated by any desire, ethical or unethical, causes rebirth, and therefore would not let its doer be liberated, since it would cause the rebirth of the doer and to be liberated means to cease to have the liability to be reborn.[48] In fact, no other Indian philosophical system than Buddhism recommends an individual's postponing attaining his own liberation for the sake of helping others to attain theirs.

The Buddhist ideal is thus straightforwardly altruistic and therefore an ethical or moral ideal, the attainment of some sort of a state of moral perfection. It is obvious, therefore, that Buddhism cannot be interpreted as recommending or requiring that ethics be transcended, that the ideal person should go beyond ethics or the zone of morality.

5.6 ETHICS' CHALLENGE TO THE *PARĀ–APARĀ* CATEGORIOLOGY

On the first blush of it ethics, quite obviously, cannot be said to be *parāvidyā*. *Parāvidyā*, we have seen in Chapter 4, is *Brahmavidyā*, the inquiry which gives the knowledge of *Brahman*, the ultimate reality by knowing which everything else is known and by realizing which the highest value is realized because *Brahman* is both the ultimate reality and ultimate value. *Brahmavidyā*, or *parāvidyā*, is thus an inquiry with a final terminus. After knowing *Brahman* nothing else remains to be known, and after realizing it no other value needs to be realized. Therefore, after one's having *Brahmavidyā*, one's inquiring into the nature of reality must come to an end once and for all because one has reached the final terminus, got the knowledge of *Brahman*, the ultimate reality. For a similar reason, since *Brahman*, the highest value, is also realized in the acquisition of *Brahmavidyā*, one's pursuit of value, one's axiological inquiry which it includes, too, must come to an end. And, *Brahmavidyā*, the highest inquiry has already been done and handed over to us, as per the *Munaka*. Therefore, no further inquiry into the nature of *Brahmavidyā* needs to be conducted; only, the *Brahmavidyā* already made available is to be understood, recounted, assimilated, digested, followed, etc.

Ethics neither gives the knowledge of such a reality nor does it claim to give a value or a set of values which can be said to have an absolutely final status as the value given by *parāvidyā* is claimed to have. Nor does ethics claim to give a set of moral principles which make any further search for another set absolutely uncalled for. Ethics is an open-ended inquiry conducted in the empirical world which never remains static, and the set of values, virtues, or principles, etc., considered desirable at any one time is not likely to be completely, absolutely, exhaustive or unalterable for all time to come. For example, even a generally accepted moral principle may have to be modified, or an exception may have to be made to it, in some circumstances without making it otiose or invalid. That is why moral principles and concepts are said to be defeasible, i.e. principles and concepts which admit of exceptions without thereby being defeated or nullified. All this is prominently highlighted in the classical Indian concept of *āpaddharma* which means that in some extraordinary, unusual circumstances an individual may do, without being guilty of doing anything immoral, a thing which is considered to be morally impermissible or forbidden in some normal circumstances. It is clear enough, therefore, that ethics is an inquiry with no final terminus. The history of ethics, replete with an exuberance of ethical theories, convincingly shows that no ethical theory can claim to have reached the final terminus of ethical theorizing and in fact no ethical theory or inquiry has made such a claim.

To clarify that matter further, with the help of an example of some unusual circumstance, be it noted that there cannot be a final list of unusual circumstances in which an exception to, or a modification in the application of, a moral principle would be permissible, nor can there be a final list of such permissible exceptions or modifications. All this cannot be done because decision-making is a very important ingredient in the process of the application of a moral principle. The application of a moral principle is not done in a mechanical, formalistic, or deductive manner. The individual concerned has to decide, whether or not the circumstances in which he is, justify making an exception and also the extent or strength of the exception to a relevant principle. He also has to see that the exception he makes does not amount to a violation of the principle, or the modification he makes does not amount to destroying the basic character of the principle. In all this he has to see that his considering an exception to a principle permissible does not amount to taking a *permissive attitude* towards the principle. For a person to take a permissive attitude towards a principle is to be fluid, or nonchalant, about it in the sense that he does not mind using it in a manner which, as per the common understanding of it, is a clear violation or misapplication of it. In all this he has to use his moral maturity, acumen, or what may be called his moral will, moral reason, or even moral intuition.

In judging whether, in a certain case, he has made a permissible exception to a principle, or has taken a permissive attitude towards it, a judger will also have to use his moral will, moral reason, or moral intuition. For example, in the *Mahābhārata* war, on Kṛṣṇa's persuasion Yudhiṣṭhira announces the lie as a truth that Aśvaṭhāmā has been killed, while adding in a subdued tone that it is the elephant, and not the man, named

'Aśvaṭhāmā'. This part of his utterance is not heard by anyone on the Kaurava side because of the simultaneous extremely loud blowing of a conch by his brother Bhīma. Yudhiṣṭhira's making this announcement is telling a lie and therefore definitely an act of going against the principle of truthfulness to which he is committed. Before telling the lie Yudhiṣṭhira thinks first that doing this will be a violation of the principle. Kṛṣṇa, on the other hand, forcefully pleads that doing that is only making a permissible exception to the principle, and not violating it. His reasoning is that only by Yudhiṣṭhira's telling this lie would Droṇa believe it to be a truth, because of Yudhiṣṭhira's reputation of being always a truth-teller, and then withdraw from the battlefield. Droṇa's withdrawal is necessary for Yudhiṣṭhira's winning the war and his winning the war is morally right and just. After Kṛṣṇa's persuasive reasoning Yudhiṣṭhira too seems to believe that by making the announcement he would be only telling a justified lie, i.e. making a justified, permissible, exception to the principle of truth-telling and not violating it. But Duryodhana, even Bhīṣma, and all those who are on Duryodhana's side, think it is a violation. Even today experts debate about the status of this lie: some think that it is a violation and that Kṛṣṇa's is a permissive attitude about the principle of truthfulness, while some think that it is only a permissible exception.

It is clear from all this, that decision-making is a constitutive feature of anyone's acceptance and application of a moral principle in normal as well as in non-normal, unusual, circumstances. The individual has to decide which principle is relevant to the situation he is in and whether it is to be applied in its usual, unaltered form, or in a form modified, augmented, or toned down in some way; he also has to decide whether or not the present situation is one which justifies making an exception to the principle. He may take the help of past precedents, or his society's ethical corpus, in making up his mind. But ultimately it is he who makes up his own mind, i.e. decides which way to go. In fact, it is his decision-making ability and its exercise by him which enable him to deserve the title of being a moral agent.

One reason for considering ethics an *aparā* inquiry is said to be its being a means to the acquisition of *parāvidyā* and therefore also a means, or nothing more than a means, to the attainment of *mokṣa*. We have seen that there are several difficulties in considering ethics as having only instrumental value which it is said to have in the footstool-or-ladder conception of ethics or morality. Moreover, to attribute only instrumental value to morality is to devalue it. And, calling it a means does not eo ipso, automatically, prove that its value is lower than the value of that, *mokṣa* or *parāvidyā*, to the attainment of which it is said to be a means. Anything's being a means by itself does not prove that it is lower in value than the end it is a means to. For example, honesty is a means to success in business. But its being a means to the latter by itself does prove that honesty is lower in value than success in business. Our moral common sense would say that honesty is of much higher value than success in business. Whether or not a means is of lower (or higher) value than its end has to be proven as an independent issue. Therefore, ethics has to be proven to be lower in value, an *aparāvidyā*, independently of its allegedly being a means to *paravidyā*.

There is another factor which also needs to be taken into account. An end does not remain untouched, unaffected, by the character of the means used to attain it. Political manoeuvring is a means used by some scholars to attain a position of power. But the use of this means reduces, adversely affects, the honour of the position attained. A means of lower value, or of disvalue, invariably adversely affects, reduces, or vitiates, the value of that which it is used to attain. Therefore, if ethics is an *aparāvidyā*, an inquiry of lower value than *Brahmavidyā*, the *parāvidyā*, and at the same time is a means to attain the *parāvidyā*, then it would surely affect, reduce, the value of the latter. The *parāvidyā* is the highest *vidyā*, an inquiry of the highest order. To reduce its value to any extent is to make it cease to be the inquiry of the highest order. It would then become another *aparāvidyā*, like ethics, because any inquiry which is not of the highest order is an *aparā* inquiry.

There is another possibility which may be used to call ethics *aparā*. The defender of its *aparā* character may proceed on some such lines:

Granted, he may say, that leading a moral life has intrinsic value, and not merely instrumental value. The attainment of *mokṣa* is also an intrinsic value. But the intrinsic value of morality is lower than that of *mokṣa*. Therefore, ethics which deals with morality is lower in value than *Brahmavidyā* which is concerned with *mokṣa*, and consequently *Brahmavidyā* is the *parā* inquiry and ethics an *aparā* inquiry.

There is more than one difficulty in this defence of the *aparā* character of morality or of ethics. Firstly, of two intrinsic values, none can be said to be inferior or superior to the other. This is so because a thing is of intrinsic value simply because of its being what it intrinsically, i.e. in itself, is, simply because of its own nature, without taking into account any one of its relations to something else or any one of its effects. The moment we take into account any one of its relations or effects, in determining its value, it becomes a thing of some instrumental, consequential, value. Therefore, we cannot state one intrinsic value to be lower or higher than another because we cannot say why this is so; we cannot say what is that which makes one of a lower value than the other. We cannot say that because nothing other than its own nature, its own being what it is, gives to it its intrinsic value and it is therefore, for that very reason, that its value is intrinsic value. Two intrinsic values, as intrinsic values, cannot be given a comparative rating.

In Indian axiological categoriology, *Brahmānanda* (pleasure or bliss in realizing *Brahman*, or Self, i.e. in attaining *mokṣa*), *Kāvyānanda* or *Kalānanda* (enjoyment of poetry or rather, artistic enjoyment of art-experience) and *Kāmānanda* or *sambhogasukha* (enjoyment of sex) are said to have intrinsic value. But Sanskrit literature does not say that any one of them has lower or higher intrinsic value than any other. It calls them *sahodara* (born out of the same womb), i.e. values equal in status. It has, however, to face the question as to which one of the three an individual should prefer if he has to make a choice. To answer this question of relative preference it brings in the notion of duration or temporality. Its answer is that *Brahmānanda* is to be preferred to the other two because it is everlasting while they are not. For a similar reason, artistic pleasure is to be preferred to sexual pleasure because it is more durable than the latter. Therefore, if morality is to be ranked lower than attainment of *mokṣa* or spirituality (because *mokṣa* is said to be a spiritual value and not a moral value), then, one way of doing that would be to say that what morality gives is less durable than what *mokṣa* gives. But Indian thinkers do not say that: rather, they emphasize that it is morality, *dharma*, which sustains the world, which keeps the world in stable order. This they say because they realize the value of morality in working as the cement which keeps the differents sectors of the world conjoined with another. This is in effect to claim that it is morality, and not *mokṣa*, which ensures the durability of the world. *Mokṣa*, or its attainment, truly speaking, cannot do that because it completely stops the possibility of its attainer's (*mukta*'s) rebirth after his (bodily) death. This amounts to making him cease to be a resident of the world and therefore implies that if all individuals get anytime liberated, then there would remain no individual in the world; that is, then there would not be a world of individuals which this world of ours is and which morality is said to sustain. Obviously, therefore, *mokṣa* cannot be said to be an agent which ensures, as morality does, the preservation of the world. It is this world in which moral life is lived and ought to be lived.

It has been held by many that all individuals can at no point of time get liberated because their number is infinite. I too have mentioned it at some peaces in this work, but I have done that as a prevalent, generally accepted, view and not as one which I myself consider defensible. In fact or rather, in point of logic, the number of individuals in the world, as conceived in Indian philosophies, cannot be infinite. This is so because all of them categorically assert that the world is finite. A finite world cannot contain infinite number of any sort of things, animate or inamimate, human or non-human. This logical fact is forgotten, or not noticed, by all those who adhere to the doctrine of the infinitude of the number of individuals, or, human beings, in the world.

To call morality *aparā*, and therefore ethics an *aparā* inquiry, or vice versa, would certainly demean, denigrate, or devalue it in the eyes of those who care for it and therefore very likely weaken their moral will. As far as those who are ethical sceptics or nihilists are concerned, for the same reason they are very likely to get encouraged to be indifferent to, or violative of, moral rules and principles. Indian thinkers realize all this; they realize that to undervalue morality to highlight the value of *mokṣa,* i.e. to undervalue the status of ethics in order to emphasize the high status of *Brahmavidyā* will be dangerous. It is because it is easier to feel tempted to flout morality than to be convinced of the value of *Brahmavidyā,* a highly abstruse kind of inquiry not within the easy reach of the common man. It is also because undervaluing ethics or moral life is likely to give at least a seeming reason to the propensity to ignore moral principles, the observance of which is essential for the preservation of social order.

All this clearly shows that there are difficulties in calling ethics *aparāvidyā* as well as in calling it *parāvidyā.* It is not feasible to do even the latter because the Indian *Upaniṣadic* tradition, which uses the *parā–aparā vidyā* categoriology, considers only *Brahmavidyā* the *parāvidyā.* To call ethics *aparā* is likely to effect social life adversely by its tendency to weaken people's moral will and to call it *parā* would affect the unique status of *Brahmavidyā* which it is said to have because of its being the only *parā* inquiry. It is clear, thus, that ethics challenges, or puts a question mark on, the viability of the *parā–aparā–vidyā* categoriology of classifying inquiries into two mutually exclusive sets or classes of *parā* and *aparā* inquiries. Perhaps it is because of these reasons that classical Indian thinkers do not put it in the list of *aparā* inquiries, nor do they give it the status of a *parā* inquiry sitting as an equal by the side of *Brahmavidyā.*

A thing of intrinsic value may also have instrumental value, as for example, honesty may be said to have both; it is a value in itself as well as instrumentally valuable because of being, for instance, conducive to success in business. Morality, too, may be said to have both intrinsic and instrumental values, since an individual's being moral is good in itself as well as conducive to making him socially respectable. Writers on Indian axiology generally speak of its admitting three sorts of values: aesthetic, ethical and spiritual, and giving to *mokṣa* the status of a spiritual value and of being the highest in the trilogy of values. When a thing has both intrinsic and instrumental values and its instrumental value is also positive, its total value would be greater than that of another thing which has only intrinsic value. Morality has both intrinsic and instrumental values and so has aesthetic experience. But *mokṣa* has only intrinsic value; it is not a means to any other value or thing which is valuable. Therefore, we cannot say that *mokṣa*'s total value is greater than that of morality because the total value of *mokṣa* is its intrinsic value alone. The same is the case with *mokṣa* vis-à-vis aesthetic value or the value of aesthetic experience.

But can we say that *mokṣa* is a higher value than the ethical, in whichever way the ethical value is conceived, in the sense that it includes the ethical value, and therefore that ethics is an *aparā* inquiry since it deals with a value lower than the spiritual value, i.e. *mokṣa*, the *parā* inquiry deals with? This too does not seem to be a defensible proposition. Firstly, some thinkers do not admit the possibility of liberation attainable by an individual while he is alive (*jīvanmukti*) but only that of liberation attainable after death, for example, the thinkers of the *Nyāya* school. They cannot admit that *mokṣa* includes the ethical value because one cannot do anything, ethical, non-ethical, or unethical, after his physical death when he is only a pure, disembodied self, and not an individual (*jīva*). Only a living individual can do anything ethical, non-ethical, or unethical. Secondly, some thinkers of devotional schools hold that god is so kind that he can liberate an individual devoted to him even if he is deprived of all ethical values, even if he is a sinner. Even such a man's *mokṣa* need not include within it any ethical value. Thirdly, if morality is conceived strictly as a means to *mokṣa* disposable after the attainment of liberation while alive, on the analogy of a footstool, then too *mokṣa* need not necessarily include any ethical value.[49] It is not safe therefore to say that the spiritual value *mokṣa* is inclusive of all ethical values and therefore is higher than the latter, and consequently ethics which deals with the lower values is *aparā*, an inquiry lower in status than the *parā* inquiry which deals with *mokṣa*, the higher-than-all-other values.

It seems to me that it is their realizing something like the difficulties which have been mentioned in the foregoing pages because of which classical Indian thinkers do not make an attempt to give a reasoning for proving that *mokṣa*, a spiritual value, is higher than any other intrinsic value, moral or aesthetic. The only reason, or that which may be called a reason, is their claim that *mokṣa* is the realization of the ultimate reality which also is the ultimate value. That the ultimate reality is also the ultimate value, or a value, too needs to be proven. But they do not think that it does. They *assume*, or hold as a *definition* of ultimate reality, that the ultimate reality is the ultimate value and that anything else, whether it is an ethical or an aesthetic value, is of a lower status on the scale of values than *mokṣa*. That a spiritual value is higher than any ethical or aesthetic value, or rather any other value whatsoever, is, thus, more of an assumption, definition, or axiom of Indian axiology or metaphysics than the conclusion of a deliberate, well-conducted reasoning. But in spite of giving this elevated status to the spiritual value, classical thinkers do not fail to acknowledge and emphasize the importance of morality and therefore of ethics.

It has been said more than once in this chapter that ethics works as the most effective social cement, that it sustains, as classical Indian thinkers, say, the world-order. To explain this point we need to discuss in some detail the place and role of ethics in the world as envisaged by moral common sense as well as by classical Indian thinkers. This topic will be taken up in the next chapter.

NOTES AND REFERENCES

1. Rajendra Prasad (ed.), 'Ethics in the Gīta', *A Historical–Developmental Study of Classical Indian Philosophy of Morals* (PHISPC, New Delhi, forthcoming) Ch. 6.
2. Rajendra Prasad, Varṇadharma, Niṣkama Karma, and Practical Morality: A Critical Essay on Applied Ethics (D.K. Printworld, New Delhi, year).
3. See Rajendra Prasad, *Dharmakirti's Theory of Inference: Revaluation and Reconstruction* (OUP, New Delhi, 2002).
4. W.T. Stace, *A Critical History of Greek Philosophy* (Macmillan, London, 1920, reprinted several times since then).
5. Ibid., p. 14.
6. Ibid., pp. 14–15.
7. Ibid., p. 15.
8. Ibid., p. 313.
9. W.T. Stace, *The Philosophy of Hegel* (Dover, 1955, reprint 1923), p. 498.
10. A.B. Keith, *The Religion and Philosophy of the Veda and Upaniṣads,* Part II (Motilal Banarsidass, New Delhi, 1998, reprint 1925). Abbreviated as *RPVU* in further references.
11. Farquhar, *The Hibbert Journal,* 1921, p. 48.
12. Sarasvati Chennakesavan, *Concepts of Indian Philosophy* (Orient Longman, 1976), p. 195.
13. Ibid., p. 470.
14. Ibid., pp. 469–71, 475–77, 584–85.
15. Haridas Bhattacharyya, 'Indian Ethics' (pp. 620–44) in *The Cultural Heritage of India,* Vol. III (The Ramakrishna Institute of Culture, Calcutta, first edition 1937, second 1953, reprint 1993), p. 635.
16. Ibid., p. 636.
17. Ibid., p. 637.
18. T.M.P. Mahadevan, 'Beyond Ethics', presidential address to the Ethics and Social Philosophy Section, in *Silver Jubilee Commemoration Volume* (The Indian Philosophical Congress, 1950, pp. 43–54).
19. Ibid., p. 43.
20. Ibid., p. 46.
21. Ibid.
22. Bertrand Russell, 'The Philosophy of Logical Afomism', in R.C. Marsh (ed.) *Bertrand Russell: Logic and Knowledge* (Allen & Unwin, 1956).
23. Ibid.
24. Ibid., p. 47.
25. Bertrand Russell, 'Knowledge by Acquintance and Knowledge by Description', *The Problems of Philosophy* (HUL, 1912); reprint. *Mysticism and Logic* (Longmans Green & Co., 1918).
26. Ibid.
27. G.E. Moore, *Principia Ethica* (Cambridge Universtiy Press, 1918) Ch 1.
28. Arthur Prior, *Logic and the Basis of Ethics* (Oxford, 1949).
29. J.S. Mackenzie, *A Manual of Ethics* (University Tutorial Press, London, 6th edition, 1929).
30. T.M.P. Mahadevan, *Outlines of Hinduism* (Chetana Limited, Bombay, 1956), Ch. 5.
31. *Leviathan* (Pelican, Harmondsworth, 1968) p. 186.
32. Mahadevan, 'Beyond Ethics', p. 52.
33. Ibid., p. 54.
34. Ibid.
35. Ibid.
36. John Mckenzie, *Hindu Ethics* (Orient Books Reprint Corporation, New Delhi, second edition, 1971), p. 205.
37. Ibid., p. 206.
38. Ibid., p. 207.
39. Ibid., pp. 209–10.
40. '*Mānusa haun to vahī Rasakhāna, basaun Braja Gokula gāon ke gvārana. Jo pasu haun to kahā basa mero, caraon nita Nanda kī dhenu manjhārana. Pāhana haun to vahī giri kau, jo dharaun kara chatra Purandara-dhārana. Jo khaga haun to basero karaun mili Kālindikūla Kadamba kī dārana*'. Quoted in *Kalyāṇa* Vol. 77, No. 2, 2003, p. 627.
41. The principle of double effect is an ethical principle which determines the conditions in which any action X is morally permissible when it has two effects, a and b, of which a is good and b is bad. According to

it X is permissible if (i) X in itself is right, or not wrong, (ii) b, the bad effect, is not intentionally produced, i.e. when it is accidental, unavoidable, etc., (iii) a itself is not the effect of b, i.e. a has not happened only because b has happened, and a and b are concordant or commensurate with each other.

42. *The Middle Length Sayings* (*Majjhima Nikāya*), Vol. I, translated by L.B. Horner (Routledge and Kegan Paul, London, 1976), pp. 173–82.
43. Ibid., pp. 173–74.
44. Ibid., p. 173. Italics mine.
45. Damien Keown, *The Nature of Buddhist Ethics* (Macmillan, London, 1992), p. 95.
46. Ibid.
47. Ibid., p. 148.
48. All this has been discussed in detail in Rajendra Prasad (ed.), 'Ethics in the *Gītā*', *A Historical–Developmental Study of Classical Indian Philosophy of Morals* (PHISPC, forthcoming).
49. This point will be further elaborated in Chapter 14.

CHAPTER 6

Theorizing in Ethics: The Indian Way

6.1 REALITY OF THE WORLD: A NATURAL PRESUPPOSITION OF THE POSSIBILITY OF ETHICAL LIFE

Without taking it as an exhaustive or a watertight definition, or even a characterization, of ethics, we can start with the understanding that ethics, as a philosophical inquiry, primarily studies, from a normative point of view, man's concern with values, virtues, obligations and rights. It explores the nature of things he should try to aim at or to make them the goals of his pursuit, the nature of character-traits he should try to inculcate, the nature of obligations or duties he should try to fulfil, and the nature of the rights he has over some others and of the rights which some others have over him, etc., along with some other related issues. All such things get their normative point, or significance, from the too obvious fact that he lives in a world consisting of other humans and non-humans, animate as well as inanimate. These inhabitants of the world, because they live in the same world and have occasions to interact with one another, form, sometimes in a loose sense and sometimes in a strict sense, some sort of a society which quite often turns into a moral community.

The summary account of the human situation, given above, as the stage on which and in relation to which ethics performs its main roles, is quite liberal. Rather, it is liberal enough to be true of ethics, ethicizing, or theorizing in ethics, done in India, classical or modern, as well as in the West. The present work is exclusively concerned with ethical theorizing in classical India, and is not at all intended to be one on ethical theorizing in general. Therefore, it is not necessary to discuss in detail here the various facets of the ethical inquiry in general. The summarily stated characterization of it, given in the beginning of this section, gives a clear hint as to what we are going to do in our endeavour to characterize the classical Indian way of doing ethical theory, i.e. moral philosophy as done by classical Indian thinkers, or available in the classical Indian corpus.

In whichever way we characterize any one of the things ethics is concerned with, it is clear that an ethical (or unethical) thing can be done only by a real, living, individual, in relation to another real individual, or a group of real individuals, or to a real non-human object, living or non-living (of course if according to the ethical perspective adopted by him such things can be done to a non-human object). For example, only a real, living person can seek, or be required or advised to seek, happiness. Only a real, living individual, or a group of such individuals, can promote, or be advised to promote, the happiness of some other real individual, or some group of real individuals. An unreal individual can do nothing. Therefore, he can do nothing of this sort, and consequently cannot be obligated or required or advised to do anything of this sort.

An unreal individual can neither be the *subject* nor the *object* of an ethical action or engagement. That is, only a real individual can be the *doer*, the *subject*, as well as the *object* of an ethical transaction. There is no point in trying to promote the happiness of an unreal individual, or to be kind to him, or to honour a right of his, etc. Ethical relations are real relations and they can exist only between real individuals, just as ethical predicates are real predicates which can be attributed only to real individuals. They are real predicates in the sense that to affirm or deny them of any individual is to assume that that individual exists.

Suppose, for example, that a childless mother believes that there is a certain god who blesses a devotee of his with a son if she performs a sacrifice (*yajña*) in his honour in a certain prescribed manner. She performs the sacrifice in the prescribed manner but does not get a son. Thereupon she feels dejected and accuses the god of being *unjust* to her. This would mean that she still believes that that god exists, i.e. is a real individual. Only an existent, real, god can be just or unjust. In believing that that god blesses a devotee with a son she believes that that god is real, and in accusing him of being unjust by not blessing her with a son also she believes that he is real. Another woman who does not believe that there is any such god, i.e. who believes that such a god is a fiction, a figment of someone's imagination, would neither call him just or unjust. She would neither affirm nor deny any real predicate of him and therefore would neither affirm or deny any ethical predicate of him. She would attach to him, or to it, only such predicates as 'being unreal', 'fictitious', or 'imaginary', etc., all of which are, in logical terminology, unreal predicates. Unreal predicates are also called non-logical predicates, just as real predicates are also called logical predicates.

It is true that we sometimes ascribe an ethical predicate to a character in a work of fiction, say, to A knowing full well that A does not denote a real individual. What happens in such a case is that A works as an individual variable, and not as an individual constant. The judgement passed on its conduct, e.g. 'A's behaviour in doing B to C is ethically condemnable (or commendable)' is really equivalent to the universal moral judgement 'Anyone's (any A's) behaviour in doing anything like B to any other individual like C is ethically condemnable'. It is this sort of universalization implicitly made by the reader of fiction which literary critics call the theory of generalization or universalization (*sādhāraṇīkaraṇa*). It is this *generalization* of A's behaviour in doing B to C which makes him feel sad, hurt, etc., say, by empathy, when, as portrayed in the work, it makes C feel sad, hurt, etc. Consequently, he experiences a feeling of moral sympathy for C and a feeling of moral condemnation or of moral anger for A. Let me illustrate all this from the portrayal of an incident by the famous Hindi fiction writer, Premchand, in his short story 'Sadgati,'[1] a powerful ethico-social satire. It runs as follows:

Dukhī, a scheduled caste (*śūdra* in classical terminology) poor labourer, more specifically a *camāra* or *carmakāra* in Hindi terminology (a shoe-maker), is overjoyed as his daughter's marriage has been settled. It is his ambition for long to get an auspicious day for her marriage determined by the highly religious (*dharmātmā*) and respected brāhmaṇ priest Paṇḍita Ghāsī Rāma. He makes a big bundle of fodder for the Paṇḍita's cow, carries it on his head early morning to his place, offers it to him as his sacramental fee because he has no money to offer, and requests him to come out, while standing outside the entrance of his house because, being an untouchable, he cannot go inside. When he comes out, Dukhī prays to him to come to his place with an almanac (*pancānga*), determine the day and bless his daughter. The Paṇḍita tells him he is free only in the evening and only then can go to his place. He curtly asks him to place the bundle in a corner, and then to clean his large, dirty compound, transport a huge pile of dry fodder to the place meant for it, and thereafter to cut a big, dry block of wood with an axe into small, thin pieces usable as fuel in his kitchen's home-made earthen oven (*cūlhā*). After assigning these tasks to Dukhī he goes inside to worship his deity, eat lunch and then take his routine post-lunch nap. Cleaning the compound and transporting the fodder by carrying in a big gunny-bag a large quantity of it on his head in several trips takes Dukhī more than half of the day. He is by then completely exhausted. But still he picks up an axe to cut the block of wood as directed. The block turns out to be as hard as a block of stone. However strongly he strikes his axe against it, it does not seem to yield. After hours of his hard labour, only a few pieces come out. The famished, heavily sweating Dukhī faints, falls down, and breaths his last then and there. When the Paṇḍita comes out and finds him dead, he waits for some time for his people to lift the dead body. But nobody comes. Then in the cover of darkness he gets a thick rope tied around the legs and drags the body—because he cannot touch it as it is an untouchable's dead body—and leaves it in a nearby orchard. Carnivorous birds and animals eat away Dukhī's body.

Any sensitive reader, after reading the story, or a sensitive viewer, after watching its dramatic version on the television screen, since it was also staged on the screen by Delhi Television's national channel some years ago, is likely to feel a strong sense of *moral anger* and condemnation for the Paṇḍita on account of his behaviour with Dukhī. He knows that neither of the two is a real individual, and the entire account is a creation of the writer's imagination. But he still condemns the one and cries for the other. In doing both he generalizes the account portrayed in the story. In fact, he condemns anyone who behaves as the Paṇḍita does and sympathizes with anyone who suffers as Dukhī does. His moral judgement, when made fully explicit would be something like this:

Any Paṇḍita-Ghāsī-Rāma-like-man's behaviour with any Dukhī-like-man is highly morally condemnable.

In abstract terms, after dropping the names of the two characters of the story, it would be something like the following:

Anyone's any behaviour with anyone else which exploits the latter's ignorance, social status and need, causing immense suffering to him, is highly morally condemnable.

I hope this short detour through a work of fiction has done its job of demonstrating that ethical predictes are attributable only to real individuals. This is a pointer to another fact. Real individuals can exist only in a real and not in an illusionary or unreal world, and only in a real world can they do anything. Whatever they do would also be real. A real man can handle only a real bow-and-arrow, or rather, the bow-and-arrow which a real man handles would be a real bow-and-arrow, and the world in which, or the battlefield on which, he handles it would also be real. If he makes anyone the target of his arrow and kills him, he would have really killed him. This means that ethical transactions can be done only in a real world. They do seem to be done, or to have been done, in the world of fiction, in a fictitious, unreal, or imaginary world, for example, in the fictitious world of 'Sadgati', the story referred to above. But then too they are about real transactions among real individuals in a real world, not in a direct way but through their fallouts in the form of universal moral judgements. These judgements, when instantiated in concrete contexts by individuals and their actions or intentions, will clearly show that a transaction which can be morally judged, to which *moral predicates* can be applied, can be enacted only in a real world among real individuals. The story yields the moral lesson that any exploitation of any lower caste man by any upper caste man because of the former's poverty and ignorance is morally wrong. It is clear that being a universal proposition, as is the case with any universal proposition, it can be instantiated only by a true singular proposition, i.e. by one which is about an instance in which a real *exploitation* is done by an upper caste man of a lower caste man on account of his poverty and ignorance and the exploitation is morally condemnable. A real exploitation can be done only by a real individual (or class) of another real individual (or class). *Ethical relations* can only be illustrated, explained, clarified, etc. by means of artificial, imaginary, examples, but they cannot hold between them.

Proceeding on these lines we can reasonably say that ethical things can be meaningfully spoken of only with reference to real individuals or objects. An unreal man can be neither virtuous nor vicious, can neither fulfil nor fail to fulfil an obligation, can neither do anything right nor anything wrong, can neither honour nor flout a right of someone else, etc. Similarly, if dirtying a river is ethically wrong, as the saint Viśvāmitra says and modern environmental ethicists concur with him, or killing an animal on a certain day at the altar of a Kālī temple to propitiate the goddess Kālī is ethically right, as a Kālī devotee would say, then we would have to grant that the dirtied, or dirtiable, river and the killed or killable animal are as real as are the human or non-human agent who dirties the river and the human agent who does the sacrificial killing of the animal. Therefore, since ethical things are things which are done, which can be done, and which are required to be done, in relation to other human beings, their groups, or to some natural objects, we have to admit that there is a real world consisting of human beings, other non-human living beings, and natural objects. This world obviously would be nothing other than the world we live in, the world we are well acquainted with, the world which in philosophical parlance is called the empirical world.

What has been said above about the logic of the use of ethical predicates and relations, and of their meaningful employment's implying or presupposing the reality of the empirical world, has been said keeping in full view the classical Indian philosophical understanding of the logic of ethical predicates and relations and of the assertions or judgements in which they are affirmed or denied. This account can unhesitatingly be said to be the account which classical Indian thinkers have in mind when they discuss any ethical issues, though they have not stated it in the way it has been stated here. This logic makes it crystal clear that ethical or moral, and consequently unethical or immoral, life can be lived only in a real world. Since Indian philosophy acknowledges, and no less forcefully than other philosophies do, that ethical life is lived in the world, that ethical relations hold good in it, it has to admit that the world is real. We shall see, as we proceed, that it does admit the reality of the world, or as already mentioned, of the empirical world. It is true that there are instances in which it *seems* to deny its reality. But it really does not even in those instances. To see how this seeming denial is to be understood or explained we have to wait for a later discussion in this very chapter. Here I would like to reiterate that there is no reason for saying that Indian philosophy has no ethics, or cannot have ethics, because it denies the reality of the world, as some thinkers like W.T. Stace hold, since Indian philosophy does not deny the reality of the world. But before discussing that issue, let us examine, of course in brief, the reason for philosophers' preferring to call the world we are ordinarily acquainted with the empirical world, which is not what we ordinarily do. We ordinarily call it the world: we simply call the world the world, a spade a spade.

The term *empirical world* has came into vogue in philosophical talk about the world because some philosophers maintain that there is a transempirical, or non-empirical, world which is the really real world, or the world more real than the world we are acquinted with. The transempirical world is said to be really real, or more real because it is claimed to satisfy some criterion of reality which the world we are acquinted with does not, or because it is claimed to be more basic, fundamental, or foundational, in the sense that it is the ground, base, foundation, etc., of the acquainted world. That is, in some sense it is the reason, or explanation of its being what it is, that it is an explanandum, and therefore needs an explanans. On some metaphysical, even epistemological or logical, grounds it is felt by the holders of this view that the acquainted world cannot itself explain its existence. In this search for its explanans, they come to the conclusion that there is another world, not experienced by us, or not ordinarily experienced by means of our senses, or even by the combined efforts of our senses and reason, which is the cause or reason for the existence and nature of the acquainted world. All this means that the world we were acquainted with is not real on its own account but still the only world we are normally acquinted with by means of our normal channels of experience, sense and reason. Hence it is referred to as the empirical world.

In its present usage, therefore, the term 'empirical world' has become neutral in the sense that the question 'Is the empirical world real? has become an open question. Its openness consists in the fact that it is left to be determined by philosophical investigation whether or not it is real, and a philosopher is free to answer it in the affirmative or in the negative depending on his philosophical findings. In the history of Indian philosophy very clearly the term has undergone such a process of evolution. For the *Cārvāka* the empirical world is not only real but the only real world, and therefore, the only world. For the *Nyāya* thinkers it is real, though not self-caused but created by God out of certain materials. For the *Advaita Vedānta*, as its position is generally interpreted, it is not real but appears to be real because of the ignorance of the person who considers it real. However, it is not as unreal as is, for example, a flower growing in the sky. Interpreters say that the *Advaita* grants to it reality of a limited or lower kind as it considers it real only for practical purposes, i.e. real only from the practical (*vyāvahārika*) point of view, but not real from the ultimate, philosophical (*pāramārthika*) point of view. Therefore, in the *Advaita Vedāntic* categoriology the term 'empirical world', they say, comes to mean the world which appears to be, or can be taken to be, real in our normal experiences, real enough for conducting our life but not found to be real when it is philosophically probed into. At one extreme is the *Cārvāka* for whom the terms 'empirical world', 'real world' and 'world' denote the same thing. This is so because the world is what it is experienced to be and there is no other world than this. For the *Advaita Vedānta,* on the other hand, as per the received interpretation, the world is not really as it is experienced to be; that is, the real world is not the same as what the empirical world is. Here the empirical world gets an ontological status different from that of the real world. The term 'the world' may then be taken to denote the real world, or to be ambiguous, denoting in one context the empirical world and in another the real world.

This sort of reality only from the practical point of view (*vyāvahārika sattā*), accorded by the *Advaita* to the empirical world, is considered by the interpreters to be sufficient, i.e. all that is required, to make worldly life and therefore ethical life in the world possible.

No modern Indian interpreter of *Advaita Vedānta*, nor any modern Indian writer on Indian ethics, has questioned the validity of the notion of being real only from the practical point of view, or has seen any difficulty in comprehending it or applying it to the world or to any inhabitant of it. The more relevant issue for Indian ethics, whether it is the world possessing only this practical sort or level of reality, or the one possessing real reality, that the possibility of ethics in the world presupposes, has not been raised and consequently it has remained undiscussed. The issue is important and needs to be discussed in some detail. Its discussion also requires reference to some other notions and views which are basic to Indian ethics. All this will be taken up in the next section.

That the world, in which ethical life is lived, is real is necessary but *not all* that is necessary to make ethical life possible. There are several other things which also need to be accepted as real. For example, there has to be in the world a real moral agent, as individual, who can do, has the ability to do, and who does moral or immoral things, and of whom it can be sensibly said that he ought to lead an ethical life. Without a moral agent there cannot be any ethical life and therefore, there would be no need of a philosophical inquiry to characterize what sort of a thing leading an ethical life is, i.e. no need of there being any ethics or philosophy of morals. Let us therefore take up first this issue of the nature of the moral agent.

6.2 THE MORAL AGENT: THE INDIVIDUAL (*JĪVA*) AND NOT THE SELF (*ĀTMAN*)

As stated above, it is an obvious truth, rather one which verges on a truism, that in order that ethical life is led in the world there must be in it human beings, or beings of a sort, who have the capability to lead this kind of life. To lead an ethical life is, as already stated, to do actions which are right, to pursue goals or values which are worth pursuing (*śreya*), to care for the welfare of others, to be sensitive not only to one's own but even to others' comforts and discomforts, to have respect for traits of character such as those of kindliness, forgivingness, etc., to enter into ethical relations like those of being obligated to, being an obligee of, being neighbourly with, being grateful to, being fair or just to someone else, etc., etc. As per Indian philosophical terminology, the above and other related ethical things, are done, or can be done, by a *jīva* for which I shall use the English term 'individual', or sometimes the term 'person'. Therefore, it is an individual (or a person) who has the capability to lead and who generally leads an ethical life. This means that the moral agent, he who does ethical things, is an individual, or in Indian terminology, a *jiva*. Consequently, to admit that ethical life is led in the world we live in, or in the world we are acquainted with, there must be individuals with this kind of capability. These individuals must be real in the sense in which we ordinarily use the term 'real'. Their reality has to be accepted because only real beings can really have the capability to do ethical things, and only those of these real beings who really have this capability can lead an ethical life.

Many scholars hold that neither 'individual' nor 'person' is a right English equivalent of *jiva.* Many scholars also hold that there is no term in classical Indian philosophical or sociological terminology of which either one of the two English terms can be called the nearest equivalent or synonym. To hold such a view is really to hold that there is no classical Indian equivalent of 'individual' or 'person'. The word *vyakti* currently used in Hindi and in some other modern Indian languages is a modern coinage for both of the English terms 'individual' and 'person'. This is more obvious from the linguistic fact that the term *vyaktitiva* (the abstract noun of *vyakti*) is used as a synonym for both the terms 'individuality' (the abstract noun of 'individual') and 'personality' (the abstract noun of 'person'). It may be true that there is no Sanskrit equivalent of 'individual' or 'person'. It is not even safe to use *puruṣa* as their equivalent, firstly because of its having been used in the *Sāṅkhya* system in a sense in which a *puruṣa* can neither be called an individual nor a person, and secondly because at places in Sanskrit *puruṣa* is used to denote a male person though sometimes it is also used, in a neutral sense, to denote both a male and a female human being, as, for example, in the term *puruṣārtha. Puruṣārtha* means any object of any human, i.e. any human being's, desire. For anything to be called a *puruṣārtha* it does not matter whether it is an object of a male person's, or of a female person's, desire. It has only to be an object of any human being's desire.

The term *jīva* certainly does not ordinarily mean what we nowadays mean by an individual (or a person). It means, as per its etymology, a living being, and in some usage even 'life', as in *sajīva,* meaning a being with life or a living being, and in *nirjīva* meaning a lifeless being or a non-living being. In this sense of *jīva* all sorts of plants and animals are *jīva*s, not only human beings. But we consider only a human being and no animal to be an individual (or a person). When a religion conceives of God as a being with traits like kindness (*dayā*), readiness to help his devotees (*bhaktavatsalatā*), etc., it treats the concept of God on the mode of an ideal human being. That is why it calls him *paramapuruṣa* or *puruṣottama* (the greatest male individual or person). That is, in its conceptual scheme God is the ideal, the highest kind of, person. This is nothing but idealizing the concept of the human person.

In spite of the asymmetry, conceded above, between the concept of a *jīva* and that of an individual, I have decided to use 'individual' (or 'person') as an equivalent of '*jīva*', and vice versa, because of a limitation imposed on the terminology of the present work by its objective. The work intends to give a philosophical account of classical Indian ethics. Any ethics any time anywhere is possible only if the reality of the moral agent is admitted. The moral agent is always a human individual with a certain level of mental and bodily or physical capability. For example, a two-year-old child is not a moral agent, nor is an adult who is in a coma, or who is insane. As will be explained a little later, on this account ethics has to be agent-centric. This I am saying with full recognition of the fact that man can enter into ethical relations with non-humans like animals, even plants, or inanimate objects like hills and rivers. This fact cannot be ignored in a study of Indian ethics which allots to nature, organic as well as inorganic, a respectable place in ethical space.

The terminological, or rather conceptual, limitation, referred to above, is constituted by the trilogy of concepts—*jīva* (embodied being), *śarīra* (body) and *ātman* (self). In any discussion of any classical Indian humanistic subject, whether it is philosophy in general, ethics in particular, psychology, political inquiry, or sociology, etc., these three terms have to be taken into account. Self, according to all philosophical systems (as usual, except the *Cārvāka*), is intrinsically a disembodied being in the sense that its relationship with any body is contingent and in no way necessary. That is, self may or may not be in, or associated with, a body. It will ontologically remain the same being, unaffected, whether or not it is in a body. Being embodied is not at all necessary for it. The relation of a body, on the other hand, to a self is not contingent. It is unbreakably necessary in the sense that without the self in it, or after the self's leaving it, the body ceases to remain alive. It then becomes a lifeless lump of matter decaying like any other material object. In fact, death of a human being simply means a state in which the self in its body leaves the body. Self itself neither dies, nor is born, neither decays nor acquires a new feature, neither does anything nor is related to anything, neither enjoys nor suffers anything, etc. That is, it is a non-agent or non-doer (*akartā*), non-experiencer (*abhoktā*), unrelated or unaffected by anything (*asanga*), etc. Therefore, it cannot be a seeker of any goal, nor can it be called a member of any society with any obligation to anyone. In fact, no ethical predicate can be attributed to it. It has to be treated as an asocial, amoral, being.

It is clear then that neither a self, nor a body, can be a moral agent. The *jīva*, on the other hand, is an embodied self (*saśarīra ātman, śarīrastha ātman*), a self in a body, with all the advantages and disadvantages which an embodied being may have.

It is this *jīva* which is a moral agent when it is equipped with a certain level of mental and bodily ability, an ability which is held to be possessible only by a human being. A normal human being is held to be a *jīva* of this type and is said to be different from other *jīvas* which lack this equipment. Therefore, those *jīvas* cannot be moral agents. It is this, the human *jīva*, the human individual, or simply the individual, which is a member of a moral community and to which moral or ethical predicates can be attributed. It is true that human beings are not the lone inhabitants of the world. But of all of its inhabitants, only *jīvas* of this human type are moral agents. It is for such a *jīva*, a human being with the required kind of ability, that I have used the word 'individual' or 'person'. This use of both the words coheres even with their ordinary use. And, it is a fitting use also because neither a self, nor a body, can be called either an individual or a moral agent. If we do not call a *jīva* a moral agent, there is no other being in the classical Indian conceptual framework to which moral agency can be attributed. Without there being any being to which it can be attributed, there can be neither any sort of ethical life, nor any discourse or talk about ethical life. This means that there cannot then be any ethics or philosophy of morals. Not only that; there cannot then be any pursuit of any sort of values, and therefore there cannot be any sort of religious or spiritual life. This would be an intellectual or axiological mishap. This mishap is bound to happen because any cognitive inquiry, any pursuit of any sort of value, ethical, religious, spiritual, or even economic or political, etc., requires beings with agency or agenthood. And, agenthood can be had neither by a self, nor by a body, but only by an embodied self, i.e. a *jīva* possessing, as already said, a certain level of maturity or competence.

All this clearly shows that *jīvas* occupy a very important—rather, a central—place in classical Indian conceptual or cognitive infrastructure. This fact is very often forgotten when scholars overemphasize the importance of the concept of self, downgrade the importance of the body, and thereby also downgrade the importance of the *jīva* or the individual. Some scholars use the term 'empirical self' for a *jīva* and 'noumenal self' for a self, i.e. for a self as it in itself, in its disembodied form, is. But this is an unnecessary, or rather a misleading, smuggling of a Kantian terminology into the Indian conceptual framework. It is misleading because a self cannot be an agent, but a *jīva* is an agent, or has to be an agent, to make ethical, or value-seeking, life possible. When a self cannot be an agent, by calling a *jīva* an empirical self we shall water down the agency aspect of the *jīva*. Moreover, it would also be misleading because when a self is naturally a non-agent, by merely qualifying it with the adjective 'empirical' we cannot do anything to it which may instil or inject into it the property of agency and thereby make it a being of which ethical predicates can be affirmed (or even denied).

6.3 THE ONTOLOGICAL MODEL ASCRIBING TO THE WORLD REALITY ONLY FOR PRACTICAL PURPOSES (*VYĀVAHĀRIKA SATTĀ*): ITS ADEQUACY FOR SATISFYING THE POSSIBILITY CONDITION OF ETHICAL LIFE EXAMINED

It has been shown in the previous two sections that the reality of the world, including naturally the reality of the individual, the moral agent, is necessary for anyone's leading a moral life, or rather for doing anything moral, or even immoral. All this is so because ethical predicates are real predicates and ethical relations real relations. A real relation can exist only between reals, and for a real relation to exist there must be at least two reals. It is obvious, therefore, that the reality of relations implies ontological pluralism, i.e. the reality of more than one thing in the world. This does not pose any problem to our common sense, i.e. to our normal, general, experience or understanding of our ethical transactions, nay, to our normal, general, experience or understanding of the nature of the world. By nature we are pluralists since we naturally believe in the plurality of reals in the world. Therefore, we do not have any difficulty in understanding the nature of our ethical transactions. It is a fact that we do ethical things and have ethical relations with others, and sometimes we do right things and sometimes wrong things. But doing something wrong, or doing something which amounts to breaking an ethical relation, like breaking a promise made to someone, also implies that there are other individuals, or other beings; that is, that there is a plurality of reals in the world.

That ethical life is lived in the world is an undeniable fact, an actuality. Facticity or actuality entails possibility, though possibility does not entail actuality. If something is actual, it must be possible. But something possible may or may not be actual. This is an obvious logical truth. Since leading an ethical life is an actuality, it must be possible to live ethically. Possibility of a thing implies that there is a condition or a set of conditions which makes it possible and therefore the condition or the set of conditions must be fulfilled in order to convert its possibility into an actuality. The condition (or conditions) which makes (make) it possible is (are) called its possibility condition(s). It is clear, therefore, that if something is actually there, then its possibility condition has been fulfilled, since if it were not fulfilled it would not have actually been there and simply remained a possibility. From all this it is clear that the possibility condition(s) of ethical life (and therefore of ethics) has (have) been fulfilled or satisfied otherwise there would have been no ethical life (and therefore no ethics), when it is a fact that men live an ethical life of this or that sort and that philosophers do ethical theorizing or ethics as is evidenced by the existence of a plethora of studies in ethics or moral philosophy.

We have seen that an unquestionable possibility condition of ethical life is the reality of a pluralistic world. Since ethical life is an actuality, it follows that this condition is satisfied; that is the world is real and pluralistic. This is also supported by common experience. A philosophical system, like the *Nyāya-Vaiśeṣika,* the ontology of which is pluralist and realist, i.e. which holds that the world is real and that its ultimate foundational realities are more than one, has no difficulty in admitting that the world really consists of many things. A pluralist ontology has to admit the reality of relations because when there are many things in the world there must be some relations among them otherwise the world would not be a cosmos, an organized, systematized, whole. The *Nyāya-Vaiśeṣika* does admit the reality of relations. Conjunction (*sanjoga*) which it lists among qualities (*guṇa*) is an external relation between two things. Inherence (*samavāya*) which is a separate category or type of reality (*padārtha*), i.e. a category of reality in its own right irreducible to any other of the seven categories the *Vaiśeṣika* admits, is also a real relation. It is an external relation since it represents an independent kind of reality different from the other kinds like substance (*dravya*), quality (*guṇa*), action or motion (*karma*), universality (*sāmānya*), particularity (*viśeṣa*) and non-existence (*abhāva*). Therefore, the *Nyāya-Vaiśeṣika* has no difficulty in acknowledging that the world is real and pluralistic and that the possibility condition of ethical life being lived in it is satisfied.

Among monistic ontologists those who hold the theory of concrete monism too have no difficulty in admitting the satisfaction of the possibility condition of ethical life because they can admit the reality of the world and its pluralist nature. An ontological theory is monistic if it holds that the ultimate reality is one in number. This monism is called concrete if it further maintains that the one ultimate reality is contentful, that it contains some diversity or plurality inside it in having in it some ingredients, constituents, elements, or parts, etc. A good example of concrete monism is Rāmānuja's qualified monism (*Viśiṣṭādvaita*). According to it the ultimate reality, God (*Brahman*) has inside it two parts, the conscious (*cit*) and the non-conscious (*acit*). Conscious beings of the world owe their origin and existence to the conscious part of God and non-conscious things owe their origin and existence to its non-conscious part. The conscious and non-conscious objects taken together constitute the entire world, and therefore basically, or ultimately, the entire world is contained, or included in the content of God, making God all-inclusive or non-exclusive. On this view obviously the world is real and pluralist containing an infinitely large number of conscious beings and non-conscious things. Equally obviously, therefore, the possibility condition of ethical life and of ethics, the reality of the world, is met with and the fact that ethical life is lived ceases to be problematic.

The other important kind of ontological monism is abstract monism according to which the ultimate reality is numerically and contentually one since it has no internal diversity or plurality, having no parts, ingredients, or elements, as its content. It is pure, absolute, unity devoid of all kinds of multiplicity; in a sense it is contentless in being just what it in itself is. It is present in all that there is, but nothing that there is, is contained in it. That is, it may even be said to be non-inclusive or all-exclusive. And, since it alone is really real, nothing else is, it is irrelational, i.e. a reality having no relation with anything else simply because nothing other than it is real. For a thing to have a relation with something else there must be some other real thing in addition to it. Since there is no such thing it is bound to be relationless. Śankara's *Brahman*, the ultimate reality for him, is a reality of this type. Therefore, his *Advaitism* is a clear example of abstract monism.

He does say that *Brahman* is *satcidānanda*, existence-consciousness-bliss (ECB). But ECB is not a compound of three things. It is a pure unity and what it is can be referred to by either of the three, existence, consciousness, or bliss because to be one is also to be the other two, or to imply the other two.

In such an ontology the world, which obviously contains an exuberant plurality of changing, impermanent things, has to be called unreal. An oft-quoted statement of Śankara, which occurs at more than one place in his writings, asserts in unambiguous terms that *Brahman* is real and the world unreal. For example, it occurs in his *Brahmajñānāvalīmālā*. There he says: 'Brahman is real (*satyam*), the world (*jagat*) unreal (*mithyā*), and the individual self [*Jīva*', meaning here the self in the individual, or the individual self] is *Brahman* itself [*brahmaiva* = *brahma eva*, Brahma itself], not anything other than *Brahman* [*naparah* = *na* + *aparah*, not other than]. The vedānta declares that the true wisdom is to be known [attained] by this [truth].'[2]

The same statement of the unreality of the world and the lone reality of *Brahman* also occurs in Śankara's *Vivekacuḍāmani* in the context of elaborating the four conditions (*sadhana catustaya*) which, any individual aspiring after knowing *Brahman*, *must* satisfy in order to be a fit person to know *Brahman*. Knowing *Brahman* is the same as attaining liberation or as properly understanding and comprehending the *Advaitic* philosophy. One of these conditions is to possess the discriminative ability (*viveka*) to distinguish between the eternal (*nitya*) and the impermanent (*anitya*), the real and the unreal. The only eternal thing is *Brahman* which alone is real, and the impermanent, and therefore unreal, thing is the world. Thus, to have a discriminative knowledge of the eternal and the impermanent is to have the knowledge of the truth that *Brahman* is eternal, or real, and the world impermanent, or unreal.[3]

Even if Śankara had not said so forthrightly that the world is unreal, the unreality of world would have been a natural consequence of his abstract monism because it is entailed by the latter. But if the world is unreal, then, as we have seen, ethical life cannot be lived in it. This consequence of the unreality of the world will not be salutary even for Śankara. He too considers it necessary to be ethical in order to properly study and understand the *Advaitic* philosophy. To properly understand and follow the *Advaita Vedāntic* philosophy is also the means, according to Śankara, to know *Brahman* which is the same as attaining liberation. One of the four conditions, referred to above, which a person is required to fulfil in order to properly study and understand the *Advaitic* philosophy is that he should acquire six attributes. They are: (1) the aspirant's self-composed concentration (*sama*) on his objective which is knowledge of *Brahman*; (2) self-control (*dama*) by withdrawing all sense-organs, cognitive, i.e. information-supplying, and conative i.e. those which are motivative of action, from their objects by reflecting over their defects; (3) cessation of all mental functions (*uparati*) by becoming unaffected by worldly objects; (4) bearing all sufferings, mental and physical (*titikṣā*) without any reaction; (5) faith (*śraḍhā*) in scriptural and teacher's instructions; and (6) constant concentration on *Brahman* (*samāḍhāna*).[4] These are not overtly ethical but religious or spiritual traits. But the cultivation of none of them, quite obviously, can be done without moral discipline. Even if that is not the case, any philosophical theory's making ethical life impossible would go against it. Śankara, being not only a philosopher but also a recluse, a saintly person, would not have denied or belittled the importance of ethical life in any world, not even in the world of his own theoretical construction or reconstruction.

Moreover, if the world is unreal then its inmates, including individuals who are required to cultivate the six traits, and to fulfil the other three conditions, would also be unreal. Unreal individuals cannot be required to do anything because they can do nothing. The other three conditions are: the discriminative ability to distinguish between the eternal and the non-eternal already mentioned; complete indifference or disinterestedness in enjoying the consequences of one's actions, here or hereafter; and lastly, the desire for liberation.[5] The satisfaction of none of these conditions can be required of an individual of this unreal world. It cannot be required of the Self, which is in an individual and is real, because being a non-agent, the Self can do nothing. Even the seeking and realization of liberation (*mokṣasiddhi*) is to be done by an individual, a *jiva*, and not by the Self because it is eternally liberated. Therefore, if the unreality of the world, a logical consequence of Śankara's abstract monism, is taken *seriously*, or, one may say, literally, then there will be an almost unsolvable problem in accounting for the possibility of leading an ethical life in the world. But it is a fact that such a life is actually lived in the world. Śankara himself lived it in this very world.

As has been said in the earlier discussions, ethical relations are real cannot be denied. Nor can be denied the obvious fact that a relation can hold only between reals and that there must be at least two reals for a relation to hold between them because a dyadic relation is the simplest one. This fact is very forcefully emphasized by Śankara himself. He is forthright in asserting that a relation can exist only between two reals, and not between a real and an unreal.[6] This obviously means that an ethical relation, say, the relation of being obligated to, can exist only between two real individuals. A student can be obligated to his teacher for imparting to him the *Vedāntic* knowledge only if both the student and his teacher are real individuals. The student can be even advised or required to be obligated to his teacher only if it is assumed that both of them are real. Therefore, it can be said that even Śankara has to admit, in some way, the reality of the world to avoid implying that his monism makes ethical life in it impossible, when it is not because it is actually lived in it.

Śankara cannot and does not deny the possibility of ethics. He cannot because the *Upaniṣads* very much emphasize the importance of ethical life and they constitute the main hinterland from which he gets the materials, the ideas, which he uses in his creative, commentarial, philosophizing. In his commentaries on them he does not question their emphasizing the importance of morality, nor is he critical of it in any way. In the *Taitirīya*, as per Śankara's own commentary, after the completion of a student's study of the *Vedas*, his teacher gives him a set of instructions which are primarily or predominantly ethical. To mention them briefly, they are as follows:

Speak the truth, behave in a moral way, do not have egoistic pride for your studies, or for your being truthful, moral, expert in any action, be dutiful to gods and parents. Treat you father as a god, your mother as a goddess, your teacher and guest as a god, do only that which is unblameworthy and not any other act, respect only those actions of your teachers which are right and not others, if you are in doubt about the rightness of an action thus follow the examples of those who are thoughtful, active, dutiful, simple-minded, etc.[7]

The *Katha* says that the desirable, the morally preferable and the pleasurable, both sorts of things are available to an individual. The well-educated selects the former and abjures the latter. Here, though this is said in the indicative mood, actually it is intended to be a normative.[8] That is, only he deserves to be considered well-educated or decent who behaves in this manner. The *Śvetāśvatara* ascribes even to God, who is taken to be beyond space and time and the creator or the ultimate foundation of this world, the attributes of being the protector or promoter of morality (*dharmāvahm*) and destroyer of immorality or sin (*pāpanudam*).[9] The *Bṛhadāraṇyaka* presents very pithily in one letter *da*, of the Sanskrit alphabet, almost a complete code of morality. When gods ask the creator of the world, Prajāpati, to instruct them what they should do, he says *da*, which is only a letter, and the same letter he utters to humans and demons who make the same request to him. By *da* gods understand self-control (*dama*), humans charity (*dāna*), and the demons kindness (*dayā*). The creator-instructor confirms that all of the three kinds of his children have properly understood his instruction. Gods are believed, in Indian mythology, to have immoderate desires for luxuries. Therefore, they are instructed to control their desires. Human beings are believed to have a love for riches. They are, therefore, instructed to do charity, to make gifts to needy people. Demons are believed to be cruel. Therefore, they are instructed to be kind.

This mythical account, when demythologized and restricted to the human world, would mean that different virtues are to be cultivated by individuals with different types of inclinations. Everyone does not need to curtail his desires, but only he who has immoderate ones. For example, there is no point in asking a poor man to control his desires when his desires are terribly limited, since he wants to have only two meals of rice and potato a day. Similarly, only he who has more than he needs to lead a happy life can be meaningfully advised to do charity; not he who is leading a hand-to-mouth life. In the same manner, only the cruel, or inconsiderate, can be sensibly required to be kind or considerate. All this could be said of even other virtues like forgiveness, honesty, truthfulness, etc.

It is clear from the few stray examples given above from some *Upaniṣads* that ethical life or morality is given in the Upaniṣadic corpus the importance it deserves. This is true even of Śankara. As we shall see in the next chapter, he believes in the classical Indian caste-system (*varṇavyavasthā*), in the hierarchical order of the different castes and in their different rights and duties (*varṇadharmas*). He believes even in the superiority of a male human over a female human. For example, in the beginning of *Vivekacūḍāmani* he says. that it is difficult to be born as a human being, and as a male person among humans, and as a *brāhmaṇ* male among human males.[10] That is why, he thinks, it is lamentable if a male *brāhmaṇ* does not seek the knowledge of the Self (or *Brahman*).

Similar things about an individual's knowing *Brahman* or for becoming a fit student of the *Advaita* are restated in Sadānanda's *Vedāntasāra* (Advaita Ashram, Calcutta), p. 9.15 and 16; and in Śankara's *Upadeśa-sahsrī* (Shri Ramakrishna Math, Madras), p. 2.2. In the latter work too Śankara is straightforward in affirming the desirability of a student of *Advaita* aspiring after *Brahmajñāna* or *liberation*, being a *brāhmaṇ*, i.e. a member of the *brāhmaṇ varṇa* or caste. All this is a clear evidence of his acceptance of the then caste-system and of the superiority of the *brāhmaṇ* caste over other castes. Thus it is clear evidence of his considering the then caste-system or social organization real, and consequently of his considering the world too, in which it existed real. A real social or societal organization, a real social hierarchy, can exist only in a real world. By Śankara's time the *varṇa* or caste-system had definitely become birth-determined (*janmanā*). Śankara himself was a *brāhmaṇa* by birth, i.e. because of being born of *brāhmaṇa* parents, much before he became a knower of *Brahman*, or the propounder of the *Advaita Vedānta* philosophy. It will be shown in the next chapter that perhaps the *varṇa* or caste of an individual was never determined by his abilities or aptitudes, or was arbitrarily determined, and soon became birth-determined. There are some conceptual difficulties in calling it determined by abilities or aptitudes, though the theory that it was originally and for a long period in the history of classical India determined by the abilities or aptitudes of individuals assigned to different *varṇas* or castes, is widely accepted by academic as well as non-academic people.

When Śankara speaks of such mundane, worldly, or even ethical, things in general, i.e. talks as a recluse (*sanyāsī*) and religious precepter, which too he is, besides being a philosopher, he speaks in the same tone or manner in which anyone who does not question the reality of the world does. In such matters he gives the impression that he considers the world to be real, or real in the same sense in which a common man considers it real. He clearly gives the impression that he does not consider it unreal. His own life-style shows that he has no doubt about the world's being real at least in some important sense. And, this is true. He grants to the world some sort of reality. We have to see what this sort of reality is and whether or not it is the sort of reality of the world which ethical life requires, the sort which makes ethical life possible in the world. The world has to be real enough not only to make possible anyone's leading a moral life but also to make possible his pursuit of *Brahmajñāna* or liberation. Even the latter pursuit can be conducted in this world only if it is a real world. No pursuit can be conducted in an unreal world, or by an unreal individual in any world, unreal or even real.

The problem the unreality of the world can cause for the possibility of ethical, and even non-ethical, normal, human behaviour must have bothered Śankara since he himself was very sensitive to the observance of moral rules and principles, very active as a teacher, propagator of *Advaitic* philosophy and religious precepter, and an astute logician. His solution to this problem is that world is not as unreal as is an illusory snake in the erroneous perception of a rope as a snake. The illusory snake vanishes as soon as the rope is veridically perceived. The illusory snake, or any illusory object of this type, has, he would say, only illusory, apparent, reality (*prātibhāsika sattā*). This kind of object is removed from sight simply by having a correct visual perception of the rope which can be easily had and in a very short time. But the world continues to appear as real till the knowledge of the Self or *Brahman*, or of the identity of the Self and *Brahman*, is attained. Attaining this knowledge is not easy as all, nor does it take place in as short a time as that in which correct perception of the rope is had. As long as *Brahman* is not known by an individual he takes the world as if it were really real, which in fact it is not. It is not, because it is destructible, sublatable, by the knowledge of *Brahman* which is never destructible by anything. The world, on the other hand, is not really real. It has what may be called an assumed reality, or an as-if reality, before *Brahman* is known. Though it is not real in its own right, we behave in it as we would have behaved in a real world.

This kind of non-ultimate, temporary, or as-if, reality of the world is enough, Śankara thinks, to make possible our behaving in it as we actually behave, and therefore to make possible our ethical behaviour and ethics in it. This is to say that as long as *Brahman*, which alone is really real, the ultimate reality (*pārmārthika sattā*), has not been known, the world remains real for all practical, behavioural, purposes. Therefore, the kind of reality it possesses can only be said to be practical, or behavioural, reality (*vyāvahārika sattā*). That is, an individual can consider it real for all practical (or behavioural) purposes. Though, after his attaining *knowledge of Brahman*, he will realize that it is not real. Śankara says in clear terms that before attaining knowledge of *Brahman* he behaves in the world taking it to be real, just as he takes to be real, before waking up, the things he dreams of in a dream. But on waking up he no longer considers them real. Similarly, after having knowledge of *Brahman* he no longer considers it real and therefore is justified to behave in the 'unreal' world in the way he has been behaving before attaining knowledge of *Brahman*.[11]

Śankara's conceding to the world reality only for practical purposes is evidence of the fact that he does not want to call the world unreal because then he cannot answer the question why anyone living in it should do anything at all, why he should, for example, do anything ethical or abstain from doing anything unethical.

Since we are dealing with only ethics in this work, let us concentrate on man's ethical behaviour in the world, and let us use PR as a short form for practical reality of the world, or its reality only for practical purposes, or only from the practical point of view (*vyāvahārika sattā*). All, or almost all, modern interpreters of, or writers on, the *Advaita Vedanta* think that PR is the kind, or level, of reality which is the kind or level of reality that is needed, or is enough, to ensure the possibility of ethical life in the world, that this kind of reality is sufficient to motivate anyone to lead an ethical life. Their thinking is that the world has to be real in some sense to make ethical life possible in it, and the notion of PR gives to the world reality in the sense required. But to me this does not seem to be so obvious a truth. Therefore, let us examine in a logical way whether or not PR has the competence to justify the possibility of ethics in the world. This needs to be done even at the possible risk of our being accused of having raised an unwarranted controversy over a well-settled issue and on that account our not being able to see the truth which is clearly visible; that is, of our being like one who himself raises a duststorm and because of the dust thrown into his eyes by his own duststorm is not able to see the elephant, an otherwise clearly visible object, standing in front of him.

There could be three types of individuals from whose side this theme could be discussed. Let us imagine an individual who has attained knowledge of *Brahman*. He would know that *Brahman* alone is real and the world is therefore, unreal. This will mean that there is no reason, or justification, for his doing anything in it, ethical, unethical, non-ethical. But he is still alive, a jīvanmukta. Therefore, he has to do certain things to avoid vegetating. He also may have to do certain things relating to some other individual or individuals which may be judged by others to be ethical or unethical. But there has to be given a reason by Śankara for his doing anything in the world which is unreal and which he knows to be unreal. He knows that it is unreal after his enlightenment, his spiritual waking up, just as an ordinary individual, after waking up from his sleep, knows that the objects which looked real in his dream are unreal. After waking up it is natural, and right, for him to think that he has to do nothing about them simply because they are unreal, that any action relating to them is uncalled for. So should be the case with the knower of *Brahman*, the spiritually awakened.

Śankara has, therefore, to give a convincing reason for a realized individual's, a *Brahman*-knower's (*Brahmajñānī*'s), doing ethical things (or anything whatsoever). A reason can be read in his commentarial elaboration of some of the things said in the *Gītā* by Kṛṣṇa about the individual who has become *sthitaprajña*, well-settled in his resolve that he is identical with *Brahman*, i.e. a realized person. Śankara's interpretation is that, according to the *Gītā* (and the *Advaita Vedānta*), he is to act, to do ethical (and some other) things and not to remain idle in order to set a good example to the *loka*, to the society, i.e. to other members of the society. His becoming totally inactive, idle, would set a bad example which, if followed by others, would lead to the disintegration of the society, of the social order organized as a system having four classes or castes of people (*caturvarṇa vyavasthā*) with their well-marked-out duties and obligations.[12] This is to say that the knower of *Brahman*, who knows that the world is unreal, should keep doing ethical things, i.e. leading an ethical life, in order that the example which he sets contributes to the preservation of the social order, or does not contribute to its disintegration. This position involves some complexities which will be discussed in a later chapter since here we are concerned only with the possibility of ethics in a world considered unreal. Therefore, we shall limit the discussion only to this theme.

It is true that leading an ethical life is promotive of the preservation of and cohesion in the society and abstaining from leading an ethical life, or leading an unethical life, instrumental to its disintegration and incohesion. But all this is true only of a real society. A real society can exist only in a real world, and not in an unreal one which the world is. That it is unreal is known to the *Brahman*-knower (*Brahmajñānī*). Therefore, the latter may not feel like doing anything ethical on the so-called ground that he would thereby promote society's preservation, etc., as Śankara advises him to do. Rather, he may feel dissuaded from promoting its preservation, etc. simply because the society, or the world it exists in, has only an as-if, practical, reality, a reality assumed for practical purposes. He may so feel because he can reasonably think that only a real society's preservation, etc., is worthy of being promoted by ethics, and not that of an unreal one. In addition, he may also think, again, quite reasonably, that the inmates of such a world possessing reality only of this level, i.e. reality only from the practical point of view, cannot be real in the full sense of being real in which they have to be real in order that ethical predicates can be attributed to them and ethical relations can hold among them.

It seems, therefore, that the reason given by Śankara or *Advaitism* for a *Brahman*-knower's leading an ethical life in the world, not having reality in the full sense of the term, but only in a diluted sense because it is real only for practical purposes, is not a good, conclusive, logical reason. It is not a good reason because he *knows* that the world is not really, fully, real and also knows that *Brahman* alone is real in this (*pāramārthika*) sense. But all this does not pose a serious problem for the possibility of ethics and of ethical life in the world we live in because the number of such realized individuals, *Brahman*-knowers, is not likely to be at any time very large in the history of the world. It was not very large even in classical India, including Śankara's India.

The realized individuals, the *jīvanmuktas*, are extraordinary persons; they may do extraordinary things. They may do ethical things even if they are not their obligations; or, they may not do them. For the people at large it does not matter much. Even for an ethicist, an ethical theorizer, what is important for an ethical theory is that it offers help and guidance to the ordinary, average, individual in deciding what is right for him to do in which sort of circumstances. Therefore, it is more pertinent to examine whether or not the Advaitic view, that the world is to be taken to be real for practical purposes and only for practical purposes though it is in fact (*tattvatah*) unreal, would matter for his leading an ethical life.

It is obvious that there would not be any serious problem caused by the above view to one who is a naturalist, for example the *Cārvāka* for whom nature, the empirical world, is alone real, and real in an undiluted sense. There is nothing besides, behind, or beyond, it which is real, or more real than it. Ethics and ethical life will certainly be possible in it because it is real in the sense in which it has to be real to make it possible. He may not have full-fledged ethical theory, even a well-structured hedonism or egoism. But that is not very relevant here.

Even a theist of the *Nyāya* or Viśiṣṭādvaita variety would not have any problem in accounting for the possibility of ethics and ethical life in the world. The obvious reason for his not having a problem on this count is that for him the world is fully real, i.e. real in an undiluted sense. It is only not self-dependent, or self-sustaining, because it has been created by God. What God creates, whether out of some materials external to him or out of some part of his own being, cannot be unreal, or real only in an as-if sense, i.e. only for practical, behavioural, purposes. An atheist too, like a Jain, or a Buddhist, would not have a problem because he as well does not consider the world really unreal and to be taken as real only for practical purposes, as the *Advaitin* does.

However, there would be an unsolvable problem for another kind of individual. Imagine a philosopher, or any open-minded, ideologically non-committed, well-meaning scholar, say, A, of something like the following characterization:

A reads Śankara's writings and those of other *Advaitins* of his ilk. He is intellectually convinced of their reasoning that *Brahman* alone is real. But he is convinced only intellectually, and has *not yet realized* in spiritual experience that *Brahman* alone is real and that he too is the same as *Brahman.* And, he has kept his own logical sense intact because he is an open-minded, culturally unbiased person. He naturally, therefore, thinks that Śankara is right in calling the world unreal, and in holding that it is considered to be real because of ignorance. His natural logic tells him that ethical life can be lived only in a real world and ethical relations can hold good only among real individuals who can exist only in a real, and never in an unreal, world. But the absolutely monistic *Advaitism* entails that the world cannot be called real. Therefore, to account for the possibility of ethical life in the world Śankara has to, he concludes, grant some sort of reality to the world. But this sort cannot be full, undiluted, reality since doing that would militate against his monism, particularly against the logic of his concept of *Brahman.* Therefore, A concludes, there is no other alternative for him than attributing to the world reality in a diluted sense, a reality, as he calls it, only for practical purposes. A sees very clearly that for Śankara the world is not real, but he advises us to go on living in it, doing ethical and other required things, by taking *it,* assuming it, to *be real as* far as our behaviour in it is concerned. Since A's natural, common-sense, logic is still intact, he would soon realize that this kind of reality is nothing but a make-believe reality. Going on doing ethical things in such a world is like journeying on a boat on the surface of a river, being intellectually convinced that neither the boatman, nor the boat, not even the river, is really real but having been advised to take all of them to be real for the purpose of his undertaking this journey. Placed in such an intellectual, ratiocinative—you may call it philosophical—situation, A is bound to be in a state of intellectual turmoil which would be something like this:

Since *Brahman* alone is real, the world cannot be real. If it is unreal, ethical life cannot be lived in it. But ethical life has to be lived. Therefore, the world is to be taken as real for all practical purposes and for practical purposes only. But this is an as-if kind of reality and the fate of living ethically in it would be like that of journeying on the boat mentioned above.

Such a situation would definitely weaken A's motivation to live ethically in the world of the *Advaitic* conception.

What has been said above and in the last few pages about the possibility and worthwhileness of doing ethical things only in a real world, and not in a world possessing only some sort of practical reality, can be further reinforced by giving a close look to the nature of our ethical dealings, relations, traits, etc., and their implications. Let us do that, of course, very briefly because here we are referring to them only to make a point about one particular classical Indian way, namely, the *Advaitic* way, of conducting ethical inquiry. We are not concerned with ethical inquiry as an independent subject.

Ethical life is led in a society which is also a moral community. A society is a moral community because its members share some values, agree in considering certain traits of character virtues and certain others vices, honour some claims as rights and treat some actions as obligatory, some forbidden, some not obligatory but still commendable, i.e. supererogatory, and some neither obligatory, nor forbidden, nor supererogatory but just permissible. This moral community is in principle taken to be the human community, and not just a localized, regionalized, group of individuals. When an individual passes a moral judgement calling an action right (or wrong), or does an act of self-sacrifice to protect a crucial interest of another individual, etc., he sets an example not only for the members of his own local community but for the entire human community, for anyone anywhere in the world. The moral community, therefore, extends to the whole world and has an undated history, with an undated past, a visible present and an unending future. All this is illustrated in our quoting past examples, precedents, of moralities and immoralities, and in our being quite often afraid of, or hesitant in, doing something wrong because of our apprehension that the future generation, posterity, would not pardon us for having done it. And, sometimes we do something morally commendable at the expense of our well-deserved rights or comforts, thinking that we would thereby set a good example, an important moral precedent or guideline, for posterity.

Reference to the moral humanity is also involved in the formulation of a moral theory or a moral principle. The Jain formulation of the *five principles* of non-injury, truthfulness, honesty, abstinence from self-indulgence, and non-attachment to sense objects is meant not only for the then Indians or Jains, but for any human being with a moral sensibility, i.e. for any member of the human moral community. Even the theory of *puruṣarthas* is meant to be a general theory of value for every human being. A moral or value theory may be found to be unsatisfactory, or be modified after its formulation, but that may happen with any theory.

All this means that for there being ethics, or for the possibility of ethical life, there has to be a moral community, a human community sharing the values and virtues the pursuit and cultivation of which are basic to ethical life. This has to be a real community, and a real community can exist only in a real world, not in a world which can be only assumed, or taken, to be real for practical purposes. Even Śankara, when he speaks of anything ethical, proceeds in a manner which shows that for him too the world is real in which exists a real moral community having a long history.

An unreal world, or a world assumed to be real, or worth assuming to be real, for practical purposes, cannot have a real history; it can also be only assumed to have a history which would not be a real history. This is evident from Śankara's accepting as valid some ethical, or axiological, concepts formulated in the past by some past thinkers and using them to substantiate his views. An instance of it we have seen in his analysis or elaboration of the *Gītā* concept of an individual who has become well-settled in his resolve that he is *Brahman* (*sthitaprajña*) and holding that, as per the *Gītā*, he should keep leading a good moral life in order to set a good example for the people. All this means that he admits that there is a real moral community which existed in the *Gītā*'s time, continues to exist in his time, and will continue to exist in future. The analysis which he gives is definitely intended by him to be accepted by the future generation. In a sense, his intention has been fulfilled because the number of people who accept it even today, in the 21st century, is legion, at least in India. The story of four *brāhmana* youths, in the famous book of moral anecdotes *Pancatantra,* ends with asserting that the small-minded person thinks in terms of mine and thine, believing that this is his and that is someone else's. A cultured, decent, morally liberal (*udāra*) person, on the other hand, considers the whole world his family.[13] This is an anecdotal way of pointing out that for leading a good moral life one has to keep in mind the fact that there is a moral community which extends over the whole world.

That the world has to be real in a full-blooded, not in an anaemic, sense in order that ethical life in it is possible is *true of the world* in which classical Indians, including Śankara himself and other classical ethicists or religionists, lived, and *true of the kind of ethical life* required by them to be lived. It is true, or has to be true, as has been shown earlier in the analysis of ethical relations and of ethical predicates, because it is a conceptual truth. Therefore, it does not matter for it whether at any point of time in the history of India (or of the world) its inhabitants lived a more or less commendable ethical life. In all such possibilities and in any other, ethical life's possibility's presupposing the reality of the world will remain intact. It seems to me that classical Indian thinkers very well realize the importance of this truth and that is why they do not even suggest that the world is unreal, or real only in a diluted sense in the contexts of their presentation of moral maxims of which classical Indian literature is full, or rather overfull. *Pancatantra,* already referred to, is just one very good specimen of the presentation of moral maxims in life-like situations depicted through interesting stories.

What has been said above and in the previous few pages about ethics' presupposing the reality of the world is not something Śankara can be said to be unaware of. In fact, his saying that the world can be considered real for practical, ethical life is a sign of his recognition of the logical fact that the world has to be real for anyone's leading, or being required to lead, an ethical life. But the logic of his monistic metaphysics does not allow him straightaway to call the world real, since only *Brahman* is real. And, led by it, he has also declared, we have seen, that the world is unreal (*jaganmithyā*). At the same time, he does not want to deny the possibility of ethics; rather, he considers leading an ethical life not only required of an aspirant for attaining liberation but also required of one who has attained it in this very life, i.e. while remaining alive. Therefore, he also wants to protect the dignity of ethical life. But doing that requires him to grant to the world reality which his logic forbids or appears to forbid. He must have felt some tension in his theorizing at this point. To release this tension he introduces the doctrine of the three types of reality (*trividha sattā*): illusory (*prātibhāsika*), practical (*vyavaharika*), and ultimate (*pāramārthika*). A snake perceived in an illusion, in an erroneous visual perception, has, according to this categorization, illusory reality which vanishes as soon as a veridical visual perception reveals that there is no snake but only a piece of a rope which was wrongly seen as a snake. The world, on the other hand, has practical reality which is seen to be unreal when the knowledge of *Brahman* is attained. *Brahman,* then, is alone ultimate reality which is never negated or sublated (*tṛkala abadhita*).

The world is not given, in this scheme by Śankara, the status of even non-ultimate, dependent, reality. Had he done that the world would have been really real. The only difference between it and *Brahman* would be that it was dependent for its reality on *Brahman* and *Brahman* would have been self-dependent, as it is in the scheme of categorization mentioned above. In this kind of world ethics would surely have been possible. In fact, in all theistic religions the world is claimed to be real but dependent for its reality on God alone, or on God and some other materials. Since the world is real, according to them, they do not have any difficulty in accounting for this possibility of ethics in it. Some of them may have some difficulty because of their God, i.e. their conception of God. But that would be another matter.

There are problems with Śankara's three-fold categorization of reality because there are logical problems in admitting degrees of reality (or existence) as well as in admitting different types or kinds of reality (or existence). But this is not the place to discuss them since our work is concerned with ethics and not with metaphysics. We can enter into Śankara's metaphysics only up to a point, namely, up to that point discussing which is necessary to clarify an ethical concern of his.

I have said that Śankara must have felt some tension because of his logic requiring him to call the world unreal and his respect for ethics requiring him to call it real. It is to relieve this tension that he calls it real but real only for practical purposes. He does not want to go the whole hog with the realist and call it unqualifiedly real. He wants to satisfy both the masters, logic and ethics, by calling it real but only for practical purposes. By calling it *real* he thinks he satisfies the demand of ethics and by adding the qualifying phrase 'only for practical purposes' to 'real' he thinks he satisfies his logic. His device is something like Yudhiṣṭhira's announcing loudly the untruth, on Kṛṣṇa's strategic persuasion, that Aśvathāmā has been killed, adding in an extremely low voice the phrase 'the elephant, not the man, named Aśvathāmā'. He thinks that by announcing the first part he will achieve that to achieve which he is required to tell the untruth, i.e. will make Droṇa lay down his arms and withdraw from the battle-field, and by adding the qualifying phrase even in a low voice he will protect his commitment to tell only a truth and never an untruth. He achieves his first objective but not the second one and is punished for this lapse by the gods in his journey to heaven (*svargārohaṇa*).

Śankara too achieves his objectives only partially. He protects the logic of his monism, partially of course, by saying that the world is not a second reality in addition to *Brahman* because, when *Brahman* is known, the world is seen to be unreal by a knower of *Brahman.* But then he has to face some extremely tricky problems about the relationship between the unreal world and the only real *Brahman* and about the cause of the appearance of the unreal world as real in normal experience. Similarly, he satisfies the requirement of the reality of the world for the possibility of ethical life but only to an uncritical mind, to one who does not see, or care to discover, the implications of ascribing to the world only practical reality destined to vanish after attaining the knowledge of *Brahman*. But for the open-minded, critical philosopher, who unpacks the implications of the notion of practical reality in a logically neutral manner, the unpacking is very likely to make him sceptical about the adequacy of the real-only-for-practical-purposes world to satisfy the possibility condition of ethics. But still it is clear that Śankara's intention in the introduction, in his ontological categoriology, of the notion of the real-only-for-practical-purposes world is to protect both, his respect for logic and his respect for ethics. And, this intention in itself is laudable.

6.4 HUMAN-CENTRICITY OF INDIAN ETHICS AS OF ANY ETHICAL INQUIRY

It has been said above that ethics is essentially an agent-centric inquiry in the sense of being man-centric or human-centric while admitting that in some Indian ethical discussions even non-humans seem to have been assigned the role of moral agents. Lest there be misread a gender bias in the discussions of this and other parts of this work, at the cost of being repetitive since I have already said it in the preface, I want to re-assert that when I use the word 'man' in a general discussion here or elsewhere, I intend to cover both a male and a female human being. Therefore, even when I say here or elsewhere in this work that ethics is man-centric I mean all along that it is human-centric, and never male-person-centric. This point is obvious since both men and women are moral agents, or can be moral agents. In fact, it is so obvious that no normal person can be oblivious of it. But it needs to be asserted, or re-asserted, particularly in a discussion about Indian ethics, because some people think that Indian ethics, or classical Indian thought in general, is biased against women.

With the above clarification about gender-neutrality, let me explain in some detail how ethics as such, and so Indian ethics, is man-centric. This, the man-centric model, is an old, one may even say an orthodox, model for explicating the nature of ethics.[14] But it is a correct or adequate model. I am saying this with full awareness of the recent resurgence of interest of moral philosophers in animal ethics and environmental ethics. The charge made by some of these philosophers, resulting out of this interest of theirs, is that these areas of ethics have been neglected, or not given until recently the consideration they deserve, because ethics has been treated as a man-centric inquiry, because philosophers have given to the concept of the human agent the place of the key, or root, concept in understanding the nature of ethics, i.e. of the nature of ethical attributes and relations, and have ignored the role of the non-human patient. They also sometimes aver that because of the human-centric bias we have not always been morally just or fair to non-humans which, unlike men, can be only patients, for example, to inorganic and organic nature, i.e. to hills, rivers, plants, animals, etc. I want to show here that ethics, as a philosophical inquiry, or a cognitive inquiry for that matter, has to be a human-centric inquiry even if we give to the concept of the patient the status of a key concept. We will see that there is nothing built into the concept of a human-centric ethics which deters us from giving to an agent, or to the concept of the patient, in any relevant ethical transaction, the importance that is due to it, or which deters us from being ethically, or morally, fair to the non-human patient. All this assumes a greater significance in the context of Indian ethics because in Indian ethical literature some non-human subjects have been given the role not only of patients but also of agents in some obviously ethical dealings. But let us first see how it can be substantiated, as a general conceptual claim, that ethics has to be a human-centric inquiry.

Ethics has to be called a human-centric inquiry because the field, using 'field' in a strictly logical sense, of any moral relation, in the ultimate analysis, is found to consist always of human beings or human things. The field of a relation is the sum or aggregate of its domain and converse domain. Therefore, what is maintained here is that, speaking conceptually, only a human being really belongs to the domain, or to the converse domain, of a moral relation. This is true even in those cases in which something non-human appears to occur in the domain or converse domain of a moral relation. The human-centric model has the flexibility or elasticity to be extended to cover even cases to which it appears to be inapplicable.

To explain the logical terms used in the above not very clear presentation of the human-centric conception of ethics, let us take, as an example of a general moral relation, the relation of being fair to. In the schematic statement involving this relation, 'x is fair to y', the name of anyone who can be fair to someone can be put in place of x and the name of anyone to whom someone can be fair can be used to replace y. Therefore, anyone who can be fair to someone would belong to its domain and anyone to whom someone can be fair to its converse domain. The field of a relation being the totality or sum of its domain and converse domain, the field of the moral relation 'fair to' would thus be the totality of all those who can be fair to anyone and of all those to whom anyone can be fair. At least a good number of moral relations are such that one can have them to oneself as well as to someone else. For example, one can be fair (or unfair) to oneself as well as to someone else and 'being fair (or unfair) to' denotes, at least in some uses of it, a moral relation.

A moral relation can operate on two levels which may be called non-participatory and participatory. It works on the non-participatory or assessive level, for example, when one judges or evaluates an action to be right or wrong, commendable or condemnable, morally relevant or irrelevant to the context in which it has been done, etc. One can evaluate in the moral sense, or from the moral point of view, not only human actions, but also human intentions, persons, groups of persons, institutions, etc. In doing this one enters into the relation of evaluating, or assessing, the moral value of the object judged. To evaluate the moral value or status of anything is to enter into a relationship with it, of course, on the mental level. The relationship is moral, whether one evaluates the moral worth of the thing in positive or negative terms. It is moral since the evaluation done may itself be morally right or wrong, justified or unjustified.

Suppose an individual A (or a social system S), following a prescription or practice mentioned in *Manusmṛti*, awards to a member of a scheduled caste a harsher punishment than the punishment he awards to a *brāhmaṇ* even though the crime committed by the former is exactly the same as the crime committed by the latter. An individual who evaluates or judges from the moral point of view, A's (or S's) method of awarding punishment to criminals, enters into a moral relationship with A (or S), no matter whether he judges the method to be morally right or morally wrong. The judgement that the method is morally right, as well as the judgement that it is morally wrong, is itself a moral judgement (and therefore subject to moral criticism which may conclude that it is right or wrong). In fact, many would say that judging the method to be morally right is itself not only logically but also morally wrong. To judge the moral worth of a thing is to adopt an attitude towards it, which may be an attitude of approval or disapproval, commendation or condemnation, praise or blame, etc. And, the adoption of this attitude can itself be morally defensible or indefensible. Therefore, to call the relation itself of judging or evaluating a moral relation i.e. a morally judgeable or criticizable relation is quite in order. To put it in another way, judging the moral worth of a thing is to do something intentionally. Rather, it is something which cannot be done accidentally, inadvertently, or in a huff, because it requires the judger to examine whether or not the thing being evaluated satisfies the relevant criterion or criteria (whatever they may be) of rightness, obligatoriness, or goodness, etc. Such an action has to be done knowingly, self-consciously, and therefore cannot be accidental or unintentional.

A moral relationship with the object morally evaluated can be held only by a person who possesses the ability of judging, who has some idea of the reasons for judging its moral status or worth in positive or negative terms. That is, he has to have a certain level of rationality or rational maturity. This means that only a human being can be such an evaluator. No plant, or non-human animal, can be credited with having the rational maturity or ability to judge the moral worth of anything. It is obvious, then, that the domain of *any (moral) relation of morally judging* must consist only of human beings possessing a certain kind of rationality, or reasoning ability.

A moral judge may not do anything besides judging the moral worth of a thing or judging and publicly expressing his judgement. Then his relationship with the thing would be, what I have called, non-participatory. But he may also become a moral activist, that is, proceed to taking necessary steps called forth by his assessment or understanding. Then his moral relation with the object or objects concerned becomes participatory in the sense that he begins to participate in a moral process or transaction.

As presented in the *Mahābhārata*,[15] the scene of Duhśāsana's trying to derobe Draupadī gives good examples of non-participatory and participatory moral relations as well as of one's being indifferent. Vidura first begins to express his reaction by condemning in strong terms the attempt to derobe her. His moral relation to it then is purely judgemental being only a relation of his moral evaluation of it. At this stage it is non-participatory. But very soon when he finds that others are silent, he begins to appeal to Bhīṣma, Dhṛtarāṣṭra, and other members of the audience to get this abominable act stopped. He now becomes a moral activist on his own level since he cannot do anything more, as he has no authority or power to stop Duhśāsana from proceeding further. Therefore, his moral relation, which was in its inception purely judgemental and therefore non-participatory, now becomes participatory. On the other hand, Kṛṣṇa's moral relation to the attempt at derobing Draupadī, immediately on hearing her wailing cry and appeal to him for help, turns into a participatory one. He uses his divine power to make her wearing apparel (*sārī*) infinitely long with the result that Duhśāsana fails to take it off from her body. Bhīṣma's moral relation or attitude to the scene, on the contrary, is one of indifference.

Yudhiṣṭhira, the eldest among the five brothers who are her five husbands, puts himself on the stakes in the game of dice played with Śakunī and loses himself, i.e., his freedom and therefore agency. A little later in the game he puts Draupadī on the stakes and again loses his chance. Draupadī asks Bhīṣma to opine whether Yudhiṣṭhira, who has already lost his freedom to do anything, had the moral right, i.e. right approved or sanctioned by *dharma* (morality), to put her on the stakes. Her own judgement is that he has no such right because he has lost all of his rights after losing his own freedom. She wants to get its confirmation from Bhīṣma, the head of the then Kaurava family, and that is why she has put her question before him. If Bhīṣma concurs with her, then it would mean that Yudhiṣṭhira's putting her on the stakes is ultra vires and therefore she has not been lost to Duryodhana and consequently is not to be derobed. Bhīṣma has here a chance to enter into a moral relationship with what is happening by answering her question in the affirmative or negative. But he does not give any answer. He says that her question cannot be answered because the concept of *dharma* is so abstruse and subtle that it cannot be said whether or not what Yudhiṣṭhira has done in putting her on the stakes is in accordance with *dharma*. By taking shelter behind the alleged insurmountable difficulty in the application of the concept of *dharma* to Yudhiṣṭhira's action, he finds, or claims to find, an excuse or pretext to be indifferent, i.e. to enter into no relation, with the entire episode of Duhśāsana's attempt to derobe Draupadī.

To conclude this theme, it is obvious that a moral relation that may be meaningfully held by anyone with anyone or anything, can be one of the following types:

(a) A substantive moral relation, like one of being fair to, being kind to, being faithful to, being polite to, being obliging or obliged or grateful to, being considerate to, being benevolent towards, being of a forgiving nature towards, etc., etc. It is clear that the opposites of these relations would also be substantive moral relations. A substantive moral relation is always a participatory, and not just a mental, passive, relation. For example, to be fair to anyone (or anything) one has to do something when there is an occasion to do that and not just to judge or think of him (or it) in a certain way, and what is to be done by him must be done intentionally, or self-consciously. For example, to be fair to Yudhiṣṭhira, Dhṛtarāṣṭra should have made him the crown prince, or when the kingdom of Kurukṣetra was divided between him and his son Duryodhana, he should have given to him a share equal in value to that which he gave his son. The holder of a substantive moral relation, one who can do what entering into such a relationship entails, must be one who has a certain level of mental and physical ability or maturity. He must have the mental or deliberative ability to decide when which sort of moral relationship in which sort of situation is appropriate and the physical ability to do at the opportune time what entering into the relationship requires him to do. This kind of twin ability can be had only by a human being. Therefore, the domain of a substantive moral relation can consist only of human beings.

The patient of a substantive moral attitude, i.e., the converse domain of a moral relation, may apparently be a non-human. For example, an animal is the patient, a member of the converse domain, in the moral relation of being kind to, when someone, say, his master, or user, is kind to him. But the animal cannot be said to be grateful to his master. He cannot be an agent, i.e. one who is grateful to someone for his doing something to it for which having a feeling of gratitude towards him is the proper moral response.

This is so because the animal does not have the mental and moral maturity to know what is gratitude, why it is morally required to be grateful to a benefactor, what is the criterion which an action of someone towards someone else should fulfil in order to oblige the latter to feel grateful towards the agent of the action, etc., etc. This is well illustrated in the dialogue between the saint Jājali[16] and the businessman Tulādhāra when the latter says that he feeds well and does not overload his animals which carry from other places the goods he stocks in his shop to sell to his customers. Feeding them well and not overloading them are signs of his being kind, or considerate, to them. But his animals cannot be said to know that he is kind to them and give a befitting moral response in return simply because they do not have the required rationality to know what is genuine kindness, how it is different from exploitative politeness, or what sort of response is a proper response to it, etc.

(b) A judgemental relation, like one of evaluating an action, intention, a policy, decision, etc. of someone as morally right or wrong, may be, as already explained, non-participatory or participatory. When it becomes participatory, it becomes, as already pointed out, a substantive moral relation because it results in, or tends to result in, some kind of action, or of a series of actions; it becomes, or tends to become, thereby a participation in some sort of an active moral transaction. It is obvious that a non-human cannot have a (b) type, i.e. a judgemental, moral relation, non-participatory or participatory, to anything, non-human or human.

A non-human's being even a patient has been qualified here with the word 'apparently' because whenever it is a patient, it is not because of its being what it in itself is. Rather, it is always a patient because of some human interest in it, and quite often because of its utility for some humans. *Tulādhāra* is kind to his animals because he has an interest in their remaining stout and healthy. Even if we say that he feels thankful or obligated to them for their services to him, it is *he*, a *human being*, who feels obligated, and does so because of their services to *him*, to *a human* being. This shows that they are made the recipient, the patient, in the relation of Tulādhāra's being kind to them because of Tulādhāra's, a *human being's, interest.* This is why it has been said above that a non-human is only apparently a patient in a moral dealing; what makes it a patient is a human being's interest in it, i.e. something human, and not something intrinsic in it, totally unrelated to anything human. All this is very clearly communicated by Tulādhāra to Jājali in his account of his *dhārmika*, moral, living in the conduct of his business.

There are also examples in classical Indian literature in which animals appear to play the role of agents. An unwary critic may see, or seem to see, in this practice an inconsistency and ask the question 'How can a non-human be an agent in a moral relation when it is not even a genuine patient in it?' He may then conclude that either Indian ethics is self-inconsistent, or if self-consistent, then it has to be conceded that it accords to a non-human the logical right to play the role of an agent as well as of a patient in a moral relationship. But this would be an unfair understanding of Indian ethics. As is the case with the occurrence of a term for a non-human, say, for some bird or birds, in the slot marked for a patient of a moral relationship, so is the case with its occurrence in the slot marked for an agent.

To give an example, a little later in the dialogue between Tulādhāra and Jājali referred to above, Tulādhāra requests Jājali to listen attentively to what some birds flying in the sky are saying to him about morality. These birds are the children and grandchildren of the birds which had lived in the nest their parents and grandparents had made in his clotted hairs, and had been begotten therein. Jājali invites them to come down and speak to him. They come down and state to him some unquestionable, sublime, moral principles, or maxims. For example, they say, the author of the *Mahābhārata* avers, in a voice similar to man's that, an action done in accordance with the principle of non-violence (*ahimsā*) and compassion (*dayā*) is productive of a good result in this as well as in the other world. If there is any inclination in the mind of the doer to cause any harm to anyone, then this inclination destroys the doer's respect for morality, or, his moral sense, and the destruction of his moral sense causes his total destruction. But if an individual is unmoved by loss and gain in leading a moral life, respectful towards morality, self-controlled, has a pure mentality, and performs his sacrifices (*yajñas*) as his duties, his *yajñas* are never unsuccessful; that is, life, lived in a moral way, is never a failure.[17]

The principles stated above, apparently uttered by the birds, are principles to which Indian ethics accords a very honourable place. If a bird, or any animal, presents them, or presents any moral principle of any level of generality, then it certainly plays the role of a moral agent. And, if superficially, or only linguistically, looked at, the above example may be cited as one in which Indian ethics makes the birds, i.e. some non-human beings, moral agents. But, as has been already pointed out, the birds have been said to have *spoken like human beings*; they have been *humanized*, i.e. conceived as having a communicative ability, like that of a human being, to state or present moral principles. In this way anything, even a rock, or a plant, can be a moral agent if it is conceived as having a communicative, ratiocinative, or deliberative, ability which only some human beings, and certainly not all of them, possess. But, then, this would mean that only those non-humans who have such abilities which are distinctive of human beings, who are like human beings, i.e. who in ethical practice behave like humans, can be moral agents. This is not very different from saying that what makes them moral agents is their possession of some human properties. Jājali's birds illustrate this point since they have the properties which make a human being a moral agent.

As per Indian theology or mythology deities too have these properties, and have done morally right as well as morally wrong things. But that is no surprise because they have been generally conceived on the pattern of what we think human beings to be, or what they ought to be. Moreover, when we discuss the nature of ethics as a philosophical inquiry, or that of any ethical issue in a philosophical or rational manner, we normally have in mind ethics as concerned with human beings, or concerned with the way or ways in which human beings deal with nature, animate or inanimate.

Classical Indian thinkers realize very well that we can have a full-fledged moral relation only with such a being with whom we can communicate and who can communicate with us, who understands the meaning of what we do and we understand what who does, i.e. we can interact with him, argue with him, try to convince him of our stand, or be convinced by his argument, etc., etc. Entering into a moral relationship is thus to participate in a social transaction in which both the parties fully participate. In what we nowadays call environmental ethics, or animal ethics, we do have cases of moral relationship in which the agent is a human being but the patient, the other party in the relationship, is a non-human, a plant, an animal, or even an inorganic object like a river, a hill, etc. Here the relationship is partial because the patient, the other party, cannot have a full-fledged moral relationship. For example, a householder may say that the cow who gives milk for his children has the *right* to be fed well, or that he, the householder, is obligated to, or has a *duty to*, feed her well. But it cannot be said that the cow too has a duty to give a good quantity of milk when it is fed so well.

But this fact does not indicate any deficiency in an ethics conceived as human-centric. Even in the sphere of ethical relations among humans, one's having a right on someone does not always imply one's owing a duty to the latter, nor does one's having a duty towards someone always imply one's having a right on the latter. A mother has no right to be fulfilled by her child daughter, though she has some duties towards her, and the daughter has rights on her mother but no duties towards her. The moral relation of being dutiful towards the child is possible because of the nature of the mother-child relationship. This relationship generates the relation of the mother's *obligation* to the child to feed her well, or the child's right on her mother to be fed well by her, even if the child has been medically declared to remain a life-long invalid. Something similar is true of the cow which has become dry and is not going to be a milch cow for the rest of its life. We say that still its owner is obligated to feed it well simply because he is its owner. Many Hindus would say that it is his duty to do that and those of them who are morally very sensitive would come forward to found centres for taking care of cows deserted by their owners. But such centres are founded, or duties towards such cows are emphasized, because of man's ethical attitude towards such sometime-useful-but-now-deserted cows, because of his interest in them and generally because of the cows' utility for him. This fact confirms our stand that ethics is basically human-centric, or that ethical relations are human-centric. All this is so, to repeat, because only a human being, or a being conceived on the model of a human being, can be the agent of a moral action, the holder of a moral attitude, and it his interest in, or attitude towards, a non-human which can make the latter a patient in an ethical transaction. This is very well testified by the way in which classical Indian thinkers conceived of ethical relations between humans and non-humans, as exemplified above.

We can say, therefore, that to adopt the human-centric approach to ethics is in no way to give less moral importance to non-humans. On the substantive level, it does not affect one's dealings with non-humans. It is not itself a substantive, or first-order, *moral*, model about how to behave with, or what to do with non-humans. Rather, it is a theoretical or metaethical concept or construct, a concept about how to understand, or conceive of, the character of ethical relations which exist or may exist between humans and non-humans. Its claim simply is that these relations can be fairly or correctly conceived of, or understood, as being human-centric in the sense explained above. An ethical theorist, a metaethicist, who considers it an adequate model, in his ethical or moral practice, may or may not be fair, or ethically respectful or caring, towards his non-human surroundings, towards the river he every day baths in or the animal on whose back he transports from one place to another the goods he sells. All this will depend on his moral nature and nurture. Therefore, simply because of being human-centric, classical Indian ethics cannot be accused of being, on the substantive, practical, moral, level, unfair to non-humans, or on the theoretical or metaethical level, of having ignored such ethical areas as environmental ethics or bio-ethics. It may be dubbed to have adopted an old-fashioned model. But that cannot be called a deficiency in it, or in any classical ethics. The human-centric model is an old model and may even be called an orthodox one. But since it has survived until date and has the built-in capability to take care of all possible sorts of ethical relations, it cannot be considered unusable simply because of its age. Rather, its survival for so long shows its theoretical, logical, strength and explanatory ability to help us comprehend correctly the nature of all possible ethical relations.

It is undebatable that classical Indian ethics, even being formulated and practised thousands of years ago, does not neglect non-humans, or non-human patients, in man's ethical transactions. Apart from their being important for human beings in so many ways, there is also another, a good, metaphysical, reason for this ethical fact. The Jaina metaphysicians, for example, hold that, among non-humans—not only animals but even plants, i.e. even objects or bodies of earth, air, fire, water, etc.—have in them life and consciousness though in a minimal or extremely undeveloped form. This means that the objects of our surrounding, organic as well as inorganic, can also be hurt or made to suffer if any damage is done to them. Doing any damage to any one of them is, therefore, to cause to it some injury and would violate the ethical principle of doing no injury to anyone (*ahimsā*). The principle of non-injury is a generally accepted principle of classical Indian ethics and its application is extended even to non-humans. For *Advaitic* thinkers, or rather, for *Upaniṣadic* thinkers in general, consciousness is taken to be present in all things, animate and inanimate, and hence almost everything would then come under the scope of the principle of non-injury. One clear effect of accepting this principle as a principle of almost universal scope would be to have a care or concern for the welfare or upkeep of even non-human objects of nature. It is this care or concern which is at the centre of environmental ethics and bio-ethics.

It is to be admitted, however, that all thinkers, or all sectors of classical Indian ethical thought, do not take the principle of non-injury so rigorously as the Jainas do. This is clear from the historical evidence that non-vegetarianism was not strictly practised in classical India and killing animals for sport (*ākheta*) was taken to be a respectable practice, or was at least not forbidden for householders. All this goes well with our characterization of classical Indian ethics or metaethics as human-centric in the sense that a non-human object, according to it, can be an object of an ethical attitude, or the converse domain of an ethical relation, only if it is an object of some human interest. It is important to remember here that to be an object of a human interest is not necessarily to be, or always to be, an object which satisfies a human need. For example, one may have the ethical attitude of being kind to an animal, say, a cow, simply because one believes that it feels hurt, or pain, if a certain thing is done to it, for example, if it is separated from its newly born calf. Kindness towards animals is therefore justified only because they are taken to possess the required sensitivity to feel pain, as a human being does. It is this sensitivity to pain which makes both, an animal as well as a human being, a fit object of the attitude of kindness. Therefore, kindness towards an animal is kindness towards a human-like object (in virtue of its potentiality to suffer pain). If this belief in an animal's sensitivity to feel pain is extended even to a plant or an inorganic substance, then kindness to it would also be a conceptually proper ethical attitude towards it. This is what Śakuntalā in Kālidāsa's famous drama *Abhijñāna Śākuntalam* does. She feels concerned or worried when she comes to her husband's house, not only about a pregnant deer in her father-like teacher's abode, which is expected to deliver its baby in a few days, but also about the plants which she used to water every morning when she was there.

In classical Indian works, particularly in the epics, as already mentioned, animals have been sometimes depicted as stating to or, reminding, human beings of, a moral principle or maxim, as, for example, the birds to Jājali. This is in a sense to mythologize the capability of the animal or animals concerned. The same may be said to be the case with conceiving a tree as the abode of a deity. Such mythologizings certainly cannot form a part of a philosophy of morals. They may even be treated by many as symptoms of a supersitious belief in the powers of nature. But the thrust, the breathing idea, behind the examples of plants' or animals' uttering moral maxims must not be left unnoticed.

It seems to be that classical Indians use these examples mainly for two, or two sorts of, reasons. One, they seem to hold that what matters, in the statement or presentation of a moral maxim, is its intrinsic worth and not the status of those who state or present it; they may be human or non-human. Two, they also seem to hold that in matters about any moral principle, there must be reached a point, the sooner the better, when debate ends and execution or implementation of the principle in conduct or actual practice begins, or the principle is shown to be inapplicable, irrelevant, or outright untenable. When an animal is depicted as stating a principle the listener cannot obviously enter into a debate with it about the reasons for or against accepting it. His debating mood is likely to become subdued or inoperative. It is very likely that he then thinks of the principle in a cool, receptive mood and without wasting much time in logically assessing its tenability, he proceeds to mould his action-pattern in accordance with it—of course, if the principle concerned is not untenable. The assumption of these two reasons behind such uses of animals is supported by the fact that generally the principles uttered by animals are obvious ones, those whose tenability is not opaque, or, does not need to be proven. All the principles which Jājali's birds utter are obviously valid moral principles which Jājali seems to have forgotten because of his pride in having done extremely arduous penances. The birds' principles make him realize the importance of some ground-level, down-to-earth, moral principles. This, the down-to-earth character of Indian ethics, or of its principles, is quite often overlooked, or, undervalued, by those who, in their characterization of it, overemphasize its alleged spirituality as well as by those who, in their estimation of it, are guided mainly by such characterizations or by the occurrence of some remarks here and there about the link between morality and spirituality. And, those who consider morality a mundane affair, and linking it with spirituality a sign of its theologization and therefore destroying or weakening its intrinsic dignity, conclude that there is no ethics in Indian philosophy. But, as has been said already, Indian philosophy, does not ignore, or belittle, the role of ethics in man's normal, earthly, life. This point will be further elaborated in the chapter dealing with the theory of *puruṣārthas* in which the relation of morality with *mokṣa* will be discussed in some detail.

6.5 ORGANISMIC CHARACTER OF INDIAN ETHICS: APPLIED AND THEORETICAL ETHICS INTERACTING WITH EACH OTHER

For the classical Indian mind there is nothing in the world of which it can be said that it is of no human interest at all. So it is today. Today too it cannot be said even of poisonous plants, dangerous animals, ravaging rivers prone to being overflooded and thereby to causing immense miseries to inhabitants of nearby areas, etc. The modern man is interested in them, and so is the classical Indian, not only in a negative sense, i.e. in that of keeping them under control or of curbing their potentialities to increase human unhappiness; he has a positive interest in them as well arising out of his curiosity to know what they are, what is it which makes them what they are, whether or not a good use can be made of them, etc., etc. Classical *Āyurvedic* practice studies quite a few poisonous plants and chemicals and makes good medicinal use of them. For example, it uses the poisonous seeds of the plant stramonium (*dhatūrā*), after subjecting it to a chemical process of purification (*śodhana*), for curing some diseases. Cāṇakya uses a *viṣakanayā*, a girl conditioned to become immune to the dangerous, fatal, effects of some poisonous substances, with her lips smeared with snake-poison, to kill Parvataka, a claimant of half of Candragupta's kingdom on the basis of a prior contractual agreement. The girl is sent by Rākṣasa, the deposed and killed king Nanda's prime minister now in alliance with Parvataka, to kill Candragupta. But Cāṇakya manages to use her to kill Parvataka. He gets her sent to Parvataka. She captivates him by her coquettish manners and as soon he moves to embrace and tries to kiss her, she kisses him and he dies instantly.[18]

An important consequence of Indian ethics' comprehending everything of human interest under the scope of ethical concern, i.e. under the field of ethical relations, is its organismic character. Without explicitly classifying ethical inquiries into normative and conceptual or metaethical, theoretical and applied, general and professional, human and environmental-bioethical, personal and social, ethics, as is nowadays done, it pays attention, in one way or another, to issues belonging to all of them. Of course, it does that in its own way, in its general philosophical framework, using the conceptual tools it has devised to handle these issues, including some others used in other related areas of philosophy. This is only to remind us of the fact that it has been cognizant of quite a few of the ethical problems which are being discussed today. However, it would be not only hazardous but also unfair to modern ethical studies to claim that whatever has been done, or is being done, in modern ethics has been already done in classical Indian ethics. Saying anything to this effect would be an affront to the creativity and progressiveness of the human mind, since it would imply that for the last few thousands of years or so, it has made no new stride in its ethical inquiries. And, to say, or to imply, it would not be in any way a compliment to the classical Indian mind, because it would mean that by its achievements it has blocked all further progress in ethical thinking.

By saying that classical Indian ethics has an organismic character it is not meant here that it has given any grand ethical theory covering every corner of the area or areas encompassed by man's ethical concerns. Presenting such a theory would amount not only to discussing in one theory an unmanageably large number of ethical issues but also a large number of metaphysical, logical-conceptual, epistemological, socio-political, botanical-zoological, geological, etc. issues.

A theory organismic in this sense is neither feasible nor is it likely to be useful in either explaining or in promoting man's ethical endeavours. No surprise, therefore, that no attempt has been made by classical Indian thinkers to present any such theory. Rather, no attempt has been made by them to present a grand ethical theory covering all aspects of man's ethical life, taking 'ethical life' to denote only a sector of his general life-style. As has been pointed out earlier in this chapter, Indian ethics abounds in piecemeal analyses of ethical issues. But almost every piecemeal analysis it offers is organismic, and not isolationist, in the sense that it is not exclusively an analysis of a particular ethical issue, problem, or theme. In discussing one theme, on the other hand, while keeping in the centre of its focus that theme, it also discusses a number of many other related themes in such a manner that in one compact account is presented a cohesive, well-structured, unified, sometimes a small, sometimes a good-sized, philosophical blue-print of an ethical theory which is normative, conceptual, applied, socio-political, metaphysical, sometimes even spiritualist, etc. I have called it *piecemeal* because it is still an account of a specific theme and *organismic* because it covers a number of other related themes, not as disparate units but as interrelated components of an organism. A good example, rather a bold one, of such a venture is Kṛṣṇa's theory of *desireless action* (*niṣkāma karma*), which will be briefly discussed in a later chapter and in detail in chapter 'of my *A Historical-Developmental Study of Classical Indian Philosophy of Morals* (PHISPC). Less detailed, and not so bold, examples of such attempts are available aplenty at so many other places. But in many such cases, more as a rule rather than as an exception, the organismic but still piecemeal character of the analysis is not visible on the surface but needs to be discovered by closely probing into it. Generally it is not visible to an unwary eye as is a fish swimming on the upper layer of the water in a pool. The nature of this kind of analysis, I admit, can be made clear only by giving some concrete examples of it. This will be done in section 6.7.

6.6 NON-RIGIDITY OF THE DISTINCTION BETWEEN APPLIED AND THEORETICAL ETHICS

Before giving some examples of it, a short general discussion of the relationship between applied ethics and theoretical ethics is called for here because it is very much in the limelight these days, and particularly because, in doing ethics in their organismic style, Indian thinkers do not emphasize the distinction. Rather they play the ethical (philosophical) game in such a way that ethicizing in their practice is always a transaction which is both practical and theoretical, applied and pure, conceptual and empirical; it is not a compound of two sorts of activities, but a single activity which is both, or one which can be called applied, practical, etc. as well as theoretical, conceptual, etc. That is why the account of any phenomenon or episode which can be cited as an example of ethicizing can also be seen as a specimen of applied, theoretical, conceptual, etc. ethics. In fact, ethicizing in concretes is always a homogeneous mass though not necessarily unanalysable, or resistant to an attempt to differentiate one component of it from another. It is almost always an exercise in theorizing/conceptualizing as well as in applying an ethical concept to an actual empirical situation and indicating what ought or ought not to be done.

The Indian way of playing the moral philosophical game is thus a natural way to play the game.

Any ethical theory, to be a worthwhile theory, must be applicable to actual ethical situations. For example, a theory about the criterion of moral rightness would be a genuine ethical theory of rightness if the criterion which it gives is applicable to concrete cases; i.e. only if it is possible to use it to decide whether or not a certain action in a certain situation satisfies the criterion and, therefore, is, or is not, right. This is so because an ethical theory is meant for enabling or helping an individual in decision-making when he is placed in a situation in which he has to decide what is morally right for him to do, or contrariwise, what is morally wrong which he has to abstain from doing. It, thus, must guide him in, or provide to him guidelines for, deciding what he ought or ought not to do, what he may do though it is not obligatory for him to do, or even may not do because it is neither obligatory nor forbidden, etc. That is, it must tell him what is morally right, obligatory, forbidden, or just permissible, etc. It is obvious that the theory, which does all this, would also enable him to pass a clear moral judgement on what someone else has done, is doing, or is contemplating doing, in a similar situation; i.e. in a situation in which he himself is not the doer but a neutral spectator or observer, who has to perform the role of a judge to decide the moral status of the latter's action.

The application of a moral theory always consists in applying a moral concept to a concrete thing, intention, motive, action, person, public agency, social institution. Every moral concept is generally both ambiguous and vague because there are some cases, or instances, of which it is not clear to say that it applies, or does not apply, to them. The larger the number of such unclear cases, the greater would be the vagueness of the concept. Therefore, if it is not possible to decide of *any* relevant case that a certain moral (or any) concept applied to it, the concept would be totally vague and therefore useless. It would be like a coin which can be used to buy nothing, i.e. one which has no exchange value. Such a concept would not be a genuine concept, and perhaps there is no such concept in any field of human concern. Something similar will be the fate of the theory which defines the criterion of an action's moral rightness in terms of its conduciveness to its doer's attaining liberation (*mokṣa*) no matter whether it is liberation attained by him while alive (*jīvanmukti*) or after his death (*videhamukti*). This point will be discussed in some detail in the chapter on liberation.

In actual communicative practice, for almost every moral concept, the range of its semantic clarity can be represented on a line. At one end of the line there would be cases or instances of which it is obvious that it does not apply to them, and at the other end cases or instances of which it is equally obvious that it applies to them. Somewhere in the middle of the line, occupying a small, or a large, part of the line there would be cases of which it is not obvious that it does or does not apply to them. It is the existence of these cases which make the concept vague. Therefore, the vagueness of one concept may be more or less than the vagueness of another, depending on the size of the area on the semantic line occupied by cases to which its applicability as well as inapplicability is unclear. Even the vagueness of the same concept may differ in degrees in the history of its usage. And, it is also possible that it may be vague in ordinary, non-technical, usage but not at all in a technical usage. For example, the concept of validity, clearly a value concept, is, at least to some extent, vague in its ordinary usage. But it is not at all vague in that of formal, deductive logic. One of the chief objectives of a theory about the use of any concept, and so of a moral concept, is to make it as precise as its nature and usage allow and thereby to minimize its vagueness. This is true of a metaethical as well as of a normative ethical concept or notion.

A word about the applicability of a metaethical theory is called for here because many think that, since it is primarily a conceptual or logical theory about the behaviour of a moral concept, it is not of any, or of much, use in ethical practice. But this is far from the truth. To give one example, metaethicists make a four-fold distinction among morally judgeable actions, in the following manner: some actions, they say, are obligatory, some forbidden, some permissible and some recommended or supererogatory. An obligatory action is one which ought to be done and not doing which is wrong. A forbidden action is that which ought not to be done and doing which is wrong. A permissible action is that which may, or may not, be done, i.e. neither doing, nor not doing, which is obligatory or wrong. A recommended or supererogatory action is, on the other hand, that the doing of which is not obligatory and therefore if an individual does not do it, his not doing it would not be wrong. But if he does it, he would be doing something commendable, something morally creditable; he would get more moral credit than he would by doing something obligatory.

To illustrate this distinction, as per classical Indian social ethics, it is obligatory for a *kṣatriya* to fight a righteous battle *dharma yuddha,* wrong to run away from a battle-field (*palāyana*), permissible to learn music, and supererogatory to pardon an unrighteous enemy. To illustrate further how this conceptual classification can be applied in ethical practice, we can easily turn to the dialogue in moral reasoning between Arjuna and Kṛṣṇa in the celebrated part of the *Mahābhārata,* the *Gītā.* Kṛṣṇa asks Arjuna to fight the *Mahābhārata* war because, he being a *kṣatriya* and the war being a righteous one, it is obligatory for him to fight it, and it is wrong for him to run away from the battle-field. Arjuna tries to prove to him that abstaining from fighting the war would be commendable and not wrong, because he would then be doing something supererogatory, something not obligatory but also not wrong; rather, his not fighting would be highly creditable because it would avoid killing relatives and respected elders. He fails to convince Kṛṣṇa, but this is the point he is trying to make, i.e. to apply the concept of the supererogatory to justify his not fighting the war. That he fails does not prove that he is not trying to apply the metaethical distinction between the concepts of the obligatory, forbidden and supereogatory, in his counter-argument with Kṛṣṇa, nor does it prove that his not fighting the war would not have been a really supererogatory step. A Mahāvīra, a Gautama Buddha, or even an M.K. Gandhi, or any individual committed to the ethical principle of non-violence (*ahimsā*) and not committed to the sacrosanctity of the then social organization (*varṇavyavasthā*), would have said that it certainly would have been supererogatory and therefore more commendable than Arjuna's fighting the war. As an example of a permissible action too we can refer to the *Mahābhārata* which records Arjuna's marrying more than one wife, since in the then Indian ethical practice polygamy was permitted. Kṛṣṇa himself does not disapprove of it. Rather, he helps Arjuna to marry his own sister, Subhadrā, knowing full well that he already has married Draupadī.

It would be relevant here to take into account the important distinction between considering an action *permissible* and having a *permissive* attitude towards it. This distinction, particularly because it brings into clear focus the nature of taking an action permissively, very aptly illustrates the untenability of claiming any hard separating line or bifurcation between applied and theoretical ethics. To put it positively, it illustrates a very intimate relationship between the two, the possibility of each one's affecting the other, like that of two rivers, each one flowing into the other at more than one point.

A *permissible* action, as already said, is definitely not wrong, since if it were wrong, it would be one which ought not to be done, and therefore would become impermissible. On the other hand, to have a permissive attitude towards an action is to be tolerant about anyone's doing it, to condone his doing it, i.e. not to mind his doing it, even though it is wrong to do it, or doing it infringes a moral principle. Since it infringes a moral principle, it is obvious that it comes under the scope of the principle, that the principle is applicable to it, because an action can infringe only a principle which is relevant or applicable to it. But when a society, or social practice, is permissive about it, it means that it does not take seriously the applicability of the principle to it and its applicability's making it wrong. This is to say that it virtually ignores it. It may be said that for the permissive society, though *in principle* the principle is applicable to the action and makes the action wrong, in *practice* it is not, and its making it wrong does not matter. It is obvious that the applied ethics of this society, as far as the application of this principle, or of the theory whose component it is, is concerned, would be different from the applied ethics of another society which is not permissive about that sort of action.

Admitting an exception to the application of a moral principle may be justified or unjustified. It is justified when it is made on a moral ground, i.e. for a moral reason. For example, an exception to the principle of truth-telling is made when it is said in its classical Indian formulation that truth ought to be total but not when it is unpleasant because of its causing some unjustified hurt to someone. This is purport of the principle in its statement as 'Truth be told, but not the unpleasant truth (*satyam bruyāt na bruyāt satyamapriyam*)'. An exception to a principle is unjustified when it is made on a non-moral ground, say, on the ground of some convenience, prejudice, or because of a prevailing social practice that has become too well-established to be dislodged though it is morally undesirable. It is on some such ground or grounds that an exception is made to a principle in a permissive society, or in a society which is permissive in respect of the immoralities that the exception makes unforbidden or condonable.

When a permissive attitude towards a wrong action, towards an immorality, becomes well-established, that sort of action or immorality begins to be considered by many as falling outside the scope of the principle which makes it wrong. This amounts to considering the principle inapplicable to it, and thereby changing the scope of the principle by taking that sort of action as falling outside the zone of its applicability. Since an action of that type still *seems* to fall under its zone, the society starts considering it an *exception* to the principle. Its stand would then be that, although the principle straightforwardly makes it wrong, it really does not do that because any action of this type is an exception to it. Here, the applied ethics of this permissive society introduces a change in its theoretical ethics. A principle, which was earlier believed to make any action whatsoever of a certain type wrong if the action infringed it, would now have to be stated in a modified form in which its infringement would not make wrong a particular sector of that type of action.

To illustrate what has been said above in a general, somewhat abstract, manner, let us take the principle forbidding any sort of adulterous relationship in the framework of classical Indian ethics. *Conjugal loyalty* is an important moral virtue in classical Indian ethics and therefore adultery an obvious moral vice. The concept of adultery is as precise in it as it is in any ethical practice, meaning a married individual's sexual relation with a woman or man other than his or her spouse. But the practice of a male person's having a sexual relation with his female servant (*dāsī*) seems to have been taken in a permissive manner. Therefore, a man having such a relation would not be accused of having committed adultery. The *Mahābhārata* very casually mentions that the born blind king Dhṛtarāṣṭra fathers a son by a young female servant of the *vaisya* caste employed in his service during the period of the pregnancy of his wife, Gāndhāri.[19] This son of his is named Yuyutsu who fights the *Mahābhārata* war along with his other sons against the Pāṇḍavas. He fights as gallantly as the others do, and, like them, is killed in the fight by the Pāṇḍavas. If such a practice in sexual ethics is taken commonly in permissive manner and becomes widely tolerated, the concept of adultery would become less stringent than it is taken to be. It would then have to be stated, in respect of a male person, in some such watered-down form as 'A sexual relation of a married male person with any woman other than his wife, except with a female servant of his, is adulterous'. This statement obviously reduces the rigour of the prohibition of adultery as a moral principle for men. Equally obviously, it lets the principle remain absolutely rigorous for a married woman.

To take another example, when the practice of female prostitution is taken permissively by a society, then a sex relation of a married male with prostitute too would have to be considered non-adulterous, or not forbidden as a bona fide act of adultery is. This has to be the case because toleration of the practice of prostitution by a society implies that that society expects and tolerates a male person's, married or unmarried, visiting a prostitute. Therefore, this society cannot call a married male's sexual relation with a prostitute adulterous and therefore forbidden. This implication is clearly visible in the law prevalent in the state of Vaiśālī of Buddha's times which required that the most beautiful young woman of the state be not allowed to get married to anyone, but be made the *nagara badhū*, the state's, the people's, wife, i.e. a prostitute. The ground given for this practice is that, being the most beautiful woman, she must be made available to anyone, but of course, not without her consent. She must not, therefore, be the property of only one person, which she would be if she is married to anyone. Then no one else would have to right to ask her for her services. It is this law, which *Āmrapālī* calls a *dhikkṛta*, condemned, law, that forces her to become Vaiśālī's *nagar badhū* in spite of her and her father's stiff resistance to it.[20]

If both the exceptions, the one suggested by the example of Dhṛtarāṣṭra and the other by that of Āmrapālī, are incorporated in a statement about what makes a sexual relation adulterous, the concept of an adulterous relation will get further loosened or watered down. It will then mean a sexual relation of a married male person with a woman other than his wife is adulterous *except* when it is a relation with a female servant of his or with a prostitute. Consequently, the moral principle forbidding adultery would also get further loosened for married males. All this illustrates very convincingly how an applied ethics of the permissive type can lead to narrowing down the scope of a moral principle or concept and thereby affect the ethical theory of which the principle is a component.

It is clear from the preceding discussion that an ethical theory, or the concept it explicates, is of no use, or is non-functional, if it is not possible to definitively affirm or deny it of anything in the range of things to which it could be affirmed or denied of without causing any semantic or logical oddity. For example, if it is not possible to affirm or deny of any action that it is morally right or wrong if the concept of moral rightness is understood or defined in a certain way, then, the concept as per that understanding or definition, or the theory which characterizes it in this way, is of no use. Therefore, the concept is not a genuine moral concept and the theory is not a genuine moral theory.

To illustrate this truth let us take the theory that an action is morally right if it is a means to procure for its doer an abode in the company of god (*Īśvara-sānidhya*) in heaven after his death and another one which holds that it is morally right if it is approved of by god. The first one is a consequentialist theory according to which the criterion of the moral rightness of an action is a consequence of doing the action. But it is a consequence of a sort which cannot be verified. We cannot verify of any action that has been done that it has produced such a consequence, nor of an action that is being done, or is intended to be done, that it will, or has a probability, low or high, of producing it. This means that this consequentialist criterion cannot be applied to any action to judge whether or not it is morally right. Therefore, the theory which offers it would be totally inapplicable and of no practical value in guiding anyone in choosing to do something morally right after ascertaining whether or not it satisfies the criterion laid down by the theory.

The other theory which presents the criterion in terms of god's approval is deontological but equally unusable in moral choice for almost the same reason. It would not be possible for anyone to know of any action whether or not god approves of his doing it. Consequently, he cannot use this criterion either, to determine whether or not an action is morally right. Obviously, then the theory which offers it would become inapplicable, and of no use to anyone in leading a moral life.

Suppose one presents a third theory which tries to incorporate both of the above two theories by holding (a) that an action is morally right if it is a means to the doer's procuring god's company after his death, or is approved of by god, and (b) that actions, which satisfy and which do not satisfy either one of the two disjunctive criteria, are listed in a certain sacred book or scripture (*śāstra*), say, in a *Veda* or a *Dharmaśāstra.* This theory may be said to be applicable if the concerned scripture lists some actions as satisfying one and some others as satisfying the other criterion. But it would be of no help in determining the rightness of an action not listed therein, and there may be many which are not included in the scriptural list. But the more serious problem with the applicability of the scriptural theory would be posed by the question of the authenticity of the author of the scripture, or of the list-maker, in ascertaining of any action in his list that it satisfies either one of the two criteria. Unless this question is satisfactorily answered, the theory would be of no help to any individual with an alert, inquisitive, critical mind. This question, being in effect unanswerable, would take away a large share of the normative, action-guiding, power of the theory.

All of the above three theories can be seen to have been suggested in some classical Indian theistic or devotional writings. An individual who is not of a critical mind may accept one or the other of them and may not see any problem in accepting it. In his application of the theory to some concrete cases, he may go by the opinion of some individual or group he considers dependable in moral affairs. Normally, such a person would be guided by the third, the scriptural, theory which combines the first and the second. Even in deciding what is in accordance with the scripture or scriptures concerned, such a person may be guided by the views held by the dependable members of his family, his kith and kin, living or dead, by the views which constitute his *familial moral code* (*kulācāra*), or by the views held by the people of his area which constitute his *region's moral code* (*deśācāra*), or by the views held by the majority of the people of his country over a long period of their history. Such views constitute the traditional or conventional moral code of his people (lokācāra). It is possible for any one of the three moral codes to be non-theological, or to contain some moral beliefs which are non-theological while some others which are theological. A non-theological moral belief may be societal or racial. For example, it may be held by the people of a certain caste that an individual's marrying within his caste preserves the purity of the caste and therefore is morally right. When a moral belief occurring as a component of anyone of the three codes is non-theological, its application would not be in principle impossible in the manner that belief in an action's being a means to procuring propinquity with god, or in the action's having been approved of by god, is. It may have some other problems, but this is not the place to discuss this possibility.

What has been said in the last few paragraphs very clearly shows that an ethical concept, or an ethical theory stating a criterion of its application or instantiation, must be usable or helpful in actual decision-making in real situations on most of the occasions it is relevant to. But in some situation or situations, for no fault of its own, it may not be *definitively* applicable, or helpful in telling an individual in an unambiguous way what he should do. This kind of uncertainty may arise in the application of any moral concept no matter whether it is the concept of rightness, obligation, value, virtue, or claim or right. This exigency is a fact of human life, or of the world in which man lives. It arises, or is likely to arise, because of the complexities of human life, the changing demands of man's private and public life on his time and energy, the changes in his social relationships and in his conception itself of what he and his world ought to be, the new kinds of benefits or burdens accruing to him from socio-economic developments. The existence of such an eventuality would not make the theory invalid or untenable.

When a situation of the above type arises, it provides to a theorizer an occasion for doing some rethinking. He may rethink about the seemingly problem-causing nature of the situation and try to reinterpret it in a certain way, or about the nature or scope of the principle for the application of which it is causing some problem. The principle of non-violence is not completely missing in Indian ethics before the rise of Jainism and Buddhism. But it is not given the paramount place in ethical living which is given to it in Jainism and Buddhism, more predominantly in Jainism which does not allow any kind of violence. *Vedic* thinkers, or people under the influence of *Vedic* ethics or traditions, consider animal sacrifice, i.e. killing an animal to propitiate a deity, a permissible or recommended practice. Jain and Buddhist thinkers do not consider sacrificial killing in any way less immoral then non-sacrificial killing. This leads to a rethinking about the nature and scope of the principle of non-violence (*ahimsā*) which now assumes the form 'Commit no violence, not even that which is sanctioned or recommended in a sacred work like a *Veda*.' The universalization of the principle also results in a rethinking about the nature of sacrificial killing, insofar as sacrificial killing now becomes non-different in ethical status from any other kind of killing. People under the influence of Vedic ethical traditions also do some rethinking. They consider sacrificial killing not reprehensible because, according to them, it causes no real violence to the sacrificed animal since the animal goes to heaven after it is killed in a sacrificial ceremony. This is expressed in the principle commonly stated, sometimes satirically, sometimes straightforwardly, as 'Violence permitted or prescribed in a *Vedic* ritual is not real violence (*Vaidikī himsā himsā na bhavati*).' But doing this also leads to a rèthinking about the principle of non-violence. If the above principle is accepted then violence committed in a sacrifice becomes an exception to the universal principle of non-violence. Now the principle of non-violence stands modified as 'Commit no violence, except when it is sanctioned or recommended in a sacred work like a *Veda*.' Sacrificial killing now would fall outside the scope or zone of the principle of non-violence.

Rethinking about moral principles or concepts as well as about things to which they are to apply is common. As already said, sometimes it is done to make more precise the ethical notion or notions involved in a principle, sometimes because of the occurrence of a situation like the one mentioned above. But an important thing to be noted is that there are certain things which are paradigmatic examples of morality or immorality. These are things which our moral intuitions, our moral common sense, untutored and unbiased, consider to be obviously moral or immoral. For example, derobing a woman in public is morally wrong, and getting it stopped or obstructed morally commendable. Our moral intuition would never consent to calling the derobing morally permissible, no matter who is the woman being derobed, who does the derobing, whatever may be the reason for his doing it, and whatever may be the place and time of his doing it. Similarly, it would never call getting it stopped or obstructed morally wrong. Such palpable, paradigmatic cases work as a touchstone for a moral theory. A theory of morality which makes derobing a woman morally permissible, even debatable or undecidable whether it is, or it is not, immoral, would eo ipso, on that very account, be a wrong or invalid theory. In such a case it is not the concerned instance of morality or immorality which needs to be rethought. Rather, it is the theory which declares an instance of a palpably immoral thing to be moral or undecidable, or one of a palpably moral thing to be immoral or undecidable, which needs to be rethought. These things will be made clearer in the coming section which presents some Indian specimens of what has been called theorizing in a piecemeal fashion.

6.7 SOME INDIAN SPECIMENS OF ETHICAL THEORIZING THE PIECEMEAL WAY: CONTENTUAL AND CONTEXTUAL

The way generally adopted by some of the best-known Western moral philosophers is to present first a general theory of moral value, of obligation or of both, depending on which one, or ones, of moral concepts the theorizer considers basic or central, and then to try to exhibit how it comprehends or explains the different themes, issues, or problems which arise in man's moral transactions. It is like first making a big umbrella and trying to include within it all the animals which need to be protected from the rains. The theorizer may in this attempt, have to modify the theory to explain a tricky problem, or to explain or analyse away a problem, not comprehensible within his theory, by trying to show that it is a pseudo-problem or a non-moral problem, say, metaphysical, psychological, sociological, etc. This way of theorizing, as it has been said earlier, does not seem to be the mode adopted by classical Indian philosophers or ethicists.

While doing metaphysics, Indian metaphysicists do adopt the above method, or a method very close or similar to it. For example, Rāmānuja first presents a general theory of ultimate reality, calling it God (*Brahman* or *Īśvara*), having two parts, conscious (*cit*) and non-conscious (*acita*), and explains the emergence of all things of the world from these two parts, the conscious things from the conscious part and the non-conscious things from the non-conscious part of the supreme being. This process of their emergence is, according to him, a process of creation by God, an act of God's will. A similar methodology in metaphysical theorizing is also adopted by other schools, like the *Nyāya-Vaiśeṣika, Sānkhya, Advaita Vedānta,* etc. We have seen that the *Advaitin* Śankara's general theory of reality being an extreme kind of abstract monism—because the ultimate reality, *Brahman,* according to it, is a pure, partless, contentless, unity—he has to call the world of multiplicity unreal, to introduce the concept of ignorance (*avidyā* or *nyāyā*) to explain why it appears to be real when it is not, and the concept of its being real only for practical purposes to accommodate the possibility of ethical life in it.

The theory of liberation in Indian axiology is, in the case of every, or almost every, school of philosophy a child of its metaphysical theory. Therefore, all the schools whose metaphysics admits it, or is congruent with it, have a *general theory of liberation.* But a theory of liberation is not an ethical theory, or, to say the same thing, liberation is not necessarily or obviously an ethical goal, because even he who does not accept any one of the various theories of liberation can also lead an impeccable ethical life.

Classical Indian metaphysical theories and therefore theories of liberation which go with them, have caught more attention of modern Western and Indian interpreters than have the other areas of Indian philosophy, including even its epistemological and logical theories. They find in its speculative metaphysics a clear presence of general theories of reality and also of liberation, but a clear absence of a general theory, or of an attempt to formulate one, in its ethics or moral philosophizing. They then conclude that there is no theory in Indian ethics, or rather, no ethics in Indian philosophy because without there being any ethical theory there cannot be ethics. They admit that there do exist in it a large number of moral maxims but also point out that a mere list of maxims cannot constitute an ethical theory or a moral philosophy.

I would like to go a little further and say that no set of moral maxims, however large it may be, can be large enough to cover all possible ethical problems or issues which may arise in all possible situations in man's private and public transactions, in his dealings with other human or non-human beings. This is bound to be so because the world, or the human world, is never static; all the possible demands of life which may necessitate moral thinking on the personal or societal level cannot be met with, or given hints for being met with, by any set of moral maxims formulated, once and for all, by any authority or set of authorities. It would be worse than chauvinism to make any such claim of any set of classical Indian set of moral maxims. Classical Indian thinkers do seem to recognize this ethical fact, and that is one of the reasons, if not the only one, or the primary one, for their theorizing in a contextual, topical, particularist manner, through, sometimes, constructing imaginatively, mythical, anecdotal, hypothetical situations, as if to remind mankind of the ethical or human truth that ethical thinking is an ever-going, unending or open-ended, process, that an individual should hope to receive from the ethical corpus they are bequeathing to him only some broad guidelines, or hints, for his *own* solving of his ethical problems, and not ready-to-use, pre-cooked, instant, solutions to them, that the solutions the corpus may suggest have to be rethought keeping in view the context, the situation, in which a problem has risen. It is to be noted that thinking on these lines does not go against the view that every moral solution is generalizable because it does not mean that a general moral principle is to be deductively, mechanically, applied to any concrete case; every application of a moral principle involves at least some amount of decision-making.

The Western or Indian interpreters are right when they say that a list of maxims do not make an ethical theory but not right when they deny the existence of ethical theorizing in Indian philosophy. They deny it, as has been pointed out earlier, because they have in their mind only one model of ethical theorizing, i.e. theorizing which results in the formulation of general theories of moral value, obligation, rightness of action, etc. They do not realize that theorizing may also be done in a piecemeal, topical, issue- or theme-wise, fashion, without putting a set of such theorizings in a general comprehensive theory as its well-linked components. All this is true not only of some Western but also of some Indian interpreters who are otherwise very respectful of what Indian ethicists have done or given. For example, Haridas Bhattacharyya begins his essay 'Indian Ethics' with the statement that 'ethics is not to be had as a separate study in Indian philosophical and religious literature'.[21] Similarly, P.S. Sivaswamy Aiyer says that 'compared with the amount of attention given by Hindu thinkers to the subjects of religion and philosophy, the scientific study of ethics has received very little attention from them'.[22] By 'the scientific study of ethics' Aiyer clearly means the construction of any systematic, general, theory in ethics. 'The *Upaniṣads*', he goes on, 'are mainly concerned with problems of metaphysics and it is only very rarely that one meets with moral rules as in the *Taittirīya Upaniṣad*.'[23] In a sense he is right, and so are others who assert that there is no comprehensive ethical theory construction in Indian philosophy. What they miss is the presence of topical, contextual, what I have been calling piecemeal, theorizing or analysis, resulting in a generalization which is expressed in the form a moral rule, maxim, etc.

The word 'piecemeal', as used here, is not to be taken in any pejorative sense, as it is sometimes taken, for example, in calling a description piecemeal because it describes a situation in unconnected bits or pieces. Ethical problems always arise in some concrete, specific, even particularized, situations, and therefore they always have their roots in some real, or real-like, situations in the life-history of an individual or of a society or group. Whatsoever solution is reached, it is reached through a process of theorizing or analysis. This process is always there though it may not be clearly visible. And, when the solution is reached, it is in principle generalizable, and therefore it is stated in the form of a moral rule, maxim, etc. It amounts to averring that in a situation *like* S any individual *like* A ought (or ought not) to do something *like* what A ought (or ought not) to do in S. The likeness meant at every point here is moral likeness, i.e. similarity in morally relevant respects. That is why piecemeal theorizing is always topical and contextual and therefore more down-to-earth than abstract, highly general, theorizing. The moral problem which generally confronts us is not 'What should I in general do?', but 'What should I do in the situation I am in (or am going to be in, in the near future)?'

When a philosopher philosophizes about a moral situation, he may himself be in that situation. But he does not have to be; he may even creatively imagine himself or someone else to be in a certain type of situation posing a certain type of problem. Therefore, he may even hypothesize i.e. construct an anecdote about, a fictional account of, a morally sensitive person facing a moral problem in a certain type of situation and via the fictional person's ratiocination reach a solution which can be stated as a moral principle. This method is very commonly used by classical Indian thinkers, as is exhibited in a work of anecdotes like the *Pañcatantra*, already referred to, and at very many places in the two epics, the *Mahābhārata*, the *Rāmāyaṇa*, and in some others.

It is a very difficult affair to theorize about the nature of ultimate reality, to give anything like *parāvidyā*, an inquiry which is the basis, or the final terminus, of all inquiries (*sarvavidyāpratiṣṭhām*). It may also be difficult to theorize on morals with the objective of presenting an ethics or philosophy of morals which may be said to have reached the final terminus of all moral inquirings. But it may not be very difficult, and may appear to be natural, to theorize on concrete, topical, ethical issues. However, classical Indians choose the latter mode of theorizing not because it is an easy affair. Choosing this alternative because of its being easier is not likely to be the reason of philosophers who take delight in philosophizing about such abstruse themes as the nature of ultimate reality and of ultimate value (liberation) which may or may not be attainable by a living individual. To me it seems that their reason for this choice is their respect for the down-to-earth character of man's ethical concerns. But all that has been said so far needs to be made clearer by means of some specimens of the Indian style of piecemeal ethical theorizing. Since only a few specimens can be given to keep this value within its planned or projected limits, I shall explain in what follows some such instances of this style which are not only important for Indian ethics but also for ethics as such.

6.7.1 Akrasia

Akrasia, moral weakness, weakness of the will, or moral failure as I have called it at another place,[24] consists in an individual's doing, or feeling inclined or motivated to do, something which he himself knows or acknowledges to be morally wrong, as well as in *not* doing, or *not* feeling inclined or motivated to do, what he himself knows or acknowledges to be morally right. It is therefore an expression or evidence of his moral weakness, failure, or of his having a morally weak will, i.e. the will to do the right and to abjure doing the wrong. In his doing the wrong while *knowing* that it is wrong, or in his desisting from doing the right while knowing that it is right, an individual can be accused of being akratic only if his knowing that it is right (or wrong) is not merely his knowing that it is considered, admitted, or held to be right by some agency which may be some other person, some society, some scripture, etc. Rather, it must be his own knowing in an admissive, convictional sense; that is, in the sense of being his *own admitting* or *acknowledging* that it is right. For example, he may say that he knows that x-ing is his duty, his *varṇadharma,* according to his society, or according to those who accept the theory of *varṇadharma,* but he does not want to do it because he himself does not consider it his duty or *dharma,* or because he himself does not consider *varṇavyavasthā* to be a morally justified social order and therefore does not accept the theory of *varṇadharma* which is a child of the theory of *varṇavyavasthā.* He would not then be an akrete, i.e. guilty of akrasia. To conclude, akrasia consists in an individual's doing, or in being inclined to do, something which, as per his own best judgement or moral assessment, is morally wrong, as well as in his not doing, or in being disinclined to do, something which, as per his own best judgement or moral assessment, is morally right.

There is another thing which too is very important to note here. Any individual can be called an akrete only when he is an agent, more precisely a free agent; i.e. one who has the unobstructed ability and power, or capability (*abādhita sāmarthya*) to do what, in his best judgement, is morally right and to abstain from what, in his best judgement, is morally wrong. One who is not an agent, not a doer, but a tool in the hands of someone else, say, a slave required to do whatever his master wants him to do, cannot be credited with having *done* something right or wrong and therefore he cannot be accused of being an akrete. Similarly, nobody can be said to be an akrete or a non-akrete on the theory which holds that no human being is a real agent, that God is the only real agent, and that therefore, whatever a human being does, it is not he who does it but it is God who does it through him; he only seems to be its doer. On a strict fatalistic or deterministic theory too, quite obviously, we can neither accuse anyone of being an akrete, nor admire him for having shown moral strength, in having done, or in having abstained from doing, something.

The issue of akrasia has not been discussed in detail by classical Indian philosophers. One reason for their not doing that is that all the schools, or almost all of them, consider self-control (*dama*) an essential moral virtue and a virtue which is possible for everyone to cultivate. Self-control means an individual's controlling his desires, inclinations, propensities, passions, emotions and feelings, which may deter him from doing what is right, from abjuring doing what is wrong, from pursuing his spiritual goal (if he believes in it), etc. Since everyone can cultivate this virtue, which he also *ought* to, everyone has in principle the *ability* to overcome, or get rid of, moral weakness, i.e. his inability or failure to do the right even while knowing that it is right, or his desire to do something wrong in spite of his knowing that it is wrong.

This is not, however, a satisfactory reason for not discussing the problem of akrasia. Even if it is admitted that everyone *can* cultivate self-control, it does not mean that everyone does, or shall, cultivate this virtue. Therefore, the phenomenon of akrasia cannot be said to be a non-problem or an unreal problem. Nor can it be said that it did not occur in classical India. As we go on, in discussing this issue as an issue in Indian ethics, we shall see that there are examples of akratic action in the classical corpus. But in saying all this it is not intended to assert or even to imply that classical thinkers totally ignored this problem. It seems to me that they were very much aware of it and their attention was directed more towards saying what one should do to overcome it than towards explaining it or towards giving a conceptual analysis of it. But even the latter kind of exercise, i.e. that of explaining or analysing it, is not completely missing. The phenomenon of akratic will or action becomes a philosophical, or ethical, problem because almost all classical Indian thinkers in their moral philosophy (as also non-Indian ones) admit to a greater or lesser extent that anyone's *knowing* what is his *dharma*, has in it at least some built-in normative force, or motivative power, that is, it does exercise some motivative influence on him to move him towards doing the right or abstaining from doing the wrong. That is why so much emphasis was laid by them on moral education. All this is only to aver that moral knowledge, i.e. knowledge of right and wrong, good and evil, etc. is not for them a neutral, *purely* fact-stating or descriptive, reportive, cognition. To adapt a little bit an *Advaitic* terminology, this is like saying that just for anyone's knowing the ultimate reality or value is to realize it, his knowing the right, the *dharma*, is at least his becoming motivated towards doing it or towards following prescriptions (and proscriptions) of *dharma*. Therefore, when one does not do what is in accordance with *dharma* or does what is *adharma*, i.e. contrary to *dharma*, while knowing that the former is in accordance with (*dharmāmukūla*) and the latter is contrary to *dharma*, becomes a philosophical, or conceptual, problem which needs to be explained.

What Duryodhana is alleged to have once said to Kṛṣṇa is often mentioned by writers on Indian ethics or philosophy as a clear expression of (*his*) akrasia and therefore as an Indian example of akrasia. However, when we consider it in conjunction with the other three lines which immediately follow it, the intent of Duryodhana's saying it turns out to be something very different. This is particularly important because the other sentences which precede and occur later are completely unrelated to this theme and to Duryodhana. Duryodhana's statement, taken in its entirety runs as follows:

> 'I know what is *morally right* (*dharma*) but I have no *inclination* to do it. I know what is vice or *morally wrong* (*pāpa*, i.e. *adharma*) but I have no *disinclination* to do it. I do as I am prompted or motivated by some god seated in my heart (or conscience). O *Madhusūdana* (Kṛṣṇa), kindly be tolerant (or indulgent) about the wrongs I mechanically do. I am a machine (*yantra*) and you are the operator of the machine (*yantrī*). Please do not blame me' (for my misdeeds because you and not I are responsible for them, since I do only what you, the god seated in me, direct me to do).[25]

What Duryodhana intends to assert is that he is not an agent, and therefore not a moral agent and therefore is not to be blamed for the wrongs he does (or praised for the right things he does). He is not, for the simple reason that he is not a real doer; the real doer, one who propels him to do, who works through him, is god, i.e. Kṛṣṇa himself. As it has been pointed out above, if an individual is not admitted to be a free agent, if god is alone admitted to be the agent, then the concept of akrasia will become inapplicable to human beings. Duryodhana can be said to be an akrete if only the first sentence of the quoted sentences is taken into account, as all those who offer his utterance of it as an evidence of his being an akrete do. But this would not be fair. The point that is made here is not to prove that Duryodhana is not an akrete. It is rather to show that if agency is considered ascribable only to a god and not to a human being then no human being can be said to be an akrete. This would mean that akrasia is not a human phenomenon. But then morality too would cease to be a human phenomenon because anything moral or immoral can be done by a human being if and only if he is a free agent, a doer.

There is some problem with the quotation given above. The *Pāṇḍavagītā*, from which it has been taken, does not mention the context in which it is uttered by Duryodhana and it is unrelated to other items mentioned in the book. The first two sentences also occur in Vidyāraṇya's Pancadasī (Ramakrishna Math, Madras, VI.176, p. 192), with only one change: in place of *pāpam* the second part of the first sentence contains *adharmam*, which is only a verbal change of no consequence. Here too the context is not given. But the surprising thing is that Vidyāraṇya does not realize that the sting of akrasia in the first two lines goes away and so does morality, both as logical fallouts of making agency a feature of some divine being seated in the human individual. In fact, he tries to argue (VI.177, p. 197) that human agency is not denied because the Lord expresses Himself in human efforts. But that would not really make these efforts human efforts. They would be the Lord's efforts appearing as human efforts. Moreover, even this Vidyāraṇya, being a post-Śankara *Advaitin*, cannot say because the *Advaitin*'s Lord, i.e. *Brahman*, being formless and featureless, is a nondoer. Therefore, he cannot express or transform Himself in human efforts.

The trouble with this quotation is that it is given in both *Pañcadаsī* and *Pāṇḍavagītā* as an isolated piece. The translator of *Pañcadasī* says that it occurs in the *Pāṇḍavagītā* which occurs in the *Mahābhārata*. But the *Mahābhārata* does not contain the *Pāṇḍavagītā* and these lines do not occur in the *Mahābhārata*. Therefore, because of their being without any context, not much philosophical use can be made of them. I have discussed them here only to dispell the aura which has gathered around them as a clear expression of akrasia in Indian ethos because of the emphasis placed on them in modern writings on Indian ethics.

A better example of akrasia containing within it a multi-faceted theory is found in the answer given by Bhīṣma to Yudhiṣṭhira when the latter goes to the former, his granduncle, for his permission to fight with him, as well as for his blessing for victory in the *Mahābhārata* war, before the war begins. Yudhiṣṭhira also meets Droṇa, his teacher, and Kṛpa, his family's preceptor, on a similar mission. The same reply is given by each one of them encoding the same theory of akrasia, or similar ingredients of a theory of akrasia. This is because all the three occupy similar positions in the set-up of the Kaurava family and are committed to fight the war from the side of Duryodhana while admitting in their heart of hearts, with conviction, that Duryodhana's is a wrong cause and Yudhiṣṭhira's a right one. That is, each one of them knows what is the morally right and what is the morally wrong decision for him to take in respect of taking sides in the war and each one decides to fight for the (wrong) side. Therefore, each takes a decision which he considers morally wrong and thereby exhibits his akrasia or moral failure. But the way he expresses it and gives his reasoning for it contains a number of things which say a lot about his ethical attitude, and therefore about akrasia. I shall analyse only Bhīṣma's reply to make my points clearer. A similar analysis can be easily constructed on a similar pattern or in a similar mode relating to the reply of Droṇa or Kṛpa in the context of their status in Duryodhana's administrative set-up. What Bhīṣma says to Yudhiṣṭhira in response to his request amounts to this:

Everybody is a slave to material conditions of comforts (*artha*); the latter, *artha*, is not a slave to anyone. I am enslaved to the Kauravas, i.e. Duryodhana, because they provide to me all the comforts of life. That is why I am speaking to you like an impotent person or a slave because I cannot fight from your side in the war, even though I know that you are going to fight for a right cause while they are to fight for a wrong cause. I am obliged to them because of the benefits I receive from them. Therefore, you should not ask me to be on your side in the war. You may ask for anything else.[26]

Bhīṣma is not an ordinary person in the classical Indian ethical corpus. Rather, he is one who has received the best education, who is famous not only for his knowledge of *dharma* or morality but also for his actually being an ideal moral individual. This is clear from the *Mahābhārata*'s presenting him as the best available knower of morality (*dharmajña*) to whom Kṛṣṇa sends Yudhiṣṭhira, after his winning the war, to receive lessons in private and public morality. And, this Kṛṣṇa does when he also knows that Yudhiṣṭhira himself is an exemplar of morality. Therefore, when such a person as Bhīṣma confesses that he cannot avoid doing what he himself considers to be wrong, it clearly means that the Indian ethos admits that akrasia is a human phenomenon. This conclusion is further strengthened when Droṇa and Kṛpa, whom too the Indian tradition considers highly morally devoted, ditto Bhīṣma's views.

What Bhīṣma says to Yudhiṣṭhira, when probed into, is found to contain elements explaining akrasia in more than one way. Firstly, if his words are taken at their face value, they say that an individual does, or may do, the wrong while knowing that it is wrong, i.e. may become akratic, because some of his desires overcome or subdue his moral sense i.e., his sense of right and wrong. This is also the common-sense view of akrasia. Secondly, they suggest that benefits or advantages received even from a person not morally upright generate an obligation for the recipient to stand by the side of the benefactor even if his is the wrong side from the moral point of view. Bhīṣma, Droṇa, and Kṛpa, all three would say that Duryodhana would be fighting for a morally unjustified cause insofar as he would be fighting the war in order to deprive, if he were to win, the Pāṇḍavas of their rightful share in the kingdom of Kurukṣetra, whereas the Pāṇḍavas would be fighting for a morally justified cause because they would be fighting only for regaining their rightful share in the kingdom. But still they feel obligated (*baddha*) to support Duryodhana because of the benefits they have received from him, i.e. because the benefits received have generated an obligation to support him in the war. This obligation to support the benefactor, who would be fighting an unrighteous war (*adharmayuddha*), may be said to be a lower, an inferior, kind of obligation than the obligation to support him whose cause is morally justified. Bhīṣma's words suggest, therefore, that akrasia also consists in fulfilling a lower grade of obligation at the cost of going against, or hurting, an obligation of a decidedly superior status. Thirdly, deciding to fight from the side of Duryodhana is considered by Bhīṣma to be a requirement of his gratitude, whereas deciding to fight from that of Yudhiṣṭhira if he had decided to do that, would have been a requirement of justice. Gratitude may be called a personal virtue because it is generally called forth, i.e. an individual is required to be grateful to someone else, when the latter has done some good to the former. Justice, on the other hand, may be called an impersonal, social, virtue because for being fair or just to someone else an individual does not need to have been benefited or helped in any way by him. Bhīṣma is preferring to be grateful to Duryodhana to being just or fair to Yudhiṣṭhira and so are Droṇa and Kṛpa. Therefore, his words also suggest that akratic behaviour may also consist in preferring a personal virtue to an impersonal or social one. We can see, it is clear from the above analysis, that several theoretical devices are suggested by Bhīṣma's (as also by Droṇa's and Kṛpa's) response to Yudhiṣṭhira to explain *why* akrasia *takes place* as well as to explain *what* it may be said to *consist* in, though one may not find these devices written in bold letters on the forehead of the statement.

The problem of akrasia is also handled, or may be seen to have been handled, by Śankara in an *Advaitic* manner in his commentary on the *Gītā*'s III.37–39. According to him, or according to the *Gītā* as per his interpretation, it is desire (*kāma*) which is the cause of all evil (*sarvānarthaprāptih*) because it alone prompts an individual to do any evil. Even anger is basically a desire since it is a desire which when frustrated (*pratihatah*) turns into anger (*krodhatvena pariṇamyate*). The evil-doers are of two kinds. To one kind belong those who do an evil as instigated by a desire without feeling any kind of compunction, agony, or repentance. Rather they feel happy in fulfilling that desire. While behaving under the influence of the desire (*tṛṣṇākāle*) he considers it to be a friend (*mitram*) of his. He feels sorry or repentant only when an unpleasant consequence of his following the desire's prompting befalls him (*tatkārye dukhe prāpte*). Only then he realizes that his suffering has been caused by his desire; not before that. Śankara calls such a person a fool (*mūrkha*), since while doing the act, i.e. while following the prompting of his desire, he does not realize that he is doing anything wrong. His realization of this fact occurs only after some suffering is caused to him as an effect of his having followed the prompting of his desire. This means that he would not realize this fact, or the fact that the desire is the source of evil, if, perchance, no suffering were to accrue to him from his desire-prompted actions. Such a man cannot be called an akrete; a victim of his own akrasia, because he does not do the wrong knowing that what he is doing is wrong.

To the other kind belongs, Śankara says, he who knows what is the right thing to do, he who knows that following the lead of a desire is to be misled to do the wrong. But his knowledge is covered, overshadowed, or overpowered by his desire, his appetitive nature, just as a fire is covered by its concomitant smoke, etc. Therefore, he knows that what his desire is motivating him to do is wrong but, since his knowledge has been subdued by the desire, he follows its lead. In following its lead he is aware that he is doing something wrong and therefore he feels sorry, guilty, or repentant, even while satisfying the motivating desire. This behaviour of the knower of the right is quite obviously akratic. Śankara's conclusion is that only a knower of the right, of the fact that desire is the cause of all evil, can be said to have knowingly done something wrong. Therefore, desire can be said to be the enemy only of a knower because it can make him akratic.[27]

A good number of other commentators on the *Gītā*, like Rāmānuja, Madhusūdana Sarasvatī, and Śrīdhara Svāmī also seem to agree with Śankara in their commentary on the *Gītā*'s III.37–39 presented above. In fact, what Śankara says seems to be the general classical Indian position about the nature of akrasia. Even while knowing what is the right and the wrong a knower may do the wrong, i.e. become akratic, when his knowledge is overpowered by some desire which prompts him to do the wrong even when his knowing that what he is doing or going to do is wrong continues to remain unaffected; it only has become ineffective.

While discussing earlier the statement which Bhīṣma has made (as have Droṇa and Kṛpa) to Yudhiṣṭhira, we have seen that Bhīṣma has admitted that he is not willing to fight the war from the side of Yudhiṣṭhira, or even to abstain from fighting on the side of Duryodhana, because of his *desire not to disoblige*, or because of his desire to remain loyal to, Duryodhana on account of his meeting all the expenses for his maintenance. This very well fits in with Śankara's analysis of knowingly doing the wrong. But it is possible that an akrete may not so straightforwardly say why he has become akratic, or may not even admit that he has become akratic when he really has become one.

If an individual entertains a desire, or has a feeling, which is morally undesirable or condemnable, but does not implement it into action, i.e. does not do what the desire, or feeling, prompts him to do, then he is not akratic. We may still say that he has a moral deficiency. But since he somehow picks up strength to avoid doing anything undesirable as prompted by his undesirable desire or feeling, we would not accuse him of being akratic or of suffering from moral weakness of the will. We may say that he exhibits an example which is not of akrasia but rather what may be called inverse akrasia. An individual exhibits inverse akrasia when he has a desire to do the wrong knowing that it is wrong, but when the occasion for doing it arrives, he does the right, or simply abstains from doing the wrong he had wanted to do.

One who considers any sort of akrasia a moral defect or deficiency would still accuse him of being akratic or of moral failure even if he does the right but entertains a desire or feeling to do the wrong, a desire or feeling morally condemnable in this or that sense. For example, as per Yudhiṣṭhira's assessment of Draupadī's behaviour with her five husbands, she has a greater feeling of love for Arjuna than she has for any other of the remaining four, though in her behaviour she has been equally affectionate to all of the five brothers. She might have controlled her feeling of greater love for Arjuna who alone has won her in the contest among the then famous princely archers for marrying her. One may even say that she has the moral strength not to let her feeling for Arjuna affect her behaviour towards her other four husbands. At the most, one may say, she may be said to suffer from inverse akrasia, i.e. of having a greater preference for Arjuna than for any other when she is expected to have equal love for all the five. But instead of treating Arjuna better than any other, she treats all of them equally lovingly and respectfully. This trait of hers, if it is a sign of akrasia, can be said to be a sign only of inverse akrasia, of being disposed to do knowingly the wrong but actually doing the right. But Yudhiṣṭhira thinks it to be a sign of her moral failing or failure, as is any case of akrasia. When the five brothers and *Draupadī*, after the end of the war, are climbing the hills in their journey to heaven, at one point of the climb Draupadī falls down. Bhīma asks Yudhiṣṭhira why she falls down when she has done nothing wrong. Yudhiṣṭhira replies[28] to him by saying that she falls because she has a warmer feeling of love for Arjuna than for any of her other husbands. That is, even having a morally unjustified feeling, not expressed in behaviour, is also for Yudhiṣṭhira as clear a case of akrasia or moral failure, as is an akratic feeling implemented into actual behaviour.

6.7.2 Obligation and Stringency

Whenever an obligation (*pratibaddhatā, kartavyatā*) accrues to a person, whatever may be its source, and he acknowledges it as his obligation, he feels necessitated to fulfil it. It is this necessitation which brings into the obligation the element of stringency. When an obligation is obvertly conditional, even then its stringency remains intact. Suppose, a Hindu becomes a Jain and therefore acknowledges that since he has become a jain, he ought not to eat any non-vegetarian food. To be a vegetarian for him is a conditional obligation. It may be for someone else an unconditional obligation, but for him it is not. The day he ceases to be a Jain and becomes a *Sākta* Hindu, he may start eating non-vegetarian food. But the stringency even of a conditional obligation, however, may be said to be absolute. As long as the individual is a Jain, it is absolutely necessary, or stringent, for him to abstain from eating any non-vegetarian food. When he ceases to be a Jain, his obligation itself goes away and therefore there is no question of its being or not being stringent, or of the degree of its stringency.

It is therefore true that every obligation, whether it is stated in the form of a conditional or categorical sentence, conceptually, or almost conceptually, possesses some sort of stringency. Hence a question arises as to whether every obligation, or only some obligations, can be said to possess absolute stringency. In Indian ethics three main types of views seem to have been prominently held. One view is that after an individual's incurring and acknowledging an obligation, the obligation is absolutely stringent or binding. The other view is that, in principle, an obligation may in some condition be infringed without incurring any moral discredit and therefore its stringency can be said be only relative or situational. The third view, on the other hand, seems to maintain that an obligation may be ambiguous in respect of stringency; that is, one may have to interpret it and examine the situation in which its fulfilment is required to determine whether its stringency is absolute or relative.

What has been said above has not been said in this cut and dried manner, in any classical work but rather has been suggested in some contextual, descriptive, account of some notable person's handling an obligational problem, or a problem of moral choice. We can illustrate the first position by analysing Daśaratha's fulfilling his obligation to his third wife Kaikeyī, to grant any two wishes of hers, by agreeing to making her son Bharat the king of Ayodhya and asking his eldest son Rāma, whom he, on his own, has decided to enthrone, to go into exile for fourteen years, the two things she wants him to do. The context of this obligation is as follows:

Sometime in the past Daśaratha gets severely injured in fighting from the side of gods in a battle between gods and demons. Kaikeyī is with him then and nurses him back to normal health. Feeling extremely pleased with her services, or rather feeling grateful to her for the trouble she has taken, he blesses her by promising to fulfil any two wishes of hers, whatever the two wishes may be. She does not ask him to do anything at that time, saying she will do that sometime later. She asks him to do the above two things much afterwards when Daśaratha has decided to enthrone his eldest son Rāma in his own place and has made all the preparations for celebrating the ceremony of Rāma's coronation.

His decision is in keeping with his family's and country's tradition of a king's, on becoming old, enthroning his eldest son.

Daśaratha has incurred the obligation to fulfil any two wishes of Kaikeyī by his own act of promising to do that. It is a blanket promise to fulfil her two wishes whatever they may be. Taking the promise at its face value, one of both of her two wishes may even be immoral. But normally whenever any such promise of unlimited or unspecified generality is made, the common assumption is that the promise would not generate for the promiser any obligation to do anything immoral. It cannot, simply because it is an *a priori* deontic truth that nobody can be obligated to do anything immoral and fulfilling anyone's any immoral wish would be doing something immoral. One implication of this truth is that if the promisee asks the promiser to do something immoral, the promiser may reply by saying that his blanket promise does not obligate him to do it because doing it would be doing something immoral. Another, similar, implication would be that the promise itself may be said to become then null and void, and therefore the obligation it generates would vanish. The promisee by asking the promiser to do something immoral has used his option to ask and what he has asked is impermissible. Therefore, he has lost his chance to get the promise fulfilled.

Both of the two wishes Kaikeyī wants Daśaratha to fulfil are immoral and therefore impermissible. But Daśaratha does not use the above-mentioned deontic, logical device to tell her that the promise made by him to her has become void or dysfunctional by her asking him to do immoral things, nor does he say that he is not obligated to fulfil these two wishes because they are immoral. He, like Kaikeyī, takes his promise at its face value or in its literal sense, and still thinks that the stringency of his obligation to fulfil the wishes is absolute. He seems to proceed on the assumption, or to hold the view, that any obligation after having been incurred is absolutely stringent. He does call the wishes cruel, unreasonable, or even immoral, but still does not think that on that account he is not obligated to fulfil them. Kaikeyī too thinks the same way: since he has promised to fulfil *any two* of her wishes, he is obligated to fulfil *these* two wishes of hers because *any two* of her wishes, conceptually, could be *any sort* of two wishes. She says to Daśaratha that he is bound by morality (*dharma*) to fulfil these wishes. Therefore, if he cares to abide by morality, she tells him, he is obligated to fulfil them.[29] Daśaratha too considers himself bound or constrained by morality to do so.[30]

When an obligation is considered absolutely stringent even if it is one to do something not morally right, the obligee can be freed or absolved from it only by the person to whom he is obligated; that is, he can be freed only if the person to whom he is obligated withdraws or takes back the demands the obligee is obligated to meet. This is what Daśaratha implores Kaikeyī to do, and when she does not, he fulfils her two wishes though the suffering caused to him by doing that is so unbearable that he breathes his last. But all along he considers the stringency of the obligation absolute, one which can in no case be toned town. In fact, as Tulsī Dāsa, in his epic story of Rāma, a later work patterned after Vālmīki's, puts it at one point when Kaikeyī questions Daśaratha's integrity and accuses him of having become akratic, he takes pride in reminding her that it is the moral tradition of the family of Raghu (to which he belongs) that one may breathe one's last but will not break one's promise.[31]

This view, which considers every obligation absolutely stringent, in whichever way it is incurred, whatever it obligates the obligee to do, makes it absolutely inviolable or unexceptionable, no matter what the consequences of fulfilling it are likely to be. Clearly, it is an example of an extreme kind of a deontological position. It has been quite often appealed to in classical writings. It may even be read into the stand taken by Bhīṣma et al., when they aver, as already discussed, that they are obligated to be on the side of Duryodhana in the war because of their being obligated to him to do that on account of the comforts he has provided to them. This they do while admitting that the objective for which he would be fighting the war is not morally defensible because it is to deprive, if he wins, the Pāṇḍavas of their rightful share in the kingdom. That is, they too consider the obligation that which has accrued to them absolutely stringent no matter how it has been generated and what may result from fulfilling it.

A slightly more liberal and conceptually well-grounded deontological position is exemplified in the stand which Karṇa takes about his obligation to support Duryodhana in the *Mahābhārata* war even after his having known that, by birth, he is a blood-brother (*sahadara bhrātā*) of the Pāṇḍavas, the other five sons of Kuntī, and the eldest of them. He is first informed by Kṛṣṇa and then by his real mother, Kuntī herself, that he is her eldest son by Sūrya, conceived and delivered by her before she was married to Pāṇḍu. Because of the fear of social and familial stigma she did not dare to keep him with herself. She, therefore, put him in a basket on the waters of a river to float with the stream. Kṛṣṇa tells him that according to the *Dharmaśāstras* the socially accredited father of a child, conceived and delivered by a girl in her unmarried state, is the man she is married to after its birth, whoever else may be its real, biological, father. The same is the practice, he says, with the child conceived by a girl before but delivered after her marriage. The first kind of child, he goes on, is, again as per social practice, called *kānīna* and the second kind *sahoḍha*. Immediately after Kuntī's revelation of the truth has been made to Karṇa, it is confirmed by a divine pronouncement from the world of Sūrya (Sūryamaṇḍala) which is really made by Sūrya himself.

The main purpose of Kṛṣṇa's and Kuntī's narrating to Karṇa the true account of his birth is to tell him that he has an *obligation* to fulfil Kuntī's, his real mother's, wish that he should come to the side of her other sons in the war with Duryodhana *simply because* she is his mother. According to both Kṛṣṇa and Kuntī the mere fact that Kuntī is Karṇa's biological mother is sufficient grounds to make Karṇa obligated to fulfil this, or any other, wish of hers.

Karṇa does not question the veracity of the account of his birth given by Kṛṣṇa and Kuntī. But he does question the alleged *grounds* of his obligation to Kuntī. He does not consider the *mere biological fact* of her being his mother a sufficient reason for his having any obligation to her. He brings in another, very basic, concept which is extremely important for understanding the generation, accrual, or ground, of an obligation. This is *the concept of role performance* which he very clearly uses in his reply to Kuntī. The substance of his reply to her is that since she conceived and delivered him, she certainly is his biological mother, but she is only his biological mother and not mother in the real sense of the term. She is not, he means to assert, because she *did not* at all perform the *role of a mother* to him. She put him in a basket on the surface of a river to float to his fate. It is Adhiratha who picked him up and played the role of a real father in bringing him up and it is his wife Rādhā who fed him her breast-milk and performed the role of a real mother. The thrust of his reply is that the mere fact of anyone's being socially or biologically related to someone is neither a sufficient, nor a necessary, reason or ground for the latter's having a social or filial obligation to the former. This is true of a biological mother and her son if she does not perform the role in relation to her child which a mother, from the ethical point of view, ought to perform. On the other hand, if another couple performs the role of real parents, as Adhiratha and Rādhā have done for him (Karṇa), he has his filial obligation to them.

Karṇa tells Kuntī in unambiguous terms that he does not think that he is obligated to fulfil her wish. And, his reason is that she did not perform a mother's role to him when he needed her care, and now she has come to remind him of his obligation to do what she wants him to do only out of her selfishness,[32] i.e. out of her earnestness to save Arjuna from being killed by him in the war and to ensure the Pāṇḍavas' victory. But he does own that he has his filial obligation to Adhiratha and Rādhā.

In a similar way, he argues about the validity of his obligation to be on the side of Duryodhana. Duryodhana, he says, performed extremely well the role of a friend by taking care of all of his needs and comforts by giving him a respectable social status, by making him a king, etc., on account of which there has accrued to him the obligation to stand by him in the war. This time he cannot, he says, desert Duryodhana and join the side of Pāṇḍavas on the tenuous ground, revealed by her just now, of having been born of the same mother they have been born of. Anyone who backs out from fulfilling his obligation to be on the side of his benefactor when the benefactor needs his help is like one, he avers, who has lived on the food he has stolen from his master's house. Such sinners can be happy neither in this nor in the next.[33]

Both of the obligations mentioned above, one to Adhiratha and Rādhā, and the other to Duryodhana, Karṇa considers absolutely stringent or inviolable. But he still grants one concession to Kuntī. He promises her that he will not kill any of her five sons except Arjuna, even if he is in a position to. This too he does because undertaking this obligation does not conflict with his promise to Duryodhana that he will do his best to defeat Arjuna by killing or capturing him alive. Karṇa's point is that an obligation undertaken earlier cannot be violated or superseded by a later one, but a new one may be undertaken which does not conflict with the earlier one while it also does not strengthen it. The new obligation he undertakes does not ensure Duryodhana's victory because it cannot be said with certainty that after Arjuna's defeat it would be impossible for the Pāṇḍavas to win. But obviously it is intended to give some solace to Kuntī even though she did not play the mother's role in relation to Karṇa who also is her son. To conclude, as per Karṇa's notion of an obligation, an obligation is, after it has been undertaken, absolutely stringent and conceptually linked with the performance of a role. He is obligated to Duryodhana because of the role of a friend which Duryodhana has played in relation to him, and he too thereby has become obligated to perform the role of a friend in relation to Duryodhana. But his notion is also liberal because it permits the undertaking of an obligation to a person, in some circumstances, irrespective of the role that person has or has not played. It is because of the introduction of the element of role-performance that Karṇa's notion of obligation has become more concrete or contentful than the one we find in Daśaratha's, though for both the stringency of an obligation is absolute.

The notion of obligation which we find in some of Kṛṣṇa's utterances and actions is more pragmatic and liberal. And, in his case too the theory involved in what he says or does is discoverable, as in the case of Daśaratha and Karṇa, from some of the contexts or incidents in which he makes use of it. On the point of stringency, in the *Gītā* which is a part of the *Mahābhārata*, he argues for the absolute stringency or inviolability of caste or class obligations (*varṇadharma*). It is on this ground that he tells Arjuna that he cannot and ought not to leave the battle-field and abstain from fighting a war, which for him is a righteous war. This he cannot, because he is a *kṣatriya* and it is the obligation of a *kṣatriya* to fight a righteous war.

The *Gītā* occurs in the *Bhīṣma-parva* of the *Mahābhārata*. In the same work, a little later, in the *Droṇabadha-parva*, he argues with Yudhiṣṭhira that he should break his general obligation to tell only the truth by declaring that Aśvathāmā, the son of Droṇa, has been killed though he has not been. His argument is that Yudhiṣṭhira can win the war only if Droṇa withdraws from the battle-field. But he will withdraw only if his son has been killed, and he will believe that he has been killed, even though he has not been, only if Yudhiṣtira makes this announcement because he believes that Yudhiṣṭhira tells only the truth and never a lie. And, Kṛṣṇa clearly means, as the context shows, that there is nothing morally wrong for Yudhiṣṭhira in telling this lie; that is, his, or anybody's, general obligation to tell the truth and only the truth, is, in some circumstances, exceptionable or violable. This amounts to conceding that a general obligation is not absolutely stringent. This point as well as the inviolability of caste-obligations will be discussed in detail in a later chapter. Therefore, only a brief account is given here to show that there also has been suggested, in a *contextual* manner, in Indian ethical literature, a theory according to which the stringency of all obligations is not absolute.

Since theory-involving things have been said in Indian ethical literature generally in some concrete, contextual, or anecdotal, description, quite often a theoretical, or substantive, ethical, idea suggested in the account is not clearly seen. For example, in the account of Yudhiṣṭhira's announcing the lie as a truth that Aśvathāmā has been killed, there is also suggested a substantive ethical truth, namely, the truth that one needs to possess oneself some greatness to appreciate a greatness in another person. In a war one enemy does not trust any announcement made by his enemy unless his own sources confirm it. But Droṇa believes that what Yudhiṣṭhira has announced is true, that his son has been killed, and as per his own prior declaration that he will withdraw from the war if his son is killed, gives up his arms and sits down unarmed. It is then that he is killed by Dhṛṣtadhyumna, a son of Drupada, as per his prior vow. Droṇa has the greatness in him to appreciate the greatness of Yudhiṣṭhira in being always truthful and therefore in being truthful even in making this announcement, though his greatness costs him his life. A Caṇakya, or, more probably, a Duryodhana, or even a Kṛṣṇa, would not have believed it without confirming it.[34]

6.8 WHY BE MORAL?

Indian ethical theorizing was done, as already said, not by first formulating an all-comprehensive theory and then testing it by applying it to concrete situations. Rather, it grew through reflecting on concrete cases and seeking solutions to the ethical problems they posed. Therefore, it always put forward that living morally well and living well in the world were something like two sides of the same coin; that is, to live a socially cohesive life was to live a moral life. That is why the question 'why be moral?' was not explicitly raised in classical Indian literature, though it was answered unambiguously by the very style of its ethicizing.

We may not locate in it a general, neatly formulated theory of obligation, for example, to the effect that what determines the nature of one individual's, say A's, obligation to another, say, B, is not B's biological, social, or professional, etc., status in relation to A, but it is B's well, or ill, performance, or non-performance, of the role which B, in virtue of his status in relation to A, ought to perform. However, the conceptual thrust, or truth, which this theory tends to highlight is very vividly, or concretely, made visible in the dialogue between Kuntī and Karṇa referred to in the previous section. Besides, the dialogue also indicates that to live well as a mother, or as a friend, is to live morally well, say, by performing well the role which a mother or a friend ought to perform. It is more accurate to say that it is this truth about the inseparability of living well and living morally well which the Indian concept of morality, or the etymological meaning of *dharma*, its Sanskrit equivalent, denotes, than to say, which modern Indian classical scholars never fail to reiterate, that *dharma*, derived from the root *dhṛ*, means that which, in a metaphysical sense, sustains the world or keeps it in order.

Indian society, it seems, from its earliest times, was structured as composed of several well-marked classes, castes, or groups. In such a society (or in any society for that matter) there are bound to be conflicts among groups or individuals because of their divergent interests, needs, or expectations. Conflicts have to be resolved and cooperation secured to ensure the members' living even a minimally peaceful, cohesive life. Morality works as a conflict-resolving, cooperation-producing agent among the constituents of any society, as the cement of social cohesion. Therefore, it is bound to be used almost always in social transactions to reduce conflict and to promote cooperation and cohesion. When it is so used, it is prone to give rise to generalizations or emergence of principles which may be used in the future, without requiring the people concerned to think afresh each time to find a way of resolving a conflict or promoting cooperation.

When generalizations or principles being to show up, it natural that theorizing, or ethicizing, takes some concrete shape. It is in this way that Indian ethical theorizing seems to have grown, and classical Indian philosophers do not seem to have disturbed this natural process of theory-emergence by giving to the then Indians a priori, neatly formulated, comprehensive, ethical theories providing clear-cut recipes to solve their multifarious ethical problems. Rather, they themselves derive their theoretical generalizations from concrete instances of people's resolving their conflicts, and illustrate them later, if required, by referring to past precedents, or, anecdotal reconstructions. This is one reason for there being available even now a rich stock of classical Indian ethical anecdotal literature, a rich treasury of moral tales. It is obvious from all this that classical Indian ethics, or moral philosophy, has from its very beginning developed in the context of the classical Indian social order which, therefore, needs to be carefully looked into. This will be done in the next chapter.

NOTES AND REFERENCES

1. Premchand, *Mānsarovara* (Hans Prakashan, Allahabad, 1965), pp. 18–26.
2. '*Brahma satyam Jaganmithyā Jivo Brahmaiva nāparah. Anena vedyam taechāstramiti Vedantadindimah,*' p. 66.20. This book has been translated by Dr N. Gangadharan. But the translation given above is mine. His translation is wrong as he translates *naparah* as 'distinct from' when it means 'not other than', as I have

done. It is a self-contradiction to say that the individual self 'is Brahman itself' and at the same time that 'it is distinct from it', as he does.

3. '*Brahma satyam Jaganmithyevanrupo viniscayah. Soayam nityānityavastuvivekah samudāhṛtah.*' *Vivekacuḍāmani* (Gita Press, Gorakhpur), p. 12.20.
The discriminative knowledge of the eternal and non-eternal is the recognition of the definitive truth that *Brahman* is real and the world unreal (translation mine).
4. Ibid., pp. 12–14: 22–27.
5. Ibid., pp. 12–15.
6. '*Satorhi dvayoh sambandhah sambhavati, na, sadsatoh.*' Śankara, *Brahma-Sūtra Bhāṣya*, 2.1.18.
It is possible for a relation to exist only between two reals, not between a real and an unreal. (It is obvious that it is not possible for it to exist between two unreals.)
7. (Gita Press, Gorakhpur), 11.1–4, pp. 68–71.
8. In the *Upaniṣad Anka of the Kalyāṇa* (Gita Press, Gorakhpur, Vol. 23, No. 1) 11.ii.2, p. 196.
9. Ibid., 6.6, p. 399.
10. (Gita Press, Gorakhpur), 2–5, pp. 8–9.
11. '*Sarvavyavhārānām prāk brahmātmātā vijñānāt satyatvopapatteh, svapnavyavahārsyeva prāk probodhāt ... Evam paramārthāvasthāyām sarvavyavahārābhāvam vadante vedāntāh sarve. Vyavahārāvasthāyām tu uktah srutāvapi īśvarādi vyavahārah.* Śankara, *Brahma-Sūtra Bhāṣya*, 2.1.18.
Before the attainment of knowledge of the identity of *Brahman* and the Self the empirical world (i.e. the world in which empirical things exist or empirical actions are done) is (considered) real, just as things experienced in a dream are (considered) real before waking up.
... And, in the state in which ultimate reality is known, the empirical world (the behavioural world) is recognized to be unreal; this all the *Vedānta* works, i.e. the *Upaniṣads*, say.
... Even the scriptures (*srutis*) say that god (*īśvara*), etc. belong to the category of the empirical world, i.e. they too remain real only as long as the empirical world is real, i.e. only before the attainment of knowledge of ultimate reality, i.e. of *Brahman*, or of the identity of *Brahman* and the Self (*Ātman*). (Translation mine).
For a detailed account of Śankara's analysis of this theme see *Brahma-Sūtra Bhāṣya*, translated by Swami Gambhirananda (Advaita Ashrama, Calcutta, 1997), pp. 326–33.
12. Śankara, *Gītābhāsya* (Gita Press, Gorakhpur), pp. 94–87, his elaboration of the *Gita*: III.20–25.
13. Viṣṇu Śarmā, *Pancatantra* (Choukhamba, Varanasi).
Ayam nijah paro veti gananā laghucetasām. Udāracaritānāntu vasudhaiva kutumbakam. Part V, story 3: 37, p. 42.
This is mine, that is someone else's, so think individuals of a narrow mind. For (morally) liberal gentlemen, the whole world is their family.
14. For a detailed statement of the human-centric model see my 'On the Adequacy of the Human-Centric Model of the Field of Moral Relations', *Philosophy and the Life-World*, Vol. III, March 2001, pp. 1–10.
15. *Mahabharata* Vol. 1 (Gita Press, Gorakhpur), pp. 894–906.
16. Ibid., Vol. 5, pp. 5093–5100.
17. Ibid., Vol. 5, pp. 5103–05.
18. Viṣākhadatta, *Mudrārākṣam* (Sahitya Bhandara, Meerut), p. 121.
19. *Mahābhārata* Vol. 1, *Sambhavapara*, p. 344.
20. For a vivid, detailed account of the life-story of Āmrapālī, see Acharya Chatursen's historical novel *Vaiśālī Kī Nagarbadhū* (Rajpal, New Delhi, 1947).
21. Haridas Bhattacharyya (ed.), *The Cultural Heritage of India*, Vol. III (Ramakrishna Mission, Calcutta, 1993), p. 620.
22. P.S. Sivaswamy Aiyer, *Evolution of Hindu Moral Ideals* (Nag Publishers, Delhi, 1976), p. 5.
23. Ibid., p. 20.
24. Rajendra Prasad, *Karma, Causation and Retributive Morality* (ICPR, New Delhi, 1989), Chapter 6.
25. *Jānāmi dharmam na ca me pravṛttih, Jānāmi pāpam na ca me nivṛttih.*
Kenapi Devena hṛdisthitena yathā niyuktoasmi tatha karomi. 58
Yantrsya mama doṣena śamytām Madhusūdana.
Aham yantram bhavān yantrī mama doso na dīyatām. 59
Pāndavagītā Evam Hansagītā (Gita Press, Gorakhpur), p. 33.

26. '*Arthasya puruso dāso dasastvartho na kasycit. Iti satyam Mahārāja baddhosmyarthena Kauravaih.* 41
Atastvam klivaved vākyam bravīmi Kurunandana. Bhutoasmyarthena Kauravya yudhadanyat kimiechasi.' 42
Mahābhārata, Vol. III, p. 2815–16. See p. 2817 for a similar statement made by Droṇa and p. 2818 for one by Kṛpa.
'O king, man is a slave of money, money is no man's slave. This is a truth. I am enslaved to the Kauravas for the money spent by them on me (for my needs and comforts). Therefore I speak to you like an impotent (enslaved) person. The sons of Dhṛtarāṣtra spend their money for my maintenance. Hence, besides asking me to fight from your side, you let me know what else you want from me.'
27. Śankara, *Gītābhāṣya* (Gita Press, Gorakhpur), pp. 162–63.
28. '*Pakṣapāto mahānasyā viśeṣeṇa Dhananjaye. Tasyaitat phlamaddaiṣā bhunkte puruṣasattama.*' *Mahābhārata*, Vol. 6, p. 6488: 6.
'(To Bhīma) O great man, she had in her mind a specially favourable attitude towards Arjuna; she is suffering today the consequence of that.'
29. '*Satyam samanuvartasva yadi dharma dhṛtā matih. Sa varah saphale meastu varado hyāsi sattama.*' Vālmīki, *Rāmāyaṇa*, Vol. I, p. 224.8
'If your (Daśaratha's) mind is seated in morality, you should follow the truth. You, a saintly person, should fulfil my wishes because you have given to me the blessing (right) to ask you do that.'
30. '*Dharmabandhena baddhoasmi.*' Ibid., p. 225–24.
31. '*Raghukula rīti sadā cali āyī. Prāṇa Jānhu baru bachanu na jāyī.*' Tuslī Dāsa, *Rāmacaritamānas* (Gita Press, Gorakhpur), p. 398.
32. '*Na vai mama hitam pūrbam mātṛvacceṣṭitam tvayā. Sā mān sambodhayasyaddya kevalātmahitaiṣinī.*' *Mahābhārata*, Vol. III, p. 2428.8. 'In earlier times you did not care for my welfare as a mother should have, and today you are pontificating to me about my duty out of your selfishness.'
33. Ibid., p. 2429. See pp. 2415–30.
34. See Ibid., Vol. IV, pp. 3692–3702.

CHAPTER 7

Ethics and Social Organization

7.1 ETHICAL LIFE AS SOCIAL LIFE: THE CLASSICAL INDIAN VERSION

The ethics of classical Indian, like the ethics of any other country, grew up in the setting of classical Indian social organization. This is true not only of ethics in the sense of ethical theorizing, or moral philosophy, but also in that of the evolution and application of practical moral principles and norms which classical Indians used, or considered worthy of use, in the conduct of their private and public life. Therefore, to properly understand the role and viability of a classical Indian ethical concept, principle, or practice, it is necessary to keep in mind the then Indian social setting. This does not, however, mean that Indian ethics was intended to be applicable to, or valid for, only the then Indian *social order*. Rather, it did offer itself as relevant to and viable for any society, though it shaped itself in the manner it did because of the distinctive nature or character of the social and societal climate in which it was born and brought up. It did claim to be a viable moral philosophy for any human society, as every moral philosophy does. Therefore, in assessing it we have to do more than to ascertain whether or not it was valid for the classical Indian society. However, it is true that if it is found not to be valid even in that society, it would almost completely lose its tenability and worthwhileness.

A theory, ethical or non-ethical, which is said to be valid in only one particular society or only in some particular period of its history, is not *really valid* even in that society or in that period of its history. The logically proper way to express this fact about it would be to say that it was *considered to be valid* in that society or in that period of its history. *Being valid* and *being considered to be valid* are two different things. A theory which is not valid but was considered to be valid in some society may be of some interest to a cultural anthropologist or a historian of morals, but it would not be of any interest to a philosopher of morals. In fact, every moral theory claims to be valid in a trans-cultural and trans-temporal sense and because of this claim it becomes worthy of a philosopher's attention and scrutiny. This is in no way less true of classical Indian ethics or ethical theories, than it is true of classical Indian metaphysics, axiology, logic, etc. It may be pertinent to point out that the concept of validity or tenability of a theory or a principle, is not a relative concept as is, for example, that of the permissibility of a practice. That is why it makes sense to say that the practice of polygamy was permissible among Hindus in classical, medieval, and even in modern India for a long time, but is not today. But we cannot say that the ethical theory which holds polygamy to be a morally commendable or permissible practice was *valid*, as an ethical theory, in classical India but is *not valid* today. Something similar is the case with the notion of being considered to be valid (or rather with that of being considered to be anything). For example, it makes good sense to say that classical Indian astrology considers the geocentric theory of the universe valid though it is not considered to be valid in modern astronomy, or even to simply say that it is not valid.

It is worse than a wild goose chase to try to ascertain when a society became ethical, or when some ethical principles or norms were introduced into it. This is so because living a social life, i.e. living as a member of a society and living an ethical life invariably go together. It is its ethics, the set of ethical principles and norms, however small the set may be, which makes a group of humans a society, or a way of living a social living. This is true of classical Indian society and ethics, as it is of any society and its ethics. By 'ethics', it is important to note, here is meant not moral philosophy or ethical theorizing but the set of concrete principles and norms which the members of the group generally use in their personal and interpersonal affairs to make them cohesive. Moral philosophy may come a little later when there arises a need for examining the justifiability of a principle or norm, or of systematizing the principles and norms into a well-knit whole, or a whole as knit as their nature or subject matter allows. Many scholars are of the opinion that Greek philosophy began with metaphysical and epistemological theorizing. Ethics, meaning ethical theorizing, or moral philosophy, was a later entrant, and logic a still later one, entering into it only with some of Aristotle's works. But this is not to say that the Greeks did not live ethically before their philosophers began to philosophize about morals.

Classical Indian philosophy, on the other hand, as is evident from a number of *Vedic* and *Upaniṣadic* speculations, seems to have begun in a much more organismic manner. This can safely be said of it because, even in its earliest stage, it is metaphysical, epistemological and axiological, and therefore ethical, all mixed together. Some scholars think that ethics entered Indian philosophy only with the stabilization of the Indian social order into one consisting of four castes or classes (*varṇāśrama vyavasthā*). In one sense it is true and in another it is not. It is true in the sense that Indian ethics is largely, though not totally, an ethics which developed with the objective of systematizing the moral obligations, rights, virtues, goals, etc., of the four stages in the life of an individual and of the four classes, to one and only one of which every individual belonged, or had to belong. But it is wrong in the sense in which it may suggest that before the introduction of four-fold division of the Indian society there was neither ethics (i.e. moral living) nor ethical theorizing in India. It is wrong because it is almost impossible to date the time when classical India did not have the four-fold social division. It is possible to date, in fact it has been dated, with a tolerably good amount of accuracy, when it was questioned, for example, by Mahavīra and Buddha, but we cannot date the period in which it did not exist, or in which it was for the first time introduced. There are not only historical difficulties, i.e. difficulties generated by the lack of adequate historical records, but also conceptual or logical difficulties which are quite serious in nature, in doing that. This will be made clear very soon.

Not only does a society need ethics in order to be a worthwhile society, ethics also needs a society to be a genuine ethics. This is clear from the fact that an ethical relation, say, a diadic one, as already shown in the preceding chapter, holds good only between two individuals who are socially related to each other, though the relation may be in some cases distant or tenuous. For example, for the relation of an individual, say A, being obligated to another, say B, for having saved him from dieing of starvation, it is not necessary that A is a cousin of B; the relation may hold good between A and B even if the two are only citizens of the same country, or even citizens of two countries having had, directly or indirectly, some interaction or communication between them, enabling one to have some soft feeling for the other. It is some such truth to which, the Indian maxim, already referred to earlier, that to have a liberal moral sense is to treat the whole world as one's family (*vasudhaiva kutumbakam*), intends to refer.

The intention of what has been said above j is not to assert or claim that in classical India everyone had a developed moral sense or did what the above maxim states or prescribes, that he considered the whole world as his family, or even all members of his own society as constituting his own family, or treated them in the same manner as he treated the members of his family. There were conflicts, strikes, divisions, or discriminations, etc., and they were not all, or always, morally justified. The stories depicted in the *Rāmāyaṇa* and the *Mahābhārata,* as well as the history of ancient India, very well testify this fact. But they also testify that classical Indian ethics, both practical and theoretical, developed in concordance with the structure of the then classical social order. In this order, every individual or group was not always morally fair to every other individual or group. But still classical Indian ethics did grow, as any classical ethics did, primarily to enable every member of the order to live a socially cohesive and personally satisfying life. Its ethical theorizing, the classical Indian philosophy of morals, too, developed in this social setting. To be specific, it developed as an organ to provide a theoretical support to the ethics in actual practice during classical times as well as to the ethics then considered worthy of being practised.

Whenever and wherever such theoretical attempts are made, some theoretical divides are brought in which generally provide a moral justification for some prevalent practices that would be justifiable in any other social order as well, i.e. justifiable on objective grounds. These devices, of course, do the work of justification in terms of concepts or categories thrown up by, or relevant to, the way or ways in which the particular social order in which they are used, functions. For example, classical Indian theoretical devices do the justificatory work in terms of such concepts as those of *varṇa* (class or caste) or *varṇadharma* (obligations which accrue to an individual by virtue of his belonging to a certain class or caste), *āśrama* (state of an individual's life) or āśramadharma (obligations which accrue to an individual by virtue the stage of his life he is passing through), *kula* (famílily) or *kulācāra* (familial obligations), *loka* (custom or convention) or *lokācāra* (customary or conventional morality), *deśa* (region) or *deśācāra* (regional morality). When such theoretical devices and the concepts or categories which go with them are used over a long period, they generate, or get congealed into, some well-marked normative structures. Then a mere appeal to, or an appeal to the conformity of a proposed course of action with, a normative structure, is considered sufficient to make that course of action morally justified, and an appeal to the disconformity of the action with it morally unjustified. To mention one instance, *varṇadharma* has become such a normative structure in classical Indian ethics. The major force of Kṛṣṇa's argument with Arjuna in the *Gītā,* to convince him that he ought to fight the war, derives from his claim that doing that would be in conformity with his, a *kṣatriya*'s, *varṇadharma,* and therefore morally justified. On the other hand, abstaining from doing that, or choosing to be a recluse, would be in disconformity with it, and therefore morally unjustified. This point will be further elaborated in a later chapter in which *varṇadharma* will discussed in some detail.

But *all* such theoretical devices, or structures, are *not* always used to do only this sort of justificatory work, i.e. the work of justifying objectively justifiable practices. *Some* of them, or all of them *sometimes*, are also used, or are usable, to provide an allegedly, or a seemingly, moral justification for some prevalent practices which are not, or cannot be, justified on objective grounds, or even on grounds intrinsic to that social order in which they are prevalent. And, this is so simply by virtue of these practices' own character, i.e. because of their being what they are.

We shall see a little later while discussing the rights and obligations of different classes or castes of people, that attempts are made sometimes to provide theoretical support, or pseudo-support, for practices which are not morally justifiable on objective rational grounds. This is illustrated, for instance, in defending the social practice of giving preference to the *parentage* or caste of an individual over his abilities in acknowledging a right of his when in the acknowledgement of that right only his abilities are relevant and his parentage or caste is not at all. This we find, as will be shown soon, in the defence given for denying the right of admission to a child in an academy for instruction because of his parentage and not on the basis of his abilities, though only his abilities, and not his parentage, are relevant to either the denial or granting of admission to him in the academy.

When such things happen, it is generally the case that the theorizers, by and large, belong to a class which occupies a higher status, a position of greater power, in the social organization than the class to which belong the *sufferers* or *victims* of unfairnesses or unfair practices, and that those who commit the unfair acts, or are the benefieries of the unfair practices, come from the former class, the class of superiors, the same class from which come the theorizers as well.

But this is not always the case. There are some notable exceptions. Mahavīra and Buddha, the founders of the Jain and Buddhist schools of philosophy, belonged to the class of *kṣatriyas*, a class which occupied the second highest social status in classical Indian social hierarchy. But they did not do such things. The reason for their not providing any theoretical justification, or even escape-route, for any unfairness done by a member of one caste to a member of another caste is their rejection of the class or caste structure, the four-fold social stratification (*varṇavyavasthā*). This stratification had become by their times a ramified caste-system (*jātiprathā*) in which the *varṇa* or *jāti* of an individual was determined by his birth or parentage (*janmanā*). In fact, it is difficult to prove, or say authentically, *when* it was not so determined. Be that as it may, Indian ethics has developed in the setting of this class or caste system, *varṇavyavasthā*, or more accurately, in the setting of *varṇāśrama vyavasthā*. This is natural because any ethics grows up in a social setting. It is a social setting which gives to ethical concepts their concrete content. This is again natural because they are formed, or get formed, in the process of man's living a social life, in the course of his interactions with other members of his society. Therefore, it is necessary to discuss in some detail the functioning of the *varṇa* system, or the way it is understood to have functioned, with our eyes primarily directed towards ascertaining its role in shaping the character of classical Indian ethics, both practical and theoretical. This will be done in the next section.

7.2 THE FOUR-FOLD SOCIAL SYSTEM (*VARṆĀŚRAMA VYAVASTHĀ*) AND INDIAN ETHICS

The classical Indian term *varṇāśrama vyavasthā* is a conjunction of *varṇa vyavasthā* and *āśrama vyavasthā*. The first means the division of the society into classes or castes, and the second the division of an individual's life into stages. Each one of the two divisions is a four-fold division; that is, the division of the society into four classes or castes and that of an individual's life into four stages. Even if *varṇa* (class) originally meant something different from caste (*jāti*), its meaning soon became identical with that of caste. It is almost impossible to date when '*varṇa*' did not mean *jāti*, though many modern scholars even today think that it does not mean *jāti* and was not originally determined by birth. They hold that the *varṇa* of an individual was determined by his abilities, propensities, etc. We shall see, as we go on in this section, that there are conceptual difficulties which block this understanding of the *varṇa* system. Most of the things which the tradition is claimed, in its received interpretation, to have said to support it, in effect support the view that it was determined by birth, or in some ad hoc, arbitrary, or circumstantial manner. However, it is true that the *varṇa* system was evolved to satisfy the classificatory intellectual propensity of classical Indians; that is, their desire or need to evolve a social order or organization in a manner as well-knit as the then social circumstances permitted. This every society needs to do, so that social life may be cohesive, and human collectivities may turn into one civil society.

Broadly speaking there are in circulation two types of accounts or theories about the origin or evolution of the *varṇa* system. One of them says, as mentioned above, that people were put into four groups, or classes, according to their abilities, equipments, propensities, etc., i.e. according to their natural capabilities, or simply their nature, to perform certain functions. This I will call the *ability account.* The other account traces their origin to the initiative of some divine agency, sometimes taking and sometimes not taking into consideration the abilities etc. of the individuals put into this or that group. Therefore, the two accounts, in some cases, flow into each other. The latter account I shall call the *mythological account.*

I shall first discuss the ability account and then the mythological one. I shall discuss the former in some greater detail than I shall do the latter. This I will do firstly because of its strong hold on the minds of almost all modern Indian writers who have written on it and secondly because its discussion will also include a large part of the *Gītā* account. The *Gītā* account is a mythological-ability account. The reason for my discussing it in some detail is that it is very often claimed to support the ability account as contradistinguished from, that which I call the *hereditary* account (*janmanā jāti*) that latter holds that the *varṇa* of an individual was determined by his parentage, i.e. it was hereditary or birth-determined (*janmanā*). But, as the discussion given here will show, the contrary is the truth: the *Gītā* account supports the hereditary account and not the ability account. Since the *Gītā* account is such that it can be implemented or executed only by a god, a Kṛṣṇa, i.e. an omniscient divine agency, I include it in the category of mythological accounts. In fact, as will be made clear when we shall discuss the mythological accounts, all of them, in effect, make the *varṇa* of an individual hereditary.

It is obvious that an ethical thinker who, or a school of ethical thought which, accepts the *varṇa*-classification will consider it important to present a theory of *varṇa*-ethics, traditionally termed *varṇadharma.* And this has really happened in the history of classical Indian ethics. Its theory of *varṇadharma* occupies an extensive sector of the space given to ethics in the classical axiological corpus. But it also follows with equal logical force that for a thinker who, or school which, does not accept the *varṇa*-classification, the *varṇavyavasthā* or caste-system, the question of discussing *varṇa*-ethics would become a non-question or, rather, a non-issue. This is what has happened with the Jain and Buddhist thinkers and schools of thought. They give general ethical theories or views, i.e. an ethics of an individual, a man as such, or of a special group. They do hold that there are differences between the obligations of householders and those of recluses. But householders and recluses do not represent two *varṇas* or *jatis*. The *Cārvākas* too do not accept the *varṇa* or caste-system and therefore they also do not consider the issue of *varṇadharma* an important, or viable, ethical one. They consider the account of *varṇa*-ethics, in circulation in their time, a device used by some clever, Brahmanical thinkers to exploit the innocent people occupying a lower status in the then social structure. But in spite of all this, the concept of *varṇadharma* occupies a very important place, rather the centre-stage, in Indian ethical thought because the large majority of classical Indian thinkers accept the *varṇa*-system. Indian ethics does discuss general ethical things, i.e. things which are independent of all *varṇa* considerations (*sāmānya dharmas* or virtues). But still the importance of *varṇadharmas* and the *varṇa*-system remains undiminished.

7.3 *VARṆA*-SYSTEM (*VARṆAVYAVASTHĀ*): THE ABILITY ACCOUNT

An accurate, or even a nearly accurate, account of the origin and development of the *varṇa*-system can be given only by a competent historian of ancient India, and not by a philosopher. Whenever a philosopher refers to its historicity, he depends on some historian's account. But historians, even those who hold that the division of the classical Indian society into four *varṇas* originally was a division of labour, i.e. based on the abilities of individuals, on the principle that rights and obligations of individuals can be determined only after ascertaining who can do what in the most effective manner, do not say in a definitive way when this division was actually done. And, they are silent about the agency which did the division. We may say that this is not a serious lacuna because there are many facts of ancient Indian history which cannot be accurately dated, or accounted for, because of the unavailability of adequate records or data. Be that as it may, all this does not pose a serious handicap for what we intend to do in this work, or more specifically, in this section.

Our interest in the ability account of the *varṇa*-system derives from the fact that it also yields a theory of *varṇa*-ethics. It not only holds that a *varṇa* is formed of the individuals who possess a certain set of similar abilities, but also that because of their possessing those abilities they are assigned some rights and obligations. These rights, obligations, etc. of theirs constitute their *varṇadharma*, or the ethics of the *varṇa* they form. A *varṇa*-ethics is a social ethics, an ethics an individual has to follow because of his being a member of a certain social group, a *varṇa*, For example, if only an individual possessing the ability to fight a battle, to rule over others, etc., and none else, is put in the *varṇa* called *kṣatriya*, them it is a natural step to assert that a *kṣatriya* ought to fight a battle when required and should have the right to rule over others if also so required. Or, if this scheme of *varṇa*-formation has been rigorously done, i.e. individuals possessing these abilities and only such individuals constitute the *kṣatriya varṇa*, then from the mere fact that one is a *kṣatriya* it can be inferred that he ought to fight a battle which has to be fought and should be allowed to rule over some others when someone has to rule over them, there being nothing else against his having been allowed to have this right. This would be true of every individual and every *varṇa*. But all this would be tenable only if the *varṇa* classification or division has been done only on the basis of the abilities of the individuals belonging to every *varṇa*. And, this would be the case only if it is *conceptually possible* to make this sort of classification.

All those who hold the ability account do maintain what has been said above of *varṇa* classification and of what follows from its having been done on the basis of the abilities of individuals. But they *only aver* that originally the classification was done on the basis of abilities alone, and not on the basis of birth or parentage. They have not raised the question of its conceptual possibility. They do not seem to realize that actuality implies conceptual possibility. That is, if it is not conceptually possible, then it cannot be an actual, or real, classification. They do not even discuss the difficulties which arise in admitting that the classification was really done on the basis of abilities. Perhaps they have failed to see all this because they have not tried to ascertain who has done it or who can be said to be capable of doing it, and how he has done it if there ever was any such agency. In the absence of authentic evidence of the historicity of this account it is very necessary to discuss the issue of its conceptual possibility. This is really a philosophical question which a philosophical study of the *varṇa*-system and varṇa-ethics must not ignore.

As generally understood and accepted, classical Indian society, because of its four-fold division, is an organization consisting of four classes, castes, or *varṇas*. Therefore, it is called a four-fold order (*caturvarṇavyavasthā*). These four *varṇas*, *brāhmaṇas*, *kṣatriyas*, *vaiśyas*, and *śūdras*. The four together form a hierarchical social order in which *brāhmaṇas* occupy the highest status, then come the *kṣatriyas*, then the *vaiśyas*, and the lowest status is that of the fourth *varṇa*, *śūdras*. Every classification or division is made on the basis of some principle or criterion. The basis of this classification, according to the ability account, is the possession of different sets of abilities by different sets of individuals. For example, those who have the ability to acquire knowledge and to impart it to others are said to compose the *varṇa* or class of *brāhmaṇas*, those who have the ability to fight a battle and to defend their country are said to compose the class of *kṣatriyas*, those who have the ability to do farming, business, etc., to compose the class of *vaiśyas*, and those who have only the ability to serve the other three *varṇas* to compose the class of *śūdras*. The rights and obligations of the members of these classes are determined keeping in view their abilities. That is, every individual is obligated to do only that which he is able to do and is entitled to the rights which he can exercise or enjoy. Since all members of a *varṇa* have, by definition, similar abilities, their rights and obligations are the same, or similar, i.e. they are also the rights and obligations of their *varṇa*, or their *varṇadharma*. This means that the *dharma* (totality of rights and obligations) of an individual is also the *dharma* of his *varṇa* and vice versa. Since, again by definition, the *abilities* of the members of one *varṇa* are different from those of the members of another *varṇa*, the *dharma* or *varṇadharma* of the *varṇa*, or of a member of it, would be different from that of another *varṇa*, or of a member of another *varṇa*. All this follows from the premise of the ability account of *varṇavyavasthā*, from the proposition that a *varṇa* is formed by putting in a class all those, and only those, who have similar abilities or capabilities.

The word 'ability' in the preceding discussion and in what follows is used in a broad sense. It is a term which includes propensities, inclinations, aptitudes, capacities or capabilities, etc. It can do this job very well because, like the latter terms, it too is a dispositional term and not an occurrent one. That is, if an individual has the ability to fight a battle, it does not mean he would always fight when there is an occasion to do so. He would fight only if certain conditions are fulfilled, for example, if he wants to fight, his body and mind at that time are in good health, he considers it appropriate, obligatory, or ethically permissible, to fight, he considers the chances of winning bright, he is not facing an insurmountable difficulty in fighting, etc. If we take all this into consideration, i.e. as comprehended in the scope of the concept of ability, there does not seem to be available any other term better than it to denote or connote the basis or criterion on which the four-fold *varṇa*-system is considered to have been formed by the account that has been called the ability account.

A clarification about the use of the term 'caste' is also needed here. In what has been said so far, the word 'class' as well as 'caste' has been used as an English equivalent of the Sanskrit word *varṇa.* This practice will be followed throughout this work. There is nothing wrong or odd in doing that. It has been done not only by Western scholars but also by some Indian ones whose knowledge of, or loyalty towards, or respect for, the classical Indian tradition and ethics is unquestionable. To give only a few examples, this practice is followed all along by Svāmī Vireśvarānanda in his translation of Śridhara Swāmī's commentary on the *Gītā* and by Svāmī Gambhīrānanda in his translation of Śankara's as well as Madhusūdan Sarasvatī's commentary on the *Gītā.* If the reader is very keen to check it, he may see, to mention just one instance from each one of the three works, page 22 of Vireśvarānanda's work, page 186 of Gambhīrānanda's first work and page 59 of his second work.[1]

Let us now turn to discussing the problems which the feasibility or possibility of the *varṇa*-system poses, or which need to be solved in order to substantiate that the ability account of the system was really implemented. That the *varṇa*-system actually existed in classical India is not questioned or doubted here. We only want to ascertain whether or not the conditions which need to be fulfilled to make possible the formation of the system, as claimed by the ability accounts, are fulfillable in practice. If they are not, or if they are extremely unlikely to be fulfilled, then the tenability of the ability account will become questionable. Even then the existence, actuality or historicity of the *varṇa*-system would not become doubtful or questionable. If would only imply that the system was formed on some basis or principle other than the abilities of individuals, or formed on the basis of individuals' abilities but not in the manner claimed by the ability account.

Let us assume, for the sake of argument, that the classification of individuals into the four *varṇas* was originally done on the basis of their abilities. Then it is natural to ask at which age an individual's abilities could or should have been reasonably considered to determine his distinctive *varṇa*—the *varṇa* which would then on be his *varṇa* and would also determine his *varṇadharma* (caste ethics). Let us transport ourselves, of course in imagination, to that period of Indian history, whatever it may be, and think seriously of the problems which surround this question. We can think of them because they are related to the concept of ability and not to any fact of Indian history. We cannot choose *any particular* age of the individual because abilities and performances of any individual may change. Sometimes they change drastically. For example, Vālmīki (6th century BC) the poet who wrote the famous epic *Rāmāyaṇa,* and is called the first poet (*ādikavi*) of India and, by some, of the world, in his early life, according to some accounts, lived the life of a thief or robber (*dasyu*), or one of a killer of birds (*vyādha*). If his propensities and performances, his abilities, his life-style, in this part of his life, are taken into account to determine his *varṇa,* he should be assigned to the *śūdra varṇa.* But in the later part of his life he becomes a great saint and poet. The tradition ignores his earlier life and calls him a great seer (*maharṣi*). But even the reverse may happen. One who is a saint in his early life, or in one period of his life, may become a corrupt or fallen individual in a later, or another, part of his life. Therefore, the abilities or performances of an individual at no particular age, or in no particular part of his life, can be chosen to determine his *varṇa* once and for all.

There is another alternative here. We may say that in case of an individual's having different sets of abilities at different periods of his life he may be put in different *varṇas* in different periods of his life. But the Indian tradition or ethos does not accept this possibility. There is no example of any one individual belonging to different *varṇas* in different parts of his life.

May we proceed, it may be asked, by averaging the quality of an individual's abilities as exhibited in his entire lifetime. This would not be a bad idea to pursue. It would be an inductive process because only after observing his career from an early age till his death can we generalize about his abilities. If this method is adopted, then only after his death, or almost at the end of his life in case of his becoming a total invalid while remaining alive, can we make a generalized judgement about his abilities. This would mean that, on the adoption of this method, his *varṇa*, and therefore his *varṇadharma*, can be declared only after his death, or after his becoming forever an invalid. This would mean that the classification of individuals into different *varṇas* would become useless for ethical or social purposes. It would not be used in anyone's active life to assign the obligations which he should fulfil, to determine the rights he should exercise, to characterize the virtues he should inculcate, or the values he should acquire. Moreover, there is no evidence in Indian history of this method's ever having been used by anyone in respect of any individual.

May it be said that, in the abilities exhibited by an individual at any particular age, a gifted person can perceive or know, in some extraordinary way, the kind of abilities he will have thoughout his life? This position would be untenable for more than one reason. Firstly, it would deny the possibility of change in an individual's abilities. Secondly, it would be difficult to say with authenticity who can do the work of reading from the kind of abilities an individual has at any one time the kind of abilities he will continue to have all through his life. Thirdly, the difficulty in locating a person who can have the above kind of extraordinary, unfaultable, cognition, may tempt an upholder of the ability account to present or accept some mythological account of *varṇa* = classification. For example, he may attribute this work to a divinity, or mythological figure. But then the theme of *varṇa*-classification would cease to be a subject of historical, sociological, study as well as of philosophical scrutiny. Moreover, as will be soon shown, a mythological account converts the ability account into a hereditary account according to which the *varṇa* of an individual is determined by his birth or parentage, and not by his abilities. Fourthly, the alleged claim of ascertaining a man's abilities all through his life only on the basis of the abilities possessed by him at any one age in his life would be a highly undependable generalization. Or, if it is taken to be absolutely unfalsifiable it would turn the empirical concept of ability into an a priori one. The concept of ability (of any individual), as already said, is an empirical concept, because only on the basis of one's experience of what another person generally does or is inclined to do, etc., can one form a dependable general judgement about the latter's abilities; and one still has to admit that one's judgement may turn out to be false some day in the future.

The *varṇa*-system is a hierarchical social order in which one class is considered higher than another, and the benefits and burdens of different classes of people are distributed among them in accordance with their position in the social order. Such a system can be formed in a fair manner on the basis of its members' abilities only if all members are given equal opportunities for growth, for equipping themselves with the abilities which matter for their placement in this or that group, or, for getting their status elevated, i.e. for being transferred from a *varṇa* of a lower status, say, the *śūdra varṇa,* to a higher one, that of the *vaiśya,* or *kṣatriya,* or *brāhmaṇa.*

But this is not true of the *varṇa*-system. An individual belonging to the *śūdra* caste is not allowed to undergo the sacred thread ceremony (*upanayana sanskāra*) in a teacher's school under the guidance of the teacher. The word *upanayana* is a compound of *upa* and *nayana. Upa* means near, close to, and *nayana* to bring, or to take, one to. It thus means the ceremony the performance of which by a child brings, or takes, him near, or close to, the teacher.[2] Only after his performance of this ceremony does a child in the classical *varṇa*-system, gain admission to a school and acquire the right to receive education. After the ceremony he becomes a twice-born (*dvija*) individual. *Dvija* is thus a metaphorical term used to highlight the importance of receiving education. As per a classical Indian social convention, the first birth of an individual takes place when he is borne by his mother. It is thus nothing but his biological birth which every human being, or rather, every animal, has. Therefore, every human being is once-born (*ekajātīya*). But so is every animal. This means that to be a once-born individual is not to have any distinctive status or importance. And, it also means, by implication, that one who does not ever become, or is not allowed to ever become, a twice-born, is lower in social status than any twice-born individual. The term *ekajātīya* is also a metaphorical one to connote the extreme insignificance, or lack-lustre character, of merely being born in the world, of being just a living being. Both the term, *dvija* and *ekajātīya* are thus highly value-loaded or evaluative, the evaluative meaning of the first being laudatory and that of the second derogatory.

In the *upanayana* ceremony, the individual who undergoes it is given by the teacher a sacred thread (*yajñopavita*) which he has to wear all his life. That is why the ceremony is also called sacred-thread ceremony. It seems to me that the thread is given, and required to be worn by everyone to whom it has been given all his life, to make any one of the three *varṇas*, *brāhmaṇa, kṣatriya,* and *vaiśya* easily distinguishable from one belonging to the *śūdra varṇa.* This can be done because no *śūdra* is allowed to undergo the sacred-thread ceremony. A clear consequence of this practice is that he is bound to remain all his life only a once-born (*ekajātīya*) individual and therefore lower than anyone from the other three *varṇas*.

That the *śūdra* is not allowed to undergo the sacred-thread ceremony is clearly mentioned in many classical works. For example, the *Brahma-Sūtra* (1.iii.36) unequivocally affirms it, and even as great a logician and ethicist as Śankara in his commentary on it not only reiterates it but also refers in his support to the *Chāndojña* (V.xi.7 and VIII.i.1.), *Manusmṛti* (X.4 and 12.6), etc. The *Brahmasūtra*'s aphoristic prohibition, 'Because purificatory rights' (*upanayana sanskāra* etc.), 'are mentioned (for others) and absence of these is declared (for the *śūdra*)', as per Śankara's gloss on it, is inviolable.[3] An obvious implication of it is that the denial to the *śūdra* of the right to be admitted in a school, or to be taught by any teacher, i.e. to be given an opportunity to be educated, is unqualified. Receiving education, or being taught by a teacher, in these days means being given an opportunity to study the *Vedas* and literature related to them. Therefore, denying them the right to receive education clearly means disallowing them to study or to be taught any one of the *Vedas*. There are clear statements to this effect in several classical works besides the *Brahmasūtra*. And, the latter in 1.iii.38 is candid in averring that 'And because the *smṛti* prohibits for the *śūdra* the hearing, study, and acquisition of the meaning of (the *Vedas*),'[4] he is not allowed to study them or to be taught them by any teacher. In his commentary on it Śankara supports it by referring to other works. He also mentions the punishments prescribed to be inflicted on the *śūdra* if he reads or even hears a *Vedic* sentence, such severe punishments as 'the chopping off his tongue if he should utter the *Vedas*, and cutting of the body to pieces if he should commit it to memory'.[5]

It is obvious that, because he is not allowed to hear them, the *Vedas* cannot be taught to him. He cannot even read them on his own, if this miracle he somehow succeeds in performing, because then he may commit them or parts of them to memory, or utter them, and would on that account have to suffer the punishments prescribed for doing committing such 'sins'.

Śankara admits that those whose actions in their previous birth have made them pure and entitled them to study the *Vedas*, can study them, or have knowledge of the *Vedas* imparted to them. This can be done because nobody can stop anyone from getting what his actions in the previous life have entitled him to get. Here Śankara simply reiterates what the *karmic* theory of the world holds. If there is any *śūdra* of this type, he would be certainly an exceptional one. Such exceptional *śūdras* are, he says, 'Vidura, Dharmavyādha, and others'. Still, *Śankara* unhesitatingly accepts the general prohibition on the study of the *Vedas* by the *śūdra* when he declares at the end of the commentary: 'But the conclusion stands that the *Śūdra* has no right to knowledge through the Vedas'.[6]

Rāmānuja's interpretation of the aphorisms of the *Brahma-Sūtra* referred to above runs on exactly similar lines as that of Śankara. In *Śrībhāṣya*, which is his commentary on the *Brahma-Sūtra*, he equally emphatically asserts that 'In the scriptures we find purificatory ceremonies like upanayana etc. prescribed as prerequisites to the study of the *Vedas* and the *vidyās* vide *Chāndojña* iv.iv.5. These ceremonies are for the three higher castes and not for the Śūdra. Their absence in the case of the Śūdra is repeatedly declared in the scriptures...' 'So they are not', he concludes, 'entitled to the study of the *Vedas* or to the vidyās'.[7] Since he is candid in including in his conclusion not only the *Vedas* but also the *vidyās*, i.e. all branches of inquiry, or knowledge as such, he is forthright in denying to the *śūdra* all rights to pursue any branch of knowledge. This amounts to denying them all rights to being educated.

Denial of education to any individual has far-reaching consequences. *Education* is, to repeat, widely accepted, effective, agent for the educatee's acquisition of new abilities as well as for strengthening and preserving his existing and desirable abilities. That is why it has become commonplace to emphasize that all individuals must be given, in a fair social order, equal opportunities for getting themselves educated, i.e. for reaping the benefits of education. This is conspicuously significant for a social order which is alleged to be formed, as per the ability account, by classifying individuals into groups, called *varṇas*, on the basis of their abilities. And, the higher, or lower, status of the groups so formed is said to be determined by the abilities of the members so grouped. In the *varṇa*-system, Śūdras are, because they are denied the right to education, bound to, or very likely to, have many disabilities and blemishes and very few desirable abilities. Consequently, because of the very manner in which the *varṇa*-system is formed, according to the ability account, they are constrained to be placed on the lowest rung of the social, the *varṇa*, ladder, though they themselves have done nothing to deserve this said fate. It is obvious that such a way of organizing the society cannot be called morally just or justified.

The admission of some exceptions by Śankara and Rāmānuja, or even by any number of thinkers, to the prohibition of the *śūdra* from receiving education, prove, as exceptions are said to prove, the rule they are exceptions to, the fact that the common run of *śūdras* have no opportunity in the *varṇa*-system to get themselves educated. And, certainly, these exceptions do not disprove the facticity of the general denial to them of the right to being educated.

But several modern Indian interpreters of Indian ethics claim of some instances, which occur in some classical works, that they counter what I have called the facticity of the denial to the *śūdra* of the right, of equal opportunity, to getting education. They maintain that these instances prove that the *śūdra* who has the ability to receive instruction in *Vedic* wisdom is taught by experts as per the then social or ethical practice. Two such instances are generally mentioned. Both of them occur in the *Chāndojña* and also in the *Brahma-Sūtra*. They have also been commented, or rather, elaborated on, by Śankara and Rāmānuja in their commentaries. If the accounts of these instances as given in the texts are looked into even cursorily, they *confirm* what I have been maintaining here and in no way counter or go against it. It is surprising why modern scholars have not been able to hear the message which they quite audibly convey to any attentive ear. The first example is that of the king Jānaśruti's having been given instruction by the *ṛṣi* Raikva, and the second that of Satyakāma Jābāla's having been admitted by the *ṛṣi* Haridrumata Gautama in his school.

7.3.1 The Example of Jānaśruti

This episode occurs in the *Chāndojña* (IV.2.1–5) and is discussed in some detail.[8] In the *Brahma-Sūtra* (1.3.34–35) it occurs almost casually but certainly in the context of asserting that *śūdras* have no right to study the *Vedas*. This amounts to, as has been shown, asserting that they have no right to education. In the *Brahma-Sūtra* the *Chāndojña* account has been simply aphoristically affirmed. Commentators like Śankara and Rāmānuja, too, in their commentaries on it have not discussed it in detail.

A brief account of the case of Jānaśruti as narrated in the *Chāndojña* and commented on by Śankara can, quite faithfully to the text, be presented as follows:

Jānaśruti is a king who leads a very pious and chaste life, makes plenty of gifts to *brāhmaṇas*, provides food to everyone who visits his house, constructs comfortable rest-houses where anybody may stay and get food and comfortable lodging facilities, etc. One night when he is on the terrace of his house, some swans are flying in the sky right over his house. One of them tells another who is ahead of it that 'the lustre of Jānaśruti, arising from the power of distribution of food, etc., spreads all around, it extends far, like (the light of) heaven, i.e. it touches heaven...may you not...get into contact with that light..., may not that light burn you up owing to contact with it'.[9] By way of uttering these words it warns the swan ahead to avoid coming into contact with the lustre of Jānaśruti's moral attainment otherwise it may get completely burnt up. The swan flying ahead replies by saying that the other swan has spoken of this man, the king Jānaśruti, as if he were like the man called Raikva who is associated with a cart, when he is much inferior to Raikva. 'It is inappropriate to speak of this one thus that he is like Raikva...'[10] When asked what kind of person Raikva is, it says that 'whatsoever good, moral, virtuous deeds all people perform in this world, all that becomes included in the virtue of Raikva.... So also anyone else who knows that which was to be known by him' (i.e. which was worthy of being known by him). And 'that which is to be known' is 'that which Raikva knew.' ...'The knower of this kind, though being other than Raikva becomes like Raikva.'[11]

Jānaśruti overhears this conversation between the two swans. To him it is like an insult and it overwhelms him with grief and agony. He gets informed of the village where Raikva is to be found as 'seated under a cart', 'scratching his itches,'[12] and runs in a grief-stricken mood to him for instruction in the knowledge which has made him so great and elevated. He has come to know of *ṛṣi* Raikva's 'desire to enter into life of a householder' (and therefore to have a wife), 'as also of his desire for wealth'.[13] Therefore, he goes to him taking along six hundred cows, a necklace, and a chariot drawn by two she-mules to offer all of them to him as gifts, and requests him to instruct him. Raikva replies, 'O Śūdra, let the chariot, together with the necklace, as also the cows be with you yourself', which expresses his refusal to instruct him.

According to Śankara's interpretation, by his refusal to accept these gifts in lieu of his imparting instruction to *Jānaśruti*, Raikva wants to convey 'O Śūdra, I have no need of this which is not sufficient for my purpose.'[14] That is, there is something lacking in the gifts. He does call him a *śūdra* but the reason for his refusal is not Jānaśruti's really being a *śūdra* but the insufficiency of the gifts or the fee.

In fact, Jānaśruti is not a *śūdra* but a *kṣatriya*. His being a *kṣatriya* has been established, by implication, on the basis of his association or close link with the *kṣatriya* Citraratha. This point has been clearly confirmed in the *Brahma-Sūtra* 1.3.35 which says that he is not a *śūdra* 'owing to his Kṣatriyahood being known later on *lingāt*', i.e. 'from the indicatory mark' (or implication) 'of mention along with a descendant of Citraratha' (who is a *kṣatriya*).[15] This issue has been very well elaborated in Goenka's *Vedānta-Darśana* (*Brahma-Sūtra*).[16]

As Śankara puts it, *Raikva* calls Jānaśruti a *śūdra* because 'From hearing the words of the swan sorrow entered into him....from hearing the greatness of Raikva he hurried to Raikva'. As explained by Gambhirananda in his annotation, the word *śūdra* is formed by combining the two words *śucā* (sorrow or grief) and *dravati* (overwhelmed with, or hurries to). Therefore, it refers to one who is overwhelmed with grief or one who hurries, or runs, to someone out of grief.[17] Both the meanings of *śūdra* are applicable to Jānaśruti; he is overwhelmed with grief and he runs to Raikva out of grief.

Śankara also points out that 'Others, however, say that he (Raikva) called him (the king) a Śūdra out of anger because he had brought insufficient wealth.' This does not seem to be a wrong or disloyal interpretation of Raikva's reason for refusal because when the king returns with more gifts, the *ṛṣi* agrees to instruct him.

It is for all, or for any one, of the reasons mentioned above, *a la* Śankara, that Raikva calls him a *śūdra* and not because he is really of a *śūdra* caste. Therefore, from the fact that Raikva, as we shall soon see, ultimately gives Jānaśruti the instruction, it neither follows that he gives it to a *śūdra*, i.e. to one of a *śūdra* caste, nor does it follow that in the *varṇa*-system a *śūdra* by caste is allowed to receive instruction.

As the story goes, Jānaśruti comes back to Raikva and offers him richer, more pleasing, gifts. He offers him one thousand cows, the earlier necklace and chariot, and, in addition, his daughter to be his wife and the village in which his place of stay is located. As Śankara puts it, 'considering her face' (Jānaśruti's daughter's face), Raikva says 'O Śūdra, you have brought these; through this very face you will make me speak',[18] i.e. I shall now, because you are giving me this girl, impart to you the instruction you have been requesting me to impart. He does, as the tradition says, then impart the desired instruction to him, though even this time he has called him a *śūdra*. But again the reason or reasons for calling him a *śūdra*, mentioned already, remain unrefuted, and the view that he instructs a *śūdra* by caste unsubstantiated. As a matter of fact that cannot be substantiated because Jānaśruti is, as already shown, not a *śūdra* but a *kṣatriya*.

Rāmānuja too in his commentary on the *Brahma-Sūtra* (1.3.33–34) totally agrees with Śankara in confirming that Jānaśruti is not a *śūdra* by caste, and his is not a case of a *śūdra*'s having been imparted instruction by Raikva.

He does not deny that Raikva calls him a *śūdra*. But he also adds that 'that Jānaśruti was addressed by Raikva as "Śūdra" is not because he belonged to that caste by birth, it refers to his grief for not having the knowledge of Brahman, for "śūdra" etymologically means "one who grieves". So Śūdras by caste are not entitled to Brahmavidyā'.[19] By *brahmavidyā* Rāmānuja means knowledge of *Veda*s and *Vedic* literature, as also knowledge of *Brahman*.

While giving an account of the conversation of swans, he says that two *ṛṣis* take the form of swans and utter those words to let Jānaśruti know that though he has led a good moral life by doing a lot of charity, etc., he does not have the knowledge of *Brahman* which Raikva has, and therefore is inferior to him. That is, they want to motivate him to go to Raikva and get instructed by him about Brahman. It is this sort of instruction which Raikva imparts to Jānaśruti and it is not to be imparted to any *śūdra*.[20]

Rāmānuja's account is not different from Śankara's because Śankara also holds that 'Either some *ṛṣis* or gods...took the forms of swans'[21] and uttered the words which prompted Jānaśruti to go to Raikva. He also avers that the instruction the king requests Raikva to impart to him is about the divine. This is clear from his beseeching 'Please favour me with the instruction about the deity'.[22] In a like manner, Rāmānuja is as emphatic as is Śankara about Jānaśruti's being a *kṣatriya* and therefore about his not being a *śūdra*. Since Jānaśruti gives a lot of gifts to people, and feeds many, he says, 'All this shows that he is a man of means, a Kṣatriya and not a low-born Śūdra.'[23] The result is that both of them hold that Jānaśruti's example does not counter the view that a *śūdra* is disallowed to receive instruction in *Vedic* knowledge which, as we have seen, amounts to saying that he is not allowed to receive education. Thus, both support the view that classical *varṇa*-system does not permit a *śūdra* to study *Vedic* literature, or to get himself educated.

There is nothing sacrilegious in saying what has been said above because it has all been said in respectable classical works and by respectable classical interpreters of those works. Nor is there any sacrilege in bringing into clear focus the fact of the great, spiritually elevated, *ṛṣi* Raikva's agreeing to instruct and actually instructing Jānaśruti only after receiving from him more wealth in the form of cows, necklace, an entire village, etc. and particularly as a result of being given a young girl to be his wife who is none other than the king's own daughter. This component of Jānaśruti's episode shows the life-affirming, positive, attitude of classical, spiritually elevated, scholars or saints. There is nothing wrong in the *ṛṣi*'s desiring to have the things he was offered by the king, not even in his having a wife with an attractive face. Rather all this counters the accusation that classical Indian scholars' attitude towards life is negative or unrealistic, or that classical Indian ethics is life-denying, or totally ascetic.

However, there is one item in the episode which must not be glossed over or overlooked in a work on Indian ethics which this is. Jānaśruti offers to the *ṛṣi*, along with other things, his daughter, as the fee, or cost of his getting instruction in *Vedic* knowledge, or knowledge of *Brahman*. And, the literature does not say that he has taken the consent of his daughter for offering her to the *ṛṣi* as his wife. Any morally sensitive person, or any moral philosopher, cannot resist the logical-ethical urge, and a well-justified one, to ask the questions: 'Is it morally right, or even permissible, for anyone to offer his daughter to attain *Vedic*, spiritual, or any sort of, knowledge?' 'Is *Vedic*, spiritual, knowledge such a thing that to attain it the aspirant's daughter can be given to the instructor in the manner in which a cow, etc., can be given?', 'Is the *ṛṣi* morally justified in accepting the girl as his wife without any moral compunction, while knowing that she has been treated, in the act of offering her, as a chattel?', etc. The answers to these questions are obvious. No traditionalist, or spiritualist, can call them irrelevant without being unfair to the *intrinsic dignity* of morality.

One thing is clear from the Jānaśruti-Raikva example of extolling Raikva's possession of *Vedic* or *Brahman*'s knowledge and considering Jānaśruti's highly moral life inferior to Raikva's way of life. In it morality is given not only a very low ranking but is made dispensable or ignorable. Jānaśruti leads a highly elevated, commendable, moral life. He is extremely benevolent because he very much cares for the well-being of others. A care or concern for the welfare of others, benevolence, is central to being moral. The *Chāndojña* does not say anything about the moral quality of Raikva's style of life. He is only referred to as the *ṛṣi* who is found sitting underneath a cart scratching his itches, who possesses knowledge of *Brahman* and accedes to Jānaśruti's request for instruction when his fee for imparting instruction is greatly augmented, more precisely by adding to it a princess as his wife. But his way of life is still rated higher than Jānaśruti's supremely moral one.

The example does not make morality a means to attain knowledge of *Brahman*; it makes morality violable, a disposable commodity. Gifting a daughter to attain anything, mundane or spiritual, is counter-moral. Jānaśruti mentions his gifts in one conjunctive sentence when he says that here are cows, a necklace, his daughter and the village, etc. Logically there is nothing wrong in listing them together because a cow, a necklace, a village, and a daughter are all substantives, particulars, i.e. all belong to the same category of substance (or individual, as used in modern logic). But ethically they belong to different categories. For example, both a cow and a daughter are living beings but, from the moral point of view, they belong to two different categories insofar as a daughter is a person, a free agent, while a cow is not. Therefore, there is nothing wrong in buying, selling, or gifting, etc., a cow, but doing any one of such things to a daughter would be morally wrong or impermissible. Jānaśruti's gifting his daughter to the *ṛṣi* is not as innocent, let alone being praiseworthy, as his giving the cows, etc. is. And, no text says that he has taken her consent before gifting her to Raikva. Giving her to him to persuade him to impart the instruction is something like selling her to buy knowledge, like using her in a barter; it is not just antifeminist. It certainly violates the morality of respecting the dignity of a person in the form of the king's daughter by using her as a mere means. Therefore, I have said earlier that Jānaśruti's example makes morality violable in the interest of elevating the status of *Vedic*, or *Brahman*'s, knowledge.

7.3.2 The Example of Satyakāma Jābāla

This episode occurs in the *Chāndojña* (section 4). The story runs as follows:

One day in his early childhood Satyakāma tells his mother Jabālā that he wants to join a school and study there observing well the discipline of the school. Therefore, he asks her his lineage (*gotra*). The lineage of an individual in the then classical Indian social structure is determined by that of his father and his lineage reveals his caste. In response to his query about his lineage she tells him:

'O my son, I do not know this, the lineage to which you belong. I got you in my youth when I was busy performing many duties and remained engaged in serving. Being as I was, I do not know this as to which lineage you belong. But my name is Jabālā and your name is Satyakāma. So you speak of yourself as Satyakāma Jābāla'.[24]

The normal practice in classical India is that a child takes the same surname which his father has, or one derived from his father's name, and his surname generally reveals his caste. Here Jabālā asks him to take the surname 'Jābāla', a word formed from her name instead of his father's surname or any word formed from the father's first name. This suggests that she does not know the exact identity of his father. This possibility is implied by her saying that in her youth when she got him she was engaged in serving, i.e. in working as a maid servant (*paricārikā*).

Only with this information about his caste Satyakāma Jābāla goes to the *brāhmana ṛṣi* teacher Gautama to get admitted in his school. Gautama, to ascertain his caste, asks him his *gotra*. Rather, as the *Brahma-Sūtra* (1.3.37) puts it, he asks his *gotra* to ascertain the absence of *śūdra*-hood (*śudratva*) in him (*tadābhāvanirdhāraṇe* = *tat* [that's, i.e. of *śudratva*, of his being a *śūdra*] + *abhāva* (non-existence in him) + *nirdhārṇe* (for ascertaining).[25] This is clear from what he concludes from Jābāla's reply to him. He replies to him by truly narrating to him exactly what his mother has told him about his caste. From his reply, Gautama concludes that since 'A non-*brāhmaṇa* will not be able to say this,' he is a *brāhmaṇa*, and decides to admit him when he, as asked by him, performs the rituals required to be performed by an aspirant in order to get admitted in his school.[26]

Gautama's reasoning behind his decision to admit him, when made explicit, stems from his sentence 'A non-*brahmaṇa* will not be able to say this (unpleasant truth)'. This is logically equivalent to 'No non-*brāhmaṇa* can say this'. Putting it in this form, his reasoning is:

> No non-*brāhmaṇa* can say this. Satyakāma Jābāla has said this. Therefore, Satyakāma Jābāla is not a non-*brāhmaṇa*, i.e. Satyakām Jābāla is a *brāhmaṇa*. Therefore, Satyakām Jābāla is to be admitted.

Thus the reason for his admitting Jābāla in his school is his being a *brāhmaṇa* as per Gautama's thinking. He does not admit him for his ability or being qualified to be taught by him, also not merely for his truthfulness. Rather, his truthfulness is a sign, according to him, of his being a *brāhmaṇ*. This is so because of his presupposition or assumption that no non-*brahmaṇa* possesses the ability to tell the kind of truth which Jābāla has told him. If he does not make this assumption, he cannot infer from his telling the truth that he is a *brāhmaṇa* and consequently cannot admit him.

It is this assumption of his which gives him a reason in Jābāla's telling the truth to eliminate the possibility of Jābāla's being a *śūdra*. Rather, it overshoots his target. It also eliminates the possibility of his being a *kṣatriya* or a *vaiṣya* because a *kṣatriya* and a *vaiṣya* are also non-*brāhmaṇa*. In his commentary Śankara also interprets Gautama's decision to admit Jābāla on the lines interpreted above. According to him Gautama's words amount to telling Jābāla 'Since you did not depart from truth, which is a virtue of the *brāhmaṇa* caste, therefore I shall initiate you who are a *brāhmaṇa*.'[27]

From the account of Jābāla's admission in Gautama's school, as given in the *Chāndojña* and commented on by Śankara, it is clear that Jābāla's admission in the school is not the admission of a *śūdra* because of his having the ability to receive education; rather, it is the admission of a *brāhmaṇa* in the school. Jābāla's case is similar to Jānaśruti's who too is instructed not because he is a *śūdra* with the ability to learn but a *kṣatriya* king who gives handsome gifts to Raikva, the teacher, and is called a *śūdra* only because of his being overwhelmed with grief. These two examples, therefore, cannot be used to prove that in the *varṇa*-system a *śūdra* is allowed to be taught *vedavidyā* if he has the ability to be taught. They cannot be used to prove either that *varṇas* are determined in it on the basis of the abilities of individuals because of the difficulties already mentioned.

By the time of the *Upaniṣads* the *varṇa*-system had become well-established and the *varṇa* of an individual hereditary or birth-determined. There is no question of the abilities of an individual coming into play in determining his *varṇa* or in assigning him to a *varṇa*. For example, Gautama is not trying to *assign* or *allot, Jābāla* to an appropriate caste by knowing his lineage; he, on other hand, is trying to *discover* it. The question of one's lineage does not arise if one does not already belong to a *varṇa* or caste, as per the classical Hindu practice. Therefore, we cannot say that Gautama *assigns* Jābāla to the *brāhmaṇa varṇa* because of his telling the truth. But assuming that every one has a caste and one of a *śūdra* caste is not permitted to be admitted in his school, he asks him his *gotra*. And, using his telling the truth, a truth not at all pleasant, as an accepted *linga*, or reason, for his, or any individual's, being a *brāhmaṇa*, he concludes, or becomes sure of the fact, that he is a *brāhmaṇa*. That is why it is not an instance of classifying an individual, Satyakāma Jābāla, as a *brāhmaṇa* on account of his truthfulness, i.e. his ability to tell the truth howsoever unpleasant it may be. That Gautama firmly believes in the sanctity of the *varṇa*-system and in its practice which does not allow a *śūdra* to be admitted in a school is straightforwardly asserted in the *Brahma-Sūtra*'s aphorism, already referred to. It unambiguously asserts that he asks Jābāla to tell him his lineage to be sure of his *not being a śudra*, and *not to test* what sort of abilities he has in order to *freshly* assign him to a caste on basis of the abilities he has.

Quite a good number of modern scholars use the statement of Kṛṣṇa in the *Gītā* that he has created the four *varṇas* on the basis of individual's *gunas* and *karmas* to support the ability account of *varṇa*-classification. Keeping in view the importance attached to the *Gītā* position it is fair to give to it a separate discussion. We shall do that below.

7.3.3 The Gītā *Version of* Varṇa-*Classification*

The *Gītā* account is very concisely stated in 4.3 uttered by Kṛṣṇa to Arjuna. Kṛṣṇa states it to him with two objectives in his mind. One of them is to let Arjuna know that the four castes and their duties or obligations have been created by Kṛṣṇa himself. This is important because it would then mean that the caste-obligations (*varṇadharmas*) have supreme sanctity derived from the most sanctified status of Kṛṣṇa who is their creator, and therefore that they are inviolable. It is very necessary for him to emphasize this point on that occasion. The reason is that Arjuna is disinclined to fight the *Mahābhārata* war, though fighting such a righteous war is a *kṣatriya*'s, and therefore his, obligation because he is a *kṣatriya,* i.e. belongs to the *kṣatriya varṇa* or caste.

The other objective of Kṛṣṇa is to tell Arjuna that though he has *done* this work of creation, and hence he may seem to be a doer, an agent (*kartā*) of it, he is not really an agent because he has done it in a completely desireless manner. Only an agent is responsible for what he does. An individual is an agent, according to him, only when he does something in a desireful manner. On the other hand, he who does anything in a desireless manner is a non-agent and therefore non-liable to earn any credit or discredit for having done it. Kṛṣṇa has to bring this point home to Arjuna because Arjuna thinks that he would be killing a number of close relatives on the battle field if he fights the war and would earn a lot of moral discredit or sin. Therefore, he does not want to fight. On the other hand, Kṛṣṇa wants to persuade him to fight the battle and fight in a desireless manner. His argument is that if he fights in a desireless manner he would be a non-agent and incur no discredit whomsoever he may kill, whatever he may do. To illustrate this view of his he says that he himself has done the *creation* of castes and caste-obligations in a desireless manner while remaining a non-agent. Therefore, he is not responsible for the results of this creation, nor culpable if any untoward consequence ever comes out of it. Here I shall discuss only the subject of the creation of the four castes by Kṛṣṇa and leave the other subject of a desireless doer as being really a non-agent or non-doer insofar as his moral responsibility, that is, praiseworthiness or blameworthiness, is concerned, for another section in the book.

In the first sentence of the *Gītā*'s 4.13 *Kṛṣṇa* asserts that 'the four castes (*cāturvarṇyam*) have been created by Me (*mayāsṛṣtam*) through a classification of the *guṇas* and duties (*guṇakarmavibhāgasah*).[28] We have to be clear here as to what we take Kṛṣṇa to be, whether we take him as the full incarnation of the god Viṣṇu with all divine powers, as the tradition takes him to be, or as a great social leader with the excellencies or powers which a human being may have. Not only the classical Indian tradition but even modern Indian interpreters take him in the former sense, i.e. as a divine being, as God in human form. To start with, let us do that and see the implications of this account of the creation of castes relevant for our understanding and estimation of classical Indian ethics. This is pragmatic to do because we are interested here in the classical Indian caste or *varṇa*-system only because of its role in the evolution of classical Indian ethics.

Since we have decided, for the time being, to follow the tradition and take Kṛṣṇa as God, or God-incarnate, it follows that he can do anything except what is logically impossible. Therefore, he can form *varṇas* in whichever way and on whatever basis he chooses to form them. One thing is clear from our assuming all this. It is that this account of *varṇa*-formation would be, because of its implementer being a divine figure, a theological, or mythological, one, and not a human, sociological, or historical, account. Therefore,

I have said earlier that the *Gītā* account when taken in a certain sense is not different from a mythological account.

The *Gītā* account has got its popularity because it has been taken by almost all interpreters as a version, or rather as the most authentic and foolproof version, of the ability account. It has been so taken because of the occurrence, in Kṛṣṇa's statement, of the phrase *guṇakarmavibhāgasah,* which means 'on the basis of the classification of the *guṇas* and duties of individuals'. The Sanskrit word *guṇa* is ambiguous. One meaning of it is quality or attribute. It is in this sense that it is used in the *Vaiśaṣika* school as one of the seven ontological categories (*padārthas*). This is also its meaning in ordinary, non-technical, Sanskrit and modern Hindi. It is in this sense that it is ordinarily understood and used in normal conversation. In the *Sānkhya* school of Indian philosophy, however, *guṇa* is used to mean a constituent or component of the primal matter, called *prakṛti,* which is one of the two basic realities, the other being the class of infinite number of *puruṣas,* i.e. pure consciousness. In the *Sānkhya* categoriology, thus, a *guṇa* does not mean quality but a substance, a thing, and a material thing since it is the constituent of matter. There are, in all, according to the *Sānkhya,* three sorts of *guṇas,* called *sattva, raja* and *tama* which constitute *prakṛti* and every material thing is composed of these three kinds of *gunas* though their proportion in any two different things is different.

The phrase 'guṇakarmavibhāgasah' is a conjunction of two terms, *gunavibhagasah* and *karmavibhāgasah,* meaning classification (*vibhāga*) of components (*guṇas*) and classification of duties (*karmas*). This will be the meaning of the conjunction if *guṇa* is taken in the *Sānkhya* sense. Famous commentators like Śankara, Madhusūdana Sarasvati, Śrīdhara Svāmī, Rāmānuja, et al., take the word *guṇa* in *guṇakarmavibhāgasah* in this, the *Sānkhya,* sense of a constituent, a substance, and not in the *Vaiśeṣika,* or ordinary usage, sense of a quality or attribute. Therefore, in this sense of the term, *guṇavibhāgasah* means classification of individuals on the basis of their components or constituents, i.e. of their constitution as formed by the way in which their component *guṇas* are organized. The fact of the matter is that, according to the *Śānkhya* ontology every individual being is a complex or organization of the three *guṇas,* i.e. three sorts of constituents. But in different individuals the *guṇas* are differently organized in the sense that in some one *guṇa* is predominant and the two others are subordinated to it, in some others another *guṇa* dominates and the other two occupy subordinate positions, in different orders of prominence in different cases.

Let us suppose that in some individuals *sattva* dominates, *raja* is subordinated to it and *tama* is minimally present; in another group of individuals *raja* dominates, *sattva* occupies the second position but in a weaker form and *tama* is minimally present; in still another group *raja* is predominant, *sattva* is present in a weaker form than in the second group and *tama* is also present in a weaker form, and in the fourth group of people *tama* is most prominent, and *raja* and *sattva* are present in the most minimal or negligible form. Let us call the first group B, the second K, the third V and the fourth S.

Every individual, or rather every object in the world, is thus, according to the *Sānkhya,* a constellation or complex. Since we are concerned in this chapter with the *varṇa*-system, the human society, let us limit our discussion only to human individuals and their groups. Then we can say that every individual is a *guṇa*-constellation. The particular *guṇa*-constellation of an individual is determined by his *prārabdha* actions, i.e. those actions which he has done in his past life and which have begun producing their effects or consequences. Their effects cannot be altered. Therefore, the *guṇa*-constellation of an individual cannot be altered according to anyone who accepts the *Sānkhya* theory or *guṇas*. Further, it is the *guṇa*-constellation of an individual which determines his nature and his nature determines what he can and what he cannot do. What an individual ought to do, i.e. his duties, obviously would be some of the things which he can do, since 'ought' implies 'can'. This means that the set of his duties, the set of actions (*karmas*) which he ought to do, is a sub-set of the actions he can do. Since all that he can do is determined by his nature, and his duties form a sub-set of all that he can do, his duties are also determined by his nature. From this it follows that his duties too are determined by his *guṇa*-constellation since his nature itself is, as said above, determined by his *guṇa*-constellation. It is this sort of thinking on *Sānkhya* lines which Śankara adopts in interpreting the *Gītā*'s 4.13 in his commentary on it.

Anyone who knows and only he who knows the *guṇa*-constellation of an individual, therefore, would know his nature and thereby his duties. Since every individual is born with his *guṇa*-constellation and continues with it all through his life, the knower of his guṇa-constellation will know his duties the moment he is born. But his *guṇa*-constellation only he can know who can know, or who knows, his *prārabdha* actions of his previous life. That is, if the duties of an individual are to be determined by his *guṇas*, then only he can know what they are who know his *guṇa*-constellation, and by implication, what he did in his previous life.

Kṛṣṇa says, as per Śankara's analysis, that he has *created* the four *varṇas*, i.e. four castes of individuals, and the reason for his putting them into four classes is their having four differing types of *guṇa*-constellations. That is, he has first done the work of classifying their *guṇa*-constellations into four types and on its basis the classification of individuals. This classification is none other than our imagined classification of individuals into four classes or castes we have called B, K, V and S three paragraphs above in which we were trying to illustrate a method of classifying people into four classes on the basis of their *guṇas* or *guṇa*-constellations. We put there Śankara's version of Kṛṣṇa's method of classification in our allegedly imaginary classification with the intention of using it later in explicating Śankara's method.

As per Śankara, our imagined type B is the *brāhmaṇa varṇa*, type K the *kṣatriya varṇa*, type V the *vaiśye varṇa* and type S the *śūdra varṇa*. Kṛṣṇa, he says, classified their duties on the basis of their nature, as he says a little later in the *Gītā* itself. Doing that means classifying their duties ultimately on the basis of their differing *guṇa*-constellations, i.e. on the basis of their *guṇas*, because they determine their nature. That is why he uses one conjunctive compound *guṇakarmavibhāgasah* to state the basis of his creating four castes of individuals with their well-defined duties. Since the *guṇas*, or the *guṇa*-constellation of *brāhmaṇas* is different from that of any other caste, say, the *kṣatriyas*, their duties are different from those of the *kṣatriyas*. On the other hand, since the *guṇa*-constellation of all *brāhmaṇas* is the same, the duties of all *brāhmaṇas* are the same.

The above method of classification of individuals into four *varṇas* and of the duties of the four *varṇas* read into Kṛṣṇa's aphorism 4.13 of the *Gītā* is not a uniquely Śankarite characterization of the *Gītā*'s version of *varṇa*-system. Rather, it is a generally accepted characterization in the classical Indian tradition. The duties of different *varṇas*, the *varṇadharmas* and problems, normative and conceptual, related to them will be discussed later in some detail.

Not only according to Śankara's interpretation of the *Gītā*, but even on any neutral interpretation of all that Kṛṣṇa says in it, or even elsewhere, it is clear that his classification of the society into four castes is not empirical, or inductive, i.e. based on the observation of what people actually do, or what kind of capabilities their life-pattern reveals. It is not, therefore, based on their actual, empirically ascertained, abilities. If it is said to be so based Kṛṣṇa would have to face all the difficulties the ability account has to face, as has been shown while examining the feasibility of the ability account.

Apparently Kṛṣṇa proceeds to present an empirical theory in an a priori, non-empirical, manner. On can say that anyone's classification of individuals into *varṇa*s, groups, on whatever basis, is an empirical, inductive, work which Kṛṣṇa does non-empirically. But a devotee of the Kṛṣṇa-cult, or he who believes in his godhood, may say that Kṛṣṇa does it empirically but in a way in which only he, a god, can. The believer may proceed on some such lines:

Kṛṣṇa does the classification on the basis of the *guṇa*-constellation of individuals. Their *guṇa*-constellation is determined by those actions (*prārabdha*) of theirs which they did in their past life and which have started yielding their destined consequences. Kṛṣṇa, being God, knows what those actions were and therefore he knows a priori the *guṇa*-constellations of all individuals. In fact he knew them even before they were born, and therefore his four-fold *classification* of individuals is *empirical* but the kind of an empirical and which only God, or on incarnation of his, can do.

For a believer, therefore, there is no problem or puzzle in Kṛṣṇa's classification, or in Śankara's and other classical Indian interpreters' interpretation of Kṛṣṇa's aphoristic statement of his procedure of classification presented in the *Gītā*. It is clear now that for a non-believer in God's existence, or in the theory of incarnation, this account of *varṇa*-formation would obviously be a mythical or mythological account and not a version of the ability account. It is unquestionable for the believer but for the non-believer it is no account at all. And, for a non-committed, rationalist, philosopher, the introduction of the belief in God in the exercise of solving the problem of *varṇa*-classification, or any problem whatsoever, may make its solution extremely easy, but only at the cost of bequeathing to it the extremely difficult problem of the existence of God itself. In this case this problem would become more difficult because of its being accompanied by the equally intractable problem of *avatāra*-hood (being an incarnation of God).

Moreover, the *Gītā* account, in spite of its being allegedly based on *guṇa-karma*-classification, virtually turns out to be a birth-determined (*janmanā*) account. Every individual is born with a *guṇa*-constellation determined by his actions in his previous birth, and his *guṇa*-constellation ultimately determines, as has been shown, his *varṇa*. Therefore, everyone is born as a member of a *varṇa*, as a *brāhmaṇa*, or a *kṣatriya*, or a *vaiśya*, or a *śūdra*. This too shows that it is not an ability account because, from an empirical, sociological, point of view, no individual's abilities can be ascertained or predicted on his birth, let alone determining them before his birth.

Secondly, since it is (allegedly) a classification by God, it has to be accepted to be free from all blemishes and therefore never needing to be improved or altered. All this follows simply from its being a God's classification. Nobody can either improve or change what He has done, nor does one need to make it better because what God has done cannot, by definition, have a deficiency or lack which a human agent can remove. A clear implication is that accepting this account would justify denial of social and societal change and keep society in a static or stagnant condition.

I mentioned in the beginning of this section an alternative way of understanding Kṛṣṇa's role in the classification of *varṇas*, namely, the alternative of taking him to be a social leader who has done the classification. But the *Gītā* Kṛṣṇa is not, as claimed by himself, just a social leader but God himself in a human form. In fact, at one point he reveals his cosmic form (*virātarūpa*) to convince Arjuna that he is really God in a man's body (*nārāyaṇa*). And, if we decide to take him as a social leader who has done the four-fold caste classification on the basis of individuals' qualities and actions which they actually do or are capable of doing, then he would have to face all the problems which the implementation of the ability account has to face. These problems are, we have seen, unsolvable. Moreover, Kṛṣṇa says that the four castes have been *created* by him (*mayāsṛṣta*), not classified, though created on the basis of their *guṇas* (*guṇa*-constellations) and *karmas* (duties determined by their *guṇa*-constellations).

All those, and all modern philosophers, who claim the *Gītā* account to be an ability account seem to have ignored, or not taken seriously, the occurrence of *mayāsṛṣtam* in the very first sentence of the *Gītā*'s 4.13 (*cāturvarnyam mayāsṛṣṭam guṇakarmavibhāgasah*). They seem to have done it perhaps in their zeal to emphasize that the classical Indian *varṇa*-system is not, in its beginning, formed on the basis of the parentage or birth of individuals but on that of their abilities. They seem to depend heavily on the occurrence of the term *guṇakarmavibhāgasah* in the *Gītā*'s 4.13, translating *guṇa* as qualities possessed by an individual, and *karma* as actions or works done or doable by him in his present life. But in this sense of the terms, *varṇa*-classification, done on the basis of *guṇa-karma*-classification, has been shown to become unimplementable. Moreover, a *classifier* of *varṇas* is not their *creator* which Kṛṣṇa claims to be saying that he has created the *varṇas*. Finally, as Śankara has shown, *guṇa* does not mean quality possessed and *karma* not action done or doable by an individual in his present life.

Even B.G. Tilak and Sri Aurobindo have translated *guṇa* and *karma* in the manner of modern professional philosophers and non-philosophers. Tilak goes to the extent of translating *mayāsṛṣtam* as 'I have made the classification or social order (*vyavasthā*) of the four *varṇas*, *brāhmaṇa*, *kṣatriya*, *vaiśya* and *śūdra*', and not as 'I have created ...'. He has completely dropped the idea of their creation by Kṛṣṇa, and interprets *guṇa* to mean qualities possessed by and *karma* to mean actions done by individuals in their present life.[29] Aurobindo admits the theory of creation of the four *varṇas* by 'the Master of existence' but still interprets *guṇas* to mean an individual's qualities and *karma* to mean work in the sense of an action which an individual does.[30]

It is not surprising that modern scholars adopt this line of thinking. It seems to me that all of them think that to propound the *varṇa*-by-birth theory is less respectable from the moral or cultural point of view than to propound the *varṇa*-on-the-basis-of-ability theory. They seem to find an easy prop for attributing the ability theory in the occurrence of *guṇakarmavibhāgasah* in Kṛṣṇa's statement. Thereby they proceed to defend that originally *varṇa*-classification was done on the basis of individuals' abilities without examining the nature of its possibility conditions, and that it got debased into the birth-determined classification only much later. They do not realize that this interpretation lacks textual support, nor that even during the time of the *Mahābhārata* war, on the battle-field of which Kṛṣṇa taught the *Gītā* to Arjuna, the caste-system had become birth-determined. Rather, some historians hold that quite early in the history of India, even before the *Mahābhārata* times, it had become birth-determined. Moreover, if the *Gītā*'s, a theological, theory makes *varṇa*-classification birth-determined as implied by its making it God-determined, there is nothing objectionable in admitting this fact.

Too much importance has been given, one may say, here to Śankara's interpretation of the *Gītā*'s 4.13, and that is unfair. But even other interpreters like Madhusūdana Sarasvati and Rāmānuja interpret it on similar lines. Madhusūdana Sarasvati's interpretation is completely similar to Śankara's.[31] But Rāmānuja's too, in spite of his propounding a different ontology from Śankara's, is very close to the latter's. Rather, he goes a bit further, to the extent of saying, while elaborating the *Gītā*'s 4.13, that 'the entire world, in which the four *varṇas* are prominent (*caturvarṇapramukham*), from Brahmā, etc., to a blade of grass (*Brahmādi stambaparyantam*), has been created by me' (i.e. by Kṛṣṇa) 'according to the classification of their components, like *sattva*, etc. (*sattvādiguṇa vibhāgena*)'.[32] It is true however that Sankara's commentarial interpretation of this issue is the most elaborate and analytical. That is why there is no unfairness involved in discussing it some in greater detail than others.

Some scholars seem to make a lot of the Sanskrit saying:

Janmanā jayate *śudrah, sanskārāt dvija ucyate.*

It may be taken to mean that every individual is a *śūdra* when he is born; he is called a twice-born only after his performance of the (*sanskāra*) sacred thread ceremony. Or that every individual is a *śūdra* when he is born in the sense of being once-born (*ekajātīya*); he is called a twice-born only on the basis of his aptitudes to behave in certain ways, i.e. on the basis of his actions. In the first sense it is a re-assertion of the birth-determined theory because, according to it too, every one, even a *śūdra*, is once-born. But a *śūdra* is not allowed to perform the sacred thread ceremony and therefore destined to remain only a once-born all his life. But every *brāhmaṇ*, *kṣatriya*, and *vaiśya* are allowed, or rather required, to undergo the ceremony. This means that on his birth itself one is either a *śūdra*, or any one of the other three *varṇas*. Only then can the prohibition for *śūdras*, and the prescription for others, to perform the ceremony be implemented. Therefore, on this interpretation the Sanskrit sentence cannot be used to disprove the birth-determined *varṇa*-theory and prove the ability-or-action-determined one.

On its second interpretation it may be used to support the ability account of the *varṇa*-theory. But it will not prove its feasibility because there is nothing in it which may be used to solve any of the difficulties in the implementation of the theory which have been already discussed. Moreover, the Sanskrit sentence does not occur in any classical work, as Nirajakant Chaudhury demonstrates in a series of articles in *Kalyāṇa*, 1970–71. Therefore, nothing substantial can be asserted about the *varṇa*-theory on its basis, whichever way we may prefer to interpret it.

Chaudhury thinks that it is an interpolation made by someone sometime much later, and that its having been repeatedly published in some works has given to it some sort of respectability. In fact, in classical times originally, he says, on conclusive textual evidence, only *brahmaṇas* had their *gotras* (lineage traced to some *ṛṣis*). Later on, even *kṣatriyas* and *vaiśyas* were allotted *gotras*, but *śūdras* never had any *gotra*.[33] Looking at the general temper of the *varṇa*-system, and the textual support he has given, there is no reason to question Chaudhury's conclusions.

This fact about the non-allotment of a *gotra* to a *śūdra* makes it clear, as we have already discussed, why Gautama asked Satyakāma Jābāla to tell him his *gotra* to ascertain that he was a *brāhmaṇa,* or at least not a *śūdra,* as the *Brahmasūtra* (1.3.37) puts it.

7.4 UNTENABILITY OF USING ETYMOLOGY TO DEFEND ABILITY ACCOUNT

Some scholars with indological or orientalist bent of mind tend to think that the ability account of the *varṇa*-system, or *varṇa*-classification, is provable from the etymological meaning of the world *varṇa. Varṇa* is derived from the Sanskrit root *vrñ* which means to choose, to select, or to opt for, etc. Therefore, they say that the *varṇa* of an individual, as per the classical Indian conception of a *varṇa,* is not determined by his birth or parentage. Rather, it is left to him to choose his *varṇa* depending on what he is capable of doing. That is, if an individual has the ability to be, for example, a warrior, then he can be a *kṣatriya* by choice. But this kind of interpretation of the functioning of the *varṇa*-system is not maintainable for more than one reason.

There is no example of any individual's belonging to a *varṇa* of his choice because of his having the abilities required of a member of that *varṇa.* Viśvāmitra has all that a *brāhmaṇa* is expected to have, still he is a *kṣatriya* and not a *brāhmaṇa* which he very much wants to be. After a lot of struggle he is called a *brahmarṣi* but not a *brāhmaṇa,* what to speak of his choosing to be one. Karṇa, is by birth a *kṣatriya* if, say, Arjuna is, but since his parentage is not known till very late in his life, he is not taken to be a *kṣatriya,* though he is a better warrior than many *kṣatriyas*. He would definitely have chosen to be a *kṣatriya* if becoming one were a matter of his choice. Similarly, Ekalavya would have chosen to be a *kṣatriya* or should have been called one at least after he exhibited his excellence in the martial skill of archery. But this does not happen, let alone leaving it to him to choose his *varṇa.* He would have been surely considered to have gone mad by Droṇa had he told him, when he refused to admit him in his school, that he chose, or had chosen, to be a *kṣatriya.* In fact, had there been available any freedom to choose one's *varṇa* on the basis of one's abilities, or even aptitudes, the same individual would have had to choose membership of different *varṇas* in his lifetime when his abilities/ aptitudes changed. And, their changeability cannot be ruled out ab initio. But Indian history does not give any instance of such an individual.

Those who adopt this method of etymological derivation to arrive at the substantive theory of *varṇavyavasthā* as based on individuals' choice, commensurate with their abilities, generally are those who hold that to attribute this account of *varṇa*-formation to classical Indians, from the moral point of view, speaks well, i.e. appreciatively or laudatorily, of what they have done. On the other hand, to attribute the birth-determined account, they think, speaks, from the moral point of view, ill or derogatorily of their practice. Apart from the fact that this approach does not realize the conceptual difficulties in the implementation of the ability account, of which the choice account obtained from etymological analysis is a variety, they also do not realize that the etymological method is a double-edged blade. Etymological analysis of, for example, the word *śūdra,* would yield a social theory which, if attributed to classical Indians, would speak, again from the moral point of view, very ill of their social practice. *Sudra* is derived from the root *śuc* which means to suffer, to experience grief (*śoka*). Therefore, etymologically speaking, a *śūdra* is he who suffers or experiences grief, i.e. one who is by definition always grief-stricken (*śokita*). Taking it to its conclusion, if we are led by etymology, we shall have to say that the classical Indian social order has a class of people who are to remain always sufferers, always grief-stricken. We have seen that this meaning of *śūdra* is exploited both by Śankara and Rāmānuja to explain why Raikva calls Jānaśruti a *śūdra* though he is a *kṣatriya.* This theory about the status of the *śūdra* puts such a thick dark paint on the of the classical Indian *varṇa*-theory that all the shine that the etymology based interpretation of *varṇa* may allegedly give to it would fail to make it lighter, let alone removing it, or making it lustrous.

The *etymology* of a word, or its grammar, is not at all a guide to understand its logic, i.e. the logic of the concept which it stands for. It is an obsolete or archaic way of doing philosophy, of presenting a philosophical theory, or of even defending or interpreting one. This simple logical point has been extremely well demonstrated by contemporary analytical philosophers, Western as well as Indian. But some of our Indian interpreters of classical Indian ideas still seem to be addicted to using etymological or grammatical analysis to make a philosophical or historical point. A satirical joke in a folklore about a verbal duet between a Sanskrit grammarian and a *Naiyāyika* very well illustrates the futility of taking a grammatical structure always too seriously. It runs as follows:

A grammarian is to play the role of a priest in performing a *śrāddha* ceremony (a ceremony performed in honour of a dead person). He asks the dead man's grandson to bring him (the dead) so that he may start the ceremony. When the *marriage ceremony of a man* is performed, he says, the man whose marriage it is has to be present. Similarly, when the *śrāddha ceremony of this man* (the householder's grandfather) is going to be performed, he must be here. The grandson feels befuddled. A *Naiyāyika* present there tries to help him out. He tells the grammarian that a *śrāddha* ceremony is not (logically) comparable to a marriage ceremony. The grammarian priest sticks to his grammar, saying both 'marriage ceremony of a man' and '*śrāddha* ceremony of a man' have the same grammar. The matter is resolved only after the *Naiyāyika* presents a detailed analysis of the two concepts 'marriage' (*vivāha*) and *śrāddha* showing that though the grammar of the words is the same, both being nouns, the logic of the concepts they stand for is not the same.

It is a commonplace of linguistics that language precedes etymology and grammar. This is true of Sanskrit as it is of any other historical language. Pāṇini had a full-fledged, well-structured, Sanskrit language much before he started ascertaining the different roots (*dhātus*) to which the formation of the then stock of words could be traced, or from which they were derived, keeping in view the meaning which the words, as per their usage, had. That is, the etymology of a word even for Pāṇini, does not *determine* its meaning; it only makes intelligible, or explains, its meaning which is the meaning it has in usage. That is why the guide to the actual meaning of a word, i.e. to the actual logical behaviour of the concept it stands for, is not the meaning of its root, but actual linguistic practice, the role the concept plays in the area of thought it belongs to.

When there is no word for a role which needs to be played in an area of thought, the grammarian, who is concerned with systematizing the functioning of the language concerned, needs to coin a new word for that role and formulate or discover a grammatical or etymological procedure, or rule, which sanctions, justifies, or explains the coinage or formation of that new word which he coins. It is said that when Pāṇini finds in the then society instances of an unmarried woman having a child before her marriage, there being available no word to denote such a child, he coins the word *kānina* to perform this role and also formulates a rule to explain its coinage. This too shows that grammar or linguistics has to follow, or serve the needs of, linguistic practice, or, we can even say, man's social, public, needs.

Returning to the child in our cradle at the moment, the concept of *varṇa,* we can conclude this short detour into the area of etymology or grammar, by re-asserting that the role of this concept, like the role of other social-ethical concepts, can be ascertained by watching its behaviour in the *varṇa*-system, including *varṇa*-ethics, and not by sticking to its etymological meaning (*dhātvartha*). Depending blindly on the etymology of a word to ascertain its meaning may sometimes cause not only conceptual but even social havoc. The word *dārā,* which means wife, etymologically means a woman who produced a son. If this is taken to be its total, or basic or essential, meaning, then a woman who is the duly married wife of a man but does not produce any son but only a daughter, would cease to be the wife of the man she has been married to. She may even be said to have become liable to be thrown out of his house because of having become thereby a non-*dārā* (non-wife).

7.5 MYTHOLOGY AND *VARṆA*-SYSTEM

There is an important distinction between classification or organization and creation. Individuals can be organized or classified into the four *varṇas* only if they are already there, i.e. only if they exist before the process of classification begins. But they can be said to be created only if they do not already exist. The already existent cannot be created. The ability account, therefore, presupposes the existence of individuals before their organization into *varṇas.* The *Gītā* account is both, a mixture of creation and organization. It involves the process of organization according to *guṇas* and *karmas* and makes it possible because it assumes the theory of rebirth and therefore admits the pre-existence of individuals in their previous birth. It also involves creation of *varṇas* because Kṛṣṇa claims to have created the individuals of different *varṇas* in their *present* life, and thereby making them belong by birth of their *varṇas.*

Other mythological accounts, on the other hand, are purely birth-determined accounts of *varṇas.* There are quite a few such accounts which we will state very briefly because, being mythological, they must not be taken seriously as far as the *varṇa*-ethics is concerned. Ethical theories can be constructed only on the basis of real character-traits of real individuals on which a mythological account can throw no light.

Some of the oft-talked-about mythological accounts are the following:

(i) As stated in the *puruṣa sukta* of the *Ṛgveda,* from the mouth of the Cosmic Person (*Virātapuruṣa*), which may be taken as God, *brāhmaṇas* are created, from his arms *kṣatriyas,* from his thighs *vaiśyas* and from his legs *śūdras.*

(ii) The *Mahābhārata* in its *Parāśaragītā* (Vol. 5, pp. 5207–8) reiterates the *puruṣasukta* account of the *Ṛgveda* but for one change: It replaces *Virātapuruṣa* by Brahmā. Manu in *Manusmṛti* 1.31 repeats the *Mahābhārata* account.

(iii) The *Bṛhadāraṇyaka Upaniṣad* (1.10–15) speaks of Brahman's projecting the four *varṇas.*

(iv) In the *Bhāgavata Purāṇa* (11.17.1–58) Kṛṣṇa avers that he himself is the Cosmic Person and has created *brāhmaṇas, kṣatriyas, vaiśyas, śūdras*, and a fifth class of people called *antyaja* who are lower in rank and merit than even *śūdras*.

The mythological accounts, all of them, are theories very similar to one another, attributing the creation of *varṇas* to some divine agent. And, all of them have made the account hierarchical, mentioning the above four (or five) *varṇas* in a descending order of status or ranking. A clear implication of these theories of the divine orgin of castes, for anyone who believes in the existence of such a divine agency, will be that this caste-organization is perfect and not to be changed, rather one that cannot and ought not to be changed, simply because the divine agent would not do anything which is defective. This implication itself is a reason for not taking them seriously because no social or social organization can be called perfect, or a never-needing-to-be-changed phenomenon.

7.6 EXPLOITING A HINT FROM MYTHOLOGY

There is a point which needs to be recognized when we try to think about the mythological accounts in a realistic, reconstructive, manner. It is true that any *mythological* account of the *varṇa*-system can be taken as a literal, factual account only by a highly orthodox, credulous or religious person with an unprobing mind, particularly when it is about a social, human, organization which the classical Indian *varṇa*-system as well as its progeny, the present multi-membered caste-system, is. But a mythological account may be taken as an allegorical one to highlight the difficulties involved in explaining the origin of the formation or structuring of a human phenomenon.

That classical India had a four-fold *varṇa* or caste system with well-defined duties is a historical fact. The ability account of its formation is an ethically reasonable one though, we have seen, it is extremely difficult to explain its implementation because of the changing nature of human conditions, particularly human capabilities. The birth-determined account is a neat one though it lacks ethical reasonableness. It is not reasonable, from the moral point of view, to aver that an individual has such and such a right or duty because of his having had a certain kind of parentage. Moreover, the birth-determined account cannot explain the original allotment of a *varṇa* to an individual because in the beginning no individual's parents would have had any caste-denomination which could have been given to a progeny of theirs.

To highlight these difficulties classical thinkers might have constructed some mythological accounts to give a hint to social-moral thinkers that it is more futile than a wild goose chase to try to explain the *first* classification of individuals into four, or any number of, *varṇas* either by following the route suggested by the ability account, or the one suggested by the birth-determined account. This hint is also relevant for the historian or theorizer of classical Indian ethics. It clearly implies that any attempt to trace the beginning, or to account for the origin, of ethics in India, or anywhere, will not have better luck than the one about the origin of the *varṇa*-system, or of any other primal grouping of human beings. This is bound to be, in the case we are concieved with, because the *varṇa*-classification is also a classification or categorization of the duties, rights, virtues, goals, etc., of the individuals allotted to different *varṇas*. In fact, it is this fact about Indian ethics and the Indian *varṇa*-system which makes study of the latter necessary for understanding the former.

Utilizing this hint, or reading this hint to have been thrown up by mythological accounts, it seems to me a good, reasonable, guess to say that the *varṇa*-classification might have begun, for the first time on the basis of individuals' abilities or competences empirically exhibited in their performances in an ad hoc, unsystematic, non-rigid, or fluid, manner. And, in this way also the then ethical codes would have simultaneously emerged and evolved. This is natural because every exhibition of ability, every performance, may be judged to be desirable or undesirable, commendable or condemnable, or neutral. Since the classification based on abilities cannot be made rigorous, or fool-proof because of the conceptual difficulties we have pointed out earlier, it seems natural that this ad hoc, but man-made, non-theological, classificatory procedure slides later into the birth-determined characterization. It is natural because of the ease possessed by the birth-determined account to name the *varṇa* of an individual after the name of the *varṇa* of his parents which might have been given to them sometime in the past on the basis of their competence and performance, i.e. their abilities or functional potentialities.

But whichever way the procedure of *varṇa*-allotment might have gone, it became the stage on which classical Indians played the moral game, both the background and the foreground of the development of Indian ethics. That is why, as we will see, classical Indian ethics is largely, or primarily, *varṇa*-ethics. This is our reason for discussing the *varṇa*-system in the manner we have done, i.e. with our eyes focused on its intrinsic, natural, link with classical Indian ethics.

It may be urged here by someone that it is unfair to give so much theoretical prominence to the *varṇa*-system and *varṇa*-ethics because neither is *āśramevyavasthā* the same as *varṇavyavasthā* nor is *āśramadharma* the same as *varṇadharma*. This issue has been so far postponed. It will be discussed in what follows.

7.7 *ĀŚRAMA*-SYSTEM AND MORAL DISCIPLINE

The *āśrama*-system is generally taken to be a scheme of life which an individual has to follow. It may be taken as a scheme which one is to follow to make one's personal life better or worthwhile. But, as we shall see, it is not a scheme which has nothing to do with the society, i.e. not a purely private concern. Even the *āśramavyavasthā* has its focus on providing to an individual a scheme of life by following which he can turn out to be a viable member of his society while getting adequate opportunities for fulfilling his own inner potentialities. The latter are, according to many classical philosophers, fulfilled when he attains spiritual enlightenment.

An individual's life is to develop through four stages (*āśrama*), or periods covering the entire span of his life, which is generally taken to be of one hundred years. The first period is that of studentship (*brahmacārya*) in which a child is admitted in a school after having performed, under the guidance of his teacher, the sacred thread ceremony. He is to stay on the school campus till he completes his education. He is required not only to acquire knowledge of the existing disciplines but also to inculcate moral culture. The primary emphasis is that he should turn into a good citizen. A student who acquires knowledge only for his intellectual satisfaction and success in wordly life and not for enabling him to become a cultured, morally descent, spiritually enlightened, person, is called a is called a brother or companion of knowledge (*jñānabandhu*), and not a genuine knower or possesser of knowledge.[34]

In any system of education everybody involved may not be fully sincere in the performance of his duties. This possibility classical thinkers acknowledge about another type of student as well. For example, a student may shift from one school to another if he finds it easier to get in this way free boarding and lodging facilities by staying in different schools for a short period only, without straining himself to grasp what the teacher teaches his students. He is very much looked down upon and is called a *tīrthakāka*, i.e. he is considered comparable to a crow who shifts from one sacred place to another to get good food, having no respect for the sacredness of the place where he stays for some time.

No mention, however, of the possibility of a teacher's being insincere seems to have been realized. Even after Droṇa's asking Ekalavya to give him his right thumb and receiving it nonchalantly after his chopping it off and presenting it to him, no condemnatory expression is used for him by anyone. He first refuses, as the story in the *Mahābhārata* goes, to admit him in his school. But Ekalavya makes an idol of Droṇa, treats it as his teacher and learns the skill of archery on his own and becomes an excellent archer even by Droṇa's standards. Since he has treated Droṇa as his teacher, and acquired the excellence, Droṇa asks him to give his right thumb as an expression of his gratitude to his teacher (*gurudakṣiṇā*). His motivation in asking for it is certainly not commendable, in fact is really condemnable, because it is to disable him from becoming an archer better than, or equal to, Arjuna, his favourite student, who is, among those he loves, second only to his son, Aśvasthāmā. The right thumb is the main finger in the exercise of archery, but still Ekalavya chops it off and offers it to Droṇa as his *gurudakṣiṇā*.

The life of a student in a school is a social life in more than one way. This is very well illustrated from certain practices. The famous auspicious vow-or-wish-expressing sentences, which occur before the actual text of the *Kathopaniṣad* begins and at similar other places, explicitly or implicitly admit that the teacher and the taught form a society and that there may occur problems between them which occur among the members of any society; for example, there may occur some disharmony, or sense of competition or rivalry, between them. The last sentence among them is a clear expression of this possibility as it is put in a form which may be taken to express a vow, a wish, or even a caution: May we not be jealous of each other (*mā vidviṣāvahai*).[35]

Children, or young men, studying in a school are required to work for their teacher, for example, to tend his cattle, to bring fuel from dry trees in the neighbourhood of their school, to go to nearby villages to collect alms in the form of raw food materials, etc. For example, when *Satyakāma Jābāla* is admitted by Gautama to his school, he gives him four hundred lean and thin cows and asks Satyakāma to follow them. He promises to his teacher that he will return to the school only when these four hundred, through their progeny, become one thousand. He stays in a forest away from the school for many years and returns, as the *Chāndojñya* (4.4.4.–5.9.3) says, only when the original stock of cows has grown into a thousand cows. The teacher, then, on his request, gives him his final lessons. All this may or may not be a historical fact. But even then it indicates that the school formed a well-knit society.

The student is expected, in this scheme only to receive his lessons from the teacher. He is not supposed or permitted to be critical of them, or of the teacher's wisdom or of his reasoning. The idea seems to be that the teacher knows the truth and therefore the student has only to grasp it, and not to question, criticize, or comment on, it. The practice of writing commentaries, or of discussing critically a teacher's views, comes in much latter in the *sūtra* period of Indian philosophy.

Generally teachers are, in classical Indian society, householders having more than one wife, and sometimes even having a wife much younger than them. This is likely because there is the custom of an old teacher's accepting a young girl as a gift from her father to become his wife. We have seen that the great saint-scholar Raikva accepts Jānaśruti's young daughter, gifted by him, to become his wife; rather, he agrees to teach Jānaśruti the knowledge of *Brahman* only after looking at the charming face of the girl. Therefore, the possibility is there of a young, grown up, student's developing an amorous attachment with a young wife of his teacher. Theorizers recognize this possibility and its gravity, or immorality as per the then ethics, and expressly require a student to avoid all likely opportunities which may facilitate the development of such an attachment. Manu severely prohibits a student from anointing, or massaging, the body of a teacher's young wife, helping her in bathing, or hair-dressing. He must not even greet her by touching her feet, but only from a distance. If she is an elderly lady, he may on the first day of his return after a long absence, pay his respects to her by touching her feet, but later on only from a distance.[36]

As already pointed out, a *śudra* child is not to be admitted in a school. Therefore, if there are many students in a school, each one of them knows that the other one is either a *brāhmaṇa*, a *kṣatriya*, or a *vaiśya*. That is, he is likely to be *varṇa*-conscious. This means that though as students they are all equal, each one of them belongs to any one of the three *varṇas*, which are not all equal in social status. Therefore, the fallouts or implications of *varṇatā*, or of the hierarchical *varṇa*-system, are very likely to be present in the student community. It is very likely, therefore, that the then student community also is a *varṇa*-system, though on a less extensive scale.

The second stage in an individual's life is that of a householder (*gṛhastha*) in which he gets married, has children, and leads a family life in a society. He is required to fulfil his obligations to all those with whom he is concerned directly or indirectly. This is the most important part of one's life because it is the householder who supports, by making donations, schools, recluses, saints, indigent people, etc. It is in this part of his life that he has to do what he is required to do to fulfil his *varṇa*-obligations as well as his general obligations. The importance given to this part of life demonstrates that the classical Indian attitude towards life and the world is highly, or rather exuberantly, positive, and not at all negative. This is so in spite of the fact that in the other, the two last, stages of his life an individual is required to retire from an active householder's life in order to devote himself to attaining spiritual enlightenment. A very clear illustration of it is found in the life of the famous saint-scholar Yājñavalkya. Only after leading a long, happy, conjugal life with more than one wife he expresses his desire to retire from the worldly householder's life in order to devote himself to the acquisition of the knowledge of the Self. This knowledge is the same as the realization of the Self, which according to him, is both the highest reality and the highest value. And, even then, before doing that he wants to divide his property in fair manner between his two wives, Maitreyī and Kātyāyanī, as stated in the *Bṛhadāraṇyka Upaniṣad* (11.iv.1). This shows that even after deciding to search for the spiritual he does not begin to attach no importance to worldly possessions.

The third stage in an individual's life is called *vānprastha*, the stage in which he leaves his hearth and home and spends his life in a forest. That is, he becomes anchorite. It is supposed to begin at the age of fifty and to last until the age of seventy-five. In this period he is required to devote himself fully to the pursuit of religious goals. Some works say that in this stage he can keep his wife with him. But in the last one, the stage of *sanyāsa* (renunciation) he is not allowed to keep her with him. The fourth stage of renunciation is a continuation of the third one of the anchorite. The only difference is that in the fourth he is to live alone, after having left his wife too. His main objective is to do all that is required to attain liberation (*mokṣa*), the highest goal of life (*parama puruṣārtha*).

In both of the last two stages the individual does not live in a society; i.e. his life is not a social one. In the third he may be said to have a society, of course a very small one, i.e., the society or company of his wife. Therefore, it may be said that he still has some moral obligations to fulfil, namely, those concerning his duties to look after her. But in the fourth he has no society; he is all alone with only one goal in mind, which is nothing other than the attainment of *his own,* and not anyone else's, liberation. He ceases to have *almost* all of his obligations to *others* in the third stage itself. In the fourth he ceases to have *all* of them. This means that he places himself outside the zone or boundary of morality or ethics. It is this *rude* fact about the concept of *sanyāsa* which is lauded by saying that the individual has reached a stage which is beyond the reach of moral life and therefore higher in merit than it. It is not realized that the concept of occupying a position outside, or beyond, morality does not imply that position is in merit higher than, or superior to, leading a morally committed life while living in a society. It may be higher, but that it is needs to be proven independently of the alleged claim that it is outside or beyond the frontiers of morality.

In the requirement or precept of adopting the *vānaprastha* and *sanyāsa* mode of life there seems to be lurking the presupposition or assumption that morality is a closed system, a finite set of a limited number of obligations, duties, virtues, goals, etc., all of which can be fulfilled, inculcated, or attained, etc., i.e. their pursuit exhausted, in the stage of the householder if it is properly lived. And, therefore, in the last two stages one is freed from all moral requirements and is at liberty to devote oneself entirely to one's religious or spiritual pursuits. This is not a fair, or healthy, conception of morality, as has been argued in the previous chapters, and will again be taken up in discussing the issue of *puruṣārthas*. Therefore, it is not being elaborated here.

Perhaps, it is the realization of this fact about morality which has motivated later thinkers to propound that even while leading a social life and doing all that morality requires, a human being can attain liberation if he does whatever he does in a detached, desireless (*niṣkāma*) manner. And, this understanding of the concept of liberation gains its prominence largely because it tries to grant to morality what is its due and gives to social life as well its due importance in the evolution of ethical norms and principles and goals and therefore in the development of ethical theorizing. That is why we have been reiterating all along the role of *social life,* or *varṇavyasthā,* in determining to a large extent the character of Indian ethics. This point will be reinforced further when we discuss in the next chapter the classical Indian general theory of values, or, of a good, decent, life.

NOTES AND REFERENCES

1. Swāmi Vireśvarānanda (trans.), *Śrimad Bhagavadgītā* (with the gloss of Śridhara Swāmī) (R.K. Math, Madras), Swāmī Gambhīrānanda (trans.), *Bhagavadgītā* (with the commentary of Śankarācārya) and *Bhagavadgītā* (with the annotation *Gūḍhārtha Dīpikā* of Madhusdan Sarasvatī) (both published by Advaita Ashrama, Calcutta).
2. Jayasankara Misra, *Pracina Bharata ka Samajika Itihasa* (Bihar Hindi Grantha Akadamy, Patna, 2002), p. 221.
3. Swami Gambhirananda (trans.) *Brahma-Sūtra Bhāṣya of Śri Śankarācārya* (Advaita Ashrama, Calcutta), p. 232. Henceforth abbreviated as *SGBSS*.
4. Ibid., p. 233.
5. Ibid., pp. 233–34.
6. Ibid., p. 234. Also see Harikṛṣṇadāsa Goendakā (trans.), *Vedānta-Darśana* (*Brahmasūtra*) (Gita Press, Gorakhpur), pp. 73–74 for various textual references. Henceforth abbreviated as *HGBS*.
7. Swami Adidevananda (trans.), *Brahma-Sūtras: Śrī-Bhāṣya* (Advaita Ashrama, Calcutta), p. 174. Henceforth abbreviated as *SABS*.
8. Swami Gambhirananda (trans.), *Chāndogña Upaniṣad* (with the commentary of Śri Śankarācārya) (Advaita Ashrama, Calcutta), pp. 251–56. Henceforth abbreviated as *SGC*.
9. Ibid., p. 246.
10. Ibid., p. 247.
11. Ibid., p. 248.
12. Ibid., p. 251.
13. Ibid.
14. Ibid., p. 253.
15. *SGBSS*, p, 231.
16. *HGBS*, pp. 70–71.
17. *SGC*, p. 253–54. *SGBSS*, p. 251–52. *HGBS*, pp. 69–71.
18. *SGC*, p. 254.
19. *SABS*, p. 173.
20. Ibid., p. 172.
21. *SGC*, p. 145.
22. Ibid., p. 152.
23. *SABS*, p. 173.
24. *SGC*, p. 265.
25. *HGBS*, p. 72.
26. *SGC*, p. 268.
27. Ibid.
28. Swāmi Gambhīrānanda (trans.), *Bhagavadgītā* (with the commentary of Śankāracārya), pp. 185–86.
29. Bal Gangadhar Tilak *Śrīmadbhagavadgītārahasya* (Tilak Mandir, Pune, 1950), p. 674.
30. Sri Aurobindo, *Essays on the Gītā* (Sri Aurobindo Ashram, Pondicherry, 1970), p. 492.
31. Swami Gambhirananda (trans.), *Bhagavadgītā* (with the annotation *Gūdhārtha Dipikā* of Madhusudan Sarasvati), pp. 282–83.
32. Harikṛṣṇadāsa Goendakā, *Gītā-Rahasya* (Gita Press, Gorakhpur), p. 146 (Translation mine).
33. *Kalyāṇa* (Gita Press, Gorakhpur), Vols. 44 and 45, 1970 and 1971. See p. 1172 of Vol. 45.9, 1971.
34. *Kalyāṇa: Yogavasistha Anka*, Vol. 35.1, p. 530.
35. *Kalyāṇa: Upaniṣad Anka*, Vol. 23.1, p. 185.
36. *Manusmṛti* (2.211, 212 and 217).

CHAPTER 8

Classical Indian Theory of Human Value: Some Structural Features

8.1 HUMAN LIFE AS PURPOSIVE: DESIRING AS VALUING

By and large, classical Indian thinkers are of the view that human life is purposive in the sense that man is a *value-seeking individual.* Though they emphasize that he should exercise almost always some control over his desires, they do not fail to equally emphasize, at the same time, that in whatever he voluntarily does, he generally tries to fulfil some purpose, to achieve some objective or goal, by trying to obtain an object he desires to have or by trying to abjure an object which he desires not to have. To desire that he does not have an object is straining a little bit our normal sensitivity to syntax, to desire to not have, or not-have, an object. To desire to have an object is to have a positive desire or to be short, a pro-desire, towards the object. Similarly, to desire to not have an object is to have a negative desire, or a con-desire, towards it. But in both the cases there exists a desire; a negative desire is obviously a desire as is a positive desire. In the case of an object of a negative desire, if an individual has somehow come to have it, he would like to get rid of it. In the case of an object of positive desire, on the other hand, if he happens to already have it, his attempt would be to continue having it, to preserve and protect it.

In this way, he tries to achieve a goal, to fulfil an objective in whatever he does, no matter whether his motivating, or operative, desire in doing it is one to attain, or one to abjure, an object. His life is thus a *purposive,* an objective-seeking, or a value-seeking, progression or procession of attempts or activities. And, it remains purposive irrespective of the nature or character, morality or immorality, of his motivating desires, of his purposes. Rāvaṇa's devilish life is as much purposive as is the saintly life of his step-brother Bibhīṣaṇa.

The classical thinkers' belief in the value-seeking nature of human life is obviously an empirical one, a belief based on their observation and understanding of how human beings, including themselves, generally conduct their life in whatever they knowingly, deliberately, voluntarily, do. It is not an a priori belief, nor a definitional one resulting out of some definition of being human, or of human life. It is also not a belief which they claim to have been given by, or to have culled from, some *śruti,* some authoritative work of some divinely gifted individual. Be that as it may, it certainly is a plausible or common-sensical belief, one which, in our day-to-day transactions, all, or almost all, of us even today consider quite innocent. Therefore, we do not need to take classical thinkers to task for holding it, and can quite justifiably proceed further to see in which direction their axiological inquiry, using this belief as its starting point, goes.

8.2 THE CONCEPT OF *PURUṢĀRTHA* AND SOURCES OF ITS NORMATIVITY

The Sanskrit word for an object of a human being's desire is *puruṣārtha.* In fact, *puruṣārtha,* as Dharmottara analyses it in his *Nyāyabindutīkā,* means *puruṣasya arthah, artha* of a human being. *Artha* from the root *arth* means in it an object of *arthanā. Arthanā* means a desire, wish, intention, etc. Thus *puruṣārtha* literally or etymologically, means an object of a desire,[1] an objective, a goal, i.e. that which a human being aims at, wants or desires to have, a purpose he wants to fulfil, etc. In its linguistic meaning, therefore, there is no restriction on the concept of an object, or on that of a desire, or on that of a person or human being an object of whose desire it is. Obviously, then, *puruṣārtha* means any object of any desire of any human being. This is what the ordinary English phrase 'an object of a human desire', or, 'a human objective (or purpose)', also means.

This *semantic* fact about the functioning of the term 'puruṣārtha', because of the term's simply meaning an object of a desire, may give the impression that the term is, or functions as, a purely descriptive one, having no evaluative meaning. This it is very likely to do to an individual who is not sufficiently sensitive to the semantic and pragmatic nuances of the psychological term 'desire' and its equivalents. Such an individual may, therefore, say that, on the analysis of the term *puruṣārtha* given above, the Indian theory of *puruṣārthas* would become a purely descriptive, a psychological, theory about human nature because of its being one about objects of human desire. It would, thus, be in no way a theory of value in the sense of being one about what a human being ought to desire or aim at, i.e. about what he values and ought to value.

Drawing the above implication would be unfair to the linguistic analysis of *puruṣārtha* given here. This analysis is linguistically completely accurate and has been approved of not only by Dharmottara but also by other classical Indian logicians and axiologists. However, it is also true that the theory of *puruṣārthas* is, in the Indian ethos, an axiological and not just a psychological, descriptive, theory. This is so because the concept of a *puruṣārtha* functions in it as an evaluative one, and it does that while functioning linguistically in the same way in which it has been claimed to be doing in Dharmottara's analysis of it. In fact, to aver that it functions as an evaluative concept is to cast not even the least doubt on the accuracy of Dharmottara's semantic analysis of the term *puruṣārtha.* To solve, or to get rid of, the puzzle anyone senses in this situation we have to do nothing more than to look a little more closely into the logic of the concept of desire, one's desiring to have or to not have, something. Since desiring to not have (or to not-have) something is as clear a case of desiring as is desiring to have something, in what follows we shall make our point only by examining the logic of desiring to have something. Even with no ingenuity a reader can apply that analysis to any example of negative desiring, i.e. to one's desiring to avoid having something as well as to get rid of something which he willy-nilly has but desires to no longer have it.

It is in the very logic of the concept of desire that, for any individual, to desire to do something, or to have something, is to like, to favour, to consider it worth his while, i.e. to *value* doing, or having, that thing. This is as well true of his desiring to continue having, to preserve or protect, something which he already has. And, it is equally true of his desiring that someone else does something, or has something, or continues to have, or preserves or protects, something which is already in his possession. All this shows that a desire has built into it an attitude of favour, a sense of considering what is desired worthwhile; that is, an evaluating attitude is a natural constituent of the concept of desiring to do, or to have, something. To desire to do or to have something is thus to value doing or having it.

It is possible that what one man desires to have and therefore values, another man considers a disvalue, or considers its opposite a value. For example, in the *Rāmāyaṇa* Kaikeyī desires that her son Bharata be put on the throne of Ayodhyā and Daśaratha desires that not Bharata but Rāma be put on the throne. But it is not possible that one desires to have something (or to have something done) and does not value having it (or having it done). That Kaikeyī values her son's being put on the throne is clear from the fact that she gets him put on the throne even at the cost of her husband's life; that Daśaratha values Rāma's having been put on the throne is clear from the fact that when his desire to put Rāma on the throne is not fulfilled, he dies of the shock the non-fulfilment of his desire causes to him. Therefore, the semantic fact that the term *puruṣārtha* means an object of a human desire does not make the term purely descriptive. It remains still an evaluative term, getting its evaluative meaning from the evaluative overtones present in the notion of desiring.

But then, it may be said, a *puruṣārtha* would only be that which is valued by the man whose *puruṣārtha* it is because, as shown above, for anyone to make something an object of a desire of his is for him to value it. His valuing it may not, however, make it *valuable*, i.e. something which *ought to be* valued simply because of its being what it is, or what it can be used to yield. But, the argument may go on, the concept of *puruṣārtha* denotes in Indian thinking not only that which *is in fact* valued, or desired, but also that which *ought to be* valued, or desired. This argument is valid but it does not destabilize the Dharmottara's type of semantic analysis which even other Indian philosophers do not dispute. In fact, nobody can dispute it because *puruṣārtha* linguistically means what Dharmottara and others say it means. It is also true that the concept of a *puruṣārtha* is normative; it is normative in the sense that for anything to be a *puruṣārtha is* for it to be something desirable or valuable, and not to be merely desired or valued. This normatively enters into the concept partly through the *content* of the things which, in the Indian theory, are considered to be *puruṣārthas*, or the chief *puruṣārthas*, and partly through the nature of the interrelations existing among the *puruṣārthas*, or among the chief *puruṣārthas*. This point will be fully clear when the different chief *puruṣārthas* will be individually discussed. But only to show what this sort of explanation means, I shall give one example and even that in a very brief manner.

Artha, one of the four chief *puruṣārthas*, meaning the totality of material conditions required for an individual to live well, *is in fact* a *puruṣārtha* in the sense that it is an object of desire for every individual. But it is also *normative*, as per the theory, in being a value which everyone *ought to* cherish because, if he does not have it, he would not be able to live the kind of life which he must live in order to attain other *puruṣārthas*. Secondly, the theory holds, this *arthas* of only the sort that everyone ought to aspire after which is approved of by *dharma* or morality. The normatively of *artha* as a *puruṣārtha* is thus a conjoint product of (a) its being what it is itself is, i.e. its being the totality of material conditions of life (which is what constitutes the content of the concept of *artha*), (b) its instrumentality in being required or necessary for the pursuit of other *puruṣārthas*, and (c) its concordance with the overall requirements of morality. An *artha* of which any one of the three features, (a), (b) or (c), is not true, will not be a *puruṣārtha* in the normative sense, though even then it may remain an actual, de facto, *puruṣārtha* of someone, i.e. someone's actual object of desire. Kaikeyī's making Bharata's enthronement her *puruṣārtha* does not have any one of the three features mentioned above, and therefore, it is not a bona fide *puruṣārtha*, a *puruṣārtha* in the normative sense, though it is her actual *puruṣārtha*, the actualization of a state of affairs she in fact desires or values. It does not have (a) because she (and Bharata) could have lived well even if Bharata were not enthroned; it does not have (b) because she (and Bharata) could have pursued all the other *puruṣārthas* even in the case of Bharata's having not been enthroned; it does not have (c) because it goes against, or infringes upon, familial morality (*kula dharma*) because, as per the royal family's moral practice, the rightful claimant to the throne is Rāma, being the eldest son of the king, and not Bharata because he is younger than Rāma. But still it is Kaikeyī's *puruṣārtha* in the sense of being the object she actually values, or aims at, and succeeds in, having.

8.3 THE THEORY OF *PURUṢĀRTHAS*: A GENERAL THEORY OF VALUE WITHOUT ANY BUILT-IN GENDER BIAS

It is a common practice among writers on Indian philosophy of morals to discuss the theory of *puruṣārthas* as a component of it. There is nothing wrong in doing that as long as it is not forgotten that the concept of a *puruṣārtha* does not, left to itself, denote an ethical or moral value, or something specifically or distinctively moral. It does denote a value, but this could be any sort of value, even a non-moral value. What kind of value it denotes, in a particular instantiation of it, depends on the *nature* of the thing it denotes in that instantiation. Vālmīki's *puruṣārtha* in writing the *Rāmāyaṇa* would be to produce a work of aesthetic value if what he aims at in writing the epic is the composition of an epic in a particular metre in elegant Sanskrit, satisfying the highest standards of the then Indian poetics relevant to epic poetry. On the other hand, it would be a work of moral value if his aim is to write out the story of Rāma as an exemplar of morality to let others have an example of what a morally upright man would do in some tricky situations in which it is difficult for an ordinary individual to decide which course of action would be the right course for him to adopt. It is also possible that Vālmīki's aim is both, aesthetic elegance and moral guidance, but still the two are different. It is possible that a work is aesthetically excellent but morally indifferent or even pernicious, and vice versa. That is why some books, of very high literary standards, are banned by some governments, or, even if not banned, are considered by many unreadable or forbidden for impressionable minds, when they are judged to be morally (or politically) undesirable.

Since a *puruṣārtha* could be any object, any desire, of any individual, the theory of *puruṣārthas* is, thus, if taken in an unqualified manner, a general theory of value or a theory of general value, rather than an ethical theory of value, or a theory of ethical value. It is true however that in it morality (*dharma*), which constitutes only one segment of it, is given much more importance than the two others, *artha* and *kāma*, and is also considered by some to be a precondition for the attainment of the fourth, *mokṣa*, which is taken to be the highest *puruṣārtha* (*parama puruṣārtha*). This fact about it has led many to conclude that the theory of *puruṣārthas* is an ethical theory of value. It is true that all of the four *puruṣārthas*—*artha*, *kāma*, *dharma* and *mokṣa*—are values. But every one of them is *not obviously* a moral value, though it has some link with *dharma* which represents moral value in the theory. Therefore, it is logically safe to call the theory a general theory of value, including within itself a theory of *dharma* which is, in the theory, the name for moral value. Since a general theory of value covers all sorts of values, it would be natural for the theory of *puruṣārthas*, then, to have within its ambit a theory of *dharma.* It is also important to point out here that a good case can be made to show that neither of the three, *artha, kāma* and *mokṣa,* taken by itself, is a moral value. Scholars may concede that this may be done in the case of *artha* and *kāma.* But they may feel sceptical of it when it is said to be the case also with *mokṣa,* largely because they consider *mokṣa* to be the spiritual value par excellence. *Mokṣa* may be a spiritual value but that would be an altogether different matter from saying that it is a moral value. All this is likely to be unclear at this place, but will become clearer as we proceed. Here an important theoretical possibility has been only introduced, or just mentioned, simply to make the point that it is conceptually more fair to call the theory of *puruṣārthas* a general theory of value than to call it a theory of ethical value.

The theory may, more accurately, be called a *theory of human* values because only a human individual deliberately seeks, or can seek, a value. Only he has the capability of having the consciousness, cognition, or assessment, of something's being an object worth seeking, i.e. a value, and of wilfully directing his efforts towards attaining it *because* of its being or having a (positive) value. The human-centricity of the concept of value and consequently of any theory of value is very well acknowledged by classical Indian thinkers. It is fully reflected in their very choice of the key word, *puruṣārtha* for value. As has been already shown, it carries its human-centricity on its face since it grammatically means an object of a human desire.

There is one misunderstanding which needs to be taken care of here. The word *puruṣa* is also taken to mean in some usage a *male* human individual. But it also means a human being, covering both male and female individuals. It is in this usage equivalent to *mānava* or *manuṣya. Puruṣārtha* is, thus, equivalent to *manavārtha* or *manuṣyārtha,* each one of which means any object of any human desire. But '*puruṣārtha*' is phonetically more elegant and easier (*sukara*) for the mouth (*mukha*) to utter than both of *mānavārtha* and *manuṣyārtha.* Therefore, the linguistic principle of smooth utterability (*mukha saukarya*) makes *puruṣārtha* preferable to both *mānavārtha* and *manuṣyārtha.* An over-enthusiastic feminist may urge that, since the term *puruṣa* is of masculine gender in Sanskrit, and in some usage means a male person, we should coin a term using the feminine term *strī* or *nārī,* with *artha,* to compensate for the gender bias lurking in *puruṣārtha* and through it in the theory of *puruṣārthas.*

It may seem to be a good retributive device to coin a term for *puruṣārtha* in the manner suggested above. But the resulting term out of *stri* + *artha,* as well as out of *nari* + *artha* would be not only not elegant. It would be (aesthetically) ugly and phonetically extremely difficult to pronounce. According to Sanskrit grammar, the term resulting out of *strī* + *artha* will be *stryartha* and that out of *narī* + *artha,* will be *nāryartha.* Both the terms are inelegant and very difficult to utter, nowhere near *puruṣārtha* which is not only soft for the tongue when it utters it, but equally soothing to the ear which hears it. Classical Indian thinkers are very careful about the choice of their terms, and they care not only for their semantic accuracy but also for their structural elegance and phonetic ease.

Whatever be the reason for the classical Indian choice of *puruṣārtha* for a human value, or even if the choice is accidental, there is definitely no gender bias involved in the choice. Therefore, no anti-feminism is built into, or ingrained in, the very concept of *puruṣārtha* or in the very theory of *puruṣārtha because* of the manner in which the theory has been formulated.

The (wrong) impression that there is such a bias may be created in another way as well. It may be created, for example, when *puruṣa* is taken to be synonymous with *puruṣārtha* as is done in the translation of same classical Sanskrit works into Hindi. *Puruṣa* is an abstract noun from *puruṣa* and it means masculinity or virility. But *puruṣārtha* does not mean any such thing. To say all this, however, is not to make the substantive claim that men and women are always treated as equal by Indian ethicists. The point which is being made here simply is that, even if they are not so treated, the use of the word *puruṣārtha* as the key word in the Indian general theory of values cannot be offered, on the grammatical ground mentioned above, as evidence in favour of the charge that they are not created as equal. Some other, more substantive, reason has to be given to defend the charge.

The general term 'value' is used in English ethical or axiological works in a broad as well as in a narrow sense. In the broad sense, it means a positive value as well as a negative value, a value which is worthy of being sought as well as one which ought to be shunned. When used in the narrow sense, it means only a positive value, a thing which ought to be sought. The word 'disvalue' is then used to denote a negative value. If a thing is a disvalue, or a negative value, then it means that we ought get rid of it if we already have it, or that we ought not to have it if we do not have it. A thing of positive value, contrariwise, would then be one which we ought to have if we do not have it, and ought to preserve or protect it if we already have it. In this work when the general term 'value' is used the context will decisively show whether it has been used in the broad, or in the narrow, sense. What is true of 'value' as known, in such respects, is also true of verbs and adjectives derived from it, for example, of 'valuing', 'evaluating', etc. and of 'evaluative', 'valuational', etc. So would be the case with other terms which may be called its synonyms, or near synonyms or equivalents.

8.4 POSITIVE *PURUṢĀRTHAS*, NEGATIVE *PURUṢĀRTHAS*, AND NON-*PURUṢĀRTHAS*

Puruṣārtha captures very well the generalities of the English term 'value'. It has the capability of being used to denote any object a human being aims at, or ought to aim at, an object of a positive desire, as well as one of a negative one. As already pointed out, a positive *puruṣārtha* is an object towards which we have a pro-desire, one which we *want* to have. Dharmottara calls it *upādeya,* a thing we consider fit or worthy to be had. Its opposite, the thing which we want not to have, or consider unfit or unworthy to be had, or rather fit or worthy of being not had, he calls *heya.* The *heya* is thus a negative value, or a *disvalue.* It is not something which merely lacks value, but something which has features on account of which we want not to have it. We have here too a desire, but a con-desire, one to not-have it. Therefore, both the *upādeya* and *heya,* are *puruṣārtha*s, objects of desire. The difference between them is that the former is an object of a pro-desire and the latter one of a con-desire. This shows that anything which is a *puruṣārtha,* has to be, as per the meaning of *puruṣārtha*, an object of some desire. This means that the concept of *puruṣārtha*, meaning any object of any desire, covers all values desirable as well as undesirable, and implies that there is nothing which is an object neither of a pro-desire, nor of a con-desire and is still a *puruṣārtha*, a value.

To value an object is to be, as per Dharmottara's analysis, interested in it in a positive or negative sense, i.e. to have an attitude of favour or disfavour towards it. This part of his analysis would be acceptable, by and large, to all classical Indian ethicists.

Dharmottara admits that there may be a third type of thing towards which we have no desire, positive or negative, towards which we are totally indifferent. Of a thing of this type it can be said that we neither want to have it, nor want to not-have it. He calls it *upekṣaṇīya*, ignorable, or a thing of no value, positive or negative, neither a value in the positive, nor a value in the negative, sense. Using 'value' in a narrow sense to mean only a positive value, or a positive *puruṣārtha*, it is neither a value, nor a disvalue, neither a *puruṣārtha* nor an *apuruṣārtha*. This is what follows from conceiving of it as *upekṣaṇīya*. But Dharmottara thinks, and wrongly, that the category of the *upekṣaṇīya* is reducible to that of the *heya* on the ground that we *do not want to have* the *upekṣaṇīya* as well as the *heya*. In doing this reduction he forgets that there is an important difference between them. It is that we do not simply not want to have the *heya*, we *want not to have* it, i.e. to avoid having it. That is, we are *interested in* not having it and therefore are *not* indifferent to it. But the *upekṣaṇīya* is that which we neither want, nor do not want, to have; it is something in which we are not interested at all, neither interested in having, nor in not having, it. That is, it does not matter to us whether we have it, or we do not have it. Therefore, it is neither a value, a *puruṣārtha*, nor an *apuruṣārtha*, a disvalue, but a non-*puruṣārtha* or non-value. This implies that the concept of *upekṣaṇīya* is not a normative or an evaluative concept. For this reason also it is not reducible to that of *heya* because the latter is normative. Its normatively is obvious from the fact that we *value* not having it and disvalue having it if perchance we are made to have it. That is what makes it a *heya*.[2]

8.5 SEEKING A *PURUṢĀRTHA*: A VOLUNTARY OPERATION

One of the important consequences of the above analysis of the concept of *puruṣārtha* is that there is an inalienable, logical or quasi-logical, link between the concept of *puruṣārtha* and that of desire. A logical fallout of this link is that the pursuit of a *puruṣārtha* has to be taken as a *motivated pursuit*, knowingly and willingly undertaken. For anyone to make something, say, wealth, a *puruṣārtha*, limiting the discussion to the concept of a positive *puruṣārtha*, is to make it an object of his desire. That would be the same thing as entertaining in himself a desire to attain it. To do such a thing for him is to choose to do it. That can be done only after his having some dependable knowledge of what wealth is. All this means that he makes wealth his *puruṣārtha* freely and knowingly, i.e. *voluntarily*; therefore, any effort to attain it would also be a voluntary affair. That is, his *acknowledging* or declaring that wealth is his *puruṣārtha* as well as *proceeding* on the path of attaining wealth is a voluntary concern of his. Neither of the two can be a reflex, or an accidental, affair.

But, it may pointed out, someone else may gift to an individual what he wants and has therefore made his *puruṣārtha*. This act of another's gifting too would lead to the attainment of his *puruṣārtha*, without his own doing anything to attain it, and therefore without his voluntarily seeking and trying to attain his *puruṣārtha.* Whatever may be the gifter's motive, selfish or altruistic, in making the gift to him, his act of gifting would cause the attainment of the *puruṣārtha.* And, this may be an *accidental* attainment, not one which is the result of any voluntary effort, or any pre-planned action, of the receiver of the gift. This, it may further be said, is illustrated in Duryodhana's gifting the kingdom of Anga to Karṇa and thereby making him the king of Anga, Angarāja. Karṇa very much *wants* to be a prince or a king, but does not know how he can become one. Becoming a prince, a king, or one related to a royal family (*rājakula*), can be called his *puruṣārtha,* an object of his wish or desire. Duryodhana's making him Angarāja, in a second, is something like a too happy accident. But it fulfils his wish, and thus, the argument against the position taken here may proceed, shows that Karṇa's *puruṣārtha* is attained in a purely accidental manner, without his having done anything to attain it. And, as far as this matter is concerned, the nature of Duryodhana's motivation in making Karṇa Angarāja would be of no consequence.

Even in this case, Karṇa's making royalty his *puruṣārtha* is voluntary and so is his accepting the kingdom given to him by Duryodhana. Here too it is his *puruṣārtha because* he has *chosen* it to be his *puruṣārtha.* Secondly, there is another, a normative, feature of the concept of *puruṣārtha,* as held by classical Indian thinkers, which needs to be taken into account at this point. It is the merit-yielding component of an individual's attaining a *puruṣārtha* by dint of his own efforts. He, who does that, earns some moral merit, some moral credit, for having done that. On the other hand, he who has it gifted a to him, does not. Karṇa becomes the king of Anga because of his having been gifted the kingdom by Duryodhana. The tradition, or Indian ethos, gives him no merit or credit for having become Angarāja. This is so because he has not acquired or attained the kingdom by doing anything to attain it. To be more precise, it may be said of Karṇa that he has not really *attained* his *puruṣārtha* but has *got* it. It is accidental that Duryodhana makes Karṇa a king to tempt him to come to his side to act as a rival of Arjuna. The tradition seems to *congratulate* Karṇa, or to call him honoured for having been made Angarāja but it does not seem to have given him any *moral credit* for having attained a *puruṣārtha* of his.

That the point made above is very clearly implied by the definition of a *puruṣārtha* as any object of any human desire, is vividly illustrated also by Dhṛtarāṣṭra in a response of his to his son Duryodhana. After his return from Indraprastha, Duryodhana expresses to him his anguish and unhappiness on account of the Pāṇḍava brothers' having developed Indraprastha, their share of the kingdom, by converting barren lands into orchards, and their having acquired by their efforts not only huge wealth but great social and political prestige as well, the *puruṣārtha*s of a royal family. Dhṛtarāṣṭra *admires* the Pāndavas for what they have acquired. But he calls Duryodhana only extremely *lucky* because of his having been given as his share the well-developed Hastināpura and thereby having been given all that a crown prince, or a king, may wish to have. Therefore, he advises him not to feel discontented or unhappy. But he does not admire him, or give him any (moral) credit, for his having all that as a result of his having been given the richest portion of the kingdom when it was divided between him and the Pāṇḍavas.[3]

The voluntariness of any pursuit of *puruṣārtha* is also obvious from the fact that classical Indian thinkers make the *knowledge of a puruṣārtha* a necessary condition for attaining it. It is common-sensical to say that unless a man correctly knows what his *puruṣārtha* in a certain situation is, he cannot know what is the means of attaining it and therefore cannot attain it. Rather, unless he knows the nature of a thing, he cannot have a desire to attain it, and therefore, then, it would not be a *puruṣārtha* of his. The question of his attaining it would obviously not then arise and he would not therefore try to attain it. This point will be elaborated further in section 8.7. Here it has been mentioned only to provide additional support to the claim, which is being made in this section, that seeking a *puruṣārtha* is a voluntary action, or a series of voluntary actions. Any such action, or series of actions, has to be intentional, well-thought out, and pre-planned, and therefore it cannot be a reflex, inadvertent, or an accidental action, or a series of such actions.

This mode of conceiving the pursuit of a *puruṣārtha* is very likely to instil in an individual a very robust, life-affirming, self-confidence-generating, attitude towards what he aims at or ought to aim at, i.e. towards his trying to attain his *puruṣārthas*. He has *first to know* the nature of his social and natural environment to determine what are the things which he ought to aim at, the things which could be his *puruṣārthas*, then to find out the means to attain them, and thereupon proceed to do so. To say that he ought to do these things presupposes that he is a free agent who can do them.

8.6 THE *NYĀYA* ELABORATION OF ROLE OF DESIRE IN SEEKING A *PURUṢĀRTHA*

That a *puruṣārtha* is an object of a desire, or that a desire plays a role on more than one level in the attainment of a *puruṣartha,* is not only emphasized but also further analysed and elaborated by some philosophers of the *Nyāya* school. Here I shall present very briefly the *Nyāya* analysis and only that form of it which has been adumbrated by Viśvanātha in his *Nyāya Siddhānta-muktāvalī*, a commentary on his own *Bhāṣā Paricchedа.* This is partly to save space but largely because in his presentation Viśvanātha also shows that the *Nyāya* position is an improvement on the *Mīmāmsa* position as held by its *Prābhākara* school. Secondly, I shall also adapt a little bit the *Nyāya* position to make it clearly applicable to the analysis of the concept of *puruṣārtha,* the theme that is presently being discussed here. The adaptation is necessary because *Viśvanātha*'s adumbration of his own position as well as his criticism of the *Mīmāmsa* position has been done overtly in the broader context of the concept of voluntary action, and not only in that of the concept of *puruṣārtha.* The adaptation is not unfair to his intention because, all along in the presentation of his position and also in his criticism of the *Prābhākara* position, he has in his mind the notion of a *puruṣārtha.* This is obvious from his admission that a *puruṣārtha* is the same as the object, in the sense of an objective or end, of an action. Therefore, his analysis of the concept of an action is, in intention, or in effect, an analysis of the concept of an action done to attain a *puruṣārtha.* His analysis of this concept too, as does Dharmottara's, includes the analysis of attaining a desirable as well as that of avoiding an undesirable object (or *puruṣārtha*). This is so because he too considers a case of effortfully avoiding an undesirable object to be a case of attaining a *puruṣārtha,* namely, attaining the avoidance of an undesirable object. All this happens because for both, Dharmottara and *Viśvanātha* an action, or attempt, to attain a *puruṣārtha* is a voluntary action or attempt.

Viśvanātha's analysis of desire, positive and negative (*icchā* and *dveṣa*), as related to its object, is as follows:

The entire world desires to have happiness (*sukha*) and the absence of pain or unhappiness (*dukhābhāva*). Happiness is yielded by moral merit (*dharma*) and pain by moral demerit (*adharma*). The desire for happiness arises from the knowledge of its object i.e. happiness, and the desire for the absence of pain from the knowledge of its own object which is nothing but painlessness. Knowing what painlessness is involves knowing what pain is because the former is nothing but the absence of pain. There are two kinds of desires: desire for the result (*phalecchā*) and desire for the means to the result (*upāyecchā*). The result is happiness and painlessness (*sukham dukhābhāvahca*). Therefore, happiness and painlessness both are, or can be called, *puruṣārthas*, or objects of human desire. This is to say that when there is a desire for happiness, happiness is the *puruṣārtha*, and when there is a desire for painlessness, then painlessness is the *puruṣārtha*. Only that object is called a *puruṣārtha*, which, when known, becomes an object of the knower's desire *because* of his own, self-assuring, understanding of what it really is, and *not because* of someone else's desiring (or causing) him to have a desire for it.[4]

It is clear now that for anyone to make an object a *puruṣārtha* of his is to have a desire for it as an act of his free choice, backed by his own comprehension of what its nature is, and is therefore a voluntary act of his. On the other hand, the desire for an object as a means (*upāyecchā*), in contrast with that for the result (*phaleccha*), says Viśvanātha, arises not simply from knowing what its nature is. Rather, in addition to this sort of knowledge, it is also necessary, for this desire to arise, to have the knowledge that this object has the capability to lead the knower to the attainment of the result, the object, aimed at by him, i.e. his *puruṣārtha*. This latter sort of knowledge he calls *iṣṭasādhanatājñāna*, knowledge (*jñāna*) of the instrumentality of the object chosen as a means (*sādhanatā*) to produce the result aimed at (*iṣṭa*). It is this knowledge which is the cause of, or reason for, considering the object in question a right means and the cause of or reason for using it to attain the end.

The desire to (try to) attain the end (*cikīrṣā*) is accompanied or caused by the individual's knowledge or conviction that it is feasible or possible for him to attain what he aims at (*kṛtisādhyatā jñāna*) by the use of the means which he considers a right means to attain it. That is, his desire to act, to actually proceed to undertaking the task, as required, for attaining the end in question is caused jointly by his knowledge that the means chosen by him is capable of yielding the intended result *and* the knowledge that by his effort he *can* attain the result.[5] On the other hand, his awareness that doing a particular thing will produce something repugnant, something which is worth not having, or is worthy of being abjured (*balvaddvistasādhanatā jñāna*), is an obstructing agent, an obstacle (*pratibandhaka*) to his having the desire to do it, or rather a cause of his having an aversion (*dveṣa*), a con-desire, towards doing it.[6] Just as there are two sorts of pro-desires, a desire for the result, i.e. happiness (*sukhecchā*), and a desire for the means to its attainment (*sukhopāyecchā*), there are also two sorts of con-desires (*dveṣa*). They are a con-desire towards the result, i.e. pain (*dukhaviṣayaka*) and a con-desire towards that which leads, or is a means, to pain (*dukhopāyaviṣayaka*). In our terminology, the former is a desire to not-have pain and the latter a desire to not-adopt or not-use anything which is a means to pain. Thus, the process of actually undertaking the task (*pravṛtti*) has the following four components: (1) the desire to undertake the task of attaining the end (*cikīrṣā*), (2) the knowledge that this task is doable (*kṛtisādhyatā jñāna*), (3) the knowledge that the means chosen is capable of yielding the result aimed at and (4) perception of the materials relevant to, or required for, undertaking the task (*samavāyi kāraṇa*) of attaining the end in question.

As presented by Viśvanātha, to put it very briefly, the *Mīmāmsaka Prabhākara* does not consider necessary for doing an action the knowledge of the capability of the means chosen to produce the result aimed at (*iṣṭasādhanatā jñāna*). According to him, for actually undertaking the task (*pravṛtti*) of attaining it, the desire to undertake the task (*cikīrṣā*) is required. For it to arise only the knowledge that the task is doable (*kāryata jñāna*, or *kṛtisādhyatā jñāna*) is sufficient. There is no need to proceed further to ascertain that the means chosen can produce the result for which the action is to be done.[7] Thus, for him *kāryatā jñāna* or *kṛtisādhyatā jñāna*, is the main thing. It alone produces *cikīrṣā* and *cikīrṣā* leads to *pravṛtti*. To put it in plain words, the root concept in the analysis of a voluntary action, say, that of attaining a *puruṣārtha*, is that of the knowledge of the doability of the task of attaining it. This knowledge produces the desire to undertake the task and this desire moves the individual to actually undertake the task.

Discussing in detail the controversy between the *Nyāya* and the *Mīmāmsa* here will be going too far afield. Therefore, I shall leave the matter at this point with the following comment:

As per the principle of *lāghava nyāya*, i.e. that of Occam's razor, the *Mīmāmsa* analysis may be called more elegant because it makes only one concept, the concept of the knowledge of the doability of an action, central to analysing the logic of an action. This concept may also have the capability of being expanded or elucidated in such a manner that it is shown to include within its range all the other factors which the *Nyāya* analysis mentions as separate items. But the Nyāya account, because of its clearly distinguishing between the various components of the process of doing a voluntary action and thereby of the process of attaining a *puruṣārtha*, is more articulate. Therefore, it is more likely to stop the occurrence of confusion in understanding and assessing the logic of the concept of voluntary action and consequently in that of the concept of attaining a *puruṣārtha*, or rather in that of the concept of *puruṣārtha* as such. Even if it does not completely stop the occurrence, it will certainly very greatly minimize it. This itself is a great philosophical advantage which the *Nyāya* analysis has over the *Mīmāmsa*'s.

8.7 *PURUṢĀRTHA*, KNOWLEDGE OF *PURUṢĀRTHA* AND KNOWLEDGE AS *PURUṢĀRTHA*

According to all Indian philosophical schools, a *puruṣārtha* can be attained only after knowing what it is. It is also good common sense to say that an individual must know what an object is before making it a *puruṣārtha* of his, and also that unless he knows what it is he cannot make the right efforts to attain it. But when this view is held by a philosopher, some problem or problems may arise because of the nature of knowledge which he considers necessary for the attainment of a *puruṣārtha*. For example, Dharmakīrti begins his *Nyāyabindu* with the assertion that *authentic or right* knowledge (*samyak jñāna*) is a precondition for the attainment of any *puruṣārtha* (*puruṣārtha siddhi*).[8] By authentic knowledge, or *samyak jñāna* he means veridical knowledge which is uncontradicted by experience and has newness, i.e. which represents a fact as it really is and is informative in the sense that the fact it is about is not one which is already known. It is to be noted here that how he defines knowledge does not matter much. What matters is the point that the knowledge which he considers a necessary condition for the attainment of a *puruṣārtha* has to be a knowledge which is authentic, cent per cent veridical knowledge, i.e. in a sense, what knowledge ought to be. This is true not only of Dharmakīrti but of most of Indian philosophers who consider knowledge of a *puruṣārtha* a precondition for its attainment.

On the other hand, when an ordinary, average, individual, a commoner, a non-philosopher, considers knowledge of an object a precondition for attaining the object, he does not mean anything like this sort of knowledge. Rather, he means by it some sort of working knowledge, some understanding, of what the object is, which gives an idea of it which is good enough for his starting the pursuit of having it. But he has an open mind. He is prepared for the eventuality that in course of his pursuit he may find that the object is not worth having, or even that some other object is better than it and therefore may have to drop this pursuit and start another for the attainment of the new object. In this way there is, for him, an interaction between the knowledge with which he starts the pursuit and the progress he makes in the pursuit. The pursuit may augment or change his knowledge, and his knowledge may prompt him to continue the pursuit, or may even require him to stop it, or to start a pursuit for another object, i.e. to make another object his *puruṣārtha*. This possibility is closed if the knowledge required is fully authentic knowledge, the kind of knowledge which a philosopher like Dharmakīrti has in mind, one which cannot turn out to be undependable, incomplete, or defective, in any manner. This kind of knowledge Indian philosophers call *pramā* or *samyak jñāna*.

On its face value, this requirement for the attainment of a *puruṣārtha* seems to be unobjectionable. It is the safest method, a holder of this view may say, to proceed ~~to try~~ to attain any *puruṣārtha* after having knowledge of this kind. Let us call it simply knowledge, and the working knowledge which the ordinary man considers sufficient to enable him to seek a *puruṣārtha* common-sense knowledge, and examine some of the implications of the Dharmakīrtian, the philosopher's, position.

One implication of it would be that knowledge itself cannot be made a *puruṣartha* for the simple reason that doing that would involve infinite regress. This can be shown in the following way: Since knowledge of a *puruṣārtha* is a precondition for attaining it, when knowledge itself is made a *puruṣārtha*, the precondition for attaining it would be knowledge of knowledge. That is, we would have first to have knowledge of knowledge, i.e. to make knowledge of knowledge our *puruṣārtha*. But then again there would be a precondition for attaining it, and this precondition would be knowledge of knowledge of knowledge. This too would require that we make knowledge of knowledge of knowledge our *puruṣārtha*, and to attain it have its own precondition, namely, knowledge of knowledge of knowledge of knowledge. This will be an infinite process which would never come to an end. That is, we would never be able to attain our *puruṣārtha*, i.e. knowledge in the philosophical sense. This would not be a palatable conclusion for any school of Indian philosophy, not even for Buddhism.

That knowledge itself cannot be a *puruṣārtha* has an implication of its own which too is not a very pleasant one. Since a *puruṣārtha* (in the positive sense) is what we ought to attain, our not being able to make knowledge a *puruṣārtha* would mean that it is not something which we ought to want to have, or ought to have. That which cannot be *puruṣārtha* cannot be a thing which we can be said to be obligated to have. This implication takes away from knowledge its normativitly, or its value-character; it would then cease to be a value because nothing which cannot be a *puruṣārtha* can be a value, or a virtue, and vice versa. All Indian philosophers would consider this implication obnoxious or mistaken because acquisition of knowledge is considered by all of them to be a thing of great value, or a great virtue. This is true even of the *Cāravākas* though what they mean by knowledge is different from what others mean by it. That a high value is attached to the acquisition of knowledge is very well illustrated in Manu's including the acquisition of *vidyā*, i.e. knowledge, in his list of ten values, or virtues, which, according to him, constitute the core of morality or moral life (*dharma lakṣaṇa*).[9] These are only a few of the implications of making knowledge, i.e. philosophical knowledge, or *samyak jñāna* a precondition for attaining any *puruṣārtha*.[10]

The general temper of Indian axiology is to treat knowledge, and therefore the pursuit and acquisition of knowledge, as a *puruṣārtha* of great importance. The highest place to it is given by the *Advaitin* for whom knowing the ultimate reality is the highest value, sine it is identical with attaining *mokṣa* which is the highest value (*parama puruṣārtha*). But even others, who do not accept metaphysical monism of the *Advaitic* variety, do not hesitate to give to the pursuit of knowledge a place of high honour. Therefore, something needs to be done on the conceptual level to ensure that the pursuit of knowledge does not lose its place of honour, or get undervalued, and at the same time some sort of knowledge of a *puruṣārtha* remains a precondition for attaining it. Both are sound propositions as per our normal intuitions about the value of knowledge as well as about the attainment of any object and therefore of any *puruṣārtha*. And, it is the concept of knowledge with which something needs to be done because it is this concept which, in Dharmakirti's and some others' similar formulations, is responsible for the problems which have been mentioned above.

In the controversy between the *Mīmāmsa* and the *Nyāya*, briefly discussed in 8.6, an attempt has been made by the *Naiyāyika* to exhibit the desirability of accepting *iṣṭasadhanatā jñāna*, the knowledge of the instrumentality of the means chosen for attaining a *puruṣartha*, or any object whatever, as a component of the process of performing successfully the act of attaining the *puruṣārtha*, the object aimed at. This device, with a very little bit of logical tinkering with the concept of knowledge, can be used to get out of the problems which making *samyaka jñāna* a precondition for attaining a *puruṣartha* creates, as discussed in the few previous paragraphs.

A *Mīmāmsaka* of the Prābhākara school would say that no individual can have at the same time both (a) the knowledge that by his efforts he can attain the object aimed at (*kṛtisādhyatā jñāna*) and (b) the knowledge that the means he has chosen to attain the object are capable of leading to the attainment of the object (*iṣṭasādhanatā jñāna*). The reason is that the former, (a), the knowledge of the possibility of one's attaining the object, can be had before attaining the object and the latter, (b), the knowledge of the *capability* of the means, can be had only after the attainment of the object. Only after our attaining the object, can we say that the means we have used have the capability or competence to produce the result, i.e. to enable us to attain the object aimed at. Therefore, the *Mīmāmsaka* can say, when (a) is admitted to be a component of the act of attaining an object, (b) cannot be; both cannot be admitted at the same time. That is why he does not admit (b), *iṣṭasādhanatā jñāna*.

Viśvanatha replies to this objection to the admission of *iṣṭasādhanatā jñāna* by distinguishing between *two ways of knowing* the capability of a means to produce a result.

In one sense of knowing, the capability of the means (*iṣtasādhanatā*) can be known only after the means actually producing the result. But in another sense it can be known even before its actually doing that. For example, by seeing someone else cooking food by using certain means, and finding the means he has chosen to be similar to that man's, he can know that his means too are capable of producing the same result, i.e. cooking food. This knowledge is certainly not as direct or conclusive as the knowledge he would have gained by himself cooking food using the means he has chosen. But it is dependable enough to justify his using his means to cook food, and also to say, as a philosopher, that the knowledge of the means' capability producing the result is also a component of the process, or act, of attaining a result aimed at.[11]

Working on this suggestion and expanding it a little bit, it can be said that pursuit of a *puruṣārtha* also can be successfully undertaken by an individual on the basis of the knowledge of it he has attained from the example of other members of his society, from hearsay, from his own common-sense understanding of what it is, etc. This ordinary man's knowledge, which I have called earlier working knowledge, would be dependable enough to motivate him to proceed on the path of pursuing it. While pursuing it he may even augment, fortify, or add to his knowledge of what the *puruṣartha* he has been pursuing is. In this way, even without having what a philosopher calls *pramā, samyak jñāna* or knowledge, he can attain a *puruṣārtha,* and can then make even the attainment of *samyak jñāna* a *puruṣārtha* of his. And, this he would be able to do without being trapped in the web of the paradoxes, already pointed out, which making knowledge, in the philosopher's sense of 'knowledge', i.e. as *samyak jñāna,* a *puruṣārtha,* gives rise to if knowledge in the same sense of the term is also made a precondition for attaining any *puruṣārtha.*[12]

We can then say that the working knowledge, or common-sense knowledge, which is a precondition of attaining a *puruṣārtha,* is something we already have, or can easily have. This working knowledge is different from the knowledge in the philosopher's sense. It is the latter which is our *puruṣārtha* in treating knowledge as a *puruṣārtha.* To start the pursuit of it we need the other sense of knowledge, the working knowledge, and not knowledge in the philosophers' sense in which it is now the *puruṣārtha.* Since knowledge as a *puruṣārtha* is now different from knowledge as a *puruṣārtha*'s precondition for its, or for any *puruṣārtha*'s, attainment, there would be no infinite regress in treating knowledge as a *purusartha.* The regress occurs, as has been shown, because knowledge which is made a *puruṣārtha* is the same kind of knowledge as is the knowledge which is its precondition. That is, *samyak jñāna* is a made a *puruṣārtha* and also a precondition for its attainment, since it is claimed to be a precondition for the attainment of every *puruṣārtha* (*sakala puruṣārtha*). It is making *samyak jñāna* a precondition for any *puruṣārtha* which is responsible for the infinite regress in making and attaining *samyak jñāna* itself as a *puruṣārtha.* The moment this condition is altered by making a working knowledge of what a *puruṣārtha* is the precondition for the *puruṣārtha*'s attainment, the cause of infinite regress in making *samyak jñāna* a *puruṣārtha* too vanishes.

8.8 OPEN TEXTURE OF THE FOUR-FOLD TYPOLOGY OF *PURUṢĀRTHAS*

Puruṣārtha is, we have seen, the Indian term for value, meaning both what human beings aim at, or desire to have, and what they ought to aim at, or desire to have. In this characterization, aiming at having, as well as desiring to have, are used in a broad sense; the former meaning both aiming to have a thing as well aiming to avoid having, or to not-having a thing, and the latter desiring to have as well as desiring to abjure or to not-have a thing. That is why a thing which one wants to have, or ought to have, as well as that which he wants to avoid having, or ought to avoid having, is a *puruṣārtha*, the former a positive and the latter a negative *puruṣārtha*. The Indian theory, as also already mentioned, arranges or classifies all *possible puruṣārthas* into four types, categories, or classes, called artha, kāma, dharma and mokṣa. Each one of them is a class of values, and neither of them is a particular, an individual, value. Each one of them can be said to be something like a basket in which values of a certain type, i.e. things valued or considered valuable and belonging to a certain class or type, have been put, or can be put. This is what a general theory of value does, or should do. It does not enumerate each and every thing that human beings value, provides in a systematic theoretical framework into which all the various types that they value, or may value, can be put or included. A theory is complete or fully comprehensive if its typology is such that everything which human beings value is characterizable as belonging to some one of the types of values it offers as the basic types. It would be a defective theory even if there is a single thing which is a value but is not included in any of its types. It would be equally defective if there is a single thing which is not a value but belongs to any one of its types and therefore becomes a value when it is really not. In the former case, it becomes incomplete, or too narrow or exclusive, because it leaves out or excludes one value. In the latter case it becomes too wide, too inclusive or accommodative, because it includes not only values but also a non-value. It would be too wide even if it makes a non-value *appear* as a value by housing it in one of its categories which is entitled to house within it only values of a certain type. In both of these respects the theory of *puruṣārthas* is non-defective. Its four-membered typology of *artha, kāma, dharma* and *mokṣa* neither excludes any value, nor does it include a non-value. This will become clear as we proceed.

There is another feature of this typology which needs to be recognized. Each one of its types is open-textured, or open-ended, in the sense that if it does not seem to accommodate something which is considered to be a value, with a little bit of conceptual or logical ingenuity its accommodative capacity can be expanded to include it. Similarly, if there is anything which is a non-value but seems to be included in any one of its value-types, we can easily find a mechanism in the general theory by using which we can say that it belongs to none of its types, and therefore is a non-value. It is for this reason that I have maintained in an earlier writing[13] that each one of its categories of value is like a proforma, and that the theory itself is like a blueprint, of human values. None of the four value-terms denotes a particular, specific, value. Rather each one of *artha, kāma, dharma* or *mokṣa* is a proforma because it can be filled in with sets of different contents, i.e. given different instantiations, if and when theoretical or practical considerations require a theorizer to do that.

The theory of *puruṣārthas* in its classical Indian form, the form in which it is available today, has been formulated by classical thinkers in the setting of the then social order. That social order, as has been already discussed, consists of four major caste-groups, called *varṇas* with each group having been assigned some specific rights, privileges, goals and obligations, and well-marked guidelines have been provided for its interactive behaviour with other groups. Similarly, in this order, the life-history of each member of the three upper class *varṇas*, is stratified is into four stages, again, with well-marked rights, privileges, obligations and goals for each stage. Classical thinkers supply contents to the four general value-categories which they consider relevant in the then social order, or which their own theological-philosophical predilections require them to do.

For example, they do not feel any moral, *dharmic*, compunction in denying to a *śūdra* child the right to be initiated and therefore to be admitted in a school to receive education; they do not think that this denial is fit to be called non-*dharmic*, that the concept of *dharma* would become vitiated if the denial of this right is retained as a *dharma*-approved denial. Similarly, the *Nyāya* metaphysics of the Self requires the *Nyāya* thinkers to fill in the concept of *mokṣa* with a content that amounts to making it impossible for an individual to get *mokṣa* while remaining alive and also entails that his Self, when he gets *mokṣa* after his bodily death, has to be a non-conscious substance. The *Advaitic* thinkers, on the other hand, because of their having a metaphysics of the Self, very different from the *Nyāya* one, fill it with, or rather have to fill it with, a content that makes it possible for him to get *mokṣa* while remaining alive and entails that after attaining *mokṣa* his Self is pure consciousness, or existence-consciousness-bliss.

All this is said to illustrate that any one of the four concepts may be given different contents by different theorizers to meet some demand of their metaphysics or axiology. Giving it different contents may also be done by different theorizers if they are theorizing in different social orders with differing conceptions of man and his relationship with his world, social or natural. Such a step may become necessary to enable the concept or concepts concerned to represent accurately what is natural or feasible for a man to aim at or to consider worthy of being aimed at in the social and natural world he lives in. If in any later period of India's, or the world's, history, nobody in his time has done this work, though it needed to have been done, the fault lies not with the concepts of the four *puruṣārthas*. That the concepts have this sort of liberal openness is the reason for my saying that the typology of *puruṣārthas* has an open texture.

The social order in the setting of which the theory of *puruṣārthas* is arrived at or matures, seems to have become very rigid quite early in its history, perhaps in its infancy itself. It seems it is born as a well-developed youth. It does get a jolt, a well-meaning jolt, in the works of Mahavīra and Gautama Buddha. But it seems that it soon becomes resistant to it and stabilizes itself. One reason for its not being shaken up seems to be the disinclination of later, technical, philosophers to write critiques of social institutions. Perhaps, because of their preoccupation with epistemology, metaphysics and spiritual axiology or theology, they find no time to realize that one of the important functions of philosophy is to keep offering off and on good critiques of social and societal institutions. Almost all of them, of course, excepting the Jainas and Bauddhas, accept the then social order and the ethics that goes with it and therefore do not change the contents of any one of the three value concepts (*trivarga*) which are basically ethical, namely, those of *artha, kāma* and *dharma*. They do change the content of *mokṣa* in accordance with the demands of their metaphysics and theology, and this they do because the concept of *mokṣa*, besides being an axiological concept is also, a metaphysical-theological, concept. But they retain the ethics which goes with the four-fold caste system, the *varṇa-āśrama vyavasthā*. All this gives the wrong impression that the concepts of *puruṣārthas* themselves are rigid, unchangeable concepts, though, in principle, they are not.

To give just one example, Śankara and Rāmānuja, the two great, most widely read *Vedāntists*, differ among themselves a lot in their ontology and axiology. But they are completely at one with each other in accepting the prevailing *varṇa*-system. Both of them model their social ethics, or ethics in theory as well as practice, in concordance with all that the *varṇa*-system stands for, good or bad, desirable or undesirable. Much before them Mahavīra and Buddha had rejected the *varṇa*-system. But this does not matter to them, rather not just to them but to members of many other philosophical schools under the fold of what are called the orthodox or Hindu system of philosophy. It does not occur to them that the rejection of the *varṇa*-system necessitates a revaluation of *varṇa*-ethics, or a re-examination of at least the concepts of *artha, kāma* and *dharma.* A glimpse of their sticking to the predominant *varṇa*-biased ethics we have already seen, in the previous chapter, in their interpretation of Satyakāma's admission in Gautama's school and in that of Jānaśruti's having been called a *śūdra* by Raikva and still being taught the knowledge of *Brahman.*

We have seen that knowledge of any *puruṣārtha* is considered necessary for attaining it even if this claim has not been made by all the schools as pointedly and forcefully as Dharmakīrti has done. This, we have said, is also a common-sense truth. But behind the claim there lurks another claim or implication, namely, the claim that the consciousness of a value is a cognitive, intellectual, or in the broad sense, a rational or ratiocinative, affair. Before attaining a *puruṣārtha* I have to have a *samyak jñāna*, a *pramā*, i.e. a veridical knowledge, of what it is. I can have this *pramā* only by the use of a *pramāṇa*, an unerring means of knowledge, because *pramā* means that which is given, or yielded only by a *pramāṇa.* Using any *pramāṇa* is a cognitive affair, not an affective or conative one, nor a reflex, automatic, or inadvertently performed operation.

Since this is so in the case of attaining a specific *puruṣārtha,* say, respecting a teacher by tending his cattle, the formulation of a general theory of *puruṣārtha*s has to be a cognitive operation on a much wider, more conscious, more articulate, level. This means that classical thinkers must have presented the categorization or typology of human values as a four-membered set (*caturvarga*) after doing a serious cognitive exercise over the course of some period of time, and not got it in a momentary flash. But it is not possible to locate any detailed account of the cognitive process as the result of which any classical philosopher has arrived at this typology. Of course, some technical philosophers give an account of the cognitive path they traverse to reach their conception of *mokṣa.* But for social life, or for social ethics, or ethics, since ethics has to be a social concern, the three-membered set of *artha, kāma* and *dharma* is more crucial and basic. That is why, as indologists agree in averring, the theory of *puruṣārtha*s first, in its original form, includes only these three. The value-category of *mokṣa* is, they say, a much later addition to them. This is natural because the concept of *mokṣa* is, for every system of Indian philosophy, a yield of its metaphysical speculation. Perhaps that is also the reason for its late entry into the Indian theory of values. It is certainly the reason for there being available in the Indian systems accounts of some metaphysical speculation as a result of which the concept is arrived at. But about the cognitive, logical, process which has yielded the three-membered set as the set of basic value-types, we can only make a guess. This is, therefore, what I propose to do here.

It seems to me that classical thinkers arrive at the typology of values—let us for this purpose take the entire theory, i.e. the theory of all the four *puruṣārtha*s—in a cognitive process which is an amalgam of both inductive-empirical reasoning and evaluative thinking. They observe what people want, desire, or prefer, to have. To *desire* to have a thing is to *actually value* it, to *like* to have it, to *consider it worthwhile* to have it. It is odd to say of anyone that he desires to have A but does not think A to be of any value. When we sometimes say it, what we mean is that we do not attach any value to A itself but desire to have it because by having A we expect to have B which we consider to be worth having. Or, we may also mean that we consider A to be not worth having for some features of it and worth having for other features of it. Cāṇakya says to Candragupta on many occasions in the drama *Mudrārākṣasam* that he wants Candragupta to befriend, in due course, Rākṣasa and to make him his prime minister, though he does not like Rākṣasa. What he means to convey is that he wants Candragupta to do that because of Rākṣasa's administrative ability and political shrewdness, but he does not like his loyalty to the slain king Nanda which he has now transferred to the king's son. Therefore, Cāṇakya manoeuvres to create a rift between the two, Rākṣasa and Nanda's son, which makes Rākṣasa change his mind, and become acceptable to Candragupta.

To find out, therefore, what people in fact value, the best way is to proceed inductively and ascertain what they generally aim at, or desire to have. Adopting this procedure, classical thinkers find that they generally, or commonly, desire to have *artha*, i.e. the material conditions for living well, *kāma*, i.e. happiness or agreeable feeling resulting out of the gratification of their desires, at least the majority of them, and *dharma*, i.e. observance of moral principles and norms. They desire *dharma* because observance of *dharmic* principles is necessary for preserving social harmony and stability which are necessary for having both *artha* and *kāma*. *Artha* and *kāma* also, in a very important sense, we shall see, are attainable only in a harmonious society, or presuppose a cohesive society. *Dharma*, by its very nature, is a social value in the sense of being pursuable in a society as well as contributive to the preservation of a good society. In this way all the three values are fundamentally, or largely, social values. The classical thinkers also seem to have realized that seeking these social values does not exhaust all that a man seeks to have. He also has some sort of a personal aspiration which remains to be fulfilled even after the attainment of the three values. Man also seeks a value which marks the fulfilment, the consummation, of this aspiration and to it they give the name *mokṣa, nihśreyas, kaivalya, nirvāṇa,* etc. That is why perhaps *mokṣa* is a late entrant in the theory of *puruṣārthas*.

It can be said, therefore, that classical thinkers found the chief types of values, goals, or objects people value by ascertaining what they generally desire, or what those, who have the maturity to distinguish between what is advantageous (*upādeya*) and what is disadvantageous (*heya*) to them, desire. And, they put these things into four categories, or types, the *caturvarga*: *artha, kāma, dharma,* and *mokṣa.* They keep them open-ended to ensure that their internal contents may be changed depending on changes in man's psychological and social resources or equipments.

To look into what human beings generally and actually desire is a good, a reasonably sound, way to ascertain what they *actually* value or are disposed to value. But what they actually or are disposed to value, may not be what they ought to value; the actually valued may not be *normatively* valuable. To identify the actually valued with the valuable, the actually desired with the desirable, would amount to, a modern ethicist would say, committing the naturalistic fallacy. But this is not what classical thinkers do. They do not equate the value with the valuable, the desired with the desirable. By looking into what human beings *actually desire* they ascertain what they *can* desire. What is desired is definitely what *can be desired,* as actuality implies possibility. They seem to be very conscious of the deontic truth that what is valuable, desirable, in a normative sense, must be a sub-class of things which can be desired; they realize that there is no point in saying to anyone that he ought to desire to have a thing which he cannot desire to have. Therefore, they look for the things which human beings ought to value among the things they can value, and they look for what they can value in things they actually value.

They seem to have found out that among the things humans value and therefore can value, those which come under *artha, kāma, dharma,* and *mokṣa* represent the kinds of things they also ought to value provided that they honour, respect, or observe a certain set of interrelations among the four. These interrelations are, according to them, very simple. For example, every pursuit of *artha* may not be desirable. Therefore, one has to have a guideline to help him to decide *which* type of *artha, how much* of it, or in *which way, artha* may be pursued in order that the pursuit deserves to be called desirable. This guideline they say, is to be obtained from *dharma.* That is, the type of *artha,* which meets with the approval of *dharma,* or is not at least disapproved of by it, they would say, is desirable, or a normative value. So is the case with *kāma.* The type, amount, or duration, of happiness or the method of acquiring it, would be desirable only if it is in concordance with *dharma.* Similarly, when there is a conflict between a pursuit of *artha* and one of *kāma,* the conflict is to be resolved in favour of that in whose favour *dharma* gives its verdict. Regarding *dharma* itself, some hold that it is desirable in itself, i.e. desirable for being what it itself is, while some others hold that it is desirable because it is a means to the attainment of *mokṣa.* About *mokṣa* there is complete unanimity among Indian thinkers that it is an end in itself and is the highest end. It is true, however, that there do arise some conceptual problems in relating in the above way the four value-types with each other. They will come up when we discuss separately, in some detail, each one of the four types.

Looking at the structure of the theory, as synoptically presented above, it may appear that it is not a logically very elegant theory. For example, it may be said that *artha* can be said to be desirable only as a means to living well, or to acquiring happiness, without itself having an intrinsic value, i.e. without any value of its own. Thus, it is only an instrumental value. But *kāma,* happiness resulting from the gratification of a desire, is an intrinsic value because it makes no sense to say that happiness or pleasure is a means to this or that thing. This is clear from the conceptual fact that we cannot ask for a reason for seeking or procuring happiness. It is, therefore, an intrinsic value, and not an instrumental value; that is, it is a value because of its intrinsic nature, i.e. simply because of its being what it in itself is. This does not, however, mean that every kind of happiness is a positive value, i.e. a positive *puruṣārtha.*

Why this is so, and what is that which makes one kind of happiness a positive *puruṣārtha* and another kind a non-*puruṣārtha* or a negative *puruṣārtha* (*heya*), will be shown later when the *puruṣārtha* of happiness is taken up for detailed discussion. Here we have only to note that it is an intrinsic value and not, like *artha,* an instrumental value. The concept of intrinsic value is not identical with that of intrinsic good. It is possible that something has an intrinsic value in a negative sense. This is the case when, using 'intrinsic value' in a broad sense, it has an intrinsic disvalue, i.e. when it is an intrinsic evil. For example, adultery is an intrinsic evil. It is an evil no matter who commits it, where he commits it, when he commits it, with whom he commits it, and for which reason he commits it. The same is true of the pleasure derived from it.

An intrinsic good also may, however, because of its association with some other factor which is in itself undesirable, become a lesser value, or even a disvalue. Worshipping a god, in any theology and so in Hindu theology, is taken to be intrinsically valuable. But it too may become a lesser value, or even a disvalue, if it is done with a sinister, undesirable, motive. For example, Rāvaṇa worships Brahmā, the sustainer of this world, with the motivation to become unkillable by his enemies, no matter what wrong or evil he does. He asks Brahmā to give him the boon that he cannot be killed by any demigod (*gandharva*), celestial being (*yakṣa*), deity (*deva*), or demon (*rākṣasa*). He does not ask for becoming unkillable by a human being simply because he thinks that no human being can kill him though he himself can kill any. His intention in asking for this boon is certainly vile because he wants to become free to commit all sorts of immoralities without being punishable or checkable by anyone. The very intention to get this sort of freedom has morally a very mean motivation and therefore, it makes his worshipping Brahmā, an otherwise intrinsically laudable thing, a disvalue. Even *Brahmā* realizes this after he grants him the boon and then finds that he misuses it in torturing saints and gods. To prevent him from going on, he along with some other gods, requests Viṣṇu to incarnate himself in the form of a human being and kill him.[14] He adopts this means to get him eliminated because it does not go against his boon which is inviolable. His boon does not make Rāvaṇa unkillable by a man, as he has not asked for it. Therefore, if Viṣṇu, in the form of a man, kills him, he is killed and the inviolability of Brahmā's boon remains intact. This is what actually happens, as per Hindu theology. Viṣṇu incarnates himself as a man in the form of Rāma, the eldest son of Daśaratha, and kills Rāvaṇa for the immorality he has committed by abducting Sītā, his wife.

Indian ethicists very well realize the point that has been made here with the help of an example from theology. They would say that it simply brings in clear focus the axiological truth that the *net value* of any transaction is not determined by the intrinsic value of any single component of it, nor by the mere arithmetical summation of the individual values of its components. Rather, it is determined in an organic, a synthetic, manner by finding out how the individual values in the transaction interact with, or affect, each other. This has a bearing on the value of the life lived as per the recommendation of the *puruṣārtha* theory. The net value of a life so lived, according to the theory, is determined by finding out how, for example, in an individual's *life-style*, his pursuits of *artha, kāma, dharma* and *mokṣa* have interacted with each other, whether or not any one has led to a weakening, or neglecting, of any other, or all have been allowed to proceed in a natural, balanced, manner. A value-seeking life is treated here as an organismic, unified, process.

Mokṣa is, we have seen, a pure intrinsic value attainable only after having led a morally commendable life, and therefore is always the highest value, and the highest positive value. *Dharma* is, in the tradition, treated by some, to be desirable because it is a means to *mokṣa,* and by some others as desirable in its own right. Therefore, it may be said, the theory of *puruṣārthas* is one consisting of a mixed variety of values, some of which are instrumental values and some others intrinsic values. It is not even a theory with one intrinsic value, *mokṣa,* with the three others all being instrumental ones, being values because of being instrumental to the attainment of *mokṣa.* Had it been of the latter type, it would have been an elegant, a neat, theory of values with only one value as intrinsic and the rest as the means or steps, for reaching it. But since it has two (*kāma* and *mokṣa*), or three (*kāma, dharma* and *mokṣa*), intrinsic values and two (*artha* and *dharma*), or only one (*artha*) in the category of instrumental value, it is like a theoretical basket the contents of which are not organized in a neat thoroughly systematic, manner. This, it may be said, is a good enough reason for saying that it is not a completely elegant theory.

The concept of an elegant theory, or of the elegance of a theory, needs to be clarified here. This notion derives from the field of logic, particularly from the notion of constructing a formal deductive, a logistic, system. A system, a theory, in this area, is called elegant if it consists of the minimum possible number of basic concepts and provides mechanisms to derive all other relevant concepts of the area from the basic one or ones. In this sense, therefore, the theory of *puruṣārthas* would have been elegant if it had only one, say, *mokṣa* as the single intrinsic value and offered mechanisms to conclusively show that all the others, *artha, kāma,* and *dharma*, derive whatever value they have from being instrumental to attaining *mokṣa* and only from being so instrumental. It could have been elegant, in this sense, even if it could have given the status of the single intrinsic value to any one of the four *puruṣārthas*, of course, if it were possible. It would have been more elegant than what it is in its present form also if it had a lesser number of *puruṣārthas* than its present four, comprehending the concept of any one of them in that of another without any logical or axiological loss. An attempt in this direction, rather an attempt of a reconstructive sort, will be made in the chapter which discusses the nature of *mokṣa*. This would be nothing more than a conceptual experiment. It may *appear*, to an orthodox interpreter of Indian axiology, as a substantive one doing some disrespect to the spiritual dignity of the great ideal of *mokṣa*, though it would not in fact do that.

However, it is worth pointing out that it is not a surprise, nor a matter of dismay, for the theory of *puruṣārthas*, rather, for any theory of values, or for any ethical theory, to be not elegant in the sense in which a logistic system can be elegant, as is, for example, the Whitehead-Russell system, as presented in *Principia-Mathematica*. This is so because man's pursuit of values is done in the world he lives in. Not only does the world change; even his aspirations, expectations, gradings, preferences, pictures of good life, etc. keep changing, depending on the changes in his appetitive, affective, cognitive, etc., nature. Therefore, his values, his grading different values, his assessment of the interrelations among his values, etc., are not likely to remain static. All this implies that his theory of value has to be liberal, *open-ended,* or even fluid to some extent, in order to remain faithful to the facts of his search for values, successful as well as unsuccessful. This is a clear enough signal to the fact that a good, realistic, or reasonably plausible, theory of value, general as well as specific like an ethical theory, cannot be a rigidly, air-tight, structured theory, which it has to be in order to be elegant in the logician's sense of an elegant theory. This feature of the construction of a value theory classical Indian thinkers seem to have very well realized. Therefore, they have proceeded, as has already been pointed out, in a mixed, inductive-empirical-normative manner, to arrive at the four-fold categories of *puruṣārthas*, and not in a formal, rigorously systematic, manner.

It is true that some classical Indian scholars, philosophers as well as recorders or compilers of Indian ethical-social norms and practices, seem to have taken the theory as a *rigid* or sacrosanct one. What they present as an account of what human beings, as required by the classical theory, ought to do, to seek, or to be, or of what well-meaning men in those (the classical) times *actually* did, does give the impression that it is a rigid, water-tight, theory. This is very obvious from the accounts available in some of the *Dharmaśāstras*, for example, in those of Manu, Vasiṣṭha, Gautama, Āpastamba, Baudhāyana, et al.[15] But this impression is created because these scholars present their accounts while themselves remaining pleasantly well-seated in the smooth shade of the then already solidified *varṇavyavasthā,* the four-fold caste-system. That is, their accounts are accounts of what human beings who are members of this solidified social system ought to, or actually, do, as required by that social system. But the theory of *puruṣārthas* itself, as a general theory of value, is not a soldified, foreclosed, theory. It is *presented* in the empirical setting of that social system, but it is not in principle conceptually bound to remain restricted to that system. In spirit, it is a general theory claimed to account for any man's axiological search, no matter to which culture or community he belongs.

There is another feature of the theory which too must not be overlooked. It is the *synthetic* character, its thesis that the four *puruṣārthas* are not alternative goals or values but a set all members of which have to be cultivated or inculcated. It is not that to lead a viable life an individual may seek one or only some of them and ignore the others. The theory has in its focus a synthetic conception of well-lived, meaningful, life. According to this conception an individual has to aim at having *dharma*-approved (*dharmānumodita*) material facilities, satisfying *dharma*-recommended or permissible desires, making his all-round behaviour concordant with the requirements of morality (or *dharma*), all this geared to his attaining the fulfilment of his personal aspiration not covered by the pursuits of *artha, kāma* and *dharma,* i.e. to his attaining his *mokṣa.* Only he whose life-style is planned in this manner would be leading the normatively ideal kind of life. Neglecting any one of the four, or pushing only some of them at the cost of some other (or others) would adversely affect the overall grandeur of his otherwise, or seemingly, successful life.

In its earlier phase in which only the first three *puruṣārthas, artha, kāma* and *dharma,* are admitted, the pursuit of *all* the three is considered to be equally important. For example, Manu in Manusmṛti (2.224)[16] very emphatically asserts that it is wrong to say that only *artha,* or only *kāma,* or only *dharma,* or even only any two of the three, are worth pursuing. All of the three are of equal importance, and one's life-style would be completely non-defective only if one sincerely pursues all of them while respecting the axiological relations among them. This is a very robust and realistic conception of life, a picture of a good life, much more robust than even that which recommends the pursuit of morality at the cost of both, or either one, of the two others.

The point which Manu makes here is the same as what we have exhibited, in the context of the four-membered *puruṣārtha* theory a little earlier. We have shown that the net value of an engagement or a life-style is determined, according to the theory, by the *net* value of its pursuit of *all* the four values taken in an interrelated, or organic, manner, and not by the intrinsic goodness of any one episode in it, nor by the mere numerical sum of the values of all the episodes taken as isolated bits or entities.

Manu's account, mentioned above, is one which even a *Cārvāka* would gladly accept. His objection to the theory of *puruṣārthas* is due only to the inclusion of the concept of *mokṣa* in it. He is averse to admitting the concept of *mokṣa* because of its being essentially rooted in a metaphysics which is, in all the Indian philosophical schools, speculative and non-naturalistic or supernaturalistic because of containing beliefs in such theories as those of rebirth, life after death, disembodied self, god, heaven and hell, etc., in some form or the other. In a sense it is true, as we shall see in the chapter on the concept of *mokṣa*, that a good moral life, covering all the corners of morality, can be lived even by one who do not believe in any doctrine of *mokṣa*, or in any of the metaphysical theories which go with it. That is, it can be lived even by him who is against metaphysicizing or theologizing ethics by conceiving an ethical goal in terms which essentially involve or presuppose some suprasensuous, suprarational, metaphysical, or theological, doctrines or beliefs. It is the feasibility of this sort of life which Manu has in mind in his 2.224 referred to above. Admitting this feasibility does not go against or conflict with the position of those who consider *mokṣa* to be the highest value. It may be said, or even they may say, that a full ethical life may be lived even without attaining *mokṣa*. But this life would not be the *best possible*, or the *most* enlightened, kind of life. That is, attainment of *mokṣa* may not be needed to make a life a good moral life, or to make it more moral, i.e. to fill in a gap in its morality. But, they may go on, it is needed to make *life as such* a completely fulfilled life, to enable the individual to have his full flourishing, the consummation of his identity or individuality.

It seems to me that this way of interpreting the *caturvarga* form of the theory of *puruṣārthas*, i.e. the theory comprising the four-membered set of values, is fair not only to the dignity of morality or ethics but also to the spirit of the Indian general theory of value. It is definitely a fairer interpretation than is the transcendental one which interprets Indian value theory as requiring or recommending that the third *puruṣārtha*, morality, or *dharma* be transcended, i.e. left behind, in seeking and attaining *mokṣa*, the fourth and the highest (*parama*) *puruṣārtha*. The latter interpretation is not fair to the dignity of morality, definitely not to its primacy, and may even lead, or mislead, an individual to consider it dispensable, as already shown in some detail in Chapter 3.

Thus far we have stated only some conceptual, or structural features of the Indian theory of value. Its complete structure will not, however, be clearly visible until we discuss in a detailed manner the nature of each one of the four *puruṣārthas*. This we shall do it in the coming three chapters, taking up *artha* in the next one.

NOTES AND REFERENCES

1. For a detailed discussion, see my *Dharmakirti's Theory of Inference: Revaluation and Reconstruction* (OUP, New Delhi, 2002), pp. 11–14.
2. Ibid.
3. *Mahābhārata* (Gita Press, Gorakhpur), Vol. I, pp. 857–71.
4. '*Yad jñātam sat svavṛttitayesyate sa puruṣārtha iti tallakṣṇāt*'. Jwalaprasad Gaud (text and trans. in Hindi) *Nyāyasiddhāntamuktāvalī* (privately published, Varanasi, 1958), p. 195. The conceptual English translation given above is that of the present author.
5. '*Cikīrṣām prati kṛtisādhyatā jñānam iṣṭasādhanatā jñānam ca kāraṇam*'. Ibid., p. 197.
6. Ibid., p. 198.
7. Ibid., pp. 200–08.
8. Dharmakīrti, *Nyāyabindu*, 1.1.
9. *Manusmrti*, 6.92.
10. For a more detailed discussion, see my *Dharmakirti's Theory of Inference*, pp. 15–20.
11. Jwalaprasad Gaud, op. cit., pp. 206–12.
12. For an elaboration of this suggestion in a more general way, independent of the *Nyāya-Mīmāmsā* controversy, see my *Dharmakirti's Theory of Inference*, pp. 18–22.
13. 'The Theory of Purusarthas: A Proforma of Human Values' in P.K. Mahapatra (ed.), *Studies in the Purusarthas* (Utkal University, 1964), pp. 35–41.
14. Vālmīki, *Ramayana*, *Balakandam*, 15: 13–18.

15. Manu, *Manusmṛti*; Patrick Olivelle, *Dharmaśāstras* (Motilal Banarsidass, New Delhi, 2000, for Āpastamba's, Gautama's, Baudhāyana's, and Vasiṣṭha's).
16. *Dharmarthavuucyate sreyah kamarthau dharma evaca. Artha evaca va sreyastrivarga iti tu sthitih.* Some say that morality and material possession are the highest values, (some) others that pleasure and material possession are the highest, (some) others that morality is the only value, (some) others that material possession is the only value. But the fact of the matter is that the highest is the (organic) set of all the three (morality, material possession and pleasure taken conjointly).

CHAPTER 9

Value as Material Well-being (*Artha Puruṣārtha*)

9.1 ACTION THEORY AND VALUE THEORY: EXPLAINING AND JUSTIFYING PURSUIT OF MATERIAL GOODS (*ARTHA*)

In the preceding chapter we have seen some of the general features of the theory of *puruṣārthas* as a general theory of value, or of human ends. The theory is certainly entitled to be given the status of the Indian theory of values. This has to be done, of course, with the awareness that it is an Indian theory only in the sense of being a theory propounded by classical Indian thinkers; it is not Indian in the sense of being intended to be valid for, or to be taken seriously by, only Indians. Anyway, in this characterization, only its concern with human ends or values gets overtly highlighted. But if we look a little more closely into the nature of its key concept, the concept of a *puruṣārtha*, we would clearly see that it can also be called a general theory of human action.

For both, a general theory of value and a general theory of action, the object aimed at by an action is its objective, goal, or end. This end is the end-state of the action in the sense that when it is achieved, the end-state of the action is reached. This means that the action which has been initiated to reach it must then automatically come to an end. But the attitude of the two theories, a general theory of action and one of value, towards the end or goal of the action is not the same. It is possible, however, for the same theory to be both a theory of value and a theory of action and thus to have a dual or multiple attitude towards the end. The attitude of a general theory of human action, or of action, is exploratory or ratiocinative. It tries to explain why anyone does any action whatsoever. For example, the *mechanical* theory of human action tries to explain every human action as an effect of certain physiological changes in the human organism. The intentional theory, on the other hand, tries to explain every voluntary action of an individual as an attempt to produce some changes in his environment in order to fulfil an intention of his. It thus attributes the initiation of these changes, i.e. the initiation of an action, to the individual's intention to achieve something. A general theory of action, thus, only explains, or makes intelligible, why an individual does an action by relating it to a *cause*, as the physiological (or causal) theory does, or by relating it to a *reason*, as the intentional theory does. But neither of them cares to *judge* whether or not an action, which has been thus explained, is *justified* or *unjustified*, worth doing or worth not doing.

The *puruṣārtha* theory is a general theory of action because, like the intentional theory, it explains why any action is voluntarily done by an individual. The explanation it offers is that it is done by him to fulfil a desire of his which may be to attain some *artha*, some *kāma*, to fulfil a *dharmic* obligation, or to attain *mokṣa*, or even to accomplish all of them together in one action, or in one series of actions. The assumption here is that whatever a man voluntarily does he does in order to attain a goal, and his goal is always characterizable as the attainment of any one, or more than one, of the four *puruṣārthas*. But it does not simply *explain* the doing of an action. It has also built into it the potentiality to *justify*, or to declare unjustified, a doing. For example, to attribute the doing of an action to the doer's desire to attain wealth, a specimen of *artha*, is to give, according to the theory, the *reason* for his doing that and therefore to *explain* it. But such an action would be *justified*, the theory would say, only if its trying to attain wealth is in accordance with the sanctions of *dharma*, i.e. morality, and it would be unjustified if it is against some moral sanction, i.e. forbidden by *dharma*. The same is the case with an action oriented towards attaining some *kāma*. A Buddhist, who entertains the doctrine of *bodhisattva*, would say that even *mokṣa* is no exception to this rule. An individual's trying to attain his *mokṣa* (*nirvāṇa*), when there exists at least one individual who has not attained his *mokṣa* and therefore needs to be helped to attain it, would be, according to the Buddhist, unjustified in doing that. And, I would like to add, even *dharma* cannot be said to be always an exception in this regard. This is clear from the classical Indian view that following a moral principle, for example, that of truth-telling (*satya*) which conflicts with, or goes against, a higher moral principle, for example, that of saving an innocent man's life (*ahimsā*), is unjustified.

We shall have occasion to come across instantiation of all such cases as we proceed on in this and the chapters that follow. Here let us be satisfied with noting the theoretical fact that the *puruṣārtha* theory explains the doing of voluntary actions as well as provides measures to determine which of these actions can be called justified and which ones unjustified. It is thus both a *theory of explanation* and a *theory of justification* in respect of man's voluntary actions. This very thing is meant by saying that it is both a general theory of action and a general theory of value. It is important to bring in this point at this stage when we are about to begin our inquiry into the nature of *artha* as a *puruṣārtha*. This is so because, quite obviously, *every pursuit* of *artha*, or pursuit of *every sort of artha*, is not morally justified. This is true in spite of the fact that to tell someone that a person does something to acquire some *artha*, or, even to retain or protect his existing *artha*, is to give him the doer's reason for his doing what he does and therefore to explain his doing it.

It is a well-known fact of ancient Indian history that Aśoka attacks the kingdom of Kalinga for doing which, then, even to his mind, the reason is his intention to extend the frontiers of his vast empire by incorporating within it that kingdom after conquering it. To say this is to admit that he has a *reason* for attacking Kalinga and therefore to *explain* why he attacks Kalinga. Even Aśoka can say this. But soon after conquering the kingdom and seeing the amount of bloodshed the war has caused, he starts assessing whether his attack and fighting the war are morally justified. He then realizes that they are not. Rather, he realizes a much more general moral truth that any venture of expanding his empire by waging a war is unjustified simply because it causes a lot of evil and therefore infringes the dignity of *dharma* (or *dhamma*), i.e. the dignity of morality. His pursuit of the goal of expanding his empire is a pursuit of *artha*. This pursuit falls within the area of human behaviour in which the issue of distinguishing between a justified and an unjustified pursuit is more important than the issue of distinguishing between a pursuit for which there is and one for which there is not a reason for engaging in it.

As a result of Aśoka's realizing the importance of this distinction and also of his realizing that he has a reason, a motivating reason but no justifying or moral reason, for waging a war and causing bloodshed to expand his empire, he stops doing all that. The Kalinga war is the last war he fights and thereafter he devotes himself to spreading the moral message of *dharma*, or morality, propounded by the Buddha, after himself becoming a disciple of the Buddha. His example very much resembles that of Yudhiṣthira after his winning the Mahābhārata war. Yudhiṣṭhira also realizes that the amount of bloodshed caused in the war does not justify his having fought it to win back his lost portion of the kingdom of Hastinâpur. But even then, after being persuaded by his brothers and wife, and above all, by Kṛṣṇa, he does not do what Aśoka does. Rather, he occupies the throne and even performs the Aśvamedha Yajña, a venture to celebrate his victory and to be accepted as the greatest of the then kings of India. In this respect Aśoka excels Yudhiṣṭhira in moral excellence, and the Buddha excels Kṛṣṇa in providing moral guidance. Had there been a Buddha in place of Kṛṣṇa, before the commencement of the *Mahābhārata* war, the war would not have been fought, and had he replaced Kṛṣṇa after the war Yudhiṣṭhira would have turned into an earlier Aśoka. But Yudhiṣṭhira does not, and even after the end of his career as a king he does not devote himself to propagating the cause of morality, or even Kṛṣṇa's teachings in the *Gītā*. Rather, he, along with his brothers and wife, starts on the great journey (*mahāprasthāna*) to ascend to heaven. Even this journey is one for familial or personal uplift and not for making the world morally better as are Aśoka's moves.

The *puruṣārtha* theory, particularly in its treatment of *artha*, gives great importance to this distinction, to the distinction between *having a reason* and *having a justification* for acquiring, or, retaining, any *artha*. The point of this distinction can be properly realized only by an individual who possesses a rationality mature enough to visualize the possibility of a pursuit's being unjustified even though there is a reason for its pursuer's engaging himself in it. All along in the application and implementation of the *puruṣārtha* theory this distinction has to be kept in mind and honoured. Since this can be done only by a rationally mature person, the theory is propounded and developed by classical Indian thinkers on the assumption or conviction that an average, educated, human being has this sort of mature rationality. It simply means (1) that a normal person is capable of using his ratiocinative, discriminative, ability to distinguish between his having a reason, i.e. a *motivating reason*, and his having a justification, i.e. a justifying reason, for pursuing what may be called a *puruṣārtha* and (2) that he has the *potentiality to mould* his conduct and character in such a way that, by and large, he is guided in his behaviour by a justifying reason and not by his *actual*, motivating, or operative, reason, if it conflicts with the former. To put the two conjointly, the theory requires that in the pursuit of a *puruṣārtha*, say, *artha*, the justifying reason be also made the operative reason.

All this is more obvious and important to remember in the context of giving to *artha* the status of a *puruṣārtha* because man has a natural propensity to pursue it, or to consider the *artha*-yielding probability of an action a good reason for doing it sometimes even if doing it is not morally permissible, as, for example, is the case of Aśoka's attacking Kalinga. This is why the *puruṣārtha* theory would not consider his conquest of Kalinga an attainment of an *artha puruṣārtha*. Indian ethics gives a lot of moral credit to him for his adopting, after the conquest, the path of peace under the influence of Buddhism, but none for his conquest. A pursuit of *artha*, as per the terms of the *puruṣārtha* theory, would be a value only if there is a moral, or justifying, reason, and not just any reason, in its favour. A moral reason for an action both *explains* and *justifies* the action and this is why to give the status of a *puruṣārtha* to *artha*, or to anything, is to aver that it *is pursued* because it is an object of a human desire, and, therefore, to explain its pursuit. In addition, it is also to aver that there is a moral reason for pursuing it and therefore that it is a justified pursuit. To say all this is what saying that it is a *puruṣārtha* connotes. To make this point clearer, we have first to see what sorts of things constitute the value category of *artha*, what is distinctive of them on account of which there could be a justifying reason for pursuing any one of them, and where this justifying reason comes from, or may come from. This task will be taken up in the sections that follow, beginning with the content of *artha*.

9.2 CONTENT OF THE *ARTHA* CATEGORY

As has already been said, *artha* is a category of certain things and not a particular thing. Keeping in view the overall intent of the *puruṣārtha* theory, or rather the general framework of Indian ethics, *artha* stands for the totality of material conditions which must be fulfilled in order to enable an individual to pursue any other value. That is, an individual must have certain things without having which he cannot successfully pursue a *puruṣārtha*. Therefore, he must or ought to aim at having these things. Since they are the necessary conditions for pursuing the other three sorts of values, they have obviously an instrumental value. Therefore, *artha*, or any particular thing which is a constituent of the *artha*-category, is said to be a value, or to have a value, only insofar as, or as long as, it is usable as a means for the attainment of any other value. As per the prevalent interpretation of Indian ethics, *artha* is a means to *kāma* and *dharma*, and *dharma* either an end in itself, or a means to *mokṣa*. That is, *artha* remains an instrumental value in both the *trivarga* or *caturvarga*, i.e. in the theory of *puruṣārtha*s conceived as consisting of only the three values *artha*, *kāma* and *dharma*, as well as in the theory conceived as consisting of the four values *artha*, *kāma*, *dharma* and *mokṣa*.

Under the totality of material conditions, which *artha* is said to be, are included not only such things as food, clothing, housing, good natural environment, normal social and societal factors, wealth, property, etc., but also the individual's bodily and mental health. One may have no objection to calling a healthy bodily condition material, but one may have an objection to calling a mental condition material. But in all Indian metaphysical systems *mind* is said to be a part or constituent of the body, that is, a bodily organ and therefore a material thing. Mind is said to be a sense organ which is claimed to be operative in the normal functioning of all other sense-organs. Since mind is a part of the body, mental health, or mental well-being, is also a kind of material well-being, or a material thing, as every bodily state or condition is.

In no Indian metaphysical theory is there any problem of body-mind duality. There is a duality of body (including mind) and self. But this duality poses no philosophical problem because the relation between the two is said to be contingent or accidental if looked at from the side of the self. The self does not need any body. Rather, in its pristine purity, in the state of liberation after the death of the individual which is really the death of the body (*videhamukti*), the self is bodiless without incurring any loss to its being. Therefore, for it the body is of no importance. For the body, of course, the self is necessary because as soon as the self leaves it, it becomes dead, or dead matter. For the individual (*jīva*) both the body and self are needed because it is nothing but an embodied self. But this fact does not alter the materiality of mind because mind remains a part of its body. Therefore, mental conditions are material conditions. It is for this reason that *artha*, meaning the totality of material conditions needed for the pursuit of values, includes mental conditions. To put it briefly, anything physical, earthly, like seeking to have a good body, a sharp mind, a loyal son, a beautiful wife, a good house, rulership of an empire, etc., if done in a certain manner, would be seeking an *artha puruṣārtha.* Vātsyāyana is most explicit about the contents of the category of *artha.* He includes under it scholarship or knowledge (*vidyā*), land (*bhūmi*), gold (*suvarna*), cattle (*paśu*), cereals (*dhānya*), utensils (*bhāṇḍa*), friend or cultivation of friendship (*mitra* or *mitrārjana*), etc.[1]

We may call *artha* an earthly, or mundane, value, in a non-pejorative sense. Indian ethics' according to the pursuit of these mundane things, the pursuit of *artha,* the status of a *puruṣārtha* or value, of a pursuit which an individual ought to undertake, is unambiguous evidence of the fact that it is not indifferent to worldly, earthly, or mundane goods which are valuable for an individual's living, or intending to live, a meaningful life in the world.

An excessive attachment to any good is likely to cause some damage to an individual's efforts to live well. This is true of an *artha puruṣārtha* as well, for example, to wealth, to one's attachment to his son, to any of one's wives, to one's property, etc. Therefore, there are statements in some classical works which in a rather exaggerated manner declare that one should have no attachment to having any *artha.* For example, Manu (*Manusmṛti* 2.12)[2] says that the knowledge of right and wrong (*dharmjñāna*) is had only by those who are not attached to having only material possessions (*artha*) and happiness (*kāma*). This should be taken only to mean that one should not have any inordinate, excessive, attachment to having *artha* and *kāma,* and not to mean that one should have no desire for them. To interpret it in the latter sense would mean that *artha* and *kāma* are not *puruṣārthas* because a *puruṣārtha* means an object of a human desire. If an individual desirous of having a knowledge of right and wrong, which he obviously needs in order to lead a moral life, is required to have no desire for *artha* (or *kāma*), then *artha* (and *kāma*) would cease to be *puruṣārthas.* This Manu, or any other classical Indian thinker, cannot say because for all of them, even for the *Cārvākas,* material well-being and happiness, *artha* and *kāma,* are *puruṣārthas.* In fact, no ethical theory, however spiritualized, can deny the value character of material well-being and happiness because the two are the most obvious things which a normal human being in the world values or seeks to have. There are, according to Indian ethics and in fact in every ethical system, certain regulative principles which need to be observed in order that a pursuit of material well-being, or of happiness, does not get infected or tainted with anything undesirable. We shall see a little later in this chapter and also in the chapter on *dharma,* that in Indian ethics it is *dharma,* or morality, which performs the role of regulating or guiding the pursuit of *artha* (and *kāma*) in such a way that its value-character remains completely intact, or at least does not get in any way watered down.

It is also worth noting that, if there are examples of statements, like Manu's referred to above, which *seem* to downgrade the value of *artha* (or *kāma*), or advise us to downgrade the value of *artha* (or *kāma*), or advise us to exercise caution in its pursuit, there are also statements by knowledgeable and morally elevated characters, in some highly respected classical works, which speak of the importance of *artha* in very laudatory terms. In assensing the importance of such statements, or in talking generally of Indian ethics, we must not forget that ethical life is an earthly, worldly, social life lived by man in a world in which material things which constitute *artha* are needed at almost every step. This fact is realized even by the thinkers who are generally considered to be greatly interested in spiritual concerns, as per the received interpretation of classical Indian thought. Views of some of these thinkers are recorded in the *Upaniṣads*, the epics, etc. In quite a few of these works we find statements or utterances expressing the high esteem in which *artha* is held as a human value. For example, in the *Taittirīya* (1.IV.1–2) a teacher is depicted as uttering an invocation, when making an offering to any god or putting some sacred materials into the holy fire, a common Hindu ritual, in some such words as 'Let me become famous among people, let me become wealthier than wealthy people,[3] etc. Not only seeking wealth, but even seeking fame is seeking some sort of *artha*. Moreover, in this invocation the teacher is praying not merely to be made wealthy but wealthier than the then very wealthy people. Therefore, this invocation or prayer to the fire-god, or to any god, is an acknowledgement, on his part, of the great importance attached by him to *artha* as a value or *puruṣārtha*. To mention one more example, as stated in the *Bṛhadāraṇyaka* (IV.1.1.),[4] when the great sage Yājñavalkya goes to the enlightened king Janaka, the latter asks him for what he has come to him, whether for some animals, i.e. cows, or for hearing some subtle philosophical, spiritual, questions put to him by Janaka, i.e. for some serious philosophical discussion with him. The reputed sage's straightforward reply is 'For both'. To get some cows from the king is definitely to get some *artha* in the form of these animals (*paśudhana*). This plain reply of the sage, devoted to spiritual pursuits, is clear evidence of the fact that even among the circle of spiritually oriented classical Indian individuals *artha* is regarded as an important value or *puruṣārtha*.

A sense of high regard for *artha* as a value has also been expressed, sometimes directly, sometimes indirectly, by quite a few of the characters considered to be exemplars, par excellence, of morality in some respected Indian classics. It has been expressed, for example, in considering it morally justified, or even honourable, for an individual to have an ambition for the possession or acquisition of his rightful property, to have a desire for togetherness of his near and dear ones, etc. Consequently, the same thing has been expressed indirectly in considering it legitimate to feel a sense of great deprivation at the loss of any of such things, i.e. of any specimen, or variety of *artha*. There is a common consensus among classical and modern scholars of Indian ethics that Rāma, Kauśalyā, Lakṣmaṇa, et al., as depicted in the *Rāmāyaṇa* of Vālmīki, are some of these exemplars. This implies that what any one of them considers to be a great positive value is indisputably a great positive value according to Indian value-theory, or the *puruṣārtha* theory.

One of the best ways to correctly understand their value-attitude towards *artha*, to material well-being, is to carefully note how they react to a situation which has the highest provability of causing to them a great deal of material ill-being because of their having been deprived of some material possession to which they have a moral or familial right. Such a situation rises when Bharata is to enthroned as the king of Ayodhyā instead of Rāma though the rightful claimant to the throne is Rāma, and Rāma is to go into exile for a period of fourteen years. Both of the two untoward things have to be done, or are being done, because of Kaikeyī's two desires which her husband, Daśaratha, the father of both Rāma and Bharata, is obligated to fulfil. Before seeing how three exemplars,

Rāma, his mother Kauśalyā and his brother Lakṣmaṇa, react to it, let us see what has brought this situation about.

As generally known, the king Daśaratha, in recognition of her services to him in the battle between the gods and demons, promises to Kaikeyī to fulfil any two wishes of hers. These are the two things which she has, in the present situation, wished him to bring about. This account of Bharata's enthronement and Rāma's exile is widely current in the circle of scholars of indology as well as in that of laymen or non-indological scholars interested in the story of Rāma, or in the Hindu ethos. But this is not the whole account. According to the *Rāmāyaṇa*, Rāma himself tells Bharata that the father of Kaikeyī, Bharata's mother, had taken a promise from their father, Daśaratha, on the very occasion of his getting Kaikeyi married to Daśaratha, that Daśaratha would make her son the king of Ayodhyā.[5] It is later that Daśaratha promises to fulfil any two wishes of hers. Rāma's point here is that even if Kaikeyī had not wished to king Daśaratha to put her son on the throne, the king was obligated to put him on the throne.

The thrust of Rāma's making known the above fact about the history of their father's marriage to Bharata is to bring out that Kaikeyī has not done anything wrong in asking the king to put him on the throne since doing that was the precondition of their father's marrying Kaikeyī which their father had promised to fulfil. This shows that there is some moral propriety in Kaikeyī's asking Daśaratha to make Bharata his successor. It also implies that if there is any moral impropriety in this regard, it lies in Daśaratha's agreeing to fulfil this blanket precondition of his marrying Kaikeyī. Generally, this precondition is not noted by scholars of indology and that is why they continue to make their account of the matter emit the unsavoury implication that Kaikeyī alone is to be blamed, if anybody is to be blamed, for Daśaratha's not making Rāma his successor.

Kaikeyī is Daśaratha's youngest wife, the last one he marries. Vālmīki records in the *Rāmāyaṇa* that he has three hundred and fifty wives[6] though only three are generally referred to in modern writings on the *Rāmāyaṇa*. It is clear thus that when he weds Kaikeyī he already has many wives, but still he wants to marry her in spite of the precondition laid down by her father Aśvapati, and agrees to fulfil it, i.e. to make her son the king after him. But the tradition does not assign any blame to him for not making Rāma the king. Had Rāma been made the king, and not *Bharata*, the question of Kaikeyī's asking Daśaratha to send Rāma into exile would not have arisen. And, had Daśaratha not agreed to fulfil the condition laid down by Kaikeyī's father for marrying her and had he not married her, neither the question of putting anybody other than Rāma on the throne, nor that of sending Rāma into exile would have arisen. But whether Kaikeyī, or Daśaratha, is blamed for depriving Rāma of his rightful enthronement, the very act of blaming implies attaching high value to Rāma's, i.e. to a rightful claimant's, being made the king or owner of a kingdom. Doing this is to attach a high value to *artha*, since a kingdom, as well as one's being made a king, is a specimen of the value category of *artha*. Aśvapati's laying down that Kaikeyī's, his daughter's, son be made the king as the condition of her marriage to Daśaratha is also a clear confirmation of the high value attached to *artha*.

We are now in a better position to assess the reactions of Rāma, Kauśalyā, Lakṣmaṇa, et al., to this situation and thereby their attitude towards the value of *artha*. That Rāma does not deny that the moral or familial right to the throne of Ayodhyā is his is expressed by him at so many places in the *Rāmāyaṇa.* So is the case about his recognition of the value of enthronement, though it is more expressed indirectly than directly, because it is generally communicated by him in his expression of unhappiness caused by the proposed enthronement of Bharata and fourteen years' exile for himself.

While informing his mother, Kauśalyā, of what has happened and is going to happen in the coming years, he does tell her that a great adversity has befallen them and that she, Sītā and Lakṣmaṇa will feel very sad to hear what he is going to tell them now.[7]

On another occasion, while trying to persuade Lakṣmaṇa not to go with him into exile, Rāma tells him with a feeling of great pathos that if Lakṣmaṇa also follows him, there would be none in Ayodhyā to look after the extremely sad and unhappy Kauśalyā (his mother) and Sumitrā (Lakṣmaṇa's mother), that Kaikeyī, the daughter of the king Aśvapati, after having got this kingdom (of Ayodhyā), would ill-treat Kauśalyā, Sumitrā and other wives of their father, that Bharata too would follow her and would not care for them, etc.[8] Three feelings of sorrow, anxiety, and deprivation expressed by Rāma very clearly indicate that he is not only not indifferent to the value of the rulership of the kingdom of Ayodhyā, i.e. to *artha,* but that he greatly values it and considers it *worth* valuing. He expresses such feelings at other places as well though he still exhibits his high regard for his father by willingly going into exile without showing any resentment.

Still more candidly Rāma expresses his grief and complaint for being deprived of the kingdom, for his being exiled, and the consequential sufferings, when the demon Virādha lifts up Sītā in his lap and utters in a threatening voice that she is fit to be his wife and not Rāma's who, with Lakṣmaṇa, is moving in a forest, both of them looking like hermits. This happens one morning when the two brothers, with Sītā, during the period of their exile, are moving from one forest to another. Rāma tells Lakṣmana in a choked voice, because of his throat being dried up due to anger and grief, that Kaikeyī has not only deprived him of the kingdom by getting it for her son but has made him witness this sad situation in which another individual has taken Sītā, his wife, in his lap.[9] All such expressions by Rāma of grief over the loss of his kingdom clearly show' that *artha* is a value, in Indian ethos, even for an exemplar of moral living. This point gets further reinforced when we see how Kauśalyā and Lakṣmaṇa react to Rāma's not being made the king and being required to go on exile.

When Kauśalyā hears Rāma's words about his deprivation of his right of kingship, which right is recognized by all of those who matter, including his father, she does not conceal her anguish. Extremely feelingly she says that all the religious things she has done for making Rāma's enthronement and kingship an extremely happy affair have become infractious. On hearing what has happened, she falls flat on the earth just as a branch of a tree, when cut, does. She very greatly values her son's becoming the king, and indirectly blames her husband for not giving to her and to her son what they have a right to get, i.e. conjugal love to her and the kingdom to him.[10]

Lakṣmaṇa's reaction to the sad news is more overt and unmodulated with familial courtesy and social convention. He considers it morally wrong and totally unjust for their father to have given such a blanket promise to Kaikeyī to fulfil any two wishes of hers, howsoever immoral they may be, and to have not refused to oblige her by declaring that both of her two wishes are completely untenable because of being immoral. He expresses his anger, which is really a moral anger, against their father, and his preparedness to fight the matter out so that Rāma is not deprived of his right to kingship and Bharata is not put on the throne. He accuses his father of being excessively sexually attached to Kaikeyī, of having lost his political wisdom and decision-making ability, and sense of right and wrong. When even a father, or a teacher, does something totally, blatantly, wrong, there is nothing wrong, he says, in killing him.[11] He shows his readiness to fight with anybody, whosoever he may be, if he is on the side of Kaikeyī. And, all this he justifies on the ground that since he is a *kṣatriya*, it is his *varṇadharma*, the moral commitment of a member of the *kṣatriya* caste, to fight a righteous battle with anybody no matter who he is or what he is.

Lakṣmaṇa's emotional reaction is an outpouring of his anger against what has happened. Rāma does not let him do what he says he wants to do as required by his caste obligation, i.e. his obligation as a *kṣatriya* youth, on the ground that caste obligation is not absolute. He appeals to the general principle of Indian ethics that a general moral obligation (*sāmānya dharma*) overrides a caste obligation. Fighting a righteous battle is a caste obligation of Lakṣmaṇa, but as a son his not doing anything disrespectful to his father is a general obligation of his and of all sons, and therefore it forbids him to fight with his (or their) father.

But in all this discussion three things are clear. One, *artha*, a material possession, is considered to be a positive value by all of them Rāma, Kauśalyā, and Lakṣmaṇa. Two, an individual's excessive attachment to *kāma*, to sex, or to any passion not necessarily sex, can endanger his sense of justice in the dispensation of material goods (*artha*). This is illustrated, according to Lakṣmaṇa, in his father's *agreeing to fulfil* Kaikeyī's two wishes, in his having *promised* in the past to fulfil any two wishes of hers, in his *agreeing to* make her son the king of Ayodhyā when it is put as a precondition of his marrying Kaikeyī, and in the consequential injustice done by him in not making Rāma his successor or crown prince. It is, according to him, his excessive attachment to Kaikeyī on account of which his father does this injustice and which Kaikeyī exploits in making him do it. Three, *artha* is a positive value but not an independent value, because it is a value only if it is in accordance with the principles of morality, or only if it does not infringe any principle of morality. Kaikeyī's asking Daśaratha to make Bharata the crown prince is to procure *artha* for her son. But it is not considered to be a bona fide, permissible, pursuit since it infringes the familial moral code according to which the eldest son of the king, and not anyone else, has the moral right to be declared the crown prince.

The positive value-character of *artha* is equally strongly emphasized in the *Mahābhārata*. Rather, the war of *Mahābhārata* is fought for *artha*. Yudhiṣṭhira and his brothers fight in order to get back their rightful share of the kingdom and therefore for them it is a righteous war. Duryodhana and his brothers fight it to retain the entire kingdom under their possession, even that portion of it which does not rightfully belong to them though they have grabbed it. For them it is not a righteous war, but that does not alter the fact that they too fight it for *artha*. What it does is to show that a pursuit of *artha*, which infringes morality (*dharma*), is not a justified pursuit of a *puruṣārtha*; rather, it becomes an immoral pursuit of an otherwise permissible *puruṣārtha*, and therefore unjustified. This illustrates the general principle of the Indian theory of value, that any one of *artha*, *kāma*, and *mokṣa* has to be pursued only in a manner which is commensurate with *dharma* or morality. This, in effect, amounts to declaring the primacy of the ethical. What is true of the pursuit of *artha*, in respect of its relation to morality, is equally true of *kāma* or happiness. This condition of *artha's* being a positive value only if it is concordant with morality does not, however, affect its character as a value. Therefore, on account of its laying down this condition Indian ethics cannot be accused of downgrading *artha*'s normative status. But leaving this issue to be further discussed in the next section, let us see here the normative status which the *Mahābhārata* gives to it.

I have proceeded in giving the *Rāmāyaṇa* account of *artha*'s importance by noting down what some of those, who are considered as exemplars of morality in it, think of it. A similar method, to keep conformity with it, will be followed in giving the *Mahābhārata* account. By almost general acceptation, Yudhiṣṭhira is an obvious exemplar of morality among the chief characters of the book. He, too, like Rāma, is not only not indifferent to *artha* but rates it as a value of great importance. When Kṛṣṇa is preparing to go to see Duryodhana to explore the possibility of arriving at a negotiated settlement of the dispute between Duryodhana and Yudhiṣṭhira about each one's share in the kingdom of Kurukṣetra, Yudhiṣṭhira very candidly expresses his unhappiness on account of his having been denied his rightful share in the kingdom. He does not mince words in telling Kṛṣṇa that *artha* occupies a very important place in the life of every human being and that he has not been allowed to have even a modicum of it to make his and his brothers' live's livable. His sense of deprivation on account of not having even a part of his due share in the royal property, even five villages, is an unambiguous confirmation of his high regard for material possession. He does not hesitate to aver that wealth is credited to be the means for the observance of the right kind of morality (*para dharma*). Everything is dependent on, or, grounded in, wealth. Only the wealth-owning man lives a meaningful life in the world. He who has no wealth is like a dead man. Those who, because of their might, deprive a man of his (rightful) wealth, they not only destroy his ethics, his property and his happiness, they destroy that man himself.'[12]

A little later in the same context he narrates some of the things which are wrong, or not worth doing, but still the deprived individual becomes prone to doing them out of discontent and anger. He even goes to the extent of saying that if no negotiated settlement is reached, war would become inevitable. Fighting the war would mean killing men on the other side most of whom are his kith and kin. That would be, he admits, definitely wrong but would have to be done, meaning thereby that it would be justified because it would have to be done to regain his lost rightful property (*artha*).[13] From such a view of a morally committed individual like Yudhiṣṭhira one may draw an inference, and not completely illegitimately, to the effect that in Indian ethics *artha*, the material or earthly condition of living, has been given such a high grade that an individual's complete deprivation of it justifies, or may justify, that individual's doing things which are otherwise wrong, to recover the *artha* he has been deprived of. Yudhiṣṭhira's mother, Kunti, is more straightforward than him. In a very curt way, conveying the agony of a mother whose sons have been afflicited with extreme penury by their cousin Duryodhana, she asks Kṛṣṇa to tell Yudhiṣṭhira to recover his share in the paternal property by using any means whatsoever. She says that Yudhiṣṭhira's fighting the war to recover his property would be absolutely in keeping with the requirements of political morality (*rājadharma*) and on no account should he keep quiet and live like a coward, remaining contented with his present deplorable condition, since that would be a dishonour to the prestige of his forefathers.[14]

To reinforce her point she asks Kṛṣṇa to communicate to Yudhiṣṭhira the historical precedent of Bidulā's asking her son not to sit idle after he has been defeated by

Sindhurāja. Bidulā exhorts him to fight fearlessly and defeat the enemy, saying that even if he dies on the battle-field, that would be more glorious than remaining contented like an impotent person. She herself would be ashamed, says Bidulā, of having produced a son like him if he does not fight with the enemy. One who is contented with the little that he has and does not struggle to regain what is rightfully his is a coward (*kāpuruṣa*). It is better to be like a short-lived blazing fire than to be a smoky one which lasts long but never has any effulgence.[15] That is, it is better to fight like a brave man and die while fighting than to live long in the manner of an invalid. Kunti's point is that on no account should one remain idle and not struggle for the *artha* which he is entitled to have. The value of *artha* is so great that even dicing in a struggle to regain it is better than remaining alive without it. Via Bidulā's example Kunti wants communicated to Yudhiṣṭhira her own ranking of the value of their share in the kingdom, i.e. of the *artha* they are entitled to have. Kunti's, a mother's, exhorting her sons to fight for a material possession which is rightfully theirs, even at the cost of their lives and even if it involves doing certain things which are not otherwise fair, shows how robust is the classical Indian conception of life and what a great value this conception attached to worldly things.

After winning the *Mahābhārata* war, when Yudhiṣṭhira has become the sole ruler of the kingdom of Kurukṣetra, he asks his brothers and also Vidura about the ranking of the three *puruṣārtha*s *dharma, artha* and *kāma*. Arjuna, who has been taught by then the *Gītā* ethics by Kṛṣṇa and has, in Kṛṣṇa's own estimation, fought the war according to the principles of morality, very candidly gives to *artha* a very high, if not the highest, place on the scale of values. His primary reason for doing that is that it is a necessary condition for doing any action in a worthwhile manner. He says that, according to the scriptural wisdom too, one cannot pursue *dharma* and *kāma* without having *artha*.[16] The tradition does not call Arjuna an exemplar of morality, and almost all modern writers follow the tradition on this point. But both, the tradition and its modern followers, have no reply to the question 'If Arjuna, who is a direct disciple of Kṛṣṇa, who has received from him the teachings of the *Gītā* and has implemented them in the war, who has not done anything disapproved of by him and excels even Yudhiṣṭhira in not having told a single lie, as per the *Mahābhārata*, cannot be called an exemplar, who else can?' That is why I say that his grading of *artha* is a grading by a classical Indian exemplar and therefore it cannot be brushed aside.

That *artha* is greatly valued in *actual practice* is admitted very clearly in the Indian ethos. Yudhiṣṭhira unhesitatingly avers that poverty is a wretched condition for any individual to be in. He even refers to *Sambara*'s, a great *ṛṣi*'s, opinion that there cannot be a more painful situation for anyone to be in than that in which he is not able to have, or provide to his family, two meals a day.[17] Arjuna too admits that *artha* is always highly valued in society. He says that just as all beings worship the god Brahmā, all human beings adore him who is wealthy. Even hermits, who lead an austere life, wear animals' skin and spend their time in religious practices, want to have *artha*. Not to accept the importance of *artha* is to fly in the face of facts. In fact *artha* is needed for doing anything. Even *dharma* and *kāma* are realized through the instrument of *artha*. The wealthy can fulfil his noble moral obligations and desires which even self-controlled, saintly, persons find it hard to do.[18]

In a later work Cāṇakya puts in a very highly impressive and metaphorical way the importance of *artha* in human life by saying that 'society would not have shown any respect for the king of gods if he were deprived of all wealth (or material prosperity).' 'The charitable man who is wealthy is considered beautiful even if he is not.' 'The wealthy man is respected by all.'[19]

The above statements or maxims about the importance of *artha* in human life, stating that *artha* is actually valued very highly by human beings, do not prove, one may say, that, according to Indian ethics, *artha* is really valuable, or a genuine normative value. This is true. The point of mentioning them here is also to show this very thing; that is, to show that classical Indians were not ascetic people, completely indifferent to worldly well-being, or to the material conditions of life. In fact the very inclusion of *artha* as a value in the Indian theory of value proves that classical Indians actually accord to *artha*, which stands for the totality of material conditions for leading a meaningful life, the place it deserves.

9.3 *ARTHA* AS A NECESSARY CONDITION FOR *KĀMA* AND *DHARMA* WITHOUT LOWERING ITS VALUE-STATUS (*PURUṢĀRTHATVA*)

It has been already said that any *artha* or material possession has only an instrumental value. This is reflected in the relationship between *artha* and *kāma* as well as in that between *artha* and *dharma* or morality. But the relationship in neither case is simple. Let us take up *artha* and *kāma* first. It is obvious that some material conditions have to be fulfilled for a person in order that he may have some happiness. But in fulfilling his material requirements, in equipping himself with them, an individual has to exert himself, sometimes lightly, sometimes very arduously. Therefore, it may happen sometimes that he has to struggle so hard to acquire a certain material possession that he has to undergo a great amount of suffering. This is likely to happen particularly when he has acquired a love or unusual fascination for the material possession concerned. It is natural for an individual to develop sometimes, by conditioning, such a great fascination or regard for a material object or condition, which is in fact only a means for the attainment of something else which is his end. He may then start valuing this means as an end in its own right. In such cases, the value attached to the end is transferred by conditioning to the means, and the means thus acquires the status of an end. This is very likely to happen in the case of one's liking for a material possession, say, wealth. Wealth can be used to buy comforts which have intrinsic value. Because of this utility of wealth one may, by conditioning, start valuing acquisition of wealth as a value in itself.

Some such explanation or interpretation may be given for Duryodhana's ambition of owning the entire kingdom of Kurukṣetra. Being the ruler of a kingdom is certainly a means to have all sorts of comforts and socio-political fame. He already has them because of his being the ruler of his share of the kingdom. But he values rulership so greatly that he takes it to be an end in itself. He is not satisfied with what he has and tries to grab even the share of his consins, the Pāṇḍavas, by hook or by crook. He has all the material possessions—a kingdom, wealth, army, many beautiful young wives, etc.—as his father Dhṛtarāṣṭra[20] himself says, but he still is unhappy. He is unhappy not because he does not have something, but because some others, the Pāṇḍavas, have something. It is this extreme sort of excessive attachment for material possessions, for *artha*, which prompts him to do things which lead ultimately to the destruction of his entire family including himself and excluding only his father and mother. In doing all that he does he has to exert himself a lot and also to undergo a lot of suffering.

According to the ethics of *artha*, Duryodhana's pursuit of *artha* contravenes two principles. It contravenes the principle that *artha* should not be pursued at the cost of *kāma* which is morally permissible or desirable happiness. Speaking negatively, it is not to be pursued if its pursuit involves a lot of suffering. This is what is meant by saying, as it has been stated earlier, that between *artha* and *kāma*, *kāma* is a higher value. Duryodhana contravenes another principle which lays down that *artha* is not to be pursued if it conflicts with any principle of morality. His attempt to have in his possession the entire kingdom of Kurukṣetra, including even the share of his consins, is countermoral (*adharma*) because it is an attempt to deprive them of what rightfully belongs to them. This makes his pursuit of *artha* impermissible because, between *artha* and *dharma*, according to the Indian ethos, *dharma* has primacy. That is, both *kāma* and *dharma* have an overriding authority over *artha*. If a pursuit of *artha* hurts any one of them, then it becomes impermissible. All this is very aptly and precisely expressed by Cāṇakya.[21]

The relation between *artha* and *dharma* too is very much like the relation between *artha* and *kāma*. *Artha* is a means to, or a precondition for, observing *dharma* in the sense that an individual must have at least some *artha*, a necessary modicum of it, in order to be able to lead a *dharma*-approved, a moral life. Secondly, it is under the control of *dharma* in the sense that its pursuit will be the pursuit of a *puruṣārtha* only if the way it is conducted does not infringe any principle of morality. Therefore, we can say that *artha* is a precondition of morality and morality is a regulator of *artha*. Let us discuss each one of these two features of *artha* or of the pursuit of *artha*.

The truth of the assertion that *artha* is a precondition of morality would need no argument the moment one realizes that only a living individual, who is physically and mentally fit, can lead, or be required to lead, a moral life. Not only to be physically and mentally fit but indeed to be alive one has to have some material facilities, or things. That is why to do something morally laudatory, for example, charity, one must have enough material goods to spare some and give it to, or share it with, some other needy person. It is true that Indian tradition gives examples of exceptionally elevated individuals who may donate whatever they have, no matter how limited, or scarce, a possession of theirs it may be. Everybody has only one anatomical, bony, structure. For any individual to donate it to someone else is to court death. But this is done, as per Indian mythology, by the saint Dadhīci. It so happens that demons under Vṛtrāsura attack Indra, the king of the gods. Vṛtrāsura is so ferocious and powerful that all the gods become afraid of his killing their god. They go to Brahmā for help. Brahmā advises them to go to the saint Dadhīci and request him to donate the bones of his body to make a weapon to be use it to kill Vṛtrāsura, since only this and no other weapon can kill him. This instruction they follow and kill the demon. This becomes possible because when they request the saint to donate his bones, he gladly courts death and relinquishes his body. The gods take out his bones, make the needed weapon out of them, and Indra uses the weapon to kill the demon.[22]

Dadhīci has only one bony structure which he donates out of benevolence and dies as a consequence of it. There is no question of anyone's having more than one bony structure so that he may donate one to someone else without loosing his own existence.

But this is a mythological example, and therefore it cannot be cited to illustrate that even if an individual does not have enough of a material possession to spare for someone else, he can do that if he is really a morally elevated person. Moreover, Indian ethical theory, like any ethical theory, is intended to be applicable to every individual, to explain the ethical behaviour even of a commoner, and therefore Dadhīci's example cannot be used to show that the *artha*, required as a precondition for being moral, may even be so minimal that one may lose his existence in doing a particular moral thing by its instrumentality. And, even if there are some such real rare individuals of this sort, they cannot be used as the data on the basis of which an ethical theory about the nature of extent of *artha*, as a precondition of morality, can be formulated.

There is a negative implication of calling *artha* a precondition of morality which Indian ethicists very rightly and forcefully draw to show, in a realistic way, that without having a certain reasonable amount of *artha* one cannot lead a moral life. This is illustrated, again negatively, in the maxim mentioned as the lesson yielded by a story about a monkey and a crocodile. The maxim says that a hungry individual may practise any kind of immorality.[23]

The story of Viśvāmitra, a great saint, entering the house of a *śūdra* to steal a thigh of a slain animal the feed the members of his family and save them from dying of starvation, in a famine-stricken situation, also illustrates the same point as does the monkey-crocodile story. Viśvāmitra's episode is also a mythological one, and therefore a fictional one, as is the story about the two animals. But both of them illustrate very well that in order to lead a moral life an individual must have certain material facilities to let him live without being put to extraordinary strain in meeting the necessities of existence. The idea behind the Viśvāmitra story is that it is his moral duty and the moral duty of every man who has a family, to make proper arrangements for the maintenance of the members of his family. He ought to arrange for them necessary eatables by adopting any means to save them from dying. This is what he tries to do when he enters the *śūdra*'s house to steal whatever foodstuff he may get hold of. [24] This example too emphasizes the importance of the human body, or bodily existence, and of the means to protect it, or to keep it in proper order, because being alive and having a healthy body are necessary for leading a moral life. All this highlights the importance of *artha*, since the human body, or any body, and foodstuff, are specimens of the value-category of *artha*. Cases like Viśvāmitra's are called *āpaddharma* (emergency obligation). But, as will be shown in the chapter on *dharma*, they all only illustrate a conceptual feature of moral obligations, namely, their feature which makes them admit of exceptions without being nullified or made violable because of their permitting exceptions.

From Indian ethics' calling *artha* a precondition of *kāma* and *dharma* it must not be inferred that *artha* is a dispensable value. Rather, what follows from it is that *artha* is indispensable because it is, in being a precondition, a *necessary* condition for leading a happy as well as a moral life. That is, the Indian view about it gives to it an honourable place by declaring that without it, since it is a necessary condition, one can neither lead a happy, nor a moral, life. This is what Cāṇakya says when he avers that *artha* is a basic value since only with its instrumentation can *kāma* and *dharma* be had.[25] Referring particularly to *dharma*, Śiva offers to Pārvati the advice that she ought not to weaken her body too much by her extremely austere religious practices mortifying it, since 'the body is the first (or primary) means, or organ, for the pursuit of *dharma*'.[26]

9.4 *ARTHA*, *DHARMA* AND *RĀJADHARMA* (POLITICAL ETHICS)

Cāṇakya in his *Śūtras* conceives of the relation between *artha* and *dharma* in such a way that this relationship provides a natural bridge to some sort of political ethics. He begins with the assertion that (1) the root of human happiness is *dharma*, or ethics. He obviously means by this that stable happiness in any society can be ensured only by the observance of certain moral principles by its members. Then he proceeds to add that (2) the root of *dharma* is *artha*. The plausible way to interpret it, while protecting its consistency with (1), is to take it as meaning that (3) *dharma*, moral living, can be ensured, or expected, only if there is no dearth or scarcity of *artha*, i.e. of the material conditions which leading a moral life requires or presupposes. To say this is, in effect, to say that these material conditions should be available to everyone. Through it he implicitly reiterates, in a straightforward manner, the principle that the monkey in the *Pancatantra* story, referred to a little earlier, states to the crocodile, namely, the obvious ethical principle that an individual deprived of the necessities of life cannot, or should not, be expected to live a morally decent, pious, life. The members of a society, however, can expect to have in a fair manner the material goods they need only if the material resources of their society are properly managed and justly distributed among them. Therefore, Cāṇakya says that (3) the root of *artha*, i.e. its proper management ensuring its needed availability to everyone, is the state (*rājya*) or good governance. (4) Good governance, or sound statecraft, he says, requires that those who govern the state or manage its affairs, or rather the people who constitute it, have control over their sense-organs (*indriyajayah*). This is to lay down that they do not have any inordinate desire for the satisfaction of any demand or propensity of any of their sense-organs. (5) Such a *sense-control*, he is right in averring, can be had by a person only if he inculcates the virtue of humility (*vinaya*). Humility can definitely be had by anyone only if he keeps his egoism or self-interest duly restrained. (6) The root of humility, Cāṇakya says, lies in serving the elders (*vṛddhopasevā*). This means having an attitude of respect towards what elder thinkers have said and done and having the willingness to implement their instructions. (7) Service to elders, he adds, yields knowledge or wisdom (*vijñāna*), i.e. makes an individual wiser or more informed. (8) Everyone, therefore, should make himself equipped or enriched (*sampanna*) with this kind of knowledge. (9) An individual equipped with such knowledge becomes a conqueror or master of himself (*jitātmā*). That is, he attains complete control or conquest over all of his desires, passions and aspirations. (10) An attainer of such a self-conquest attains or acquires all kinds of material facilities or goods (*sarvāstha*) (11) This kind of material achievement (*artha sampadā*) makes the state, or its people, happy in a natural manner. (12) A state whose people are happy can very well administer or govern itself even without a leader to guide it.[27] The principles 1 to 12 stated above very clearly encapsule an ethics which the people and managers of a state (*rājya*) should follow to let the state run on the right lines. That is why this ethics can very well be called political ethics (*rājadharma*).

But the way Cāṇakya proceeds in analysing the relationship between *artha* and *dharma*, particularly by calling *artha* the root of *dharma*, may give the impression that his is a materialistic interpretation or explanation of morality, that he considers morality to be solely determined by the material conditions of human life. This is not, however, the case. Instead of making morality determined by material conditions, by drawing attention to the hard fact that morality needs some material conditions, he draws our attention to what the morality of human beings in fact is, or to what morality as a human affair is. By using metaphorically the word 'root' (*mūla*) in calling *artha* the root of *dharma*, he points to the reality that moral issues arise always, or almost always, because of the problems posed by man's desire for *artha* or because of problems arising in course of the management, distribution, or production of material goods. For example, had Duryodhana let the property of the kingdom of Kurukṣetra be properly distributed between him and Yudhiṣṭhira, the *Mahābhārata* war would not have taken place, and had Kaikeyī not entertained the inordinate desire to make her son the king of Ayodhyā, Rāma would not have been required to go into exile.

The moment the close relationship between material goods and morality is accepted, it becomes easier to realize that the formation of a state, or of a governing agency, is necessary. This is so because no individual, left to himself, can manage to have all the material goods which he needs in order to lead a morally decent life. That he may not be allowed to have the material good which he needs and which it is his right to have or receive, or that he may not be allowed to retain what he already has, is an obvious truth. It is to ensure that everyone has the material goods he needs or deserves that a state is required. That is why Cāṇakya says that the root of *artha* lies in the state or good governance. His concept of state is not a non-normative one since he locates the root of statehood or statecraft in control of all the senses. Since mind is also, in Indian philosophy, a sense-organ, and it is mind which entertains desires, control of sense includes control of desires as well. Therefore, it means a complete control of man's appetitive nature, a control of all of his desires and passions and inclinations. To achieve this kind of control is to achieve a highly elevated moral condition. This shows that *artha* itself is now said to be rooted in something moral, something *dharmic*. This process of grounding *artha* in *dharma* is reinforced when Cāṇakya says in the next sentence that sense-control is rooted in humility because humility is considered to be a great moral virtue by all Indian ethicists. Even in the later sentences the reinforcement continues, and he reaches a point where he says that an individual who has conquered his own ego attains all sorts of *arthas*. Then, he says, the state, or its people, would become naturally happy. And, when they are happy, the state, or the people, can live well, i.e. without anyone disturbing anyone else, even without a leader, or ruler, that is, without a governing-guiding agency. Such a world would be an ideal moral world, something like a paradigmatic example of the rule of *dharma* in a human world.

It may appear from the way happiness (*kāma*), material goods (*artha*) and morality (*dharma*) have been related to one another in the above account that Cāṇakya is arguing in a circle. He roots, one may say, happiness in *dharma*, *dharma* in *artha*, *artha* in *dharma* and *dharma* in happiness (since he says that when the people are happy they can live well in a *dharmic* way without any external help). But no circle is involved here. What he is doing is to show that all the three values, *artha*, *kāma*, and *dharma*, are interrelated. That is, they function as normative *puruṣārthas* only if each one of the three functions cohesively, i.e. in unison with, the other two. The hidden truth, the importance of which writers on Indian ethics do not seem to have adequately realized, is that according to Cāṇakya, or Indian ethics as such, anyone who pursues any one of the three goals in the way it ought to be pursued, would be pursuing the other two as well. If, for example, *a la* Cāṇakya's account, he pursues happiness, he has to follow *dharma*, or the relevant moral principle otherwise his pursuit of happiness may be obstructed because of its collision with the pursuit of some other value. When he pursues the path of *dharma*, he has to have some material goods (*artha*) for which again he would require ultimately to follow *dharma*. Since every individual pursuing happiness in this world would have to ultimately follow *dharma*, the pursuit of none would collide with anyone else's pursuit. This would mean that there would be no collision or clash of interests. That would mean that, then, everyone would be happy and therefore would not disturb, or clash with, another's pursuit of any one of the three values. This would obviously imply that each one would be leading a *dharma*-concordant life. And, then again, each one would require some material goods (*artha*). In this way, man's value-seeking life would go on and on. If there is a circle here, it is not a vicious but a virtuous one because it simply shows that no matter which value one starts in search of in one's axiological journey, if it proceeds in the right way, one would miss neither of the remaining two values. This is because of the nature of the three human values (*trivarga*). We are bound to meet this cohesive nature of value-seeking in the coming chapter which discusses the nature of happiness (*kāma*), as well as in the next one which discusses the nature of *dharma*, the other two components of the three-fold (or the four-fold) set of *puruṣārthas*.

NOTES AND REFERENCES

1. *Vidyābhūmi hiraṇya paśudhānya bhāṇḍopaskara mitrādīnāmarjanamarjitasya vivardhanamarthah.* Vātsyāyanamuni, *Kāmasūtram* with Jayanangatā, translated by Parasnath Dvivedi (Chaukhamba, Varanasi, 1999), 2.9, p. 24. *Artha* consists of knowledge, land, gold (or golden ornaments), cattle (animal wealth), cereals (food materials), utensils (articles of domestic use), friends, etc. and augmenting or adding to each one of them (if already had).
2. *Arthakāmeṣvasaktānām dharmajñānam Vidhīyate.* Knowledge of right and wrong can be had only by those who are not attached (or addicted) to material things and happiness.
3. *Yaśo janeasāni svāhā. Śreyan vasyasoasāni svāhā.* May I become famous among people, *svaha*. May I become great among (i.e. wealthier than) the (other) wealthy people, *svaha*. (The Sanskrit word '*svaha*' is an ablative expression, uttered before making an offering to a god in a Hindu religious ritual or religious ceremony.)
4. *Yājñavalkya, kimarthamacāroh, paśūnichhan, aṇvantāniti.*
   Ubhayameva, samraḍiti hovāca.
   Yajñavalkya, what is the purpose of your coming here? To get some animals or to be asked some subtle questions? Both, O great king, replied Yājñavalkya.
5. *Purā bhrātah pitā nah sa mātaram te samudvahan.*
   Mātāmahe samaśrausīd rājyasulkamanuttamam. Rāmāyaṇa, Ayodhyā Kāṇda, 107.3.
   Brother, this is a matter of the past. When (our) father was married to your mother, at that very time he had accepted your maternal grandfather's noble condition of giving the kingdom to her son (i.e. to you).
6. (Context: After getting ready to go into exile, in a hermit's dress, Rāma comes to his father's Daśaratha's, house and requests Sumantra, his charioteer to tell Daśaratha that he has come to see him before leaving Ayodhyā to go into exile. Sumantra informs the king and the king responds by ...)
   Sumantrānaya me dārān ye Kecidih māmakāh.
   Dāraih parivṛtah sarvaidrastumicchāmi Rāgham. Ibid., 34.10.
   Sumantra, call all of my wives who are here. I want to see Rāma with all of them.
   (Context: After getting the king's instruction, Sumantra goes to that part of palace where his wives reside and informs them of the king's, their husband's, wish to see all of them. Thereupon all of his wives ...)
   Ardhasaptaśatastatra pramadāstāmralocanāh.
   Kauśalyām parivāryātha sanairjagmudhṛtavratāh. Ibid., 34.13.

A little red-eyed three hundred and fifty young women, devoted to their husband, surrounding Kauśalyā, came and entered that (Daśaratha's) house.

7. *Devi, nūnam na janīṣe mahad bhayamupasthitam Idam tava ca dukhāya Vaidehyā lakṣamaṇasya ca. Gamiṣye dandakāraṇyam Kimanenāsanena me. Vistarāsanayojño hi kāloayam māmupasthitah caturdaśa hi varṣāṇi vatsyāmi vijane vane. Kandamulaphalairjīvan hitvā munivadāmiṣam.* Ibid., 20: 27-28-29.
   Devi (mother addressed as a goddess), certainly you are not aware of these; there has come to happen a highly fearful situation for you. On hearing what I am going to tell you now, a lot of unhappiness will be caused to you, Sītā and Lakṣmaṇa. Still I will tell it.
   Now I shall go to forests. Therefore, there is no need of such a precious material for me to sit on (which you are offering to me). The time has come for me to sit on a straw mattress. Relinquishing the use of things fit for a royal prince, I shall live in uninhabited forests for fourteen years, eating roots and fruits and no meat, as hermits do.
8. Ibid., 21.12–14.
9. Ibid., *Aranya Kānda*, 2.13–21.
10. Ibid., *Ayodhyā Kānda*, 20.32–55.
11. *Na rocate mamāpyatadārye yad Rāgavo vanam. Taktvā rājayaśriyam gacchet striyā vākyavaśangatah. Viparītaśca vṛiddasca viṣaiśca pradharṣitah. Nripah kimiva na brūyaccodyamānah samanmathah.* Ibid., 21.2–3.
   Elder mother, I do not like respected Rāma to relinquish his right to the kingdom and go into exile. The king is under the influence of that woman (Kaikeyī). Therefore, his mind has become misdirected. Firstly, he is old, secondly, he is attached to sex. Therefore, being possessed by sex, the king under the influence of Kaikeyī, can do anything.
   Protsāhitoayam Kaikeyyā santuṣto yadi nah pita. Amitrabhūto nihsangam vadhyatām vadhyatāmapi. Gurorpyavaliptasya karyākaryamajānatah. Utpatham pratipannasya kāryam bhavati śāsanam. Ibid., 12–13.
   If our father on the instigation of Kaikeyī and being pleased with her, has become our enemy, then we should also, brushing aside our love and attachment, arrest him or kill him. (This is justified) because it becomes necessary to punish even a teacher who, after losing his sense of what he ought and ought not to do, starts moving on a wrong path.
12. *Danamāhuh param dharme dhane sarve pratiṣthitam. Jīvante dhanino loke mṛtā ye tvadhanā narah. Ye dhanāda-Sakarṣanti naram sabalamāsthitāh. Te dharmārtham kāmam ca pramathnanti naram ca tam. Mahābhārata, Udyogaparva,* 72.23–24.
13. Ibid., 25–50.
14. Ibid., 132.32, 34.
15. Ibid., 135.5–15.
16. Ibid., *Śāntiparva*, 167.12.
17. Ibid., *Udyogaparva*, 72.22.
18. Ibid., *Śāntiparva*, 167.12–20.
19. *Mahendrapyarthahīnam na bahumanyate Lokah. ... Virūpoarthavān surūpah. Arthavān sarvalokasya bahumatah. Cānakyasūtra* (Radha Pocket Books, Meerut), Chapter 2: 5, 7, 8, pp. 16–17.
20. *Mahābhārata, Dyūtaparva*, 49.6–11.
21. *Atikleśena ye cārthā dharmasyātikramena tu. Śatrūnām praṇipātena te hyarthā mā bhavantu me. Cāṇakyanīti* (Manoj Pocket Books, Meerut), 16.11, p. 148.
   A material good (*artha*) is not to be acquired if acquiring it involves great suffering, infringing morality, or genuflecting before an enemy.
22. *Mahābhārata, Vanaparva*, 100–01.
23. *Bubhuksitah kim na karoti papam, Kṣīṇa janā niṣkaruṇā bhavanti. Pancatantra*, IV.1.16.
   Which sin is there that a hungry man may not commit? Extremely poor people are merciless.
24. *Mahābhārata, Śāntiparva*, 141.13–35.
25. *Artha eva pradhāna iti Kautilyah. Arthamūlau hi dharmakāmaviti. Arthaśāstra* 3.6.1.
   (In the three-fold scheme of *puruṣārthas*) *artha* is basic. *Dharma* and *kāma* are dependent on it.
26. Śarīramādyam khalu dharmasādhamah. Kālidas, *Kumārasambhavam*, 5.33.

27. (1) *Sukhasya mūlam dharmah.* (2) *Dharmasya mūlam arthah.* (3) *Arthasya mūlam rājyam.* (4) *Rājyamūlam indriyajayah.* (5) *Indriyajayasya mūlam vinayah.* (6) *Vinyayasya mūlam vṛddhopasevā.* (7) *Vṛddhasevāyā vijñānam.* (8) *Vijñānena ātmānām sampādayet.* (9) *Sampāditātmā jitātātma bhavati.* (10) *Jitātmā sarvārthaih sanyujyet.* (11) *Arthasampat-prakṛtisampadam karoti.* (12) *Prakṛtisampadā hyanāyakamapi rājayam nīyate.*
Vachaspati Gairola (ed. and trans.), *The Arthaśāstra of Cāṇakya with the Cāṇakyasūtra* (Choukhamba, Varanasi, 1984), p. 775.

CHAPTER 10

Value as Appetitive Well-being (*Kāma Puruṣārtha*)

10.1 *KĀMA* AS APPETITION (*KĀMANĀ*)

The *kāma puruṣārtha* denotes human well-being, feeling well, or happiness, resulting out of the gratification of a desire for an object, external or internal. 'Desire' is used here in a broad sense including all sorts of wants, wishes, aspiration, passions, etc. Therefore, the term will cover in the present discussion, or rather in this work all along in the context of *kāma*, even feelings and emotions. If an individual entertains a feeling of kindness towards a thirsty animal and feels happy after pouring some water into its dry mouth, then his happiness too would come under *kāma*, as would his happiness resulting out of satisfying his anger against a child-killer leopard by killing the leopard. It is common for a king in ancient India to go on a hunting expedition in a forest, kill some animal or animals, and in the same trip to distribute, out of a feeling of charity, some items of daily needs among the saints living in that area. Both the acts he enjoys. His appetitive urge in both the cases, though the motivating feelings in the two cases are different, come under the category of *kāma*. The tradition considers both sorts of activities as socially permissible. Hunting, killing an animal as a sport (*akheta*), as well as distributing things of need among saints, are considered desirable acts for a king, or, rather, for any *kṣatriya*. The *enjoyment*, or *the feeling of well-being*, resulting out of the gratification of both of the two appetites, the appetite for hunting and that for doing charity, and of many others, come under the category of *kāma puruṣārtha*.

The word *kāma* (from the root *kām*) means *kāmanā*, desire, or more appropriately, any appetition, since *kāmanā* is used here, as mentioned above, in a very broad sense. It covers any motivational, appetitive, urge the satisfaction of which yields some enjoyment or feeling of well-being. That is why this feeling or experience of well-being may better be called appetitive well-being. It does not cover, as we will soon see, only sensuous pleasure. But *kāma*, it is important to note, does not only mean *kāmanā*. It also means the object or objective (*abhīṣṭa padārtha*) of a *kāmanā* or of appetition, as well as the feeling of well-being resulting out of the gratification of a *kāmanā*. We have, therefore, to examine closely how these uses or *meanings of kāma* operate in the notion of *kāma* as a *puruṣārtha*. Only then shall we be able to properly understand the full import of *kāma* in Indian value-theory.

Let us first see the role *kāma* as *kāmanā* (desire) plays or can play in the theory. We have seen that every *puruṣārtha* is an object of a desire, and the pursuit of a *puruṣārtha*, therefore, is a motivated pursuit, that there has to be a motivation, a mover or moving force, behind the pursuit. Indian thinkers are forthright in admitting that this moving force is desire, that there has to be a desire, or, will to do anything, to enable a man to seek any object. Every action is thus a motivated action with a desire as its motivating force. This admission is very useful and important because it distinguishes an action from an event as well as from such things as those which are inadvertently or accidently done. Though we call them inadvertent or accidental actions, they are not really actions; they are more like happenings or events than like actions. Ethics or value-theory is concerned with actions and not with happenings or events. This is the case because only actions, their motivating desire, or their results, can be morally evaluated, and only for them can a doer be held responsible, or praiseworthy or blameworthy. By defining an action as necessarily involving a desire, an appetition, the area of ethical evaluation is, thus, made well-demarcated because events and inadvertent doing are shown then as automatically falling outside it.

That every action involves a desire, or, that there is a desire behind every action working as its motivating force, is averred by Manu in an unqualified manner.[1] Manu's point clearly is that no action of whatever type, worldly, religious, ritualistic, ethical, etc., is possible without its doer having a desire to do it. By an action he undoubtedly means a voluntary action done by a free agent. Keeping in mind this general feature of an action, he says that the desire to do an action generates in the doer's mind the will to do it which moves him to do it. Therefore the performance of a sacrifice, observance of vows, cultivation of self-control, and religious duties are possible because of, or are the result of, the doer's will to do them (*sankalpasambhava* or *sankalpaja*).[2]

Anyone's being obsessed with a desire (*kāmātmatā*) is not, Manu says, commendable. But it is also true that it is not possible for anybody to have in him complete absence of all desires, i.e. desirelessness (*akāmatā*). Manu also seems to think that it is not desirable to be completely desireless. This is so because the knowledge of the *Vedas*, cannot be acquired without a desire for its acquisition. Nor can the rites recommended or prescribed by the *Vedas* be performed without a desire to perform them.[3] Desires are, thus, the prime movers in a man's appetitive life, in his performance of the multifarious types of actions he has to perform in a value-seeking life. Manu's point is valid because no value can be sought without a desire for it, nor can a moral regulation be implemented by an individual in his behaviour without his wanting to do that. It is obvious that he can neither seek a material facility (*artha*), nor follow a moral rule (*dharma*), not can try to attain liberation (*mokṣa*), without having a desire to do that. Therefore, to lead a good life as recommended by the theory of *puruṣārthas* he has to be desirous of acquiring the material conditions needed for leading such a life (*artheccu* or *arthakāma*), desirous of observing moral principles (*dharmeccu* or *dharmkāma*) and desirous of attaining libration (*mumukṣu* or *mokṣakāma*).

Kāma not only means *kāmanā*, desire, but also being desirous of, as it does in the compounds *arthakāma*, *dharmakāma*, and *mokṣakāma*. Therefore, *arthakāma* means *arthecchu*, desirous of *artha*, *dharmakāma* means *dharmecchu*, desirous of *dharma*, and *mokṣakāma* means *mokṣecchu* or *mumukṣu*, desirous of *mokṣa*.

There is nothing odd in this linguistic fact because to have a desire (*kāmanā*) for a thing is to be desirous of having it, of seeking it, or of observing it, depending on what kind of a thing it is. The upshot of all this is that *kāma*, meaning *kāmanā*, is involved in the pursuit of all the other three *puruṣārthas*, *artha*, *dharma*, and *mokṣa*. Even that of *mokṣa* cannot, in point of logic, get rid of it. To put it a little more accurately, the concept of *mokṣa* necessarily involves the concept of desire if *mokṣa* is posited as a value which an individual ought to seek, simply because he cannot seek anything without a desire to seek it, without a motivation to do that. Although all this is being said here in the context of elaborating some of Manu's views about the relationship between desires and actions, or voluntary actions, saying all this is nothing but stating the common-sense logic of the concept of value-seeking. It is a logical or conceptual truth that for an individual to seek anything presupposes or implies that he has a desire to have that thing. Therefore, Manu cannot be taken to task for considering a desire basic to the performance of any action, or to the pursuit of any goal, even if this view of his conflicts with a view on that subject held by some other classical Indian thinker, howsoever venerable the tradition may hold this thinker to be.

The role of *kāma*, meaning desire or appetitive motivation, in human action, as its moving agency, is recognized even by the *Bṛhadāraṇyaka* (I.iv.16–17) as per Śankara's commentary on it. For Śankara, as it is well known, knowledge of the Self is the only means for the attainment of liberation. Rather, to have it is the same as having liberation. Doing any kind of action or series of actions cannot enable its agent to attain liberation which is the highest value. It may, on the other hand, detract him from the path of knowing the Self, and therefore from that of attaining liberation. But still man indulges in all sorts of actions, including ritualistic ones. In reply to the question of an imagined adversary as to why he does that, what is the source of all human activity when it is not going to liberate him, Śankara's response, while commenting on I.iv.16, is that it is desire. As the Katha *Upaniṣad* (II.5) says, fools under ignorance which is natural to man are outgoing in their tendencies and pursue objects of desire. And the *Smṛti* also says, 'it is desire, it is anger' etc. (G.II.37). And the *Manu Samhitā* (II.4) also describes all activity as being due to desire'.[4]

We have already referred to Manu on this matter. The *Katha* too, which Śankara refers to in his support, in II.4 avers that ignorant (*mūḍha*) people indulge in actions prompted by desire, as one blind man is led by another blind man on a rough road and suffers a calamity. The *Gītā*, which the abbreviation 'G' in the above quotation stands for, in III.37, considers anger as a derivative of desire because it is, according to it, nothing but an obstructed or a frustrated, desire. That is why it says that desire and anger (*kāmah krodha*) are non-different. Śankara takes both, the *Katha* and the *Gītā* as holding desire to be responsible for all evil.

Whether or not the *Katha* and the *Gītā* hold the view Śankara attributes to them, it is clear that Śankara himself holds that desire is the cause of all actions. It is evidenced by the fact that he recommends the cessation of all desires in order to achieve the cessation of all actions, i.e. to abstain from doing all actions except those which are absolutely necessary for keeping the doer's body in a minimally functional condition. The background of this position of his is his excessively ontologized axiology according to which liberation can be attained only by knowing the Self and not by any sort of action. Not even desireless, benevolent action is sufficient to enable its doer to attain knowledge of the Self. Rather, since a life of action lived by an individual may deflect him from the path of knowing the Self, it is desirable or necessary to stop doing all but the minimal, necessary, actions. In order to be able to achieve this sort of actionlessness, Śankara says, an individual has to eradicate all desires because, if he has a desire, it would be a desire to have some object, and to have that object he would have to indulge in doing some action or actions. To cut the root of actions, all desiring has to be cut off since it is desiring which is the root of all actions. A desire is always for some means to attain some ends and not for anything more or anything else. This sort of means-ends pursuit cannot yield liberation or knowledge of the Self. Therefore, in commenting on the *Bṛhadāraṇyaka* I.IV.17 he says that 'Desire consists of the two hankerings after the ends and means, visible or invisible, which are the special sphere of an ignorant man. Hence the wise man should renounce them' (i.e., the two hankerings).[5] To renounce 'the two hankerings after the ends and means' is to renounce all desires because, for Śankara, it is they which constitute a desire, or it is of them that a desire consists.

Whether or not Śankara is right in requiring an individual to renounce all desires, it is clear from what he holds of the nature of a desire and of an action that he too, like Manu, maintains that every action has as its mover some desire. He recommends renouncing all desires, not because his conception of a desire, or of an action, is different from Manu's. Rather, it is because of his ontologized axiology, as mentioned above, according to which to get liberated an individual has to have only the knowledge of the Self, and not to pursue any course of action, not even actions which the *Vedas* prescribe.

Let it be noted here that though Śankara refers to the *Gītā* as attributing all actions to the promptings of a desire, the *Gītā* admits the possibility of a desireless action. Still, Śankara's interpretation of it and of the two *Upaniṣads*, the *Bṛhadāraṇyaka* and the *Katha*, as attributing all actions to *kāma*, positive or negative, confirms the view that not only Manu but even other classical Indian thinkers consider *kāma* or *kāmanā* to be the motivating force of human actions. The Indian value-theory definitely does that as is clear from its calling a human value a *puruṣārtha*, an object of a human desire. To attribute to desire the role of the prime motivative force in the performance of any voluntary, goal-seeking purposive action is, as already said, quite common-sensical. Therefore, Indian ethicists cannot be said to have gone astray for their holding such a theory of action, particularly because they use the world *kāma*', the Sanskrit equivalent of 'desire', in a broad sense to include all forms of appetition.

Kāma, meaning *kāmanā*, a desire or an appetitive motive, cannot be called a *puruṣārtha*. But from this is does not follow that it is of no importance or value. We have seen in the preceding discussion that it is a precondition for all the (other) *puruṣārthas*. Unless an individual has a desire to attain *artha*, to follow *dharma*, or to attain *mokṣa*, he cannot have *artha*, *dharma*, or *mokṣa*. Therefore, though it cannot in itself, or by itself, be called a *puruṣārtha*, it still has prime importance in any endeavour to attain any of the other three *puruṣārthas*. Cāṇakya calls *artha*, we have seen, the basic (*pradhāna*) *puruṣārtha* simply because it is a precondition for the attainment of the (other) three *puruṣārthas*. Following him, even if we do not call *kāma*, meaning *kāmanā*, the basic *puruṣārtha*, since there is no point in calling a desire a *puruṣārtha*, we can definitely call *kāmanā basic to all the puruṣārthas*.

10.2 *KĀMA* AS ALL-COMPREHENSIVE WELL-BEING

Kāma not only means *kāmanā*, appetition, but also *abhīṣta*, objective, which is nothing but the gratification of a desire. To gratify a desire is to attain its object, and the gratification of every desire yields happiness, pleasure, or a feeling of well-being. Therefore, *kāma* is quite often taken to denote happiness as a *puruṣārtha*. This happiness, or feeling of well-being, is not something external to its seeker or enjoyer. It is an *experience* which is yielded by the gratification of some desire of his. In this respect it is different from *artha* and *dharma*, and similar to *mokṣa* as conceived by some thinkers. It is not the same as the object of a desire. For example, the object of a desire may be wealth. But the end-product of the attainment of wealth, of the gratification of the desire for wealth, the experiential condition in the mind of the desirer resulting out of the attainment of wealth, would be happiness or *kāma* as a *puruṣārtha*. Happiness is a *puruṣārtha* because we want, *desire*, to have it and it is desirable, morally right, to have it because there is nothing built into, or intrinsic to, the notion of happiness which may make it undesirable, a disvalue. If sometimes an experience of happiness is considered undesirable it is because of, as we shall see later in the chapter, its discordance with some moral principle or value.

Vātsyāyana, therefore, in his *Kāmasūtram* calls *kāma* (as happiness) a mental phenomenon (*mānasa vyāpāra*). It is, he says, the pleasant experience which an individual has as a result of any one of the five types of sensuous experiences, generated by any one of the five sense organs, ear, skin, eye, tongue, and nose, with the cooperation of the internal sense, mind. A sense organ generates a pleasant experience if the object it comes into contact with, or it receives, is agreeable to it.[6] For example, the sense of hearing does that when the words or sounds heard, or received, by it are soothing, pleasant, and not jarring, or disagreeable, to it.

Something very similar to Vātsyāyana's has been said, much earlier than it, in the *Mahābhārata*. *Kāma* denotes, it says, the agreeable experience, or pleasure, generated by the contact of any one of the five sense organs with an external object congenial to it, or by a mental operation satisfying to our cognitive, conative, or affective nature.[7] Like Vātsyāyna's, this account of *kāma* also denotes all kinds of pleasant or agreeable experiences occasioned by our sensuous, emotional, or intellectual operations. That is why it can fittingly be called the experience of appetitive well-being, as it is these operations which constitute our appetitive nature.

Since *kāma* denotes all kinds of pleasures resulting out of any sensuous-mental operation, it also denotes all sorts of aesthetic pleasures, i.e. pleasures obtained from, or occasioned by, an individual's aesthetic experience of any sort. It thus includes the pleasure obtained from watching an object of natural beauty, as well as the pleasure obtained from the appreciation of a work of art, an object of beauty created by man. For example the pleasure obtained from seeing the rising sun from the top of Tiger Hill in Darjeeling, or from seeing a beautiful woman's spontaneous smile, as well as one from witnessing a dramatic scene on a stage, say, the scene of Duṣyanta's standing still, wonder-struck, on looking at Śakuntala's beautiful, deer-like eyes, in one direction, while aiming his arrow at a deer in another, or that from reading poetry, listening to music, seeing a work of painting or sculpture, etc., will all alike come under the value-category of *kāma*. In all of these pleasures the use of an attentive mind, an appreciative, sensitive, affective nature, and some sense organ is necessarily involved. A person who is in an inattentive mood, or has no, or a very weak, aesthetic sensibility, or whose concerned sense organ is impaired, cannot have the concerned aesthetic experience and therefore the concerned experience of aesthetic pleasure. For example, a deaf man cannot derive any pleasure from a musical performance, nor can a blind man from the performance of a dramatic scene. Aesthetic pleasure has been given in Indian value-theory a very high status on the scale of values. Viśvanātha in his work *Sāhitya-darpaṇa* (3.2) declares aesthetic pleasure (*rasānubhūti*) as having the same axiological status as that of *Brahmānanda* (*Brahmānanda-sahodarah*), the experience of bliss present in an individual's realization of *Brahman*.

10.3 *KĀMA*, SEXUAL PLEASURE, AND GENDER ETHICS

Since *kāma* as a value includes all sorts of pleasures derived from any sensual experience, it is natural for it to include sexual pleasure as well. Sexual pleasure is used here in a broad sense. It denotes all sorts of pleasures experienced by one or both of two individuals of opposite sexes as a result of emotional, passional (*ragatmaka*) interactions, mental as well as physical, between them, the consummation of which is effected in sexual union. *Kāma* does not mean, as we have seen in the preceding discussion, only sexual desire or sexual pleasure. Therefore, it is wrong to take it to mean only sexual pleasure, or desire for sexual pleasure, as several students of Indian value-theory do. The fact of the matter is that the concept of *kāma* is so liberal in its coverage of human pleasures that its proponents do not shy away from talking about and including sexual pleasure in this value-category. They unhesitatingly recognize its importance in human life and give to it the status of a respectable specimen of the *kāma-puruṣārtha*, a status in no way less respectable than that of any other specimen of *kāma*, or appetitive well-being.

The importance of *kāma* as sexual pleasure in Indian ethos is also testified by the fact that just as there is a classical treatise on *artha* (*Arthaśāstra*) and several treatises on *dharma* (*Dharmaśāstra*), there is Vātsyāyana's *Kamasūtram*, a treatise mainly on *kāma* as sexual pleasure. Vātsyāyana admits, as we have mentioned earlier, the generality, or open-texture, of the concept of *kāma*, denoting pleasure derived from all sensuous experiences. But he devotes his book primarily to the discussion of sexual pleasure and to that of the techniques of having it to the maximal degree. He even narrates the sexual practices prevalent in different parts of the country in the manner of an empirical sociologist of the then Indian sexual culture.

While tracing the genealogy or ancestry of the works on the *puruṣārtha* of *kāma*, Vātsyāyana says that for the first time Brahmā writes a massive treatise on *dharma*, *artha* and *kāma* for the guidance of mankind, i.e. for all human beings, and not just for Indians, since Brahmā is the caretaker of all living beings, and not only of those living in India. This treatise consists of a hundred thousand chapters. In course of time, out of it Manu produces a shorter work dealing with matters relating to *dharma*, or ethico-social behaviour of man. It is this which is called *Mānavadharmaśāstra* (or, in brief *Manusmṛti*). On matters relating to *artha*, Bṛhaspati writes a shorter work called *Arthaśāstra*. Similarly, taking out of Brahmā's classic matters relating to *kāma*, Nandi writes a shorter one called *Kāmasūtra* which consists of one thousand chapters. Śvetuketu further shortens Nandi's work into another consisting of five hundred chapters, and Bābhravya shortens Nandi's into a still briefer one consisting of one hundred and fifty chapters. After Bābhravya, Vātsyāyana says, several other sages, like Dattaka, Cārāyaṇa, Suvarṇanābha, et al., write several manual-type works on some specific topics, as and when required by people. The result is that the original work gets divided into several treatises dealing with several topical issues discussed in the original. These works dealing with specific topics are not able to give a comprehensive account of *kāma* and even Bābhravya's briefer one, because of its size (running into one hundred and fifty chapters), is unusable. Therefore, taking this comprehensive but brief work of Bābhravya he has brought out his *Kāmasūtram* in a much shorter and manageable form so that an ordinary individual may study it and conduct his life-affairs in the manner outlined in it, i.e. in keeping with the intentions of Brahmā, the divine caretaker of the world and the original author of the ethics of *kāma*.[8]

This account of the ancestry of his *Kāmasūtra* given by Vātsyāyana, is definitely mythology. But even this mythology has an important lesson to yield. Its point is towards the importance of the pursuit of *kāma* as a *puruṣārtha* and towards the respectable character of anyone's studying matters relating to *kāma* and the methods or techniques of attaining the kind of well-being which *kāma*, as a value, denotes. All this is true of the concept of *kāma* even in that instantiation of it in which it means sexual pleasure, i.e. is true of *kāma* as sexual pleasure. *Vātsyāyana's* objective, thus, clearly is to aver that the pursuit of sexual pleasure in the most effective way and to the greatest possible extent is as respectable a human value as any other human value may be, i.e. that there is nothing profane, or intrinsically evil, in pursuing it. That for some other, extraneous, reason it may become undesirable is another matter since that can also happen with the pursuit of any other human value. How this issue is tackled by Vātsyāyana and Indian ethics in general we shall see a little later in the next section.

That sexual pleasure is not shameful or dirty and studying it and the methods of attaining it not a mean intellectual exercise is further highlighted by Vātsyāyana at the end of his book.

The last thing which he says on the last page of *Kāmasūtram*, as per the interpretation of his commentator Yaśodhara in his commentary called *Jayamangalā*, is that, according to Vātsyāyana himself, the account of sexual pleasure and sexual practices which he has given in this book, he has received, after practising extraordinary celibacy (*lokottara brahmacarya*), in a direct experience (*sākṣātkāra*) in an unmediated concentration of his mind (*nirvikalpaka samādhi*).[9] Saying this seems like offering a rock-bottom justification of the authenticity as well as the normativity or desirability of his ethics of sex. Giving any account of sexual behaviour is an empirical matter, a subject which can be described only on the basis of empirical data. It is not something which can be done on a non-empirical basis, even on the basis of *yogic* concentration, or meditation or spiritual cognition. Vātsyāyana, therefore, may quite reasonably be taken to have said what has been mentioned above only to add to his account a *yogic* authority, since it might have been believed in his time that what was received in a state of *yogic* concentration could neither be anything questionable nor anything undesirable. Or, perhaps it was customary in his time for a scholar to claim of any piece of knowledge or of a theory, that it had been received by him in a *samādhi* or spiritual experience in order to persuade people to believe that it was something too sacrasanct to be questioned. Otherwise, the kind of description of sexual practices, or suggestions, or sex-medicines, which Vātsyāyana gives in the book are too empirical, i.e. sense-mind-empirical, that it seems completely odd to declare them to have been known by him in his *samādhi*. It is the empirical character of this book which gives the impression that it is an erotic work or one on sexology, and that is the reason, and not a completely unjustified one, for a householder to consider it not worth keeping in his domestic library, or even for a librarian not to keep it in his public library.

But in spite of all this, Vātsyāyana's declared objective in writing the book is only to help a man to lead a happy, successful sexual life in a morally desirable and balanced manner. At many points he emphasizes that the pursuit of *kāma* has to be done only in a manner which is concordant with the pursuit of *artha* and *dharma*, and not in a manner which is sexually reckless.

The anecdote about Śankara's acquiring knowledge of sex to answer a question relating to sex put to him by Bhāratī, the wife of Mandana Mishra, is worth mentioning here. It may be just an anecdote, and not a matter of real history because it is not mentioned in any historical account of Śankara's life. It occurs only in the introduction to *Amarūśatakam*, a work by Amarūka. It runs as follows: Śankara has a debate with Mandana Mishra and he, in the debate, defeats the latter. Then Mishra's wife, Bhāratī, comes forward and says that her husband cannot be declared defeated because he and she, a husband and his wife, make a unity. He can be declared defeated by Śankara only if she, his wife, is also defeated by him. Therefore, there has to be also a debate between Śankara and her and Śankara has to defeat her too to celebrate his victory over her husband. Śankara agrees to this condition and asks Bhāratī to put a question to him. Bhāratī is a clever woman and she puts to him a question which is not one pertaining to a philosophical issue but to a matter of sex. Śankara, being a life-long celibate, has no sexual experience and therefore is unable to answer it. He realizes, as any logician like him would, its empirical character and the epistemic-logical truth that an empirical question can be answered only on the basis of empirical knowledge of the relevant facts. He is also cognizant of the other, consequential, truth that it cannot be answered on the basis of spiritual, mystical, experience. Therefore, he, unlike Vātsyāyana, does not lay any claim to knowing its answer on the basis of his spiritual experience. Rather, he chooses the empirical path though in a very difficult, unusual, manner. He comes out of the arena of debate, relinquishes his body, enters into the dead body of a king, and the king (i.e. Śankara in his body) all on a sudden becomes alive. This king, or really Śankara in the king's body, receives education on sexual matters from an authoritative scholar of sex, then relinquishes the king's body, enters his own which he had relinquished, appears before Bhāratī and answers her question.

This anecdote cannot be taken to be an account of what really happened because it is based on something like a miracle. But its importance is in no way diminished on that account. Its importance consists in highlighting the fact that, sex being an empirical matter, anything can be said of its character, utility, or ways of satisfying it, only on the basis of facts about sexual experience. Vātsyāyana's claiming to have known all that he has said about sex, sexual experience, techniques of heightening sexual pleasure, etc., in his meditative experience in a life of complete celibacy can be taken, as already said above, to lend some sort of unquestionability to his account. But it is questionable whether people in his time believed in his account's having been a result of this experience. Perhaps, in those times too, discussing sex in the manner he has discussed it was not considered respectable for a saint which he is, according to the tradition. This may be the case in spite of the fact that classical Indians, including classical Indian saints and teachers, lived a rich, sometimes free and luxurious, sexual life by having more than one wife. This sort of a social stigma about discussing sex, or even sex-ethics, is predominantly existent among philosophers of India even today. That is why very little has been done in this area by them. But even then classical Indian philosophers are very liberal and fully cognizant of the value of sex in human life which is exhibited in their inclusion of *kāma* among the four basic objectives of man and more specifically in their inclusion of sexual pleasure in the concept of *kāma* as a *puruṣārtha*.

The recognition of the moral value of sexual activity by Indian ethics is further testified by the fact that it is considered by it a duty or obligation of a householder to produce children, preferably male, by his wife i.e. by the woman or women he has married in a socially approved manner. That is, it is an important component of the ethics of a householder (*gārhasthya dharma*). There are three obligations which every individual has to fulfil. The first is the obligation to the teachers, the scholars (*ṛṣi ṛṇa*) who teach him in his student life (*brahmacarya āśrama*) the wisdom contained in the *Vedas*. This obligation is fulfilled, the debt to scholars repaid, by receiving the instruction in the manner required and paying to the teachers their honorarium. The second is the obligation to parents or ancestors (*pitṛ ṛṇa*) which is fulfilled by entering the householder's stage, getting married and producing children. The third is the debt to deities which is fulfilled by performing religious sacrifices and rituals.[10]

It is the second obligation which makes sexual union a duty because without it no procreation can be done. Classical Indian thinkers realize that pleasure and procreation go together. That is why they make procreation a duty the fulfilment of which goes with the attainment of pleasure. Since it is a consequence or accompaniment of the fulfilment of a duty, sexual pleasure becomes, as are other sensuous pleasures, a value (*puruṣārtha*). All this again shows that the classical Indian conception of life is not only a realistic, down-to-earth, conception but also a robust or generous one, and not at all a dull dry dreary, or life-negating, one. As some classical books show, classical Indians, particularly the three upper classes, lived a very rich, joyous, life, rich even in sexual enjoyment one sign of which is the prevalence of polygamy among them.

Sanskrit literature is full of works which paint the romantic and sexual life of their characters, even of some deities. For example, the eighth canto of Kalidāsa's *Kumārasambhava*, portraying the love life of the venerated god Śiva and his spouse Pārvatī is worth reading in this regard. Āyurvedic medical science abounds in prescriptions for sex medicines and even names some of these medicines in highly romantic, sex-related, terms, for example, *kāminī-mada-mardana vaṭī*, the pill for vanishing the sexual power of a woman. Even some books have been given romantic, or sex-loaded, titles, for example, Jagannātha's *Manormā-Kuca-Mardinī*, a commentary on Vattojidikṣita's *Praudha Manoramā*, a work on grammar. Nowadays one may think twice before uttering such names in a mixed gathering. The point of mentioning these literary, or naming, practices is only to show that classical Indian scholars are not averse to talking about sex or to speaking in sex-loaded terms. This means that for them neither sex nor sex-talk is a prohibited zone.

Returning to *polygamy* in classical India, we may not approve of it; but we must appreciate classical Indians' not making celibacy a virtue for all. They seem to have realized that doing that would have been destructive. If everybody becomes celibate, procreation would stop, and a time may come when there is no human being on this earth. But if procreation is made a duty, even if some fail to fulfil it, or only some fulfil it, the continuation of the human species will not be endangered. However, in all this talk about *kāma* in the sense of sexual participation, there is a male-centric bias because there is always shown a bias for fathering a male child. Even Vātsyāyana's description of man-woman union, even of the prevalent or recommended techniques, is more from the point of view of the male than from that of the female.

In fact, the gender ethics of classical India is generally male-centric. Polygamy is quite common and not condemned or looked down upon. Among moral exemplars Rāma is monogamous but Vālmīki does not at any place in the *Rāmāyaṇa* paint this aspect of his life in bold colours, or highlight it as a great moral virtue. Nor does he highlight Lakṣmaṇa's leading a celibate's life for fourteen years while accompanying Rāma all along in the period of his exile. Nor does he make even a slightly critical remark about Daśaratha's having many wives. On this point of the practice of polygamy, even the *Mahābhārata* is not different from the *Rāmāyaṇa.* Most of the important characters of it are polygamous, and like Vālmīki, its author or compiler Vyāsa does not consider being polygamous in any way morally derogatory. Pāṇḍu, the socially accepted father of the Pāndavas, after whose name they are called Pāṇḍavas, has two wives, Kuntī and Mādri. Among the Pāṇḍavas, Arjuna has married, besides Draupadī, three others, Ulūpī, Subhadrā, and Citrangadā, and Bhīma has married one more, Hiḍimbā. Karṇa himself admits that Adhiratha, who has brought him up, has arranged for his getting married to so many women of his own (*sūta*) caste. Dhṛtarāṣtra too admits that Duryodhana has many beautiful young wives. Even Kṛṣṇa, the propounder of the venerated ethics of the *Gītā* himself has many and instead of considering polygamy in any respect wrong, considers it commendable. This is clear from his helping Arjuna to marry his sister Subhadrā, when he finds Arjuna attracted towards her.[11]

Polyandry does not seem to be very common but also not disallowed in classical India. The example of it most commonly referred to is that of Draupadī's having been married, at the same time, to all the five Pāṇḍava brothers.

The *Mahābhārata,* which depicts the story of which Draupadī's marriage constitutes an important event and of which Draupadī can be said to be the heroine, or one of the most important female characters, does not anywhere consider it wrong or unjustified. Rather, it tries to extol or justify it. Many modern scholars believe that this story is a part of Indian history and Draupadī's polyandric marriage a real historical event. Be that as it may, what is important for a work on classical Indian ethics, which ours is, that, like polygamy polyandry is also not considered in it morally unjustified or unfair to the fair sex. Taking Draupadī's case, it is not only not considered morally wrong, but also is justified on some palpably not very strong grounds. The ground which is generally taken, by the classical ethos as well as by a good number of modern writers, to be a morally sound one is that all the five brothers marry Draupadī because this is what Kuntī, their mother, asks or instructs them to do. This act of theirs is considered morally right, or even laudatory, it is said, because a mother's instruction or order is inviolable for all of her children.

It is true that in classical Indian ethos a mother is to be revered like a goddess and obedience to her order or wish by a child of hers is considered to be an absolute obligation, or a great moral virtue, of the child. But when the incident of Draupadī's polyandric marriage, or Kuntī's instruction, is examined comprehensively and contextually in an objective manner, the aforesaid moral justification of it does not stand the test of logic. Perhaps that is why in the attempt to justify it appeal is also made to some other factors, like preservation of unity among the five brothers, past precedents of polyandric marriages in respectable upper caste Indian families, and also to mythology. It may not be trouble-free to call any one of these factors morally relevant, i.e. relevant for morally justifying an action or practice. But before we take up this issue let us first look at the context of the marriage and its alleged moral justification on the ground of its being a case of obedience to a mother's order or instruction. It can be briefly put as follows:

As per her father's, king Drupada's declaration, Draupadī is to choose as her husband only him who hits with his arrow the cornea of the eye of a fish kept in a moving disc, located at some height, by looking at the image of the fish reflected in a liquid placed on the ground. Only Arjuna is able to perform this tricky feat of archery and therefore she chooses him as her husband. He and his elder brother Bhīma, with Draupadī, return in the evening of the same day to their cottage. Their eldest brother Yudhiṣṭhira along with the two youngest ones Nakula and Sahadeva had earlier left the place of the contest, leaving Bhīma to defend Arjuna if attacked by any unsuccessful contestant. At the time when Arjuna and Bhīma with Draupadī reach the cottage, Kuntī, their mother, is inside the cottage and is not in a position to see who or what is with Arjuna and Bhīma. This time of their return is the time when they ordinarily return after collecting alms, consisting of eatables and some other materials for their daily needs. Kuntī is expecting them to come home even today with similar things. Being naturally jubilant because of having got Draupadī, to inform Kuntī of their success: they say 'Mother, we have brought the alms (*bhīkṣā*).[12] They do not say that they have brought a young beautiful princess, let alone saying that Arjuna has won her in a contest to be his wife. And, Kuntī is neither expecting it, nor does she come out to see what they have actually brought. Without seeing Draupadī and assuming that the alms they have brought today, as they do every day, are some material, edible or usable daily needs, she responds to their announcement by saying 'All of you (brothers) together partake of (enjoy, or use) it'.[13] But immediately, on turning towards them and seeing Draupadī, she becomes greatly worried for what she has uttered and expresses her mistake by saying feelingly 'Oh, an extremely wrong thing has come out of my mouth'.[14]

It is clear from the context that Kuntī's asking her sons to share or enjoy all together, what Arjuna and Bhīma have brought, has been done by her not only under the veil of complete ignorance about the identity of what they have brought, but also because of her expecting them, on good grounds, to have brought some material thing which can be shared by all of them without any impropriety done to anyone, including the thing asked to be shared. Her *intention* is not at all that they share Draupadī, a woman. And, that she has committed a grave moral error in asking them to do what her words, if taken at their face value, require them to do, is expressed by her very clearly in her feeling sorry or repentant for what has come, inadvertently, out of her mouth. In the case of every utterance, or speech-unit, its *real* meaning is not always what it, as a verbal unit, means, i.e. what its constituent words mean. That is, its verbal meaning is not always either its real meaning, or its *speaker's* meaning. And, all this is generally true of an utterance made by a speaker who is ignorant of the identity of the thing the utterance is about. This means that if Kuntī's, the Pāṇḍava's mother's, asking them all to share what Arjuna and Bhīma have brought, is taken as an order given by the mother, Kuntī's intended meaning of this order is not that all of them share Draupadī, i.e. that all of them marry her. Therefore, even if a mother's order is taken to be inviolable, this order of Kuntī does not require that Draupadī is made the wife of all of them simply because it is *not an order to do that*; it is an order to the effect that if what has been brought is a material thing, edible or usable in some other way, then they all should partake of it. Secondly, if a particular order of a mother requires that some immoral thing be done, then it would cease to be inviolable plainly because no order or prescription to do anything immoral can be inviolable. Rather, it would become morally obligatory to violate it, as it is a deontic tautology that it is obligatory to abjure doing what is immoral or morally forbidden. But Kuntī is not so ratiocinative as to tell the Pāndavas in clear terms that her asking all of them to share what has been brought does not mean that Draupadī be made the wife of all of them. And, to save her soul, or conscience, she is forthright in confessing immediately that she has asked them to share without any knowledge of the facts and is sorry for that. Therefore, she leaves the matter to Yudhiṣṭhira to decide what they should do. She does that because, like others, she too believes that he is not only the eldest and the wisest of the five brothers but also an individual possessing a thorough knowledge of morality and an impeccable moral character. Her worry, after seeing Draupadī, because of her having asked all of them to enjoy what they have brought, indicates that she does not want that Draupadī be shared by all of them. It would not be too hazardous, therefore, to guess that she has the hope that Yudhiṣṭhira would not decide that she be married to all of them.

Yudhiṣṭhira is thus referred to by Kuntī to decide, as a moral judge, what should be done in the circumstances in a manner which does not result in any injustice to any one of the persons concerned, more particularly, to Kuntī and to Draupadī. No injustice would obviously be done if no disrespect or disobedience is done to Kuntī, the mother, and no infringement is done to the dignity of the personhood of Draupadī, the person *about* whom the decision is to be taken. If no disrespect is to be done to Kuntī *because* she is a mother, no infringement of her dignity is to be done to Draupadī because she is a *person* and not a *thing*, not a shareable *commodity*. In his adjudication, Yudhiṣṭhira does take into account the fact that *Arjuna alone* has won Draupadī in the contest, among the assembled youths, for being *chosen* by her as the person to whom she should be married, and says that, therefore, he alone is the person who should marry her. Arjuna does not disown his moral right to marry her. But he points out that since Yudhiṣṭhira and Bhīma are elder than him, as per familial practice, they should get married earlier than him, and he should wait until then. He does not say, however, that they too should get married to Draupadī, nor that he is unwilling to marry her. On this matter, however, Yudhiṣṭhira does not feel the need of consulting Draupadī, as if her consent does not matter, though it matters very importantly. It does matter because she has *chosen* Arjuna in the contest, in a *svayamvara*, a ceremonial occasion given by her father to her with the freedom to choose her husband. It is by exercising this freedom of hers that she chooses Arjuna who alone meets the condition of being chosen, and does not allow Karṇa to participate in the contest on the ground of his being the son of a *sūta* and not being an upper caste prince. Yudhiṣṭhira's ignoring her consent, therefore, goes against the very principle of letting a girl choose her husband in a *svayamvara*, a form of marriage prevalent in classical India in which a girl herself (*svayam*) makes the choice (*varana*) of the person fit to be her husband.

In his interpretation of his mother's words, he takes her words, as explained, in their literal meaning and not in the meaning in which she intends them to be taken. Her intended meaning is very different from their literal meaning. He does not even give due consideration to Kuntī's admission that she has uttered those words without knowing the identity of what they have brought as alms (*bhīkṣā*) and that she therefore expresses her feeling of sorrow for having uttered them. This admission of hers she makes to indicate that she has asked them all to use or enjoy what they have brought because she did not expect them to have brought a girl, a human being, as a girl is not a thing to be given as alms by anyone to anyone else. Yudhiṣṭhira, even then, in spite of her admission, does not realize that words uttered, or any order given, without knowing the nature of the relevant facts, lose their prescriptive force, that *ignorance of the relevant facts* takes away all the moral strength or obligational power which the issuance of an order or prescription may have for the person or persons by whom the order is to be obeyed. That is why he gives the verdict that Draupadī be married to all the five brothers doing which would make her shareable by all of the brothers. This, he seems to be claiming, is some sort of a *moral* solution or justification on the ground that doing it is what the mother's words require them to do, i.e. that all the brothers share or enjoy together what they have brought as alms. Some modern writers call it laudatory on the alleged ground that it is done, that Draupadī is married to all the five brothers, in order to fulfil the mother's wish or order, and is therefore an expression of the Pāṇḍavas' very high degree of devotion to their mother (*mātṛbhakti*). But as the above analysis has conclusively shown, it cannot be called even justified, let alone laudatory, on this ground *because* the mother's intention is not that Draupadī, a human being, be shared by all of them.

There is another, very important, issue, popping up its head here in a very conspicuous manner. This is an issue concerning the resolution of conflict between two moral principles. It can be demonstrated as follows:

Let us assume that Kuntī's words mean that Draupadī should be shared by, i.e. married to, all the five brothers. Then as per the moral principle that a mother's wish be always fulfilled, Draupadī should be married to all the five brothers. But there is the other moral principle that no indignity be done to any individual or to any individual's personhood. This principle requires that Draupadī be married only to Arjuna as per the principle of the *svayamvara* form of marriage, and not to anyone else, let alone being married to five individuals at the same time. And, to get Draupadī married to all of them is to do indignity to her *personhood.* It may even be said to be immoral because it amounts to treating her, a person, as a property or thing, to commodify her, by considering her to be a shareable thing even if doing that is to fulfil the mother's wish. Here the two principles conflict with each other since following one amounts to flouting the other, and this actually happens. Yudhiṣṭhira does not feel even the existence of the conflict, leave alone realize the need of evolving a method to resolve it. The great knower of all *dharma* (morality) though he is said to be, he does not seem to recognize the sanctity of the moral principle of honouring the dignity of the personhood of a woman, or the immorality involved in treating Draupadī as a commodity. This principle as well as the immorality resulting out of its violation is an important concern of gender ethics since each one of the two refers to the dignity of a woman. But it is not just that. The principle concerned in this theme is only a specification of the general moral principle that no indignity be done to any person's personhood. But the great moralist Yudhiṣṭhira does not seem to be sensitive to these issues in the context of his deciding that Draupadī be married to all the five brothers. Even the tradition does not raise these issues, nor does it question the morality of Yudhiṣṭhira's decision. All this may be taken as a bias against women in respect of considering them equal to men in moral matters. That is why I have said that the classical Indian ethos—perhaps all classical ethics—is male-centric.

We cannot even defend Yudhiṣṭhira's decision on the ground that Draupadī herself does not mind whether she is married to Arjuna alone, or to all the five brothers. This we cannot do because she gives a clear hint that she is against polygamy when she expresses her anger against Arjuna when he marries Subhadrā. After the marriage, when he enters Draupadī's bedroom, she expresses her wifely anger against him and jealousy against Subhadrā. She very emotionally asks him why has he entered her bedroom, and tells him that now he should go to the bedroom of Subhadrā. She tells him in clear words that his love for her must have got loosened by now after his having another wife. In a very poetic and pathetic way she says that when a bundle is tightened a second time, after having been already tightened once earlier, its earlier binding is sure to have become loosened (*pūrva bandhah slathayati*).[15] That is, a husband's love for his first wife is bound to have become weaker after his having loved and married another woman. A woman who is against her husband's polygamy cannot be expected to have favoured her own polyandric marriage.

There seems to be another reason also, as per the *Mahābhārata*, which has worked in Yudhiṣṭhira's mind in deciding the way he has done. But even this reason is not pro-feminist. After Arjuna's saying that he would like to wait until the elders get married, he looks at his other brothers. He notices that all of them are very greatly attracted by Draupadī's extraordinary beauty and are feeling highly sexually excited. Realizing that if Draupadī is married only to Arjuna, then since all the others are sexually attracted towards her, the marriage may cause disunion in the family. Therefore, to protect unity among the brothers, which is very badly needed, he declares that Draupadī be married to all the five brothers.[16] This reason too has male gender bias, or is anti-feminist, because it amounts to sacrificing the dignity of a woman to preserve unity in the family. At best it can be called a *pragmatic* reason, and is not at all a moral reason. In fact, there *cannot be* a *moral reason* for marrying any one woman to more than one man and that too without taking her consent. This practice infringes the dignity of the woman's personhood. It goes against a basic, fundamental, principle of morality that no person should be treated as a means. But even this infringement, caused by Yudhiṣṭhira's decision, is not strongly, or, openly, questioned or criticized by anybody in the tradition.

However, there seems to be present a lurking feeling in the tradition that this pragmatic reason too is not a conclusive justification for the polyandric marriage. To fill in the logical gap between the reason and the decision, or to give a (seemingly) incontrovertible reason, an appeal is made to mythology. Vyāsa drops in and reveals what happened in Draupadī's previous birth. He says that in that birth she requested Śiva five times to bless her with a very good husband. Because she requested five times, Śiva blesses her with five very good husbands. On account of this blessing she is fated to have five husbands. Therefore, nobody should be surprised, or feel sorry, about her being married to all the five brothers. This is something which cannot be avoided. This legendary logic of appeal to mythology offered by Vyāsa, can explain or justify nothing. His appeal to Śiva's blessing is of no justificatory significance. Moreover, if it is taken seriously, it would adversely tell on the godhood, *Śivatva*, of Śiva because a woman's making five times the same request, i.e. the request for a good husband, is not at all a reason for blessing her with five husbands. One may even say that anybody who does not see that it is not a reason for giving this kind of blessing cannot be called a god, a Śiva. Or, that one who uses any such reason, or any reason whatsoever, for sanctioning polyandry, or making a woman fated to be married in a polyandric manner, cannot be called a god.

Vyāsa's referring to this mythology to silence all questions about the propriety of this polyandry also raises some serious doubts about the role of the great *ṛṣi* in the then moral climate. Instead of helping the Pāṇḍavas to solve their problem without taking recourse to this unethical polyandric device, he declares it is to be something which is fated, or necessitated, to happen. This shows that he does not play the role of a moral guide by providing moral solutions to moral problems. And, since Draupadī's polyandric marriage is an anti-feminist step, Śiva by ordaining it and Vyāsa by justifying it seem to put a divine stamp on this unethical practice. Thereby they also seem to lose their own moral status, if this piece of mythology is taken seriously and in a secular, non-partisan, manner. It may be that in the then society polyandry was an acceptable practice and Yudhiṣṭhira takes the decision simply because, or mainly because, it is socially acceptable. Even then, had Vyāsa questioned it on moral grounds and forbidden him from taking it he would have shone as a moral reformer and added a new lustre to his sainthood. Perhaps such great spiritually oriented saints did not bother about mundane, social matters, which moral issues are. But it is more surprising that even modern writers on Indian ethics do not raise the question of the morality of Yudhiṣṭhira's decision, let alone talk about it in a critical manner. Rather, most of them do not seem to see anything objectionable in it.

Historians say that polyandry was then in vogue in the region in which, as per the *Mahābhārata* story, the marriage of Draupadī is said to have taken place. Some of them say that even now in the northern hilly parts of India polyandry is present though it is not very common. Therefore, they say, there is nothing unusual in Yudhiṣṭhira's deciding the way he does. But it is not too much to expect a great saint-intellectual like Vyāsa to question the legitimacy or *desirability of this social* practice. It is one of the obligations of an intellectual, and definitely of an enlightened one like Vyāsa, to provide a critique of social institutions. And, it is in no way a commendable move to justify it by making an appeal to a mythology or to fate, or even to a divine dispensation. Doing any one of these things can an best be called using, as already said, a legendary logic which is no logic at all. It is largely by providing critiques of prevailing social institutions that an intellectual, or a saint, contributes to making a society progress by getting rid of its undesirable institutions and replacing them with desirable ones.

Indian gender-ethics, i.e. ethics pertaining to the man-woman relationship, is thus in a sense liberal, or too liberal. In its liberalism too it is, as is clear from the above, male-centric, that is, more liberal in respect of the male partner than in that of the female one. It was not customary in classical India for an unmarried girl to produce a child, but was not rare. And, it was not considered desirable or socially respectable. But the father of such a child was not condemned or looked down upon. For example, the saint Parāśara for fathering Vyāsa in unmarried Satyavatī does not lose even a tint of his spiritual lustre on account his having done that.[17] But Satyavatī keeps it concealed, out of social shame, for a long time. She reveals this information only when she needs Vyāsa to produce sons by her two childless, widowed, daughters-in-law, Ambikā and Ambālikā. But even this incident reveals the male-centricity of Indian ethics. Vyāsa is called to produce sons and not any child, male or female, by each one of them. The consent of neither of the widows is taken; rather, both are unwilling to be made a mother. Vyāsa himself does not bother to take their consent, or to inquire from his mother whether or not they have given their consent. He does as asked by his mother Satyavatī, and produces by Ambikā the blind Dhṛtarāṣṭra and by Ambālikā the weakling, yellow-complexioned, Pāṇḍu.[18] The former is born blind because his mother closes her eyes out of fear on seeing Vyāsa approaching her. The latter becomes yellowish because his mother turns yellow, again out of fear on seeing the man going to be her son's father. All this is done because of being in accordance with the then socio-ethical practice or principle of *niyoga*, the principle which permits, requires, or justifies, a brother to produce a son by a childless widow, or widows, of a dead brother of his. Vyāsa does not question the moral validity or justification of this principle, nor does he mind the unwillingness of the two widows. Had he done that not only might he have ushered in a great moral change in the then Indian society but he would surely have added an extra shine to his sainthood. But the *Mahābhārata*, or Indian ethos in general, does not raise any such issue, nor does it make any adverse remark about Vyāsa for having done what he does by gladly proceeding as his mother asks him to do as per the principle of *niyoga*.

Preference for the male child is a typical classical Indian phenomenon, as it is even today. All along in the above example, this preference is visible, and it is a common, universal, phenomenon even in some later examples. Bhīṣma gets his blind nephew, Dhṛtarāṣṭra married to Gāndhārī, the daughter of the king Subala, because she has been blessed by the god Śankara to have one hundred sons.[19] The literature pertaining to the story of Rāma also shows this preference. Rāma is not mentioned anywhere as having a daughter, nor are any of his brothers. His father, the king Daśaratha, is also not mentioned as having one. But Vālmīki does mention that he performs a horse-sacrifice (*aśvamedha yajña*) to get sons and as a result of it gets four sons. There is not mentioned anyone performing a sacrifice for getting a daughter and no specific sacrifice (*yajña*) is named as one the successful performance of which by a daughter-seeking individual is sure to enable him to have one, just as there is named one which is to be performed with the desire to get a son (*putreṣti yajña*) and which surely enables the performer to have the number of sons he wants to have. Thus, in respect of having marital-relations, or sexual relations even without entering into marriage, as well as in that of having progeny, classical Indian ethics may be said to be liberal, even to extent of being permissive, for males.

For a man even visiting a prostitute is, Vātsyāyana says, natural and not forbidden. He seems to hold that it is not even immoral, even if the visitor is a married person. Here too he lays down some rules about what a prostitute should and should not do in her dealings with her customers. But he is not so restricted about the male visitors. He devotes six chapters in his *Kāmasūtram* (pp. 454–526 of the edition already referred to) on the institution of prostitution. This means that it was a socially accepted institution in classical India.

Notwithstanding what has been said above, there is no denying the fact that there are in some classical works statements or maxims according to women a respectable status. For example, it is a common saying by many classical thinkers that a wife is her husband's life-long partner, half of his being (*ardhāngini*), because without her he cannot produce a son, and therefore a successor. He cannot also get the fruits of his offerings made in a religious ceremony unless she accompanies him in performing the ceremony. That is, both should jointly perform the ceremony. This implies that she is indispensable to him. There is also a statement, very often quoted, which mentions six qualities which a good wife should have. It does add that it is rare, or very difficult, to have one who has all of the six qualities. But it also suggests that it is possible for a woman to have them and that it would be real good luck for a man to get a wife who has them. 'It is rare', it asserts, 'for a man to have a wife who acts as an adviser in whatever he does, as a slave in obeying his orders, as a mother while serving him food, as a prostitute while sharing her bed with him, as one who always behaves in a morally right manner, and who is of a forgiving nature as is the earth'.[20] This is certainly a list of very stringent qualities. But it does indicate that classical Indians very highly prized having a good wife. Manu too at places accords a very honourable place to woman. For example, he says that gods are very pleased with the household in which women are worshipped, i.e. respected. On the other hand, the actions of those, in whose household they are not respected, do not yield their fruits. The former household is prosperous whereas the latter gets dissolved or destroyed.[21]

But the same Manu, in the same work, says at another place that the performance of the marriage ceremony of a woman with a man is what the performance of the sacred thread ceremony of a male by his teacher is and her stay in the service of her husbands similar to a male's stay in his teacher's school for receiving education. The obvious implication of it is that a female is not to be admitted in a school for education. Manu also thinks of a female as a defiling, corrupting, agent and therefore advises that a wise man should not be attracted by her, nor should he be incautious in his dealings with her. This advice he considers very appropriate or justified because man, he says, is naturally subject to being sexually attracted towards her and to feel angry if he is obstructed in his venture, and women are expert in exploiting this weakness of even wise men. That is why one has to be watchful. He should not meet in a lonely place even with his own mother, sister, or daughter. To say this is to go much farther than Manu needs to, but he does not hesitate to state it with as much firmness as he says the other things about the man-woman relationship. As regards the duties of a married woman, Manu is very strict and rigorous. A chaste wife must always serve her husband as if he were a god, even if he is devoid of education, moral character and conjugal loyalty. After becoming a widow, she must control her passions and desires by living on flowers, roots and fruits and should never even dream of another man. If a woman leaves her inferior husband and marries another, a superior person, she becomes socially condemnable and is called a wife who has been already enjoyed by someone else.[22] Rules for men are extremely liberal if compared with these rules meant for women. And, these are only some of such rules.

Perhaps because of her built-in, natural, defects, or inferiority to man, Manu holds that a woman, in no period of her life, childhood, youth, or old age, is to be left free to do anything according to her own sweet will. In her childhood she is to be under the control of her father, in her youth under that of her husband, and after the husband's death, in her old age, under that of her son.[23]

It has been said above that, as per Manu's account of the classical gender ethics, a woman does not seem to have been given adequate opportunities for receiving education in a school. This seems to be supported by his saying that she is not to undergo the sacred thread ceremony, or any similar one, in a school, but her marriage is taken to be its equivalent. This is not strange because almost no classical society is recorded to have given to women educational opportunities on a par with those given to men. Some scholars mention the examples of intellectually alert women—Gārgī, Maitreyī, Kātyāyanī, et al.—as evidence against the view that women in classical India do not enjoy educational facilities, or facilities equal to those enjoyed by men. It is true that such examples illustrate that classical India does have some scholarly women, but certainly not that men and women are *generally* treated equally in respect of their right to receive education. Altekar[24] gives some examples, from the early *Vedic* period, of some women participating in educational activities. These examples too are very scanty, and he admits that in the later *Vedic* period women's position in educational and other activities seems to have got weakened. Be his interpretation taken as it may, it remains true that gender equality, *in all* respects, is not a characteristic feature of classical Indian ethics. But as already said, this is not true of classical Indian ethics alone, and therefore cannot be claimed to be its distinctive deficiency.

Before we conclude this section, it is worthwhile to take note of Rāma's waging war against Rāvaṇa of Lankā to free his wife Sītā, abducted by Rāvaṇa, from his clutches, as depicted in the Rāmāyaṇa. This is relevant to bring out the importance of love, or conjugal love, an expression or instantiation of the *kāma puruṣārtha,* even for a moral exemplar as well as to provide a bridge to the next section. All along in his separation from Sītā Rāma is candid in expressing his love for her. His waging a war against Rāvaṇa does show his high regard for womenfolk. But he too fights shy of admitting that he has fought the war because of his love for her when at the end the war, after Rāvaṇa has been killed, Sītā is freed, and is brought before him by Vibhīṣaṇa. This is a most pleasant moment for her because she has been yearning for all these years to meet him whom she treats as her god. But when she appears before him, Rāma, in stead of expressing his happiness, or sympathy for all that she has suffered, tells her in a curt manner, that he has waged the war to free her not out of his great love for her. Rather, he says, he has done that to fulfil his obligation (*dharma*) as a husband. It is his obligation to protect his wife and she had been abducted when she was in his care during his exile. Therefore, to free her from the abductor is his duty, his *dharma.* To fulfil this *dharma* he has done all that he has done, and not out of any love, or emotional attachment, for her.[25] This seems to give the impression that he does not consider a husband's love for his wife, or a man's for a woman, a good moral reason for doing the kind of things he has done. On the other hand, fulfilment of an obligation or *dharma* is such a reason, and *dharma* is a higher value than *kāma.* Be that as it may, *dharma* does occupy a higher status on the scale of *puruṣārtha*s in the Indian ethos. Therefore, let us see how the two are related with each other.

10.4 APPETITIVE WELL-BEING AND MORAL REGULATION (*KĀMA* AND *DHARMA*)

Kāma, as an experience of pleasure, or well-being, as we have seen, is the resultant of the satisfaction of an appetite or desire (*kāmanā*). It does not matter what sort of a desire the satisfied desire is. As an *experience,* the experience of pleasure is, as has been said earlier, an intrinsic value in the sense of its being a value not because of its being a means to the attainment of another value, or in the sense of its being a value for which there is no need to give a reason for its being a value. Rather, it is a value because of its being what it in itself is. But still it may be the case that a certain experience of pleasure, or, to be brief, a pleasure, may not be a positive value, or may be a lower value than some other value. This is natural because of a complexity in the concept of a desire.

The concept of a desire by itself is not a complete concept. It does not make complete sense for anyone to say that he has a desire. His utterance would make complete sense only when he adds a word or phrase to denote the object of his desire. When he adds that he has a desire, or the desire, to obtain x, or to cause x to happen or come about, etc., his utterance becomes completely, or adequately, sensible. It is the *object of desire* which distinguishes it from another desire whose object is different. The desire-for-*artha* (*arthecchā*) is different from the desire-for-*mokṣa* (*mokṣecchā*) because *artha* is different from *mokṣa*, and not for any other reason. Even the *experience* of desiring *artha* is different from the *experience* of desiring *mokṣa*, for this very reason. As *objects of a desire*, the two, *artha* and *mokṣa* are categorically, conceptually, of the same order or status; each one is an object of a desire (if it is the actual object of someone's desire). Their value-status may be different, i.e. one may be a higher, or a lower, value than the other. But that would be for some different reason. Therefore, if one desire is rated to be a better, a higher, a more desirable, desire than another, it would be because the object of the former is of a higher value than that of the latter. A complete description of the identity of a desire can thus be given only by including in its description a reference to its object.

As an illustration of what is being maintained here, let us go back to what Rāma says to Sītā, as mentioned in the previous section, when she is presented before him after being freed from her confinement in Rāvaṇa's Aśokavātikā (garden). He admits that he had, in doing all that he has done to free her, the *desire to extricate her*. But it was not his desire to extricate his beloved wife, a desire to free his object of love. Rather, it was his desire to fulfil his obligation (*dharma*) because he thought that it was, and still thinks that it is, his duty to free the woman who (had) has been abducted by Rāvaṇa while under his protection during his exile. His stating his desire this way may appear harsh to Sītā and to all those who are there when he makes the statement. Speaking from an emotive point of view perhaps it really is harsh. But looking at it from a logical angle, it is very pointful. By stating this way his desire in doing all that has been involved in extricating her, Rāma makes complete and precise the description of the identity of his desire. He very successfully demonstrates that it is not a desire to get the woman he loves but to protect the dignity of his *dharma* though a consequential result of it is also the freedom of the woman who is his wife. It is this way of identifying the desire behind the war which makes his war against Rāvaṇa a war to preserve *dharma* or morality (*dharmayuddha*) and not just a man's war for a woman. The dignity of the war is thus elevated to a much higher level. It is a similar point which Kṛṣṇa makes all along in the *Mahābhārata* war and more specifically in the *Gītā* portion of the epic. Before the war begins, he succeeds in convincing Arjuna that if fought it would be a moral war, one for protecting morality, and not simply a war for property. It is the moral content of the desire to wage the war which makes both the Lankā war and the Kurukṣetra war a moral war.

Had there been no moral content in the desire behind the two wars, the victors would have been happy at their end and thus would have gratified their desire (*kāmanā*) or attained their *kāma*. But we would not call this *kāma* or happiness of theirs a *puruṣārtha*, or the Indian theory of *kāma* as *puruṣārtha* would not allow us to do that. The reason is obvious. Since a desire has always to have an object in order to be a desire, since there cannot be a desire which is not a desire for having something, what makes a desire a commendable or a condemnable desire is the nature of its object. More specifically, as per the *kāma* theory of Indian ethics, if the object of a desire is morally commendable, then and only then is the desire a commendable (or even a permissible) desire and the feeling of appetitive well-being resulting out of its gratification a commendable (or a morally permissible) feeling of well-being. To put it in a more liberal manner, *dharma* or morality is the determiner of the positive value (*puruṣārthatva*) of a *kāma*, of the experience of well-being resulting out of the satisfaction of a desire.

Thus morality works as the regulator of desires or objects of desires. It regulates the pursuit of *kāma* in the sense that the pursuit of an object of desire is *permissible* if the object is not forbidden by, or in discordance with, any moral principle; it is *commendable* if it is prescribed or required by a moral principle, and it is forbidden if it contravenes a moral principle. The role which a moral principle plays in regulating the pursuit can also be played by a moral value, a right, or a virtue. The *puruṣārtha* theory admits that the gratification of any desire yields happiness and that any experience of happiness is a value in the sense that it is actually desired or valued by human beings. But it introduces the requirement that the pursuit of happiness be regulated by morality since it can become a *puruṣārtha*, a valuable value, or more accurately, a positive *puruṣārtha*, only if it is regulated or guided by a moral concern. The relation of *kāma* to *dharma* is thus similar to that of *artha* to *kāma* and to *dharma*. It is to be noted that the Indian theory of value does not rule out the satisfaction of any desire unconditionally. It simply requires that the object of a permissible desire must not be one the pursuit of which, for one reason or another, is forbidden by any moral principle.

It is, therefore, quite reasonable, Vātsyāyana says, to consider sexual pleasure also, like any other pleasure obtained by the gratification of a non-sexual desire, a *puruṣārtha*. Against the objection that an excessive indulgence in sex leads to several kinds of physical and mental illnesses, he says that excessive indulgence in satisfying a desire for some tasty food, or excessive eating, also causes such illnesses. But we do not stop eating, or advise anyone to stop eating, all kinds of food.[26] What we need is to regulate properly our sexual desire, or desire for food. His point is that this is a general truth about all desires, or, rather, about our trying to gratify any desire whatsoever. We cannot live a desireless life because without a desire we cannot do anything. Gratifying a desire yields pleasure, but exceeding a certain limit in gratifying it causes evil effects. It is therefore that we do not need to stop gratifying our desires, even sexual desires, but to regulate them, or regulate our efforts to attain any kind of appetitive well-being. It is here that morality comes to our help by providing the needed regulation. It offers the guidelines as to which sort of desires are worth satisfying and which sorts are not.

Gratification of a desire is to be regulated not only *because* an excessive indulgence is hurtful, but *also because* of a social reason. One man's attempt to satisfy a certain desire of his may also come in the way of another man's attempt to satisfy a desire of his and therefore cause social conflict, in some cases even leading to disturbing social or societal equilibrium. Anyone's going beyond a certain limit in satisfying a desire of his, say, a desire for a woman, or some property, may result in depriving another man of his wife, or his property, and thus cause social injustice. In such cases too our appetitive pursuits are to be regulated. This work of social or societal regulation is also done by *dharma* or morality. This is natural because care and concern for the welfare of others is the essence of morality. That is why Indian ethics as such considers morality as the guide or regulator of *kāma* or of the pursuit of *kāma* as a *puruṣārtha.*

Adopting this method solves many problems which hedonism as commonly understood finds difficult to do. For example, like hedonism it grants to pleasure or happiness the status of an intrinsic value. But unlike hedonism, it is not faced with the problem of distinguishing between desirable and undesirable pleasures, and is not left with only the alternative of grading one pleasure higher than another in quantitative terms, like intensity, duration, etc. It can, on the other hand, say quite cogently that a pleasure the attainment of which has been done in a manner concordant with morality is higher than another the attainment of which has not been done in that manner, or done in a manner discordant with morality. All this it can do because it does not consider every sort of pleasure or happiness a *moral* value or *puruṣārtha,* but only that which is acceptable to morality, or, is at least not considered impermissible by it.

The inclusion of happiness (*kāma*) in the Indian theory of values is largely the result of looking at the world, particularly the social order, or society, from the point of view of the individual. Whatever be the source of happiness, the object of sensual enjoyment, the experience of appetitive well-being is personal, the individual's private experience. The inclusion of *dharma,* morality, on the other hand, is largely the result of looking at the individual from the society's point of view. This has to be so because the essence of an individual's moral being lies in his having, or cultivating, an interest in the welfare of others (*paropakāra vṛtti*). Even *artha* can be said to be primarily, though not totally, the result of looking at the individual from the society's point of view that *dharma* is credited with the role of regulating the pursuit of *kāma* as well as that of *artha.* Even *mokṣa,* as will be shown in the chapter dealing with it, may be said to be very greatly, if not absolutely, the result of looking at the individual and the world from the viewpoint of the individual, i.e. the result of making the individual the central point from which the individual himself as well as the world is looked at. This is clear from the obvious empirical, or quasi-logical, fact that a particular individual's experience of happiness is his, and not anyone else's experience. One man's experience, in point of logic, cannot be another man's experience in spite of the fact that the latter too may become happy by knowing that the former is. One cannot feel another's feeling, though another's feeling may generate in him his own feeling. But then it would be his private feeling and not the feeling of the man whose feeling has generated it or provided the occasion for it. Similar things can be said of *mokṣa.* But to see how or why it can be said we have to wait for the chapter on *mokṣa.* And, now is the time to discuss the nature of morality or *dharma,* as conceived in the Indian theory of values. This the next chapter will do.

NOTES AND REFERENCES

1. *Akāmasya kriyā kāciddṛśayate, neha karhicit. Yaddyaddhi kurute kincittattatkāmasya ceṣṭitam. Manusmṛti,* 2.4. No human action without any desire is found in the world. Whichever action a man does is the result of an effort involving a desire of his.
2. Ibid., 2.3.
3. Ibid., 2.2.
4. *The Bṛhadāraṇyaka Upaniṣad* with the commentary of Śankarācārya, translated by Swami Madhavananda (Advaita Ashrama, Calcutta, 1993), pp. 131–32.
5. Ibid., p. 144.

6. *Kāmasūtram*, 2.11 (pp. 25–26 of the book with *Jayamangalā* commentary of Yaśodhara, trans. by Parasanath Dvivedi, Choukhamba, Varanasi, 1999).
7. *Indriyāṇām ca pancānām manaso hṛdayasya ca. Viṣaye vartamānām yā pritirūpajāyate. Sa kāma iti me buddhih karmaṇām phalamuttamam. Mahabharata, Vanaparva*, 33.37.
8. *Kāmasūtram*, pp. 7–12.
9. Ibid., p. 552.
10. *Manusmṛti*, pp. 35–38.
11. *Mahābhārata, Ādiparva*, 218: 14–20.
12. ... *Bhikṣetyathā vedayatam narāyyau.* Ibid., 190: 1.
13. ... *Bhunkteti sametya sarve*, Ibid., 190: 2.
14. ... *Kaṣṭam mayā bhāṣitamityuvāca.* Ibid., 190: 2.
    I am sorry (worried) that an extremely wrong (highly improper) thing has come out of my mouth (been uttered by me).
15. Ibid., 220: 17.
16. Ibid., 190: 13–16.
17. Ibid., 63: 70–86.
18. Ibid., 104–105.
19. Ibid., 109: 9, 10.
20. *Kāryeṣu mantrī vacaneṣu dāsī bhojyeṣu mātā. Dharmānukūla, kṣamayā dharitrī, bhārya ca sāgunyavatīha durlabhā.* Quoted in Nirupama Vidyalankar (trans.), *Mudrarākṣasam* (Sahitya Bhandar, Meerut, 1992), p. 15.
21. *Manusmrti*, 3.56, 57.
22. Ibid., 2.67, 213, 214, 215; 5.154, 157, 158, 163.
23. Ibid., 5.147–49.
24. A.S. Altekar, 'Vedic Society' in *The Cultural Heritage of India* (R.K. Mission), Vol. I, pp. 222–23.
25. *Ramayaṇa, Yuddha Kanda*, 115.15, 16. See also 115.1–14.
26. *Kāmasūtram*, 2.37.

CHAPTER 11

Value as Living a Morally Good Life (*Dharma Puruṣārtha*)

11.1 MORALITY AS THE CORE OF *DHARMA* IN ITS MULTIFARIOUS MEANINGS

Dharma, in the Indian ethos, is a key term and so is the concept it stands for. But it is a term which is really multivocal or omnifarious. This feature of it gives it some advantages as well as some disadvantages. Because of this, it has the advantage of possessing the potentiality of being used to cover a wide range of phenomena, human as well as non-human. The result is that, in some sense of it, both a human being and a non-human thing can be, equally meaningfully, said to have a *dharma* of its own. One of the disadvantages is that sometimes debates about its application turn out to be unenlightening because different debaters use it in different senses and it becomes undecidable which particular sense of it is the most relevant in the context in which the debate takes place, or impossible to identify a particular sense to which all of them should agree. Another disadvantage, quite often visible in classical Indian literature, is that sometimes a clever man gets at least a seemingly tenable reason to say of a situation that it is not possible to decide whether the situation is or is not concordant with *dharma,* or which course of action in that situation would be concordant with it and therefore should be taken.

A *multivocal* term also, quite often, becomes vague, even though being multivocal and being vague are two different sorts of semantic defects. A term is multivocal if it has many meanings. It is vague in those cases in which it is not decidable whether or not it is applicable to any one of them. In fact, most of our common terms are vague but not completely or absolutely vague. If a term is absolutely vague it is unusable in any linguistic transaction, like a coin which has no purchasing power, i.e. which cannot be used in any commercial transaction. *Vagueness* admits of degrees in the sense that one term can be more or less vague than another. The semantic range of a term can be divided into three parts, one part which has objects to which it is clearly inapplicable, and the middle part which has such objects about which it is not clear whether or not the term is applicable to any of them. A term is more vague than another when its middle range—the range of undecidable referents—is wider or more commodious than that of the other. *Dharma* is both a multivocal and a vague concept but neither of the two deficiencies are so great or extensive as to make it unusable. This is testified by the fact that it is a concept which has been successfully used in classical Indian practices, both intellectual and practical, and is being equally successfully used in modern Indian practices, intellectual as well as practical.

It is true, however, that in both classical and modern times clever people exploit its two deficiencies to their advantage. But this is something which has to be only noted for being what it is and not left to mislead us into thinking that the concept is too deficient, or even too complex and difficult, to be used by an ordinary individual. *Dharma* is a concept of use in any ordinary, normal, man's life, a coin which any normal individual needs to use and uses in his normal social, practical, communicative transactions. This itself is a proof that it cannot be too difficult or unmanageable a piece for him to handle.

Dharma's multivocal character is evidenced by the fact that it has been used to denote such widely different things as nature, law, custom, religious rituals, or religion, rules pertaining to education, marriage, conjugal relationship, professional practice, morality, rules and strategies fit for use in administration and governance, etc. This is so because it covers the entire range of a man's life, private and public, as well as the functioning of societies and their interrelations. But behind all these dimensions of it there is a normative cone. Of almost all of the specimens or manifestations of the normativity of *dharma* morality constitutes the central core. This is so because anything normative is ultimately justified on the putative ground of its being morally right or at least permissible. Therefore, it would not be too wide of the mark to say that, in the most dominant sense of it, it stands for morality as such as well as for the distinctive morality of the different sectors of the society. That is why *dharma,* as a human value or *puruṣārtha,* can be said to be the value which consists in, or is constituted by, living a morally good life, a life which is in concordance with the requirements of morality appropriate to a man's just being a human being as well as to his role in his society or to his being a participant in interpersonal transactions. In this chapter and all along in this work *dharma* is used to mean morality. That is why *dharma* as a value is taken to denote moral value, or more precisely, value as moral living or living a morally commendable (or permissible) life.

Before we proceed further it is important to point out that *dharma* does mean religion also, along with several other things as mentioned already, in the classical ethos, as it does in modern times in modern Indian languages. It is important to remember this fact because some Indology-oriented philosophers and Sanskritists do not tire of repeating that *dharma does not* mean what religion means. That it does mean religion in the classical Indian ethos is clear from its having been so used at so many places. This is not to say that it is an equivalent of the English word 'religion', but only to bring out that religion also is one of the several things it denotes. In the *āśvamedhikaparva* of *Anuśāsanaparva* of the *Mahābhārata* there is a long section called *vaiṣṇavadharmaparva* in which Kṛṣṇa adumbrates the principles of *dharma* in the sense of religion. He also tells the Pāṇḍavas that he himself has founded a religion which he calls *vaiṣṇavadharma.* At many other places in the *Mahābhārata,* the Rāmāyaṇa and several *purāṇas* as well *dharma* is used in the sense of religion. The *Bhāgavata Purāṇa* is an example par excellence in this connection. In it *dharma* is used more in the sense of religion than in any other sense and the book is taken by the Hindus as a religious work, given more religious importance than even the *Gītā.* It is a common belief among orthodox Hindus that listening to its recitation for one week by a *brāhmaṇa* priest, along with the performance of a prescribed set of rituals, will fulfil the desire of the listener to fulfil which the ceremony is performed. This kind of listening for seven days is called *saptāh śravaṇa,* and the entire ritual is called a seven days' sacrifice (*saptāha yajña*).

However, in this work we shall deal only with that sense of *dharma,* as already announced, in which it means morality or moral ethos. This we shall do while admitting that there is no classical Indian book which discusses exclusively *dharma* and different aspects of it in the sense of morality so that it can be handed over to anyone to be read as a book on classical Indian philosophy of morals. Not one of the *Dharmaśāstras* does this kind of work. All of them take *dharma* in its multivocal sense and present prescriptions and prohibitions on a large variety of themes, legal, political, familial, religious, dietetic, conjugal, social, ethical, etc. Vātsyāyana is more topical than the authors of compilers of the *Dharmaśāstras*, Since he concentrates primarily on sexual relationships. But it is true that even he, like the authors of the *Dharmaśāstras*, does not present an account which can be called a philosophical account of some moral issues involved in men's sexual participation with and attitude towards women and women's with and towards men.

11.2 *DHARMA* AS THE SUSTAINER OF THE HUMAN WORLD: IRRELEVANCE OF ETYMOLOGICAL ANALYSIS

Quite often *dharma* is said to be the sustainer of the human world, or the world, on the basis of an etymological elaboration or derivation of the term '*dharma*'. Several such elaborations from the root (i) '*dhṛyate lokoaneneti dharmah*', meaning *dharma* is that by which the society, or the world, is sustained. In other words, *dharma* is that which sustains the world. Or (ii) '*dharati lokam yah sa dharmah*', or '*dharati visivamiti dharmah*', which means *dharma* is that which holds the society, or the world, together, i.e., which does not let the society, or the world disintegrate or get dismembered. Or (iii) *dhṛyati janairiti dharmah*'. It means that *dharma* is that which is inculcated or practised by human beings. All of these derivations seem to emphasize that '*dharma*' means that which sustains, maintains, preserves, or protects the world, or the human society.

An obvious implication of the emphasis on *dharma*'s power to hold the world as it is, is that it preserves the world's identity, and therefore does not let it be changed, altered, or modified, that is, if it does not let it degenerate, it also does not let it get improved or bettered. This is to say that *dharma* is a protector or preserver of the status quo. This implication is generally not seen by those who think that these etymological derivations of *dharma* give to it a very high status, though they do not really do that. Rather, they paint it as an agent of status quoism, and therefore as one which blocks the possibility of social change. Moreover, if they give to it a sacrosanct, honourable, status as etymologists think, they make it a ground for declaring all social change undesirable. For example, if the human society is a system of four classes or castes (*varṇas*) of people, and *dharma* or *varṇadharma* sustains it, then, whatever it is, it is not to be altered, and any action, intentional or unintentional, which is likely to disturb it, or cause some change in it, would be un*dharmic* and therefore wrong. It is on some such lines that Kṛṣṇa seems to think in the *Gītā*. This is clear from the arguments he gives to Arjuna to fight the *Mahābhārata* war. Most of his arguments are based on the premise that it is Arjuna's *dharma,* i.e. *varṇadharma* (or *svadharma* since the two are identical with each other) as a *kṣatriya,* to fight a righteous war whatever be its consequences, good or bad. He ought not to go against it because doing that would disintegrate the social order. He must not do that and never follow the *dharma* of someone else, of a non-*kṣatriya,* even of a *brāhmaṇa,* even if his following his *dharma* causes his destruction. The breathing idea behind this view of Kṛṣṇa about *dharma* is its (alleged) power to protect or sustain the then social order, the status quo. It is obvious that the conception of *dharma* as a sustainer of the world (*viśva*) or the social world (*loka*) as it is, if strictly adhered to and actually implemented in practice, would block social progress, or progress as such. Had Mahāvīra and Gautama Buddha adhered to it, as Kṛṣṇa asks Arjuna to do and as Arjuna does, neither of them would have ushered in a social revolution by working for a casteless society.

Dharma is taken in the sense of morality in the classical Indian ethos more prominently than in other senses of it. That is why we are justified in taking it in this sense in the present work and so are other works on classical Indian ethics which do that. But if *dharma* stands for morality and its being the sustainer of the world order is taken to be its essential, constitutive, property, then morality too, as conceived in the Indian ethos, would become an agent or champion of status quoism and therefore a block in the way of social reform.

Moral rules, principles ideals, virtues, etc. are, in any society, codified or given cogent shape by its elite which belong to its upper strata. This is true of classical Indian society as well. Its ethical codes for different classes of its members have been given concrete shape largely by its elite, the intellectuals belonging to the uppermost classes of it, the *brāhmaṇas*, though to some extent also by some members of the next class, the *kṣatriyas*, and to a still smaller extent by some members of the *vaiśya* class, occupying the third rung of the social ladder. The *śūdras*, the class occupying the fourth, the lowest rung, have played no role in the shaping of the codes. Therefore, if (*dharma* or) morality is the sustainer of the human world, it would be the sustainer of the four-fold social order in which the fourth class is given a very low place and almost no rights. A member of the then fourth class may say that morality in its Indian conception is an exploitative tool devised by some upper class people to protect their interests and to keep the members of the lowest class under their permanent service and subjugation. And, he may go on, this they would justify on the alleged ground that morality requires or demands it, that it is this kind of social and societal arrangement which morality sustains, preserves or protects. If he does not do that some members of the modern backward, suppressed, class of Indians very vocally and forcefully do. And, the classical *Cārvākas* certainly do that in their own way.

An obvious lesson of this implication of the conception of morality as the sustainer of the social order is that it does not deserve to be emphasized the way, or to the extent to which, it has been. In modern writings on classical Indian ethics it has been overplayed because their authors do not realize what it implies, nor do they realize that a healthy morality not only sustains the social order but also provides reasons for questioning some aspects of it as well as for introducing changes in it to make it better. And, it also offers reasons for not letting this process of betterment stop once and for all because no human society can be perfect.

It seems to me that it is not the *classical Indian* consensus that *dharma* sustains the social order which they then had and that therefore it does not need to be, or cannot be, changed. Manu does appear at some places in his *Manusmṛti*, to hold this view and so do the authors of some other *Dharmaśāstras*. But in several other works the sustainer-conception of *dharma* is underplayed even by the writers of some of the *Dharmaśāstras* including Manu. They realize that unless some empirical content is added to its characterization, the concept of *dharma* can perform any useful role neither in practical, moral, life, nor in the characterization of Indian ethical theory or philosophy of morals.

But before illustrating how they do that, it is worth while to mention a congenital feature of any etymological derivation of a term which makes it a futile, or an almost futile, exercise in the charting out of the nature or actual functioning of the phenomenon which the term in question denotes or is concerned with. It is in the process of charting out what morality, or *dharma,* does in man's life that a good number of philosophers give the etymological derivation from the root *dhṛ* to declare that *dharma* is the sustainer of the world. But any etymological analysis gives the etymological meaning of a word and not of the thing which the word denotes or stands for, if it denotes or stands for something. Coming to dharma, its *etymological* analysis only states the plain linguistic fact that, because of its root being *dhṛ,* the word *dharma* means that which sustains. From this analysis it does not follow that there actually exists a thing, an object, a phenomenon, called *dharma* because there may be a word with an etymology which is a non-denoting one, i.e. one which denotes nothing existent or real, which has no referent. There exists in the present case a phenomenon, or an institution, called *dharma,* the referent of the term *dharma.* But its characterization can properly or fairly be done by finding out what kind of phenomenon it is, what morality does to man, or what kind of life a moral, *dharmic,* life is, and why it is to be lived. This characterization or analysis may, in principle, confirm or disconfirm the etymological analysis. For example taking up the classical Indian practice of *dharma* as *varṇadharma,* one characterizer may say that it does not sustain the social order because, if it does, then, Ekalavya's right thumb would not have been chopped off to be given as honorarium to the teacher who refused to teach him and Sambūka would not have been killed by the moral exemplar Rāma for his being engaged in rigorous religious practice (*tapasyā*). Both of these acts in the name of morality or *dharma* are disintegrative, and not at all protective, of social order. On the other hand, another characterizer may say that it does sustain and he may offer the example of Aśoka who, because of his agreeing to lead a moral life as preached by the Buddha, gives up warfare and works for people's welfare and world peace both of which are protective of a very healthy type of social order. The upshot of all this is that in stating what morality does, what morality really is, one has to be guided by one's understanding of what kind of life a life lived in accordance with morality is, and not by any etymological analysis of any moral term, even of the term 'morality' or *dharma.* Any etymological analysis can take the philosopher of morals only a very short distance. And, even in that short distance, it may mislead him, as, for example, it misleads many who consider Ekalavya's and Sambūka's cases and others like them as examples of the sustaining power of *dharma.* This obviously merits the (philosophical or) moral retort (or even rebuke) that if these are examples of *dharma*'s sustaining power, then *dharma* sustains an immoral social order.

It may not be unfair to *dharma* not to have mentioned so far one sense of it in which it sustains that of which it is the *dharma.* It is not unfair because this sense of *dharma* does not counter what has been said above since it is an existential, a completely non-moral, non-normative, sense of the term. This is the sense in which the *dharma* of a thing means its nature or the set of its essential property or properties. Since the essential properties of a thing constitute its nature, let us examine this sense of *dharma* of a thing as meaning its nature.

To say that the *dharma* (as the nature) of a thing, non-living or living, sustains it is true because it is a tautology. Everything is what it is because its nature is what it is. To destroy its nature is to destroy it, and to change its nature is to change its identity which is the same thing as destroying it as the thing which it originally (while having the nature now destroyed) was. For example, if the *dharma* or nature of fire is to burn, then, if x is a fire, it must have the power to burn and if it is divested of its power to burn, then it is no longer a fire, and therefore no longer x (with the power to burn). x is now destroyed and in its place something else, some y, which is not identical with x, has come into being.

Dharma as a moral category can be predicated only of an individual, a human being. And, it cannot be called his *nature.* To say that he has such and such a nature is to make a purely factual, descriptive, non-normative, statement. Every object, living or non-living, and among living objects human or non-human, has a nature of its own. Rather, it has to have a nature in order to be what it is. Therefore, to say that A has such and such a nature is to say nothing about his *dharma,* his morality or moral sense, his moral obligation, goal, virtue or right. Only an adult, mature, normal, individual, a human being of this type, can be said to have, or even to lack, morality, whereas everything can be said to have a nature since it cannot be anything without having a nature.

Since anything is, truistically or tautologically, what it is only as long as its nature is not destroyed or drastically changed, it can also be said, as we have seen, that the nature of a thing sustains it, or to be more precise, its identity. This logical feature of the concept of the nature of a thing seems to have tempted the proponents of the *dharma*-as-the-sustainer view to hold that *dharma* (as a moral category) sustains the human world or the world as such. They do it by committing the mistake or fallacy of semantic transfer. This fallacy consists in transferring what is true of one sense of a term to another sense of it though the two senses of it are entirely different from each other. It is true that *dharma*-as-the-nature of a thing, i.e. *dharma* in its factistic sense, sustains it. From this it does not follow that *dharma*-as-the-moral expectation from, or performance of, an individual sustains his existence. It may or may not. And, that it does, if it does, does not follow from the factistic sense of *dharma.* The factistic sense is entirely irrelevant to the moral issues. That *dharma* also means nature and that as nature it sustains the thing whose nature it is are entirely different facts about *dharma* from the putative fact that *dharma* as a moral category sustains the thing whose *dharma* it is. That is why it is wrong to make the semantic transference of what is true of the former sense to the latter sense of *dharma.*

Be it also noted that we cannot even make a blank statement that the nature of thing sustains it. The burning power of a fire certainly sustains its identity as a fire. But it does that, or can do that, only as long as there does not exist another object which absolutely stops it from burning, for example, only as long as no downpour of heavy rain occurs as soon as a fire is lit on a dry object fit to burn in normal circumstances. Therefore, whenever a statement is made to the effect that *dharma,* meaning the nature of a thing, sustains it, it must be added, or kept in mind, that it sustains it subject to the condition that there does not exist another, countervailing, factor which does not let it do what it normally, in the absence of any countervailing object or occurrence, does.

The sustainer conception of *dharma,* as we have shown in the foregoing discussion owes its origin very greatly to the etymology of the word *dharma* and its semantic versatility in referring to several things. Therefore, to eliminate the possibility of being misled in characterizing *dharma* as a value, as a normatic concept, we have to shift our analysis from the etymology of the word to some non-linguistic, empirical, features of the concept the word denotes, i.e. of *dharma* as morality. Only then would its characterization be substantival or contentual as it should be in any philosophical account of it. Only then alone would it be of any practical value or guidance to anyone who wants to shape his life-style in accordance with the guidelines provided by the Indian theory of *dharma* or morality. The classical Indian ethos is well aware of the importance of this fact. That is why at several places in classical ethical literatures immediately after, or even before, saying that *dharma* sustains the social order, the writer or characterizer adds some empirical features of what it does in human life when it is correctly practised. This method or procedure makes the characterization contentually richer and lifts it much above the verbal or grammatical level of the etymological analysis of the word *dharma*. It is these contents of *dharma* which make the discussion a discussion of *dharma* as a value, or of the concept of *dharma* as morality.

11.3 CONTENT OF THE CONCEPT OF *DHARMA* (MORALITY): WELL-BEING OF ALL

A characterization of *dharma* as being contributive to the well-being (*hita*) of all concerned is very persuasively presented by Kṛṣṇa to Arjuna in the *Mahābhārata* through some tales illustrating the morality, or the morally high status, of one's doing something to protect or to promote the well-being of other individuals. He gives the example of Balāka, a tiger who kills a blind animal while it is drinking water in a pond to quench its thirst. Apparently, it is morally wrong to kill the animal who cannot see and therefore cannot protect himself from his enemy. But, instead of being censured for killing him, Balāka is given an honourable place in the heavens. Flowers are showered on him from the sky, a beautiful vehicle attended on by angels descends on the earth and takes him to the heavens. All this happens because that blind animal, as a result of his austere religious practices in his previous birth, had acquired a boon to be able to destroy all living beings. That is why Brahmā, the creator, makes him blind. By killing him Balāka saves the entire living world, i.e. protects the well-being of all, by eliminating a potential cause of their destruction.

Kṛṣṇa gives another example in which an apparently right act is considered morally wrong or condemnable because it leads to the destruction of some innocent individuals. A group of individuals hide themselves in a corner of a forest to save themselves from some dacoits who are chasing them to kill them. The saint Kauśika knows the location of the place of their hiding. The dacoits ask him and he tells them the location of that place because he has cultivated the virtue of always telling the truth and only the truth. That is why he is called a teller of truth (*satyavādī*). The result of his telling the truth is that the dacoits find them out and kill them. Kauśika's ordirnarily considered morally right act of telling the truth is considered to be a misuse of a virtue, declared morally condemnable and on account of it Kauśika is sent to hell.

Kṛṣṇa concludes his illustrations by very briefly stating that *dharma* consists in safeguarding, caring for, or contributing to, as far as one can, the well-being of all others. It is in this sense that a *dharmic*, morally upright, life is a life devoted to the good of all; consequently, an otherwise morally right act, like telling the truth, may become wrong, and an otherwise morally wrong act, like killing someone, may become right, when we lead our life with an eye on this goal of morality. Any act would thus be concordant with morality (*dharma*) only if it is a means to this goal. An ordinarily right act's failing to be that would then make it wrong, as is the case with Kauśika's telling the truth. It is an ordinarily right act but becomes morally wrong because it leads to the killing of some innocent men. Similarly, an ordinarily wrong act, like Balāka's killing a blind animal, becomes morally right because it saves the life of many thousands of living beings. Morality or *dharma* thus aims at the preservation or promotion of all beings' well-being. It is because of this feature of it that *dharma* is (called) *dharma* (sustainer)[1] of all beings or of the universe.

An expansion of the above way of providing concrete content to the value-category of *dharma* is done, in a more comprehensive and purely philosophical, non-anecdotal, manner, by Kaṇāda in the second canon (*sūtra*) of his *Vaiśeṣikasūtra.*[2]

According. to him morality (*dharma*) leads to the moral man's total well-being or flourishing (*abhyudaya*) in his worldly life as well as to that of his highest objective (*nihśreyasa*). Let us take each one of the two attainments one by one.

Abhyudaya means total or overall well-being or flourishing and the well-being or happiness meant here is not only that of the person who leads a *dharmic* life. Rather, if means the well-being of all those with whom his leading this life is concerned, directly or indirectly. And, since it leads to happiness in this life, in this world, it protects and promotes social harmony, or rather, harmony of one man with the rest of his universe. To be modest in our statement of this conception of morality, we can say that, according to it, living a moral life makes the life of the moral man happy in all respects and it does that by establishing a harmony between his and others' interests. Moral life is, thus, not a selfish life. The *abhyudaya*, the total well-being, which it yields is not the total well-being of any one man at the cost of the well-being of any other person. And, it is a well-being which is attained by the moral man in this very life. Therefore, morality, or living a life in accordance with the principles of morality, pays in that very life itself. To live morally is thus to ensure that one leads a happy life.

The other thing which morality, as already said, does is to lead to the attainment of *nihśreyasa*. *Nihśreyasa* means the highest value, literally, that than which nothing else is greater or better in value, or as a value, i.e. as a *puruṣārtha*. Generally this value is said to be *mokṣa* or liberation. Liberation, according to some Indian thinkers, is attainable in this life also, while according to some others it is attainable only after death. But all of them admit that it is a state of being in which there is complete absence of pain or suffering. This state is generally taken to be a spiritual state and then it is called spiritual well-being.

It is possible, however, that a philosopher takes the concept of *nihśreyasa* in a sense broad enough to denote any kind of perfection or consummation, spiritual or non-spiritual, which is not ordinarily required or considered necessary for living a happy life. It may be the consummation of his spiritual aspiration to attain *mokṣa* as conceived by any one of the philosophical schools. But it may also be the consummation of some other kind of aspiration or aptitude of his. For example, it may denote his poetic, musical philosophical, scientific creativity like Kālidāsa's poetic, Tānsen's musical, Dharmakīrti's logical, or Ārya Bhaṭa's scientific, genius. It may even denote an individual's aspiration for social service, for serving and uplifting the condition of the downtrodden, suffering, even depraved and fallen, sections of the society, or for protecting neglected or vanishing species of some animals, or flora and fauna. This, latter, kind of aspiration may be called ethical or moral but in a highly extraordinary, or supererogatory, sense. But to be a poet, a scientist, a logician, etc. is certainly not a moral requirement. A non-poet, or a poor poet, may be more moral, or even happier, than a Mirzā Ghālib. What I mean to emphasize is that the concept of *nihśreyasa*, though rooted in some sort of spiritual metaphysics or ontologized axiology, does not have to be so rooted. In modern times it may be conceived in a broad sense, or freed from its classical rooting in theology or spiritual axiology. Then even one who does not accept such a theology or axiology may find the concept a useful one in explaining the role of morality in human life, viz. the role of contributing to the overall well-being of man which may be conceived either as having both spiritual and non-spiritual components or as having only non-spiritual ones.

It may be asked what is the need for adding the concept of *nihśreyasa* to that of well-being as the end of morality. It seems to me that there is a very important reason for doing that. Well-being or happiness may be taken by a layman, or a particular kind of theory-oriented individual, in a crudely materialist, earthly, sense, thereby implying that the other kinds of pleasures, like those which are experienced in artistic, intellectual and religious pursuits, are of no value, or of value lower than the value of morality or values with which morality has nothing to do. By adding *nihśreyasa* as a conjunct of *abhyudaya* Kaṇāda eliminates this possibility. There is also a second reason for doing that and this reason is no less important than the first reason. Suppose morality is said only to ensure social harmony and thereby the happiness of the moral individual. The personality of a moral man would obviously be graded as higher than that of an immoral or amoral one. But if a moral man is also, say, a good poet, the *total* grade we would award to him as an individual would, again, obviously, be higher than that which we would award to him who is moral but has no sense for poetry. Similarly, the total grade we would award to the personality of one who is a good poet but is immoral, or indifferent towards moral matters, would be lower than that which we would award to the good poet who is morally sensitive as well. To grade the personality of an individual in an organismic, all-comprehensive, manner we need to take into account all of his accomplishments and achievements. Keeping this point in mind, it is conceptually as well as axiologically more accurate to link morality with both happiness and *nihśreyasa*. This is so because to *grade* a man as moral would then be to grade his total personality, and not only some aspect or aspects of it. What has been said of the accomplishment of being a poet can also, *mutatis mutandis*, be said of the accomplishment of being interested in attaining *mokṣa*.

To conclude, the central point of the *Vaiśeṣika*'s explication of the role of morality is that it is a precondition for leading a life which is desirable in all respects, hedonistic as well as non-hedonistic. It is, in fact, a precondition for leading such a life in a much more important sense than in the sense of being a necessary condition of it. It is, because it is said to *ensure* its achievement, as it is said to be that which effects its *siddhi*, i.e. its *realization or attainment*, the *siddhi* of both *abhyudaya* and *nihśreyasa*. This view explicates the concept of morality as well as *justifies* leading a moral life. It answers both the questions, 'What does morality (*dharma*) mean?' and 'Why should one be moral?' with a single answer. We can now say in a more contentual way that *dharma*, if followed by men, sustains or preserves the world, particularly the social world, or society, in such a way that in it leading a life desirable in all respects becomes not only possible but a surety.

As an aside, we would like to point out that the *Vaiśeṣika*, or the *Nyāya-Vaiśeṣika*, philosophers would be confronted with a problem which it is almost impossible for them to solve if the concept of *nihśreyasa* is taken to denote *mokṣa* as conceived by them. *Mokṣa*, according to them, is attainable only after death and a self which is liberated (*mukta*) is non-conscious or devoid of consciousness. This has to be so because consciousness is only an accidental property of self. It is conscious only when it is an embodied being, i.e. an individual (*jīva*). When the body dies, the self becomes disembodied and therefore non-conscious. After attaining *mokṣa*, since *mokṣa* is attained only after the death of the body, the self is in the state of its pristine purity, i.e. in a state in which it is non-conscious. A non-conscious substance can neither have any pleasure nor any pain. Therefore, the *Nyāya-Vaiśeṣika* philosophers say that the liberated self is completely free from pain or suffering, though it is not blissful. But a non-conscious substance cannot even be said to be painless; only a conscious one, which can experience pain and pleasure, can be said to have no pain or pleasure, i.e. no experience of pain or of pleasure. It is a point of logic that a stone-breaker cannot say that the block of stone he is breaking into pieces feels no pain however hard he strikes his hammer on it. And, if he says it, he can say it only in a highly denuded, rarified, sense. If a liberated self of the *Nyāya-Vaiśeṣika* conception can thus be said to be painless, it can be only in the sense in which an object like a block of stone can be. It would be very odd, many would say, to give such a state the status of the highest value (*nihśreyasa*) and to make it one of the objectives, or end-points, of morality, or of our moral pursuits.

Postponing for the chapter on *mokṣa* the detailed discussion of the problems arising from linking morality to *mokṣa* as its means, we can very briefly mention another problem in the *Nyāya-Vaiśeṣika* way of doing that. According to it, as already said, *mokṣa* is attained by an individual only after his (physical) death. Therefore, the proposition that morality leads to *nihśreyasa*, meaning *mokṣa*, becomes one which can neither be proved nor disproved in any empirical or logical manner. This means that no one can decide what is morality (or *dharma*) or morally right (or *dharmānumodita*) because no one can decide of any course of life, or of any action, what it will lead him to have after his death. This incurable inability of man implies that he cannot lead a moral life simply because he cannot know what sort of life is a moral life. That is why it has been suggested earlier that it would be more elegant to take the term '*nihśreyasa*' in a broad sense, and not to restrict it to denote *mokṣa*. If the belief in the link between morality and *mokṣa*, as conceived by the *Nyāya-Vaiśeṣika*, is still retained, it can be retained only as one for or against which no reason can be given. It is such a belief which we call a dogma. Moral life is lived in the world we live in. To hook it up with anything other—worldly, or non-worldly—is bound to create some problem for it.

The Indian account of the nature of morality contributing to man's total welfare, as elaborated above, is clearly altruistic or universalistic, as the welfare it contributes to is not only of the moral individual as an individual, but of all concerned. The emphasis in it on altruism, or benevolence, is very forcefully expressed in a maxim which occurs in so many works though only as a maxim or principle. Perhaps it is a maxim which had attained the status of the people's maxim (*lokokti*). That is why it is not a statement made by any particular moral thinker in a particular context. It runs as follows: 'The essence of the teachings of the eighteen *purāṇas* is that doing good to others is the highest good or virtue and causing any suffering to anyone else is the greatest vice or sin.'[3] At some other places it occurs in a slightly different form though saying essentially the same thing. In place of 'The essence of the teachings of the eighteen *purāṇās*' it has 'The two (central) teachings of Vyāsa in the eighteen *purāṇās* are...'.

In fact, Indian ethics is altruism of a universalist type. According to its *karmic* theory, which will be discussed in a later chapter, because of his having done actions of a certain type a human being may be reborn as an animal, or a plant, or may be cursed to become a block of stone. For example, as per its mythology, Jatāyū, an eagle, who fights with Rāvaṇa to extricate Sītā from his clutches and dies in the battle, after his death goes to heaven where highly moral men go after their death. Ahilyā, a woman, is turned into a block of stone because of her having been duped into commiting adultery, and again becomes the same woman she originally was after Rāma touches the block of stone with his feet. It is not that we are asked here to believe in such mythological tales. But we have to take note of the fact that, because of their *karmic* worldview which is said to make possible the rebirth of man into another kind of organic being, or even in the form of an inorganic substance, classical Indian thinkers have a reason to believe in the unity of organic and inorganic nature, the unity of the human world, the plant-animal world, and the inorganic world. This belief in the unity of the universe gives them a reason to aver that we do not have to have ethical attitudes only towards other humans, but rather towards all the beings and things in the organic and inorganic sectors of the universe. That is why there are maxims to the effect that we ought to be considerate or kind towards all beings or things of the world.

Manu (*Manusmṛti*, 1.48–49) says that even plants are sensitive to pleasure and pain though their consciousness is minimal. His implication obviously is that we ought not to hurt them in any manner. To have such an ethical attitude towards all things, living or non-living, i.e. one of not hurting any of them, is thus an obligation, a moral requirement, a demand of *dharma*, for all of us. And, to follow *dharma* is not a thankless job. Rather, it alone ensures our well-being.[4] It is an oft-quoted saying that there is victory, prosperity, or all-round well-being only where *dharma* is followed or respected (*Yato dharmah tato jayah*). The same thing is asserted by Manu in a slightly different but more emphatic manner. He says that he who destroys, or disrespects *dharma*, is himself destroyed by *dharma* and he who follows, or preserves it, is protected by it.[5]

This conception of *dharma* really presents a very optimistic and encouraging account of morality, building into the very concept of it a powerful motivational pull. Everyone wants his own all-round well-being. Therefore, if being moral is the surest way to have it, he does not need any other reason for being moral, i.e. for being what he ought to be. That is why it is being maintained in this work all along that the classical Indian ethos avers the primacy of the ethical, or of being moral for everyone interested in leading a viable life. This point is reaffirmed in declaring morality to be the regulator of *artha* and *kāma*. Each one of them, we have seen, is a value, a *puruṣārtha*, only when its pursuit is in accordance with, or regulated by, *dharma* Kṛṣṇa in the *Bhāgavata Purāṇa* (11.23.17–19) says that one who pursues *artha* (material prosperity), with no regard for morality, suffers from fifteen evils. He becomes disposed to commit theft, use violence, tell lies, feel conceited, to have inordinate desires, to feel angry, proud, egotistical, to have a divisive intellect (*bhedabuddhi*), to feel animosity, distrust, sense of competition, to cheat, to gamble, and to become addicted to drinking. It is the regulation or guidance of *dharma* which makes the pursuit a desirable one.

Yāska, a grammarian, calls *dharma* a synonym of *niyama* (regulation).[6] This shows that by his times the regulative function of *dharma* as a value or a social institution—since morality is also social institution—had received so much popular acceptance that this meaning of the word *dharma* had entered into common usage. As examples of the evil that befalls an individual who pursues *kāma* by flouting *dharma*, Vātsyāyana mentions the cases of Indra, Kīcaka and Rāvaṇa. All of the three get destroyed; Indra is destroyed because of his immoral behaviour with Ahilyā, Kīcaka destroyed because of his with Draupadī, and Rāvaṇa because of his with Sītā.[7] This very point, namely, the point that both material and appetitive well-being (*artha* and *kāma*) can be successfully and desirably attained only by pursuing them in a *dharma*-concordant manner, is asserted very forcefully at the end of the *Mahābhārata* by its poet. He says in an emotionally surcharged voice: "Raising my hand up I very loudly announce but nobody listens: *artha* and *kāma* are attained by means of *dharma* (i.e. by leading a moral life); why is that *dharma* not inculcated?'[8]

In spite of the great emphasis on the importance of *dharma*, however, the *concept of dharma* is at numerous places said to be extremely subtle, or rather too subtle. This allegedly extremist kind of subtlety causes some problems, not only conceptual but moral as well. Let us therefore examine it in some detail.

11.4 OVEREMPHASIS ON THE SUBTLETY OF THE CONCEPT OF *DHARMA*: ANALYSIS AND ADVERSE IMPLICATION

A concept is subtle when in some situations it is difficult, sometimes extremely difficult, for an intelligent layman to apply it affirmatively or negatively to a certain case. In such a case he has to make a *decision*, taking an overall view of its role in the language-game it belongs to, as to whether or not the concept is applicable to it, or the case falls outside the zone of things to which the concept can be affirmatively or negatively applied. But the latter type of cases have to be very small in number. If their number is very large, it would mean that the concept is not of much use in our social or communicative life. Further, in the life-history of every concept there are also some clear cases to which it is obviously applicable. And, in the difficult cases too, the experts in the field must he able to help others, laymen, in deciding which way a putative subtle concept is applicable. Coming back to the concept of *dharma*, and assuming that it is a very subtle concept, any layman, using only his common sense, would say that Rāvaṇa's abducting Sītā by adopting fraudulent means when she is unprotected is morally wrong, or *adhārmic*. Similarly, he would say, again using only his moral common sense, that Rāma's getting her freed from Rāvaṇa's clutches, even by killing him since he is unwilling to free her in a peaceful manner, is morally right or *dharmic*. But if anyone says that the concept of *dharma* is so subtle that it is difficult to decide whether the former is morally wrong, *dharma pratikūla*, and the latter morally right, *dharmānukūla*, then it would mean that there is something wrong with the man who holds this view of *dharma*, or something wrong with the concept of *dharma* itself, implying that it is a non-viable or dysfunctional concept.

Taking only two cases of the claim to the extreme subtlety of the concept, to save space, let us see what the attribution of this level of subtlety to it amounts to. As the first instance, we shall take up Yudhiṣṭhira's making the claim to the *yakṣa* in answering his question about which one is the morally right way to go, *Kah panthāh*,[9] i.e. what should one do to conduct one's life in morally right ways. The question is thus about how to know the *dharmic* way of living. In telling him the ways to know *dharma*, or the *dharmic* mode of living, he tells him that reason or intellect is ununiform in the sense that people of differing levels of rational maturity may give different judgements about it, different sacred works (*srutayo*) are of different views, there is not a single seer whose view can be said to be more authentic than the views of other moral experts, and the essence of *dharma* is concealed in darkness and therefore not discenerable by ordinary men. Therefore, the ways great men, i.e. the accredited exemplars of morality, have gone, the ways in which they have behaved, are the right ways, the ways of *dharma*, which we should follow.[10]

The view expressed here about the path of morality or the source of moral knowledge will be discussed in the next section in some detail. Here we are concerned only with the emphasis that has been put on the subtlety of the concept of *dharma*, or on the extremely difficult nature of the method of accertaining what is and what is not morally right. But in the example this difficulty is only mentioned and a way out is suggested; no illustration is given, and no implication from the allegedly extremely difficult nature of *dharma* is drawn.

The other example of such an emphasis on the extremely intricate or subtle nature of *dharma* is found in the scene of Draupadī's being derobed in public by Duryodhana's brother Duhśāsana. The context is as follows:

A game of dice is played between Yudhiṣṭhira and Duryodhana's maternal uncle Śakuni as Duryodhana's proxy. In the game Śakuni uses fraudulent means as a result of which Yudhiṣṭhira goes on losing at each step. He first loses his kingdom, then his brothers, one by one, thereafter himself and in the last stage he stakes their wife Draupadī and loses her too. This is the last chance he gets and thereupon the game ends because he has nothing left to put on the stakes. Duhśāsana drags Draupadī from her chamber by her long hair and brings her into the hall in which the game has been played before the assembly of a large number of learned and considered-to-be highly morally elevated individuals like Bhīṣma, Droṇa, Kṛpa, Vidura, and many others. These moral stalwarts, or *mahājanas*, i.e. moral exemplars, are still present when Draupadī poses some extremely pointed and relevant moral questions.

The *Mahābhārata* presents a very detailed account, with a good amount of literary flavour, of all that happens there. That is why all of her questions have not been presented at one place but at several places and generally in a roundabout, and not in a cut and dried, manner. Each question is a moral question with a moral answer obvious to any layman with an objective moral common sense. But the majority of the members of the august assembly keep mum. Bhīṣma breaks his silence once or twice but, as will be shown here, does not opine on any of the questions in a definitive way. Only two, Vikarṇa, another younger brother of Duryodhana, and Vidura, the prime minister of his father, the king Dhṛtarāṣṭra and the son of a maid-servant, give straightforward, appropriate, answers.

Draupadī's *first* question is a factual one but with a very important ethical implication. She asks the assembly whether Yudhiṣṭhira loses himself before, or after, putting her on the stakes and losing her. Everyone present there has seen that after losing himself, Yudhiṣṭhira puts her on the stakes and loses her. The clear implication of this fact is that she has been lost by him and won by Duryodhana in an unlawful, immoral, manner, i.e.

her having been lost to, or won by, Duryodhana is morally indefensible. This implication can be demonstrated in the following manner:

For Yudhiṣṭhira (or any other individual) to lose himself is to lose his agency, his freedom to do anything on his own initiative. Since Yudhiṣṭhira has already lost himself he has no moral right to stake Draupadī. This means that his putting her on the stakes is morally wrong and consequently his losing her, or Duryodhana's winning her, is also morally wrong. This amounts to the (moral) fact or truth that she has not been really lost to, or won by, Duryodhana and therefore all the insult, suffering, and torture that have been inflicted on her are immoral or against *dharma.* But this fact is not recognized by the great men present there except by a brother of Duryodhana, the villain of the piece, and the helpless prime minister son of a maid-servant, the two acknowledgedly not as great and powerful as the men mentioned above.

Draupadī's *second* question is whether or not it is morally right to treat her as a property that can be put on the stakes. The moral implication here is that she, being a woman, a wife, is a person, and not a property, and therefore cannot be treated as a part of Yudhiṣṭhira's kingly property which can be put on the stakes. She also suggests that being a person she cannot be treated as an object to be used in commerce, i.e. gambled with in an attempt to recover all that Yudhiṣṭhira has so far lost in the game. This implication is moral and obvious since it shows that her having been lost and won is morally wrong. It shows this because it is a moral truth not only of gender ethics but of ethics that a person is not a property. But this question too receives no answer from the audience except from the two not so powerful men.

Her *third* question is whether or not Yudhiṣṭhira has the moral right to put her on the stakes even if it is morally right (in the then gender ethics) to treat her, a wife, as a property. Even this question's answer is very obvious even to a layman who knows that she is not the wife only of Yudhiṣṭhira but also of his four other brothers whom he has lost in the game much earlier. Therefore, he is not the whole and sole owner of the property Draupadī. Only a whole and sole owner of a property has the moral (and legal) right to sell it, mortgage it, gift it, or even to put it on the stakes, and not anyone who is only a partial owner of it. Yudhiṣṭhira has only one-fifth of the ownership of Draupadī (if she is a property) and therefore it is against *dharma* for him to have put her on the stakes. All this is known to the great men there but still they do not opine on her question.

Her *fourth* question is expressed more by her tears and crying and wailing and seeking protection from every possible source when Duhśāsana drags her by her hair and tries to derobe her when she is in the state of her monthly period and has only one piece of clothing on her body. To any ordinary individual, who has even a minimal moral sensibility, and modicum of moral knowledge, what is being done to her is not just morally wrong, not just against *dharma* but morally abominable, a clear case of killing *dharma* (*dharmahanana*). Her tearful eyes and cries very powerfully pose to the assembly the question, 'Is what is being done to me in your presence not against *dharma*?'

Vikarṇa has the moral courage to answer all her questions. He declares in a forthright manner, in clear and strong words, that the answer to each question of hers is that what has been done to her is morally wrong. He avers that since Yudhiṣṭhira first loses himself in the game and then puts her on the stakes, his doing that is not morally right, that a woman is not a property but a person who ought not to be used as a commodity, that Yudhiṣṭhira has no right to put her on the stakes because he does not have the complete ownership right over her even if she is a property, and that in any case what is being done to her by Duhśāsana is totally wrong. His clear judgement is that she has not been lost to and won by his eldest brother Duryodhana in a manner concordant with *dharma*. He even implores Duryodhana to get all this stopped and to free Draupadī.[11] But he is silenced by Duryodhana and Karṇa and accused of being disloyal to his family.

Vidura too declares in unambiguous and emotionally surcharged words that immoralities are being perpetrated on Draupadī. He has been pleading, since much before the ghastly scene of Draupadī's being dragged to the court and the attempt to derobe her takes place, to Dhṛtarāṣṭra to get the game of dice stopped. He appeals to the other learned men present there to condemn the grave injustice that is being done to Draupadī. He even goes to the extent of reminding all present there that when an injustice is being done at any place by someone to someone else and the members present there do not condemn it, they are also guilty of committing injustice, maybe a little less guilty than the man who is actually committing it. His appeal is directly and more pointedly addressed to Dhṛtarāṣṭra and Bhīṣma to condemn the injustice and torture that are being done to Draupadī and to get the immoralities being perpetrated on her immediately stopped.[12]

Dhṛtarāṣṭra's silence is intelligible because it is his sons who are committing the immoralities. But even Bhīṣma does not answer Draupadī's questions, and does not opine on the issue of whether what is being done is in accordance, or in discordance, with *dharma*, i.e. morally right or wrong. He takes shelter behind the veil of the extreme kind of subtlety and depth of the concept of *dharma*. His response to her is that it is not possible for him to say definitively either that what has been done, or is being done, to her is morally right, or that it is morally wrong, because of the subtlety and depth (*sūkṣmatvāt gahanatvāt*) of *dharma*.[13] He adds that Yudhiṣṭhira is an excellent knower of *dharma* and therefore he may answer her questions. This is a good example of what is called passing the buck, something like a judge's passing the onus of deciding the legality of an issue in a dispute to a man who himself is very importantly responsible for the birth of the issue in question. Yudhiṣṭhira himself is also, to a large extent, responsible for the suffering and insult caused to Draupadī by first agreeing to play the game of dice with Śakuni and then, after losing his property, four brothers and himself, putting Draupadī on the stakes and losing her too.

Bhīṣma forgets that, if the concept of *dharma* cannot be used, because of its subtlety and depth, to declare morally wrong such obvious immoralities as those which are being perpetrated on a woman who has done nothing wrong, it becomes a totally dysfunctional one. That it is not at all difficult to use it to call them morally wrong, that the concept is not too subtle to be unusable here, has been already demonstrated before him by Vikarṇa who is an ordinary, educated and morally sensitive, young man, in no way comparable to Bhīṣma in wisdom and moral expertise as per the high status given to Bhīṣma in the Indian ethos. And, Vidura, whom even Bhīṣma acknowledges to be a great scholar and expert on moral matters, has found no difficulty in using the concept of *dharma* to call what is being done to Draupadī blatantly wrong.

What is happening here is that the subtlety, etc., of *dharma* is used by Bhīṣma as a pretext to defend his silence, or indecisiveness, about the immorality of these acts. Why he takes this stand will be analysed soon. But here we must highlight the danger to morality, to *dharma*, itself which may be caused by emphasizing too much the subtlety, etc., of the concept of *dharma*. If this is done, then any clever man can escape his responsibility of opining on an issue whose morality or immorality is in question. He may thereby let an immorality be perpetrated, or a morally desirable action not be initiated, even when he is in a position to get the immorality stopped, or the desirable action initiated. Bhīṣma alone in the Kaurava family occupies such a position. He could have stopped all that happened to Draupadī had he condemned it and asked Duryodhana to stop executing his immoral plans.

It is, therefore, not worthwhile, either normatively and conceptually, to emphasize too much *dharma*'s (or any moral idea's) subtlety. This has been seen above in Bhīṣma's non-committal stand. That it is not conceptually correct to do so is the case because *dharma* is not really too subtle. This also we have seen in Vikarṇa's and Vidura's straightforward declaration of the immorality of what is being done to Draupadī. They have used the concept of *dharma* and this shows that they do not find it too subtle to be used in declaring the immoral to be immoral. *Dharma*, or rather every moral term, is a term of daily use in the life of an ordinary individual in the normal conduct of his life, private, public, and professional. He does not find any of these terms too subtle to use in the general run of his transactions. Sometimes he does find it difficult to decide what is right and what is not. But even then, by thinking more and more on the issues concerned, he is able to go ahead.

It does happen sometimes that he does not call the morally wrong wrong (or the morally right right) because of some non-conceptual or selfish reason, or because of his being akratic. All this has nothing to with the subtlety or clarity of the notions of right and wrong. Duryodhana does not call, for example, Draupadī's being derobed wrong because of his desire to take revenge on her for having once called him blind as he is a blind man's son. But this is a selfish reason. Vikarṇa, on the other hand, has the moral courage, a strong moral conscience, to call it wrong even though he is also a brother of Duryodhana. Vidura too declares it to be wrong because of his moral strength even though he is an employee of Duryodhana being his father's prime minister. Neither of the two, Vikarṇa or Vidura, is akratic.

Bhīṣma, though the eldest member of the Kuru family, is one who gets all the expenses of his life met by Duryodhana. It is on this account, this, as has been said in an earlier chapter, that he does not oblige Yudhiṣṭhira by agreeing to fight the *Mahābhārata* war from his side even though he thinks that his cause in the war is a morally right cause. Admitting that Duryodhana's cause in the war is not a right cause, he fights it as his commander-in-chief. This, we have said earlier, is a case of his akrasia, his weakness of moral will, i.e. a case of doing the wrong thing while knowing that it is wrong to do it. His present attitude towards Draupadī's questions and not answering them on the alleged ground of *dharma*'s extreme subtlety or abstruseness, on the ground of its functioning in a manner extremely difficult to decipher (*dharmasya paramā gatih*),[14] is also describable as a case of akrasia on his part: a case of the weakness of his moral will not allowing him to answer Draupadī's questions by declaring that what has been as well as what is being done to her is morally wrong; i.e. in order to avoid displeasing Duryodhana, he does not declare them wrong. There is a good reason for describing it this way. Bhīṣma cannot be accepted to have truthfully said that he considers *dharma* to be too subtle to be used to answer Draupadī's question, because it is the same Bhīṣma who agrees to teach and teaches Yudhiṣṭhira the principles of morality (*dharma*) from his deathbed after Yudhiṣṭhira has won the war and become the king, and Duryodhana and all his brothers and friends have been killed. At that time he does not decline to give moral lessons on all sorts of problems. Yudhiṣṭhira goes to him for the lessons because Kṛṣṇa asks him to do that. He calls him a man of great moral wisdom (*mahāprājña*), a treasure house of morality (*dharmamayo nidhih*).[15]

When Kṛṣṇa says that Bhīṣma is such a great possessor of moral knowledge, it must be true because Kṛṣṇa, an incarnation of God as per the tradition, cannot tell an untruth. And, since Bhīṣma agrees to impart and actually imparts all sorts of moral lessons to Yudhiṣṭhira, it shows that he himself accepts, and knows, that he is a knower of all morality (*mahāprājña*). It is unbelievable that such a man does not know what is morally right or wrong when Draupadī asks him to adjudicate, and it is strange to hear him say that Yudhiṣṭhira, his would-be disciple, is a better judge than him. Therefore, his confession of ignorance or inability can be taken as an expression of his having an akratic will, i.e. a will too weak to let him express an opinion which he knows to be the right opinion but does not want to express because it goes against the interests of Duryodhana whom he does not want to displease as he is living a comfortable life on Duryodhana's largesse. Or, his confession can be taken as a strategic, or, diplomatic, admission of ignorance to conceal his unwillingness to tell the moral truth though he knows what it is, again, for the same reason. Whether he is akratic or strategic, he tries to conceal his inability or unwillingness, his akrasia or diplomacy, behind the veil or cloak of the alleged extreme kind or subtlety and depth of the concept of *dharma* or morality.

Through Bhīṣma's example, Indian ethicists demonstrate in a very concrete manner that the subtlety, etc., of an evaluative, practical, concept must not be given too much prominence. If it is, it may be used sometimes even by a man of acknowledged moral excellence, like Bhīṣma, to conceal his own moral weakness or failure and prompt him to do nothing to stop the commission of an immorality which he can stop, or to help the commission by not taking the moral stand which he otherwise could and should have taken.

This is the lesson which Bhīṣma's example yields and which the *Mahābhārata* intends its readers to draw from it. There is simply no logical point in mystifying the concept of *dharma* by claiming it to be too subtle to *apply* even to a visibly clear case of immorality as that of the attempt to derobe Draupadī and all that which proceeds it. One has to call it immoral, or discordant with *dharma*. There is also a practical, or moral, point against mystifying the concept of *dharma* because it may help perpetrate of immoralities. But quite a good number of modern writers on classical Indian ethics do not draw this, the right, intended, lesson. Rather, they do the opposite. They think that by overemphasizing the extreme subtlety and unfathomable depth of the classical Indian concept of *dharma*, or morality, i.e. by mystifying it, they put it very high on the axiological ladder. But in effect they do just the reverse. They subject classical Indian ethicists to the ignoniminy of not being able to realize the actual role of *dharma* in an ordinary man's daily life and make the concept of *dharma* an unusable (conceptual) tool. Moral concepts are like current coins in a monetary system. Any moral concept, if mystified, becomes something like a coin whose exchange value becomes unknown to the common man who *needs to use it* in his normal, everyday, moral commerce, i.e. practical life.

A genuine ignorance of morality, of what is and what is, not, right, is a different matter. No one can be blamed for not expressing his moral opinion on an issue if he does not really know what is right or wrong in a given case. His ignorance here is virtually his innocence. Sometimes a man has the required moral knowledge but is ignorant of some relevant facts. In such a case his ignorance of the facts disables him from expressing his moral opinion on an issue to which the facts concerned are relevant. This is uncontestable. But there is another question which arises here, namely, the question 'May, or may not, a person be held morally responsible for having done an action without knowing, i.e. being completely ignorant of, some relevant facts about the situation in which he has done it?' This question is closely related to another which may be put in some such form: 'May a person be held morally responsible for having done an action accidently, inadvertently, or unintentionally?' This question also *involves ignorance of some facts about* the situation in which the action is done, or *ignorance of the identity of the action* that is done, otherwise the act of doing it would not have been accidental, etc. Such questions are pointers to some central issues in moral philosophy or ethical theory. Let us discuss them in the next section by examining what classical Indian ethics or ethical practice has to say about the role of ignorance in the determination of moral responsibility.

11.5 IGNORANCE OF FACT AND MORAL RESPONSIBILITY

Before we proceed to the exact theme of this section let us distinguish between the issue of anyone's general responsibilities and that of his being responsible for having done something specific. When we ask what are the general responsibilities of a teacher, or of a *kṣatriya*, we normally intend to know what are the duties or obligations of a teacher, or of a *ksatriya.* But when we ask who is responsible for a certain action, or for something which has been caused to happen, we generally ask it when something untoward, undesirable, unwanted, or at least not morally approvable or commendable, etc., has been done, or has happened as a result of some human agency. Here we intend to determine or assign responsibility in the sense of apportioning some blame, culpability, moral accusation or disapprobation, etc. to the doer. The role which ignorance of a fact, or inadvertence, etc., may play in the assessment of an action, or in the assessment of the character of an agent, from the moral point of view, needs to be studied only in respect of determining responsibility in the second sense, i.e. in the sense of culpability or blameworthiness of the action or the agent. Quite obviously, it is not to be studied in respect of determining responsibility in the former sense, i.e. in that of the duty or obligation of any agent. Quite obviously, again, ignorance of any sort, inadvertence, etc., involved in the doing of an action can make the action neither a duty, nor a forbidden action or anti-duty (or con-duty).

Classical Indian ethicists discuss the issue of an individual's responsibilities, in the sense of his duties, in terms of his obligations as a human being (*sāmānya dharma*) and according to his stage in his life (*āśrama dharma*) and his place in the social order (*varṇa dharma*). These duties, obligations, or virtues, etc. we shall discuss in some later chapters. Here we shall concentrate on the role of ignorance, inadvertence, etc. in respect of determining responsibility in the sense of culpability, blameworthiness, etc. This use or sense of the concept of responsibility, or of being responsible, is common-sensical, and not at all a technical, philosophical, one imported into either of the concepts. Rather, on some occasions, even the word 'do' and its grammatical derivatives, chosen in accordance with grammatical suitability, can do the work of the word 'responsible' or 'responsibility'. For example, when a mother finds the bottom of a door curtain dirtied, her asking her servant who did it (or who dirtied it) can very well do the work of the question 'who is responsible for dirtying it?' Similarly, the servant's saying 'I did not do that because I was not in the house' can very well do the work of 'I am not responsible for it because ...' or of, 'You cannot hold me responsible for it because ...' or of 'You cannot blame me for it because ...' etc. The servant may also say 'Please do not put the responsibility (blame) for having done it on my head because ...'. Which mode of speaking would be appropriate would certainly depend on the context and speaker-hearer social relationship.

Normally when something desirable, right, or likeable, has been done, we do not ask who is responsible for it. The president of a political party does not appoint a committee to determine the responsibilities of those who have made the party the winner in an election and his doing that would be conceptually odd. But it would be quite in order, of course, conceptually, if he appoints one to determine the responsibilities of those who have led to its failure to win if it has been a failure. Similarly, in case of its failure, his saying that he is responsible for the failure, or his taking the responsibility for the failure entirely on his head, would also be conceptually in order. In the case of some desirable or happy result, occurrence, phenomenon, we give the *credit* to some one or ones for having made it possible; we do not hold anyone responsible for it. These things are true not only of the English words 'responsible' and 'responsibility' but also of their equivalents in all languages because they are truths about the behaviour of the concept of being responsible, or of the concept of responsibility, and not merely grammatical truths about the usage of the words concerned.

We are now well set to discuss the role of *ignorance* of some relevant fact, inadvertence, etc., in holding anyone responsible for having done something untoward. Take ignorance first. Normally, when a person does something wrong, whose consequences are not to any great extent grievous, painful, or costly to anyone, we do not punish him, or accuse him of a serious moral lapse. Suppose a person fails to attend a birthday party of a friend of his, though he has promised to do that, simply because he wrongly thinks the party is to be held on the coming Sunday while it was actually held on the preceding Saturday. Certainly the friend would call it a lapse, feel unhappy, or even annoyed because of his lapse. But he would not consider it a hostile or unfriendly action, and the faulting person's sincere expression of being sorry for the lapse would satisfy him. On the other hand, if the lapse caused by an agent produces some grievous, seriously morally wrong, consequences, then too, if, he has done it because of being misled by his ignorance of some relevant fact, our accusation of him, or the punishment awarded to him, would be toned down when we come to know that he has done it because of his ignorance, i.e. unknowingly and therefore unintentionally.

Suppose, under the cover of darkness, a man shoots an arrow at a black animal and kills it, under the impression that it is a black bear roaming the street for its prey and likely to kill a child if it comes across one, but the animal really is a black cow without horns owned by a neighbour. The fact of the matter now is that he has killed a cow and caused a great loss to his neighbour. But when the neighbour is convinced of the fact that he has done it in complete ignorance about the identity of the animal he shoots at and there is a good reason for his ignorance as it is completely dark then, he would tone down his accusation. In such a case, if the wrongdoer repents, expresses his apologies, and compensates the owner of the cow for the financial loss, normally our moral common sense would tell us that the owner should now exculpate him from having committed the wrong.

One may even say that the killer of the cow is not at all responsible or guilty for the wrongdoing because he is justifiably ignorant that the animal targeted by him is a cow and not a black bear. Even this stand is not totally unmaintainable. But even if we do not go that far, we would definitely say that moral punishment, or censure, which a man, ignorant of a relevant fact about the wrong action done by him, would have deserved had he not been ignorant, has to be toned down because of his ignorance. That is, we would consider it justified to say that ignorance of a relevant fact is a good reason for toning down or reducing the culpability of the wrongdoer, i.e. for toning down, or reducing the extent of responsibility ascribable to him for having done the wrong thing.

What is true of ignorance of fact reducing the rigour of responsibility is also true of inadvertence in having done something wrong, or of the wrong thing having been done accidently. For example, suppose an arrow, shot at a point in the trunk of a tree by an archer to test his skill in archery, hits a calf which strays, unexpectedly, into the path of the arrow and gets killed. It would make a good moral sense to say that the *archer is not* responsible for killing the calf, and therefore not at all culpable or censurable for having done a morally wrong thing. One may say this even while admitting that a *morally wrong thing has been* done or has happened and the archer is associated with it as he has played some role in it. And, here again we may say that the maximum we can require of the archer is that he repents for it and compensates for the loss caused to the owner of the calf by offering him something in cash or kind equivalent to the material value of the calf.

Returning to the stand taken in classical Indian ethical practice on issues like the ones mentioned above, i.e. the role of ignorance or accident in reducing the rigour of responsibility, we find that it sometimes does and sometimes does not consider them to be a reason for reducing the gravity of a wrongdoing and consequently for reducing the severity of the blame or punishment due for it. That is, its position on this theme is ambivalent, since it sometimes concedes and sometimes does not concede that a wrongdoing done ignorantly or inadvertently is not culpable to the same extent as one which is done with full knowledge of relevant facts and therefore done intentionally. Only two examples will be mentioned below, one to show the former stand and another to show the latter. The former example is from the *Rāmāyaṇa* and the latter from the *Mahābhārata.* Since these issues have not been discussed by classical philosophers or theorizers, there is no alternative here to depending on examples which may even be called by some mythological or ancedotal. This is true of many ethical issues in respect of the stand or stands taken on them in classical Indian ethical or social practice.

As stated by Vālmīki in the *Rāmāyaṇa,*[16] the king Daśaratha in his youth unknowingly kills Śravanakumāra, the only son and support of his blind father and blind mother. The king has the skill to hit with his arrow a target only on the basis his hearing some sound coming from the spot where it is located (*śabdavedhi vidyā*), even though the target is completely invisible to him. One night, in the rainy season, when nothing is visible, while standing at a place a little away from the bank of the river Sarayū, he hears a sound coming from a spot in the river which resembles the sound made by an elephant while filling her trunk with water from the river. Using his skill he shoots at the target thinking it is an elephant. He has no reason to expect a human being to be filling his pitcher with water in the river at that untimely hour. But the target is a human being, Śravanakumāra, the young son of his blind thirsty parents who are waiting in their hut for water. Daśaratha hears his dying cries of pain, rushes to that place, and on his request takes out the pierced arrow from his body to relieve him of pain. As a result of that he dies, after requesting him to give the pitcher of water to his parents to quench their thirst. The king rushes to their hut, breaks the news of the sad death of their son caused by him unknowingly (*ajñānād*). The parents cry and wail, ask him to take them to the river so that they may touch their son's body, and after touching the body they die because of the grief caused by his having been killed.

Before dying, the old father tells Daśaratha that his crime is so grievous that the right punishment for it is to curse him to be burnt to death then and there. But since it has been done unknowingly (*ajñānāddhi kṛtam*), he tones down the punishment and curses Daśaratha to die, as he and his wife are, due to the pangs of suffering caused by the separation of his son from him. This actually happens. Daśaratha lives for a long time after the death of the old couple and their son, rules over his kingdom, marries many women, gets four sons, enjoys all royal splendour, name and fame, but ultimately dies because of the agony caused by his eldest son Rāma's being separated from him when he goes into exile for fourteen years. Certainly this is a punishment much milder then being burnt to death immediately after the commission of the immorality. And, this softening, or reduction of severity, of the curse is due to the fact that he has committed the immorality unknowingly and therefore unintentionally. It can also be said to have been done accidentally because it is an accident, and unexpected thing, that the target hit by his arrow is a human being and not an elephant as expected or calculated by him.

The other example pertains to an incident in the life of Karṇa as given in the *Mahābhārata*.[17] One day in the course of practising archery he is moving around in a forest, shooting his arrow to hit difficult targets to perfect his skill in archery. In one attempt of his the arrow he shoots hits a calf which strays into the path of his arrow and gets killed. The animal belongs to a *brāhmaṇa* named Vijaya. Karṇa has shot his arrow without expecting, and without knowing, that a calf, or any living being, may stray into its path. He has, therefore, killed the animal but entirely unknowingly (*ajñānenahi*) and therefore accidentally or inadvertently, without any intention of killing it. But Vijaya gives him for it the curse (*śāpa*) that when he is in the most fearful condition on the battlefield, while fighting a war, a wheel of his chariot will fall into a ditch. Karṇa offers him six oxen, seven hundred elephants, hundreds of male and female servants, fourteen thousand cows, his grand palace, all his wealth, etc. He very greatly repents for the wrongdoing and beseeches Vijaya to pardon him. But the *brāhmaṇa* does not relent, and he says that he has cursed him to protect morality (*dharma*). It is this curse which later, in the *Mahābhārata* war, costs Karṇa his life. His wheel does fall into a ditch at a crucial moment, and when he gets down from his chariot unarmed to lift it up, Arjuna, under Kṛṣṇa's instigation, kills him, though attacking an unarmed combatant is against the ethics of the war agreed upon by the two fighting armies.

What is important to note here is that the *brāhmaṇa* curses him, i.e. awards this punishment, in the name of morality and does not tone it down in spite of the fact that the killing of his calf by Karṇa, the moral wrong, has been done by him unknowingly. Neither his ignorance of the fact that calf is coming in the path of his arrow, nor his not intending at all to kill or aim at it, is considered by the *brāhmaṇa* a reason for reducing the extent of his responsibility for the killing, or for toning down the punishment which it, according to him, deserves.

11.6 SOURCES OF MORAL KNOWLEDGE: THEIR EPISTEMIC COMPETENCE EXAMINED

Whether or not ignorance of a fact relevant to an action has any role in our determining the responsibility of an agent for having done the action, he must have some knowledge of what is right or wrong in order to be able to do the right, or to avoid doing the wrong. In fact, moral life consists in doing the right and abjuring the wrong. Knowing the right and the wrong is not a rare or extraordinary trait. Leading a moral life itself is not a rare or extraordinary or supraordinary affair. Most normal individuals lead such a life and in most cases know what is right and wrong, though they may not always do the right and avoid doing the wrong. Were this not the case, it would not have been possible for anyone to lead a normal life. This is as true of classical Indians as it is of any people of any time and country. It may, however, be true that in some period of the history of a country or in some part of the world at any one time, the number of people leading a moral life is larger or smaller than what it is in another period of their history, or in another part of the world. But this possibility, or fact, does not controvert the fact that most men know the right and the wrong at least to the extent to which they need to in order to lead a satisfactory moral life in a general or life-facilitating sense. Normally one does not need to consult a philosopher of morals to tell one what is right or wrong in a certain situation.

An ordinary individual, however, may not be able to state what is the source of moral knowledge, or even that of *his* moral knowledge. This kind of ability he does not need to have in order to lead a moral life; if he has it, it may equip him better, or perhaps may not, because, as some philosophers say, he may be an expert in moral epistemology but still may not be an unerring person in leading a moral life. But the fact of the matter is that this task of stating and explaining the source or sources of moral knowledge, in classical Indian terminology, the way or ways (*mārga*) of *dharma*, or of getting *dharmajñāna*, is the philosopher's task, particularly the task of the philosopher of morals, or of extremely gifted and intellectually alert individuals. This is what one may expect the writers of the various works called the *Dharmasūtras* or *Dharmaśāstras* to have done. In a sense they have, but not in the sense in which a philosopher of morals should have done. They have, rather, stated in a descriptive manner the acknowledged or generally accepted ways of knowing *dharma* (morality or moral propriety), or in a preceptorial manner what one should do to know what is morally right and wrong.

The classical Indian position, or the predominant position, seems to have been summed up well, or tolerably well, by Manu. According to him, *Veda*, *Smṛti*, principles exemplified in the behaviour of moral exemplars or morally impeccable individuals, and an action's satisfying one's own conscience (moral sense or moral intuition), these four are, as wise men say, the determiners (criteria) of the morality (*dharmatā*) of any issues'.[18] The *Vedas* are taken by classical *Brāhmaṇical* thinkers to be infallible documents, either revealed by a divine being, or eternally valid works. *Smṛtis* or *Dharmasūtras* are taken to be memorial records of principles or truths given to us by highly gifted and elevated scholars called *ṛṣis* (seers). Both of them are considered to be unquestionable or unfaultable. The two sets together may be called scriptural authorities, i.e. works which state what is morally right or wrong, obligatory, forbidden, or just permissible, virtuous or vicious (along with truths of many other kinds), etc., etc. Therefore, Manu and many others would say, one source of moral knowledge is constituted by them. The other source is the behaviour of moral exemplars or heroes. The assumption is that there are some individuals who are morally perfect or incorruptible and their behaviour can also function as certifiers of morality. That is, if they have done something, or called something forbidden, then that thing is morally right, or wrong. The other organ of certifying the morality of an action is its satisfying, or having been approved of by, our moral sense or sensibility. The intention of describing the sources of moral knowledge in this way is that when we need to take a decision about the rightness of an action, we can appeal to any one of them. This intention is combined with the (unargued) assumption that these organs taken together are sufficient, or adequate, to give us all the help we need, or may ever need, in solving any problem in moral decision-making.

Manu's list of sources, mentioned above, is generally accepted by many others with minor variations. For example, Gautama in his *Dharmasūtra* (1.182) mentions only three, *Vedas*, *Smṛtis* and behaviour of moral exemplars. *Āpastambasūtra* (1.1–2) mentions only the approval of those who know *dharma* and the *Vedas*. The *Vaśiṣṭhadharmasūtra* (1.4–7) says the *Vedas* and the *Smṛtis* are the (chief) sources. When they do not deal with an issue then the conduct of morally elevated individuals may be referred to. A morally elevated one is he who has no .desire or motivation. The *Yājñavalkyadharmasūtra* (1.7.3–5) adds to Manu's four—the *Vedas*, the *Smṛtis*, behaviour of moral exemplars, and approval of moral conscience—a fifth one, namely, the desire born out of right moral will (*samyak sankalpaja kāma*). The fifth may simply be called moral goodwill. We have seen a little earlier that Yudhiṣṭhira considers knowing the way morally great men behave as the most dependable way of knowing what is morally right. But that seems to have been uttered by him more with the motivation of emphasizing the extreme kind of subtlety of the concept of *dharma* than with that of stating or describing the methods or ways of knowing it.

It is important to note that the Jaina and Bauddha thinkers do not accept the authority of the *Vedas* and *Smṛtis*, the *Brāhmaṇical* scriptures, in respect of any subject. Therefore, obviously, they do not accept them as givers of moral knowledge. But in course of time the words and opinions of the founders of the two schools, Mahāvīra and Gautama Buddha assume an authoritative character for their religious disciples as well as for scholars and philosophers including ethicists, belonging to these schools of thought. But still there is an important difference between their authoritativeness and that of the *Veda-Smṛtis*. The *Vedas* from whose views and teachings the *Smṛtis* get formed or compiled by some scholars—are said to owe their origin to some divine source, or to be eternal. But the words and opinions of Mahāvīra and the Buddha are human thoughts, expressed by the individuals as a result of their experiences and thinking about the empirical conditions of human existence and how suffering can be ameliorated. The other two organs of moral knowledge, the conduct of morally elevated individuals and satisfaction of our moral conscience (or enlightened reason) Jains and Buddhists would accept without a murmur.

The *Brāhmaṇical* account of the organs of moral knowledge raise some very tricky conceptual or philosophical questions. Take, for example, the moral authority of the *Vedas*. If a certain thing is considered morally right or obligatory by some *Veda* or *Vedas* which is not right or obligatory, or is palpably morally wrong, then the fault lies not with that morally wrong thing, and the morally wrong thing does not become morally elevated, i.e. right, or even permissible, because of its occurrence in a *Veda*, or its having been prescribed or recommended by it. Rather the *Veda* concerned gets de-sanctified or morally de-authenticated. For example, it is common knowledge that the *Vedas* prescribe some animal sacrifices to propitiate gods to get benefits. And, an orthodox believer in the authority of the *Vedas* thinks, or may think, that killing an innocent animal when prescribed by a *Veda* is not doing any injury to the animal and therefore is not morally wrong. As the saying goes, he may aver that a *Veda*-prescribed killing is not really a killing (*vaidikī himsā himsā na bhavati*). But killing an innocent animal cannot be made morally right no matter who does it, when and where he does it and how he does it. Similar questions have been raised by the *Vedic* attitude towards women and *śūdras*.

Behind such issues there lurks a very important conceptual question which may be said to be a cousin of what is called in modern ethical literature, the (platonic) Euthyphro question. This question may be put as follows: Is a moral opinion held by a *Veda* morally right because it is held by it, or it is held by it because it is morally right? If it is said that it is right because it is held by it, it becomes a definition of moral rightness to the effect that a morally right opinion is that which is held by a *Veda*. In that case the view that the *Vedas* constitute one source of our knowledge of what is morally right becomes a mere definition of the notion of moral rightness and therefore ceases to be a substantive statement of a source of moral knowledge. If the question is answered in the other way by saying that a *Veda* offers a moral opinion because it is morally right, then it is clear that its occurrence in the *Veda* concerned *does not make* it right but only records this morally right opinion. This obviously entails that a *Veda* is not a source of any moral knowledge and that there is some other source from which it is obtained and then recorded in it.

This may be an aside but it is also worth mentioning that when a god is said to be one which can be propitiated by killing an innocent animal in its honour, i.e. one which can be propritiated by doing an immorality, this destroys its godhood since it goes against our notion of what it is to be a god. And, this means that a work which glorifies such a being as a god cannot itself be, without a prick in our moral conscience, considered a glorified, sacred, scriptural, document.

To the question why a *Vedic* injunction should be called morally right simply because it is a *Vedic* injunction, it does not seem to be possible to give a logically defensible reply. Normally those who hold the unquestionability of *Vedic* ethics hold it simply because it is *Vedic*, a view for which no reason need be asked, i.e. as a dogma; or hold it on the ground that the *Vedas* are divine, god-given, documents. The introduction of the concept of God, or a god, in any philosophical controversy solves it only for him who believes in the god concerned and who is not willing to listen to problems which this belief itself gives rise to, or who does not have the logical sophistication needed to be aware of them. Moreover, when an obviously immoral injunction, like that of sacrificing an innocent animal to please a deity, is found in a *Veda*, it does have an adverse bearing an the godliness of the god itself who is said to be the giver of the *Vedic* ethics. A god who has issued such an immoral injunction cannot be called a perfectly moral god, and a god who is not perfectly moral would not be a god, as per any sensible moral conception of a god. Secondly, the Euthyphro question can be raised even about the morality of an injunction issued by a god itself. For example, if a *Vedic* injunction (about sacrificing an animal in a religious ritual) is said to be morally valid even if our moral sensibility calls it morally wrong, one can very well ask whether it is right *because a god has originally issued it* (and then it has been recorded in the *Veda* it occurs in), or whether the god has issued it *because it is right.* To choose the first alternative is not logically trouble-free, as has been already shown. But to choose the second one also is not. We shall explain why below.

If a *Vedic* injunction is in itself morally right and therefore has been given by a god and then recorded, it means that there is an independent, a separate, criterion of moral rightness by satisfying which it is morally right. This implies that its being a god-given principle, or its being a *Vedic* principle, is not the reason for its rightness. It further implies that our finding it in a *Veda,* or our ascertaining what a *Veda* enjoins or forbids, is of no avail in ascertaining what is morally right and what is morally forbidden. The logical consequence of all this is that then no *Veda* can be called a source of moral knowledge, as is claimed by all *Brāhmaṇical* thinkers. And since no Veda can be, no Smṛti (or Dharmasīra) can be.

Let us now come to *sadācāra,* or the behaviour of moral exemplars (*mahājanas* as Yudhiṣṭhira has called them). But in this case too we face problems because we find that some of the individuals acknowledged by the tradition to be *mahajanas* have done things which are morally wrong, or at least not morally right. We shall take only a few examples. That will suffice because even if there is one *mahājana* who has done something wrong, or is not different from an ordinary (moral) individual, then it cannot be maintained that from the behaviour of a *mahājana* we can learn what is right, or that we should go in our moral life the way a *mahājana* has gone.

Let us take the example of Rāma. There seems to be complete unanimity in the tradition that he embodies *all perfections* relevant to a man and therefore *all moral perfections.* But we find that he too does certain things which are morally wrong or at least not morally impeccable. To mention just one example, he contracts a friendship with Sugrīva in order to get help in freeing Sīta, his wife, from Rāvaṇa who has abducted her. He promises to help Sugrīva by killing Vāli, his eldest brother, because Vāli has taken away Sugrīva's wife. Vāli has done no wrong, or nothing hurtful, to Rāma himself or his family. Still he kills Vāli when Sugrīva, on his advice, has engaged him in a combat. He kills him concealing himself behind some trees. For anyone, killing anyone else who has done him no wrong is wrong, and is doubly wrong if he does it without attacking him in a face-to-face fight, but rather keeps hidden, and kills him when he is already in combat with another individual.

Vāli asks Rāma why he has killed him though he has done no offence to him. None of the reasons Rāma offers in response seems to justify his doing that. One reason he offers is that this part of the land comes under the jurisdiction of the king Bharata, his brother, whose representative he is. It is his duty, as Bharata's representative, to punish anyone who has committed a crime in his kingdom. Vāli's crime was to take away his younger brother's, Sugrīva's, wife. But it is right for a king, or his nominee, to punish any accused only after giving him a chance to explain his conduct and finding him really guilty with no justification for having done what he has. But this Rāma has not done. He himself has not asked Vāli to appear before him and present his version of the case. He has killed him after hearing only Sugrīva's version.

Rāma's second reason is that he has contracted friendship with Sugrīva and promised to him to kill Vāli, his enemy. He says he is a *kṣatriya* and a *kṣatriya* never backs out from fulfilling any promise made by him. Therefore, to fulfil his promise to his friend he has to kill him. But, Vāli says, he did not try to befriend him who had greater might than Sugrīva to defeat Rāvaṇa and extricate Sītā. This is true because, as per mythology, Sugrīva has defeated Rāvaṇa once. Here Rāma admits to having proceeded on the twin principles, as ordinary individuals do, that a friend's enemy is an enemy whoever he may be and that a promise to a friend has to be fulfilled whatever its fulfilment may amount to.

Rāma's third reason is that *kṣatriyas* do kill animals in sport by concealing themselves from them or by entrapping them. So do human beings who eat the meat of animals. Vāli, being a monkey, is an animal. Therefore, in killing him, while concealing himself, he has done nothing wrong. But, Vāli points out, a monkey's meat is not eaten by human beings nor is the skin of a monkey used as a dress material. To this Rāma has no reply. In fact, the tradition does not consider a monkey to be an animal killable in sport. *Kṣatriyas* or kings have been portrayed as killing lions, other ferocious animals, deer, some birds, etc., but not any monkey.[19]

It does not need much thinking to see that none of Rāma's replies can be said to be cent per cent morally impeccable or justificatory. This is not to say that his killing of Vāli is wrong but only to suggest that his reasons for doing that are not completely convincing. Moreover, they are reasons of the type which even an ordinary individual, if he had killed Vāli in a similar situation, could have given. Also, there is nothing in them which makes Rāma shine as a moral exemplar. Further, from this 'moral behaviour' (*sadācāra*) of Rāma an ordinary individual can derive no help or guidance in knowing what is right for him to do if he is faced with a similar problem which he solves as Rāma does. Some of these problems are: Is it morally right to punish an accused without giving him a hearing, even if the accusation is very serious and so is the punishment deserved by him? Is it always right for one to treat a friend's enemy as an enemy? Is it always obligatory to fulfil any sort of promise? Is it right for a morally upright man to kill an enemy while keeping himself hidden from him? etc.

As another example of an acknowledged moral exemplar's conduct not helping us to know what is morally right, we can very well take Kṛṣṇa's replies to Karṇa when Karṇa asks Arjuna not to assault him while he is unarmed because he is engaged in lifting up the wheels of his chariot which have sunk into a ditch. Karṇa's reason for asking this is a moral one because, as per the *Mahābhārata* war ethics, it is immoral to attack an unarmed combatant. It is a principle of that ethics to which even Arjuna and Kṛṣṇa have agreed. But Kṛṣṇa asks, or rather instigates, Arjuna to shoot him with his arrow at this very time. He replies to Karṇa by enumerating some of his own immoralities. For example, he points to his having been on the side of Duryodhana when he tried to get the entire *Pāndava* family burnt alive by arranging to set on fire the lac house in which they are staying; when Yudhiṣṭhira was being cheated by Śakuni in the game of dice; when an attempt was made on his instruction to derobe Draupadī; when the teenaged Abhimanyu was attacked by stalwarts and killed, etc. And, then, he reports to Karṇa, he, who has done so many immoralities, has no moral right to remind Arjuna of the war ethics that attacking him when he is unarmed is morally wrong. The clear implication is that attacking an enemy like Karṇa who himself has done so many immoralities, even when he is unarmed, is not unethical.[20]

Kṛṣṇa proceeds here on his conviction that it is morally right to take revenge on an individual who has done an immorality (or a set of immoralities) by doing an immorality to him; i.e. the principle that it is morally right, or not wrong, to do a moral wrong in response to a prior wrong. But this is a principle which even an ordinary individual many times accepts and works on, and one which some morally more mature ordinary individuals consider untenable. This is only to bring out that, like the incident of Rāma's killing Vāli, even this reply of Kṛṣṇa shows that, if he is a moral exemplar, as the tradition claims, not all the principles on which he acts, or causes to be acted upon by others, can be accepted as morally impeccable. This means that not all of even his behaviour which he himself, or the tradition, considers morally right (*sadācāra*), or exemplary, can always be taken to be impeccable, or even morally unquestionable. Therefore, his 'moral behaviour' cannot always be of great help in our deciding, or knowing, what is really right from the moral point of view.

As a third example of a moral exemplar's behaviour not proving to be of any help in moral decision-making, we may recollect Bhīṣma's strategic expression of his inability to reply to Draupadī's questions, on the plea of *dharma*'s, or morality's, being extremely subtle and deep, as already discussed.

Such examples from the life of traditionally acknowledged exemplars can be narrated galore, but that is not necessary at all. Even these few examples are enough to show that it is not logically or morally completely safe to depend on the behaviour of traditionally declared moral exemplars.

Sometimes it is suggested that we should not take everything which an exemplar does as morally right, or exemplary, but only that which really is. But this would mean that we must have, independentlly of moral exemplars, the knowledge of what is and what is not morally right, in order to be able to choose from their actions only those which are right and use them as our guides. But, then, we cannot say, nor can a Yudhiṣthira or Manu say, that one of the sources of moral knowledge is the behaviour of individuals who are considered moral exemplars in our ethos. Yudhiṣthira himself is almost unanimously considered to be one. But even he is addicted to playing dice and it is this addiction of his which is very largely responsible for the miseries and ignominies suffered by his family. Not only that, it is Droṇa's taking him to be an unfailing teller of truth and of only truth which costs Droṇa his life. Droṇa believes that Aśvathāmā, his son, has been killed when this is announced by Yudhiṣthira though it is not true. Droṇa gives up his arms, and then his head is chopped off by Dhṛṣtaddyumna. This example of telling of an untruth by a moral exemplar will be further discussed, in another connection, in the chapter that follows.

In spite of giving so much importance to *mahājanas* or moral exemplars, classical Indian thinkers do not state in clear terms the criteria which an individual should fulfil in order to be a *mahājana*. There seems to a good reason for their not doing this. If the criteria are stated in terms of non-moral attributes, then one can very reasonably ask why a person fulfilling them, one who has these non-moral attributes, should be called a moral exemplar, or why the behaviour of such a person be called *sadācāra*, or exemplary moral behaviour. On the other hand, if they are stated in terms of moral attributes, such as benevolence, justice, forgiveness, etc., then one must know in an independent manner when somebody can be called benevolent, just, forgiving, etc. This means that he would not need to consult a moral exemplar, or to consult an ethical treatise recording how he behaves, in order to know how a moral exemplar behaves when he behaves justly, benevolently, etc., when he himself is in a situation in which he is expected to behave justly, benevolently, etc. It seems to us that this is the reason for classical thinkers' not defining or explicitly describing the properties which make one a *mahājana.* They go by the tradition. i.e., leave it to the tradition to tell who such exemplary individuals are.

It is very relevant here to point out that a moral exemplar cannot be defined as one who is well-equipped with the wisdom, which is claimed by *Brāhmaṇical* thinkers to be stored in the *Vedas* and *Smṛtis*. Doing this will entail, by definition, that Mahāvīra and Buddha are not moral exemplars, and consequently that no Jain or Buddhist saint is, not to speak of a *Cārvāka* thinker. Each one of them would be, by definition, disqualified from being a moral exemplar because he does not accept the authority of the *Vedas, Smṛtis,* etc. But this would be a travesty of truth. The basic thrust of Mahāvīra's and the Buddha's philosophy is moral, and the life-style of each one of them outshines, in moral respects, (almost) any individual claimed to be a moral exemplar in the *Brāhmaṇical* literature. But this is the mistake which Udayana commits when, in his *Ātmatattvaviveka* (Chaukhamba, pp. 431–38), he defines a *mahājana* in terms of his having thoroughly understood and grasped the wisdom of the *Veda-Smṛti* literature. In fact, he does not conceal his intention of eliminating the possibility of Mahāvīra's or the Buddha's being called a *mahājana.* But a modern student of Indian ethos can justifiably retort to him by offering the counter-fact that if neither Mahāvīra nor the Buddha is a *mahājana,* then none else is.

Coming back to the *Brāhmaṇical* position, or the topic, we can say that the thinkers of this orientation seem to go by the tradition in their entire approach to the sources of moral knowledge. They mention the *Vedic* ethos, or works considered ethically authoritative, behaviour of *mahājanas*, satisfaction of moral conscience or moral reason, etc., as the generally or traditionally accepted organs of moral knowledge. It is this approach which explains their saying at several places that sometimes an individual may derive help even from customary morality in deciding what he ought to do. This he may very well do, or does, by consulting the ethos or ethical customs of his family (*kulācāra*), or of his region (*deśācāra*), or of his community or society (*lokācāra*). The purport all this is, to put it briefly, that one can solve at least some of one's moral problems, or problems in moral decision-making, by consulting one's ethical heritage, a good part of which can be found to have percolated into the life-style of every mature individual.

Classical thinkers would not deny that *Vedic* ethics, or *mahājana*'s behaviour, may not render every time all the help one needs; or that these two sources, or any two injunctions, may sometimes conflict with each other. It is in such cases that *ātmatuṣṭi,* or a deliberation which satisfies one's moral conscience, alone can help one out.

Ātmatuṣṭi, satisfaction or conviction of moral conscience, is not a sensuous, or merely affective, satisfaction. It is the satisfaction of man's moral propensity or sensibility, his moral reason, or moral earnestness, however may we may nowadays like to name it. It is bound to be a reflective, deliberative, process conducted in a cogitative, ratiocinative, manner. This is, in effect, what we call moral thinking or deliberation, an exercise undertaken by an individual's intellect, his moral reason, or moral will (*sumyaka sankalpa*), and therefore a rational process. It is clear now that, notwithstanding Yudhiṣṭhira's overall condemnation of reason, in a huff, as unstable or undependable, the importance of reason, or moral reason, in man's moral life is appropriately recognized by the inclusion of *ātmatuṣṭi* (self-satisfaction) in the list of organs of moral knowledge. We can, therefore, conclude this section by saying that the Indian general theory of morality, while admitting the great role of man's ethical heritage in his moral life, is not anti-rational, since it accords to reason, or moral reasoning, the authority to adjudicate between two conflicting sectors of the heritage or two moral principles, if they ever conflict with each other.

This general theory of morality (*dharma*) outlined in this chapter concretizes itself through its elaboration of some of the general virtues or character traits (*sāmānya dharma*) which an individual ought to inculcate, the obligations he ought to fulfil as a member of his class or caste (*varṇadharma*) and the highest value (*mokṣa*) he ought to attain. The first of these three will be taken up immediately in Chapter 12, the second in Chapter 13 and the third in Chapter 14.

NOTES AND REFERENCES

1. *Mahabharata, Karnaparva*: 39–62.
2. *Yatoabhyudayanihśreyasasiddhih sa dharmah.* Morality (moral living) is that which leads to the attainment of the well-being and highest objective (of all these who cultivate it).
   Vaiśeṣikasūtropaskāra, Vaiśeṣikasūtra with Śankara Miśra's commentary Upaskāra, trans. by Dhundhirāja Śāstrī, ed. by Nārāyana Miśra (Choukhambha, Varanasi), p. 11.
3. *Aṣṭādaśa purāṇānām sāram sāram samuddhṛtam. Paropakārah puṇyāya pāpāya parapīḍanam.* Quoted by B.G. Tilak in his *Gitārahasya*, p. 90.
4. See *Kaṭhopaniṣad*, I.ii.1–3.
5. *Dharma eva hato hanti, dharmorakṣati rakṣatah. Tasmāddharmo na hantavyo, māno dharmo hatoavadhīt. Manusmṛti.*, 8.15.
   When *dharma* (morality) is destroyed, it destroys (its destroyer). When *dharma* is protected, it protects (its protector). Therefore, *dharma* ought not to be destroyed, may not *dharma* destroy all of us (who destroy or violate it).
6. *Kāmasūtra*, p. 23.
7. *Kāmasūtra*, 2.36, p. 39, also see 2.37, p. 41.
8. *Mahābhārata, Svargārohaṇaparva*, 5.62.
9. Ibid., *Vanaparva*, 313.114.
10. Ibid., 313.117.
11. Ibid., 68: 12–26.
12. Ibid., 68: 59–90.
13. Ibid., 69: 16.
14. Ibid., 69: 14.
15. Ibid., *Sāntiparva*, 50.19.
16. *Ayodhyākanda*: 63 and 64.
17. *Karṇaparva*, 38–49.
18. *Vedah, Smṛtih sadācārah svaysya ca priyamātmanah. Etaccaturviddam prāhuh sākṣāddharmasya lakṣaṇam. Manusmṛti*, 2.12.
19. Vālmīki, *Rāmāyaṇa, Kiṣkindhā Kānda*, 18.1–28.
20. *Mahābhārata, Karṇaparva*, 91.1–30.

CHAPTER 12

Morally Good Life through Inculcation of Virtue (*Sāmānya Dharma*)

12.1 VIRTUE AS CHARACTER-TRAIT: A COHERENTIST APPROACH

It has already been shown in this work, and is an acknowledged fact of history, that Indian ethics, or ethical theorizing, has developed, by and large, in the context of a social order consisting of four main *varṇas* or castes. Even the philosophical-theological schools, like the *Jaina* and *Bauddha*, or the neglected *Cārvāka*, which do not accept the caste-system, have developed their ethics in that very context, not only in the sense that they have tried to antidote some of the prescriptions and prohibitions prevalent in the *varṇa*-system ethics, but in the positive sense that they accept, or do not outrightly reject, some of the things prevalent in the ethics given by the philosophies which accept the caste-system. Among these things are what the *varṇa*-ethics calls *sāmānya dharmas*, i.e. virtues which, at least in principle, are worth inculcating by every individual irrespective of the caste to which he belongs. The common assumption here is that to live well in a moral sense, i.e. to lead a morally good life, is to live through the inculcation of a set of virtues. A morally good life, or, to be brief, a good life, is thus conceived as a virtuous life, and the latter is said to consist in respecting, cultivating, or inculcating, certain morally desirable traits of character. Traits are called *sāmānya dharmas*, i.e. *common* or general virtues, because they are not caste-bound or caste-restricted; rather, they are common or universal in the sense that everyone is free and advised or required to have them to make his life morally good.

A *sāmānya dharma* is a trait of character because it is a feature of the character of the individual who has inculcated it, and not an external object like the *artha puruṣārtha*, wealth, i.e., wealth which he has honestly acquired, nor like a pleasure (*kāma puruṣārtha*) he has experienced. It is a trait of character also in an ethically richer, or more contentual, sense that its possession adds to the morality of the possessor's character, or heightens the moral value of his character. That is, its possession can very well be said to be a constituent of his moral character, and in some cases even of his having a commendable character in a more general sense. That is why, using a somewhat cumbrous phaseology, it may be said to be a characterological property in the sense of being a morally good-character-making property, just as a woman's naturally possessing the property of caring for her newly born child may be said to be a biological property in the sense of a biologically good-mother-making property. Because of this feature of it, the inculcation of such a trait of character, or virtue, may be said to be an obligation of an individual in the sense that he *ought to* inculcate it. But even then a virtue will remain a character-trait of the individual who has fulfilled this obligation and not the attainment of an external good. All this will be clearer as we proceed in elaborating the nature of some of the virtues, or even when we mention the things which are generally accepted as virtues, or *sāmānya dharmas*, in Indian ethos.

Some generally accepted virtues are benevolence, hospitality to guests who may even be strange and not necessarily known or friendly people, feeding stray animals, respecting elders, offering homage to dead forefathers, kindness, patience, forgiveness, promise-keeping, honesty, non-violence, non-stealing, truth-telling, self-control, controlling or subjugating disposition for sensual enjoyments, charity, courage, attentiveness to what one does, sexual purity, cleanliness, pursuit of knowledge, non-attachment, absence or complete control of feelings like those of anger, greed, lust, pride, envy or jealousy and hatred for anyone, etc. Manu has arranged in a string ten virtues which he calls the ten components or constituents of *dharma*, meaning by *dharma* general morality which everyone has to honour and practice in his life. He does not add a closure clause to his list of virtues to the effect that nothing other than the ten is a virtue. This is natural because he is aware of the other virtues which are mentioned by other thinkers or occur in other works. The ten constituents of morality, according to him, are patience (*dhṛti*), forgiveness (*kṣamā*), self-control, i.e. control of mental propensities (*dama*), non-stealing (*asteya*), cleanliness (*śauca*), control over senses (*indriyanigraha*), morally commendable development of intellect (*dhī*), scholarship or knowledge (*vidyā*) truthfulness (*satya*), and non-anger (*akrodha*).[1]

A *sāmānya dharma* or virtue, being a trait of character, obviously is, as has been said, a component of an individual's character, or rather, of good character. 'Good character' sometimes is used in a very exclusive sense in which a man is said to have a good character if he simply possesses sexual purity, i.e. if he does not commit any sexual lapse. Then, in spite of his having several other virtues, if he is loose in his sexual behaviour, he would be, in this sense of good character, a man of bad, or loose, character. And, in spite of his not having some other virtues, if he leads a sexually pure life, he would be a man of good character. His sexual purity is enough to make his character good and sexual impurity enough to make it bad. There is also a second, a little more inclusive, sense of good character in which one needs to have, besides sexual purity, some other virtues as well to be a man of good character. These virtues are generally those which we nowadays call moral virtues, like those of honesty, dutifulness, gratefulness to benefactors, truthfulness, promise-keeping, respect for parents and elders, benevolence, etc. This is the general, normal, sense in which the term 'good character' is ordinarily used. There is also a third, a still more inclusive or comprehensive sense than the second, in which to have good character one needs to have, in addition to moral virtues, some other virtues as well which may be intellectual, aesthetic, or prudential or pragmatic, in a positive normative sense.

In Manu's list of *virtues*, there occurs the names of virtues which, some would say, are not necessary for having a morally good character. For example, there is mentioned in the list *vidyā* which means scholarship or knowledge. Many would say that an individual may be a very good scholar and yet his character may not be morally good. For example, Rāvaṇa, the tradition says, is a very good scholar but his life-style is not only morally not commendable but, rather, highly condemnable. The same is true of Duryodhana. Even Bhīṣma, Droṇa, Kripa, et al., are good scholars but still fail to have the moral strength to tell Duryodhana not to ask Duhśāsana to derobe Draupadī. Similarly, one may not be a scholar and yet have a good moral character. For example, Vibhīṣaṇa, the step-brother of Rāvaṇa, is, as claimed by the tradition, much inferior to Rāvaṇa in scholarship but in morals very superior to him. The *Mahābhārata* mentions one Dharmavyādha, a meat-seller, nowhere near any *ṛṣi* (saint) in wisdom, but still leading a life morally very commendable. This example is also relevant for an issue in the theory of *varṇa* ethics. Therefore, it will be discussed in some detail in the next chapter. Perhaps Manu's or other thinkers' treating knowledge as a virtue relevant to morality is meant to suggest that one must have enough epistemic ability in the sense of rational maturity in order to lead a morally good life. In this sense *vidyā* can definitely be said to be a constituent of good moral character. It is obvious that one must have a sufficiently good moral common sense, or rationality, to have an understanding of what is, and what is not, morally right in order to do the former and abjure doing the latter.

It also seems possible, in fact extremely plausible, to hold that Manu and other writers on the *Dharmasūtras* have in mind what has been called above a very comprehensive view of good human character. That is, Manu's ten virtues, or the other virtues mentioned before, are considered in classical Indian ethos necessary in order for any individual to have an all-round good or commendable character. That is why if knowledge (*vidyā*) is called an intellectual virtue, patience (*dhṛtih*) may be called a pragmatic or prudential virtue, and telling a truth in a pleasant or elegant manner an aesthetic virtue. We can thus say that classical ethicists' list of virtues cover not only the constituent virtues of a morally good character but of good character per se, i.e. of one in a very comprehensive sense covering all, or almost all, aspects of human life. That patience may not be called a moral virtue in a restrictive sense of the term is obvious from the fact that a highly moral man may not be patient. Rather, he may even be extremely impatient to get an immorality immediately stopped, as is Vidura to get the attempt to derobe Draupadī immediately stopped. His impatience not only does not lower the morality of his character but in fact heightens it. And, that it is a prudential or pragmatic virtue is clear from the fact that an individual's patience may reduce the intensity of his own moral tension and may also dissuade him from rushing in to get a moral decision implemented and thereby land him in some trouble On the other hand, his impatience may sometimes be counterproductive by annoying the other person or persons who are to implement the decision he wants to be implemented in the soonest possible time. It may also give rise to a feeling of anger, which is considered to be a vice, in both the man who is impatient to get the decision implemented and in him who is to implement it. Therefore, by and large, patience remains a general virtue, not necessarily moral, and so is the case with knowledge and many other traits of character considered virtuous or desirable in Indian ethics.

Normally, general virtues, in the Indian ethos, are such traits of character which are supposed to make a man's character good in an *organismic* sense. It is possible that the specific traits which constitute what we call good moral character in a restrictive sense, form a subset of these traits. Rather, it is assumed in Indian ethics that this is always the case. This point will become clearer if we expand a little further the notion of a character being good in an organismic sense. From what has been said so far, it is obvious that the virtues of a man make his character good (and therefore their opposites, vices, make it bad). But simply the possession of some *virtues* as isolated, independent, traits do not do that. The virtues do that only if they are organized in such a coherent manner that none of them is so greatly inflated that it hurts some other important virtue and leads to some obviously evil consequence or consequences. This is illustrated very well by the *ṛṣi* Kauśika's extremist kind of fascination for telling the truth and only the truth, no matter what his truth-telling results in.

We have seen that because of Kauśika's telling the truth about the place where some innocent men are hiding themselves, their marauders find them out and kill them. Here the *ṛṣi* has an excessive, or rather a fanatic, attachment to truth-telling without care for whether or not it conflicts with some other virtue in any particular case. In the present case it conflicts with the virtue of saving some innocent people's lives. This means that his set of virtues is not well-ordered, i.e., his virtues are not related with one another in such a manner that they form an organismic or coherent set. His virtue of truth-telling hurts the virtue of non-injury or non-violence (*ahimsā*). He possesses a lot of other virtues as well, like knowledge, patience, self-control, non-anger, non-stealing, etc., etc. But because of the non-organismic or non-coherent natural of the set they make, and the resulting character of his which they constitute, his character's total rating is not very high. Rather, it seems to be very low because, on account of his truthfulness's causing the murder of the hidden innocent people, he is sent to hell after his death. This example may be called mythical. But it is a good enough instance substantiating our claim that the Indian theory of virtues, or *sāmānya dharma*s, is one of *virtue coherentism,* some sort of an organismic virtue-theory.

Virtue-coherentism, to be made practical, requires that some ordering or relative grading of virtues is provided; that is, when a list of virtues is given, a principle is also given showing which virtue is higher than which other or others so that an individual may prefer the higher to the lower if the two conflict in any situation. But classical thinkers do not seem to have provided a list fortified with such a principle.

Arranging virtues on a ladder or scale is a philosophical, theoretical, largely conceptual, exercise. It can be done properly only by a conceptually sophisticated philosopher, and not by a writer of mythology or a chronicler of moral or practical principles. But classical Indian technical philosophers do not seem to have taken up this task and the writers of the *Purāṇa*s and *Dharmasūtra*s are not interested in such a conceptual, logical, exercise. Perhaps this is the reason that we do not find a scalar organization or systematization of virtues; only contexts are available which show that sometimes one particular virtue is to be given preference over some other or others.

The *Jain*s do seem to maintain that non-violence is the highest virtue to which all others are subjugated. But this is, as we shall see a little later, a fallout of their metaphysics and not the result of a conceptual grading of virtues by examining pro and con reasons for not treating any other virtue higher than, or equal in moral merit to, non-violence. They too do not, like others, provide a scalar ordering of virtues, mentioning the criterion or criteria which make one virtue higher than another. It is true of many works which talk about virtues, or about this or that particular virtue, that when they talk about *any* specific virtue, say, kindness, forgiveness, non-violence, etc., they extol it so much that they seem to put it at the pinnacle of the ladder of virtues. It also happens sometimes that the same work in another context, or another work in a similar context, does the same thing in its praise for another virtue. Such cases make the task of the modern conceptual philosopher extremely difficult in determining any scalar arrangement of virtues in Indian virtue theory. But it would not be proper to conclude from this practice of theirs that classical thinkers are not aware of this problem. It seems to me that they consider all virtues to be, prima facie, i.e. in principle, worth cultivating. But the issue of determining which one should be given preference over which other in a context of conflict, they leave it to the judgement of the individual who has to make the decision. And, they seem to assume that by analysing the relevant facts of the case, appealing to any one of the sources of moral or normative knowledge given by them and considered by the individual most appropriate in that context, and by using his rational equipment (*vidyā*), he can generally make the right decision. Perhaps this is why they consider knowledge (*vidyā*), an intellectual or conceptual virtue, a necessary constituent of good character, or rather of good personhood.

To leave this matter to the individual is not, speaking philosophically, a reprehensible device. Whatever sources of moral knowledge may be available to him, which one is relevant in which situation and how it is to be used, only he has to decide because only he is to use it in his moral deliberation. His moral deliberation is *his* deliberation, and he can conduct it only in the way he is capable of doing, i.e. only in the way his *vidyā*, his intellectual equipment, enables him to do. If he blindly decides as advised, or dictated, by someone else, it ceases to be his decision and therefore his moral decision, and therefore he deserves no credit or discredit for it. Anybody's moral decision, to be a moral decision, has to be a process of free decision arrived at on the basis of *his* own understanding of the nature of the relevant facts of the case and his application of the available relevant moral principle of grading, or even his own grading, of the relevant virtues if more than one virtue is relevant in the situation. This is so because moral, or any evaluative, decision-making, is a non-*mechanical* process, something like what is called chewing the cud. That is why we have said that classical Indian thinkers' not giving a scalar account of virtues to be mechanically implemented and leaving it to the individual to decide which virtue to exemplify when, i.e. to himself do the act of chewing the cud, is quite fair to the character of moral or evaluative, or in fact any sort of genuine decision-making.

12.2 SOME SPECIMENS OF VIRTUES (*SĀMĀNYA DHARMAS*): COMPASSION (*KARUṆĀ*)

Any one of the terms 'compassion', 'kindness', 'mercy', etc. can be taken to mean *karuṇā*, which in the Indian ethos, is used as an equivalent of the Sanskrit words *dayā*, *kṛpā*, etc. A devotee addresses his god equally correctly when he calls him *karuṇasāgara*, *dayāsāgara*, or *kṛpāsāgara*, etc., each one meaning an ocean of compassion (or of kindness, mercy, etc.). In the present discussion we shall follow the some linguistic convention.

Compassion is not explicitly included in Manu's list of virtues. But it would not be inappropriate if his list is expanded to include it. This we say because there is nothing in his list with which it would not cohere, or with which it would collide. In fact the entire corpus of classical Indian ethical thought, or rather culture, Brāhmanical as well as non-brahmanical, considers compassion as an important virtue, though Buddhism has emphasized it perhaps more than other systems have. The Jains put non-violence at the apex of the system of virtues. But the concept of non-violence is very closely connected with that of compassion. He who wants to be non-violent cannot be unkind and the kind man cannot be violent. This is so because to do any violence to any creature is to do something unkind to him, and vice versa.

Even Indian poetry very greatly honours the virtue or value of kindness. As already referred to in an earlier chapter, the first Indian poet (*ādikavi*) Vālmīki spouts spontaneously the first two lines of his poetry out of his intense feeling of compassion. They are not composed by him through an exercise of his poetic or scholarly will, because at that point he is not a poet. As the account goes, one day he sees a pair of birds engaged in sexual union hit by a fowler's arrow, which kills the male bird. The female starts crying at her partner's death and her cries arouse in Vālmīki a deep sense of pathos or compassion. This experience of compassion gets spontaneously expressed in a couplet, the first two lines of Indian poetry, which comes out of his mouth automatically without any effort of will on his part (*Rāmāyaṇa, Bāla Kānda*: 2.15). It is after this that he writes the famous epic, the *Rāmāyaṇa*, the first example of Indian epic poetry. This example of his experience of compassion leading to the blossoming of his poetic genius is very relevant in a discussion of virtues, because it illustrates the aesthetic, i.e. normative, ennobling character of the experience of compassion. So it is no wonder that classical Indian ethos gives compassion a place of great honour in man's moral life, or rather in leading a noble life per se.

The experience of compassion consists in feeling sad, or in having an experience of suffering, because of knowing in some way that another creature, human or non-human, is experiencing some suffering. In Vālmīki's case, the suffering creature is a bird and not a human being.

Limiting the discussion to human beings, we can characterize the essence of the feeling of compassion by saying that the suffering felt by a man on account of the suffering of someone else would be compassion only if that someone is not related to him in any intimate manner. Gautama's feeling sad on finding mankind suffering a lot on account of disease, old age, death, etc., is the clearest example of compassion. The sufferers are not related to him in any close manner. The only relation that exists between him and them is specific, i.e. the relation of belonging to the same species since they too are human beings. That is why Gautama's feeling of sadness is unquestionably one of compassion. Rāma's feeling of suffering on account of Sītā's suffering caused to her by Rāvaṇa's abducting her is not a feeling compassion. Her suffering is virtually Rāma's own suffering because she is his wife, because there is an intimate bond of relationship between the two. Nor is Rāma's feeling sad for Sugrīva's suffering caused to him by his elder brother Vāli's abducting his wife a feeling of compassion, because Rāma has contracted friendship with Sugrīva and promised to kill Vāli and free Sugrīva's wife in return for which Sugrīva has promised to help him in freeing his wife Sītā from Rāvaṇa. One friend's unhappiness virtually becomes the unhappiness of the other friend if the friendship is genuine and sincere. It is this feature of compassion, i.e. its being a feeling of suffering caused in the compassionate by the suffering of any other human being who has no personal tie with him, which makes it a moral virtue. It is for the same reason rated higher than the feeling of suffering experienced by a man for some other man's suffering when the other man is his kith and kin, or related to him because of some contractual agreement between the two.

Compassion, like any other virtue, has built into it a great motivational pull which is fundamentally an ethical pull. It motivates the compassionate to do whatever he can to alleviate the suffering condition of the other. Since he is another person, not his kith and kin, or related to him on account of any contractual relationship, alleviating, or even trying to alleviate, his condition is a benevolent work. That is why the feeling of compassion is an ethical motivative feeling. Therefore, it can be very well said to be an agency contributive to the production of social and societal well-being. For the same reason of its being an aid to benevolence, it also works as an agent of social control in the sense that it restrains the compassionate man from doing anything which hurts the interest of the other or others towards whom he feels compassionate. In this way it can be a good agent for producing social cohesion. These two features, i.e. those of being promotive of social well-being and protective of or contributive to social control of the individual, are the common features of all general virtues (*sāmānya dharmas*). *Compassion*'s possession of these two features is conclusively demonstrated by Gautama's own example. Because of his compassion he gives up his kingdom, his princely status, his wife and sleeping baby son, and embarks on the spiritual path of searching for a permanent solution for the elimination (or reduction to the maximum) of all sorts human miseries. The result is his giving to the world what we call his Buddhist ethics which provides not only ways to individuals to lead a suffering-free life but also ways and grounds for reconstructing a casteless human social order.

The strongest opposite of compassion is cruelty which is taken to be an intrinsic evil or vice. But even indifference to the condition of an individual, the proper response to which is compassion, would also be a moral deficiency. For example, the indifference of Bhīṣma, Droṇa, et al, to the wailing of Draupadī when she is being derobed, which definitely deserves compassion or even active intervention, to get the derobing attempt stopped, is felt by every morally sensitive individual to be a sign of a great moral lapse on their part.

It is obvious from the above discussion that the feeling of compassion as well as acting as prompted by it presupposes a social order with different strata of people. He who suffers and deserves compassion for his suffering naturally occupies a lower stratum on the social ladder than he who is kind to him and in a position to do something to ameliorate his condition. That is why had there been only one individual and no other, he would have got no opportunity to experience kindness towards another individual. Doing charity (*dāna*) is a common way to express one's kindness to the individuals to whom it is done, and it is very highly valued in the classical Indian ethos. We have seen that Jānaśruti is treated as a highly morally elevated person because of his charities. But charity is also a social virtue which can be practised only in a society which has some rich and some poor, needy, people to whom the rich can give something to enable them to meet at least some of their needs. A society which has only affluent, self-supporting, people will have no place for kindness or charity. Classical Indian society had different strata of people, a good number of them belonging to the lowest, poorest, class of *śūdras*. But it is strange that when kindness or charity is talked about, it is seldom mentioned that one should be kind towards them or do charity to help them. Charity is generally recommended, or sometimes prescribed, to be done to *brāhmaṇas* or hermits who too are generally *brāhmaṇas*.

Some virtues, we shall see, admit of exceptions in the sense that the principles requiring them to be practised may not be considered violated if an exception is made to them in certain situations. It seems to me, however, that the Indian tradition does not *require* that we should feel no compassion towards someone's suffering in some specific situations. As a mere feeling, it may not be improper, according to it, to have compassion towards even a recidivist, i.e. a person who continues committing crimes even after having been punished, or pardoned, for some earlier crimes or crimes of his. But whether or not in the dispensation of legal justice the punishment deserved by a criminal should be tempered with mercy and therefore waived, or toned done in its severity if his circumstances arouse compassion in the mind of the judge, is an issue which does not seem to have been discussed by classical Indian philosophical ethicists. Whether or not the classical jurists have discussed it and taken some definite position on it, it is difficult for a philosopher to opine on. But it seems, and there is a good ground to say, that it is highly probable that they would not like to let compassion affect the severity of a punishment considered legally proper for a certain kind of crime. If the general condition of any class of people in classical India deserved compassion, it was the condition of the *śūdras* whose only *dharma* (obligation) was to serve the members of the other three upper classes. They had no right to own any property, and the use of sexually their women for sexual gratification was permissible for members of the upper classes. But instead of recommending compassion towards them, the law-givers prescribe a severer punishment for a *śūdra* for having committed a crime than the one they prescribe for a similar crime committed by a member of any of the upper classes. Manu, for example, says that if a *śūdra* abuses any twice-born individual, i.e. any member of the *brāhamaṇa, kṣatriya,* or *vaiśya,* caste, then his tongue should be chopped off; if he abuses him by naming his caste, then a ten-finger-long red-hot iron rod should be forced into his mouth; if he egoistically preaches moral precepts to a *brāhmaṇa,* then the king should get boiling oil dropped into his mouth and ears, etc. (*Manusmṛti,* 8.270-71-72). No such harsh punishment is prescribed for any non-*śūdra* for a similar, or even a greater, crime.

It is also worth noting that even the preaching of a moral precept by a *śūdra* is considered to be a crime and a serious one, not an ordinary lapse, extremely severely punishable. By no standard, even in Indian ethics, is the act of preaching a moral precept as such a crime, as is killing an innocent person, or even telling a lie. But it becomes a crime, as per Manu, if the act is done by a *śūdra.* This is a strange doctrine, a doctrine which makes an act a crime not for there being any criminality or wrongdoing in the act itself, but for the simple reason of its doer's belonging to a certain class or caste. And, the doer belongs to that caste not because of his own choice but because of society's, more specifically the society of the three upper castes, putting him in that caste.

It is not only the *Manusmṛti* which records a prescription for such punishments to *śūdras*. Even some other respectable works do the same thing. *Āpāstambadharmasūtra* (1.27.14–17) says that if a *śūdra* abuses a twice-born, his tongue should be chopped off; if while speaking, walking, remaining on his bed, or sitting, he poses to be equal to him, he should be beaten (or caned); if he kills someone, steals someone's property, he should be killed and deprived of all of his belongings. If a *brāhmaṇa,* on the other hand, commits any one of these crimes, only his eyes should be bandaged (so that he may not see). The *Gautamadharmasūtra* says (1.12.1–7) that if a *śūdra* abuses or physically hurts a twice-born, the part of his body used in the crime should be chopped off. If he indulges in sex with a twice-born woman, his sexual organ should be cut off and his belongings taken away. If that woman has a husband or son, the *śūdra* should be killed.

If he listens to a *Vedic* recitation, then some hot molten metal or glass should be poured into his ears. If he himself recites it, his tongue should be cut off, and if memorizes it, his body should be cut into pieces, etc.

If, in the administration of criminal law and dispensation of justice in order to punish a criminal, any tempering of justice with mercy to make the punishment a little lighter were allowable, it should have been so in the case of a *śūdra* criminal. It should have been, because of his backwardness, lack of education, unavailability of opportunities for inculcating virtues, etc., i.e. his having been the victim of what modern moral philosophers call moral bad luck. But what we find is that the Indian legal ethicists, instead of prescribing some leniency in awarding punishment to him, are more stringent and require him to be severely, indeed cruelly, punished, even for doing something which is no crime at all, for example, listening to, repeating, memorizing, etc. a *Vedic* teaching. Therefore, it seems to me that Indian ethicists, or law-makers or law-users, are not in favour of tempering justice with mercy. It may be urged that they are in favour of doing that in the case of the upper castes. For example, they do hold that a *brāhmaṇa* is not liable to capital punishment whatever be his crime, as is evidenced by the *Manusmṛti* 8.380, *Baudhāyanadharmasūtra* 1.18.17, and many other works. But this is not tempering criminal justice; it is really tempering it with what I call *varṇa*-bias or brahmanical bias of *brāhmaṇa* ethicists or legal experts.

For anyone who does not subscribe to the view that such an apparently unjustified dispensation of the award of punishment to a *śūdra* is due to any brahmanical bias, it remains an almost unsolvable problem why, after all, this system of criminal justice is promulgated or approved of by the then law-givers who are also considered to be great *ṛṣis* or morally elevated individuals. The *karmic* worldview of Indian philosophy seems to solve it definitively. But if it is admitted or claimed that it does, it solves it by making totally *unjustified* and *futile* the very experience of compassion as well as the steps it may motivate the compassionate to take. According to it the suffering (or happiness) which an individual undergoes is the consequence of some action or actions (*prārabddha karma*) of his done in his previous birth, which have matured and started yielding their results. These results or effects he *deserves*, i.e. is *obligated*, to experience, and he necessarily has to undergo this experience. Since he deserves it, it is morally wrong and therefore unjustified to do anything which comes in the way of his undergoing it. Since it is also *necessary* that he undergoes it, it is futile to take any step to reduce his suffering. Therefore, on account of an unavoidable emotional push, like an urge to scratch an itch, caused by our sensitivity, we may feel compassion for him, but we ought not to, and cannot, take any step, prompted by our compassion, to help him out. In fact, the general question of tempering justice with mercy in anybody's case by any judge becomes now a non-question. The general problems which the *karmic* worldview raises for ethics in Indian ethos will be discussed in some detail in Chapter 15.

Whatever the *karmic* worldview may imply about the justifiability and practical utility of our experience of compassion, it is a moral fact, i.e. a fact of moral living, that compassion is a commendable moral trait of character, a trait that at least is one of the chief features which distinguish between a man and an animal, or even between a cultured, decent man and an ill-bred, insensitive one. Therefore, if the *karmic* worldview has the implication mentioned above, the implication tells on the viability of the *karmic* theory itself because of its disloyalty or insensitivity to the nature of morality, to the hard facts of moral life.

It is feelings like those of compassion, benevolence, liberalness, etc. which nourish the moral calibre of man by motivating him to care for the welfare of others and generate in him the necessary motivative desires to take appropriate steps for others' welfare. That is why any philosophical, religious, or (allegedly) ethical theory, which prescribes that all feelings, emotions, and desires be gotten rid of, is bound to impoverish man's moral equipment and thereby the quality of his entire life. We shall see in Chapter 15 that the theory of *niṣkāma karma* also has to face some problems if it is taken to mean a theory which prescribes the elimination of all desires.

It is true that compassion, when used injudiciously or indiscriminately, can produce morally undesirable consequences. For example, if one is kind even to a recidivist and lets him off unpubished, one may encourage him to go on committing crimes. This will be a misuse of compassion. It is possible to misuse any moral virtue, and the misuse of any virtue may cause undesirable results. But all this does not negate the fact that some feelings and desires enrich man's moral sensitivity and the quality of his life. It is for this reason that the great Hindi writer Ramachandra Shukla says that 'the ethicists' and theologians' precept of getting rid of all feelings and desires is sheer hypocrisy or pretentiousness'.[2]

It is proper to emphasize, thus, the appreciation of the value of compassion as a virtue. But it is also important to realize that its value must not be described in hyperbolic terms, as the *Padmapurāṇa* (*Pātālakhaṇḍa* 98.15,27,23) does. It says that 'to compassion no other virtue is equal or comparable in merit, neither an austere religious practice (*tapa*), nor any charity, nor any friend. Only he is a morally elevated person who helps suffering people. He is to be treated as a god's man. In our view, neither the happiness one gets in heaven, nor the bliss he gets in *mokṣa* equals the happiness he gets as a result of relieving anyone's suffering (out of compassion).'

Buddhism too extols the value of compassion to the highest extent. While discussing the issue of whether or not a *bodhisattva* can violate any one of the general Buddhist precepts, there occurs in *Bodhicaryāvatāra* (V.84) the following: '... a *bodhisattva* should always be diligent in the interests of others. Even what is forbidden is allowable for one who seeks the welfare of others with compassion.[3]

This style of characterizing compassion in such bold colours as if it were the highest, or supersessive, of all virtues, is not to be taken literally. Rather, it seems to be a style which classical writers generally use in characterizing a virtue in order to emphasize its importance. It is not that the *Padmapurāṇa* does not realize the importance of other virtues because it talks about compassion in glowing terms. The same is the case with Buddhism. Though it emphasizes compassion quite often, it does not ignore other virtues. In fact, for the Indian ethical tradition no virtue can be realized in full by completely ignoring any other. Good moral life has to have an equilibrium of its own which suggests that in some condition some virtue may have to be given preference over some other virtue in order to maintain moral equilibrium which is nothing but cohesion in personal and public life. This implies that no virtue is categorical or unconditional in the sense that it is to override all others in all conditions. The obviousness of this point will be further strengthened when we consider the nature of some of other virtues according to classical Indian ethics.

It is important to remember here that no conceptual, philosophical, or theoretical, analysis of any virtue is available in any classical work. That is why a good amount of reconstructive analysis and reorganization of the ideas classical works needs to be done when attempting to give a philosophical account of Indian virtue ethics. This we have done in our account of compassion and shall be doing all along in the account of the other virtues presented in this chapter.

But before we take up another virtue, one general feature of all virtues has to be taken note of. We have been speaking of the feeling of kindness (or compassion) as the virtue of kindness. This mode of speaking is quite in order, as it is to say that a man who has inculcated the virtue of kindness feels kind towards a suffering creature. But to understand the real *intent* of it we have to be aware of the fact that just feeling kind on a particular occasion will not entitle a man to be called one who has inculcated the virtue of kindness. There would hardly be a man who does not feel kind at least once in his life towards someone. Though to be kind is to feel kind, it is not to feel kind in a merely episodic manner. It is rather to have cultivated the *disposition* to feel kind in appropriate conditions. That is why classical Indian thinkers speak of the virtue of kindness as *dayabhāva, karuṇāpravaṇatā,* which signify the *attitude to feel kind* on suitable occasions. Thus, every virtue, or *sāmānya dharma,* is a disposition, or attitude, to feel a certain kind of feeling and to be prone to act in a certain way as prompted by that feeling on that occasion. It is in this sense of feeling that Buddhism speaks of the *bodhisattva* as motivated to work for the welfare of others out of his feeling of compassion for them. Even the *Padmapurāna*'s *dayā* (kindness), so much eulogized, is a disposition to feel kind and not merely to experience the feeling of kindness in one, or a few, episodes in one's life. Keeping all this in mind we can now turn, in the next section, to forgiveness, another important virtue in Indian ethics.

12.3 FORGIVENESS (*KṢAMĀ*)

Kindness, as we have seen in the previous section, is a man's reactive attitude towards the suffering of someone else. Forgiveness too is a man's reactive attitude but one towards the wrong done to him by another individual, subject to the wrongdoer's satisfying certain conditions. A reactive attitude is reactive because it is formed and activated by a person as a reaction or response to something pertaining to another person or to some action done by him. It is an attitude in the sense that it is a well-seated disposition of his to feel a certain kind of feeling or emotion towards some condition of, or some action done by, the other person *and* to *act* in some appropriate way in relation to him. For example, kindness is one's reaction to some suffering, or painful condition, of another person and a disposition to *feel* sad for him and to take some appropriate steps to end or reduce his suffering. Similarly, forgiveness is also *reactive* in the sense that it is a *reaction* to someone's wrongdoing, and *attitudinal* because it is a *disposition to act* in relation to the wrongdoer, for example, to stop taking any action against him for his wrongdoing, or to free him from the agonizing feeling of repentance he is experiencing on account of his wrongdoing, etc. Therefore, forgiveness, too, like *kindness,* is a *social virtue,* i.e. a virtue which can be cultivated or exemplified only in a society consisting of at least two members and which has some institutions or norms according to which some doings are wrongdoings and justify or call for some punitive steps or revengeful actions in response to them. We shall see soon that kindness and forgiveness are very closely related to each other, and both of them are equally closely related to non-violence. In fact, all general virtues are interrelated or related very closely with each other. The result is that if, in a list of virtues given by a philosopher, a particular virtue does not (visibly) appear, we cannot blame him for not including it or for not considering it a virtue. We cannot do that because, by analysing the scope and working of some other virtue on his list, he can, if he has the needed logical acumen, show that the virtue not visibly present in his list is comprehended in the content of some other virtue visibly present therein and therefore it has not been ignored. It is true that the classical list-makers do not do such an exercise and therefore have been accused of ignoring some virtues by some modern, particularly Western, interpreters. But an unbiased analyst can show the baselessness of this accusation with only a little bit of logical ingenuity. We shall show, briefly, after a little while, by choosing only a few examples, how this can be done. But let us first see the conceptual framework of the working of the virtue of forgiveness.

Every general virtue is, we have said in 12.1, a trait of character. This mode of speaking is not a purely Western, or, as some would say, an Aristotelian, mode, though even its being Western would not entail its inapplicability to the description of the identity of a human quality considered to be a virtue in the classical Indian ethos. In fact, some of the classical works come very near calling, or even do call, a virtue a character-trait of a certain type. When we have said that it is one we too have meant that it is a character-trait which exercises some restraint or control over the behaviour of the individual whose character-trait it is. And, since every virtue plays a social role, or is exercisable in a society or social context, this self-control of the individual, which a virtue as a character-trait of his is, also becomes a principle or motivating agent of social control. It is a principle of self-control or self-restraint in the sense that through it the individual *himself* controls or restrains his behaviour in relation to some other member or members of his society. For example, a kind man, i.e. one who has the virtue of kindness, *himself* restrains his behaviour in relation to a suffering man by *not* letting himself remain indifferent to his suffering and by shaping his behaviour in such a way that it reduces his suffering, or if that is not possible, at least expressing the kind man's sympathy for him.

Therefore, every virtue may be called a principle or agent of self-restraint or of social control, a *yama*, since '*yama*' also means self-restraint or principle of self-restraint. '*Niyama*' on the other hand is used in classical Indian ethical language to mean a lesser restraint or a principle having lesser stringency, restraining power, or authority. In a broad sense, both, *yama* and *niyama* are restraining agents in the character of an individual and both are his character-traits. It is possible that one ethical system treats one virtue as having greater stringency than another and calls the former a *yama* and the latter a *niyama*, while another system does vice versa. But for both of the systems both of the virtues remain character-traits.

While saying all this, it is to be noted that *niyama* is also used sometimes to denote an external rule, i.e. a rule of action prescribed by some agency other than the individual who uses it as a rule having some authority to regulate his behaviour. Sometimes *niyama* is used to mean a virtue as a character-trait no doubt, but a trait mostly of his bodily behaviour, whereas *yama*, then in contrast with it, is used to mean largely a mental trait. But this distinction is fluid and we treat both *yama* and *niyama* here as character-traits of equal categorial status. Our main intention here is to show that the classical Indian ethos does use the mode of speaking adopted here, which calls a virtue a character-trait by calling some virtues *yamas* and some *niyamas*. For example, the *Skandapurāṇa* says that 'According to *Smṛtis* truthfulness, forgiveness, simplicity, meditation, non-cruelty (or kindness), non-violence, control of senses (mind and bodily senses), joyfulness (*prasāda*), sweet behaviour and politeness (or polite behaviour towards all), are the ten *yamas*. Cleanliness, bathing, austere religious practice (*tapa*), charity, silence (*mauna*), performing sacrifices, self-study, observance of religious vows (*vrata*), fasting, and suppression (or complete control, *damana*) of sex organs are the ten *niyamas*.'[4]

A statement, only slightly different from the *Skandapurāṇa*'s, is found in *Yājñavalkyasmṛti* (3.313) which asserts that 'celibacy, kindness, forgiveness, charity, truthfulness, cleanliness, non-evidence, non-stealing, sweet behaviour and self-control, etc. are the *yamas* according to the *Smṛtis*.' Some works mention only five *yamas* which comprise non-violence, truthfulness, celibacy, cleanliness, and non-stealing. In fact, the number of virtues given in any work need not be taken as sacrosanct. Different classical ethicists mention different sets of virtues with some common members in the sets, which appear to them basic in the contexts they present their list. They do not convey any implication to the effect that no other virtue is important. Moreover, each one of the virtues mentioned in every list is conceptually open-ended. Therefore, by analysing the conceptual content of some virtue in the list, a virtue not mentioned in the list can be shown to have been implicitly included in it, or the list can be shown to be capable of comfortably accommodating it without causing any disfigurement to its own structure. I think that classical thinkers realize very well that there is no point in trying to give a list of virtues claiming to be inclusive of all virtues and exclusive of none because in different contexts, or different ages, some virtues may become more or less important than some others, or even some new virtues may come up.

Returning to the virtue of forgiveness, the main theme of this section, we find that forgiveness too at many places has been presented in highly laudatory terms which seem to give the impression that it is the highest virtue in Indian ethics. For example, the widely read Buddhist work *Dhammapada* (6.2) says that one's inculcating sincerely the virtue of forgiveness is the highest religious-moral, the most austere, virtue (*tapa*). In later Buddhism, when the concept of *bodhisattva* gets formulated as denoting the highest human ideal before attaining *nirvāṇa*, forgiveness is considered to be a necessary character-trait of a *bodhisattva*. It is necessary for him in the sense that he has to have it in order to be a *bodhisattva*.[5] The *Bhāgavata Purāṇa* (1.7:41–48), through Draupadī, presents an example of forgiveness which gives the impression that forgiveness is the most lustrous of the general virtues. Her five sons have been killed by Aśvathāmā and she is grieving over the tragedy. Arjuna promises to her that he will kill Aśvathāmā and present to her his chopped off head. He catches hold of him, ties his body with a rope and produces him before her, ready to chop off his head. Aśvathāmā is standing before her with downcast eyes, visibly feeling guilty and repentant and sad and ashamed, as if not daring to ask her to forgive him. Draupadī sees all this in him, pardons him and asks Arjuna to let him free (*mucyatām mucyatām esa*). Even though he does not verbally ask to be pardoned, out of shame, she reads in his sorrowful eyes his prayer and gets him let off. Draupadī tells Arjuna and Kṛṣṇa that just as she, is crying for the killing of her sons, his mother, Gautamī, too, would cry if he is killed. This act of forgiveness definitely exhibits her extraordinary regard for forgiveness and thereby her highly elevated moral character.

By this example, as already said, the tradition's objective is simply to signify the place of honour which it gives to forgiveness. The highly laudatory way of saying it should be taken, as already pointed out, not literally, but only as a device to show the importance of forgiveness and not to say that it is the topmost virtue. This is what has been done in the case of kindness as shown in the preceding section.

It is to be noted here that the above example of Draupadī's forgiveness may well be taken as an exhibition of her kindness. This would not be wrong because the whole account in the *Bhāgavata Purāṇa* is presented in such a literary manner that one can do that without being unfair to the text. But there is also a good conceptual justification for doing that. The concept of kindness and that of forgiveness are so closely linked that we can easily go from one to the other. An unkind (*nirdaya*) man cannot be forgiving (*kṣamaśīla*) and an unforgiving (*kṣamahīna*) man cannot be kind. In fact, the Indian virtue-concepts are so open-textured, or contentually rich, as already shown, that its virtue-ethics cannot be accused of having ignored any viable virtue in its composite set of virtues even though its name may not appear in any individual set. We can easily show that the said-to-be-missing virtue is present in its womb. This exercise would not be very different from what Socrates does with some of the ancient Greek concepts, an exercise to which he gives the colourful name of philosophical midwifery.

To demonstrate what we have been maintaining here, we can right now dispose of the accusation made by quite a few *Christian writers* on Indian ethics that it does not give to social service the status or importance which it deserves as a moral value or virtue. This view is held even by those who wrote their works in India. For example, S. Cromwell Crawford, who was trained in a Christian theological seminary in Serampore in Bengal, does not find the virtue of social service even to have been mentioned in Manu's list. He admits that Praśastapāda recognizes it by including non-violence (*ahimsā*) and doing good to all creatures (*bhūtahitatva*) in his ethical theory. But still, Crawford feels, he does not attach to it the importance he should: to be more specific, the importance which Christianity attaches to it. I am not surprised at Crawford's not realizing that the virtue of social service can be analysed or drawn out of more than one virtue mentioned in this or that classical list of virtues by doing some sort of logical, Socratic, midwifery. The reason for my not being surprised is that *Crawford* is a scholar of theology or religion, not a philosopher, and therefore his not being able to *see* the logical capabilities of Indian virtue concepts, or moral concepts, is not something strange.[6]

A very similar position, rather more forthright in accusing Indian ethics of being non-cognizant of the moral value of social service and of definitely being for this reason weaker than Christian ethics, is taken by John Mckenzie who taught in Wilson College, Bombay, and was also more of a theologion than a pure philosopher.[7] As we have shown, the virtue of social service can be drawn out of any one of the concepts, kindness, forgiveness, charity, non-anger, non-stealing, non-violence, etc. And, if one does not want to do any conceptual analysis, if one simply remembers the Indian emphasis on the moral value of benevolence (*paropakāra*), one can say only on the pain of self-contradiction that Indian ethics ignores the value of social service, or does not give to social service the importance it has the right to have. It is important to note here that such virtue-terms as non-anger, non-stealing, non-violence, etc. are negative only in their linguistic form and not at all in their ethical content, or conduct-regulating-or-guiding role. For example, non-anger's positive content is sympathy or love, non-stealing's is respect for the other's property, non-violence's is respect for the dignity of the life of every living being. Even this much understanding of their positive content or intent is enough to exhibit that anyone who cultivates any one of these virtues cannot abstain from social service while sincerely conducting his life in a manner required of him by his adherence to this virtue.

Since forgiveness is exemplified only in a social context, in a society or social set-up consisting of at least two persons, let us note the general framework of this contextual set-up in its simplest, clearest, form. It is obvious that for the exemplification of this virtue, there must be at least two mature, adult, normal individuals sharing some common moral ideas, norms, values, etc., in such a manner that they can be said to form a moral community, or can be treated as members of the same moral community. Of the two, one does some moral wrong, or wrong, to the other, knowingly, intentionally, and freely, i.e. not inadvertently, accidentally, or pressurized or forced by someone else, and therefore can be held responsible for the wrong done. The wronged person takes or considers this action to be a wrongdoing and feels hurt, damaged, insulted, or disrespected, etc., and therefore resents or strongly disapproves of the person who has done wrong to him. He considers the wrongdoer guilty and may even avenge him for his having done it, of course, if he has the power and authority to do so. The social relation between the two is thus soured or ruptured. But if the wrongdoer, on later thinking, realizes his guilt, repents for having done it, and directly, or by his behaviour and appearance, expresses that he is sorry for having done it and requests the wronged person's pardon, the latter, on being convinced of his sincerity, forgives him. As a result of his forgiveness the social relation between the two may thus become normal as it was before the wrongdoer's wrongdoing.

A wronged person who is very weak, timid, or powerless, and therefore not at all in a position to avenge or punish his wrongdoer, therefore, may never have any opportunity to forgive his powerful wrongdoer. He has no alternative but to suffer the pangs of having been wronged and his wrongdoer may never repent for having wronged him and ask for being forgiven for his wrongdoing. If, on the other hand, the wronged weakling, on his own initiative, says to the masterly wrongdoer that he has forgiven him, the latter may take it to be a sign of his *weakness or cowardice.* Therefore, the issue of granting or not granting forgiveness takes its full-blooded exemplification only if the wronged person has the power and authority to avenge and punish the wrongdoer. That is why we admire him if, instead of punishing him, he forgives him and lets him go unpunished or gives him a lighter punishment than his wrongdoing requires him to undergo. This is the reason why forgiveness in the Indian tradition is said to be the ornament of the brave (*kṣamā vīrosya bhūṣaṇam*).[8]

What has been said above is well illustrated in the case of Draupadī's forgiving Aśvathāmā, in the example already given, even though he has committed the grievous crime of killing her five sleeping sons. Arjuna, her husband, has caught hold of him and is both able and willing to chop off his head as he has promised to do. She and Arjuna are thus in a position to avenge and give him the severest punishment which he also deserves. But they do not; on Draupadī's forgiving him, he is allowed to remain alive. The virtue of forgiveness is thus a fitting virtue of the powerful; that is why it is standardly, ordinarily, exemplifiable only in a society in which there is at least one man who has both the power and authority to punish one who has wronged him or any near and dear one of his, or in some cases, anyone. The *Mahābhārata* very aptly states this feature of it, or its fittingness for the powerful who has a genuine respect for morality, when it avers that the powerful always forgives while the powerless is always angry (because he has no power to avenge his wrongdoer).[9]

Draupadī, through Arjuna, and Arjuna himself, have the power to punish Aśvathāmā even by killing him. And killing him would have been retributively justified. But Arjuna does not kill him because Draupadī forbids him to do that when she sees Aśvathāmā in that condition and pardons him. For pardoning him, or for showing mercy towards him, she offers two reasons: his being the son of Arjuna's, or their family's, teacher, and the suffering that his death would cause his mother. She reminds Arjuna that it is the great skill in archery which his father Droṇa imparted to him which enabled him to win her in her *svayamvara* as well as to win the *Mahābhārata* war. Therefore, killing his son, the teacher's son (*guruputra*) would go against the important virtue (*dharma*) of gratitude and devotion to the teacher. Secondly, to kill him would make his mother Gautamī suffer grief of the kind she herself is undergoing as a result of her sons' having been killed. Therefore, letting him free, forgiving him (or being merciful to him), is concordant with the two other virtues, namely dutifulness-devotion to the teacher and abstinence from causing suffering to another (*ahimsā, paradukakātaratā*), whereas killing him, and therefore not pardoning him, would be discordant with both of them.

Arjuna had promised to Draupadī that he would present her with Aśvathāmā's chopped-off head. But he became convinced by her two reasons for letting him free without chopping his head off. This implies that the two reasons also justify his not fulfilling his promise. The clear meaning of this implication is that even promise-keeping is not an absolutely inviolable moral principle; that is, sometimes when promise-keeping is discordant with some other virtue, it may become exceptionable in spite of the fact that there are statements in Indian ethical literature which give the impression that it is never violable. This episode thus highlights two important features of Indian virtue ethics: The first is that the cultivation and exemplification of a moral virtue or principle has to be done in such a manner that, as far practicable, it is concordant with other virtues relevant in the situation concerned. The second is that to protect this concordance an exception may be made to the exemplification of a virtue or to the observance of a prior commitment if demanded by some moral features of the situation concerned.

Draupadī's asking Arjuna to let Aśvathāmā free unhurt, and Arjuna's unhesitatingly agreeing to do that on her asking, bring to light the very high moral character of both of them. Kṛṣṇa reminds Arjuna of his promise and the sanctity of it. But he too does not insist on Arjuna's fulfilling the promise literally, or in full. On his hint Arjuna does not chop off Aśvathāmā's head but only his hair along with the jewel placed on his head when he was born on account of which (jewel) he has his power and lustre. Therefore, his power is gone but he remains alive. Even this modified or milder way of fulfilling the premise shows that, according to Kṛṣṇa (or Indian ethics, since he is taken to be an exemplar of it), the rigour of promise-keeping is not always absolute, because in some circumstances it can be softened. But from all this it is also obvious that Draupadī, by asking Arjuna to let Aśvathāmā go free on the ground of the two good moral reasons, and Arjuna, by agreeing with her, shine in better moral light than does Kṛṣṇa. He thus loses at least a bit of his moral lustre by asking Arjuna to chop off Aśvathāmā's hair with the jewel and by getting his behest implemented by him. He seems to be different from them in being an ethical pragmatist and not an idealist. But then the difference between him and them would be a distinct kind of difference from that which can protect or preserve his moral dignity vis-á-vis theirs.

The issue which has become prominent here, with regard to the moral status of forgiveness, is that it is to be pursued only in a manner which is not glaringly discordant with some other virtue. This means that its moral value is conditional since it is to be pursued only if this condition, i.e. absence of discordance and presence of concordance with other virtues, is fulfilled. In fact, this is an important issue about all *samanya* (general *dharmas* virtues). Most, or almost all of modern interpreters think that every *sāmānya dharma* is categorical, i.e. a virtue never to be violated or transgressed. Let us therefore discuss this issue in the next section.

12.4 CONDITIONAL OR UNCONDITIONAL VALUE OF FORGIVENESS AND SOME OTHER VIRTUES

Before we take up this theme, let us make it clear right here that calling forgiveness, or any trait, a *sāmānya* or *sādhāraṇa*, i.e. general, virtue is *intended* to mean, as its grammatical form suggests, a virtue which *everyone* ought to inculcate. Modern interpreters also take the term *sāmānya dharma* to denote a virtue required of all human beings. But that is not really, in practice, the case. Every virtue which figures in this or that list of *sāmānya dharmas* cannot be required of everyone in the classical Indian social order. For example, in the *varṇa*-system, knowledge, which occurs in Manu's list of general virtues, cannot be required of a *śūdra* since he is not allowed to be admitted in a school for receiving education. Even forgiveness cannot obviously be required of him because he does not have the power to retaliate against or punish any member of the three upper castes. Even if it is required of him, this requirement may become defunct in his case. We have seen that forgiveness is a reactive response of a person to a moral wrong done to him by someone else if (a) the wrongdoer satisfies certain conditions, (b) the wronged person has the moral sensitivity to feel that something morally wrong has been done to him, and (c) the wronged person has the rational maturity to ascertain that the wrongdoer is genuinely repentant, etc. If anyone does not satisfy the conditions (b) and (c) he cannot be required to respond to the wrongdoer by forgiving him. A *śūdra*, as generally depicted in classical Indian literature, is not expected to satisfy these two conditions because of his not having been given adequate opportunities to be properly educated. And if, even then, he or anyone else who does not satisfy the conditions, is required to inculcate forgiveness, the requirement is bound to be defunct or infructuous.

The above general observation about forgiveness, or rather any general virtue, clearly signifies that forgiveness is a conditional virtue because it can be required not of everyone but only of those who possess certain abilities. But this is too general a condition. The question whether forgiveness is a conditional or unconditional, i.e. categorical, virtue has its arrow directed in a different direction. It queries whether or not, granting that one is competent to respond to a wrongdoer by forgiving him, it is morally right for one to forgive the wrongdoer, no matter who the wrongdoer is, why he does the wrong, what his mental condition is before and after the wrong done by him, whatever may happen as a result of forgiving him, etc. To give a positive answer to this query is to hold that forgiveness is a virtue in *all* conditions, i.e. an unconditional, or categorical, virtue. On the other hand, to give a negative answer, i.e. to hold that it is morally right to forgive him only if he satisfies a certain set of conditions, is to hold that it is only a conditional, non-categorical, virtue.

In the Indian ethical tradition both the positions have been held, the position that forgiveness (or every character-trait called a general virtue) is an unconditional virtue, and the opposite one that it is only a conditional virtue. From the implications of the episode narrated in the preceding section a glimpse of the latter view has been given via an analysis of what the wronged Draupadī and Arjuna, and their moral guide, Kṛṣṇa, have said and done about their wrongdoer, Aśvathāmā. Draupadī is the main person through whom this position has been suggested or adumbrated. In the discussion that follows also we shall examine this position, the view that forgiveness is a conditional virtue, by analysing some other things which the tradition has held and expressed through her words. All this is said only to bring into clear vision what in fact it is we are talking about. We are talking about *an Indian* theory of forgiveness as a conditional virtue (which is expressed in Draupadī's words), and not the view of an individual, an unhappy, wronged princess, and queen, which Draupadī is.

We shall adopt the same procedure in discussing the opposite view to the effect that forgiveness is a categorical virtue, i.e. discuss it as an *Indian* view about the moral status of forgiveness (though, again, expressed through some words and thoughts of an individual who, now, is Yudhiṣṭhira). Both Draupadī and Yudhiṣṭhira are to be taken as the vehicles or media used to convey to the world that both the views have been held in the Indian tradition. It will be also shown through their examination that the Indian tradition's inclination is more towards the conditional-virtue-status of forgiveness (and other general virtues) than towards the categorical-virtue-status view, though many interpreters consider *sāmānya dharma*s to be both universal and categorical. Perhaps they are led or misled to think that they are universal in sense of being obligatory for all human beings because of the linguistic fact that they are called *sāmānya* or *sādhārana*, i.e. common or general virtues. But we have seen that that is not the case. They are common *dharma*s only in the sense that they are required of all members of the three upper castes. That they are not categorical is yet to be seen, as we are yet to present an analytical discussion of it.

One of main reasons, or the primary reason, for assigning to forgiveness the status of a categorical virtue seems to me a great prejudice against, or a great injustice done to, the concept of anger (*krodha*) and through it a grave devaluation of the positive value of anger, which too is a grave injustice done to its positive normativity. This is clear from the fact that Manu and many others have given to the complete absence, negation, or abnegation of anger (*akrodha*) the status of a general virtue, implying thereby that feeling any anger in any condition for any reason for any person's having done anything is a vice.

To hold any such view is totally untenable. It is held because the concept of anger as well as the morally positive role which anger can play and plays in human life has not been given its due either by classical thinkers or by their modern, devoted, committed-admiring, interpreters. To be fair to anger as well as to those who plead for its absolute abnegation, it is necessary, therefore, to analyse in some detail the concept of anger to ascertain what an individual's feeling of anger, or becoming angry, may incline, provoke or enable him to do, and whether all these doings are likely to be morally undesirable, or if some of them may also be morally permissible or commendable.

Such an analysis needs to be done before ascertaining whether forgiveness is an unconditional or conditional virtue. This is so because one of the chief reasons for assigning to forgiveness a very high moral status as a virtue is the alleged belief that anger is a vice, or a feeling which can prompt its experiencer to commit many moral vices, and that forgiveness is its antidote, a counteractive trait of character, which saves the individual from committing those vices. Therefore, we shall take up the concept of anger in the section that follows and only after its analysis come back again to forgiveness. We hope to show therein that not only it is sometimes not wrong to be angry but it is sometimes wrong not to be angry, i.e. it is sometimes morally wrong to have the virtue of angerlessness, as prescribed by Manu and others. If this analysis is sound, then it would also imply that the oft-quoted classical Indian aphorism, as a moral truism, that all anger is a root of sin (*krodhah pāpasya mūlam*), is not even a sound empirical induction.

12.5 CONCEPT OF ANGER: ANGER'S IMMORAL AND MORAL POTENTIALITIES

That anger is a morally as well as a pragmatically bad feeling has been incessantly emphasized by classical Indian thinkers. Writers of the *Dharmasūtras* and other classical thinkers list it among the things a man is forbidden to have and its absolute absence, or complete elimination, is generally listed among the great virtues. We have already seen Manu listing *akrodha* (absence of anger) among the ten primary virtues. Doing that obviously means that *krodha* (anger) must be gotten rid of. The *Āpāsṭambadharmasūtra* (1.3.22) lists among the rules required to be strictly observed by a student that he be 'not given to anger'. The householder who is the central figure in any society, as far as moral living to concerned, is required by it to abstain from 'anger and whatever would provoke someone to anger' (2.18.2). The *Baudhāyanadharmasūtra* (1.15.30) requires that he should never 'become angry'. The *Gautamadharmasūtra* (2.13) says that he must not feel angry. The *Vasiṣṭhadharmasūtra* (4.4) too avers that 'refraining from anger' like truthfulness, charity, non-violence, etc., is a virtue required of the members of all classes of people. Yudhiṣṭhira too, when he pleads for the view that forgiveness is an unconditional virtue, begins with first narrating the evils which anger can cause.

Through Yudhiṣṭhira, the tradition, before averring that forgiveness is a categorical virtue, presents a picture of anger as a cause of many evils. The underlying idea is that anger is aroused in an individual in response to something hurtful done by another individual. Its very nature is to prompt the angry man to do many evils if it is not controlled. Therefore, it has to be controlled and ultimately completely eliminated, making the individual absolutely unprone to feel angry, whatever is done to him. To achieve this state of mind is to become completely tolerant of even an extremely hurtful thing done to him. The acquisition of such a state, or the inculcation of this disposition or trait of character, is what the tradition calls forgiveness (*kṣamā*) and considers to be an intrinsic categorical virtue. It gets adumbrated through Yudhiṣṭhira's words, uttered in response to Draupadī, who holds that forgiveness is only a conditional virtue. Since anger provokes its experiencer to oppose or resent any wrong done to him, it is obvious that it may not let him forgive the wrongdoer even if he may sort it out with him in a befitting manner. Therefore, if every non-forgiveness is morally wrong, anger would have to be absolutely abnegated, i.e. complete absence of anger (*akrodha*) would have to be inculcated. And, every non-forgiveness would necessarily be morally wrong if forgiveness is on unconditional, a categorical virtue. Therefore, a logical gateway to arrive at the view that forgiveness is an unconditional virtue is, the tradition thinks, as is clear from (the *Dharmasūtras*' statements referred to above and) Yudhiṣṭhira's words, to narrate the evils of anger. But it does not realize that this gateway can be used to reach this view if and only if there is nothing morally desirable which anger can lead to.

Let us first see what are the evils of anger which Yudhiṣṭhira mentions. Be it noted that he only mentions, or narrates, them, as truths about anger; he does not present them on the basis of any logical analysis of what anger may yield under which conditions, nor on that of any sound empirical generalization about its actual consequences. He begins[10] by saying that anger kills or destroys the angry man himself, that conquering it is promotive while yielding to it destructive of his interests. It prompts him to commit sins, to kill even his teachers or elders, to disrespect others by uttering harsh words; it blinds his vision and does not let him see what is right and what is wrong, speakable and unspeakable, and may lead him to kill the innocent and worship him who should be killed. A weak man who is angry with another man more powerful than him, being blinded by anger may attack him and be killed by him. The angry man does not know the limits beyond which he must not go in taking revenge on his enemy. Therefore, good, wise men have given up anger. He who is not angry and therefore does not attack another man, saves both himself and the enemy. He who is more powerful than the man angry with him but himself is not angry and does not attack the angry, goes to heaven. Saints say that the conqueror of anger always progresses. Anger is revengeful, i.e. it prompts the angry man to abuse him who abuses him, to beat him who has beaten him, and thus promotes enemity.

What has been said above about anger is true but not the whole truth about it. To see the whole truth about it, let us see what in fact it is and all that it may do.

Anger is a reactive feeling. Its stimulus is the other individual who has caused some suffering to him in whom this feeling is aroused. It is thus a feeling aroused in reaction to the suffering caused and its target is the cause of the suffering, the individual who has caused it. This feeling of anger has a great moving, or motive power in it in the sense that it motivates the angry man to avenge the wrong, to harm or hurt the other who has caused the suffering. Yudhiṣṭhira is right in pointing out that any attempt to attack a man more powerful than the avenger may be self-destructive because it may destroy the avenger himself or increase his existing suffering. But this only shows the pragmatic disutility of the avenging attempted and not its ethical impropriety. The ethical impropriety or propriety of any move depends on something other than its pragmatic disutility or utility.

There are some distinctions, very important for understanding the ethical-unethical role of anger, which do not seem to have occurred to Yudhiṣṭhira or to the classical ethicists as whose mouthpiece or spokesman he has presented his one-sided account of the role of anger. Firstly, the suffering caused to the angry man may be morally deserved or undeserved by him. For example, it may be the punishment given to him because of his having committed a crime and his criminality may have been conclusively proven. Then his feeling angry is morally unjustified and so is his move to avenge his suffering. His anger therefore is immoral anger. Consequently, if his move to avenge goes against his own interests, or increases his suffering, it gives a moral lesson to his society that a move, prompted by immoral anger, to avenge the giving of a morally deserved punishment, is not worth the trouble.

In some cases, the suffering caused to the angry avenger may be morally undeserved, which it would be for example, if it is the result of the suffering individual's having been deprived of his rightful share in his parental property by his deceitful cousin. Then the suffering is undeserved, its infliction immoral, and the inflicter's act of causing it also immoral. The upshot of it is that the causation of this suffering is a moral wrongdoing and the anger felt on account of it is a moral anger, i.e. a morally justified anger. Not to feel it, or to defend the view that it should not be felt, would be morally wrong, and any move to avenge the wrongdoing by trying to recover the lost property would also be morally justified or right, whether or not it is pragmatically paying. This moral truth Yudhiṣṭhira does not clearly see at this stage of his career, when his own name may very well replace the suffering individual in the above imagined example. The point of this example is that some anger may be *moral anger* and therefore ought not to be gotten rid of. Only for immoral anger a case may be made to get rid of it.

In yet another case, moral anger may be felt by an individual on account of his own undeserved suffering, as has been illustrated in the above example, as well as by the undeserved suffering of another individual totally unrelated to him. Rāma's moral anger against Vālī, first aroused on account of the suffering against Vālī has inflicted on his young brother Sugrīva by taking possession of his wife, is of a higher value since no self-interest is involved in it, since it is an anger aroused by the suffering of an individual unrelated to him. But only a very little later he contracts friendship with Sugrīva on the terms that Sugrīva will help him in rescuing his wife from Rāvaṇa and he will kill Vālī for his injustices to Sugrīva. Even then his anger against Vālī remains a moral anger but its value-status becomes a little reduced since it has become, at least to some extent, an anger against his own undeserved suffering. This is so because a man's suffering is also the suffering of his friend if the friendship between the two is sincere, as Rāma's friendship with Sugrīva is said to be.

What is obviously true, as shown above, is that anybody's anger, against any injustice done, or any unjust suffering caused, to anybody, is a moral anger and therefore not to be abjured. Rather, not to feel it on an appropriate occasion would be morally wrong. Any individual's not feeling it and not taking steps against the person responsible for the injustice done would be a sign of his moral insensitivity, or even depravity. It is this truth which Vidura very ably demonstrates when he pleads to the members of the audience, including Bhīṣma and Droṇa and Dhṛtarāṣṭra to stop the injustice being done and suffering being caused to Draupadī by Duhśāsana's attempting to derobe her. And, Bhīṣma's, Droṇa's and Dhṛtarāṣṭra's not feeling *moral anger* and not acting accordingly does not show their moral greatness even if we assume that they have conquered anger and have inculcated absolute non-anger (*akrodha*). Rather, any normal moral man's (moral) consciousness would say that, by not feeling moral anger against Duhśāsana and therefore not stopping him from derobing Draupadī, all of them exhibit moral insensitivity or depravity. The upshot of all this is that not all anger is a vice, nor is all non-anger a virtue, as classical Indian moralists say directly, or through any of their spokesmen like Yudhiṣṭhira.

There is another feature of anger and so of moral anger which makes it an augmenter or promoter of the moral value of some other virtue or virtues. This point has been very well made by Ramachandra Shukla, a great Hindi critic and scholar of the classical Indian ethos, in a very forcefully logical manner. As he argues, anger provides the motive, or moving, power to other virtues, like mercy. This can be shown as follows: Suppose a wicked man is torturing a helpless woman. A bystander feels mercy towards her. His mercy can enable him only to do some charity to her or express his sympathy for her. But the agent of her suffering is present there and needs to be stopped from torturing her. This can be done only by anger which would obviously be moral anger. The moral anger of the bystander would move him to take steps to stop the wrongdoer and save the woman. Here the work is done by anger, but anger is so liberal that it leaves the credit to be given to mercy. People will say, says Shukla, that he saved the woman's honour by his mercifulness towards her. They will not say that he saved her out of his anger against the wrongdoer.[11]

What Shukla says about the moving, or motivating, power of anger is very well illustrated by the behaviour of Bhīṣma and Rāma in the instances already given. The *Mahābhārata* at so many places indicates that Bhīṣma is sympathetic towards the Pāṇḍavas and feels that they should be allowed by Duryodhana to have their share of the kingdom. But his sympathy and good wishes do not move him to stop Duryodhana from grabbing their share. His kindness for them is ineffective because he does not have the needed moral anger against Duryodhana. Thus, kindness becomes impotent because of having no moral anger to support it and to do what has to be done. Rāma, on the other hand, has both sympathy for Sugrīva and anger against Vālī for having taken away his wife. His anger, no matter whether it may or may not be called moral anger, makes his sympathy effective. It is anger which moves him to kill Vālī and recuse Sugrīva's wife, not his sympathy by itself, i.e. without being accompanied with anger.

The way Yudhiṣṭhira depicts anger as an agent of evil, and the writers or compilers of the *Dharmasūtras*, the classical Indian ethical codes, list it among forbidden fruits, may give the impression that anger is by and large a condemned thing in classical Indian social practice as well. If it is, at least the individuals rated to be morally elevated and the *ṛṣis*, the seers of spiritual truths, must have been completely angerless or unprone to feel angry. But, as we have seen above, anger is not all evil; it has also the potential of being a promoter of morality by providing a helping hand to an undisputed virtue, like mercy or a sense of justice. Therefore, Indian social, meaning socio-political, life would have not been effectively conducted had anger been completely gotten rid of by the then great men. Even socio-political life has to have a system for awarding punishment to criminals or wrongdoers (*dandavyavasthā*). No system of punishment can function if anger, including moral, legal, anger, is considered to be a pure evil and therefore to be abjured. This practical truth Indian social practice very well recognizes and honours. The result is that in spite of the moralists' forbidding it, in actual practice great men and *ṛṣis* have exhibited anger and acted as prompted by their feelings of anger and the Indian ethos does not condemn them for all that. We shall mention below some examples in the next section in support of it.

12.6 INDIAN ETHICAL PRACTICE NOT AN ECHO OF INDIAN ETHICAL THEORY'S GENERAL CONDEMNATION OF ANGER

Classical Indian ethical practice is more natural in its attitude towards the role of anger, and therefore more faithful to facts of social moral life, than is its virtue ethics. Great men and great *ṛṣis* have exhibited anger as normal human beings and they have not been, as already said, looked down upon by the tradition for having done that. The *ṛṣi* Durbāsū is more famous for his proneness to anger and for cursing those who displeased him, rightly or wrongly, than for anything else and his sainthood has not been in any way diminished on that account. He is always addressed as a practitioner of great austerities (*mahātapasvī*) and a great moral soul (*mahādharmātmā*). Because of his angry temperament he is a very difficult guest. Knowing his nature, Duryodhana pleases him by respectfully attending on him, ungrudgingly tolerating all of his idiosyncracies. When he is pleased Duryodhana asks him for a blessing, requesting him to visit Yudhiṣṭhira at a time when all members of his family have eaten their food. Yudhiṣṭhira is then in the forest in exile. Duryodhana's intention is that at that time there would be no food in Yudhiṣṭhira's kitchen and therefore he would not be able to serve any food to the saint. The saint would then naturally be angry and give him a severe curse. Durbāsā does go to Yudhiṣṭhira, as requested by Duryodhana, with several others, and asks for food at a time when there is really no food in his kitchen. His honour is saved because Kṛṣṇa does the miracle that causes the saint and his companions to all feel their bellies are too full to receive any additional eatable, and therefore they do not return to Yudhiṣṭhira's hut after their bath, as they have promised.[12]

Another greatly venerated *ṛṣi* Yājñavalkya loses his temper in a debate with Śākalya on matters of great spiritual importance. When he finds that Śākalya is doing very well in the debate, at long last he asks him if he knows 'that Being who is to be known only from the *Upaniṣads*, who definitely projects those beings (which exist) and withdraws them into Himself, and who is at the same time transcendent'. He then gives him the curse, out of anger, to the effect that 'If you cannot clearly tell me of Him, your head shall fall off'. 'Śakālya did not know Him, his head fell off, and robbers snatched away his bones, mistaking them for something else.'[13] The irony is that in this debate Yājñavalkya, being an accredited knower of that Being, the Self, which the *Upaniṣads* claim to be the ultimate reality, intends to prove that the claim is valid, and Śākalya being not convinced of it goes on questioning him further and further. Yājñavalkya is not happy with his argumentative skill and unpreparedness to accept his position without his proving it in a logically sound manner. Being unhappy with his incessant questioning, instead of using better logic to prove the reality of the *Upaniṣadic* Self, of which Śākalya admits he is not yet convinced, but will be convinced of it if it is conclusively proven to him, Yājñavalkya asks him if he knows it. And, since he does not, curses him, causing head to fall off. But in spite of all this he is still accepted as a venerable seer of truth and a great philosopher too, even today by the majority of modern *Upaniṣadic* scholars. *His anger* thus is not at all a vice and he is not accused of having not inculcated the virtue of angerlessness (*akrodha*).

Among the *ṛṣis* Vasiṣṭha is characterized as one of the most peace-loving and quiet-tempered saints. But even he becomes angry when Viśvāmitra requests him to give his spiritually gifted cow which can fulfil any desire (*kāmadhenu*), and on his refusal to part with it tries to forcibly take possession of it. Viśvāmitra is willing to give, in exchange for the cow, a lot of other things, but still Vasiṣṭha does not agree to part with the cow. The fight between the two *ṛṣis* becomes very fierce and both of them exhibit great anger against each other and use extremely powerful, even divinely received, weapons. Vasiṣṭha ultimately wins, but for our present purposes that does not matter much, What matters here is that the two *ṛṣis* are not angerless and their not being angerless does not affect their sainthood. Vasiṣṭha's anger may be called moral anger because it is directed against the man who wants to take away his cow though he has no legal or moral right to do that. Viśvāmitra's anger is unjustified. Even then it does not diminish his saintly importance. But even Vasiṣṭha's anger, though moral, is aroused because his own self-interest, his ownership of his cow, has been threatened; it is not because someone else's interest is in danger.[14] Viśvāmitra has been portrayed in the tradition as an anger-prone saint, though not to the same extent as Durbāsā has been. For example, Viśvamītra asks Daśaratha to hand over his two dear sons, Rāma and Lakṣmaṇa, to be trained by him and also to help saints in forests to perform their religious rituals and austerities by saving them from demons' onslaughts on them. Out of sheer love for them, Daśaratha first declines and then Viśvāmitra becomes extremely angry, his anger being as flaming as fire is when melted butter is poured into it.[15] This anger may or may not be called moral anger. It may not be called moral because he has no moral right to deprive an old father of the company of his sons. It may be called moral because Viśvamītra wants to take them away for their benefit, i.e. their education, and also for the protection of other saints. Be that as it may, our concern here is only to show that anger is not considered in classical Indian practice a pure evil as some theorizers, or Yudhiṣṭhira, posit it to be.

Yudhiṣṭhira himself, who condemns anger as an unmixed evil, is also not completely angerless. At one point of time during the *Mahābhārata* war, Arjuna is not able to check Karṇa from advancing further and killing Pāṇḍava combatants. For strategic reasons, he also has to go to another front which has become more vulnerable for the Pāṇḍavas, and leaves the Karṇa front to be handled by Bhīma. Yudhiṣṭhira himself is no match for Karṇa and has already been defeated in an earlier encounter with him. When they meet in the evening of that day, Yudhiṣṭhira flares up at Arjuna for leaving Bhīma to fight Karṇa and accuses him of being disloyal to his brother. He calls Arjuna dull-headed, too weak to face Karṇa and therefore only boasting falsely of defeating him, and not deserving to handle the great bow Gāndīva. His anger knows no limits since he now feels that he will lose the war very greatly because Arjuna is not skilled enough in archery to kill Karṇa. He goes to the extent of asking Arjuna to give the great bow to Kṛṣṇa to fight the war and himself become his charioteer.[16]

Yudhiṣṭhira's anger is natural because he now is losing hope of winning the war since his hope is very greatly based on his belief that Arjuna would be able to kill Karṇa. This anger cannot be called moral anger because the reason for it is not moral; it is only the fear of losing the war. But still his status as a morally elevated person is not considered by the tradition lowered because of it. To any individual committed to upholding at any cost the view that all anger is a vice, it may look strange to see one of the greatest champions of that view becoming so blinded by his anger as to call Arjuna disloyal and unfit to handle Gāndīva, and still not losing even a tint of his glory as a moral exemplar of the Indian ethos.

We have already seen Rāma's anger against Vālī. That is not the only occasion when he is angry. He is also angry with the sea when it does not give way to let his army cross over it in order to reach Lankā. His eyes become red with anger, he shoots an extremely powerful arrow into it, and threatens to dry it up. The sea-god then appears, apologizes, and tells him that one combatant monkey in his army has the power to make solids which will hold on to the surface of the sea-water, so a bridge can be constructed on the sea which the sea will support, and thus his army can walk over the sea and reach Lankā. This anger of Rāma's is a result of his self-interest in reaching Lankā to fight the battle with Rāvaṇa.[17]

Kṛṣṇa does condemn anger in the *Gita* (2.63) calling it a source of many evils, as causing delusion which causes loss of memory which produces loss of understanding which makes the angry man perish. But he himself exhibits his anger at many places in the *Mahābhārata* and incites some key Pāṇḍava combatants, particularly Bhīma and Arjuna, to be angry. Doing the latter shows his belief in the moving power of anger. Had he not done his best to make Bhīma extremely angry when fighting a duel with Duryodhana, Bhīma would not have killed him—of course, also not without Kṛṣṇa's indicating to Bhīma to hit his opponent hip-joints which was against the agreed ethics of the duel.[18]

The stray examples given above are not intended to prove that anger is not considered to be undesirable in any sense by Indian practice. They have been given, on the other hand, to show that Indian practice is more realistic in its attitude towards human feelings, emotions, passions, inclinations, etc., than some statements of moral theorizers make it appear, or require it to be. It realizes their value as well as disvalue and its use of them is guided more by its sense of realism than by the absolutist prescriptions of theorizers. It may also be said that theorizers offer these absolutist views, like the one characterizing anger as totally forbidden, more as guiding stars in the sky than as lanterns we can easily use as instruments of illumination. Rather, they are meant to function as pole stars guiding us from a distance in respect of matters for which no handy lighting instrument is available.

The long detour through anger, in our journey primarily undertaken for locating wherein lies the actual place of forgiveness in a virtuous life, can very well end here with the conclusion that forgiveness cannot be called an unconditional virtue on the mere ground that when cultivated it amounts to the complete absence of all anger. Let us see if any other ground is given in the Indian ethos to safeguard its right to be an unconditional virtue.

12.7 RETURN TO FORGIVENESS'S CLAIM TO BEING AN UNCONDITIONAL VIRTUE

In this exploration too we shall follow the same method which we have so far followed. We shall take Yudhiṣṭhira as a spokesman of the Indian ethos and examine the ground or grounds, if any, on which he defends the unconditionality of this virtue. He states this view mainly at two places: first in a dialogue with Draupadī who holds the opposite view that it is only a conditional virtue, and second, in his response to Virāṭa's requesting Yudhiṣṭhira to forgive him for his having hurt him with a dice piece. But in neither case does he offer any ground or reason for holding his view.

In the dialogue with Draupadī he praises this virtue in hyperbolic terms, some of which do not convey any precise sense if taken literally. In the *Vanaparva* of the *Mahābhārata*, section 29, already referred to, he says that forgiveness is morality (*dharma*), the religious ritual of sacrifice (*yajña*), *Veda*, and recorded knowledge (*śruti*). He who knows this truth about forgiveness becomes able to forgive everything (29.36). Forgiveness is, he proceeds, Brahmā, truth (*satya*), past (*bhūta*), future (*bhaviṣya*), practice of austerity (*tapa*), and cleanliness (*śauca*). It is forgiveness which sustains the world (*dhṛtam jagat*) (29.37). The forgiving individual attains a higher, i.e. a better, world (after his death) than does the performer of sacrifices, a knower of Brahman, and practitioner of austerities (*tapasvī*) (29.38).

It is very difficult to make sense out of these utterances by understanding their key words in their literal senses, or even in some metaphorical sense if they can be given a metaphorical sense. It is obvious that to be a forgiving person is not to be a knower of the *Vedas*, and also equally obvious that to be a knower of the *Vedas* need not amount to being a forgiving person. Durbāsā is a knower of the *Vedas* and so is Yājñavalkya. But the former is more apt to curse anyone who annoys him even by doing a minor lapse, and Yājñavalkya, instead of forgiving Śākalya for not knowing what the *Upaniṣads* consider to be the highest reality (which is not obviously a crime), causes his head to fall. This amounts to causing his death, i.e. to killing him. And certainly, forgiveness is not the whole of *dharma*, i.e. morality; there are many other virtues than it. With a little conceptual ingenuity used with a logically open mind, without being infected with ancestral prejudice, one can very easily see that Yudhiṣṭhira's statements about forgiveness, giving to it the status of an unconditional, or rather the highest, virtue, can at the most be taken as emotive utterances about it, without any communicative competence to prove that it is such a virtue.

In the other instance Yudhiṣṭhira's statement about the great value of forgiveness is still more cryptic. There it occurs in response to the king of Matsya Virāṭa's requesting Yudhiṣṭhira to forgive him for his hurting him with a dice piece when the two are playing dice. Yudhiṣṭhira is staying there with his family, all incognito. He has assumed the name Kanka, and his duty is to entertain the king by working as a partner in playing the game of dice with him, since both love to play the game. One day in the game, on account of certain words uttered by him in praise of his brother Arjuna as a charioteer, there staying in the garb of a woman called Bṛhannalā, the king gets angered. He hurls a dice piece at Yudhiṣṭhira's nose which starts bleeding as a result. Later the king realizes his mistake, and apologizes, beseeching Yudhiṣṭhira to forgive him. Yudhiṣṭhira responds by saying that even before his realizing his fault and apologizing, he has forgiven him. He has done that, he says, because 'since long in my life I have taken a vow to forgive everyone (whatever be his crime). Therefore, your fault has automatically been forgiven by me (without and before your apologizing). I have no complaint against you' (Ibid., *Virātaparva*, *Goharaṇaparva*, 68.63).

By making this reference to his blanket vow to forgive any crime committed by anybody whosever he may be, without his repenting, apologizing, promising not to commit this or any sort of crime again, etc., Yudhiṣṭhira seems to hold that forgiveness is an intrinsic, unconditional, irrelational virtue. Perhaps there is a trend of thinking in the classical Indian ethos assigning this status to forgiveness. But no logical or normative analysis of the concept of forgiveness, which may validate this claim of it, or of any virtue, is available anywhere. In fact, no sector of Indian virtue ethics has been given a conceptual treatment in any detail, though it constitutes a very important part of the Indian philosophy of morals. It has to be an important part because *sāmānya dharmas*, general virtues, are given in it the place of character-traits which everyone of at least the three upper castes of the then society is obligated or recommended to cultivate.

The fate of the view that forgiveness is a conditional virtue, i.e. a virtue which has to be exhibited only in some and not in all conditions, is a little better. Even though it too has not been presented in a tightly argued-out fashion, the tradition seems to be more in its favour than in that of the categorical view, its opposite. Perhaps that is why to present it, it chooses as its spokesperson Draupadī, a lady who has suffered a lot of injustices and troubles for no fault of her own and very largely due to the weakness of the moralist Yudhiṣṭhira for gambling. The view which in the Indian ethos gets expressed through her words is down-to-earth and much akin to our common-sense understanding of the conditions in which a fault should be forgiven and of those in which it should not be.

Keeping in mind Duryodhana as an example of an individual who has done a lot of injustices and thereby caused a lot of suffering to her and her family, she points out to Yudhiṣṭhira that a wrongdoer deserves to be forgiven only if he shows genuine repentance (*paṣcātāpa*) for his wrong doing. The conceptual as well as normative truth which she has in her mind is that even forgiveness may be given judiciously as well as injudiciously. To forgive Duryodhana would be injudicious since he does not repent for his bad deeds. Similarly, not to forgive him who does repent would be injudicious or wrong (Ibid., 27.4,40). Forgiving an unrepentant, undeserving person and not forgiving a genuinely deserving one are specially to be avoided by a *kṣatriya*, which Yudhiṣṭhira is. Here she has in her mind the duties assigned to individuals or different castes. To be a *kṣatriya*, she says, means to be one who causes the destruction (*kṣarana*) of the wicked, the perpetrators of injustices. Her appeal here is to the etymology of the word '*kṣatriya*' as a *kṣatriya* is he who destroys (*kṣarate eti kṣatram*) the wrongdoer. This is another argument for those whose duty is to punish the wrongdoer and to forgive the innocent.

As male scholars generally do, Draupadī too fortifies her view of forgiveness by referring to the lessons on it given to Bali by his grandfather Prahlāda. The latter very forthrightly says that it is an indubitable truth that neither power (*teja*) nor forgiveness (*kṣamā*) is always, in all conditions, or in all uses of it, good or commendable (Ibid., 28.6). He who forgives in all conditions has to bear a lot of ignominies. His servants, enemies, and strangers, all, disrespect him. Nobody behaves with him politely or respectfully (Ibid., 28.7 and 8). Others try to take away from the always-forgiving person even his wives and the unwise wives of his tend to become disloyal or self-willed. The irascible man also suffers from several defects. Therefore, Prahlāda's advice is that neither forgiveness nor non-forgiveness is an unconditional virtue or vice.

Draupadī also mentions the conditions, as laid down by Prahlāda, in which a criminal may or should be forgiven. They are:

(1) If somebody has earlier done some good to an individual, then, keeping in view his earlier record, his crime should be forgiven by the latter. This is, in effect, the moral demand of gratitude to one's benefactor.

(2) Any crime done inadvertently, or unknowingly, should be forgiven. This is, as we have said, due to the moral fact that a person is responsible only for what he has knowingly and willingly done. But, Prahlāda adds, if a criminal lies and declares a crime to have been inadvertently done when it has really been done knowingly, then he should be punished even if his crime is not a serious one.

(3) The first crime of everyone deserves to be forgiven. But if the criminal, after being forgiven for it, does another crime, which means he is ungrateful to the forgiver or wants to take advantage of his forgiving nature, he should be punished even for a minor crime of his.

The net conclusion which Draupadī, through Prahlada, or the Indian ethical theory, through Prahlāda and Draupadī, arrives at is that forgiveness is a great virtue by which a lot of good can be achieved, aggressive as well as quiet enemies can be won over. But one has to use it carefully and cautiously, not to forgive everybody, or anybody in all conditions. Forgiveness has to be used only after duly considering the appropriateness of the time, place, and one's strength and weakness. By an indiscriminate, unconditional, use of it no good can be achieved (Ibid., 28.6–33).

This presentation of the status of forgiveness as a conditional virtue may not be taken as a foolproof account. It is a mixture of conceptual, normative, as well as pragmatic reasons for calling forgiveness a conditional virtue. But this is in no way strange. Moral life is a life in a social practice and every virtue is a practical virtue, i.e. a practisable trait of character. Therefore, in characterizing it, it is natural for all these reasons or elements to come in. It is not a purely conceptual, or logical, account. But to me it seems to be a good, workable one, and may be taken as an account favoured by the Indian ethos more than the hyperbolic one presented through Yudhiṣṭhira. Perhaps the latter has been given only to let Draupadī's account shine better in sharp contrast with it.[19] Draupadī's account has the advantage of not having any metaphysical-theological dross; that sort of dross has been burnt in the fire of the suffering the heroine of the great epic has undergone in spite of her having five mighty husbands.

To hold that the virtue forgiveness is conditional, in logical terminology, is nothing but to say that the concept of forgiveness is a flexible, defeasible one. It has been maintained in this work that all, or almost all, moral concepts of Indian ethics, or ethics as such, are flexible. To call a moral concept, say, the concept of a virtue, flexible is only to say that there are some conditions in which an individual may do something which is incommensurate with it and still what he does may not be morally wrong or forbidden, or it may be even morally commendable, or more commendable than doing something commensurate with the virtue would have been. And, also because of his doing the incommensurate thing the doer cannot be said to be violating the dignity of the virtue it is incommensurate with. When we recognize properly the full import of a moral concept's flexibility, we shall see that the concept of *āpadharma*, i.e., that of morality in an emergency condition, can very well be explained in terms of the flexibility of the virtue or principle seemingly violated in that condition. This would show that there is no need for a separate category of morality which the concept of *āpadharma* is claimed to be. There may not even be a genuine gap in ethical theory which *āpadharma* is claimed to fill in. All this will be shown in the next two sections.

12.8 BUILT-IN FLEXIBILITY OF A GENERAL VIRTUE ILLUSTRATED

In the above discussion it has already been shown that there are certain conditions in which forgiveness may not be granted to a wrongdoer without any implication about lowering the value of this virtue. One example is not forgiving a recidivist who repents and apologizes for his present crime but has been found in the past to have continued to commit crimes even after having been forgiven for an earlier crime. One may even say that forgiving such a man would be a misuse of the virtue of forgiveness, whereas not forgiving, or punishing him, would be a fitting response to what he has done.

The exceptionability of the concept of a virtue we have already exhibited, maybe indirectly, earlier in 6.7.2 and in the section 12.2 of this chapter as well. But in all these cases the reason for making an exception to a virtue is not the same or of the same type.

The reason suggested in 12.2 for not forgiving a recidivist, even if he repents, etc., is retributive. The repentance of a man, who is prone to commit crimes even after having been forgiven, or after having been punished, does *not deserve* to be trusted. Therefore, he does not *deserve* to be forgiven, or rather, *deserves* to be denied forgiveness, i.e. to be punished. In 12.2 Kauśika is considered to have committed a great moral lapse by *not making* an exception to his well-established virtue of truthfulness, or to his principle of always telling the truth. That is, his situation is considered to be a fit one for making an exception to it, i.e. a fit case for not telling the truth about the location of the place where the innocent men, chased by the dacoits, are hiding themselves. The reason for making the exception, for telling an untruth or not telling the truth by, say, feigning ignorance about the place, etc., here is the damage caused by the exemplification of the virtue of truthfulness at the expense of another virtue, the virtue of causing no injury to any innocent creature, a variant of the virtue of non-injury to any creature (*ahimsā*). This is a moral-consequential as well as a coherentist reason. It is a moral-consequential reason because telling the truth causes the morally undesirable consequence of causing the killing of some innocent men. It is a coherentist reason because it goes against the principle of Indian ethical theory to the effect that any virtue has to be inculcated and practised, as far as possible, in such a manner that its practice coheres with the practice of other virtues, i.e. does not cause any damage to any other virtue.

The reason given in 6.7.2 for Yudhiṣṭhira's telling the untruth—that Aśvathāmā has been killed—and therefore for his making an exception to his always practising the virtue of truthfulness, is on the face of it, pragmatic or strategic. It is pragmatic because it is necessary, as per Arjuna's and Kṛṣṇa's assessment of the situation of the war, that Droṇa withdraws from the battle-field because, if he does not, the chance of the Pāṇḍavas' winning the war is nil or extremely bleak. And, to make him withdraw, this is the only way because he would withdraw only if he is made to believe that Aśvathāmā has been killed and he would believe that only if it is announced by Yudhiṣṭhira. But Kṛṣṇa, in his presentation of it, gives to it a moral colour and perhaps that colour is its natural colour. Like the other examples from the *Mahābhārata*, which I have presented in this work as well in some others of mine as ethical or philosophical-conceptual examples, the morally coloured presentation of this reason also has been given in a long-winded manner. What Kṛṣṇa has said in a long-winded way to convince Yudhiṣṭhira that there is a good reason for him to make an exception to his practice of being always truthful and to tell this untruth can be briefly stated as follows:

This war which is fought between the Pāṇḍavas and the Kauravas is a *righteous* war for the Pāṇḍavas because they are fighting it only to take back from Duryodhana's possession the portion of the kingdom which is *rightfully* theirs. Therefore, it is morally right for them to win the war. It is true that only impeccably right means should be used to win even a righteous war. But when that is not possible and it is necessary to use an untruth to win it, it is morally right to do that. It is morally right because it is to do a tiny little piece of immorality in the service of an unquestionably right larger moral cause. On the other hand, the consequence of not using this untruth is likely to be a moral catastrophe. Therefore, he concludes, Yudhiṣṭhira ought to announce that Aśvathāmā has been killed (though it is not the case).

Kṛṣṇa seems to be doing here something like an ethical cost-benefit analysis, proceeding on the assumption that where we cannot attain a right cause by using only cent per cent right means, we are morally right in using the least possible immorality to attain it. Or, he can also be taken to assume that what is normally an immorality may not be one in some unusual situation, for example, in a situation in which something highly moral is in danger and can be rescued only if this normally-considered-immoral thing is done.

The argument is forceful, it persuades Yudhiṣṭhira to announce the untruth, and things follow as anticipated. The war is won by the Pāṇḍavas. The situation in which the untruth is told is an emergent one for the Pāṇḍavas. Kṛṣṇa's point is that in such a situations making an exception to a moral principle or virtue does not, in the long run, devalue that principle or virtue.

Kṛṣṇa's his words which express, or contain, reasoning do not carry it visibly on their face. But such reasoning is one which in practical moral life most of us normally use. We do that not only to meet emergencies, but also many times in not such urgent situations. This we are able to do, and classical Indians were able to do, because of what we have been calling the built-in flexibility of moral concepts.

The flexibility of moral norms Kṛṣṇa exhibits further by citing a number of situations in which a morally upright man may tell an untruth, i.e. seemingly abjure practising the virtue of truthfulness, without being accusable as having inculcated the vice of being untruthful. He says that 'If it is necessary to tell an untruth to save anyone's life, then the untruth (and not the truth) should be told (by the virtuous man).' 'Where the consequence of telling an untruth is as beneficial as that of telling a truth normally is, or where the consequence of telling a truth is as harmful as that of telling an untruth normally is, there the untruth, and not the truth, is to be told'. Covering some cases, which sombre-looking philosophers do not like to talk about, he adds that 'on the occasion of getting married, of having sexual union with a woman, of anybody's life being endangered, of one's entire possessions being snatched away, and for the benefit of a *brāhmaṇa*, if required, untruth should be told. Telling an untruth on these five occasions does not constitute a vice.' He concludes his account by asserting that 'only he who is a fool thinks that the virtue (or principle) of truthfulness as used in general practice is to be necessarily used at all places' (or in all circumstances).[20]

Manu's aphorism that 'truth is to be told but not an unpleasant truth, nor be told a pleasant lie', also proceeds on a track similar to Kṛṣṇa's.[21] It also aims at indicating that the virtue of truthfulness is not to be taken in an absolutist sense; rather, it should be practised in such a manner that its practice coheres with that of other virtues. By saying that unpleasant truth be not told, he only means that in the practice of truthfulness one must not forget the virtue of causing no hurt to anybody, i.e., that of *ahiṃsā*, or benevolence. Similarly, in saying that even a pleasant lie be not told, he simply means that the virtue of non-injury or of benevolence must not be allowed to make one underplay the virtue of truthfulness. Basically what he means is that, by using his moral maturity and experience the virtuous man should adjust his practice of a virtue in an appropriate manner in different circumstances, normal or abnormal. He assumes that this is possible because of the flexibility of moral norms or virtues (*dharmas*).

What has been said of the flexibility of the concept of forgiveness and of that of truthfulness can also be said to be true of other virtue-concepts. We shall do that very briefly for non-violence, the central moral notion of Jainism and in some way accepted by all other systems as well. It is one of the five great vows (*panca mahāvrata*) of the Jain ethics. One sect of it goes to the extent of holding that no injury be done to any living being knowingly or even unknowingly. But finding that this is not possible for an ordinary individual, in course of time the absoluteness of the virtue of non-violence becomes binding only on monks and not on householders. The other systems, all the *Vedic* ones and even Buddhism, also consider non-violence to be a great virtue but do not consider it absolutely inviolable. This is clear from the fact that none of them requires every individual to abstain from eating meat. The *Mahābhārata* presents Dharmavyāhda, who runs his business of selling the meat of animals killed by others in accordance with the ethics of his profession, as a morally elevated person who is said to excel even some great saints.[22] Even the *Gītā* can be read as justifying killings in a war, or even generally, on allegedly some metaphysical grounds. Both of these examples will be discussed in some detail in the next chapter.

The *Vasiṣthadharmasūtra* (14.1–48) mentions the items of food which are permitted and which are forbidden, and among the permitted items includes some varieties of meat. So do some other *Dharmasūtras*, including *Manusmṛti*. We need not discuss them here because our aim here is not to discuss the permitted kinds of animal food. Ours is only to show that Indian ethics considers the concepts of general virtues flexible in the sense that it allows an exception to the normal practice of a virtue, or to the normal application of a moral principle, and thereby does not consider the resulting diversion to be an immorality.

Classical thinkers might not have said all this in clear terms. But it seems to me that this is what they do through their introduction of the concept of *āpadharma*, which may be taken to mean moral permissibility of and use of a *dharma*, a virtue or principle, in an emergency, an abnormal situation, in a manner which may appear deviant if we use the standard of moral permissibility for normal situations. The introduction of this concept is a sign of classical thinkers' moral, or rather, conceptual, sensitivity to changing nuances of social reality and the complexity of moral living. But even if this concept had not been introduced in Indian ethics, it could have handled the problems the concept is supposed to handle by means of the notion of flexibility built into the notion of a moral virtue or principle. To clearly see this, let us examine the concept of emergency ethics, or rather, of ethical emergency, which *āpadharma* stands for.

12.9 FLEXIBILITY OF A GENERAL VIRTUE AND ETHICAL BEHAVIOUR IN ADVERSE CONDITIONS (*ĀPADHARMA*)

In some modern discussions the concept of *āpadharma* is interpreted in a manner which suggests that Indian moral philosophy admits of, or presents, two types or kinds of ethics: one for normal times and the other for abnormal, adverse, times, implying further that the entire *ethics* meant for normal times may be violated if need be, in abnormal times, without causing any kind of immorality, or that it may be considered irrelevant for abnormal times. But this is not the purport of introducing the concept. There are not two such kinds of ethics; there is one and only one ethics which has to be used in normal as well as in abnormal times. Secondly, this ethics, in its entirety, can neither be violated, nor can it be considered irrelevant, in abnormal times. What may happen in abnormal times is that some virtue or virtues may, because of what we have been calling built-in flexibility of virtues, be subordinated, or made to yield, to another virtue because of special needs of an abnormal situation. The sanctity or equilibrium of the entire system of ethics remains undisturbed; only an internal readjustment is made to meet the emergency. This is very well illustrated in the *Mahābhārata* in the example of the saint Viśvāmitra's stealing a block of the flesh of a thigh of a dog, killed by a member of the caste called *cāndāla*, a subclass of the class of *sudras*, from his house in an abnormal situation when a devastating famine has been caused by a severe drought. Viśvāmitra himself and all others of his family have had no food for some days and are likely to die of starvation. Therefore, to procure any eatable material he enters the house of a *cāndāla*, finds the thigh of a killed dog, and wants to steal it, and takes it after a long argument with the *cāndāla*. The *cāndāla* using his ethics, which is also Viśvāmitra's ethics, and therefore their ethics, the ethics of all humans, offers his reasons to prove the immorality of what he is trying to do, implying that he should be punished for this attempt of his to steal. The *cāndāla*'s reasoning, to make it brief and to make its point clearly visible, can be presented as follows:

That (a) stealing anything from anybody's house is wrong, (b) stealing by a saint from a *cāndāla*'s house is more wrong than stealing by someone else and from somewhere else, (c) stealing any part of a killed animal from a *cāndāla*'s house by a saint is more wrong than any other kind of stealing, (d) any part of any killed animal is profane as an eatable (*abhakṣya*) for a saint like Viśvāmitra, (e) a dog's meat is more profane than any other animal's meat, and (f) its thigh's meat is more profane than the meat of any other part of its body. Therefore, his stealing it is morally the worst, i.e. the most immoral kind of stealing. Therefore, he ought not to do this extremely immoral thing and try to find some other kind of eatable which is morally permissible. Rather, he adds, since he has been found trying to steal this leg of the killed animal, he should be killed by him, the owner of the killed animal.

The *cāndāla* is arguing with the saint, a man belonging to a higher caste, higher than the caste of the *cāndāla*, within the framework of the Indian ethics meant for normal times, considering it fully relevant for the time when Viśvāmitra is trying to steal the block of meat. According to this ethics stealing is morally wrong, a vice, and non-stealing a virtue. He also appeals to caste ethics which lays down the norms for different castes and the ethics which grade the immorality of stealing different types of goods from different places and persons. Using this ethics he proves that stealing a block of meat of a killed dog is the meanest kind of stealing and therefore an extreme kind of vice.

Viśvāmitra does not question the sanctity of this ethics, nor its applicability to his behaviour. He admits that the stealing he is trying to commit is of the types the *cāndāla* says it is. He also admits that it is the gravest kind of moral vice he claims it to be. But, he argues, this is an abnormally troubled time of famine when no other food is available to him. If he does not steal, or get this block of meat, to feed himself and other members of his family, then all of them will die of starvation. That will in itself be a moral vice, in fact a greater vice for him to commit (by letting them die, amounting to causing their death) than is the stealing he is trying to commit.

Protecting his life and the life of others under his care is the moral responsibility of every individual. To do anything to keep alive himself, or another under his care, even indulging in the vilest kind of vice, like stealing a block of this meat, for him is morally right. This is so because only a living man can do anything moral or inculcate and practise any virtue. Therefore, only a living individual can ultimately help, or contribute to, the maintenance of the moral order, the ethical system, to which the *cāndāla* is appealing in calling his stealing this block of meat a great vice. The same system permits or allows this act of stealing in this abnormal time of famine because of its having posed a great threat to human survival. If he remains alive by eating a part of this meat, then by leading a highly moral life he can compensate for this vice of his. But if he dies of starvation, there would be no question of anything moral being done by him. Thus, he admits that the general principle of ethics that stealing is wrong is valid even now. But because the lives of some individuals are endangered in this abnormal time, this moral principle is to be subordinated to the higher principle that an individual's existence, if endangered by factors not under his control, ought to be protected. This can be done by admitting, not that stealing is never a vice, but that an abnormal situation like the present one is a fit situation in which stealing any eatable to save anyone's life must not be called a vice, i.e. it is to be considered an exception to the principle 'stealing is wrong', or to the principle that non-stealing is a virtue, without invalidating the principle (*dharma*). This is like bending the concept of the virtue of non-stealing in the interest of the higher virtue of protecting the individual's, the moral agent's, existence. This is possible because of the built-in flexibility of the concept of the virtue of non-stealing, and this is necessary to keep in proper health the system of virtues, or, morality as such, i.e. to keep *dharma* stable.[23]

The *cāndāla* agrees with his reasoning, is convinced of the moral justification of his taking the meat, of this kind of stealing's not being a vice because the times are abnormal, and lets him have it, no longer considering it to be a vice and punishable as normally stealing is. The point of the dialogue between the two could have been made in a purely conceptual, logical, way by Indian ethicists. But this style of presenting a theoretical claim through anecdotes, concrete dialogues, is a peculiarity of classical Indian ethicizing. It is not a fruitless venture because it shows the roots of morality in real life much more vividly than a purely abstract, conceptual, way would have done. The point of the dialogue is thus, to conclude, that there are not two kinds of ethics, but only one—what we call general, or commonly used, ethics with built-in flexibility or potentiality to take care of even abnormal, troubled times in a man's or a society's life.

This dialogue has also a mythological accompaniment. Normally we do not care for such frills. But a lesson can be seen as an implication of it. This implication can be drawn as follows:

After taking the meat, Viśvāmitra cooks it, and prepares a dish fit to be offered to the gods including Indra, before he himself eats any portion of the cooked meat. As soon as he offers it to them, they get pleased with him and Indra sends good rainfall which makes available all kinds of food. People eat the food, so do Viśvāmitra and the members of his family, and they are thus spared of eating the forbidden food, the stolen dog-meat. Everybody is thus happy and the moral-social order is restored and continues in the normal manner.

This mythological frill of the dialogue may be taken allegorically. It may, I think, be allegorically taken to imply or suggest that if, in adverse times, when there may arise a temptation not to care for the distinction between right and wrong, if people apply a normal ethical virtue or rule by bending it only at the right point in the interest of a higher value, thus keeping the entirety of the moral system undisturbed, this effort of theirs would be rewarded, i.e. would contribute to the upkeep of their moral-social order. It may thereby bring back the peace and security which leading a moral life is meant to provide them with. An adverse time may thus be taken as one which tests the ability of a moral man to use and apply his moral code in the right way, i.e. in this case, not by totally flouting it but by adjusting or bending it only for some moral reason, in a manner which only bends it without breaking it. It is something like this which the saint-poet Tulsīdāsa says, proceeding on the lines of classical ethicists, in his *Rāmacaritamānasa*, when he avers that 'the four (ethical) things of a man, (the virtue of) his patience, his (commitment to) ethics, (the loyalty of) his friend, and (the faithfulness of) his wife are tested when he is passing through an adverse (or troubled) time'.[24]

In his argument, the *cāndāla*, we have seen, has raised a question about not practising, or doing something incommensurate with, a general virtue, namely, the virtue of non-stealing, as well as one about what a man of an upper caste ought, or ought not to do, and how is he related to a man of a lower case in respect of moral matters. We have discussed in this chapter general virtues (or *sāmānya dharmas*). We have yet to discuss caste-virtues, or *varṇadharma*, i.e. the ethics pertaining to different castes, classes, or *varṇas*, of society. This we shall do in the next chapter.

NOTES AND REFERENCES

1. *Manusmṛti*, 6. 92.
2. *Cintāmani* (Lokabharati, Allahabad, 2004), p. 30.
3. Quoted by Damien Keown in his *The Nature of Buddhist Ethics* (Macmillan, London, 1992), p. 151.
4. *Satyam, kṣamā ārjava dhyānamānṛśansyam ahimsānām.*
   Damah prasāde mādhuryam mṛduteti yama daśa.
   Saucam snānam tpo danam maunejyādhyayanam vratam.
   Upoṣaṇopasthadandau daśaite niyamah smṛtah. (5.19–21).
5. For a detailed account of the moral traits of a *bodhisattva*, see Keown, *The Nature of Buddhist Ethics*, pp. 138–41.
6. See S. Cromwell Crawford, *The Evolution of Hindu Ethical Ideals* (Firma K.L. Mukhopadhyaya, Calcutta, 1974), pp. 222–23. Until very recently he was, and perhaps is still, a professor of religion in Hawaii University.
7. John Mckenzie, *Hindu Ethics* (Oriental Books Reprint Corporation, New Delhi), pp. 214–15.
8. *Kalyāṇa Nītisāra, Anka* (Gita Press, Gorakhpur, 2002), p. 421.
9. *Śaktastu kṣamate nityam aśaktah krudhyate narah. Adiparva, Sambhavaparva*, 87.5.
10. *Mahābhārata, Vanaparva (Arjunābhigamanaparva)*, 29.1–51.
11. Ramachandra Shukla, *Cintāmaṇi*, Part I (Lokabharati, Allahabad, 2004), p. 78.
12. *Mahābhārata, Vanaparva (Draupadīharaṇaparva)*, 261.
13. *Bṛhadaraṇyaka Upaniṣad*, translated by Swami Madhavananda (Advaita Ashrama, Kolkata), II. IX. 26, pp. 387–88.
14. *Rāmāyaṇa, Bāla Kanda*, 53–55.
15. Ibid., 20.28.
16. *Mahābhārata, Karṇaparva*, 68 and 69.
17. *Rāmāyaṇa, Yudha Kanda*, 21 and 22.
18. *Mahābhārata, Śalyaparva, Gadāparva*: 56–58.
19. For a detailed, non-regional conceptual analysis of forgiveness, see Chapter 7, pp. 151–230, of my *Varnadharma, Niskama Karma and Practical Morality: A Critical Essay on Applied Ethics* (D.K. Printworld, New Delhi, 1999).
20. *Mahābhārata, Karṇaparva*, 69, 23, 32, 33, 34.
21. *Manusmṛti*, 4.138.
22. *Varṇaparva, Mārkandeyasamasyaparva*, 208: 1–29.
23. *Śāntiparva*, section 141. The entire section is worth reading for seeing the ethical-conceptual point of the argument between Viśvāmitra and the *cāndāla.*
24. '*Dhīraja dharma mitra aru narī. Āpada kāla parīkhiahin cārī*'. *Rāmacāritamānasa, Āraṇya Kānda*, 117.4.

CHAPTER 13

Morally Good Life through the Performance of Caste-duties (*Varṇadharma*)

13.1 *VARṆA* AND *VARṆADHARMA*

The concept of *dharma* or morality has been developed, as we said earlier, through the characterization of the concepts of general virtues (*sāmānya dharmas*), obligation in troubled times (*āpadadharmas*), caste-duties or virtues (*varṇadharmas*) and one's own duties (*svadharma*). We have explained and illustrated the concepts of *sāmānya dharma* and *āpadadharma* in the preceding chapter and shown that the concept of *sāmānya dharma* is logically capable of taking care of all that *āpadadharma* is claimed to do. Therefore, though there is nothing wrong in Indian ethical theory's having propounded or postulated it, the theory would not lose anything even if it does not have it, or drops it.

We shall show in this chapter something similar to be true of the concept of *svadharma*. This concept also is not an independent concept different from that of *varṇadharma* because, on analysis, it turns out to be non-different from the latter. This is so because ultimately it turns out to be nothing but *svavarṇadharma*, the *dharma* or set of obligations which an individual has in virtue of his being a member of a *varṇa*. But this is what every *varṇadharma* is. Therefore, although we shall also discuss the role of *svadharma*, our primary task in this chapter is to explain and illustrate the nature of the concept of a *varṇadharma* along with the problem or problems, if any, its introduction in the Indian ethical theory gives rise to.

As its verbal form suggests, *varṇadharma* means the *dharma* of a *varṇa*. A *varṇa* as we have seen in some detail in Chapter 7, is a class of people, a sector of society, as per the Indian theory of social organization according to which society consists of four classes, or sectors, of people, called *brāhmaṇa, kṣatriya, vaiśya* and *śūdra*. Therefore, the *varṇadharma* of an individual is the set of obligations he is obligated to fulfil on account of his belonging to, or being a member of, the class or *varṇa* he is in fact a member of. It is clear from this, and is also a social fact, that it is not that he first has earned or acquired a certain set of obligations and is engaged in fulfilling them and thereupon, or on account of all that, he becomes a member of a particular *varṇa*. Rather, the fact is the other way round. As per the Indian theory, he is first a member of a particular *varṇa* and simply on account of this membership of his he has to have a particular set of obligations, more specifically, the set of obligations which every member of that *varṇa*, by definition, has to have.

Every individual has to belong to a *varṇa* and to only one *varṇa*. This is so because the Indian social or ethical theory does not admit the possibility of there being anyone who belongs to no *varṇa*, who is some sort of unaligned person, nor the possibility of one who belongs to more than one *varṇa*. But in whichever way we think of a *varṇa* and a *varṇadharma*, fulfilling one's *varṇadharmas* is a necessary component of living a full moral life. All this is, of course, true of the ethical theory of only those philosophical schools of India which believe in the *varṇa*-system. The Jains, Buddhists, and *Cārākas* are not committed to holding this view of living a good moral life.

A *varṇadharma* is, thus, not the same as what we call professional morality or obligation. It is possible that an individual may not be a member of any professional group and therefore may not have any professional obligation. Secondly, it is also possible that he belongs to more than one professional group. For example, he may be a philosopher, a politician, a businessman, etc., and therefore may have different sets of professional obligations. Thirdly, since he may *choose* a profession, he may as well change his present profession, and opt for another. For example, he may first choose to be a philosopher, then leave philosophy completely and opt for being a full-time politician. This means that he can change his set of professional obligations. After giving up philosophy and becoming a full-time politician, he is no longer obligated to doing philosophy in a creative, or any, manner. We have seen in Chapter 7 that change of *varṇa* is (almost) impossible and that one does not *choose* one's *varṇa*. We shall see in this chapter that the Indian tradition insists that every individual sticks to his own *varṇadharma* and should not try to opt for, or practise, the *varṇadharma* of any *varṇa* other than his own. At the least, it does not consider change of *varṇadharma* desirable.

We have also seen in Chapter 7 that, to all intents and purposes, every individual is considered to be born belonging to a particular *varṇa*, i.e. born as a *brāhmaṇa*, or a *kṣatriya*, or a *vaiṣya*, or a *śūdra*, and therefore born as occupying in the social order a position higher or lower than someone else's. This has to be the case because the *varṇa*-system is a hierarchical system. A *brāhmaṇa* is higher than a *kṣatriya*, a *kṣatriya* higher than a *vaiśya*, and a *vaiṣya* higher than a *śūdra*. Such a conception of the *varṇa*-system is bound to affect the Indian theory of *varṇadharma*.

As per Śankara's commentary on it, even the *Bṛhadāraṇyaka Upaniṣad* (1.iv.6) presents an account of the origin of the four castes which is almost the same as what we have called in Chapter 7 the mythological account. It attributes the origin of the *brāhmaṇa* from the mouth of Virāj, the origin of the *kṣatriya* from his arms, that of the *vaiśya* from his thighs, and that of the *śūdra* from his feet. A little later, while commenting on this upaniṣad (1.iv.11), Śankara clarifies that Virāj is non-different from *Brahman.*[1]

In order to ensure that a powerful caste may not unreasonably dominate over, or oppress, a weaker caste, Śankara says, 'He specially projected that excellent form' called 'righteousness' or *dharma*, i.e. morality. Righteousness controls, or regulates the behaviour of the members of the four castes[2] and thereby ensures harmony or cohesion among them. Righteous practice or conduct is one which is in accordance the *dharmas* as recorded in the scriptures. What members of the four different castes ought (or ought not) to do, i.e. their moral codes, or morality, their *dharmas* or *varṇadharmas*, are thus said to be determined by the scriptures. This means that any member of a *varṇa*, as a member of that *varṇa* ought, or ought not, to do only that which the scriptures say that he ought, or ought not, to do. Śankara, while interpreting 1.iv.13 of this *Upaniṣad* does not raise the question whether the scriptures prescribe (or proscribe) something because it is morally justified to prescribe (or proscribe) it, or whether it is morally justified to prescribe (or proscribe) it because they prescribe (or proscribe) it. He does not, in fact, even raise the more general question why any scripture prescribes (or proscribes) anything at all. For him and for many others of his ilk the mere fact of any prescription's, or proscription's, being in accordance with a scripture is a sufficient condition of its being morally right or justified.

Since Śankara does not admit the reality of the world and therefore the real creation of anything in it, he cannot consider the creating of the castes as real. It is therefore that he interprets the *Bṛhadāraṇyaka* to mean that Virāj or Brahman only 'projects' the four castes and does not really create them. This means that none of the individuals belonging to any of the four *varṇas* has real reality; he has only *vyāvahārika sattā*, empirical or behavioural reality, which is enough to enable him to perform his *dharmas*, i.e. his duties in the world.

For our present purposes, it does not matter whether the *varṇas* are really created or only projected. What matters is that they are brought into being by a divine, a non-human, non-societal or non-social, agency. Explaining their origination in this way, we have seen in Chapter 7, amounts to holding that an individual is born as a *brāhmaṇa*, a *kṣatriya*, a *vaiśya*, or a *śūdra*. He does not become one *because* of what he does in his life-time. This implies that his *varṇa*hood (*varṇatā*) is not determined by his performance of a certain set of *dharmas* or moralities, but by his birth.

To illustrate what is said here, if one is, say, a *brāhmaṇa*, he is because he is born as a *brāhmaṇa*, and not because he has led his life in a certain way. The specific set, of *varṇadharmas* which are his *varṇadharmas*, i.e. those of a *brāhmaṇa*, accrue to him *because* he has been born as a *brāhmaṇa*; *his brāhmaṇatva* (his being a *brāhmaṇa*) does not accrue to him because of his having performed what may be called *brāhmaṇa*-making obligations, or *varṇadharmas*, which one ought to perform in order to be a *brāhmaṇa*. Therefore, in effect, this theory of *varṇadharmas* holds that if an individual is of a certain *varṇa*, then his *varṇadharmas* are such and such. It does not hold that if he performs a certain set of *dharmas*, then he would be, or should be, called a member of a particular *varṇa*. It is this theory of *varṇadharmas* which is implied by the Indian theory of *varṇas* as divinely created.

That this is obviously the case with the divine account is further supported by Śankara's saying that Virāj projects *dharma* also when he projects the four *varṇas*. '*Dharma*' here definitely means the four sets of *varṇadharmas* for the four *varṇas*. This implies that the *varṇas* are created along with their respective *varṇadharmas*; that is, when one is born, say, as a *śūdra*, he is born with the *varṇadharma* of a *śūdra*, i.e. is already, by birth, obligated to serve some member or members of the three upper castes.

A similar account of an individual's *varṇadharma* as something like his innate set of duties or obligations is found in the *Gītā*'s 4.13 when Kṛṣṇa tells Arjuna that the four-fold *varṇa*-system (*cāturvarṇyam*) has been created by him (*mayāśṛṣṭam*) by classifying human beings into four groups in accordance with their guṇas and karmas (*guṇakarma-vibhāgasah*). The Sanskrit term *guṇakarmavibhāgasah* is a conjunction of *Guṇavibhāgasah* and *karmavibhāgasah*. The word *guṇa* means here a component or constituent, and not a quality or attribute. More specifically, it refers to *sattva*, *rajas* and *tamas*, the three elements which according to the Sānkhya metaphysics, are the components of everything, living as well as non-living. By classifying humans in terms of their *guṇa* is meant classifying them in terms of their dominant *guṇa*. Of the three *guṇas*, all are present in every human being but some one of them is dominant in some, and some other one in some others.

As elaborated by almost all the famous commentators on the *Gītā*, like Śankara, Madhusūdana Sarasvatī, Rāmānuja, Śridharasvāmī, et al., in *brāhmaṇas satva* is predominant. Therefore, their duties or *varṇadharmas*, are the control of mind and body (*sāma* and *dama*), austerity, etc. In *kṣatriyas rajas* is predominant and *sattva* is secondary. Their duties as *kṣatriyas* are courage (*śaurya*), valour (*tejah*), etc. The duties of *vaiśyas* are to engage themselves in agriculture, etc., because in them *rajas* predominates and *tamas* is secondary. In *śūdras tamas* predominates and *rajas* is secondary. Their only duty, therefore, is to serve the other three classes. These duties are the *varṇadharmas* of the four *varṇas* or castes assigned to them by Kṛṣṇa, or God, simultaneously with their creation. That, is, in this account too, the *varṇas* are created with their *varṇadharmas*. This is made possible because, as per this theory, *varṇadharmas* are duties assignable to individuals on the basis of their ontological composition, the nature of their *guṇa*-complex made up the three components, *sattva, rajas,* and *tamas,* and in differing order of dominance, known to their creator.

According to classical Indian metaphysics or ontology of *sattva, rajas* and *tamas,* the being of every individuals is composed of these three elements and the order of predominance of one element over another is never the same in two individuals. The order does not change anytime and therefore two different individuals are bound to remain always different. This means that the four *varṇas*, which are determined by the component *guṇa*-complex of the individuals composing them, would always remain the same four *varṇas*; and, so would remain their *varṇadharmas* because they too are determined by the same unchangeable *guṇa*-complexes.

A logical fallout of this view would be that no individual of one *varṇa,* say, a *kṣatriya,* can ever give up his *varṇadharma* and opt for that of another, say, of a *brāhmaṇa.* If, perchance, anyone is able to do that, that would be a counter-instance to this theory and therefore would invalidate it. The theory is offered as a universal, incontrovertible, one, being propounded by a god, Kṛṣṇa. A divinely propounded theory has to be incontrovertible because a god, its propounder, cannot, by definition, commit a mistake, i.e. cannot give a falsifiable theory. And, if it is found to be falsifiable, then it would mean that either it is not a divinely propounded theory, or that its propounder is not a god. This would be a catastrophe for both, the theory and the god who claims to be the theory's propounder; a catastrophe for the theory because it would be disproven and for the god concerned because he would lose his godhood.

The history of India does offer two very clear counter-instances to the divine theory, or Kṛṣṇa's theory of *varṇadharma* or of *dharma* briefly given above. Both Mahāvīra, the founder of Jainism, and Gautama Buddha, that of Buddhism, are *kṣatriyas* by birth. But they give up the life-style of a *kṣatriya* and adopt that of a recluse, a *brāhmaṇa,* very successfully and do the like of which no bona fide *brāhmaṇa* saint has been able to do. This means that *varṇas*, or *varṇadharmas*, are not as unalterable as Kṛṣṇa's theory entails them to be, nor is adopting another *varṇadharma,* a *dharma* other than one's own, as dangerous or fear-generating as he claims it to be when, in the *Gīta* 3.35, he forbids

Arjuna to give up his, a *kṣatriya*'s *varṇadharma* of fighting a righteous war and adopt that of a recluse or *brāhmaṇa*, even if the former looks unattractive to him.

Even if we ignore the reference to the role of any divine agency in the *Bṛhadāraṇyaka-Gītā* theory and take the theory only to mean that human beings are *born as* members of different *varṇas* with their *varṇadharmas* or duties already assigned to them, the theory's account of our *varṇadharmas* would not be a realistic account of them. *Varṇadharmas* are nothing but our social, interpersonal, obligations or duties. Very few obligations are those we are born with, if there is any such given-with-the-birth obligation.

It may be said, as some say, that to be born as a child of some parents is to be born with the obligation to support the parents in their old age, or to fulfil their wishes, obey their orders, etc. But even this obligation cannot be safely said to be an entirely given-with-the-birth obligation. There is a strong view to the effect that this obligation very much depends on whether or not the parents, after the birth of the child, perform well the role of parents; that their merely being the parents, merely occupying in the society the position of parents of the child, does not generate the child's obligation. The concept of the role one does or does not play towards someone, as a determiner of the latter's obligation towards one, is very much there in Indian ethics. We have seen that Karṇa does not accept his full obligation to his mother Kuntī to fulfil her wish to come over to the Pāṇḍavas' side on the ground that she has not fulfilled her role as a mother to him.

Obligations, like those which *varṇadharmas* are, are *generated* in the network of relations we have in our social life with other members of the society. That is why they change when a relevant social relation changes. The *Bṛhadāraṇyaka-Gītā*'s given-with-the-birth account of obligations, if taken as a general theory of obligations, or even of social obligations, entails that neither can our obligations change, nor can we incur a new obligation. It does this because it makes *varṇas* and therefore inter-*varṇa*, interpersonal, relationships unchangeable. Therefore, it may be said that the theory is counter-intuitive or incommensurate with the facts of moral life. This implication can be gotten rid of by modifying, or restructuring, the theory as maintaining that the different *varṇas* of classical times emerged in the course of social-societal *evolution* and therefore they may change when this evolution takes a new direction. We can then very well say that *varṇadharmas* may also change, some prevalent ones may atrophy and in their place some new ones may get generated when social-societal relationships change.

Some modern scholars take mistakenly the *guṇa* of *guṇakarmavibhāgasah* to mean qualities of individuals forming a *varṇa*, and the *karma* of it to mean the actions they perform in their present lifetime. Then, by committing the second mistake of ignoring the term *mayāśṛṣṭam* (created by me), they interpret Kṛṣṇa's 4.13 of the *Gītā* to mean that individuals have been grouped or classified into four *varṇas* on the basis of the qualities they actually possess and the actions they perform. Therefore, they take the *Gītā*-sentence[3] to mean that *varṇas* are not determined by birth (*janmanā*) but by their qualities and actions. It has been shown in some detail in 7.3 that this account not only suffers from the two mistakes mentioned above but also makes the task of putting any individual in any *varṇa* insoluble. Therefore, the reasoning is not repeated here.

The classification of individuals into four *varṇas* on the basis of their constitutive *guṇa*-complexes links the classification inexorably with the *Sānkhya* metaphysics. According to the latter the three *guṇas*, *sattva*, *rajas* and *tamas*, are the components or constituents of *prakṛti*, or matter, which is one of the two ultimate realities, the other being *puruṣa*, or pure consciousness. This metaphysic is speculative or a *priori*, not empirical, and has been severely criticized and shown to be defective by several non-*Sānkhya* philosophers. Therefore, to link the *varṇa* theory and therefore the theory of *varṇadharma* with it may be said to make it vulnerable to such defects which accrue from the defects of the *Sānkhya* metaphysics, particularly its theory of *prakṛti*. But since, this work is not concerned with Indian metaphysics, going into the criticisms of the *Sānkhya* theory of *prakṛti* would amount to going far afield. However, there is one redeeming feature of the theory of *varṇadharma*'s basing the *varṇadharmas* of different *varṇas* on the *guṇa*-complexes of the individuals composing them. It is the theory's introducing the concept of nature (*svabhāva*) as the connecting link or intermediary between *guṇa*-complexes of an individual and his *varṇadharma*. As interpreted by almost all important commentators of the *Gītā*, the *guṇa*-complex of an individual determines his nature and his nature determines his *varṇadharma*. That is why the *Gītā* calls every *varṇadharma svabhāvaja* i.e. born out of, or determined by, the nature of the individual or individuals whose *varṇadharma* it is. This claim is a pointer to a larger issue in ethical theory, namely, the issue of ascertaining how is a man's nature related to his obligations or duties. Therefore, we shall take it up in the next section.

13.2 HUMAN NATURE AND *VARṆADHARMA*

Even if the general theory of *guṇas*, or *guṇa* theory as holding that the *guṇa*-complex of an individual determines his nature, is unmaintainable, if the theory that the nature of an individual determines his *varṇadharmas* or obligations is maintainable, then the *Gītā*'s, or the Indian, theory of *varṇadharma* as nature-born (*svabhāvaja*) would be maintainable. Rather, it may even be taken as a valid general theory of obligation. But let us see how the commentators go from *guṇas* to nature to morality in order to examine in a logically fair way the propriety of calling a *varṇadharma* nature-born. Among the commentaries on the statements of the *Gītā* relevant to this issue, Madhusūdana Sarasvatī's commentary is most elaborate. We shall make use of it in our discussion, using those relevant points of it which are acceptable to thinkers of both *Advaitic* and non-*Advaitic* persuasion.

For the first time the *Gītā* presents in 18.41 the view that *varṇadharmas* of an individual are determined by, or born out of, his nature. In it Kṛṣṇa says to Arjuna.

'O scorcher of enemies, the duties of the *brāhmaṇas* the *kṣatriyas* and the *vaiśyas*, as also of the *śūdras* have been fully classified according to the *guṇas* which are the sources of disposition.'[4]

According to Sarasvatī, summarizing his analysis, this statement may be taken to mean one of the following, each one asserting that the individual's nature is the source from which his *varṇadharmas* are born, or generated:

(i) The word *svabhāva* in 18.41 may be taken to mean a man's nature is the totality of his dispositions. His *varṇadharmas* are the obligations he is disposed to fulfil, i.e. a set of dispositions to do certain things. Anything which is unnatural for him to do cannot be a *varṇadharma* of his. Therefore, his *varṇadharmas* have been said to be determined by his dispositions or nature. That is why individuals having different natures have been assigned different sets of *varṇadharmas*. For example, *brāhmaṇas* have a preponderance of the *sattva guṇa* due to which their nature is to be peaceful or peace-loving. The *kṣatriyas* have the preponderance of *rajas* with *sattva* being secondary. Their nature is to be domineering. The *vaiśyas*' nature is to be diligent because in them *rajas* is preponderant and *tamas* is secondary. The *śūdras*' nature is to be dull because in them *tamas* is predominant.

(ii) *Svabhāva* or nature can be taken to mean *prakṛti*, the primal matter with the *guṇas* as its components. Since a man's *guṇas* determine his dispositions, i.e. human nature, and dispositions determine his *varṇadharmas*, *prakṛti* can be said to determine *varṇadharmas*. This is non-different from (i) because according to it also a man's dispositions or nature determine his *varṇadharmas*.

(iii) *Svabhāva* may also be taken to mean a man's *sanskāra*, the set of his pre-existing impressions, his *prārabdha karmas*, the set of those actions performed by him in his past life which have begun to produce their effects in this life. It is these impressions which determine his present dispositions or nature in the sense of human nature, which in their turn determine his *varṇadharmas*. In this interpretation too a man's nature determines his *varṇadharmas*. Therefore, in the following sentences, 18.42–44 *varṇadharmas* are explicitly said to be nature-born (*svabhāvaja*).

Sarasvati refers, and rightly, to the *Dharmasutras* of Gautam, Vasiṣṭha, Manu, et al., about the four *varṇas*' *varṇadharmas*, as stated by them, to have been determined by their nature. As per the *Gītā* (18.42) 'The natural duties of a *brāhmaṇa* are control of the mental and external organs, austerity, purity', etc. Those of 'a *kṣatriya* are heroism, boldness, forfitude', etc. (18.43). The natural duties of 'a *vaiśya* are agriculture, cattle-rearing, trade' etc. and 'of a *śūdra* too the natural duty is in the form of service' (18.33).[5]

The theory of *varṇadharmas*, which is a major, or the widest, sector of the Indian ethical theory, thus derives, or more appropriately, claims to derive, all *varṇadharmas* from human nature. The Indian ethical theory also claims, we have seen, to have classified human beings into four varṇas on the basis of their nature, or because of their having the nature they actually have and would continue having during their entire lifetime. It thus assumes that the nature of a man can be determined once and for all. Those, and their number is very large, who think that *varṇadharmas*, or man's obligations, virtues, etc. can be, without causing any philosophical problem, conceptually derived from his nature, and that his nature can be ascertained for all time to come, hail this theory of morality as a completely accurate, or faultless, one. But this is not really the case. That it is not we shall try to show in the next section in some detail.

13.3 THE INDIAN ETHICIST'S DERIVING HIS ETHICAL THEORY OF CASTE-OBLIGATIONS FOR HIS THEORY OF HUMAN NATURE: A MOVE APPARENTLY ATTRACTIVE BUT CONCEPTUALLY UNTENABLE

We have seen in the previous section that Kṛṣṇa, as per the *Gītā*, derives the theory of *varṇadharmas*, the obligations of the different *varṇas* or castes, from his theory of human nature. The theory determines the nature of an individual in accordance with his *guṇas* and *karmas*. Therefore, it can be called the *guṇakarma* theory of human nature. It involves the *Sānkhya* theory of *prakṛti* as constituted by the three *guṇas*, *sattva*, *rajas*, and *tamas* and the theory of rebirth as well as that of *karma* according to which actions done by an individual in his previous birth determine the character of his present life. All of the three theories, which go into the making of the *guṇakarma* theory of human nature, are metaphysical theories. Therefore, there is nothing wrong in calling the *guṇakarma* theory a metaphysical theory.

The theory of caste-obligations, on the other hand, is an ethical theory, since it is one about what an individual, by virtue of his being a member of a certain *varṇa*, i.e. of his *varṇa*hood (*varṇatā*), ought (and ought not) to do, seek to have, to be, to claim as his right, etc., etc. Therefore, Kṛṣṇa's attempt to derive the theory of caste-obligations from, or to found it on, the *guṇakarma* theory of human nature, is one to derive an ethical theory from a metaphysical theory, to derive a theory about what a man *ought* to do, seek, or be, etc. from what his nature is, i.e. what he is fact *is*. Thus to discuss it is really to discuss a very important and topical issue, namely, the issue of whether or not Kṛṣṇa or other Indian ethicists have been really successful in deriving 'Ought' from 'Is', an ethical from a metaphysical, i.e., a non-ethical, theory. A good number of present-day moral philosophers, having a strong logical sensitivity, would say that nobody can achieve this philosophical feat. Therefore, if Kṛṣṇa has really succeeded in achieving it, we can boldly say that Indian ethics has offered a way of doing it which some modern thinkers believe is impossible. This is a very good reason for giving to his, the *Gītā*'s, ethical theory of caste-obligations a serious, unbiased, scrutiny.

There is another, an equally good, reason for giving this attention to Kṛṣṇa's theory because it is not only his, a uniquely personal theory, but has become one acceptable to almost all classical Indian thinkers who accept the four-fold caste-system. Even the Jains and Buddhists who do not accept the caste-system do not seem to have questioned the central principle of the *Gītā* theory, the principle that the moral obligations, or oughts, etc. of an individual are determined by his *nature*, by what he, in fact, by nature, has been equipped to do or be. This is largely so because they too accept the metaphysical theory of rebirth and that of *karma*, or the *karmic* worldview.

The *Cārvāka*s have the boldness to reject both of these theories because they find them unprovable. But even they do not seem to have questioned the role of human nature as the determiner of ethical obligations. Rather, they seem to have accepted it because their hedonism is based on it. The only argument which they seem to have offered for it, or to have had in their mind, is that man's nature is such that, or nature has made him such a being that, he seeks pleasure in whatever he does or seeks to have. Therefore, pleasure is his final end, and not heaven, or another, better, birth or anything like what is called *mokṣa*, etc. None of these is his end because he seeks none of them in a *natural* manner, i.e. if he is allowed to proceed in an untutored manner. I do not say or suggest that their view of human nature is philosophically sound, nor do I say that it is not. I am not concerned with its evaluation. My plain and simple objective here is to point out that they too accept the role of human nature in determining human obligations, a position which is one of the basic tenets, if not the most basic one, of the theory of caste-obligations presented in the *Gītā* and accepted by the majority of classical Indian thinkers. Therefore, the *Gītā* theory of caste-ethics, as determined by human nature, can very well be taken as the classical Indian theory of caste-obligations.

Since it has been shown above that the central feature of the theory is the role it assigns to human nature as the sole determinant of anyone's caste-obligations, we shall take up below a brief examination of what role a man's nature can really play in determining his moral obligations of *any sort*. Since caste-obligations are moral obligations of a sort, what is said in a general way of the relation between human nature and obligations will as well be true of the relation between human nature and caste-obligations.

It is apparently, on the face of it, very attractive, to think that anyone's obligations are very closely related to his nature, to the kind of person he is. There is a good reason for this attraction and it is a short step from this attraction to go to the view that his nature is the sole determinant of his obligations. Let us first see the reason for the initial attraction and examine how far it can justifiably take us in the direction of constructing, or arriving at, an ethical theory of obligation. It is necessary to keep this end in view because the *Gītā*'s, or Indian, ethics considers its theory of human nature competent to yield its theory of caste-obligations. But if it turns out, on good, or even plausible, logical grounds, that no theory of obligation can be yielded by a theory of human nature alone, it would eo ipso be shown that no theory of *caste-obligation* can be derived from it.

The reason for a theory of human nature being considered very closely related to human obligations, or human values, etc., is the fact that the theory sets the limit of the zone of human obligations, values, etc. This is so because the limit of what a man *can* do, or is able to do, is the limit of what be may be said to be obligated to do. This a plain conceptual, deontic, truth, or fact, about human obligations, and not a normative, or any contentual, ethical principle. It is a conceptual truth that we can say of anyone and of any action that he ought to do it if and only if we know, or at least assume, that he can do it. Therefore, to ascertain what one ought to do, or can be said to be obligated to do, it is very important to know what one can and what one cannot do.

The nature of an individual is the totality of his dispositions, as, we have seen, Madhusūdana Sarasvatī puts it. His dispositions are his aptitudes or abilities to do certain things (or to abstain from doing some others). If it is known or proven that a *śūdra* cannot acquire knowledge of any scripture, there is no point in telling him that he ought to do that. But if we know that he can serve others, it does not follow that he ought to do that. This is so because serving others may not in itself be a thing worth doing, or the others may not deserve to be served. All this is obvious because it is not true that one ought to do all that he can do; we can morally require or ask him to do only that which satisfies our criterion of moral rightness, duty, value, etc.

To root the caste-ethics of an individual in his nature may seem to empower an upholder of this theory to give a very simple answer to the question of why an individual belonging to a caste should follow his caste-ethics. The answer, one may say, is that he is to follow it because he has such and such a nature. This would mean the same thing as saying that he should because he belongs to the caste (*varṇa*) concerned, since every caste is claimed, in the *varṇadharma* theory, to have been formed on the basis of the nature of the individuals put into it. This answer, thus, clearly gives to the nature of an individual the logical right to justify his caste ethics. But this cannot, in point of its own logic, be done. An appeal to his nature can authorize anyone only to know or aver what he *can*, or has the ability to, do, and not to know or aver what he ought to do. And, what he can do and what he ought to do, need not always coincide or cohere with each other. For this very reason the appeal to nature cannot entitle this theorizer to decide what is even permissible for him to do, even though not obligatory; that is, what he may do without incurring any moral impropriety. Even the permissible and the natural, the doable, are not conceptually identical with or non-different from, each other. An appeal to his nature does authorize a theorizer to know or decide what he must not, or rather ought not to, consider obligatory for him to do; namely, not to tell him to do something which he knows his nature, or natural equipment, does not allow him to do. But this is not to know anything normative or ethical about him, anything about his *varṇadharmas*. It is something logical or deontic, though it may seem to be ethical. It is, in fact, to say only that he cannot meaningfully consider something to be his *dharma* or *varṇadharma*, an obligation, or a duty, if he cannot do it. It has no implication about what he ought or ought not to do. That is why to assert it the theorizer, or anybody else, does not need to apply, or to have, a criterion of obligatoriness. But still what the appeal to a man's nature authorizes the theorizer to do is very important and makes it extremely relevant to the construction of a theory of obligation, or rather, of morals as such.

We can assert without having any criterion of obligation that what a man's nature does not permit him to do, i.e. what he cannot do, cannot be obligatory for him to do, because it only requires us to know the *meaning* of 'ought' or obligatoriness, and not the content of it. That is why we call it a deontic, or semantic or logical, truth, and not a moral one. This is obvious from the fact that whatever be the criterion of obligatoriness a man cannot be said to be obligated to do what he cannot do.

Therefore, while admitting that the knowledge of an individual's nature is very relevant, or rather unavoidable, for ascertaining his *dharmas* including his *varṇadharmas*, we can say that from it alone we cannot derive any knowledge or account of what his obligations are. This means that we cannot use a theory of human nature to yield a theory of *dharmas*, and therefore of *varṇadharmas*. But this is what Kṛṣṇa seems to have done in the *Gītā* and other Indian ethicists seem to have followed him without any logical or moral murmur.

All of them seem to have been misled by the initial attraction which a theory of human nature has for a moralist concerned with determining the content of man's moral obligations, i.e. with formulating an ethical theory. They seem to have concluded that a theory of human nature, which is necessary for ascertaining what may or may not be a man's obligation, is also *sufficient* for ascertaining what in fact *is* or *is not* his obligation. This is clearly visible in their theory of varṇification and of *varṇadharmas*. It not only holds that the members of a *varṇa* have such and such *varṇadharmas* because they have such and such a nature, but also that a *varṇadharma* derives all of its normative force, or obligatoriness, from the *fact* they it is natural, or born from the nature (*svabhāvaja*) of the individual whose *varṇadharma* it is.

Of the things a *brāhmaṇa*, for example, can do, some may be obligatory, some permissible, and some forbidden. The tradition would say that it is obligatory for him to teach the art of archery to an eligible student and permissible to ask the student to pay his sacred fee (*gurudakṣiṇā*). We may also add here that anybody can say that it is morally wrong, or forbidden, for him to ask the student to pay as his honorarium his chopped-off right thumb. But the knowledge of the nature of a *brāhmaṇa*, or a theory of human nature applicable to a *brahmana*, alone cannot entitle anyone to say all this; that is, it would not be sufficient to enable him to construct a theory about the *varṇadharmas* of a *brahmana*. It has to be aided by a separate theory of morality—more specifically, one of what is morally right, obligatory, desirable, etc.

From a theory of human nature we can neither infer what a man of a certain *varṇa* ought to, or may, do nor what he ought not to, or may not, do. In order to infer even the latter we need an ethical theory about the criterion of obligatoriness which, we have seen, a theory of human nature by itself cannot provide.

The *varṇadharmas* of the different *varṇas* constitute, in effect, the social ethics of the different social groups. They are claimed to have been ascertained, or determined, on the basis of the nature of the individuals put into four different *varṇas* or castes.

The two processes, that of classifying them into four castes and that of determining their ethical roles, are simultaneous, and not successive; they really coalesce into one and the same process. To call an individual a *brāhmaṇa*, to put him into the *brāhmaṇa varṇa*, or to be brief, to varṇify him as a *brāhmaṇa*, is also to assign to him a specific sort of moral code or role pertaining to his personal and social life. Thus his being put into a particular caste, his *varṇatā*, and his having been assigned his caste-ethics, his *varṇadharmatā*, both are based on the kind of nature he has.

The nature of an individual, in the context of the theory of *varṇadharmas*, means the nature he is born with, and is called *sahaja* which means *saha janmanā utpanna*, the nature which is born with the birth of the man whose nature it is.[6] Since it is this, inborn, nature of his which is claimed to determine his *varṇadharmas* or caste-ethics, it follows that he cannot get rid of his caste-ethics, or change it because he cannot get rid of or change his nature. To do the latter would mean he would cease to be the man he is because it is his nature which makes him the individual he is, which determines his identity as the person he is.

We have seen that the nature-born-ness, or naturalness, of a *varṇadharma*, its *sahajatā* (the property of being born to an individual together with his birth, i.e. biological birth) has been repeatedly emphasized[7] and said to be *svabhāvaja*, i.e. born out of the nature of individuals. Calling a duty nature-born may be said to have one (apparent) advantage. It may make the performance of a duty appear to be a smooth affair. Since it is the natural duty of a *kṣatriya* to fight a righteous battle, when the occasion of fighting one arrives, it may be said that he would naturally fight it.

Nay, to call it nature-born may even imply that he would necessarily do what his nature prompts him to do; i.e. he would necessarily fight it. That the *Gītā* does take it to have this implication is clear from what it says at one place. Here Kṛṣṇa tells Arjuna that he, because of his indiscrimination, his befogged understanding, asserts that he would not fight the war. But he shall ultimately fight it because, he being a *kṣatriya*, and it being the natural duty of a *kṣatriya* to fight such a war, he would be impelled, necessitated, or bound, by his nature (*svabhāvajena nibaddhah*) to fight. This means that an individual is bound by his nature to fulfil his *varṇadharmas*.[8] That is, the nature-born-ness of a *varṇadharma* not only makes its fulfilment smooth but unavoidable or unfree. Neither Kṛṣṇa, nor any commentator on the *Gītā*, Seems to realize how an individual can get any moral credit for having done a duty of his if he does it unfreely. Rather, Kṛṣṇa unhesitatingly avers in the next two lines[9] that no individual is free to do what he chooses to do. God, he says, resides in the heart of all creatures and moves them or makes them do whatever (they think) they do. The gravity of the problem with regard to how then it could be said of anyone that he ought (or ought not) to do this or that, i.e. about the possibility of ethics, is not felt by him, or by any writer on the *Gītā*, classical or modern.

But there is another fallout of a man's nature's necessitating him to fulfil his *dharmas*. If this is a fact, then there is no need of any moral argumentation, reasoning, or dialogue to persuade anyone to fulfil any *varṇadharma* of his in case he shows unwillingness to fulfil it. We can say that then there is no need for Kṛṣṇa's argumentation or dialogue with Arjuna to persuade him to fight the war. This means that Kṛṣṇa's undertaking the task of uttering all that he has said in the *Gītā* is not called for, because the primary objective of this classic is to persuade Arjuna, or speaking in a more general way, any individual whatsoever, to fulfil his *varṇadharmas*, and Arjuna, or everyone, is already bound by his nature to fulfil it. A third obvious fallout of an individual's being bound by his nature to fulfil his *varṇadharmas* is that akrasia, or moral deviation, becomes impossible.

There is one likely interpretation of the Indian ethic's making a caste-obligation nature-born which may be claimed to take away the normativity of the theory of caste-obligation as an ethical theory. This interpretation may be done by taking the relation between a man's nature and his caste-ethics as a causal one. The incentive to do that may arise because of the *Gītā*'s calling a *varṇadharma svabhāvaja* i.e. nature-generated, which may appear similar to a classical Indian physician's calling a body-pain *vātaja* i.e. generated, produced, or caused, by an excess of wind in the body of the patient. In the medical case both, excess of wind in the body and the experience of pain, are events, the former is the cause and the latter its effect. On this analogy, or grammatical similarity between the words *svabhāvaja* and *vātaja*, a *varṇadharma*, or caste-obligation, becomes an event which is an effect of another event, the nature of an individual, as it is generated by the latter. And, then, one may say, this nature-born (*svabhāvaja*) theory of caste-obligation is untenable because it makes caste-obligation an event. But no obligation is an event; it is, on the other hand, an action or a series of actions done or to be done. When an obligation is fulfilled, it is an action or a series of actions done, and before its fulfilment it is an action or a series of actions which ought to be done, i.e. which is yet to be done. Before Arjuna fights the *Mahābhārata* war, his obligation as a *kṣatriya* to fight it is a series of actions he ought to do, and when he has already fought it out, it is a series of actions already done because his obligation to fight, his *varṇadharma*, has been fulfilled by him. Therefore, the objection, which this interpretation gives rise to, is to the effect that the *Gīta*, or the Indian, theory of caste-obligation is untenable because it makes the concept of obligation isomorphic with that of an event. But it is wrong for the theory to do that because obligation comes under the concept of an action which is categorically different from that of an event.

This interpretation also indicates, maybe indirectly, that the *svabhāvaja* theory makes an obligation a one-place, a monadic, predicate when it is a relational one, and the two, a monadic and a relational predicate, are categorically different from each other. Kṛṣṇa, we have seen, says in the *Gītā*, that he has created the four *varṇas*, i.e. the individuals belonging to them. For anyone to belong to a *varṇa* i.e. for Arjuna to have been created as a *kṣatriya*, is to be created having been already assigned the *varṇadharmas* of a *ksatriya*. This means that his *varṇadharmatā* is a predicate of his since his birth, i.e. a monadic predicate, and not the result of his having entered into a set of relationships with other individuals belonging to a social network, a moral community, to which he also belongs. But this is counter-intuitive, incongruent with our normal, unbiased, understanding of the concept of an obligation. An obligation is a relational predicate or concept, a liability which accrues to an individual because of his having been related to some other individual, or a group of individuals, in lieu of his having done something to him or them, or of the other individual's, or, group's, having done something to him.

To come back to Arjuna, again to exemplify the above point, his obligation to fight the *Mahābhārata* war is a relational predicate, and not a monadic one. It is relational because it involves more than one term. To see this let us see what it is. To put it briefly: It is *his* obligation or duty to *fight the war* with *Duryodhana* for recovering from him his ancestral property which Duryodhana has wrongfully grabbed. One term of it is Arjuna himself as the agent or owner of the obligation; the second, fighting the war, as the means; the third, recovering his lost ancestral property, as the objective; the fourth, Duryodhana as the agent of the action which makes the fighting with him his duty; and the fifth, Duryodhana's wrongfully grabbing the property, as the action done by Duryodhana on account of which the obligation to fight him accrues to Arjuna.

Both of these objections against the Indian account of caste-obligation as nature-born are grave. But the tradition does not seem to have attended to them with any seriousness. However, if anything can be done by a traditionalist to defend the nature-born theory against them, it may be done on the lines below, though we have to admit or confess that it is not an irrefutable defence. The traditionalist may possibly proceed as follows:

The four *varṇa*s, and therefore the individuals who compose them, are created by god (Kṛṣṇa) and their nature too is determined by him on the basis of their *guṇa*-complex, i.e. on the basis of which one of *sattva, rajas*, and *tamas* predominates in which individual *and* on the basis of the *karmas* they have done in their previous life. Therefore, neither their having come into being, nor their having the nature they have, is an event; rather, each one of the two is the result of divine action. Their *varṇadharmas* are, of course, nature-born, *svabhāvaja*, i.e. they are what they are because of their having the nature they have. But they too may not be said to be events because of the individual's nature's not being an event. A *varṇadharma*, it may be added, remains in the theory a relational predicate because god does not create an individual as an isolated being but as a member of a *varṇa*, a caste, a person in a social network, in a *varnavyavasthā*, which is a four-fold social order.

It is obvious to any critical, open-minded, reader, that this defence is vulnerable at many points. Moreover, it depends on the (a) belief in theism, (b) belief in creationism, (c) belief in the organization of social order as an act of divine dispensation, (d) belief in the *Sānkhya* theory of three *guṇas*, (e) belief in the theory of rebirth, (f) belief in the *karmic* worldview, (g) belief in the doctrine that what emerges out of an action, a non-event, cannot be an event, and (h) belief in the doctrine that the *varṇadharma* of an individual can be called a relational predicate *accrued* to him even when it is his *varṇadharma* as a result of a divine action. Each one of the beliefs (a) to (h) can be shown without much difficulty to be unmaintainable, or at least unprovable. The reader can very easily do this exercise and satisfy himself of the extremely shaky character of these beliefs.

13.4 *VARṆADHARMA* AS *SVADHARMA*

Any *varṇadharma* is an obligation of an individual as a *member* of the *varṇa* he belongs to. But its fulfilment is to be done by him, and not by the *varṇa* concerned, or by any *varṇa* whatsoever, because a *varṇa* is not an entity, a being. That is, a *varṇadharma* is not a *dharma*, obligation, of any *varṇa*, but always of some individual. Therefore, it can as well be called his, the individual's, own *dharma*, i.e. his *svadharma*. This is what the term *svadharma* means. This is also the sense in which the *Gītā*, or Indian ethics, uses this term. It does not mean by it a *dharma* different from *varṇadharma*. It is the same as *varṇadharma* spoken of from the point of view of its fulfilment by an individual since only he can be said or required to fulfil it.

But a large number of modern writers take it to stand for a *dharma* different from *varṇadharma*, meaning by it the *dharma* of an individual as a unique person. Perhaps they are misled by the grammatical forms of the terms *varṇadharma* and *svadharma*. They seem to think that *varṇadharma* means the *dharma* of a *varṇa*, or of an individual as a member of a *varṇa*, and *svadharma* an individual's own, personal, *dharma* not shared by, or obligatory for, any other individual. Treating *svadharma* as a *dharma* obligatory for one and only one individual is both conceptually and textually incorrect. Let is first see the conceptual impropriety of thinking of it as a separate category and thereupon the textual impropriety of doing that.

The concept of a *dharma*, or obligation, like any other moral concept, is universalizable. If an individual with the ability to fight ought to fight a righteous battle, if this sort of fighting by him is an obligation of his, then it is also the obligation of any other individual who is similar to him in morally relevant respects. In the present, oversimplified, case only one feature of the individual is morally relevant, namely his ability to fight a battle. But generally more than one feature of an individual is morally relevant to attributing any obligation to him. Whenever an obligation is attributed to an individual, some respects or features of his personality, his status in his society, his relationship to the individual he is said to be obligated to, etc., constitute the ground or reason for attributing it to him. We can call them obligation-making features, conditions, or attributes of the obligation concerned. For attributing any obligation to any individual there must be some obligation-making, or obligation-justifying, attribute or attributes. This is a logical, conceptual, feature of the act of attributing an obligation to anyone. It is this feature of it which always makes it sensible for a person to whom an obligation to do such and such is attributed, or of whom it is said that he ought to do such and such, to ask why it is his obligation, or why he ought to do it. It is this logical feature of the act of attributing an obligation, or, a *dharma*, to him which makes the act of attribution a rational act, and the concept of obligation a rational concept. This is true of all moral concepts and therefore of all *dharmas*.

It follows from what has been said above that when anything is said to be a *dharma* of an individual, he must be one who fulfils or satisfies those *dharma*-making conditions which are required for the attribution of that particular *dharma* to him. It also follows then that the *dharma* can be attributed to any other individual who fulfils those conditions. For example, the *Gītā* requires that Arjuna ought to fight the *Mahābhārata* war because (a) he is able to fight it, (b) it is a righteous war because it is to recover his rightful property from Duryodhana who has immorally grabbed it, (c) all other means of recovering the lost property have failed, (d) if he fights it as a duty with no desire or attachment for its consequences whatever they may be, he would incur no sin even if he kills in the war otherwise respectable, or innocent, people, etc. And, Kṛṣṇa calls it Arjuna's *svadharma* to fight this war, obviously, on these grounds. It is clear that it would be then the *svadharma* not only of Arjuna alone, i.e. of Arjuna as a person distinct and different from all other individuals. Rather, it would be the *svadharma* of all those who satisfy the conditions (a) to (d), and therefore the same as the *varṇadharma* of all *kṣatriyas*. Every *kṣatriya* is said to have the obligation to fight a righteous war on the grounds on which, or in the manner in which, Arjuna is required to fight. What the *Gītā* calls a *svadharma* of Arjuna is, thus, his *dharma* as a *kṣatriya,* and not as a person totally different from all others. But this is what his *varṇadharma,* or any *kṣatriya*'s *varṇadharma,* is. All this is true of all *varṇadharmas*.

The *varṇadharma* of any individual belonging to any *varṇa* is, thus, his *svadharma,* and vice versa. Therefore, *svadharma* really means *svavarṇadharma,* the *dharma,* or set of obligations, which any individual belonging to any *varṇa,* ought to fulfil by virtue of his belonging to that *varṇa,* i.e. that which he ought to fulfil *as* a member of that *varṇa.* We can, therefore, conclude that the concept of *svadharma* is the same as that of *varṇadharma,* and vice versa. There may be an emotive advantage in calling a *varṇadharma* a *svadharma* because, on account of the syllable *sva,* meaning one's own, occurring in it, it may suggest to an individual that it denotes a *dharma* which is his in a much more intimate sense than the sense in which his *varṇadharma* is his *dharma.* It may thereby be used by a clever argumentator to win over a person unwilling to fulfil a certain *varṇadharma* of his and make him willing to fulfil it. Perhaps this is the reason for Kṛṣṇa's using it at a crucial point in his argumentation with the unwilling Arjuna to convince him that he ought to fight the war. But that he succeeds in winning him over does not imply that he succeeds simply because of the use of this emotive device, since he offers so many other reasons as well, and, to crown all, reveals himself in his divine form to Arjuna to convince him that what he says is unquestionable.

The purport of what has been said above is not to aver or suggest that Kṛṣṇa does not realize that the two terms, *svadharma* and *varṇadharma* denote one and the same moral concept. He very clearly admits their non-difference. In fact, no classical thinker makes the mistake of considering *svadharma* as the *dharma* of an individual as a unique person, non-attributable to any other individual. Only some modern writers have made this mistake and without even giving a supporting reason to make it appear as a tenable view.

What has been said above is fully supported by what Kṛṣṇa has actually said in the *Gītā.* His treating svadharma to be the same as *varṇadharma* is crystal clear when he says to Arjuna[10] that he, taking into account his own duty (*svadharma*), should not hesitate to fight the war because nothing is better as a duty for him as a *kṣatriya* than fighting a righteous war which this war is. He thus identifies Arjuna's own duty, *svadharma,* with his duty as a *kṣatriya,* i.e. as a member of the *kṣatriya varṇa,* his *varṇadharma* or caste-duty. Nowhere does he mention any duty which can be called a *svadharma* but not a *varṇadharma,* or vice versa, nor does any other thinker do that anywhere. In the same context he further emphasizes the importance of *svadharma* as *varṇadharma* by averring that if Arjuna avoids fighting the righteous war, i.e. fails to perform his duty as a *kṣatriya,* he would fail to perform his own duty (*svadharma*) and to protect his reputation as a fighter, and would consequently incur sin. He reinforces his emphasis further[11] when he says that even if one's performance of *svadharma,* as one's *svavarṇadharma,* is defective (*viguṇah*) and a *paradharma* (another man's *dharma* i.e. the *varṇadharma* of a man of another *varṇa, paravarṇadhavema*) is non-defectively or impeccably done (*svanuṣṭhitāt*), the former is higher in value (*śreyah*) than the latter. Nay, it is preferable to die while performing one's *svadharma,* rather than performing another man's *dharma* which is fear-producing. The context of these utterances of Kṛṣṇa make it fully clear that by *svadharma* he means the *dharma* of one's own *varṇa* and by *paradharma* the *dharma* of another *varṇa.* This is because he utters them to Arjuna to persuade him to fight the war on the ground that it is his obligation as a *kṣatriya,* i.e. his *varṇadharma,* and not to commit the mistake of leaving the battle field and think of becoming a peace-loving mendicant, because doing the latter is a *brāhmaṇa's varṇadharma,* and therefore for Arjuna a *paradharma* or *paravarṇadharma.* But nowhere in the *Gītā* nor in any commentary on it, is a reason given to explain why one's own *varṇadharma* or *svadharma* is given such an honour, nor to explain why even performing another man's *varṇadharma* in a faultless manner is bound to cause fear in him who does that.

Kṛṣṇa knows very well that Droṇa is a *brāhmaṇa,* a non-*kṣatriya* and an extremely skilled and able fighter as an archer, i.e. an excellent performer of a *paradharma,* since fighting a war well is a *dharma* of a *kṣatriya* and not of a *brāhmaṇa* and therefore a *paradharma* for a *brāhmaṇa.* In fact, the history of the *Mahābhārata* war conclusively shows that in the war he proves himself to be the best archer or the second best only to Bhīṣma, if Bhīṣma is considered the best one. Droṇa's not being a *kṣatriya,* or performing a *paradharma,* does not produce any fear in him. And, the irony is that Kṛṣṇa never tries to convince him of the superiority of *svadharma* or *svavarṇadharma.* A similar thing may be said of Mahāvīra who founds the ethic-religious system of Jainism and of Buddha who founds the similar system of Buddhism. Both are *kṣatriyas*, but both abjure what Kṛṣṇa would have called a *kṣatriya*'s *varṇadharma* and adopt what he would have called a *brāhmaṇa*'s *varṇadharma,* since both become recluses and evolve ethico-religious codes which, according to them, everyone ought to adopt. They not only reject the division of human society into four castes or *varṇas*, which Kṛṣṇa says, he himself as a god has created, but even reject the existence of any god. None of these things cause any fear in either of them, nor can either of them be said to have failed in his mission, or committed a sin by doing a *paradharma.*

At one point[12] Kṛṣṇa says that everything which has a beginning, as has every action, and therefore every action, is accompanied by, or involves some evil, as is every fire accompanied with some smoke. This means that one's own *dharma,* or *varṇadharma,* i.e. caste-duty, which is the *dharma* one is born with (*sahaja*), as well as another man's *varṇadharma,* or caste-duty, involves some evil. Consequently, by giving up one's *dharma* and adopting the latter, a *paradharma,* one does not get freed from all evil. Hence, one should continue doing one's own *dharmas* or caste-duties.

The above may be claimed to be offering a reason for preferring to do one's own caste-duties rather than to do someone else's. But if it is claimed to be doing that, the reason it is alleged to offer cuts both ways. If both involve some evil, and there is nothing else in either of the two which makes it morally better than the other, then there exists no moral reason for preferring one to the other. This means that the choice between them has to be arbitrary, i.e. without any moral reason; or it may be made on some non-moral ground. And, then, an individual may choose either one, his own, or someone else's, *svadharma,* or *varṇadharma,* which his non-moral reason or consideration favours or supports. For example, Droṇa may say that he has chosen to acquire excellence in archery, a *kṣatriya*'s *dharma* and therefore a *paradharma,* and not to acquire excellence in *Vedic* scholarship, his *svadharma* or *svavarṇadharma,* because the *paradharma* is more advantageous or paying because it has procured for him royal patronage and a style of living which only a king can have. Whether or not Droṇa's reasoning is valid, Kṛṣṇa's theory, as readable in what he says in the *Gītā*'s 18.48, cannot be used to prove its invalidity. Rather, it may be used to prove its validity or acceptability, as has been shown above.

Buddha can be said to have given to Kṛṣṇa a good moral reason for choosing a *paradharma* in some of his remarks. But it has been more vocally and forcefully asserted by his life than by any one of them. He may be taken to have replied to Kṛṣṇa, or to a champion of the *varṇadharma* theory, that he has chosen to be a recluse in order to find out for everyone a way of getting rid of, or minimizing, his suffering. He has given up his *svadharma*, in Kṛṣṇa's scheme his *varṇadharma* of ruling over his kingdom and fighting a righteous war if necessary, because removing or minimizing human suffering is *intrinsically*, as a moral value, superior to doing his *svadharma*. To this no reply can be given while remaining confined within the framework of the *varṇadharma* theory of ethics. What has been demonstrated through the works and life of Buddha can equally well be illustrated through Mahāvīra's.

Another serious problem arises for the Indian *varṇadharma* theory when we reflect on the nature-born-ness, *svabhāvajatā*, of a *varṇadharma* as a *svadharma*. From what has been said so far about it, it is clear that, according to the *varṇadharma* theory, every *varṇadharma*, or *svadharma*, is *svabhāvaja*. While always keeping in mind that the concept of *svadharma* is non-different from that of *varṇadharma*, let us limit the present discussion mainly to the concept of *svadharma*.

We have seen that the *guṇa-karma* of a individual determines his nature (*svabhāva*) and on the basis of, or in concordance with, his nature, his *varṇa* and *varṇadharma* are determined. Therefore, every *varṇadharma*, or *svadharma*, is called *svabhāvaja*, or *sahaja*, determined or generated by, or born with the birth of, the individual whose *svadharma* it is. This means that *svabhāvajatā* is a necessary condition of *svadharmatā*. That is, if doing anything is a *svadharma* of an individual, it is also *svabhāvaja*, a natural thing for him to do. No other condition is mentioned in the *Gītā*, or in any other classical work, as another necessary condition of it. A clear implication of this fact is that, according to the Indian theory, *svabhāvajatā* is the one and only condition of *svadharmatā*. From this it follows not only that every *svadharma* is *svabhāvaja* but also that every *svabhāvaja* action has to be called a *svadharma* because nothing other than, or in addition to, *svabhāvajatā* has been said to be required of, or necessary for, a thing in order to be a *svadharma*. To put all this in a briefer way, *svabhāvajatā* turns out, in the adumbration of the (*varṇadharma*) *svadharma* theory to be, virtually, or, in effect, both the necessary and sufficient condition of *svadharmatā*. This interpretation has to be accepted as legitimate because the theory's non-mention of anything other than *svabhāvajatā* as a necessary condition of (*varṇadharmatā* or) *svadharmatā* has to be taken seriously.

We have seen earlier that what is natural need not always be moral, or, even morally permissible or non-condemnable. Therefore, to make *svabhāvajatā* the criterion of *dharmatā* or *svadharmatā*, i.e. moral rightness, or obligatoriness, is neither normatively nor logically a safe procedure for any ethical theory. We see a clear demonstration of it in what Rāvaṇa says to Sītā in response to her moral rebuke to him for having done the moral evil, or vice, of having abducted her who is another man's, Rāma's, wife. Rāvaṇa admits that he has done the act of abducting her but refuses to call it a moral evil, or a moral wrongdoing. Rather, in abducting her, he says, he has done nothing wrong but a right thing because doing an act of adultery or abduction is his *svadharma* as a demon (*rākṣasa*), i.e. the *svadharma* (or *varṇadharma*) of all demons. It is their *svadharma*, he goes on, because it is their nature to do such acts; that is, in terms of the *varṇadharma* theory, they are their *svabhāvaja* acts and therefore their doing anyone of them is not a moral wrong (*adharma*) but their *svadharma* or *dharma*.[13]

It may be said by someone from the side of the *varṇadharma* theory that, since *varṇadharmas* or *svadharmas*, are determined by a divine agent, such an agent would never make such acts anyone's *svadharma*, not even a demon's. But a Rāvaṇa may rejoin by reminding him that the divine agent has to determine these *dharmas* in concordance with the nature of the individuals whose *dharmas* they are. Their nature it determines not arbitrarily but, on the basis of their *guṇa*-composition and their karmas done by them in their past life. It is possible then that the *guṇa-karma* constitution of all demons is such that they have to have such a nature which makes them fit or empowered to do such acts. Therefore doing them is natural, *svabhāvaja*, for them and consequently their *svadharmas*.

The above, which may be called a hypothesized, or an imaginary, account justifying an act like that of abduction as a demon's *svadharma*, has been given not to defend Rāvaṇa's having abducted Sītā. Rāvaṇa's act of abducting her, or anybody's abducting anyone, male or female, anywhere at any time or place in any condition is an abominally immoral act. This judgement of our moral common sense is unquestionable. Therefore, any theory which makes it a *svadharma* of anybody must be declared untenable for that very reason. But if we make the *varṇadharma* theory our standard, which makes *svabhavājatā* of an action the sufficient condition for its *svadharmatā* or *dharmatā*, we cannot call Rāvaṇa's theory untenable because it too makes *abduction* a *svadharma* on that very basis, i.e. on that of its *svabhāvajatā*. Nor can the kind of nature which Rāvaṇa's theory attributes to a demon be said to be impossible, because it is not impossible that the *guṇas* and *karmas* of an individual entitle him to be only a demon with this sort of nature.

What has been shown above makes it clear that as long as we are hooked to the *varṇadharma theory* as given to us by the tradition, we cannot prove the untenability of any *Rāvaṇa*-type theory. We have to modify the *varṇadharma* theory at least by recasting it so as to clearly aver that *svabhāvajatā* of an action is only a necessary condition, and not a sufficient condition, for making its doing a man's *dharma* of any type, be it a *sāmānya dharma*, or a *varṇadharma-svadharma*. This is merely to say that only that can be meaningfully called his *dharma* which his nature, or natural capabilities, make it possible for him to do, though everything which his nature makes possible for him to do need not be his *dharma*. Be it also noted that this alone is not enough. We would also have to specify what else is needed to make a natural action morally right or a *dharma*. That is, we would need to incorporate into the theory a statement of the conditions which, together with *svabhavājatā* of the action, would make it morally right, if the action satisfies them. This is only to say that the *varṇadharma* theory has to be modified to include both the statement of necessary and that of sufficient conditions of *dharmata* and *varṇadharmatā-svadharmatā*. All this cannot be done merely as a sporadic or episodic addition to the theory. It would require the introduction of some further, more fundamental, or foundational, changes into it. Obviously, all this cannot be done in a work of the present type.

It is also to be noted that the *guṇa-karma* metaphysics, which the theory claims to be supplying the material ground for the determination (by a divine agent) of everyone's nature, is not trouble-free. Nor is the theory's attribution of the determination of everybody's nature and *dharma* to a divine agent any better. Both these assumptions or beliefs are full of almost irremediable defects. But we cannot discuss them here. Discussing the former would require us to examine in detail the tenability of the *Sānkhya* metaphysics and discussing the latter would require us to go into the heart of Indian theology since it assumes the existence of a divine being, a god. We cannot take it up here as we are primarily concerned with Indian moral philosophy and not with Indian theology.

13.5 CASTE-ETHICS AND GENERAL ETHICS (*VARṆADHARMA* AND *SĀMĀNYA DHARMA*): THE ISSUE OF PRIORITY

In any ethical theory which admits of more than one sort of virtues or obligations, the issue of priority becomes important. Speaking more specifically, in the Indian ethical theory this issue is that of priority between a *varṇadharma* and a *sāmānya dharma*, for example, a caste-virtue or obligation and a general virtue or obligation. Most of modern works on Indian ethics interpret Indian ethical theory as holding that whenever there is any conflict between a *varṇadharma* and a *sāmānya dharma*, the *sāmānya dharma* is to be preferred, i.e. to be given priority over the *varṇadharma*. To say this is not totally untrue. There are instances of this position available in classical Indian works and in the Indian ethos. For example, both Mahavīra and Gautama Buddha abjure doing their duties as householders as well as the duties they are required to do because of their caste. Both of them devote their life to doing what may be called a *sāmānya dharma*, more accurately, a *sāmānya dharma* higher than the *dharmas* mentioned in most of the lists of *sāmānya dharmas* given in some important works. Each of them becomes a recluse and take up the cause of finding a way to free mankind from all possible kinds of suffering. This non-*varṇadharmic* goal of theirs is, rightly, not considered morally wrong in the Indian ethos. And, it can quite fittingly be called a very high, or the highest, kind of *sāmānya dharma*.

It may, however, be urged here that the issue of priority between a *varṇadharma* and a *sāmānya dharma* does not arise in their cases, or does not apply to what they do, because they do not accept the *varṇa*-system and therefore the theory of *varṇadharmas*. It is true that they do reject the *varṇa*-system and therefore the question of anything's being a *varṇadharma* does not arise for them. But what is important to note is that even those thinkers who accept the *varṇa*-system, and therefore the theory of *varṇadharmas*, do not question the high moral quality of Buddha's or Mahāvīra's objective, or the moral excellence of their life-style. That is why we say that general Indian ethos does not consider them to have done anything wrong in not attending to their *varṇadharmas* and devoting their life to propounding and propagating a scheme of life which would help everyone to get rid of all sufferings. This objective of theirs is a non-caste, a *sāmānya, dharma*, a general and high noble moral virtue, or, ideal, because, according to them, everybody, without any caste-discrimination, is entitled to pursue it. Both of them are fully aware of the things which are called the *varṇadharmas* of the different *varṇas*. But still they prefer to pursue this general value the morality of which can surely be seen to be much higher than that of fulfilling any of the *varṇadharmas*. This value or virtue which they seek is much higher, for example, than a *kṣatriya*'s fighting a righteous war even for recovering his lost property, a *varṇadharma* of a *kṣatriya*. It is for fulfilling this *varṇadharma* that Kṛṣṇa presents to Arjuna his ethical theory in the *Gītā* to persuade him to fight the *Mahābhārata* war.

Another example of according priority to a *samanya dharma* we find in the *Rāmāyaṇa.* Kaikeyī asks the king Daśaratha, her husband, to enthrone her son Bharata on the throne of Ayodhyā in place of Rāma, his eldest son, the rightful claimant of the throne, and to send Rāma into exile for fourteen years. This she does based on the king's earlier blanket promise to her to fulfil any two of her wishes. In order to let his father not be accused of breaking his promise out of love of him, Rāma willingly agrees to go into exile. Both of the demands of Kaikeyī are morally wrong, the king knows that they are, and so does Rāma. The king does not ask Rāma to go into exile, but still Rāma gets ready to go because he considers it, and so does Indian ethics, a *sāmānya dharma,* a general virtue or duty, of a son to respect his father and his wishes. It is to fulfil this duty of his that he readily agrees to go into exile. His other younger brother, Lakṣmaṇa, too, considers Kaikeyī's demands wrong but he also considers wrong the king's, their father's, non-rejection of her two demands which implies his unexpressed or unuttered (*anuccarita*) wish or order that Rāma go into exile. Since it is the *varṇadharma* of a *kṣatriya* to fight anyone who does such a wrong, he tells Rāma that, as a *kṣatriya,* he ought to fight and he would therefore fight out the issue with the king and his army and get him (Rāma) enthroned. But Rāma forbids him to do that because the *sāmānya dharma* of his and Lakṣmaṇa, as sons, is to respect their father's wishes whatever they are and whether or not they are verbally announced or expressed. A *sāmanya dharma* is to be given priority over a *varṇadharma,* and therefore Lakṣmana, he says, ought not to think of fighting or of doing anything disrespectful his father, even if his *varṇadharma* may prompt him to do any such thing.[14] Lakṣmaṇa agrees with him and puts down his bow and arrow. This position taken by Rāma to aver that a *sāmānya dharma* supersedes a *varṇadharma* is very much admired in some classical, and even modern, Indian ethical literature. Many modern writers on classical Indian ethics, keeping some such cases in mind, take it to be the general stand of classical Indian ethics and ethos.

But it is not fair to interpret Indian ethics in this manner. If the Rāma tradition, as stated above, pleads for the priority of *sāmānya dharma* over *varṇadharma,* the Kṛṣṇa tradition, as presented in the *Gītā,* strongly pleads for the priority of *varṇadharma* over *sāmānya dharma.* And, the *Gītā* ethos is not in any way less respected than the Rāma tradition in Indian ethos. Arjuna is unwilling to fight the *Mahābhārata* war because, if fought, it would require him to cause a lot of bloodshed by killing some innocent combatants fighting from the other side, and also to kill or injure some of his elders and teachers whom he ought to respect. It is not that he does not know that his *varṇadharma* as a *kṣatriya* is to fight a righteous war which this war would be. But he still prefers to desist from causing bloodshed, killing or injuring elders and other respected persons. In his reluctance to fight the war Arjuna very clearly shows his according priority to some *sāmānya dharma*s over his *varṇadharma* as a *kṣatriya.* Abstinence from causing bloodshed, as well as from hurting, or disrespecting, elders, whatever may be their fault, is a laudable general virtue (*sāmānya dharma*). But Kṛṣṇa argues for the priority or primacy of *varṇadharma* over *sāmānya dharma.*[15] He ultimately succeeds in making Arjuna agree to fight and he actually fights the war. What Arjuna is afraid would happen does happen, for example, a lot of blood is shed, innocents are killed, elders are killed or severely injured, etc. But Kṛṣṇa is satisfied that he has succeeded in getting *varṇadharma* fulfilled and thereby keeping the *varṇa*-order intact.

The Kṛṣṇa tradition is as prevalent as is the Rāma tradition in the Indian ethos. It would, therefore, be fair only to say that Indian ethics considers neither *sāmānya dharma* to have *overall* priority over *varnadharma* nor *varṇadharma* to have this over *sāmānya dharma*. Its attitude in this regard may be called either ambivalent or indecisive, leaving it to the individual to use his moral maturity to decide in which situation which one of the two should be given priority over the other. In making up his mind he may sometimes be guided by some knowledgeable person he respects and trusts, as Lakṣmaṇa is guided by Rāma and Arjuna by Kṛṣṇa, with the possibility that he even sometimes may make his decision himself. This seems to be a fitting characterization of the Indian position and is in keeping with its not considering any *sāmānya dharma* a categorical, or an unconditional, virtue or obligation, as we have shown in 12.4.

13.6 MORALLY GOOD LIFE AS NOT THE COMPLETELY GOOD LIFE: A HINT FROM THE INADEQUACY OF THE *VARṆADHARMA* THEORY

A large, or the largest, sector of Indian ethical theory, seems to accept the *varṇadharma* theory as propounded in the *Gītā*. To get the theory accepted and implemented in social practice seems to be the primary objective of its defence which has been elaborated in it in some detail, perhaps in more detail than anywhere else. Arjuna may be taken as representing an initially critical, well-educated, individual, feeling disinclined to follow the *varṇa*-ethics in a morally sensitive situation, and Kṛṣṇa as the most committed champion of the *varṇa*-ethics. That he succeeds in converting Arjuna to his position does not mean that he succeeds in proving the validity of the theory on purely logical or morally impeccable grounds. An important ploy of his in support of it is his giving to *varṇadharma* the name of *svadharma*. But it breaks down the moment it is shown, as has been done in the preceding discussion, that, *svadhama*, in his account of it, simply means *varṇadharma*, and is not a new concept. The result is that the term can at best have an emotive appeal but no logical, probative, power.

A little later in the dialogue with Arjuna Kṛṣṇa avers[16] that whenever there is decline of virtue (*dharma*) and increase of vice (*adharma*) then he appears in the world, i.e. incarnates himself in order to protect virtuous, saintly, people, to punish the vicious, and to get virtue re-established, or rejuvenated. In this pronouncement of his as well *dharma* does not denote morality or moral virtue as such, nor does *adharma* denote immorality or moral vice as such. In it too *dharma* denotes *varṇadharma*, caste-duty, the duties of the four castes and *adharma* violation of, or transgression from it by members of the four castes by not performing their caste-duties, or by performing some duty or duties of a caste other than theirs. This point has been very forcefully and candidly made by Śankara[17] in his commentary on the *Gītā* while commenting on Kṛṣṇa's pronouncement made in 4.7, 8. This is also clear from the context of the pronouncement because it is made when he is trying to convince Arjuna that he ought to fulfil his *varṇadharma*, as a *kṣatriya*, of fighting a righteous war, and is narrating the evils which would follow if he, or anybody else, fails to do what is prescribed by his caste-ethics, and the advantages which would result when he fulfils them.

Generally *dharma* and *adharma* in this pronouncement are wrongly referred to as denoting morality and immorality as such. That this interpretation is totally wrong is amply testified by the fact that, as the *Mahābhārata*, of which the *Gītā* is a small fragment, shows, in conducting the operations in the war, as Arjuna's charioteer and guide of the Pāṇḍavas, Kṛṣṇa advises them to do and gets done by them more than one thing which can quite reasonably be said to be against morality (*dharma*) as such, i.e. *dharma* not glued to the *varṇa*-system and its ethics. To mention only a few such instances, we can refer to his getting killed unarmed Jayadratha and Karṇa by Arjuna, unarmed Droṇa by Dhṛṣṭadyumna, Duryodhana by instigating Bhīma to hit him with his weapon (*gadā*) at his hip-joint which the *Mahābhārata* war ethics does not allow, by getting Bhīṣma put in a situation in which he cannot use his weapons even to defend himself and thereby enabling Arjuna to so heavily injure him that he has to withdraw from the battle-field.

None of the above-mentioned acts can be called right in a general, non-*varṇadhārmic*, sense of morality or *dharma*. If anyone wants to call any one of them morally right, he can do that only if he accepts the principle that it is morally right to use any means, even if it is in itself morally wrong, to win a war he considers righteous, a clear version of the principle that end justifies the means howsoever vile the means may be. Working on this principle may be all right for one who is an opportunist or a pragmatist in moral matters but it would not become a moral idealist. It cannot be a principle, therefore, of a general theory of morality, though it may be an acceptable one in a theory of *varṇadhārmic* ethics. Kṛṣṇa has been all along, in the war, after having taught the *Gītā* ethics to Arjuna, telling him that whatever he asks him to do in the actual fight is his duty as a *kṣatriya*, i.e. his *varṇadharma* and therefore morally right. Such an argument would never have convinced a Gautama Buddha and stopped him from going on his ethical-religious mission on the ground that ruling over his kingdom was his *varṇadharma* as a *kṣatriya* prince. This is because the Buddha freed himself from the *varṇa*-system and *varṇa*-ethics.

The Buddha and Mahāvīra are good examples of the truth that every aspect of an individual does not reach its complete fulfilment by his doing only that and even all that social ethics, or ethics, requires him to do. There is something in him which inspires him to do something more than just leading a good moral life. It is this inspiration which makes him leave his home and hearth to become a wondering mendicant in search of finding out the cause of suffering and a way of getting rid of it. When he thinks he has fulfilled his mission, he thinks, and the tradition thinks, that he has attained his full flourishing, his liberation in this very life. It is his desire for this flourishing which has prompted him to leave his family and devote himself to finding out a permanent solution to the problem of freeing mankind of all kinds of suffering. This objective itself is a highly noble ethics one and therefore his going out to seek it is not to leave, or go beyond, ethics, or ethical life. It is rather to seek his complete flourishing or fulfilment which encompasses or comprehends within itself living a good moral life. Any such attempt by a classical Indian thinker is born out of the conviction that leading a good moral life is good but not the complete good. Therefore, it is not to be transcended or left behind, but supplemented or made richer.[18]

The Buddha and Mahavīra do what has been stated very briefly above by rejecting the theory of society as consisting of four *varṇa*s or castes. But even the thinkers who accept the four-fold caste-system also agree with them in admitting that something more than living a good moral life is to be done by man to attain his full flourishing. It is this goal which is the fourth *puruṣārtha*. It has several names, like *nirvāṇa*, *kaivalya*, *mokṣa*, etc. But, as we have said at the very beginning of this work, we use the term *mokṣa* for it. It needs a separate discussion and therefore will be taken up in the chapter which follows.

NOTES AND REFERENCES

1. Swāmī Mādhavananda (ed.), *Bṛhadāraṇyaka Upaniṣad* with the commentary of Śankarācārya (Advaita Ashram, Calcutta, 1993), 1.8v.11–14, pp. 119–24.
2. Ibid., p. 123.
3. '*Cāturvarnyam mayāśṛṣṭam guṇakarma vibhāgasah*'. 'The four *varṇas* have been created by me through a classification of the *guṇas* and duties.' Swāmi Gambhīrānanda (trans), *Bhagavadgīta* with the commentary of Śankarāchārya (Advaita Ashram, Calcutta), 4.13, pp. 185–86.
4. "*Brāhmaṇakṣatriyaviśām śūdrānām ca parantapa. Karmāṇi pravibhaktāni svabhāva.* Madhusudana Sarasvatī, *Bhagavad-Gītā* with the annotation Gūdhārtha Dipikā, trans. by Swāmi Gambhīrānanda (Advaita Ashrama, Calcutta, 2000), pp. 951–54.
5. Ibid., pp. 955–58.
6. Ibid., 18.48.
7. Ibid., 18.42–44.
8. Ibid., 18.59, 60.
9. Ibid., 18.61.
10. Ibid., 2.31, 33, 35.
11. Ibid., 3.35.
12. Ibid., 18.48.
13. Vālmīki, *Rāmāyaṇa, Sundara Kanda,* 20.4–7.
14. Ibid., *Ayodhya Kanda,* 21.40–48.
15. *Gītā,* 1.20–48 and 2.3–6.
16. Ibid., 4.7, 8.
17. Swāmī Gambhīrānanda (trans.), *Bhagavadgītā* with the commentary of Śankarācārya (Advaita Ashram, Calcutta), pp. 180–81.
18. For a slightly different and more analytical and critical discussion of the *varṇadharma* theory from the point of view of its applicability in modern times see Chapter I of my *Varnadharma, Niskama Karma and Practical Morality: A Critical Essay on Applied Ethics* (D.K. Printworld, New Delhi, 1999), pp. 3, 32.

CHAPTER 14

The Highest *Puruṣārtha*: Liberation (*Mokṣa*)

14.1 FULFILMENT OF THE PERSON: THE END-POINT OF PURSUIT OF VALUES

The discussion of the three *puruṣārthas*, *artha*, *kāma* and *dharma*, that has been presented in the previous chapters clearly shows that the pursuit of each one of them is social or society-centric. This is to say that the pursuit of each one of them derives its significance from the fact that it is done, or is doable, by an individual in a society, i.e. in a social context in which he has to interact with some other individuals, or, members, of his society or moral community. This point is obvious not only in the pursuit of *artha* and of *dharma* but also in that of *kāma*. Any attempt to satisfy a desire and thereby to attain some pleasure or agreeable experience derives its ethical content or relevance from the fact that it involves some interaction with some others. This interaction may be in the form of receiving, directly or indirectly, cooperation from them or in that of conflict with some of their interests. This is true of the pursuit of *artha* as well. It is this fact on account of which *dharma* has to have the role of a social-moral regulator of the pursuit of *artha* and *kāma* as *puruṣārthas*. This regulation is largely needed to make one man's pursuit cohere with the relevant or related pursuits of others in the interest of protecting and promoting social cohesion and harmony. In the case of *dharma*, too, whether as *sāmānya dharma* or *varṇadharma*, its social role or socio-centric nature has been made amply clear in the discussion of general and caste-virtues or obligations.

The pursuit of the three values, in the manner prescribed in the theory of *puruṣārthas*, i.e. conducting one's life in such a way that the pursuit of *artha* and *kāma* is done in concordance with *dharma* and moral (*dhārmic*) obligations, general and caste-relative, are fulfilled, may be said to be, as per the Indian ethical theory, all that leading a good moral life consists in.

It is possible that this life still turns out to be not completely impeccable, or fully moral. But that would be due not to any lapse on the part of the person leading it, but to some defect in the Indian theory as an ethical theory. In fact, it has been shown in the previous chapters that the Indian theory is not completely faultless and that there are things which it permits or even requires which our moral sense, or moral common sense, does not approve of, or consider morally right. But in spite of all this, the point which is being made here is that a elaboration of the content of each one of the three basic concepts of *artha*, *kāma* and *dharma* and of their interrelations may be taken to be all that is required to present the Indian ethical theory. This means, then, that if a characterization of the Indian ethical theory stops after having done this, it need not be accused of being an incomplete account of the theory. Saying this would have the implication that an account of it in order to be complete does not require to be augmented with a characterization of liberation (*mokṣa*), which is generally said to be the highest value and has also been considered so in this work. In a sense it is and in a sense it is not true.

It is true if we take Indian ethics as being an ethics primarily concerned with man in his social order, in whichever way that order is conceived to be, whether as an order consisting of four castes or caste-groups as Hindu thinkers do, or as a casteless order consisting of individuals related with one another in many different but morally relevant ways, without being classifiable or varṇifiable into well-marked caste-groups, as the *Cārvākas*, Jains and Buddhists do. A non-traditionalist, open-minded, study of the basic things Indian ethics says does give this impression. Depending on it a interpreter can very well think that a characterization of the three *puruṣārthas*, *artha*, *kāma* and *dharma*, is all that needs to be made to give an account of Indian ethics. It is also worth noting that an account of the set of these three *puruṣārthas*, called *trivarga*, (three-membered set), gives the major part not only of Indian ethics, but of any ethics, if we drop those aspects of the three which are hooked to the Indian theory of the four-fold division of the span of an individual's life (*āśrama vyavasthā*) and to the four-fold division of society (*varṇa vyavasthā*). Perhaps that is why in the early part of its history Indian ethical theory mentions only these three *puruṣārthas*. The fourth one, *mokṣa*, is added to them later. Many scholars, quite knowledgeable ones, are of the view that the concept of *mokṣa* does not occur in the *Ṛgveda*.

But in spite of all this, it is also true that stopping with the account of the three values or *puruṣārthas* will not be fair to the temper of Indian value-theory which considers *mokṣa*, the fourth *puruṣārtha*, to be the highest one.

We have hinted at the end of the last chapter that Indian thinkers feel that all normative, value-seeking, aspirations of an individual are not fulfilled by leading a moral life alone. There is something else too which he seeks to have; there is in him some propensity, or aspiration, other than that for being moral, which too he wants to satisfy. This aspiration is not social as the moral one is; the moral one is satisfiable only in a social life but this one is personal. It is satisfied by an individual when he accomplishes his full flourishing, the fulfilment of the person he is. Perhaps when this trend of thinking becomes amply prominent or powerful, the concept of *mokṣa* is added to the *trivarga* theory of *puruṣārthas* which then becomes the *caturvarga* theory, i.e. a theory of four values or *puruṣārthas*. It is this theory which is, as we have called it, the Indian general theory of value, or Indian value-theory.

The Indian general theory of value, thus, considers *mokṣa* to be the highest value the attainment of which completes man's quest for values. This final quest for *mokṣa* is personal because *mokṣa* itself is, we shall soon see, a personal value. Man's leading a moral life, his successful quest for the values of *artha*, *kāma* and *dharma*, fulfils the aspirations he has as an individual-in-society, whereas his attainment of *mokṣa* fulfils the aspiration he has as the person he is when left to himself, or his aspiration to just be the person he really is.

Perhaps it is only when the importance of *mokṣa* as the highest but also a personal value is realized and added to the *trivarga* theory that the last two stages in the life-span of an individual, namely those of *vānaprastha* and *sanyāsa*, the stage of living in a forest and that of renunciation are added. In the last two an individual is supposed to leave his family and society and to devote himself completely to attaining *mokṣa*, shunning all his familial, social, responsibilities, obligations and duties. When we attend to this aspect of Indian value-theory, we have to admit that an account of it is not complete if an account of only the first three *puruṣārthas* is given.

Indian ethics, or ethical theory, is a sector, perhaps the most important, or at least a very important, one of the Indian general theory of value. Therefore, what the latter considers to be the highest value, namely, *mokṣa*, must have some relevance to it. This means that a discussion of its nature and role in man's life is very likely to throw some new light on Indian ethical theory. That is why it would not be fair to close the ethical theory's characterization with only that of *trivarga*, i.e. of *artha*, *kāma* and *dharma*, even if it is true that only these three constitute the stock of ethical values. That is why we have said that to call complete an account of Indian ethical theory limited to that of *artha*, *kāma* and *dharma* is true in one sense but not in another. It is true if we take ethical theory in the sense in which it is ordinarily understood, i.e. in the sense in which its function is to present a systematic account of the moral values an individual-in-society should pursue, the virtues he should inculcate, the obligations he should fulfil, the rights he should claim or allow others to claim, etc. But it is not true in the philosophical sense in which, to be complete, it should also include a discussion of the theory's place or role in the general theory of value in which it is housed. That is why a discussion of the Indian concept of *mokṣa* is very relevant for a proper understanding of Indian ethical theory because, as we have said, though *mokṣa* denotes a personal value, it is this value which is the highest value according to the general theory. In fact, even discussing the relation of Indian ethical theory with Indian aesthetic theory would contribute to sharpening our understanding of both of them. But we will not do that here to avoid making the work too large. We shall remain satisfied with only discussing the nature of *mokṣa* and that too with a view to ascertain what could, or could not, possibly be the relationship between *mokṣa* and morality.

Classical Indian thinkers' realization that leading a good moral life does not *exhaust* the content of a good life, that an individual's fulfilling all of his moral obligations is not all that he aspires after, that even after that there is *something left* in him which he has to fulfil to derive complete satisfaction, shows their great insight in respect of what he *can be* or *wants to be.* This left-over aspiration of his can be conceived in more than one way. For example, an aesthetic theorist may conceive it as one which is fulfilled by an artist in creating a work of art, or in cultivating or maturing his propensity to get absorbed in enjoying a work of art. This point is very ably made by Indian aestheticians when they declare that the value of *kavyānanda*, enjoyment of poetry, is equal to that of *brahmānanda*, blissfulness experienced in realizing *Brahman.* It is true for example that Kālidāsa would not have been satisfied with only having led a good moral life; an important part of his personhood would have remained unfulfilled had he not written his great literary pieces. Similarly, a mathematician, a philosopher, a scientist, etc., with a rich creative talent, would not think of himself as having got his full flourishing without developing his talent, a fulfilment of his personal aspiration, of his personhood, had he merely led a good moral life. Neither would a devoted religious theist, believing in a personal god or *avatar*hood (incarnation), be fully satisfied with only leading a good moral life; rather, he may wish to dance out of love for his deity in a temple, or even in a crowded corner of a busy market.

Classical Indian axiologists or ethicists have adumbrated their conceptions of *mokṣa* in the manner suggested by their metaphysical-theological theories. Since different philosophical schools have different metaphysical-theological theories, their accounts of *mokṣa* also are different, or not identical in all respects. But all of these accounts agree in holding that termination of the liability of an individual to be reborn is a necessary feature of the attainment of *mokṣa* by him. It may even be said to be the only feature commonly present in all the different accounts. This feature conclusively shows that *mokṣa* is a personal value since, by attaining it, an individual terminates only his and his own, personal, liability to be reborn, and not anyone else's. It may equally well be said that, according to all of them, only by terminating this liability of his and his alone does he attain his *mokṣa* or become liberated (*mukta*).

We have said above that the primary reason, or at least one of the important reasons, for adding the concept of *mokṣa* to the *trivarga* theory of value is that *mokṣa* is a personal value or goal and therefore its inclusion in the theory compensates for the lack of adequate emphasis on the importance of, or *concern for*, the person as he himself, or left to himself, is. This statement is liable to be misunderstood or wrongly interpreted by taking it to mean that it makes *mokṣa* a selfish or an egoistic value. This is not at all what we intend to convey by calling it a personal, as contrasted with a social, value which each one of *artha*, *kāma* and *dharma* is.

Different philosophical schools do give different accounts of *mokṣa* but, in effect, according to all of them, it is a return of the self of an individual to its original, natural, state. As already said at the beginning of this work, it is the individual, the *jīva*, who is liberated. The individual is an embodied self (*saśarīra ātmān*) and when he is liberated, the self in him is in its original state, or seated in itself (*ātmastha*) in its unpolluted pristine purity. Since different schools differ in their conception of the self, their conceptions of *mokṣa* also differ. But they all agree in averring that the state of *mokṣa* is the original state of the self. This means that the self in the individual's *mokṣa* does not become anything other than what it in itself is, or does not acquire anything new, any new attribute which it did not originally have. Therefore, it is wrong to say that the self attains its perfection in the state of *mokṣa*, as Hiriyanna and many others say.[1] The self is, for all the schools, something non-developing, non-evolving; therefore, the question of its becoming perfect, or attaining perfection, any time, or in any condition, does not arise.

In the case of the three values, *artha*, *kāma* and *dharma*, we have seen, they are required to be pursued because their pursuit is needed to make man's life in the world happy and socially cohesive. But, the ethicists say, there is in man a desire for getting rid of all kinds of his suffering, the absolute absence of pain of any kind. For anyone to live in the world is to experience at least some kind of suffering at some time. A state of complete painlessness cannot be had by him as long as he is in bondage. To be in bondage is to bound by the chain of birth-death-rebirth; i.e. to be bound to die at the end of his present life, to be reborn in a form determined by the actions done by him in his previous life, to die and to be reborn again and till he is freed from bondage, i.e. from the chain of birth–death–rebirth. This freedom from the chain is his *mokṣa*. That is, to get rid of all possible kinds of suffering, he has to attain emancipation from his bondage, to attain *mokṣa*.

All these things will be critically discussed in the next chapter. Here they have been briefly mentioned to draw the attention of the reader to the fact that *mokṣa*, for all philosophical schools which accept it as the fourth, the highest, value, basically denotes that sort of freedom. In fact, the word *mokṣa* means freedom. The advocates of the *mokṣa*-theory give a content to it by precisifying it as the individual's freedom from the liability to be reborn after his death. There are some other things as well which they say of it, and followers of different schools differ in specifying them. But there is complete unanimity among them in calling it the termination of the liberated individual's liability to be reborn. Therefore, the termination or cessation of this liability is a necessary feature of the concept of *mokṣa*. It is obvious that this termination is attained by an individual, a person, and is the termination of his own, his personal, liability, and not anyone else's. Nobody else can attain the termination of his liability, nor can he attain anyone else's. And, the termination frees him, and none else, from all kinds of suffering. All this shows that it is completely conceptually fair to call *mokṣa* a personal value, a value sought, or worth seeking, for satisfying an individual's desire to completely free himself, and not anyone else, from all kinds of suffering. To be *mukta* is, thus, to be free from all kinds of suffering which is the same thing as to cease to be reborn again. We can rightly, therefore, say that *mokṣa* necessarily is freedom from all kinds of suffering, or freedom from the liability to be reborn, as well as say that freedom from all kinds of suffering, or from the liability to be reborn, is *mokṣa*.

It is the individual who is liberated even if someone else helps him to attain his state of being liberated; his helper helps him to attain *his own*, the attainer's personal, liberation. If a man, on the other hand, inculcates the moral virtue of kindness, and exercises his virtue in saving a child from sinking into a pond, his exercise of a *dharma*, kindness, saves another person and not himself. In fact, we would not credit him with the virtue of kindness if he is kind only to himself. We would call him then a selfish or egoistic. i.e. an immoral person. Even if we considered it harsh to say that, we would certainly not call him a very moral person. But if an individual attains *his mokṣa*, as per any Indian conception or characterization of it whatsoever, we would have to call him, according to the Indian theory of *mokṣa*, liberated. Were it possible perchance for anyone under any condition to attain *mokṣa* even if he flouted, or was indifferent to, morality, then too he would have attained this personal value of being liberated. And, those who still stick to calling *mokṣa* the highest value, would have to declare that he has thereby attained the highest value. It seems, in order to rule out this eventuality, the Indian tradition considers morality, or living a good moral life, a precondition for attaining *mokṣa*. I shall explain a little later how calling it a precondition is different from calling it a means to *mokṣa*, as modern interpreters generally do.

An Advaitin may object to calling his conception of *mokṣa* a personal goal on the ground that it is the realization of the identity of the self with *Brahman*, which identity is the ultimate reality. It is not something to be attained because it is something that already is, or rather, because it is the only reality, or the only thing, that there is. It is true that the *Advaitin*'s *mokṣa* is such a thing. But still it can be said to be a personal goal attained by an individual, a *jīva*. An individual is not the self but an embodied self, a *jiva*, under the influence of *māyā*, or, ignorance, unaware of the identity of the self (in him) with *Brahman* and therefore he is in bondage, or unliberated. He has to attain the knowledge of this identity by getting rid of his ignorance. But to attain that knowledge is also to attain *mokṣa.* It is a verbal matter whether we call it his attaining the knowledge or his getting rid of his ignorance or his attaining *mokṣa.* In either case it is he who gets the knowledge which is his knowledge, or who gets rid of his ignorance. Since it is this, *his* knowledge, or *his* getting rid of *his* ignorance, which is *his mokṣa,* this *mokṣa* too is his personal goal or achievement. By doing all this he attains his own *mokṣa,* and does not lead to anyone else's getting it. Attaining knowledge (of the identity of the self with *Brahman*) is attaining something, and getting rid of ignorance is also attaining something because it is attaining the absence of ignorance. And, all this is done by the individual for himself. Even when a spiritual teacher helps him to attain *mokṣa,* what happens is that it is he, the attainer, who in the end attains freedom from his ignorance, i.e. his *mokṣa* which also means freedom (and here, freedom from ignorance).

The point of calling *mokṣa* a personal value is to contrast it with social value or values and draw attention to an individual's concern for his own upliftment or consummation of the best in him as a person. Doing this is in no sense a misreading of the import of the concept of *mokṣa.* Hiriyanna, a scholar very knowledgeable and respectful of the classical Indian tradition and value-theory, also calls *mokṣa* a personal value.[2] This is not, however, to suggest that his treatment of the concept agrees in toto with the present analysis. In fact, his philosophical attitude towards it is not like ours, that of a critical analyst but of a loyal exegete of what the tradition, according to him, thinks of it. His calling it personal is mentioned here only to bring home to the reader the fact that calling it personal is in keeping with the way even traditionalist scholars look at it. Our calling it personal need not imply, as we have already said, that we are degrading it to the status of a selfish goal, i.e. one pursued by a selfish person, because, as has been mentioned above, living a good moral life has been made by the Indian tradition a prerequisite or precondition for attaining it. A precondition enters into the very being of what it is a precondition for. Therefore, this personal goal, *mokṣa,* cannot be a selfish one because that in which morality has entered cannot remain anything selfish. The essence of being moral is to have a care and concern for others' welfare. A goal for the attainment of which moral living is a precondition, therefore, cannot be selfish, i.e. cannot be a goal of a man whose interest is limited to his own welfare.

There is also a concept of *sarvamukti* which verbally means liberation of, or for, all. But in no way does it tend to signify or even suggest that anyone can, or should, procure, or try to procure, another man's liberation, let alone suggesting that one person's liberation is also another's. We shall very briefly discuss, in the section that follows, some of the contexts in which the question of *sarvamukti* has been raised and the answers given to it. This will be done only to ward off the possibility of the existence of this concept's being used to disprove our characterization of *mokṣa* as a personal value or goal.

14.2 THE CONCEPT OF LIBERATION OF ALL (*SARVAMUKTI*)

Of each one of the three *puruṣārthas* it can be said that it can be sought or attained by all, or at least by everyone belonging to the three upper castes. It can, in the same manner, be asked if it is possible for everyone to attain liberation. The *Yoga* school, or the *Sānkhya-Yoga* school holds that everyone cannot. That is, it is not possible that at any time in the history of the world all individuals in it are liberated. This is so, firstly, because the number of individuals is infinite and, secondly, because the world (*sansāra*) itself is also endless (*ananta*). For the world to be existent all the time it is necessary that there are at least some individuals in it. If at any time all individuals become liberated, then after their death they would not be reborn. This would mean that there would be no individual and therefore no world. But this is not possible because the world is endless. Hence, it is not possible ever for all individuals to become liberated.

The *Dvaita Vedānta* school also holds that all are not competent to attain liberation. This means that some individuals are bound to die and to be reborn again and again. Hiriyanna[3] interprets even the *Mīmāmsa* school to hold that all cannot at any one time become liberated because the world is endless or changeless. The other schools hold that everyone is, in principle, entitled to seek liberation and can attain it if he follows the right path prescribed for its attainment. Therefore, for them *sarvamukti* is possible but only in the sense that the attainment of *mokṣa* is possible for each and every person. In this sense of it each man's liberation would remain his personal liberation.

There is another sense of the doctrine of *sarvamukti* in which to uphold it is to aver that any individual can be liberated only when all others are liberated. Here too, of course, all would be liberated at the same time, but anyone's liberation would be his personal, and not any other's, liberation, though when his liberation is attained, others' also is attained at the same time. This is like saying that one man smiles only when all others do; but saying it does not deny that each man's smile is his and only his smile. This it has to be because it is logically true that one man cannot smile another's smile.

Some thinkers hold that there is only one self which imagines or dreams that there are many selves. They, therefore, maintain that when this real self is liberated all others are also liberated. But here too the one self's liberation is its own liberation, as it is the only real self. The dream-selves cannot be said to be really liberated because they themselves are not real. We can speak of their liberation only as one that is dreamed of and therefore not as a real liberation.

The doctrine of *sarvamukti* is generally attributed to Bhartṛpanī. According to him there is only one self which is partially present in the individual selves. Only this self is to be liberated, but that is done when all other, individual, or finite, selves are liberated. This means that all, the real or cosmic self and finite ones, are liberated at the same time. According to this view, too, we see that liberation of each self, cosmic or finite, is its own liberation, though the liberation of any two selves is simultaneous and not successive.

The Buddhist concept of *bodhisattva* also cannot be said to maintain anything which goes against the interpretation presented here, that *mokṣa* is a personal goal. The doctrine only holds that he who is a *bodhisattva*, though fit to attain his *nirvāṇa*, i.e. *mokṣa*, postpones its attainment by him in order that he may help others to get theirs. This only shows, as we have already explained earlier in this work, that the *bodhisattva*'s act of postponing his own *nirvāṇa* is an act of a great moral sacrifice, a highly altruistic act. But it does not in any way imply that one man's *nirvāṇa* is any other man's *nirvāṇa* as well. The *bodhisattva* aims at only helping another man to attain his own, his personal, *nirvāṇa*; the *bodhisattva* does not himself attain the *nirvāṇa* of any other man whom he helps.

The Indian *karmic* worldview puts something like a final seal on the view presented in this work, making it impossible for anyone to attain, not only another man's liberation, but anything pertaining to him or to his life-style. According to it, everyone's life, what he is, or would be, here or hereafter, in his lifetime or after his death, is solely determined by his and only his actions. A clear logical corollary of this view is that every individual's liberation, if he ever attains it, would be the result of only his personal actions and therefore a result which he alone has to experience. Thus, it rules out the possibility of one man's experiencing another man's liberation which is the result of the latter's own actions. In such a *karmic* world there cannot ever be anything like the *sarvamukti* which means that one's liberation is not only one's own personal liberation but also that of someone else. The *karmic* view, however, does not go against, but seems to affirm, the view that everyone can in principle attain liberation. But this sense of the concept of *sarvamukti* does not controvert our view that each man's liberation is his own liberation and therefore that liberation is a personal value, clearly unlike *artha* and *dharma* because they are social values. In a slightly modified sense, it is unlike *kāma* as well because *kāma* can be both a social and also a purely personal value depending on the nature of the object of a *kāmanā* or desire that is sought to be attained in a particular situation. This point will be further elaborated a little later in this chapter.

We can now safely conclude that the existence of the concept of *sarvamukti* in Indian ethical literature does not, when the various senses in which it is actually used in it are examined, refute the present interpretation of *mokṣa* as a personal value.

We have not said much so far which can be called very contentual about the concept of *mokṣa.* We shall do that in the next section but only to the extent to which, or in respects in which, it is relevant for having a proper understanding of the role of *mokṣa* as a human value.

14.3 SOME GENERAL FEATURES OF LIBERATION (*MOKṢA*) BASIC TO UNDERSTANDING ITS PLACE AS A MORAL VALUE IN INDIAN ETHICS

Mokṣa, we have said, is the return of the self to its original, primal, state according to all the classical Indian philosophical schools. But to say this is not to say much about what this state, or *mokṣa*'s nature, is. Their theories of *mokṣa* differ because their theories of the self differ. For the very same reason they characterize the state of *mokṣa* in different ways. For example, for Buddhism, *Sānkhya-Yoga* and *Pūrva Mīmāmsa* it is a state of absolute absence of all kinds of pain or suffering (*sarva dukhābhāva*). Even the *Nyāya-vaiśeṣika* school, in common Indian philosophical usage, is claimed to hold this view. But there are some problems in doing that which will be explained very soon. The other two schools, Jainism and the *Vedānta,* call it a state not only of absolute absence of suffering but also a state of pure, permanent, undisturbable, pleasure or bliss (*ānanda*).

All these schools of both the groups, however, believe that suffering is an unmixed evil, something which nobody wants to have, and everybody wants to get rid of, as well as an evil from which everyone ought to free himself. That is, it is both a positive and normative evil (*heya*) and therefore a thing not fit for being a positive *puruṣārtha,* a disvalue, i.e. a negative *puruṣārtha.* Happiness, pleasure, or bliss, on the other hand, is both a positive and a normative *puruṣārtha,* a value, in the sense that it is not only desired to be had by all human beings but also fit to be, or worthy of being, desired by them. This claim about suffering and bliss is taken to be too obviously valid to need any elaborate reasoning for its validation or vindication.

There is another assumption made about bliss or blissfulness. It is that the more lasting it is, the more valuable, or greater as a value, it is. Proceeding on the same lines, it is said that, therefore, to be the absolute, supreme, value a bliss must be not only an unmixed bliss but also an indestructible or everlasting one. That is, if a man once attains it, it must become impossible that he is ever deprived of it. In a similar way it is said of the absence of suffering that the more lasting it is, the greater value it is. Therefore, those who take *mokṣa* to be only a state of absence of suffering hold that, since it is the highest value, it is an unending, permanent, absence of suffering. The claim that the state of permanent bliss, of the permanent absence of suffering, is the highest value, is also said to be too obvious to need any argument in support of it. This view of *mokṣa*'s being a permanent state, never coming to an end, entails that once attained, it is attained for ever. That is, a liberated, *mukta*, individual, never loses it, he never becomes again one in bondage, i.e. de-liberated (*boddha*, or *amukta*). That is why there is no concept of de-liberation in Indian ethical or even metaphysical literature so far as my knowledge of it goes.

There is a concept of re-death applicable to a person who, after his death in this world, as a result of his good actions, gets a place in heaven. If he there commits a sin, does anything grievously wrong, then he dies in his heavenly abode, and is reborn in the mundane world where he has to suffer the punishment he deserves for his evil deed there. Since he has gone to heaven only after his death in this world, his death in heaven is re-death. But after his becoming once liberated, there is no possibility of his again becoming an individual in bondage. That is why one's attaining *mokṣa* is said to be a higher value than one's getting a heavenly abode. Had the heavenly abode been a permanent one, it would have been (almost) impossible for *mokṣa*-theorists to prove *mokṣa*'s superiority to it because to reside in heaven is to lead a life, as believers in heaven say, extremely happy and free from all kinds of suffering. Perhaps that is why the possibility of a heaven-dweller's committing a sin is admitted which, in its turn, makes possible his getting the retributive punishment of re-death in heaven and rebirth in the human world to experience the suffering he deserves on account of his sin. This reason for re-death and consequent rebirth may be said to be a mythological reason. But any talk about heaven and hell is mythological and therefore there need be no wonder in anyone's giving a mythological reason for defending a mythological claim.

I have mentioned this belief in anyone's getting a heavenly abode and then re-dying to suffer a retributive punishment not because in itself it is of any great philosophical relevance. This belief was quite current and prominent in classical India and it is still so in modern India. The classical Indian philosophers, on the other hand, put *mokṣa* in the place of the highest value. Therefore, they have to show its superiority to the value of getting a heavenly abode. They have to because the believers in the doctrine of an individual's getting a heavenly abode after his death as a result of good works done by him in his lifetime, believe that getting a heavenly abode is the highest value. To prove the superiority of *mokṣa* to it, it seems, philosophers use this mythological reason of the possibility of re-death if it is already there in mythology, or invent it in case it is not there.

The emphasis on the *permanence* of the *mokṣa*-state and the *impermanence* of the heavenly life, as well as considering permanence of a pleasure as a feature of it which heightens its value, entails that classical Indian ethicists accept the reality of time. Permanence as well as impermanence is a temporal notion. Anything can be called permanent or impermanent only if it exists in time which it can be said to do only if time is real. To say that *mokṣa,* when attained, is attained forever also assumes that time is real even for the liberated (*mukta*) because only then we can say that he is liberated forever, i.e. for all time to come.

Before I leave this issue of *mokṣa's* being a state only of painlessness or one of blissfulness, I must explain why I find it difficult to accept the prevalent interpretation of the *Nyāya-Vaiśeṣika* conception of *mokṣa* which presents it as holding that *mokṣa* is only a state of painlessness and not of pleasure. This interpretation is based on the *Nyāya-Vaiśeṣika* conception of the self. The self, according to it, is a substance with consciousness as an attribute of it. The relation between a substance and attribute of it is of only one-way dependence in the sense that an attribute depends for its existence on the substance whose attribute it is, but the substance concerned does not depend on the attribute for its own existence. Therefore, a self can exist even without consciousness but consciousness cannot without a self. A self becomes conscious only when it is embodied, i.e. only in its existence as a *jīva* or an individual. An individual, we have seen, is nothing but an embodied self. According to the *Nyāya-Vaiśeṣika, mokṣa* is attained by him only after his death. After his death he is only a disembodied, pure, self because in death only the body dies and the self in it exists as it in itself is. With its disembodiment its consciousness is also gone. Therefore, in its state as a pure self it is a non-conscious substance. It is this state of it which is the state of *mokṣa,* i.e., *mokṣa* attained by an individual after his death (*videhamukti*). Such a non-conscious state (of the self) cannot be said to be a state of pleasure because a state of pleasure is a state of consciousness, as is a state of pain. Only a conscious being can be said to feel pleasure or pain. Therefore, the upholders of the prevalent interpretation claim that they can say of the state of *mokṣa,* which is a non-conscious state, that being a state of a non-conscious substance, a self, it is only a state of painlessness.

This interpretation of the *Nyāya-Vaiśeṣika* conception of *mokṣa* has been current for ages and therefore has gathered great respectability in philosophical literature. But when we look at it from the point of view of the use of the concepts of pain and pleasure in any language, whether it is English, or Sanskrit or its child, Hindi, we notice that we affirm, or deny, only of a conscious object that it has or does not have pleasure or pain. Limiting the discussion only to the predication of pain or painlessness, we do not speak of a non-conscious object as having or not having pain. When a blacksmith cuts an iron rod into pieces, we not only do not say that the rod feels pain but we also do not say that it feels no pain. We do not even speak of its being painless when it is lying untouched somewhere in a pile of iron rods. We would call it logically odd if a blacksmith says that he is cutting an iron rod into pieces by striking hard at it with his big hammer because it feels no pain. The question of calling a non-conscious object painless (or painful) does not arise because there is no possibility of its being painful (or painless). There seems no point in calling, therefore, a non-conscious self painless because it is not possible for it to be painful (or to have any pain). To say that it is painless seems to be as pointless or meaningless as it is to say of an eyeless child that he does not have an ugly eye. It may be said that since he has no eye, it is true that he does not have an ugly eye. Yes, it is true, but too trivial a truth to be stated. Similarly, since a non-conscious self cannot feel any pain, it is true that it is painless. But this truth also is, as in the case of the eyeless child, too trivial a truth to be stated, and therefore too trivial a truth to be included in an account or interpretation of the *Nyāya-Vaiśeṣika* theory of *mokṣa* (which it calls *apavarga*). However, if we have to put the *Nyāya-Vaiśeṣika* concept of *mokṣa* somewhere in the two major groups of views about it, we can put it only in the group of those which consider it to be only a state of painlessness, of course keeping in mind the point made above about the implication of calling it a non-conscious state.

Apart from the division among Indian philosophers about *mokṣa*'s being a positive state of bliss, or one of only a negative state of absence of all kinds of suffering, there is also another division. This division is on the issue of whether *mokṣa* can be attained by an individual while he is alive, in the very life in which he tries to attain it, or only after his death, i.e. when he becomes disembodied (*videha*) because, we have seen, only his body dies and not his self. Philosophers of some schools, namely, those of Jainism, *Sānkhya-Yoga*, and *Advaita Vedānta* hold that attaining *mokṣa* in life, *jīvanmukti*, is possible, while those of the *Nyāya-Vaiśeṣika*, *Mīmāmsa*, *Viśiṣtādvaita* hold that only *mokṣa* after death, *videhamukti*, is possible.

Liberation-only-after-death is a state about which, one would say, nothing can be said. Nobody knows, or can know, what would happen to him, or to anybody else, after his death. Therefore, such a state, even if there is one, cannot be a sensible moral ideal or value because nobody would be able to decide what would help him to attain it, or what would stand in his way of attaining it. Therefore, the belief in it would not help him in deciding what is right or wrong for him to do in order to attain this moral ideal, if it is accepted to be one. If anyone believes in it, he can believe only on the basis of some mythology or what has been said of it in some religious or theological work. Moreover, he has to accept it only as an article of faith and not as one based on reason. Therefore, the belief in it, in whichsoever a way it is characterized, whether as a state of bliss, or as one of painlessness, can at the most be a religious one, or one of some religious utility. This is possible because every religion has some beliefs which it accepts as not amenable or open to reason's scrutiny. And, whenever a theologian offers something in the name of a so-called rational justification for any one of them, it is very likely to be a rationalization and not a reasoned defence of it.

This is an issue of which we cannot afford a detailed analysis here because doing that would take us far afield. Moreover, in a philosophical work on morals, like the present one, it is more realistic to restrict the discussion of *videhamukti* only to mentioning that it is offered as one of the forms of *mokṣa* by some philosophical schools. They do that because it is the way they conceive of the nature of the self and of that of *mokṣa* which makes it impossible for anyone to attain *mokṣa* while he is alive. For example, according to the *Nyāya-vaiśeṣika*, the self in the state of the individual's *mokṣa* is non-conscious. But it cannot be non-conscious as long as he is alive, that is, the self in him is embodied. Therefore, the state of *mokṣa* would be attained only after his death, that is, when the self in him gets disembodied.

Living a moral life, as generally understood, is a *rational affair*. It is concerned with what a person *does*, gains or loses in the life he lives, how his actions affect, or are affected by, other living members of his society, etc., and not with what *happens* to him after his death. If he wants to set an example for posterity, it is for those who would live in the world after his death, and not for himself after his death. For these reasons, the concept of liberation-only-after-death does not have much significance in a work on morals. Therefore, and also because of the difficulty in talking about *videhamukti*, we shall primarily be concerned here with liberation-attainable-in-life (*jīvanmukti*).

Roughly summing up what has been said so far about *mokṣa,* it can be said that the necessary or essential, the most common, feature of it, according to all Indian philosophical schools, is its being a state of permanent absence of suffering. This is true even of those views which call it a state of permanent bliss because there cannot be any pain in such a state. But to say this is not the whole, or the most basic, truth about it. There is an assumption made by Indian philosophers which we have not so far properly highlighted. It is to the effect that as long as an individual is liable to be reborn after his death, i.e. as long as he lives in the world, he is bound to experience some suffering. The individual who has become liberated while alive also experiences some bodily sufferings, i.e. sufferings his body is subject to, like those due to hunger, thirst, disease, natural calamities like an earthquake, landslide, flood, famine, drought, etc., though he does not mind them because he has acquired complete self-control over his bodily and mental functions. That is why as long as he is liable to be reborn, he is said to be in bondage and bound to be afflicted with some suffering. Any complete absence of suffering, the ultimate value a man seeks and ought to seek, can thus be attained when he is liberated, i.e. frees himself from bondage, from the chain of birth–death–rebirth. He is, thus, really liberated only when he has terminated his liability to be reborn after the death of his present body.

Permanent freedom from suffering can be called a moral value, or even a great moral value. And, when we do that, we can fairly call *mokṣa* a moral value. But the basic, foundational, truth about *mokṣa* is not that it is permanent freedom from suffering, but that it is the termination of the liability to be reborn because it is this termination which gives freedom from suffering. Thus, its necessary, essential, most common, feature, as has been repeatedly said, is its being the liberated person's termination, or cessation, of this liability. This point has been noted by modern interpreters but its implications have not been fully or correctly drawn. That is why they all extol classical thinkers for characterizing *mokṣa* as freedom from rebirth in the manner they do.

The primary purpose of the institution of morality is to help everyone to have an interest in the well-being of others and the most obvious way for anyone to express this interest is to help someone to get rid of at least some of his sufferings. But a down-to-earth moralist, or moral theorist, would not pitch his aim at so high a point as to make his own, or anyone else's, permanent freedom from all possible kinds of suffering his moral ideal. He would be satisfied with making his goal minimization of suffering, as much as possible, keeping in view our resources, our existential and circumstantial conditions, and limitations in the world we live in. He would also proceed with the assumption that we can achieve this goal in due course, or come nearer and nearer to achieving it with the help of our natural, mental and material, resources and capabilities if we lead a moral life. He would also feel that it is morally more important to emphasize minimization of others' sufferings than the minimization of the one's own sufferings because every moral agent, or everyone, normally, or naturally, is interested in minimizing his own, personal, sufferings. He would thus be satisfied with the possible minimization of sufferings which may only by the best possible, and not the best, state of affairs attainable by man with his natural resources. But classical Indian moralists are not satisfied with the *best possible*; they want the *best* state of affairs to be attained. The best state would obviously be the permanent freedom from all possible kinds of suffering. Īśvara Kṛṣṇa's *Sānkhyakārikā* very forcefully asserts that right knowledge, or moral knowledge, or rather philosophical knowledge, must help man to get rid of all possible kinds of sufferings, yielded by bodily, mental, natural, supernatural, etc., causes.[4]

Indian thinkers, however, unlike ordinary moralists, in pleading for *mokṣa* to be attained as man's highest value, make it an *agent's* goal to attain *his own mokṣa*, since he *can* attain only his own *mokṣa*. He may advise someone to seek his *mokṣa*, or give him some lessons about what to do to attain it. But he cannot do anything more than that. Only that person can take the necessary steps to attain it. Helping him to attain it is not like a kind man's helping him to get rid of his pangs of hunger by giving him an adequate quantity of food to eat which relieves him, even though he himself does nothing to procure or earn the food. It is this feature of *mokṣa* which makes it a personal and not a social or moral value and helping anyone to attain it is different from helping him in any moral way, i.e. by doing something morally good to, or for, him. That is why it is the objective of everyone to attain his own *mokṣa* i.e. to free *himself* from all kinds of suffering. On the other hand, the highest moral value, as averred by almost all great moralists, consists in his pursuing the development of his own talents and in promoting the well-being of others.

This may appear to imply or suggest that the seeker of *mokṣa* may very well not have any care or concern for the welfare of others, which morality requires him to have, when he does his best to attain his *mokṣa*. Even after attaining it, he may not have this care and concern since he would have then attained the highest value. Even the question of doing anything moral after attaining *mokṣa* would arise only for him who has attained it while alive. For him who attains it after his bodily death, on the other hand, it would be nonsensical to raise it since a dead man can do nothing. After attaining *videhamukti* the attainer is a pure self and a self is a non-doer, a non-agent. All this is *apparently* implied by the theory of *mokṣa*. Taking all these things as *really* implied by the theory of *mokṣa*, some critics have said that it encourages indifference to morality, or even immorality. But, as we shall see, classical thinkers try to take care of the problem raised here and to ward off any undervaluing of morality.

It is, thus, the two emphases, one on permanent freedom from all possible kinds of suffering and, the other on freedom from *one's own* sufferings, which leave no alternative to classical Indian thinkers except to make use of the theory of rebirth available in the then ethos and require the individual to take steps to terminate his liability to be reborn. This is so because, if he continues to be reborn, he would not be free from all sufferings. And, if he is not reborn after his death, he would not be, or exist, in the world, would no longer be an individual of this world, and therefore would not have any suffering which an individual living in the world has necessarily to experience. He would then just be a self which is either only free from all possible suffering, or is also blissful or simply bliss. But in any case he would not be a being of the world we live in. A moralist who does not have a metaphysics which accepts the theory of rebirth, the theory of self as a being which in itself is disembodied and only contingently related to a body, and the theory of *karma* as holding that an individual would continue to die and to be reborn unless he does in a life all his actions in a desireless (*niṣkāma*) manner, would not have any reason to say that one has to terminate one's liability to be reborn to be absolutely and eternally free from all kinds of suffering. But then he would also not be able to hold that it is possible for anyone to be free from all kinds of suffering for all time to come.

The two doctrines, the one of rebirth and the other of *karma,* have not been so far discussed in any detail. They will be discussed in Chapter 15.

A moralist of the common-garden variety who does not have the above sort of metaphysics may consider complete freedom from all sufferings not only unattainable but also not a tenable moral value. He may say, against those who consider *mokṣa* to be only a state of absence of suffering, having no pleasure, that this is a bleak and barren ideal and in no way attractive. Against both, this view and the other which considers it also to be a state of pleasure, he may say that the ideals of both are not only personal values but also values which are finally attained by an individual only after he ceases to be a creature of the world, i.e. ceases to exist as an individual. In his *videhamukti,* he would say, he obviously ceases to exist. Even in his *jīvanmukti,* as long as he is alive and therefore has a body, he will, willy-nilly, have to bear some bodily sufferings. He too would be finally free from all sufferings only after his (bodily) death. Therefore, both of the two conceptions of *mokṣa* make it a value unattainable by an individual as long as he is an individual, a member of the world or of any society. It therefore ceases to be a social value and consequently a moral value. Moreover, he may go on to say that the ideal of making the world better and better in order that we have, while we are alive, the maximum level of happiness and minimum of unhappiness in a socially cohesive manner, is a much more desirable ideal, a social and therefore a moral ideal, than *mokṣa* is. And, if he is a tough-minded optimist, he may even say that it is humanly possible to make such a world real, maybe in the far future. A thinker of this type may even say that Gautama, the prince and heir-apparent of the kingdom of Kapilavastu, would have done a better moral service to the world by devoting his life to the actual amelioration of the conditions of his people by opening good schools, good hospitals, making needed reforms to promote production of food materials and generation of wealth, etc., than he did by becoming a recluse, himself a Buddha, and giving to the world a religious ethics which presents a theory of *nirvāṇa,* i.e., *mokṣa* in the terminology of this work, claiming it to be the highest moral (or religious) ideal.

About the reaction of our imagined, hypothesized, critic of *mokṣa* as the final moral ideal, we can say that classical Indian philosophers do not seem to be unaware of it. Classical Indians are as much interested in making their earthly life better and better as moderners are. This is clear from the fact that political governance and social arrangements in classical times are intended to make worldly life happier and happier. However, classical Indian moralists or axiologists seem to have the feeling that man is not finally satisfied, that even his *moral sense* is not satisfied, unless he attains what they call *mokṣa.*

The theory of *mokṣa* has been propounded by them with a worldview as its background, as something like a prompter in the green room of the drama of Indian axiology providing support, without visibly coming on the stage. This worldview is not clearly stated at any one place. But from ideas strewn here and there in classical ethical-aesthetic, or general axiological, literature anecdotes, mythologies, etc., it can be stated or reconstructed in some such way as the following:

The life of a man does not end with his death, as his death does not terminate his existence. It is only the end of his body. Every individual is either in bondage, or liberated, or ready to be liberated after the death of his present body. There is no station for him in between bondage and liberation. If he is in bondage, he is re-born after his death, and goes on for ever and ever to be reborn, to die, and again to be reborn. If he is liberated in life, after his death he gets finally liberated and is never reborn. If he is not liberated in life but ready to be liberated, he is liberated after his death and is never reborn. His bondage has no beginning but it has a final end after his liberation. Neither his bondage nor his liberation admits of degrees; at any time he is either in bondage or liberated, and never partly in bondage and partly liberated. In his state of bondage, in his life in the world, he can prepare for being liberated by leading a moral life. This moral life does not end with his getting liberated but becomes a component of it, or enters into it, since living a moral life is not a means but a precondition of it. This means that without being moral he cannot be a liberated being, as nothing can exist if its precondition is removed. Since one can never cease to exist because he has to be reborn after his death, one cannot hope to end one's existence, as a man committing suicide thinks, by committing suicide. This is so because he would be reborn and would have to bear the consequences of the sin of suicide added to be consequences of his other actions done in the life which he had hoped to end by his act of suicide. He is bound to bear them because no consequence of an action can be evaded. This is a very good argument against suicide, of course, if one believes in the theory of rebirth. Since moral living is a precondition of attaining *mokṣa*, it is necessary to lead a moral life one of the aims of which is to make the living conditions of others as well as one's own better and better by reducing or minimizing suffering in the world. An individual may become satisfied with its minimization and not try to attain complete freedom from it. But this is not the best ideal, though it may be called a good enough ideal. The best life would be that which is completely free from suffering. This may look impossible if he is appalled by the size of the world he lives in. But it is possible because the root of suffering lies primarily in the individual and it is possible for him to destroy this internal root by following a schedule of living a moral life and knowing the nature of ultimate reality. By following this schedule he himself can be free from all suffering while alive (or after his bodily death). A suffering-free man's world is a suffering-free world, or a good man's world a good world. He does not have to do the stupendous task of first making the entire world sufferingless or happy to be himself sufferingless or happy. Rather, to make the world sufferingless or happy he has to make himself sufferingless or happy by leading a moral and enlightened life, an ideal not at all selfish or self-centred. Since to achieve this *best state of affairs* he has to work largely on improving or changing his own internal being for which he has the capability, there is no reason to remain satisfied with only the *best possible* or a *good enough* state of affairs for which a moralist of the common garden-variety pleads. This is what Gautama does by becoming a Buddha, and it is therefore no wonder that he is applauded as an ideal moral person and an ideal moral guide for all.

Anyone who keeps in mind this worldview would not have any difficulty in understanding the classical Indian thinkers' giving to *mokṣa* the most elevated status as a value. This is not, however, to say that it is a logically airtight view with no crack in it. Even this work has shown and will show again some problems with the rationale of including in it some of its components. It has been mentioned here only to make intelligible the approach of *mokṣa*-theorists towards morality.

With a view escape the difficulties raised in the criticism, mentioned earlier, of the theory of *mokṣa* as the highest moral, or the highest overall, value, instead of pointing to the worldview which is behind its formulation, some interpreters take it to be a spiritual or religious value transcending the sphere of moral values. This amounts to saying that it is not a moral value. Such scholars seem to think that interpreting it in this way gives to it the status of a higher value than calling it a moral value does. But this way of thinking is conceptually untenable. Anything which is not morally desirable, not a moral value, cannot be a spiritual, or any sort of, value. It is rather better, fairer, to the spirit of Indian ethics to say that *mokṣa* is intended to be a moral value even if it is a value of some other sort as well. This needs to be said even if it is admitted that in the actual adumbration of the theory of *mokṣa* certain things have entered which make it extremely difficult for the *mokṣa*-theorist to exhibit that it is the highest *moral* value or *puruṣārtha* (in addition to being the highest value in other respects as well). To understand the source, or one of the sources, of this difficulty we shall examine in the next section what may be called the necessary or essential, the central, feature of *mokṣa* according to all the schools. This is what we have called the cessation of the liberated individual's liability to be reborn after the death of his present body.

14.4 TERMINATION OF LIABILITY TO BE REBORN AS A NECESSARY FEATURE OF LIBERATION (*MOKṢA*): PROBLEM OF INSTANTIATION

From what has been said so far, it is clear that the most common, necessary, feature of being liberated is to be freed (*mukta*) from the chain of birth–death–rebirth (*janma-marana-punarjanma-śṛnkhalā*). It is this feature of a liberated individual which I have called the termination or cessation of his liability to be reborn after his death. It is a necessary feature of both the types, *jīvanmukti* and *videhamukti*, and one that is accepted to be so by all Indian philosophical schools except the *Cārvāka*. In spite of its playing so important a role in the theory of *mokṣa*, it has not been given the serious attention and scrutiny it deserves. We shall try to do that in this section.

The question of the *Cārvāka*'s accepting the importance of it does not arise because he does not accept *mokṣa* to be a value, or, rather, the possibility of anyone's attaining it. He does not, because he does not accept the duality of the body and the self, and therefore the reality of a self intrinsically independent of the body. Therefore, for him the question of the self's being freed forever from the body does not arise. An individual's life ends with the end of his body, i.e. with his death. His consciousness or self is nothing but a set of functions of his body. Therefore, when he dies, his body ends, everything in him comes to an end. There is neither a possibility of his being reborn, nor of his being liberated.

All the other schools accept the doctrine of rebirth and that of *mokṣa*. Different schools of Indian philosophy do differ in some details about *mokṣa*. Buddhism calls it *nirvāṇa* and for it it is the end of the stream of conscious or cognitive states, something like the blowing out of a lamp. The *Nyāya-Vaiśeṣika* calls it (*apūrva*) and describes it as the return of the self to its original state of a non-conscious substance. The *Sānkhya-Yoga* calls it *kaivalya* which, according to it, is a state in which the self considers itself completely different and distinct from and unrelated to *prakṛti*, the primal matter. Early *Mīmāmsa* considers *mokṣa* to be the attainment of an adobe in heaven by performing sacrifices in the manner prescribed in the *Veda*s. The liberated individual stays in heaven (*svarga*) as long as the effects of his good actions, his merits, last or as long as he does not do there anything wrong on demeritorious. Thereafter he re-dies and is reborn and returns to this, the mundane world. For later *Mīmāmsa* it is not attaining a heavenly abode but the return of the self to its natural state in which there is no pain but also no pleasure. For the *Advaita Vedānta mokṣa* is self-realization, i.e. realization of the self as being existence-consciousness-bliss which is the same as realizing the identity or non-duality of the self and *Brahman*. According to Jainism the self is unchanging consciousness of the same size as the body in which it resides. Liberation is attained by leading a life of self-discipline when all the effects of all actions (*karma*) are exhausted. In the liberated stage it is in a state of perfect knowledge and bliss. According to the *Viśiṣṭādvaita* school of Rāmānuja, to attain *mokṣa* is to reside in the kingdom of God as a part of God. This school does not admit the possibility of *jīvanmukti* which the *Advaita Vedānta* admits. The position of the *Dvaita* school of Mādhava is not very different from Rāmānuja's. According to it, in the state of *mokṣa* the self is free from all suffering and enjoys bliss in the company of God, remaining always devoted to God and worshiping him.

In spite of differences in their theories of *mokṣa*, arising primarily from their differing metaphysical theories, all the schools agree that for an individual to be liberated is to terminate his liability to be reborn.

According to those who accept only *videhamukti*, i.e. liberation only after death, this termination can be attained by him only after he dies. For ordinary people, including philosophers, it is not possible to say anything about what happens or may happen to a person after his death. If anything has been said in a work about it, only he can take it to be a true statement who is so credulous as to accept that every statement made in the work is true without requiring any evidence for its truth. This a philosopher of morals, or any rationally mature person, cannot do or cannot be expected to do. Therefore, if it has been said therein of a man that after his death his liability to be reborn has been terminated, that he has become videhamukta, liberated after death, nothing can be opined about it by him. Since it can be neither confirmed nor disconfirmed, silence is the only rational response to it. One cannot give any example of a (dead) person of whom it can be said that he has, or has not, terminated his liability to be reborn.

The difficulty mentioned above points to what may be called the difficulty, or rather, impossibility, of instantiating, or, exemplifying, the concept of *videhamukti*, of giving an example or instance of a person who has actually become a *videhamukta*. This difficulty or impossibility, we shall soon see, pertains to the very concept of *mokṣa* because it is equally difficult or impossible to give an instance of a person who can be said to have become a *jīvanmukta*, i.e. liberated while alive. This we shall show a little later. Let us discuss first the importance of instantiating a concept.

Whenever a concept is introduced in the adumbration of a theory, the concept must be intelligible. To show that it is intelligible, the safest and surest way is to give an instance of a thing to which it applies, or is applicable, or, to give a set of realistic conditions to which the concept can be applied. The set of conditions must not contain any condition about which it is impossible to say of any object that that object satisfies, or does not satisfy, it. A concept, the set of conditions of whose application contains any such condition, would be unusable in the language-game to which it is said to belong. It would be then like a coin in a currency which has no exchange value. For an example, we may take the *concept of the greatest number* as one which cannot be instantiated and therefore cannot play any viable role in the language-game of arithmetic. If any number is given as one which is said to be the greatest number, we can produce by adding the number 'one' to it another number greater than it. Therefore, we can say that there cannot be any instance of this concept and that, consequently, this concept is of no use in the language of arithmetic. Something similar to, or worse than this, would be the fate of the concept about which it is *impossible* to say that it applies, or does not apply, to anything whatsoever. Of the concept of the greatest number we can at least say that no number can be said to be the greatest number. Had it been the case that we could not say of any number that it is not the gratest number, the concept of the greatest number would have met an even worse fate.

To return to the concept of *mokṣa*, we have seen that it is possible neither to say of anyone who is dead that he has, nor to say that has not, attained *videhamukti*. The same is the case with the concept of *jīvanmukti*. It is equally impossible to say of anyone alive that he will, or that he will not, be reborn after his death, even if we know that he has followed the path recommended for attaining *mokṣa*. There are several things said to be true of the state of *mokṣa*. But the cessation of the liability to be reborn is the most common or necessary condition, or rather, the distinguishing condition, or constituent, of *mokṣa*. If a man is still liable to be reborn, or if it is not known that he will not be reborn after his death, we cannot say of him that he has attained *jivanmukti* or *mukti*. Besides, if we cannot definitely know that he will or will not be reborn, we cannot say either that he has, or that he has not, attained *jivanmukti* (or *mukti*).

The Indian tradition considers some individuals, like Vyāsa and Janaka, to have become *jīvanmukta*. It is very difficult to decipher how could anybody know that they were not reborn after their death. Even if it is true that they exhibited some *other*, empirical, features that a *jīvanmukta* is claimed to have, like Janaka's having complete detachment, it is not impossible that they were born again unless there was another, an independent, piece of evidence that they were not. But no such evidence is given simply because it is not possible to do that. Merely on the basis of anyone's having the *other features*, or, on that of his having followed the recommended path for attaining *jīvanmukti*, we can say that he will not be reborn if and only if we make it true by definition that he will not. But doing that would make it a verbal, non-substantive, truth. A verbal truth cannot have any axiological, or normative, significance; it cannot have any normative force, or appeal, to move anyone to make *jīvanmukti* his final goal, or, goal. Perhaps this is why Indian ethics, or axiology, does not make it a definitional, verbal, truth. It is emphatic in calling it an empirical, ontological-axiological, i.e. a substantive, truth, and offer in its support the alleged fact that men like Vyāsa and Janaka are instances of individuals who have attained *jīvanmukti*. But it does not seem to realize the difficulty or impossibility involved in knowing, and therefore in affirming (or denying), that someone will not be reborn, and consequently in citing any example of a person who has attained *jīvanmukti*. It does not seem, thus, to realize the importance of the fact that unless it is *known* that an individual will not be reborn, it cannot be said that he has become *jīvanmukta*.

Moreover, if an individual is mentioned as an example of one who has become *jivanmukta* on the ground that a scriptural work says that he has, a religious person may take it to be true. He may then have no doubt about the empirical possibility of attaining *jīvanmukti* and therefore about the exemplifiability of the concept of *jīvanmukti* and of that of anyone's non-liability to be reborn. But to take this stand on the basis of faith in a scriptural authority is not to solve the *philosophical* problem of how we can know the termination of anyone's liability to be reborn in an empirically or logically defensible manner.

A philosopher of morals, or any philosopher, cannot take such a stand because he would not fail to see that it does nothing to solve the logical hurdle involved in applying to anyone the concept of having become non-liable to be reborn, and therefore in applying to him the concept of *jīvanmukti*. This hurdle cannot be taken lightly because unless it is solved, we cannot call anyone a *jivanmukta* and therefore cannot instantiate the concept of *jīvanmukti*. This handicap has a serious normative or moral implication because it would adversely affect our ability to convince anyone that *jīvanmukti* is a realistic, actually attainable, moral, or general, value of the highest kind as is claimed by Indian axiology.

The difficulty of instantiating the concept of *jīvanmukti*, or *mokṣa* itself, arises, as is clear from the above, because of its having been defined in terms of the termination of the liability of being reborn. Doing that is ultimately to hook the concept of *mokṣa* to the theory of rebirth. The latter is, in its turn, hooked to the theory of *karma*. It is true that it is also said that he who does desirelessly all that he does is not reborn after his death, i.e. he is liberated. Even on this account of *mokṣa*, it is difficult or impossible to instantiate the concept of *mokṣa* for the same reason. If we know that someone's actions are all desireless, even then we are in no better position to know that he will not be reborn, unless we take it to be true by *definition* and thereby make it a trivial truth. All this is true because of the same difficulty, i.e. because of our not having any means to know, or to be sure of, the termination of the desireless agent's liability to be reborn. If we take this difficulty too seriously, we would have to say that the concept of *mokṣa* is uninstantiable and therefore of no use. But this concept occupies such an important place in the Indian theory of value that it may appear too cruel or harsh to treat it as one of no use, or of not much practical or normative use.

The fact of the matter is that the two doctrines of rebirth and *karma* in the context of which the concept of *mokṣa* is housed, are taken as postulates or foundational principles in the Indian ethos. Philosophers, who use the concept of *mokṣa* as denoting the highest value, take these two doctrines as given or available to them, and do not try to validate or prove their authenticity. And, when they accept them as unquestionable, they experience no difficulty in elucidating the concept of *mokṣa* in terms of them and, therefore, in considering it to be obviously a genuine one. Both of the two doctrines are, we have seen, constituents of what we have called the worldview which provides the general conceptual framework in which the concept of *mokṣa* occurs. All *mokṣa*-theorists accept or presuppose this worldview. Therefore, we need not feel surprised to see that no classical Indian thinker realizes any difficulty in using the concept of *mokṣa* in its *jīvanmukti* or *videhamukti* form.

It may also be that classical advocates of the doctrine of *jīvanmukti*, as well of *videhamukti*, are aware of the fact that the concept of the non-liability of anyone to be reborn, no matter whether he is alive or dead, is uninstantiable. Therefore, while holding that to be liberated is to cease to be reborn, they do not even try to prove of anyone alive that he will not be reborn, or of any dead person he that has not been reborn. They remain satisfied with referring to some text they consider to be authoritative (*śruti*). For example, Sadānanda Yogīndra remains satisfied with quoting *Katha Upaniṣad* (5.1) as asserting that the liberated (*vimukta*) is freed from (*vimucyate*) further rebirths.[5] This can be taken as an example of using *śruti pramāṇa*, scripture, as a source of knowledge of things not empirically or rationally knowable. Saying this is not very different from saying that this practice is an example of admitting the possibility of freedom from rebirth as a corollary of having accepted what we have called a certain worldview.

It is really surprising, however, that among modern writers on classical Indian moral philosophy, none has realized it, raised any question about the concept's instantiation, or given any justification of its being a usable concept without being instantiable.[6] The importance of the concept of *mokṣa*'s instantiability for its functioning as a viable concept in the Indian theory of value does not seem to have occurred to them. They do not realize the importance of the fact that it would be instantiable only if the concept of the termination of anyone's liability to be reborn is instantiable and that to show the instantiability of the latter is well-nigh impossible, unless one takes the doctrines of rebirth and *karma* as unquestionable, unarguable, articles of faith.

Non-liability to be reborn, or freedom from rebirth, may be said to be a negative feature of *mokṣa*, as it appears to be. Really it is not, because it signifies the negation of bondage which is a negative state. Even a negative feature, of it is antidote to something negative is a positive one. However, it may be said that it is not instantiable because it is in spirit a negative state. Therefore, we shall take an obviously positive characterization of *mokṣa* and see if it can be said to instantiable. We shall, to be fair to Indian axiology, take a feature, or rather what may be called the essence, of the concept of *mokṣa* according to some, to instantiate or exemplify which an attempt has actually been made in the tradition. Our task here will thus be to examine whether this attempt is successful, and if it is how far it can take us in understanding the status of *mokṣa* as the highest value. This we shall do in the next section.

14.5 DREAMLESS SLEEP (*SUṢUPTI*) AS GIVING A SHORT GLIMPSE OF THE STATE OF LIBERATION (*MOKṢA*)

The attempt to use the example of dreamless sleep, or deep sleep (*suṣupti*), as giving something like a genuine peep into the nature of *mokṣa*, has been largely made by some *Advaitic* philosophers. The idea of it first occurs very prominently in the *Māndukya Upaniṣad* and the *Bṛhadāraṇyaka Upaniṣad*. This feature of it has been forcefully emphasized by Śankara in his commentaries on them. Another work in which also it occurs in a very significant way is Vidyāraṇya's *Pancadaśī*. It may also be traced in some other works. But I shall limit the present discussion only to these works primarily because what they say about it adequately serves the specific purpose for which I am discussing it here. Secondly, I do this because discussing it in a comprehensive manner, taking into account its occurrences in other works as well, would unnecessarily lengthen the discussion. My present purpose is only to exhibit how it is used to exemplify, or to give an authentic idea of, the kind of experience *mokṣa*-experience is, as claimed by the *Advaita*. The *Advaita* also uses it to show that the self is only a witnessing consciousness (*sākṣī caitanya*) and not a participating one, not one which participates in any experience of an individual (*jīva*), i.e. not one which enjoys or suffers what the latter does.[7] But I shall not take up this theme of *Advaita*, nor this use of the concept of dreamless sleep. I shall not do that because my objective is not here to discuss the general topic of the *Advaitic* concept of self. Discussing it would amount to discussing the *Advaitic* philosophy in its entirety.

The *Advaitin* admits that dreamless is only a temporary phenomenon and it gives only a glimpse of the experience of *mokṣa*, at least of a basic, positive, feature of it. It resembles *mokṣa*-experience to an extent good enough to give an authentic idea to its experiencer of what *mokṣa*, as conceived by the *Advaitin*, is. He also thinks that this resemblance is very likely to motivate him to try to attain *mokṣa*.

The Advaitin admits the possibility of an individual's attaining *jīvanmukti*, i.e. *mokṣa* while he is alive. Therefore, for any individual it is the highest value which he can and ought to attain. He can attain it by leading a faultless moral life and attaining knowledge of the ultimate reality. To be more precise, his leading a good moral life is a precondition for knowing the ultimate reality which is the same as becoming liberated (*jīvanmukta*). The ultimate reality is *Brahman* which is the same as the self in the individual. The two words '*Brahman*' and '*Atman*' (the Self) thus refer to the same entity. Therefore, for an individual to know the ultimate reality is to know the self in himself, i.e. what he himself really is, which he has forgotten, or does not yet know, because of ignorance. To know what the self is, is thus to get rid of this ignorance.

The moment ignorance is removed, he knows what the self (in him) is. Since he already, really, is the self thus revealed, knowing the Self is realizing, or experiencing, what it, or he, really is. This realization of the Self, or self-realization, is the same as realizing *Brahman*, or the identy of the Self with *Brahman*, because the two are numerically as well as qualitatively the same entity. This realization is *jivanmukti* when attained by an individual while he is alive. According to the *Advaitin*, this state can be called the highest moral value since morality, or living a good moral life, gets consummated in it and thereby blessed with itself becoming the highest value per se because there is nothing else which is higher than it in value.

Since to attain the highest moral value is to know, to realize, what the individual really is, it is only to be, or to re-become, or to return to being, the self (one already is). This self, according to the *Advaitin*, is eternal existence-consciousness-bliss (*satchidānanda*). It is important to note here that it is not an existent being who is conscious of something and who is also blissful. Rather, it is not an existent being but existence itself, not a conscious being but consciousness itself, and not a blissful, or happy, being but bliss itself. Secondly, it is not a composite thing composed of three things, existence, consciousness and bliss, but a pure, *irrelational*, unity. Therefore, any one of the three terms can singly be used to name it, since to call it any one—existence, or consciousness, or bliss—is to refer to or mean the same reality, existence-consciousness-bliss. To attain *mokṣa* or *jīvanmukti*, for a person is thus to realize, or re-become, forever or eternally existence-consciousness-bliss and not to realize that he is an eternally existent and conscious being enjoying bliss. If he is once a *jīvanmukta*, he is forever in his lifetime a *jīvanmukta*, until his bodily death when he becomes a *videhamukta* (liberated after death).

This ideal is said to be very attractive for every man. But it may appear to be so only as long as one does not try to take it seriously or with understanding. For a philosopher who has intellectually become an *Advaitin* by accepting every doctrine of it to be invulnerable, it may naturally look attractive or free from every type of objection, because he has already given credence to everything which the *Advaita* holds. Also, since he is an *Advaitin* only on an intellectual plane and is not yet a practising one, i.e. not one who tries to realize that he is existence-conscious-bliss, his mind would be at rest with his conviction. He would defend it intellectually and remain unbothered by any problem thrown up by it. Another man, who is a practising *Advaitin* having accepted *Advaita* as his religion—let us not forget that *Advaita* has also given rise to a religious sect of Hinduism and has an order of monks—too would not bother to probe into the concept of existence-consciousness-bliss and therefore would not have any difficulty with it. He would follow the discipline which his religious preceptor asks him to follow. And, the third type of individual, who has actually, in his life, realized the *Advaitic* moral ideal of Self-realization, of course, if it is a realizable one, would also have no problem with it.

But a fourth type of person, as open-minded, logically sensitive, moral philosopher, who wants to understand this concept, not just for defending it committedly but to determine whether or not it is fit to be accepted as the highest, or even a working, moral value in practical life, may not feel as comfortable with it as the first three types of individuals may. The reason for his not feeling comfortable, or feeling uncomfortable, with the characterization of self-realization as existence-consciousness-bliss is his difficulty in comprehending or understanding the concept of anyone's realizing or being existence-consciousness-bliss. His difficulty is also the difficulty of an intelligent layman. The reason is that we understand what it is for anyone to exist or not to exist, i.e. to be existent or non-existent, to be conscious of something, as well as to be not conscious of it, to be blissful or unhappy, i.e. to enjoy bliss, or to be deprived of it, or, to experience some pain, etc. But it is difficult to comprehend what it would be like for anyone to be existence, or, consciousness, or bliss. In the concept of existence-consciousness-bliss, existence does not mean some existent thing, consciousness not someone's consciousness of something, and bliss not someone's experience of some bliss. And, existence-consciousness-bliss is said to be fully homogeneous, unified and irrelational. When all these facts are taken into account, one finds it difficult to comprehend what it would be like to be such a thing. Then even the attractiveness of this ideal starts waning because one finds that to be existence-consciousness-bliss is not to exist forever, to remain always conscious of everything, and to remain always blissful. This is so because to be existence itself is not the same as becoming an existent thing, to be consciousness itself not the same as becoming a conscious being, or to be bliss itself is not the same as becoming a blissful being. Rather, our normal way of speaking and thinking starts strongly resisting when we try to speak or think of existence as an existing thing, of consciousness as a conscious being, or of bliss as a blissful being. It is obvious that we like to exist, to be conscious, to be blissful, but it is not obvious that we like to be existence, consciousness, bliss. Therefore, the ideal of realizing existence-consciousness-bliss may not, at least at its first blush, attract many.

It seems the *Advaitin* apprehends that such a difficulty may arise in many a sensible mind. Therefore, he tries to give what he considers to be an empirical example—citing the experience of dreamless sleep as illustrating, of course in a limited, modest, but authentic manner, what the experience of *mokṣa* or *jīvanmukti* is like in being a homogeneous, undifferentiated, unified experience in the realization of the individual as being existence-consciousness-bliss. It illustrates the experience in a limited way because it lasts for a very short duration whereas *jīvanmukti* is permanent. The *jīvanmukta* (liberated), on the other hand, does become disembodied after the demise of his body; but even then he does not lose his liberation. He never again incurs bondage, or gets de-liberated. Dreamless sleep is claimed to give an idea of what the experience of *jīvanmukti* is like. Therefore, anyone who realizes its value, the *Advaitin* thinks, is likely to feel motivated to realize *mokṣa* in *jīvanmukti* because it gives to him on a permanent basis what dreamless sleep gives to him for a few moments.

Dreamless sleep, or deep sleep, *suṣupti*, is said to be as the English phrase indicates, sleep without any dream. In any sleep, the *Advaitin* believes, the sleeper is conscious. In dreamful sleep the objects he is conscious of are his dreams, or dreamed objects. He conscious because he remembers after he wakes up at least some of the things he has dreamed of while he slept. Dreaming, therefore, for the *Advaitin*, is also experiencing, or having some experience, because the sleeper can remember what he dreamed of only if he experienced of what he dreamed. This is because memory or recollection presupposes a past experience of recollected things. Whether or not dreaming can be called an experience is a debatable issue. But let us not go into it here because at the moment we are concerned with dreamless sleep and not with dreams or dreamful sleep.

Dreams are the only things which can be said to be the objects of awareness in a sleep and that too only of a sleep which is dreamful. In a dreamless sleep there is no dream and therefore, if there is some awareness in it, that awareness is bound to be objectless. An enthusiastic follower of *Advaita* may add here, though the classical *Advaitin* does not say it, that in a dreamless sleep there is no self-awareness in its experiencer, the sleeper, that he is having it, or is its experiencer, because, if he had this awareness, he would not then be sleeping and therefore not be sleeping dreamlessly. Therefore, the follower may go on, dreamless sleep is without any object as well as without any subject, and consequently it resembles, exemplifies, or is like, the consciousness of existence-consciousness-bliss because that consciousness is also said to be objectless and subjectless.

But this is not the case. Not having the awareness that he is sleeping is true even of him who is having a dreamful sleep. If he is conscious of the fact that he is sleeping, whether dreamlessly or dreamfully, he is not sleeping. Any sleeping person cannot say or think that he is sleeping. If he does, for example, if he utters 'I am sleeping', or thinks, i.e. utters sub-vocally, in his mind, 'I am sleeping', he is not sleeping. But for this reason neither dreamless nor dreamful sleep can be said to be subjectless. That is obvious from the fact that after waking up both the sleeper who had dreamful sleep and the other who had dreamless sleep own that they had slept, dreamfully or dreamlessly, as the case may be. Both of the two kinds of sleep, thus, have a subject, a person who has them, to whom the experience or ownership of the sleep can be attributed. But in the case of consciousness of the Self, there is no subject whose consciousness it is, who can be said to have its ownership. However, if dreamless sleep is possible, and there is awareness or consciousness in it, then it can be said to partially resemble the consciousness of existence-consciousness-bliss in being objectless like the latter.

As far as existence as such is concerned, it is (almost) impossible to find anything empirical, i.e. anything in the external or internal world, i.e. in human mentation, which can be said to resemble it. Anything which we experience, or may experience, is an existent object, or an existent experience, and not anything which can be said to be in any way just existence. It seems to me that the *Advaitin* cites the example of dreamless sleep to primarily exemplify, or make intelligible, to us the completely homogeneous, undifferentiated, non-dual, tensionless, etc., character of *jīvanmukti*, i.e. bliss. This is clear from the account of dreamless sleep which some classical works give. For example, the *Māndukya Upaniṣad* describes it as an experience completely unified (*ekibhūta*), homogeneous, undifferentiated, a mass of consciousness (*prajñānaghana*), completely non-dual, tensionless and effortless, and therefore, of the nature of bliss. There exists no desire in it. Therefore, there is no effort or tension to fulfil it, no sense of frustration because of the failure to fulfil it. In waking and dreaming experiences the real reality, which is the Self, is miscognized but in dreamless sleep there is no object of cognition and therefore there is no danger of micognizing it. It is mere consciousness as such, not consciousness of this or that thing as there is no object that is being experienced in it.[8] Since thee is no effort, tension, frustration, duality, etc. it is of the nature of pure bliss.

The *Bṛahadāraṇyaka Upaniṣad,* attempts to make the undifferentiated, unified, blissful character of *suṣupti* and thereby that of *jīvanmukti* further clear to us by comparing its non-dual, homogeneous, nature with that of the most intimate union in mutual embrace of a husband and his beloved wife: 'As a man fully embraced by his beloved wife does not know anything at all, either external or internal, so does that infinite being (self)' (i.e. the individual) 'fully embraced by the Supreme Self, not know anything at all, external or internal. ...and...is free from desire and devoid of grief.'[9] Commenting on it Śankara says that in profound sleep (i.e. *suṣupti*) the self in the individual, although always conscious, does not know anything at all because this state 'is pure unity, as of a couple fully embracing each other'.[10]

Here too the emphasis is on the unity or unified nature of the experience of profound sleep, or of intimate union of a lover and his beloved. That is, neither of the united couple, while united in the most intimate mutual embrace, knows anything of the world because each of them is deeply engrossed in enjoying embracing, and being embraced by the other. But this experience of union in mutual embrace is not devoid of duality. Each of the couple is aware of the fact that he (she) is embracing and is being embraced by *her* (him), the other *partner,* and enjoys embracing her (him) only because he (she is aware of the fact that she (he) also enjoys being embraced by him (her). This duality is the bedrock of enjoyment or bliss in human love as well as in the divine love of a devotee for God. In loving Kṛṣṇa the Maiden of Vṛndāvana believe that Kṛṣṇa is someone other than each one of them. It is because of their presupposed duality of the lover and the beloved that the great scholar Uddhava fails to convince them of the superiority of cultivating detachment and adopting the method of knowledge (*jñānamārga*) over that of devotion (*bhakti*), and therefore fails to persuade them to stop grieving over their separation from Kṛṣṇa caused by his going away from Vṛndāvana to Dvārkā. That is why the example of human love cannot exemplify the experience of *jīvanmukti* or *mokṣa* in which there is no duality at all, since in it the Self realizes only what it itself is, though it may exemplify to some extent the element of bliss in *jīvanmukti.*

What is true of the experience of enjoyment in an experience of amorous union is also true of that of poetic pleasure (*kavyānanda*) which too is said to be, by some classical Indian aestheticians, similar to the bliss of *jīvanmukti* (*brahmānanda* or *ātmānanda*). In it also the duality of the enjoyer, the human individual, and the object enjoyed, the poem, or work of art, is there. The enjoyer of a poem enjoys reading the poem, and not something of his own being, and he knows that the poem is a different thing from him. It is true that he is deeply engrossed in, or taken by, the experience of enjoying it. But that does not mean that there is nothing other than him when he is enjoying the poem. The moment he comes to believe that there is nothing, his enjoyment will vanish into thin air. Similarly, in the case of human love, the moment the enjoyer realizes that the object embraced by him (her) is not someone other than him (her) but a part of his (her) own being, or his (her) own being, as does the *jīvanmukta* when (he) the Self in him realizes that what (he) it realizes is (himself) itself and not any other being, the lover's (or the beloved's) enjoyment will vanish in a moment. Another important thing to be noted is that in neither of the two enjoyments, amorous or artistic, does the enjoyer *become* the enjoyment or bliss; rather, he has it, or is the experiencer of it. But in *jīvanmukti* the liberated is bliss as he is existence-consciousness-bliss, and not its experiencer. It is thus impossible to exemplify this feature of *jīvanmukti*. However, both amorous and poetic enjoyment can be taken to exemplify a completely tensionless bliss or blissfulness of *jīvanmukti*. If that is the intention of citing them, we can say that the citation serves some purpose. But this is a very scanty kind of help to be giving to any critical, not-committed-to-*jīvanmukti*-doctrine, person in understanding the nature of *jīvanmukti* as the realization by an individual that he is existence-consciousness-bliss. It is very difficult to say that this scanty help would motivate him to make *jīvanmukti* his moral, or even spiritual, ideal.

After this very relevant detour it is now time return to the concept of dreamless sleep. In it, we have seen, the sleeper has no object of cognition, no dream, nor is he aware of himself as its experiencer or owner. Let us first take up the notion of bliss. We cannot nonchalantly say that there is bliss in dreamless sleep. The experience of bliss can be had only when the experiencer's mental state is cognitively articulate or alert and not merely a state of undifferentiated mass of consciousness, or that of indifference. His post-*suṣupti* mental state, however, may be, or may taken to be, a pleasant or blissful, one. And, if it is, it can very reasonably be taken as the after-effect of the dreamless sleep. But it can be said that the after-effect of any sound sleep, even of a dreamful one, is pleasant or blissful. And, then a dreamless sleep would not be even a limited analogue of *jīvanmukti* because *jīvanmukti* itself, and not its after-effect, is claimed to be bliss. Rather, there is no after-effect of the state of *jīvanmukti*, because existence-consciousness-bliss, the realization of which it is, does not produce anything. It is itself the last, final, state of being. Obviously, then the concept of dreamless sleep would not fare better than sound dreamful sleep.

There is another logical point which needs to be taken into account. In a sleeping state we do not, or rather *cannot*, do anything. In a dreamful sleep one may *dream of* doing something, say, of climbing on a hill, or of having some enjoyment, say, in meeting one's beloved. One may even describe such experiences by saying that one climbed a hill in last night's dream, or enjoyed the company of one's beloved. This locution is used in some languages, say, in Hindi. Rather, people also speak of having *seen* a pleasant, or terrifying, dream the previous night. All such modes of speaking are not considered odd or impermissible. And, if they are taken literally, they illustrate or testify analytic philosophers' now trite claim that language does sometimes mislead an unwary philosopher and prompt him to construct some baseless philosophical theories. When looked at with a philosophically alert or critical eye, such expressions mean something different. For example, such expressions as 'I *climbed* on a hill in my dream last night', 'I *enjoyed* he company of my beloved in my dream last night, 'I *saw* a pleasant dream last night', etc., really mean 'I dreamed of having climbed a hill last night', 'I *dreamed* of enjoying the company of my beloved last night', 'I *had* a pleasant dream last night', etc. An ordinary user of the language is not misled by them; only an unwary, or *logically insensitive*, philosopher is. The latter is, because he is too keen to construct a new-fangled philosophical theory, though in his common-sensical, normal, behaviour, he would not be guided by what he '*did*', or '*saw*' in a dream of his.

The above analysis has been given only to suggest that it is not common-sensical, or normally sensible, and consequently not logically on empirically safe, to speak of having done, or having experienced, something in a sleep, whether dreamful or dreamless. It seems some classical Indian philosophers do not realize this fact about sleep. A good example of this realization is found in Vidyāraṇya's method used in his attempt to prove that there is an experience of bliss in dreamless sleep. He says that after having slept very soundly in his dreamless sleep, when he wakes up. 'A man from deep sleep remembers his happiness and ignorance and says: I was sleeping happily; I knew nothing them.' It is incumbent on us now to analyse this statement and see where it takes us in illustrating that dreamless sleep is an exemplification of the state of *jīvanmukti.*

Let us grant that the sleeper of a dreamless sleep on waking up says 'I was sleeping happily; I knew nothing then' and abbreviate it as HI for convenience in referring to it. The first part of HI, the abbreviation H of 'I was sleeping happily', Vidyāraṇya considers to be a memorial, or recollective, statement, reporting, on the basis of his recollecting, what the sleeper felt in his dreamless sleep. Every recollection presupposes or implies that there was a past experience in which what it reports, i.e. its content, was experienced. H reports that the sleep was happy. Therefore, there was happiness or bliss in the dreamless sleep. If this understanding of H by Vidyāraṇya is granted, then there is bliss in dreamless sleep and therefore it exemplifies *jīvanmukti* as a state of bliss. He takes the second part of HI, 'I knew nothing them', abbreviated as I, to mean that there was complete ignorance, or complete absence of knowledge or awareness, in the state of dreamless sleep. This implies that the sleeper knew nothing, i.e. he had no experience of anything and therefore no experience of happiness, in his dreamless sleep. But then how does he recollect that he slept happily? This problem Vidyāraṇya tries to solve by invoking the *Advaitic* doctrine of witnessing consciousness (*sākṣī caitanya*). He proceeds as follows:

Since the sleeper has no awareness of there being happiness in his dreamless sleep, and he recollects it even then, there must be an agency which watches what happens in it as an witness without participating in it. This witnessing consciousness is nothing but the self. It is this witnessing consciousness or awareness of his happiness which enables him to recollect that he slept happily in his dreamless sleep.

In this way Vidyāraṇya uses the recollection of happiness by the sleeper, who is unaware of it, to allegedly prove the necessity of admitting that the self is a witnessing consciousness, and uses the witness's awareness of the happiness to explain the recollection of it by the sleeper.[11]

It is not very difficult to see how sloppy this explanation or defence of the doctrine of the sleeper's recollection of his happiness in his dreamless sleep is. The sleeper who is said to recollect is the individual, *jīva,* the embodied Self, and not the pure Self. He sleeps dreamlessly and recollects that the sleep was happy when he wakes up, though he was unaware, or ignorant, of it when he was actually sleeping, and thus had no experience of it. The happy nature of the dreamless sleep is known to another agency, the witnessing consciousness, the Self. It is another agency, though it is also in the individual, because the individual has not yet realized it and only on realizing it is he the pure Self. Therefore, the agency which knows that the dreamless sleep is happy, and the agency whose dreamless sleep it is and which recollects that it was happy when it had it, are two agencies. But this is conceptually impossible. Only that agency which had dreamless sleep can recollect that it was happy. No agency can recollect what another agency is or was at any time aware of, or has at any time the experience of. This is nothing but to bring to our clear vision the fact that one cannot have the memory or recollection of something one was unaware of when it occurred or happened even though it occurred or happened to oneself.

There is another way in which the sleeper's saying 'I was sleeping happily; I knew nothing then', after his having a dreamless sleep, can be interpreted. In this way it can make it unnecessary to presuppose the reality of any witnessing consciousness and to attribute to it the watching of the dreamless sleep and cognizing it to be bliss, or a blissful experience. It may be said that H, the first part of the sentence, is a report of the sleeper of the effect, or rather of the after-effect on him of having had a dreamless sleep. That is, it is not a memorial or recollective statement but one stating what he, after the sleep, feels. Similarly, the second part, I, may be taken in a non-assertional, metaphorical, sense, i.e. as a sentence conveying only the intensity of the sleep. That in a very sound sleep one is, as a natural effect of it, unaware of one's surroundings, and of what happens therein, is well-known and is very well expressed in the phrase 'sleeping the sleep of the dead', i.e. being sound asleep. This interpretation is very-much common-sensical and down to earth. But it would not appeal to an *Advaitin*, or to any speculative philosopher, because then dreamless sleep cannot be used as a limited analogue, or exemplifying tool, to help anyone, particularly any intelligent layman, to understand, or to form an idea of, what *jīvanmukti* or *mokṣa* is like.

Apart from such difficulties as have been mentioned above, the use of the example of dreamless sleep to give an idea of *jīvanmukti* has another, something like a congenital, disadvantage. Dreamless sleep is something which happens, or occurs. It cannot be had at will by an ordinary person, even by a great philosopher. Therefore, we cannot tell anyone that *jīvanmukti* is a perfected state, or a consummation, of what he has experienced for a very short while and in a scanty manner in his dreamless sleep. We cannot do that because he might not have had so far any dreamless sleep and we cannot give him any recipe by using which he can have it. Therefore, he may not be assured even of its possibility. It is necessary that an exemplifying or instantiating feature of any concept must be a paradigmatically unquestionable feature, one in the reality or availability of which there should be no doubt at all. The examples of amorous and poetic pleasure have these features but they do not have the kind of non-duality which *jīvanmukti* is said to have. Moreover, the concept of dreamless sleep has to face another danger from science. Neurologists are not yet decisive about its empirical reality, about whether or not sleep is ever dreamless. Psychologists are united in saying that most dreams are forgotten on waking up, and therefore give the hint that what a person considers to be a dreamless sleep may well be one whose dreams have all been completely forgotten on waking. It may also be said that while he was sleeping, due to fatigue, or some other physical factor, the awareness of the dreams he had, or might have had, was so thin or weak that, on waking up, he has no memory even of the fact that he had any dream. The *Advaitin* thinks that the common man has sometimes at least some dreamless sleep. This is an empirical belief and if it is found, on scientific, or on good empirical, grounds, to be false or doubtful, the utility of dreamless sleep as an example of any sort for making the concept of *jīvanmukti* intelligible will be greatly reduced.

Some scholars think that dreamless sleep is, or can be, had only by those who have undergone some process of spiritual disciplining. This claim would meet neither the scientific, nor the empirical, challenge, nor would it have any effect on the logical difficulties which exist, as shown here, in using the concept of dreamless sleep even as a working example of *jīvanmukti.* It would also not have much point. It is not the spiritually oriented person but the common man who needs to understand the notion of *jīvanmukti,* the doctrine which avers that realizing that he is really existence-consciousness-bliss is the highest value. The spiritually oriented one might have already accepted that it is the highest value, or have become a disciple of *Advaita* and therefore accepted the *Advaitic* theory. Invoking spiritual experience or orientation would therefore be not very relevant to solving the problems which the nature of the concept of dreamless sleep raises in considering it to be an exemplifying device for the concept of *jīvanmukti.* The common man, and not the spiritually oriented person, or one who is committed to *Advaita,* needs to understand what being existence-consciousness-bliss is like in order to make its realization his highest moral or spiritual value.

The aim of an ethical or xiological theory is also to present only that as the highest value, or even a value, the concept of which can be made intelligible to every mature person and not only to the spiritually oriented one, or to him who has already accepted the theory. This it can do only if the instances it uses to explain, or make clear, the concept of the value, are down to earth, instances which are themselves clear and unquestionable and within the easy approach of every mature person. Only then will the ethical or axiological theory be a down-to-earth, genuine, theory. If we keep this fact in mind, we are bound to have some problems in understanding the concept of *jīvanmukti* and using the concept of dreamless sleep as an exemplifying agent for it. This difficulty is compounded many times when we remember the difficulty or difficulties, already discussed, in instantiating the liberated person's non-liability to be reborn after the death of his body. Perhaps for these reasons classical as well as modern scholars have desisted from discussing the *concept of mokṣa* and concentrated on describing what *mokṣa* is and are satisfied with mentioning the names of individuals taken by the tradition to have become *jīvanmukta,* without caring to discuss how they are known to have ceased to be liable to be reborn after their bodily death. It is very important to realize that discussing the logical behaviour or status of the *concept of mokṣa* is very different from describing the *nature of mokṣa* according to this or that school of classical Indian philosophy. It is the former which needs to be done to characterize Indian ethical or axiological theory. The latter sort of discussion would only be Indological. If this term is not very respectable, we can say that it would be an exercise in the history or anthropology of morals or values, and not in moral philosophy.

In spite of all this, *mokṣa* has been figuring in classical Indian philosophies and theologies, as well as in modern discussions of them, as the highest value to which morality has been claimed to be closely related. Even we have said that, if we take into account that feature of *mokṣa* which consists in effectuating freedom from suffering, it is a moral value, and when this freedom is taken to mean or denote freeing all being from suffering and for all time, it can very well be called the highest moral value. Be that as it may, the role of the ideal of *mokṣa* in moral life is an important theme in the Indian philosophy of morals or values, and therefore needs to be discussed. This will be done the next section.

14.6 LIBERATION (*MOKṢA*) AND MORALITY: A PROCEDURAL CLARIFICATION

It has been said on some occasions in this work that *mokṣa* is not a moral value or goal. It has been pointed out in support of it that even if an individual does not try to attain *mokṣa*, or does not believe in any doctrine of *mokṣa*, his life-style may be perfectly moral. This point has not been noted, or given the philosophical attention it deserves, by many writers on Indian ethics. But they too cannot deny the brute fact that there are some highly moral persons who have no time to think of *mokṣa*, or have not bothered to know what it is. This cannot either deny that in our actual evaluative practice, more often than not, we seldom try to ascertain whether or not a person has attained, or is trying to attain, *mokṣa*, in order to judge the moral worth of his character.

On some other occasions in the work, on the other hand, we admit, we have called *mokṣa* a moral value, or even a high, or the highest, moral value. We have done this apparently self-inconsistent thing because of certain potentialities in the concept of *mokṣa*, or in the different ways in which the concept has figured, or been characterized, in some classical works and in some modern interpretations of it. Some of these potentialities tend to lend support to the view that it is not a moral value, or is a value indifferent to morality. Some others of them lend support to the other view that in its heart of hearts it is a moral value, or has to be first a moral value even if it is said to be something more, whatever that something more may be. We hope to make all this clear in this section.

We have also said more than once that the Indian ethos gives to *mokṣa* the status of the highest value, as it places it on the highest rung of the ladder of values in the structure of its general theory of value, the theory of *puruṣārtha*s. This is clear from the fact that it calls it *parama puruṣārtha*, the highest or greatest among the objects of a positive human desire. Classical Indian ethical theory, i.e. the theory of moral value, virtue, obligation, etc., is generally taken to be included in, or constituted by, the Indian theory of *dharma*, in the general, conceptual, framework of the Indian general theory of value. In our presentation of the general theory, *dharma* has been treated as its third component, though not as the third in rank or status. Rather, we have shown that the Indian value theory can very convincingly be interpreted as admitting the primacy of the ethical over all other values or value-considerations. This point will be further strengthened in this section. If the Indian conception of moral value, virtue, etc. is taken to be equivalent to the Indian conception of *dharma*, then *mokṣa* being the highest among all values, has to be taken as higher, or more important, than *dharma* or morality. In that case it may seem justified to hold that, according the Indian general theory of value, *mokṣa* is a higher value than any moral value, and therefore higher than even the highest moral value whatever that may be. This strand of thinking can be read into some accounts of *mokṣa* available in some works. It is that strand of thinking which prompts many a thinker to say that morality, in Indian value-theory, is only a means to *mokṣa*, or that it is the pursuit of *mokṣa* which justifies leading a moral life, or that the concept of *mokṣa* transcends, or goes beyond, the zone of morality, etc. But there is also a strand of thinking which can be, reconstructively of course, taken to suggest that *mokṣa* does not transcend morality but consummates it by incorporating it within itself. It does this because it is itself the moral man's all-round fulfilment of his desirable potentialities. It thus turns out to be moral perfection plus something more than moral.

These are some of the possible ways in which the relation between *mokṣa* and morality may be understood. Some of them are also the prevalent ways in which this relation has been characterized by interpreters of Indian ethics theory. Without prejudging which one of them characterizes this relation correctly, or fairly, it can be said that the very possibility of there being more than one characterization of the relation is a good evidence of the fact that it is not a very simple one; i.e. one which is clearly written on the face of the concept of *dharma*, or on that of *mokṣa*, which anybody can easily read. Realizing this fact convincingly shows that merely to emphasize that *mokṣa* is, according to Indian ethical theory, the highest value (*puruṣārtha*), does not say much about the theory or about its conception of what a life ought to be in order to be a good moral life. To clarify a few of these issues we shall discuss hereafter, in some detail, some of the ways in which the relation between *mokṣa* and morality may be, or has generally been, understood.

14.7 MORALITY AS A MEANS TO *MOKṢA*: AN UNWORKABLE POSITION

Since *mokṣa* is according to Indian value theory the highest value, it seems truistic to many to say that morality has the value it has only because it contributes to its attainment; that is, it is, or has to be, a *means* to the attainment of *mokṣa*. Excepting the *Cārvāka* and one school of the *Mīmāmsa*, all the remaining schools of Indian philosophy are interpreted as holding that position. The *Cārvāka* does not accept anything like *mokṣa* and, therefore, for him the question of there being, or there not being, any relation between morality and *mokṣa* does not arise. That school of the *Mīmāmsa* which accepts *dharma* to be autonomous, and not a means to *mokṣa*, means largely by *dharma* performance of rituals and sacrifices as prescribed in the *Vedas*, and not what we mean by *dharma*, that is, *dharma* as morality. Therefore, it is not safe to say that it upholds the autonomy of morality or of ethics.

One of the obvious implications which may be drawn from considering *mokṣa* the highest value, or standard, of morality and morality a means to it, is that all other moral predicates be defined in terms of their conduciveness or instrumentality to the attainment of *mokṣa*. Many writers on Indian ethics think that doing that would be all right, or cause no problem for ethical theory and practice. For example, Crawford nonchalantly asserts that '*mokṣa* serves as the ultimate standard of right conduct. It measures the value or disvalue of an act by the extent to which it helps or hinders the attainment of freedom,' i.e. *mokṣa*.[12] He does not realize that difficulties are bound to arise in using the concept of *mokṣa* as a measure of the morality or immorality of an action. It is not, then, only the moral rightness of an action, but the moral status of all other moral things, like virtues, rights, etc. that would have to be judged in terms of their conduciveness to *mokṣa*. The moral worth of an obligation, a character-trait's property of being a virtue, or a claim's being a moral right, etc., would be determinable only in terms of its instrumentality in attaining *mokṣa*. For example, an action would be morally right if and only if doing it is conducive to its doer's attaining *mokṣa*; when more than one action is conducive in a certain situation, then that which is the most effective would be obligatory; similarly, a character-trait would be a virtue if an only if its cultivation helps its owner in attaining *mokṣa*, and this would be the case with any claim's being a moral right. Only that claim would be a moral right which would help the claim-holder to attain *mokṣa*. To say these things may look very simplistic but none of them is. Rather, each one of them makes the concept it is about indeterminable or undecidable, i.e. inapplicable or unusable in actual practice.

Let us take one example, namely, the notion of a morally right action. What will be said of it would be true of all other notions mentioned above and even of other moral terms whose criterion would be their conduciveness to the attainment of *mokṣa*. Whenever anything is held to be the highest value by a theory, conduciveness to its procurement or promotion becomes, according to it, the criterion of the application of other value notions or concepts. Therefore, when *mokṣa* is taken to be the highest value, an action would be morally right if and only if doing it helps the doer to attain his *mokṣa*. For any property of any concept to be a criterion for the concept's application to anything, it is necessary that it is possible for any normal user of the concept to decide, in finite time and in a finite number of steps in his thinking, whether or not the property belongs to a certain thing in a certain situation. Only then can he decide whether or not the concept, whose criterion this property is, can be applied to that thing. If the aforesaid property does not satisfy this condition, it would become disqualified to be a criterion of the concept concerned. This condition for being a criterion of a concept's application is a logical or semantic one, true of the very concept of being a criterion. Therefore, it cannot be questioned or rejected on any empirical or regional ground which may even be said to be a distinctive feature of the classical Indian ethos or social order.

Secondly, ethical concepts are used and required to be used by ordinary, normal, individuals in normal as well as not so normal, i.e. difficult, unusual, circumstances. Therefore, their criterion or criteria, must be such that an ordinary person can generally decide their applicability, and only in a very few cases have to take help from some moral expert (if there is any). They are not like legal concepts for help in the application of which there are readily available legal experts, nor like ritualistic ones in respect of which a normal individual can nonchalantly depend on his family's priest. They are also not like abstruse, speculative, metaphysical ones in the application of which a philosopher may claim to be an expert and in which a normal individual is not interested because the correct or incorrect application of these concepts does not matter much to him. Therefore, if an ethical theory offers a criterion of moral rightness the application of which is undecidable, or undecidable for a normal person, then there is something wrong with the theory and not with the normal person.

The criterion of the moral rightness of an action, entailed by the Indian ethical theory, interpreted as considering *mokṣa* to be the highest value, as Crawford, for example, does, is the conduciveness of the action to the attainment of *mokṣa*. *Mokṣa* may be taken to mean liberation attained after death or attained while alive. It is obvious that it is not possible for anyone to decide what an action done by him now will be conducive to liberation, or even to decide whether or not it would have any effect at all, after his death. Therefore, the notion of moral rightness would become then totally dysfunctional for anyone for whom only *videhamukti* is possible. It may be said, and it is said by even some modern philosophers, that to know what it would produce after his death, he has to depend upon some theological, taken-to-be-sacred, books by some allegedly divinely gifted individual, called *ṛṣis*, seers of eternal truths. To adopt this remedy is to leave the zone of morality which is a zone of free rational choice about what is right, or not right, to do, and land oneself in a zone of theological authoritarianism. To have this fallout is no laurel to the theory of moral rightness we are presently considering, or to the general ethical theory which yields it.

Alternatively, *mokṣa* is also taken to be attainable in life. Even this conception of it does not fare better in respect of the issue we are presently discussing. The criterion of moral rightness, according to it too, would remain the same, i.e. conduciveness to the attainment of *mokṣa.* A necessary feature of a person liberated alive is that after the death of his present body he would not be reborn. Therefore, to be morally right, an action done by a person must satisfy the condition of being conducive to terminating his liability to be reborn after his death. But it is not possible for any person to know of any action that it satisfies the condition which is now the criterion of moral rightness. This is so because it is not possible for any person to know of himself, or of anyone else, that after his death he will not be reborn. This means that the theory of *mokṣa,* which admits the possibility of liberation while alive, i.e. of bodily liberation (*jīvanmukti*), too, makes the moral rightness of an action undecidable, as does the theory of liberation after death, i.e. bodiless liberation (*videhamukti*). In the case of *jīvanmukti* too we would have to land in, what I have called, some sort of theological or scriptural authoritarianism. The upshot of this analysis is that fixing the criterion of moral rightness of an action in terms of the action's conduciveness to *mokṣa* will make moral life (almost) impossible if one sticks to using this criterion in making one's decisions about what is and what is not morally right for one to do, while keeping one's rationality and freedom in moral-decision-making intact.

It may be urged that termination of the liability to be reborn is not the only feature of a person who is liberated while alive. That is true. But the termination of the liability to be reborn being a necessary condition of being liberated, whatever other laudable features a man may have, if after his death he is reborn, he would not be a liberated person. A believer in this theory cannot console himself by holding a second belief that a man who has the other features of a *jīvanmukta,* mentioned in some books, would automatically, as a matter of necessity, cease to have the liability to be reborn. He cannot, because the second belief too is neither confirmable nor disconfirmable. Nobody can know that a man who has cultivated such and such traits of character in his lifetime will not be reborn after his death nor can anybody counter a claim that the man will not be reborn. The belief, that anyone with such and such moral accomplishments would not be reborn after his death, in the case of a man who is already dead as well as in that of one who is alive, is bound to remain, thus, always a belief which can be held only on some theological, scriptural, i.e. non-rational, ground, or as one considered to be too sacred to be subjected to rational scrutiny. Theologies do have such beliefs. But an ethical theory cannot afford to have any of this type because ethical issues are rationally arguable or debatable. Moral reasoning is as respectable a rational thing as is non-moral reasoning.

Let us look at some of the features of a bodily liberated person other than the termination of his liability to be reborn. The *Yogavāśiṣṭha,*[13] in the later half of the section which discusses the nature of bodily liberation, mentions several features of the bodily liberated. For example, it says, he has no desire except the desire to do good to those who are ignorant or unenlightened; while doing all types of commendable things he is not a doer of anything; though bereft of all kinds of feelings, like fear, grief, fatigue, etc., he is unhappy to see someone else unhappy; he neither feels pleased to have something nor grieves over having been deprived of something; he knows the eternal truth, and never does any wrong thing, etc.

However, the *Yogavāsīṣṭha*[14] does not hesitate to add that it is not possible for everybody to know who is and who is not bodily liberated. It candidly says that just as only a snake knows how to identify, or identifies, the footprints of another snake, only a *jīvanmukta* knows how to identify, or identifies, one who is a *jīvanmukta.* This is to admit that even if an ordinary person decides to ignore non-liability to be reborn and restricts his attention to some other features of being a *jīvanmukta,* it is not possible for him to know who is a *jīvanmukta.* This means he cannot know, or know easily, what it is to be a *jīvanmukta,* and therefore which action is conducive to his becoming one, i.e. to his attaining the state of *jivanmukti.* Apparently, then, he cannot know, or know easily, whether or not an action is morally right. But it is the ordinary individual who has to decide, and generally to decide in a short time, what is morally right for him to do. And, many times he must decide and choose to do one of two, or of more than two, actions open to him because the situation he is in is such that he cannot either wait for long or remain completely passive. Therefore, giving to morality the status of only a means to the attainment of *mokṣa* cannot work because it entails making conduciveness to attaining *mokṣa* the criterion of moral rightness. And, this criterion is unusable because it makes it impossible, or almost impossible, for an ordinary (or rather, any) individual to decide which action is right and which is not. It is obvious that this will make moral life itself impossible, or the very institution of morality dysfunctional.

The ethical standpoint, which makes *mokṣa* the highest value, is obviously *teleological* because, then, any of the notions of moral rightness—obligation, virtue, claim, etc.—are to be interpreted in terms of its conduciveness or instrumentality to attaining the highest value. Morality would thus be a means to *mokṣa.* In this approach it is one central component of the concept of *mokṣa,* i.e. non-liability to be reborn, which makes it impossible to apply any one of these other notions. It is important to think over the possibility, if there is any, of some small tinkering with the concept of *mokṣa* to let morality remain a means to *mokṣa* without being thereby made inapplicable or dysfunctional. This possibility we shall explore in the section after the next one along with discussing some other issues, as whether or not *mokṣa* has to be the highest moral value when it is considered to be the highest value, whether or not it is fair to the status of morality to call it a means to *mokṣa,* whether or not any classical thinker has realized the problem which the non-liability to be reborn gives rise to in making conduciveness to attaining *mokṣa* the criterion of the application of a moral concept to anything, etc., etc. In the next section we shall discuss another important fallout of making morality a means which does seem to have occurred in some classical thinkers' understanding of *mokṣa* and which seems to threaten the very existence or identity of morality as a socially useful institution.

14.8 MORALITY AS EXTERNALLY RELATED MEANS TO LIBERATION (*MOKṢA*): MAKING MORALITY DISPENSABLE FOR THE LIBERATED

The concept of means-end relationship is not as simple as it seems to be because it can be of different types, depending on the differing nature of the things which function as means and ends in different cases. We shall mention here two of such types, both of which are illustrated in classical Indian ethical theory's allegedly considering morality as a means to the attainment of *mokṣa*. I shall call them (i) *normatively external* and (2) *normatively internal*. In this section I shall discuss the first type and in the next the second type.

Speaking more specifically, the relation of a means to its end is *normatively external* when it is of such a sort that the object functioning as the means gets its entire value from the object which functions as its end or objective, while adding nothing of its own to the value of the end. It is this view which is generally held, though wrongly, to exhaust the meaning of anything being a means to something else. It is also this view which seems to be prominently present in the ethical theory which holds that the end justifies the means; that is, if the end is good, any means used to attain it is ethically a right means. A teleological ethical theory is quite often taken to involve this conception of means-end relationship.

The classical Indian position which considers morality to be a means to *mokṣa* does contain, as one strand of it, this view. Therefore, the upholders of this view consider *mokṣa* to be the justifier of morality. For them, to the question 'Why should one be moral?', the right answer is 'One would get *mokṣa* by being moral.' One consequence of this conception of means-end, or morality-*mokṣa*, relationship, is that a means, after having been used to attain what it is a means to, becomes a disposable, dispensable, or unwanted, commodity. It is this view of means which is expressed in the analogy of calling morality a foot-stool, or ladder, which is used to reach, or climb, to the state of *mokṣa*.

After attaining *mokṣa*, the liberated individual would, carrying the analogy further, need to use the foot-stool, or ladder, only if he has to come down to his earlier, pre-liberated, state of bondage, i.e. to the stage of unliberatedness. But liberation is attained, we have said so many times, once and for all. There is no question of any liberated person's becoming de-liberated. The obvious fallout of this is that for the liberated person morality is not at all needed, or that he no longer needs to be moral. Stretched further, this line of thinking would lead or authorize its upholder to say that the liberated has transcended the zone of morality, or, that moral predicates no longer apply to him. This fallout thus threatens the sanctity of morality. It does because morality is considered to be a means to *mokṣa* and the means-end relationship is conceived in a manner which is what I have called normatively external to the end in the very *specific* sense in which the means totally depends for its value on the end, though it does not depend on the end for its existence. This is to say that *mokṣa* justifies morality because morality is worth cultivating if and only it is a means to attaining *mokṣa*. If it exists without being instrumental to *mokṣa*, then it would have unjustified existence. On the other hand, *mokṣa* does not get even a fraction of its value from morality, though to attain it the *mokṣa*-aspirant needs to use morality as a means.

If morality is a means to attain *mokṣa* and of no use after its attainment, a stand may be taken that the liberated may justifiably become indifferent to morality, or may not care for what is morally right or wrong. To put it differently, it does not matter to him whether what he does is right or wrong. This mode of thinking is visible in certain accounts of the state of *mokṣa*. For example, while discussing the nature of deep sleep (*suṣupti*) as a limited analogue of the state of *mokṣa*, the *Bṛhadāraṇyaka Upaniṣad* says that in this state, the individual is beyond all human relations and therefore beyond all social and moral relations. 'In this state,' it says, 'a father is no father, a mother no mother, worlds no worlds, the gods no gods, the Vedas no Vedas. In this state a thief is no thief, the killer of a noble Brāhmaṇa no killer, a Cāndāla (*śūdra*) "no Cāndāla, a Pulkasa (another kind of *śūdra*) no Pulkasa, a monk no monk, a hermit no hermit. (This form of his) is untouched by good work and untouched by evil work, for he is then beyond all the woes of his heart (intellect)."[15] The state of *mokṣa* is a stabilized, eternal, state of this kind. It is obvious that a man who is in such a state, a bodily liberated person, will be beyond all moral relations, duties and obligations, values and virtues, i.e. beyond all moral goods and evils. Neither does he need to have any care for morality, nor can anyone else accuse him of having done any moral evil, or praise him for having done anything morally right or commendable, as he is untouched by good and evil. He is, thus, no longer a member of the moral community.

Emphasizing further the same implication of making morality a means to *mokṣa*, a fallout which has been stated above, Vidyāraṇya goes to the extent of saying that a liberated person may do anything, even the vilest kind of immorality, without incurring any moral demerit or deserving any moral censure. He says that 'Before realization' (i.e. before he attains (*jīvanmukti*), 'one has many duties to perform in order to acquire worldly and celestial advantages and also as an aid to ultimate release; but with the rise of knowledge of Brahman' (with the attainment of *jīvanmukti*), 'they are as good as already done, for nothing *further remains to be done*'[16] (italics mine). What he wants to bring out here is that since the highest value has been achieved by achieving *jīvanmukti*, now there is no duty left to be done, i.e. there is no obligation left to be fulfilled by the liberated. He may, therefore, retire from moral life; he may, as a matter of courtsey, continue doing what his society calls morally right or required, but if he does not, he would not be accused of having done any moral omission or commission.

Thus if a liberated person does something which, as per the normal conception of morally, right and wrong, is of the vilest kind, even doing it would not tarnish the glory of his high status. This is bound to be so because he has now gone outside the boundary of morality, the zone only within which moral predicates are applicable. Just as the predicate of being a square, or of being a square-root, can be applicable only to a number or of a variable whose values are numbers, the predicate of being morally praiseworthy or of blameworthy is applicable only to him who is a member of the moral community, i.e. inside the zone of morality. Therefore, we cannot give any credit to the liberated for having done anything morally right, or discredit him for having done anything morally wrong. This point is clearly made in the lines of the *Bṛhadāraṇyaka* also which have been quoted earlier. Vidyāraṇya reinforces the same point when he, quoting the *Kauṣitaki Upaniṣad* (3.1) approvingly says 'that killing of parents, stealing, causing abortion and such other sins do not effect his (the liberated person's) illumination' 'nor is the colour (serenity) of his countenance marred.'[17]

To hold such a view about morality, or an axiolgoical theory giving to *mokṣa* this kind of status, is plainly to admit that morality loses all importance for the liberated. Treating morality in this way certainly goes against our normal understanding of its role and status in our life. We do not consider it to be a disposable commodity at any time, which it is, as per Vidyāraṇya, for a *jīvanmukta*. This is a necessary fallout of making morality a means to *mokṣa* and considering the relation of means to its end to be, what I have called, normatively external, a relation in which morality is to be used as an external tool, a foot stool, or, ladder, to attain *mokṣa,* without entering into the very being of *mokṣa,* i.e. without becoming internal to, or, integrated into it.

14.9 MORALITY AS INTERNALLY RELATED MEANS TO LIBERATION (*MOKṢA*): BECOMING A PRECONDITION INTEGRATED INTO LIBERATION

The means–end relationship, more often than not, is of a type that the means and end form a whole in which the means contribute to the distinctive character of the whole. This happens invariably when the end is a value-carrying object. In such a case the means becomes indispensable for the end, particularly for the value, positive or negative, that it has. The fact of the matter is that sometimes the value of the end of determined in a significant way by the value of the means. This shows that it is not the case that the end always justifies the means by lending to the means from its own source whatever value the means is said to have. Rather, the reverse of the latter view may be said to be exhibited by such cases. The show that sometimes the means–end complex has to be judged as an organic whole, and not as a compound of two separable or separate things, the means and the end, in which the means is instrumental to the being of the whole but derives all its value from its instrumentality to the production of the end. In the case of the means–end complex being conceived as an organic whole, if the means is altered, the value of the end is also altered. It illustrates the normative truth that not only does the end (sometimes) justify the means, but the means too (sometimes) justifies the end. The relation of the means to the end in these cases is such that the means plays some role in determining the value of the end. Because of this nature of the relation I call it normatively internal. It is *normative* because it is a relation which matters for the value of the end and it is *internal* because the means, or the value of the means, enters, or, gets integrated, into the value of the end, and thereby makes the means indispensable for, or inseparable from, the end. This is to say that the whole, that is, the end, would cease to retain its value if it dispenses with the means. In such a case of means–end relationship it may even sometimes be true that the value of the means is greater than that of the end, or, that the value of neither the means nor the end can be stated by taking either one of them in isolation from the other.

To illustrate what has been said above in an abstract manner, let us come back to our theme of *morality-mokṣa* relationship. Before doing that it is worth noting that it is an intrinsic feature of morality that whichever end is achieved in a morally right manner, it is better than the same end achieved in a morally wrong, or indifferent, manner. That is, anything, in favour of attaining or doing which there is a moral consideration, has a greater value than that in favour of attaining or doing which there is no moral consideration, or there is only some non-moral or immoral consideration. The point that is being made here is that the morality present in achieving or doing anything always adds to, or heightens, the positive value of it and immorality present in the attempt lessens its positive value, or adds to its negative value.

Fighting the *Mahābhārata* war for the Pāṇḍavas is fighting a righteous war because they fight it to recover their rightful share in their paternal property presently in the unjustified possession of Duryodhana. On the other hand, fighting the same war for Duryodhana is fighting an unrighteous war because he fights it to retain in his possession of that portion of the kingdom to retain which he has no moral right. Victory in a war is *prized* by any fighter. But it becomes *worth prizing*, or prizeworthy, i.e. morally prizeable, only for him for whom the war fought is a righteous, i.e., a moral, war. But the moral value of the victory remains intact, or gets heightened, if in the actual fight only morally right means are used. The opposite is the case if even one immoral means is used. Had the Pāṇḍavas used only morally right means in the actual combat, the moral merit of their victory would have been much greater than it in fact it is. Their morally right end, the recovery of their rightful share, gets polluted by their using some means morally not impeccable, like telling a lie in getting Droṇa killed, killing Karṇa when he is unarmed, etc.

It is for the above reason, i.e. not using any morally not right means, or using much fewer morally not right means, in attaining victory in his war with Rāvaṇa than those used by the Pāndavas, on Kṛṣṇa's persuasion or instigation, in winning the *Mahābhārata* war, that the Indian ethical tradition rates Rāma's victory higher in moral merit than Pāṇḍavas' and Rāma as a greater moral hero, or exemplar of morality, than Arjuna or Kṛṣṇa. All this makes it clear that in the Indian ethical tradition the morality or immorality of a means is admitted as playing an important role in determining the value of the end it is used to attain and that a desirable end does not justify the use of an undesirable means. This is so because, according to it, the value of the means enters, or, gets integrated, into that of the end, making it brighter or darker, depending on the nature of the value it itself has, whether positive or negative.

When a means is internally related to the end, as illustrated above, it becomes a *precondition* of the value of the end. A precondition enters into the being of that of which it is a precondition, and therefore it can never be dispensed with by the conditioned. We may continue to call it a means still, if we do not forget that it is indispensable for the end. For example, wetness of the fuel may be called a means for getting smoke out of it on burning it. But it is a means internally related to causing it to produce smoke because the fuel has to be wet all the time it emits smoke. The moment it gets rid of its wetness, i.e. becomes fully dry, it stops emitting smoke. Therefore, I call wetness of the fuel internally related to, or a precondition of, the fuel's emitting smoke. The relation between the fuel's wetness and its emitting smoke is factually (not normatively) internal because the relation is factual or causal. Such a relation in evaluative or moral cases I have called normatively internal because here the relation between the means or precondition, and the end or the conditioned, is normative or evaluative since the value of the means affects the value of the end.

The relation between the morality of a means the value of its ends thus being normatively internal, the morality of the means is a precondition of the value of the end. A victory, in the moral value of which the moral value, or morality, of the means used to attain it has a share, cannot retain its value if, after its attainment, in further using or utilizing it, the victor starts using undesirable, or immoral, means. For example, the moral merit of Rāma's victory would have become greatly reduced, or its moral image greatly darkened, had Rāma started adopting undesirable means in his post-victory practice, say, in using the rights which accrued to him as a result of his victory, for example by mistreating his brother Lakṣmaṇa, his friends who fought the war from his side, etc. etc. And, in fact, the tortuous ordeal to which he subjected his wife Sītā and his killing Śambūka do take away some of the moral merit of his performance as the king of Ayodhyā, though he gets his kingship in a commendable manner and as his moral right. Therefore, we conclude that moral means, or the morality of the means, used to attain an end does not become dispensable after the attainment of the end, whatever the end may be and howsoever great its value may be.

Can what is true of the morality of the means used to attain an end judged to be morally commendable, also be said to true, according to Indian ethical theory, of the use of morality as a means to attain *mokṣa*? That is, can we say that the morality used as a means to attain liberation works as a precondition for its attainment in the sense that it enters into it with the result that the liberated person too leads a moral life and that leading it for him carries in no way a lesser value than it does for a non-liberated one? It seems to me that we can, because this trend of thinking is also present in the classical Indian conception of the morality-*mokṣa* relationship. For example it can very well be seen in Śabjara's commentary on the first canon of the *Brahmasūtra.* He says therein that it is a prerequisite, i.e. a precondition, for the desirer of the attainment of knowledge of *Brahman,* which is the same as *mokṣa,* to first have 'discrimination between the eternal and non-eternal (value), dispassion for the enjoyment of the fruits (or works), here and hereafter, a perfection of such penances as control of the mind, control of the senses, and organs, etc. and a hankering for liberation. Granted the existence of these, Brahman can be deliberated on or known...' To fulfil these prerequisites or preconditions is obviously to have a perfectly moral temper or style of living.[18]

A worthwhile discussion of this theme can be done only if liberation is taken in the sense of liberation attained while alive. There is no point in talking about, or rather, we cannot talk about, the role of morality for a person liberated after death. A dead man can do nothing and therefore can do neither anything moral, nor anything immoral. The person liberated after death is the self in its original state and the self is a non-doer and non-experiencer. In respect of post-mortem liberation morality can be only a means to attain it and a means to be used only before attaining it since the moment it is attained the attainer is dead, or, it is attained only when he is dead. This point is conceded by all the schools of Indian philosophy which admit the possibility of liberation only after death.

The bodily liberated individual does use morality as a means, in his pre-liberated state, to attain liberation. But he continues to live, after becoming liberated, in the same world in which he lived in his pre-liberated state. In this world living a moral life is necessary for an ordinary, unliberated, person, and so it was for the liberated-in-life in his pre-liberated state. Therefore, it becomes an important question to ask if the liberated-in-life, for short, the liberated person, also has to live a moral life, i.e. to keep doing all the moral things which an unliberated person ought to do, and which he himself was obligated to do in his pre-liberated state. One implication of treating morality as a means to attain *mokṣa* is that, after the attainment of *mokṣa,* its use becomes redundant. This implication seems to be drawn, as we have seen, in some versions of the morality-*mokṣa* relationship. But it can be drawn only by those thinkers who consider morality as a means externally related to the attainment of *mokṣa.* For them the liberated person is no more interested in leading a successful worldly life for which leading a moral life is necessary. And now, since he has attained *mokṣa,* he does not need it to attain it. Therefore, he can dispense with it. He may still lead a minimally moral life in order to physically survive in the world as long as he is alive. But this will not mean that morality has any great value for him. And, even that he would need to do only if he wants to physically survive.

On the other hand, for those who hold that morality is a means but an internally related one, and therefore a precondition, for attaining *mokṣa*, it becomes integrated into the liberated state (*muktāvasthā*). Obviously, then, morality, or, living a moral life, would not become redundant even after the attainment of liberation. For such thinkers, since morality gets integrated, or enters, into the state of *mokṣa*, it does not have only instrumental value but also some intrinsic value, or a dignity of its own. *Mokṣa* is an intrinsic value par excellence. Had morality no intrinsic value at all, it would not have been integrated into the state of *mokṣa* on its attainment. This version of the morality-*mokṣa* relationship is found in some accounts of the life-style of the liberated person given at some places in the *Gītā*, *Yogavāsiṣṭha* and Vidyāraṇya's *Jīvanmuktiviveka*.

In these accounts it is stated that the *jīvanmukta* naturally does what is morally right or commendable and abjures doing what is morally wrong or forbidden. The accounts differ only in their verbal presentation; contentually they are very similar to one another. For example, all of them, in substance, say that the *jīvanmukta*, whom the *Gītā* calls the *sthitaprajña* (a man of steady knowledge of the Self), has given up all of his desires, has no attachment for anything, is friendly with every being or thing, has conquered all of his feelings and passions, remains undisturbed when anything is taken away from him, never feels obligated, required, or necessitated, to do any duty since he spontaneously or naturally does what others feel obligated to do as their duties, does not feel to be an agent, an enjoyer, or a sufferer, etc., etc. The *Jīvanmuktiviveka* extensively quotes from the *Yogavāsīṣṭha*.[19]

The point which such accounts seem to make is that since an individual has to lead an impeceable moral life as a means to attain liberation, the kind of strict moral discipline he inculcates in this preparatory period makes morality, or living in a morally perfect manner, a constituent of his nature, or his second nature. Therefore, this natural propensity of his to do all that is morally upright continues to be a part of his nature even when he attains liberation. This is to say the same thing as I have been trying to bring out by saying that, according to this trend of thinking, morality enters, or gets integrated, into the state of liberation. But in none of such or other accounts is any criterion of moral rightness, obligation, etc., given.

In the *Gītā* and another work of Vidyāraṇya, *Pañcadaśī*, as we have already pointed out, there are statements which give the impression that, according to Indian ethical theory, the liberated person has no duties to fulfil, i.e. he has gone beyond the frontiers of ethics or of morality. This implies that morality has lost all its charms for him. It seems to me that Indian ethicists exhibit both trends of thinking, this one and the one stated above, because of a problem generated by the conceptual structure of their general theory of value, i.e. the theory of four types of *puruṣārthas*, which gives to *mokṣa* the status of the highest intrinsic value. In their zeal to highlight this status of *mokṣa* they tend towards the view that morality is only, what I have called, an external means to it and, therefore, loses all its importance for him who has attained it. This is natural to think because when the highest has been attained, everything which is lower than it is *superseded*, left behind, or transcended.

But they also seem to realize that any state of affairs, the attainment of which implies ignoring, undervaluing, or devaluing morality, would on that very account lose at least some of its shine. Then they try to rehabilitate morality by tending towards giving to it, more indirectly than directly, the distinctive status of, what I have called, an internally related means to the attainment of liberation. This character of it ensures its entry or integration into the state of liberation and thereby saves it from the risk of being ignored or devalued when liberation is attained.

The problem which Indian ethicists face naturally arises in any general theory of value which gives to anything, *contentually* different from morality, the status of the highest value. *Mokṣa* is *contentually* different from morality (or *dharma*) because of its being the ontological state of the return of the self to its original state along with being the cessation of the liberated person's liability to be reborn (i.e. of the self's being re-embodied).

Mokṣa would have become a completely non-moral, or amoral, value had it been claimed to be only such a state. And then it would have been extremely hard for its proponents to provide to a person a *moral reason*, or motivation, for attaining it. But it is also said to be a state of permanent and complete freedom from all kinds of suffering. It is this feature of it which seems to save it from becoming absolutely non-moral, or from its totally losing its affinity with a moral value. This is so because suffering is a moral evil and therefore freedom from it a moral good. But this conceptual gain the *mokṣa* theory does not fully utilize, or sometimes loses, because it greatly emphasizes, and generally too much, the ontological status of *mokṣa* and considers its being freedom from suffering a consequence of its being the ontological state it is said to be, more particularly, its being freedom from rebirth. Therefore, the mention of its moral character generally gets overshadowed by the excessive emphasis on its ontological character. Hence also the problem of ambiguity in tending to consider morality sometimes as an externally related means to *mokṣa* and thereby becoming dispensable after attaining it, and sometimes as an internally related means to *mokṣa* and therefore as a precondition and consequently getting integrated into the attained *mokṣa*-state. However, it is because of its being also claimed to be freedom from suffering that I have called *mokṣa* a moral value wherever I have done that. And, wherever I have said that it is not a moral value, I have done that keeping in mind the depiction of it primarily as an ontological state.

Of the two ways of looking at the relationship between morality and *mokṣa*, i.e. maintaining that the liberated has no duties, or, that he naturally does all the duties which the unliberated does with a feeling or awareness of being obligated, the latter does give more honour to morality than the former does. But both give the impression that there is a limited or fixed set of duties which an individual has to do, because only then can we say of anyone that he has done, or does, all his duties, or even that he has no duties. This goes against our normal understanding of duties, or of our moral life. As per this understanding, duties keep arising, even changing, and new ones come up, all through our life because of newer and newer demands of life and of our social relationships. Perhaps Indian ethicists have in their minds only the duties or obligations of different classes or castes of individuals set forth in the scheme of four-fold division of the society and of a man's life (*varṇāśrama-vyavasthā*) generally taken to have been listed in the various works called *Dharmasūtras*. Perhaps this is also the reason for not stating or discussing the criterion or criteria of moral rightness, duty, obligation, virtue, etc.

It is also surprising that, in spite of the fact that cessation of an individual's liability to be reborn is said to be the distinctive feature of his having been liberated, nowhere is any moral concept defined in terms of its being a means to the termination of this liability. Perhaps the Indian ethicists realize that it is not possible to empirically ascertain which action will contribute to it. They seem to remain satisfied with making the blanket assertion that a desireless action does that, without giving any argument in support of it. We shall not pursue this topic any further here because we shall take it up again in the next chapter. Desirelessness is thus given an honourable place in Indian ethics since all desires are said to cause bondage, the opposite of liberation. But an exception is made in the case of *mumukṣā*, the desire for *mokṣa*. What exactly it is and what its admission in ethical theory leads to, or may lead to, we shall discuss in the following section.

14.10 LIBERATION (*MOKṢA*) AND DESIRE FOR LIBERATION (*MUMUKṢĀ*)

Mokṣa is a *puruṣārtha*, or rather, the highest *puruṣārtha*. To be a *puruṣārtha* is to be an object of a human desire. Therefore, *mokṣa* must also be one. Indian ethical theory admits that it is, and calls the desire for it, as we have mentioned at the end of the last chapter, *mumukṣā*. The word *mumukṣa* (or its synonym *mokṣecchā*) means nothing but a desire of yearning for *mokṣa*.[20] Therefore, there is nothing very distinctive in giving to the desire for *mokṣa* the name *mumukṣā*. The grammatical rule of Sanskrit language, which has been used to form the word *mumukṣā* (*mua* + *san* + *a* + *tāp*) meaning the desire for *mokṣa*, has also been used to form *bubhukṣā* (*bhuj* + *san* + *a* + *tāp*), meaning the desire for eating, partaking, or enjoying, an object. And, the way the word *mokṣecchā* (*mokṣa* + *icchā*), a synonym of *mumukṣā*, has been formed is the same in which, for example, *arthecchā* (*artha* + *icchā*) can be formed to mean desire for *artha* (something material).

What is important to note is that when all desires are considered to be bondage-causing,[21] the desire for liberation is not, though conceptually this desire is as good a desire as any other. The conceptual structure of every desire involves three terms: (1) the desirer who is the individual, the subject, (2) the act or experience of desiring, the yearning, for having owning, acquiring, etc., something in the case of a positive desire, for short, a pro-desire, and that of not having, disowning, getting rid of, etc., something in the case of negative desire, for short, a con-desire, and (3) the object desired to be had or to be not had. As per Indian ethics even the desire to do something morally commendable, say, to help a hungry man by giving him food, or to recover one's rightful property grabbed by someone else, is not exempted from having a bondage-causing effect. Therefore, it is important to know why the desire for liberation is considered exempt from causing bondage. It is this feature of the desire for *mokṣa* on account of which Śankara calls a man who does not have it dull-headed and a destroyer of himself.[22]

This point does not seem to have been even noticed, let alone discussed, by classical Indian thinkers. Perhaps the reason for their not doing this is that their attention is primarily directed towards emphasizing the highest status of *mokṣa* among the *puruṣārthas* and therefore the importance of the desire to attain it. Their zeal for doing that is so great that it makes them indifferent to the importance of this purely conceptual, logical, issue generated by their theory that all desires (and therefore desire-motivated actions) cause bondage. If all desires, good and bad alike, cause bondage, there must be some reason for according this role to the desire for liberation and considering it an exception to this general accusation regarding all desires. However, keeping in mind the general temper of Indian ethical theory, the following explanation of making the exception may be reconstructed:

A desire prompts the desirer to do the action required to fulfil it. That action produces some result or results which its doer has to experience, i.e. to enjoy or suffer. To experience that portion of the results which he does not experience in his present life, he has to be reborn after his death in order to experience it in his next life. In this way the cycle of birth–death–rebirth goes on and on until the doer is freed from it, i.e. gets liberated. In the case of the desire for liberation, too, when the required things to get this desire fulfilled are done, the object of the desire, liberation, is attained. Since liberation is necessarily the cessation of the liberated person's liability to be reborn, along with some other things, the liberated person is not reborn after his death, no matter whether he is liberated while alive or after his death. The termination of this liability to be reborn ends the cycle of birth–death–rebirth which is bondage. Therefore, the desire for liberation, too, when fulfilled, has its result and this result is not bondage but the termination of bondage. To conclude, it can, thus, be said that the desire for liberation, unlike other desires, does not cause bondage because its very object is the end of bondage, i.e. liberation.

While discussing the nature of a *puruṣārtha* it has been pointed out that a *puruṣārtha* is, by definition, an object of a human desire. It has also been held that in its early career the theory of *puruṣārthas* admits of only three types of *puruṣārthas*, *artha*, *kāma*, and *dharma*, with the normative regulative principle that *artha* and *kāma* be pursued under the overall guidance of *dharma* (morality). At this stage of the theory the emphasis on the binding, or bondage-causing, nature of each and every desire either does not exist, or wherever it does, it is in an extremely weak, or not very noticeable, form. This is so in fitness with the logic of the concept of a *puruṣārtha*. Since every *puruṣārtha* is an object of a desire, to call all desires bondage-causing would be to call the pursuit of each and every *puruṣārtha* bondage-causing. This would amount to recommending, or, prescribing, that no *puruṣārtha*, not even *dharma*, be pursued or cultivated, and therefore to destroying the theory of *puruṣārthas* itself, or to making it self-destructive. Doing this would be equivalent to depriving the then social set-up of any regulatory framework for the preservation and promotion of coherence in it because the theory of *puruṣārthas* has been given for performing this very task, i.e. for keeping the then, or, any society, in proper order. How far it has, or has not, succeeded in performing this task is another matter.

The emphasis on the bondage-causing nature of all desires, thus, seems to have been emphasized in the later part of the career of the theory of *puruṣārthas* when *mokṣa*, as the fourth and highest *puruṣārtha*, is added to it. And then the great importance of the desire to attain liberation, along with the overall accusation that all desires are bondage-causing, to maintain its superiority to all of them, also gets emphasized or overemphasized.

Mokṣa-theorists seems to feel that to say that it is the desire to attain the highest value is all that is needed to prove that it is the most important desire. That may be the case but still it remains to be shown, on a conceptual level, why it too does not cause bondage and therefore is not required to be gotten rid of. What is true of *all* desires must be true of each and every desire. It has to be because it is a plain logical truth that what is true of all members of a class must be true of each and every member of it. If there is something which is not true of any putative member, then either that putative member is not a bona fide member of that class, or, if it is, then there must be some special feature of it which is not a feature of any other member, on account of which that thing is not true of it, though it is true of all other members of the class. In such a case, it also would have to be shown that in spite of its being different from all other members in this particular respect, it is similar to them in enough number of respects on account of which it is a member of the same class of which the others are. This kind of analysis is not available, to the best my knowledge, in any classical work to show that though *mumukṣā* is a desire, being a desire for attaining *mokṣa,* as is any other desire a desire for attaining something, it is different from all others in not being bondage-causing when all others are. The reconstructed explanation, or analysis, which I have given above, seems to me to do quite well the job of accounting for giving to *mumukṣā* or *mokṣecchā* the exceptional status of not being bondage-causing by the theory which considers all desires to be bondage-causing.

Some modern interpreters of Indian value-theory do maintain that *mumukṣā,* the desire for liberation, is *totally different* from all other desires and therefore there is no discrepancy in calling it not-bondage-causing while holding that all other desires are, and therefore in requiring it to be had while requiring that all other desires be abnegated. They do not realize that in holding this view two very important but obvious things are not recognized and therefore two very serious mistakes are committed by them, or if their interpretation is correct of the classical Indian position, then by the classical thinkers whom they themselves adoringly consider to be *ṛṣis* i.e. unerring seers of truth. The first one of the two is concerned with the logic of attributing a class-character to a thing. When any class-character is attributed to a set of things, then all of the things in the set must have something common; i.e. each and every one of them must have something in common with every other. If any putative thing is totally different from all other members of the set, then it is obviously not a member of that set, i.e. not a thing of the type that members of the set are. If the set is the set of all human desires, then it is not a member of that set, which means that it is not a human desire. *Mumukṣā* is *mokṣecchā,* as Sadānanda says, which means nothing but a desire for *mokṣa* (liberation). Therefore, for any interpreter to assert the *conjunction* that *mumukṣā* is a desire for liberation and that it is totally different from all other desires would be a serious logical mistake. To hold that the assertion of the above conjunction is the correct interpretation of the classical Indian concept of *mumukṣā* would then amount to attributing that mistake to the *ṛṣis* who explicate the concept of *mumukṣā* in this manner.

The other thing they ignore is a mixture of something substantive and something logical. The substantive thing is about the classical Indian conception of the role of a desire in causing bondage. According to it the mere fact that some propensity is a desire does not make it bondage-causing. Rather, what happens is that a desire prompts the desirer to do some action (or actions) to get the object he has to get in order to fulfil the desire. This action has some consequence (or consequences) which he has to bear. If any fraction of the consequence is not borne by him in the present life, then he has to be reborn after his death to bear it in the next life. It is this type of a desire which in this way causes rebirth which is the same thing as causing bondage. To put it in a shorter way, it is not a desire's merely being a desire but its leading to the production of some sort of consequences in fulfilling it which causes bondage. The interpreters who claim *mumukṣa* to be different from all other desires, on the other hand, think that merely considering it to be like any other desire would make it bondage-causing because they take the classical Indian position to hold that the very fact of its being a desire would entail that it is bondage-causing. They do not realize that it is logically possible that a desire may lead to only such consequences all of which are borne by the desirer, in his present life. In that case this desire itself would not be rebirth-causing and therefore bondage-causing. Moreover, if the object itself of the desire is *mokṣa,* as it is of *mumukṣā,* when the desire is fulfilled, it would lead to *mokṣa* and not to bondage. Therefore, calling *mumukṣa* a desire does not entail that it is bondage-causing because to be a desire is not equivalent to being bondage-causing.

Their logical mistake is that they fail to notice the similarity in the conceptual structure of all desire-statements, statements about someone's having a desire of any sort. Every desire-statement has some such form as 'A desires to have B (or to not have B)'. As it has been said earlier, two different desires can be distinguished only in terms of their different objects. Of the three factors in the conceptual structure of a desire, in the case of all desires, the desirer is the subject of the desire and the act of desiring is the experience of wanting or yearning to have the object desired. These two factors are common to all desires. Desires differ from one another, when they do, only when the objects desired in them are different. For example, the desire for wealth is different from that for liberation only because in the former desire the object desired is wealth and in the latter it is liberation. Secondly, if we rate the desire for wealth inferior in value to the desire for liberation, we do that because we rate wealth inferior in value to liberation. But it does not mean that the desire for liberation is not a desire, or is conceptually, in point of logic, different from all other desires. All this only shows that it is a desire conceptually like other desires, and is different from them, i.e. from all those whose object is something other than liberation, because its object is liberation. It means, therefore, that desires are graded to be lower or higher in terms of the grading of their objects. For example, desire for wealth would be graded lower than desire for knowledge if knowledge is graded higher than wealth. Indian ethical or value theory grades the desire for liberation to be the best, the most honourable, among all the desires simply because it rates liberation to be the highest among all the objects a human being can or should desire.

There seems to be also lurking another fear, a logical but a false one, in the minds of interpreters who call *mumukṣā* totally different from all (other) desires. This fear is that if they call it a desire, conceptually like other desires, they would not be able to attribute to it a feature which no other desire has, i.e. the feature of emancipating the desirer (*mumukṣu*) when he fulfils it. But this is a false logical fear. One member of a class may have a feature which no other member of that class has, while still remaining a member of that class because it has all or some of the other features which the other members have. All members of a class do not have to have the same, identical, kind of features, and it is possible that one member has a feature which no other member has. For example, only Bhīṣma of the Kuru family is said to have the unique freedom to die only when he intends to die (*icchā mṛtyu*). No other member has it. But still he is a member of the class of human beings who compose the Kuru family. To take another example, it is logically as well as empirically possible that a fabric manufacturing company makes only one *sārī* with a particular kind of border for the lady prime minister of its country. This feature of having a unique border would not make that *sārī* a non-*sārī*. Still that *sārī* would be a member of the class of *sārīs*, i.e. would conceptually be a *sārī* like any other *sārī*.

Giving to the desire for liberation the kind of importance it has been given, i.e. treating it as not bondage-causing but as emancipating or liberating, while calling even a morally commendable desire as rebirth-causing or bondage-causing, may give the impression that the *mokṣa* theory undervalues morality or living a moral life. An individual's getting liberated, i.e. achieving the termination of his liability to be reborn, is his personal achievement, a personal good, or value. It has nothing to do with anyone else's welfare, even with his liberation. On the other hand, his desire to feed a hungry man, a moral desire, as well as his fulfilling this desire by actually feeding him, is concerned with someone else's welfare. Therefore, the latter is a social, à moral, good, and not a personal one. But normally we consider a social, moral, good higher than a personal good. Therefore, the emphasis on the desire for liberation and *liberation* itself may be, as we have said even earlier, taken to imply underrating a moral value in comparison to a personal one which may even encourage someone to ignore morality.

Those who take the *mokṣa* theory as transcending morality may not mind this implication on the ground that liberation is higher than any moral value and, therefore, they may go on, there is nothing wrong in morality being ignored in the process of, or as a result of, attaining liberation. But nothing, we have seen, which ignores or devalues morality can keep its own value intact, and so would be the case with liberation and the desire for it. The above implication of *mokṣa*-theory, to repeat, can be taken care of, or made ineffectual, by pointing to, as has been done in this chapter, morality's being a precondition for fulfilling the desire for liberation. That is, by saying that since it is a precondition, morality gets into the life-style of the aspirant for liberation (*mumukṣu*) and, therefore, neither in attaining liberation nor after attaining it could he be negligent of anything morality requires, or considers desirable.

A desire is graded, we have seen, in accordance with the grading of its object. Therefore, when an object is considered to be one which everyone ought to desire to have, the desire for it also can, quiet legitimately, be said to be one which everyone ought to have, or acquire if he does not have it. This is why Indian upholders of the *mokṣa*-theory consider it obligatory for everyone to have the desire for liberation. This way of thinking is quite natural. We do consider it desirable to have some desires and undesirable to have some others, and many times we do follow in practice the principle underlying it; i.e. we learn to acquire some desires and to give up some others. Therefore one may say that there is nothing unusual in classical Indian thinkers' prescribing the acquisition of *mumukṣā* and in our agreeing to follow their prescription.

All this is plain logic if liberation is the highest *puruṣārtha*. But it is not as easy to have *mumukṣā* as it may seen to be on the face of it. *Mumukṣā* is an individual's desire for *mokṣa* which is to get terminated his liability to be reborn. Therefore, to have this desire the individual must believe in the theory of rebirth. Anyone's rebirth is caused, according to classical Indian philosophy, to put it cryptically, by those of his actions whose consequences he has not been able to bear in his present life, and is caused to enable him to bear them in the next life. All this is the case because of the way the law of *karma* operates in the world. Therefore, he has to believe in the theory of *karma*. That the law operates the way it does, and rebirth takes place for the reason it does, assumes that there is a self in every individual which is in itself disembodied but gets embodied and has different bodies in different births in the being of different individuals, and returns to its original nature when the individual gets liberated. The individual should, it is said, try to get liberated because only then can he be absolutely and eternally free from all possible kinds of suffering, since to live in the world is necessarily to have some kind of suffering or pain. We see, thus, that only he can be expected to have a desire for liberation who believes in the theories of rebirth, *karma*, disembodied self, life in the world being essentially painful at least to some extent, and in the fallouts of these theories. It is obvious that these theories constitute a worldview. It is also obvious that what has been said here is opaque and far from giving even a tolerable, or working, understanding of any one of the theories mentioned therein, or of the worldview they constitute. Therefore, they need to be explained in some detail. This we shall do in the next chapter, the last one of the book, and call it, for short, the *karmic* worldview. We shall see therein that it works as both the conceptual and substantive background of the classical Indian philosophy of morals.

NOTES AND REFERENCES

1. M. Hiriyanna, *Indian Conception of Values* (Kavyalaya Publishers, Mysore, 1975), p. 249.
2. Ibid., pp. 249–50.
3. Ibid., Chapter 13 for some more details.
4. *Sānkhyakārikā*, 1.1.
5. *Vedāntasāra*, VI.227.
6. For a slightly different and more critical account of the difficulty in instantiating the concept of *mokṣa* see my earlier work, *Varnadharma, Niskama Karma and Practical Morality: A Critical Essay on Applied Ethics* (D.K. Printworld, New Delhi, 1999), Chapter 3.
7. For a comprehensive but slightly different and more logical and critical analysis of the nature and philosophical utility of the concept of dreamless sleep, see Chapter 4 of my *Varnadharma, Niskama Karma and Practical Morality*, already referred to.
8. *Māndukya Upaniṣad* with Karika and the commentary of Śankarācārya, in *Eight Upanisads*, Vol. II, Chapter 1.5, translated by Swāmī Gambhīrānanda (Advaita Ashrama, Calcutta).
9. *Bṛhadāraṇyaka Upaniṣad* with the commentary of Śankarācārya, IV.III.21, translated by Swāmi Mādhavānanda (Advaita Ashrama, Calcutta).
10. Ibid., p. 461. Also see Ibid., IV.iii.19–20, pp. 455–59.
11. *Pancadaśī* (Sri Ramakrishna Math, Madras), XI.58–60.
12. S. Cromwell Crawford, *The Evaluation of Hindu Ethical Ideals* (Firma K.L. Mukhopadhyaya, Calcutta, 1974), p. XIV.
13. *Yogavāsīṣtha, nirvāṇa prakaraṇa, uttarārddha*, 102.6–12.
14. Ibid., 102.25.
15. The *Bṛhadārṇyaka Upaniṣad* with the commentary of Śankarācārya, trans. by Swāmī Mādhavānanda, (Advaita Ashrama, Calcutta), IV.III.22, pp. 462–63.
16. *Pañcadaśī*, VII. 253.
17. Ibid., XIV.17.
18. Swāmi Gambīrānanda (trans.), *Brahma-Sūtra-Bhāṣya* of Śrī Śankarācārya (Advaita Ashrama, Calcutta), p. 9. The same point has also been made in *Kathopaniṣad* 1.11.24.
19. See *Gītā*: 2.54–56, 5.19, 13.16, 15.10; *Yogavāsīṣṭha*: the later part of *Nirvāṇaprakaraṇa*; *Jīvanmukti-viveka*: *Jīvanmuktilakṣaṇa prakaraṇa*.
20. Sadānanda, *Vedāntasāra*, 1.25.
21. *Bṛhadāraṇyaka Upaniṣad*, Śankara's commentary on 1.iv.16; *Katha Upaniṣad*, IV.5; *Gītā* III.37.
22. *Vivekacūḍāmaṇi*: 4.

CHAPTER 15

The *Karmic* Worldview: The Theoretical Background of Classical Indian Ethics

15.1 THE WORLD AS AN ORDERLY WHOLE: THE CONCEPT OF *ṚTA*

Moral life is lived by a living individual in a social world. He has to live it because only then can he live as a viable, or even an acceptable, member of his society. That is why every society virtually becomes a moral community. It is in such a community, or such a world, that the individual pursues a set of values, performs a set of actions which may be right or wrong, fulfils certain obligations or duties, exhibits certain reactive attitudes which constitute his virtues, makes certain moral claims which constitute his genuine rights, etc. Morally upright behaviour is considered commendable and its opposite condemnable or undesirable. It is natural for an individual to wish for, or expect, some reward, appreciation, commendation, or at least a pat on his back, for his morally right behaviour and so it is for other members of his moral community. Vice versa is the case for morally bad behaviour. Though a moral wrongdoer may not wish to be punished in any way for his wrongdoing, he cannot deny that his punishment, if meted out to him, would be justified. In fact, that morality, as well as immorality, ought to pay, morality in a pleasing and immorality in a pinching way, for the individual who does it, is taken to be, in all cultures, an unquestionable, or a priori, ethical truth. It is this truth which is expressed in the common-sense saying that the moral man deserves to be rewarded, or at least admired, and the immoral punished, or at least condemned.

Classical Indian ethicists not only accept and emphasize the sanctity of the above ethical truth but go to the length of averring not only that it is not to be transgressed, but also that it can never be transgressed, that it is not only an obvious, but also a *necessary*, truth. This they do because they ethicize under the assumption of a worldview according to which the world is so constituted that every action done by an individual unfailingly has a consequence morally *commensurate* with it, i.e. pleasurable or painful, depending on the action's own merit or demerit, which its doer must enjoy or suffer. This consequence is in no way arbitrary or accidental because it is what the doer deserves to experience on account of having done the action. The world is of this nature because it is governed by the law of *karma*, or *karmic* law, which ensures that nobody absconds from experiencing any consequence of any of his actions. That is why we have called this view of the working of the world the *karmic* worldview. This worldview is at the back of the mind of every Indian ethicist, no matter whether he is a Hindu, a Jain, or a Buddhist thinker. It functions as the foundation, the general theoretical background, or the unquestioned premise, of the entire Indian ethicizing, both conceptual and practical.

The law of *karma* is said to be derived from the *Vedic* law of *ṛta*, or an application of it, in the realm of morals, or, in that of the socio-political-moral functioning of the human world. The word *ṛta* means order, regularity, or course, which enables it to denote a principle or law to the effect that there is complete order or orderliness, regularity, or uniformity in nature, which even gods are not allowed to disturb. Rather, they are said to be its guardians or protectors. In this sense it means a law of nature stating that things happen in the world in a uniform, and not in a haphazard, manner. A law of nature is a factual law stating how nature, in a certain area, or in all areas of it, in fact or actually functions. Considering this aspect of *ṛta*, it can be said that it is a fact-stating law about the entire cosmos and therefore may be called a cosmic law. But it is more than a merely fact-stating law because it is also said to be inviolable or unexceptionable, that is, a law which none can violate or break. And, it is further said that no one should try to violate it. The law is thus claimed to have a normative force, or normativity, which makes it a normative law as well. This means that there is some moral or axiological propriety in the way the law operates in, or governs, the world; that is, the way it regulates the functioning or working of the world is also the right or righteous way for the world to function.

To incorporate all these elements in the concept of *ṛta* is, howsoever greatly we may respect the classical thinkers for having formulated it in this manner, certainly to put into it contents of diverse types all of which are not compatible with each other. For example, a natural, fact-stating, law, simply because it is fact-stating, cannot be a necessary law for the reason that facts may change in future and therefore they may not behave at some later time the way they behave at an earlier time. Therefore, *ṛta* cannot be a law which is both natural and necessary. Secondly, if it is a necessary law, i.e. one which can never fail to hold good, then violating or breaking it is impossible. But then there is no point in requiring that none *should* violate it, since none *can* violate it because of its being a necessary law. It is pointless to prohibit anyone from doing something which he cannot do. The upshot of all this is that the same law cannot be a natural, a necessary, and a normative, law. A normative law, to the effect that one ought, or ought not, to do something implies that one can do it which implies that one may, or may not, do it. Such possibilities do not hold good of a necessary law and therefore a necessary law cannot be called a normative law. A natural law, which is not necessary, too, cannot be called normative. It may not hold good at some time but that would be because nature, the set of facts to which it applies, has changed and not because someone has gone against it while the zone of the facts it applies to have remained unchanged. But even if these sophisticated distinctions are not made or recognized by classical formulators of *ṛta*, we need not blame them. We can still appreciate their insight into the working of nature and formulating, in effect, what is called nowadays the law of uniformity of nature which is a principle basic to making any generalization about the world or about any sector of it.

Since the entire cosmos is orderly, the human world, which is a sector of it, must also be, and for the same reason. More specifically, the human world's orderliness is the result of its governance by the law of *karma*. This law is, as already said, an application of *ṛta* in the human world. It operates in the realm of human actions in such a comprehensive way that whatever a man is or has is determined by it. The result is that the world of man, to all intents and purposes, becomes a *karmic* world, i.e. a world shaped in accordance with the requirements of this law. To show how this world functions, or what kind of worldview this view of the world as the *karmic* world is, we have to explain the nature and the working of the law of *karma*. But before we do that it is necessary, as an ancillary to it, to state some of the ways in which classical thinkers classify human actions because the concepts of some of these actions would off and on figure in our characterization of the law.

15.2 CLASSIFICATION OF HUMAN ACTIONS

(1) In the context of the working of this law, and even otherwise, classical Indian ethical theorists first make a distinction between two kinds of actions, desireful (*sakāma*) and desireless (*niṣkāma*). A desireful action is one which is done with a desire to produce a result, i.e. to obtain an object, to get rid of an unwanted object already in possession, or to stop the possibility of being made to have an unwanted one. It is clear that, of the three cases, the desire in the first case is a positive one, and that in the other two cases a negative one. As I have done in the previous chapters and in some earlier works of mine, I shall continue to call a positive desire a pro-desire and negative one a con-desire. An action done with a *pro-desire*, or with a *con-desire*, would, therefore, be a desireful action. A desireless action, contrariwise, would be one in the doing of which no desire is involved. Sometimes, or by some scholars, it is said that by desireless action, which is contrasted with an action done with a desire as its motivating agent, the Indian ethicist does not mean an action in the doing of which no desire is involved, but that in the doing of which there is no desire to produce a particular result, or, no attachment for any result producible by it. But I shall show a little later that an action done with no desire to produce by it any result, or with no care or attachment for any result it may produce, turns out conceptually, or, on logical analysis, to be a desireless one. Therefore, even such actions are better called desireless actions. That is why I take classical thinkers to first broadly classify actions into desireful and desireless ones.

(2) Actions are also classified from the point of view of their effectuating potential, their effect-producing, or consequential, preparedness or readiness. The above classification in (1), into desireful and desireless ones, we have seen has been done from the point of view of the motivation, or motivating agency, of actions. From the point of view of effectuating, actions are first said to be of two broad types, (i) *prārabddha*, already-effectuating-actions and (ii) *anārabddha*, not-yet-effectuating-actions. The second is further divided into two types, (iia) *sancita*, already-done-but-not-yet-effectuating-actions and (iib) *sancīyamāna*, actions which are being done. Of these three types, the effects of (i), a major part of the tradition says, cannot be stopped by any means. Whatever an individual may do, howsoever enlightened he may be by attaining the knowledge of highest reality, or howsoever a rigorous moral life he may lead, he *cannot* avoid experiencing these effects or consequences. Moreover, since he *deserves* to experience them, it is also wrong for any power, if there be one, even to try to help him out because it would amount to trying to interfere with the moral governance of the world. Moreover, since no agency can succeed in doing that, the moral governance is ensured. The effects of both of (iia) and (iib) types of actions can be, according to the entire tradition, stopped or counteracted,

by an individual's attaining knowledge of reality and leading a good moral life if he wants to be freed from experiencing them.

The *Mundakopaniṣad* does say that 'when that Self, which is both the high and the low, is realized, the knot of the heart gets untied, all doubts become solved, and all one's actions become dissipated'.[1] These lines may give the impression that by attaining knowledge of the self, the highest reality, the knower not only gets enlightened and freed from all ignorance and doubts, but also nullifies the effectuating power of all of his actions, i.e. of all the three types of actions. But that is not the case according to most of the prominent classical philosophers. For example, Śankara, while commenting on those lines, says that as a result of an individual's attaining the knowledge of the self, the highest knowledge, is destroyed the effectuating power only of those actions which have been done and got accumulated, or are being done, but which have not yet ripened to be able to effectuate. Then he adds that 'but not so' (is the case with) 'the actions that produced the present life, since they have already begun to have their fruits' (i.e. have become *prārabddha*).[2]

The *Brahma-Sūtra* too confirms the same point and Śankara makes it more explicit in his commentary, on the concerned aphorisms of it.[3] 'After the acquisition of knowledge, those virtues and vices,' he says, 'that have not begun to yield their fruits and that were accumulated in earlier lives or even in this life before the dawn of knowledge are alone destroyed but not are those destroyed whose results have already been partially enjoyed and by which has begun this present life in which the knowledge of Brahman arises.' Śankara also refers to the *Cāndojña* VI.xiv.2 in support of this interpretation of his of the *Brahma-Sūtra's* IV.i.15.[4] A little later, while commenting on IV.i.19 of the text and referring again to the *Cāndojña*'s same statement, he straightforwardly asserts that 'the other virtues and vices that have already begun to fructify are exhausted through experiencing the results.'[5] That is, there is no way to get freed from experiencing the results of *prārabddha* actions, i.e. those which have begun to fructify. Only those of *anārabddha* actions, i.e. the actions called *sancita* and *sancīyamāna*, which have not yet begun to fructify, can be gotten rid of.

Even Rāmānuja, who very widely differs from Śankara on many issues and is said to be the founder, or one of the founders, of the devotional method of attaining liberation, does not hold a view different from the one stated above about the nullification of different kinds of actions. While commenting on IV.i.15 of the *Brahma-Sūtra*, he expressly says that 'only those previous deeds are destroyed, the effects of which have not yet begun to bear fruits'. Quoting the *Cāndojña*, VI.xiv.2, in the manner of Śankara, he too says that, as far as those actions which have begun to bear fruits are concerned, their effects have to be experienced and cannot be nullified before attaining liberation. About the unliberated, he quotes the *Cāndojña* saying, 'For him there is delay as long as he is not liberated from the body.' That is, as long as he is alive, he has to experience their consequences; only by experiencing them can he exhaust them. In his commentary on IV.i.19 he unequivocally says that 'the deeds which have begun to yield fruits have to be destroyed solely through experience'.[6]

The point which Śankara and Rāmānuja make, as stated above, represents the position generally accepted by classical Indian philosophers. It is also accepted to be such by modern writers on Indian philosophy and ethics, and is quite often said to be the position held by the Indian theory of action as far as an action's moral effects, or effects relevant to man's moral life, are concerned.

In fact, no classical Indian philosopher expressly says that any *prārabddha karma* can be made ineffectual, or that a doer of it can be freed from experiencing any consequence of it. Moreover, in general works at places some statements may be found to the effect that it can be stopped from effectuating. For example, the *Mahābhārata* says that 'even after committing a lot of sins if a man engages himself in doing benevolent (i.e. morally commendable) actions, then he is absolved of all of his sins in the manner in which the moon gets freed from the clouds which had covered him. Just as the rise of the sun destroys the pre-existing darkness, the desireless agent of morally good benevolent actions gets freed from all of his past sins.'[7] Some theistic, devotional, thinkers who believe in the unfailing instrumentality of their love for, or devotion to, god in liberating them, or in granting them divine company, feel that their god can do anything and therefore can wash them of their past sins, including their past sinful *prārabddha karma*'s and their effects, when their love for him is genuine. Such assertions have been generally made by poets who present them more out of an exuberance of their devotion to god (*bhakti*) than as a component of a theory of moral action or of moral desert. For example, a modern saint-poet Tukārāma, in a very telling couplet, addressed to god, asks him what good he (god) does to him (the devotee) if he (the devotee) gets his liberation only because of his own actions, i.e. not because of any favour or kindness of god.[8] But by and large, the Indian philosophical or ethical tradition, as shown earlier, maintains that the effects of a *prārabddha* action can by no means by antidoted, nullified or escaped from.

(3) From the same effectuating point of view, but taking into account the felicific and infelicific nature of their effects, actions are classified into four types. The earlier classification is also according to actions' effectuating potential but it is based on the temporal dimension of their actual effectuation. *Prārabddha* actions are those which have begun to effectuate, while *sancita* and *sancīyamāna* ones are those which are still waiting to ripen, i.e. which have not yet actually begun to produce their effects. And, we have seen, their effectuating power may be thwarted and then they would not produce any effect. The present classification does not take into account the temporal dimension but the moral quality of the actions and of their effects. From this point of view they are said to be of four kinds: white or morally right (*śukla*), black or morally wrong (*kṛṣṇa*), partly morally right and partly morally wrong (*śukla-kṛṣṇa*), and neither morally right nor morally wrong (*aśuklakṛṣṇa*).

Each one of these four types of actions produces its effects, as already said, only when it has ripened or matured. A morally right action produces for its doer pleasurable consequences. On the countrary, a morally wrong one produces painful consequences. One which is partly right and partly wrong, similarly, produces some pleasurable and some painful consequences. An action which is neither right nor wrong, as per ordinary usage, means one which is morally indifferent, i.e. which falls out of the purview of moral assessment, for example, the act of my choosing the pen I am using at the moment to write out this four-fold Indian classification of actions. There is a large number of such actions which we almost every day do. They are, thus, morally indifferent because the question of calling them morally right or wrong does not arise. But classical Indian ethical theory does not mean this sort of morally indifferent actions by their fourth class, i.e.

aśuklakṛṣṇa actions. Rather, it ignores them, though they constitute a major bulk of the stock of human actions and for a general theory of the concept of action they are, as actions, no less important than my other type of actions which are morally relevant or assessable. As per Indian ethical theory an *aśuklakṛṣṇa* action is that which produces for its doer no (moral) consequence at all, i.e. one which its doer deserves and is bound to experience. Under this category, according to it, comes only that sort of an action which is done with no desire for fulfilling any objective, or with no attachment for the *natural* result, whatever that may be, which it is expected or assumed to produce, or actually produces. Being an action, a thing of the natural world, it may produce some result but that has no binding or obligation-generating effect on the doer. This notion of a desireless action is fraught with some quite tricky problems for Indian ethical theory and the theory's very conception of a human action. Therefore, we shall discuss it a little later in some detail.

(4) There is a fourth kind of classification of actions which basically is a classification of actions considered doable by the scriptures and held to possess differing degrees of stringency. This is a four-fold classification into *nitya, naimittika, kāmya* and *pratisiddha.* Under the *nitya* category are put those actions which are to be done simply because a scripture requires that they be done and no reason be asked to justify why they should be done. By doing such an action an individual does not earn any reward or moral merit but by not doing it he does incur some demerit. For example, taking a daily bath and some special kind of bath on certain special occasions are said to be *nitya* actions for a student. *Naimittika* actions are those which are to be performed when some special things happen, like the birth of child, or the death of someone, in the doer's family. Generally, these actions are ritualistic. The third kind of actions are called *kāmya.* They are to be performed when an individual wants to achieve some objective, for example, to have a son, to defeat an enemy, etc. Under the fourth, the *pratisiddha,* class we have actions the doing of which is disallowed or prohibited by a scripture, like a *brāhmaṇa*'s associating himself with a *śūdra.*

This classification derives its sanctity from its scriptural rooting and therefore would have none for him who does not accept the authority of any scripture in moral decision-making. But we can divest the concepts of these four types of actions of their scriptural moorings and can make them profitably usable in our ordinary moral discourse. For example, what is called a *nitya* action can be taken to denote the normal duty of an individual which he himself acknowledges to be his normal, usual, duty, for example, the duty of a teacher to teach the subject assigned to him with his consent and for doing which he is paid his salary. A *naimittika* action may be taken to denote a seasonal, circumstantial, one, for example, the duty of a teacher to do invigilation work in an examination hall in which his students are taking their annual examination. A *kāmya* action may, similarly, be taken to denote any action, which is not immoral, that he needs to do to fulfil a desire of his, for example, his taking lessons in vocal music to develop his musical talent. A *pratisiddha* action, obviously, would then be any action which he ought not to do because it is contrary to, or obstructive, of, any action belonging to any of the above three types and therefore can be called a prohibited one. In fact, for actions of the first three types we do use in our common moral terms, life's regular duties, occasional duties, prudential duties, etc. Those which belong to the fourth types we simply call wrong or forbidden.

15.3 THE LAW OF *KARMA*: STATEMENT OF AUTONOMY

Though the law of *karma* is one of the basic laws or principles arching over the entire classical Indian ethical, or axiological, thought, like some other such principles, it has not been discursively stated and explained, and its various implications drawn, in any classical work. This point has been acknowledged by several knowledgeable modern scholars of Indian philosophy who have talked about it in one context or another. This has been done even by those of them who consider it a matter of great insight on the part of classical Indian thinkers to have offered it as a basic principle of both ethical theory and practice. For example, G.R. Malkani admits that it 'is rarely discussed in Hindu or allied circles. Hinduism, Jainism, Buddhism, etc., all take for granted the truth of the law—so you sow, so shall you reap.'[9] But even modern scholars have not philosophically discussed or examined its role, whether or not it has the conceptual capabilities needed to let it perform the role it is said to perform in ethical theory or practice.

It is true that in classical works only some statements or remarks testifying its importance and overall authority in shaping man's worldly, i.e. ethical, as well as his post-mortem, i.e. theological or spiritual, destiny are available here and there. The clearest statement of it is found in the *Bṛhadāraṇyaka* which says that 'what it (the individual) desires, it resolves; what it resolves, it works out; and what it works out, it attains'. It goes on in the next set of lines to assert further that 'exhausting the results of whatever work he did' (in the previous life), 'in this life he returns from that world to this for (fresh) work. Thus does the man who desires (transmigrate). But the man who does not desire (never transmigrates). Of him who is without desires, who is free from desires, the objects of whose desire have been attained, and to whom all objects of desire are but the Self, the organs do not depart. Being but Brahman, he is merged into Brahman.'[10]

When elaborated, the above lines mean to assert that of any motivated action, i.e. of one which is done in order to attain an object, desire is its root cause. When a man desires to attain an object, he wills, or has the determination to do it, and then he does it. When he does it, he gets what the action results in or leads to. This is to say that every desireful action produces a result, an effect, i.e. it effectuates. The results of (at least some of) the actions done in his previous life he bears in his present life and (at least some of) those done in this life in the next life. This means that he had a life previous to the present one and would have a next life after the expiry of his present one and all this happens because of his *desireful actions.* To say this really amounts to saying that desire plays the main role in the drama of man's destiny and transmigration. Therefore, he who in a life does not have desires, all of whose actions, if any, are desireless, does not have another life, i.e. a rebirth, because there is nothing for him to bear or experience for which he needs another life or transmigration. His liability to be reborn is thus terminated, which means that he becomes liberated.

The analysis and evaluation of the law is bound to be protracted and deserves to be given in some detail. Therefore, I shall first take up the issue of its autonomy since that will be a short one. After that I shall come back to its analysis and evaluation.

As per the general temper of Indian ethics, the *karmic* law is usually considered to be autonomous in the sense that it operates on its own without there being any ordainer or formulator of it, i.e. without there being a law-giver who has ordained it or who administers it. There are some philosophers who hold that God plays some role in its administration. But that role does not affect its autonomous character because neither does it make the law dependent on God's will for its existence, nor does if allow him any freedom to operate it as he pleases to do.

The Jain, Buddhist, *Sānkhya,* and *Mīmāmsa* philosophers straightforwardly call it an autonomous law, taking its own course in deciding the life-style and fortunes of individuals. The theistic *Nyāya, Advaita Vedānta, Viśiṣṭādvaita,* and *Dvaita* philosophers do hold that God plays some role in its administration. But this role only helps and does not hinder the law in its functioning. Rather, it may even be taken as limiting not the autonomy of the law but that of God itself. For example, Śankara, in his commentary on the *Brahma-Sūtra,* says that individuals in the world differ in their experiences of pleasure and pain because God has created them in this manner. But he has not done that arbitrarily or indiscriminately; rather, he has done it because of their virtues and vices, merits and demerits, which have accrued to them on account of the actions they did in their previous life, i.e. in accordance with what they deserve as ordained by the law of *karma.* This is only to confirm that God too follows the law of *karma.* He only facilitates the working of the law. Śankara compares this process of God's making individuals have different kinds of experiences or fortunes with what rainfall does to different kinds of plants like paddy, barley, etc. The rainfall is the same which showers on all plants but plants get diversified into different kinds because of the different kinds of their seeds.[11] Exactly the same thing on this point is said by Rāmānuja in his commentary on the same item, i.e. the same *sūtra* of the book, using the same analogy of what rains do to different plants because of their having different kinds of seeds. In fact he forthrightly says that there being in the world individuals leading different styles of life, 'The Lord is only the operative cause in the creation of beings; the main cause is the past karma of the beings'.[12] The *Nyāya* position in this regard is also similar to that of Śankara and Rāmānuja and so is the case with the *Dvaita* thinkers, though all of them differ in their metaphysical views in more than one respect.

15.4 THE LAW OF *KARMA*: ELABORATION AND EVALUATION

Keeping in mind the various ways in which actions have been classified in the Indian ethical tradition, the *Bṛhadāraṇyaka* account of the law of *karma* needs to be stated in a neat, propositional, form in order to make clearly visible its conceptual structure. We have to do it in order to assess whether or not all constituents of it are fully concordant with one another and non-discrepant with its status as a moral law. We can then very smoothly draw out its implications and properly ascertain whether or not, so stated, it can perform the role or roles in ethical theory and practice which it is generally assumed, or claimed in classical thinking, or in its modern, received, interpretation, to play.

We did give a summary elaboration of the *Bṛhadāraṇyaka* account after stating it. But that was done only to show its general character, freed from classical Indian metaphysical frills. Therefore, it is not adequate for enabling us to do what we want to do, as suggested above, in the present section. Consequently, we shall present a more analytical characterization of the law, or the worldview it represents in an almost embryonic form, as holding that (a) every desireful action has a set of effects or consequences; (b) the set is *necessarily* produced by it in the sense that it is not possible to do it without having the set; (c) this set, in its turn, depending on its own moral quality, requires the doer to experience some pleasure or pain in his lifetime, or in his next birth; (d) his experiencing this consequential pleasure or pain is morally justified because he deserves it; and (e) in the case of a *prārabddha* action there is no means at all for the doer to use in order to avoid experiencing the consequences it has already begun yielding to him.

In the above characterization we have left out what the law considers to be the role of desireless actions because, as already said, this aspect of it will be treated separately.

The above propositional characterization consisting of the five components, (a) to (e), is in no way novel or bizarre. Rather, almost all modern historians of, or writers on, Indian philosophy have described the working of the law in an exactly similar manner, though they have not drawn out, or cared to draw out, the logical implications of any one of (a) to (e).

What is asserted in (a), by calling every desireful action a cause of some consequences, makes the law of *karma* a causal law, or an instantiation of the general law of causation. The (b) component makes it a necessary causal law, the (c) component assigns to every such action the power to produce some pleasure or pain for the doer which is claimed by (d) to be morally justified. Thus it turns out to be an amalgam of a law which is causal, necessary, and moral, all mixed into every operation of it. This character of it is affirmed by Malkani when he calls it 'the law of causality in the moral sphere' whose 'scope extends beyond our present life', i.e. covers even our past and next life, what we were, are, and will be when reborn.[13] Hiriyanna dittoes Malkani and adds that it operates in such a way that 'as every event in the physical world is determined by its antecedents, so everything that happens in the moral realm is preordained.'[14] By assigning to it the role of preordaining everything in the moral realm, which means nothing but man's moral life, he puts the emphasis on its *necessitarian* character. This is to aver that whatever happens in man's moral life, the accrual of his moral merits and demerits, his moral deserts, i.e. rewards and punishments, in short, his moral destiny, is preordained, or necessarily determined, by the law of *karma*. That is, the law disallows the possibility of any diversion, of anything which has happened to have happened in a way different from the way it has actually happened, or of anything ever happening in future in a way different from the way required by the law. The law must have a moral character in order that it may be called an extension of the law of causation in moral life. This point is clarified by Dasgupta when he says that every 'action done by an individual leaves behind it some sort of potency which has the power to ordain for him joy or sorrow in the future according as it is good or bad'.[15] This is what we have stated in the (d) and (e) components of our propositional characterization, which assert that a morally good action yields to its doer some joy and a morally bad one some sorrow. The joy and the sorrow are thus what he *deserves* because the former is the result of a morally good, and the latter of a morally bad, action of his own. He has a right to have them and this right can never be infringed by anyone, i.e. he cannot fail to have the joy or sorrow because the law is inviolable. All these elements are very neatly and pointedly stated by D.M. Datta when he says that it is this law the operation of which equips the individual with the body and the environment which his past career' (i.e. his past actions) 'entitles him to'. The natural surroundings, and everything good or bad in their world 'which form the common background of the people of an age or a country are just what are deserved by all of them according to their common moral worth'[16] i.e. which they have earned as a result of their past actions and of nothing else.

The upshot of all this is that whatever an individual has, his physical and mental equipment, his capabilities, his goals and aspirations, his virtues and vices, his suffering and happiness, his family, society, environment, i.e. in brief his world, is due to his past actions as their effects. His existence, as per the Indian tradition, is beginningless, his present life is the successor of his previous one, and the previous one that of the one which preceded it, and so on ad infinitum backwards. Therefore, there never was a time when anything which he had was not the result of some action done by him in his past life. This means that it is impossible to locate, in the case of any individual, a life of his which he lived for the first time, without having had a previous one, and therefore one in which he conducted his life freely in a manner guided only by his own plans and projections, with no determination or control exerted on it by any action done by him in a previous life since he had no previous life until then.

In its operation the *karmic* law is, thus, primarily a causal, fact-stating, or naturalistic, law, of course, subject to the condition that there is such a law which actually governs the working of the world in the alleged manner. It is important to note here that the major part of its characterization does not make it a moral law, or a law with some moral relevance. But, as we have seen, the way the law is said to govern the world is also said to be the morally right way in the sense that it ensures that whatever a man gets as a result of his actions he *deserves*, or has a moral right, to get. In fact, he gets, it is claimed, only that which he deserves, *all that* he deserves, and never gets anything which he does not deserve. Since the law permits no digression, failure, or excess, in the dispensation of his deserts, it works in a completely necessitarian fashion. Nothing deserved by a man is denied to him, nor is anything undeserved by him given to him, no matter whether the deserved thing is pleasurable or painful, of the nature of a reward or a punishment. There is thus no loss of moral value in the world governed by the law of *karma*, i.e. the *karmic* world, or, the world. That is why, following Radhakrishnan, Chatterjee and Datta call the law of *karma* a law of conservation of moral values.[17] Hiriyanna avers the same thing in a slightly different manner by saying that there is complete justice in the world because the law of *karma* governs it in such a way that everyone gets the reward or punishment he deserves because of his actions.[18]

15.5 LOGICAL CONSEQUENCE OF MERGING WHAT OUGHT TO BE WITH WHAT IS IN AN EFFORT TO IMPROVE WHAT IS

The *karmic* world is thus a world in which an individual necessarily gets what he ought to get. This is so because the law of *karma* governs it in such a manner that his life in it is totally the *result* of his actions, that it is *necessary* that it is what it in fact is, and that what it in fact is, is also what it ought to be. The law, therefore, has all of the three features of being a causal law, a necessitarian law, and a normative law. Writers on Indian ethics generally consider the ascription of these features to it as highlighting its grandeur and majesty. But when looked into very closely they turn out to be not completely cohesive with each other. For example, a causal law, as understood today, is a *factual* law in the sense that if an event is generally, in fact, followed by another and wherever it is absent, the latter too is also absent, the preceding event is called the cause of the succeeding one. There is no implication here that the succeeding event must, or necessarily, follow the preceeding one. But the *karmic* law is said to be a causal, as well as a necessary, unbreakable law.

Secondly, a causal or factual law states what actually happens and not what ought to happen. But the *karmic* law is said to ordain both what actually-necessarily happens and what ought to happen by further ordaining that what actually-necessarily happens is also what ought to happen. It is a built-in, conceptual, feature of a factual law that it may not always hold good and still remain unfalsified, and of a necessitarian law that it can never be broken without being thereby falsified. That is why to call the *karmic* law both causal, i.e. factual, and necessary is not completely congruous. But one may say that, according to the classical Indian conception, a causal law may also be a necessary law. One would then need to be reminded that the attribute of being necessitarian can belong, strictly speaking, only to a conceptual, or logical, law, and not to a factual law which a causal law is. Classical Indian scientists were fully aware of this fact and that is why they did not consider a causal law to be a necessary one, or causation to be the same as necessitation. For example, Āyurvedic, medical, scientists did not say that what they held to be the cause of a certain disease necessitated the occurrence of the disease but only that it generally led to it.

Thirdly, a normative law is conceptually not a factual law because even if an action is not in fact done it may be said to be one which ought to be done. Even if people more often tell a lie than a truth, it can be said that truth ought to be told and no lie ought to be. Classical Indian philosophers did know that most men had several passions, feelings, temptations, etc. to which they generally succumbed; still, they adumbrated the normative law that passions, feelings, etc. ought to be controlled. Rather, when things which ought to be done are generally not done, or people do not generally get what they ought to get, moralists emphasize it more that such and such things ought to be done or that such and such people ought to get such and such things. The conceptual truth which this feature of a normative law highlights is that the non-observance of it does not invalidate it whereas there cannot be a non-observance of, or an exception to, a necessary law. This can be said in another way as well by saying that a normative law can be violated without being disproven, whereas a necessary law cannot be, and if it is violated, or falsified, even in a single instance, it would be thereby proven that it is not a necessary law. Therefore, to characterize the law of *karma* as factual-clausal, necessary and normative is not to do an honour to it or to its propounders.

Further, characterizing it in this way not only makes it imbued with incoherent features, as shown above, but also loaded with some implications, to be shown soon, on account of which a belief in it would create some serious normative problems, i.e. problems for moral living. In all likelihood, classical thinkers did not realize that it would then meet this fate. Rather, it seems that they expected it to become then more effective in persuading or motivating the believer in it to lead a good moral life.

To see how it fails to fulfil their exceptation, let us analyse its working as a law, assumed for the sake of argument, or for this analysis, to actually possess the above three features. According to it, then, everyone's present living, or life's condition is the effect of his actions which have begun yielding their effects (i.e., of his *prārabddha* actions). It is a necessary effect of theirs because no effect of a *prārabddha* action can be nullified or modified. There is no question of any *sancita,* or *sancīyamāna* action's having played any role in its being what it is because the action has not yet started producing any effect. The effectuating power of only these two kinds of actions can be nullified or modified. Everyone's present living condition is also what it ought to be because it is what he deserves it to be. Therefore, the condition in which anyone lives is morally the best possible condition for him to live in. Since it is necessarily what it is and morally the best condition, it cannot be changed and therefore cannot be ameliorated even if it is miserable. Secondly, it does not need to be improved because it is the morally the best, or what it ought to be. Therefore, even trying to improve it would be morally wrong because it would amount to trying to alter the character of what is the morally best for the man to have, and thus to interfere with the moral course of the world-process. Moreover, since it cannot be altered, and therefore cannot be bettered, any effort to better it is bound to be dysfunctional.

The lesson the above account yields is that a believer in the *karmic* worldview ought not to do and cannot do anything to better the condition of a sufferer. If it were somehow made possible for him to perform the miracle of making his condition better, it would amount to snatching away from the sufferer the chance of his having what he deserves to have because of his *prārabddha* actions. He deserves to live in a miserable condition but now is made to live in a comfortable one. But this is not possible, the believer would say, because no effect of a *prārabddha* action can be nullified. Therefore, he would go on to add, there is no danger to the dignity of the law of *karma* and to the world it governs.

There is another fallout of this view which also needs to be taken note of. In conformity with his belief in the *karmic* theory, if the believer does not try to improve the condition of the sufferer, that would obviously be antithetical to the practice of the moral virtues of benevolence and compassion. Both of these virtues are highly prized in Indian ethics. It would also be contrary to the moral principle that we ought to try, to the best of our abilities, to ameliorate a deplorable human condition. This is, according to Indian ethics, a laudable moral objective for us to pursue and so it is according to our present-day moral common-sense. But our belief in the *karmic* view would not allow us to do that.

If the sufferer himself believes in the law of *karma* he may remain satisfied with his lot and not feel restless or resentful. But he may then not also feel motivated to do anything to improve it. And, another person, even a moralist, who believes in the law, too, may not feel disturbed to see him suffer because he would consider it justified, or deserved by him, by attributing it to his past actions of the *prārabddha* variety.

For example, M.K. Gandhi, a moralist greater than whom it is difficult to locate in the modern world, reacted in some such manner when a large number of people in Bihar suffered a lot due to the devastating earthquake that occurred in 1934. On March 25, 1934, in a meeting at Motihari he said that 'the earthquake being God-sent should be welcomed and that people should regard it as a punishment for observing untouchability.' The same remarks he repeated at Muzaffarpur. In a meeting at Mangles Tank, Patna city, also he reiterated his opinion that the earthquake was a 'punishment for the sin of untouchability'.[19] Gandhi's remarks characterize a natural calamity which an earthquake really is, as a punishment inflicted on the sufferers on account of their having practised the sin of untouchability and therefore as one that they deserved. This view of his springs obviously from his belief in the law of *karma* and in the *karmic* worldview. They were very strongly criticized by Rabindranath Tagore, a great admirer of Gandhi. He felt pained and surprised at his having attributed the earthquake and the miseries it caused to people to the working of the law of *karma* when they were really caused by certain physical factors. This is very clear from Tagore's saying that:

'It is all the more unfortunate because this kind of view of things' (i.e. the view Gandhi's remarks express) 'is too readily accepted by a large section of our countrymen. I keenly feel the indignity of it when I am compelled to utter a truism in asserting that physical catastrophes' (like this earthquake) 'have their inevitable and exclusive origin in certain combination of physical facts. Unless we believe in the inexorableness of the universal law' (i.e. the law of *karma*) 'in the working of which God Himself never interferes, we find it impossible to justify His ways on occasions like the one which has surely stricken us in an overwhelming manner and scale.'[20]

If Gandhi is right in his view, then the natural conclusion from it is that no relief should have been provided to the sufferers because they deserved the miseries caused by the earthquake. But this was not done by the workers engaged in relief work under the overall direction of Rajendra Prasad and the result was morally commendable. They would have been *logically* right had they stopped relief work if Gandhi was right, but any morally sensitive person would say that they would have then been *morally* wrong. It is true that Gandhi's intention was not to get the relief work stopped, nor to exploit people's belief in the *karmic* view to let them suffer without a murmur and not to complain if no relief was supplied to them. His intention was to arouse in them the feeling that treating anyone as an untouchable was morally wrong. But his reason or ground for doing that was, as Tagore says, *factually* wrong. It was also *morally* wrong because explaining a suffering as a retributive punishment caused by the *karmic* governance of the world, which is unverifiable and the suffering is actually due to something else, in the present case due to some physical causes, can very easily be used by people in power to exploit credulous, poor, sufferers' belief in the *karmic* view in order to absolve themselves from performing their moral duty to reduce their suffering. That this happened in classical, and even in modern India before its independence, in letting the extremely poor people, particularly those who were in the *varṇa*-system called *śūdra,* live a miserable life.

Moreover, working on the assumption that the world, or our social order, functions as the *karmic* view of it claims, is not always practisable because it is not possible, in a large number of cases, to know which suffering (or happiness) is due to which action of the suffering (or the happy) individual. And, it is definitely not when it is attributed to some action done by the sufferer in his previous birth or births, or by his forefathers. In Gandhi's case, he definitely means by the sin of untouchability committed by the sufferers, not sins committed by them immediately preceding the occurrence of the earthquake but for long, in this life or their past life, or by their ancestors. But if he were questioned on what ground he believed that it was due to their *sin of untouchability and not to any other sin,* or to any other kind of action, or actions, of theirs, or of their forefathers, he could not have answered. He could not have, because nobody could have answered, nor can anybody answer a question of this type even today simply because it is impossible to do that.

This situation, in which any evil, or suffering, can be justified, and therefore making an effort to get rid of it, or to alleviate the resultant condition, becomes infractious as well as unjustified, is due to the karmic view's merging 'ought' with 'is' and considering the 'is' as inevitable, i.e. due to considering the functioning of the law of *karma* as unexceptionable, or as Tagore puts it, inexorable. This is clear from the fact that, according to the *karmic* view, a desireful action done by an individual necessarily produces a result which he must experience and ought to experience because he deserves to. That is, what he in fact experiences is also something he *must* experience and he ought to experience. Therefore, the victims of the calamity, which the earthquake was, should, according to Gandhi who believed in the *karmic* view, have welcomed their miseries caused by the calamity because they were given thereby an opportunity to have what they ought to have had.

That this is a logical consequence of the *karmic* theory is undeniable if we take seriously into account the unnullifiable or unalterable character it ascribes to the effects of *prārabddha* actions. And, when it is so taken, it may quite justifiably be taken as a *reductio ad absurdum* argument against the *karmic* theory, as has been shown above in Gandhi's justifying the miseries of the victims. It is a *reductio* because a moral theory, which the *karmic* theory is, or the worldview which it generates, that justifies such moral evils like the miseries of the earthquake victims, cannot be called a valid moral theory, or a valid moral worldview. These miseries our untutored moral intuitions consider paradigmatic examples of moral evils. Any moral theory which justifies them, or their kind, cannot, therefore, be called a valid, or viable, moral theory.

It is the role assigned by the karmic theory to *prārabddha* actions which is largely responsible for the theory's having an implication yielding such unpalatable results for it. This role, therefore, needs to be given a little more detailed treatment. This task will be taken up in the next section.

15.6 *PRĀRABDDHA*, FREEDOM OF WILL AND STATUS OF HUMAN INITIATIVE

Some writers on Indian ethics make the claim that the implication drawn and discussed in the previous section, namely, that the *karmic* worldview makes an individual's effort to improve his, or anyone else's, existing condition dysfunctional, is not really yielded by the *karmic* theory. Their contention is that though a man's present is determined by his *prārabddha* actions, his future can be made better. It can be said to be in his own hands and also that someone else as well can help him in doing that, for example, by giving him right moral instruction, by being benevolent, or, compassionate, to him, etc. Let us restrict our discussion to the status of the individual's, i.e. the agent's, own initiative and see whether or not this claim is in keeping with the role of the *karmic* law as conceived in the Indian tradition. This discussion can also, with some adjustment, be used by the reader to decide whether or not another person can help him to have a better future in the *karmic* world.

An individual may, as the claim goes, be presently, or in his present life, in an abominable condition, but by doing morally right actions and acquiring right knowledge, he can get rid of it and make the later part of his present life, or his future, i.e. the next, life (after death) better. The claimant forgets that, according to the *karmic* theory, the *entire course* of his present life is determined by his *prārabddha* actions done by him in his previous life or lives and on their effects he has no control. Since they do that, he cannot do in his present life anything which they do not allow him to do. If they dispose him to do ameliorative actions he would *automatically* or necessarily do them, and not otherwise. It is not that he can choose to do something irrespective of what his *prārabddha* actions dispose him to do. Were it the case that he can freely do certain things and therefore can do things in order to better his future, it would mean that his *prārabddha* determines only some aspects or spheres of his life and leaves some others to be freely determined by him in a manner he chooses to. But it is not possible to know or decide which aspects of his life are *prārabddha*-determined and which others are not. That is, we cannot say what is the zone or range of the effects of *prārabddha* and what is the free zone in which the individual can act as he wills. For example, we cannot say which suffering of his is the effect of his *prārabddha* and therefore a suffering he ought not to try to get rid of, and which suffering is non-*prārabddha*-determined and therefore within his powers to be gotten rid of. The Indian ethical tradition says nothing about the zone of the effects of the *prārabddha* in a man's life because it does not exclude anything in it from his *prārabddha*'s control.

The fact of the matter is that according to the *karmic* theory every action originally, when it is *sancīyamāna* (being done) or *sancita* (already done and accumulated along with others of its kind), is *anārabddha*, or non-effectuating. When its potentiality to effectuate is not nipped in the bud by the agent's good moral work and knowledge, and it becomes ripe to produce its effects, it becomes a *prārabddha* action with indestructible power of effectuation. But no method is given, nor any can be given, by any classical Indian thinker, to let anyone know which particular *anārabddha* action of an agent is going to be, or has become, a *prārabddha* action. Nor has any method been given, or can any method be given, to help anyone know which particular *prārabddha* action exercises, or does not exercise, if the *prārabddha* does not determine everything in a man's life, control over which side of his life. For an agent to act freely is to act without being determined by his *prārabddha*. But since we have no means to know that any action of his is not *prārabddha*-determined, even if it is a free action, we cannot say that it is not *prārabddha*-determined and therefore that it is free. We cannot go by the agent's personal feeling that he has acted freely because he may feel that way even if he is not free. Therefore, an upholder of the view that the *prārabddha* determines all behaviour of the agent can very well say that this action too is *prārabddha*-determined.

Moreover, the tradition does not say much about the constituents of the *prārabddha* and does not even raise issues like the ones mentioned above. To all intents and purposes, it seems to hold that it determines everything in our life. Therefore it does not need to demarcate the zone of the effects of *prārabddha* in our life, i.e. the zone it determines from the zone it does not, implying thereby that our present life in its entirety is determined by it. This understanding or interpretation of it is confirmed by all the modern historians of Indian philosophy, as we have referred to earlier. It can thus be said that, according to the *karmic* worldview, whatever a man is, has, or can have, or can intend, or try to have or do, is determined by his *prārabddha*. The obvious logical consequence of it then is that in the *karmic* world man has no *freedom* at all to do anything he chooses to do.

Kalidas Bhattacharyya is candid enough, among modern scholars, to admit the denial of human freedom in the *karmic* theory of the world. He unhesitatingly avers that 'In a sense, in traditional Indian philosophy there is, of course, no room for "freedom of will": every detail of man's life, including even the activities (that lead willy-nilly to some enjoyment or suffering) is determined'.[21] He does seem to think of it as a deficiency in Indian philosophizing. But he tries to justify it on the ground of his belief that even in Western philosophy there are thinkers who deny freedom of will. This is more like a solace than like a justification. It very much resembles a man's considering a leak in the roof his own bedroom not worth bothering about because of his belief that the roof of his neighbour's bedroom also has a similar leak. Still, it is creditable for Bhattacharyya to have acknowledged this truth about classical Indian philosophy which is, according to him too, a logical fallout of its *karmic* worldview.

The denial of freedom of will by the *karmic* theory is not admitted, or is slurred over, by those who do not clearly see the implication, drawn here, of the overall governance of the world by the *karmic* law. They do not realize that when the present of a man is fully determined by his *prārabddha*, his present disposition to better his future would also be so determined. Consequently, then, his future cannot be said to be fully in his hands to be shaped in a form he wants it to be. But classical thinkers are well aware of this implication. It is their realization of it which prompts them to hold that an individual can get liberation *only after* exhausting the effects of his *prārabddha* actions by actually experiencing them, i.e. by suffering or enjoying them. It is necessary that he also stops his *anārabddha* (*sancita* and *sancīyamāna*) actions from bearing any fruit by dint of his good works and knowledge. But it is to be noted that they do not realize the important fact that he can do good works, or acquire knowledge, only if his *prārabddha* disposes, allows, or prompts, him to do so. This means that nullifying the effects of even *anārabddha* actions is also under the control of *prārabddha* actions.

This notion of the *prārabddha* creates a serious problem even for the general precept of classical thinkers that an individual ought to try to attain *mokṣa*. The attempt to attain it is to be made here, in the *karma*-governed world, by the individual in his present life which is under the control of his *prārabddha*. This means that he can make the attempt only if his *prārabddha* actions allow him to do it. That is, if his *prārabddha* is of such a type that, as an effect of it, he cannot take any initiative to attain it, he would not attain it. The precept for him would thus be otiose because his *prārabddha* disallows him to follow it. Similarly, if his *prārabddha* is such that, as an effect of it, he deserves to get *mokṣa* in this very life, he would automatically or necessarily get it, and therefore does not have to make any effort to get it. These are the only two possibilities. Therefore, if the *prārabddha* works, as it is said to work, it makes it a necessary truth that an individual either cannot even try to get it, or, that he automatically gets it without making any effort, depending on the nature of his *prārabddha*. Such a position would surely make all talk about trying to attain *mokṣa* pointless because trying to get it is either impossible or unnecessary.

Vidyāraṇya seems to be aware of the problem which the classical Indian philosophical practice of doing both, acknowledging the overall primacy of the *prārabddha* and at the same time pleading for the desirability of making an effort to attain *mokṣa*, may have to face. Referring to a possible objection, like the one mentioned above, he tries to defend this practice in his own way. Let us see what his attempt amounts to.

The objector, Vidyāraṇya says, may urge that a *prārabddha* action of an individual requires him to experience some pain or pleasure as an effect of it. This he can do only if he has intact his passional nature, his *cittavṛtti*, i.e., his sensitivity to the experience of pain and pleasure. But the pursuit of *mokṣa* requires him to get rid of his feelings, desires, cravings, etc., i.e. his passional dispositions (*cittavṛtti-nirodha*), by practising *yoga* or spiritual-moral discipline.

No effect of a *prārabddha* action can be gotten rid of. Therefore, one's passional nature too cannot, because, if it is, then one cannot experience any of its effects. This is so because to experience an effect of it is to have an experience of some enjoyment or suffering. But one can have such an experience only if one has a passional (*rāgātmaka*) nature, i.e. a nature prone to enjoy or suffer. Consequently, the precept, too often given by Indian ethicists, to get rid of one's passional nature in order to attain *mokṣa* becomes infructuous. Either no attempt to implement it can be made, or if made, it would necessarily fail. The result would obviously then be that *mokṣa* cannot be attained.

To this Vidyāraṇya's reply is that the pleasure which the attainment of *mokṣa*, or *jīvanmukti*, yields to the individual, being one of a sublime kind, can also be taken as an effect of his *prārabddha*.

The objector may give a rejoinder to his reply, Vidyāraṇya says, by pointing out that the *prārabddha* of the individual makes him experience automatically its effects, i.e. without his making any effort to experience them. Therefore, if *mokṣa*, or the pleasure of it, is also an effect of it, there is no need for him to make any effort to attain or experience it.

Vidyāraṇya replies to the rejoinder by pointing out that the *prārabddha* of any individual is unseen or invisible (*adṛṣṭa*), i.e. concealed. Being concealed, it needs some visible, empirically observable (*dṛṣṭa*), effort, or agency, to enable it to effectuate because, while remaining unseen, it cannot do that. Therefore, the agent needs to make an effort to let his *prārabddha* yield the pleasure of *jīvanmukti* which he has called an effect of it. That is why making such an effort, as well as pleading for it, is neither infructuous nor unneccessary.[22]

This defence of Vidyāraṇya is not foolproof, for more than one reason. Firstly, he does not deny that the *prārabddha* of an individual determines the entire course of his life. Therefore, it can be said to *determine* even his *effort*, or initiative, to attain *mokṣa*. This means that if it does not allow him to do that, he would not, and if it does, he would, no matter whether or not a philosopher tells him that he ought to. That is, either he cannot take the initiative, or he would necessarily take it, i.e. necessitated by his *prārabddha*. Thus, the same problem which the objector raises about the attainment of *mokṣa* occurs about taking the initiative to attain it. It is taking this initiative which Vidyāraṇya calls the *dṛṣṭa*, visible, factor, which enables the *adṛṣṭa*, unseen, *prārabddha*, to effectuate. Secondly, the *karmic* theory, as we shall see in a coming section, maintains that every action, being a temporal thing, terminates within a short time though it effectuates sometimes after a long gap. In the gap, though the action has terminated, its potentiality or power to effectuate persists, and through this power of its own it effectuates. This power is also called *adṛṣṭa*, *apūrva*, etc. This power does not need any other, presently active, i.e. *dṛṣṭa*, agency to enable it to effectuate. Thirdly, if the *prārabddha* needs the assistance of another, a visible, agency in the form of a presently made effort by the individual, in order to actually effectuate, it may as well be said that the effect which then occurs is the result of that presently made visible effort alone and that there is no need to believe in anything like an unseen *prārabddha* or *apūrva*. Fourthly, if another agency is needed by the *prārabddha* to be able to effectuate, its primacy, or autonomy, is gone. It cannot then be said that it necessarily produces its effect which the doer must experience because, if he does not make the needed effort, or take the needed step, the *prārabddha* would not effectuate and he would not therefore experience its effect. It would then become a contingent matter that a *prārabddha* action effectuates because it would be contingent or dependent on that other, visible, agency, or effort, brought into being, or made, by the doer of that *prārabddha* action.

It is true, however, that classical Indian thinkers do plead for attaining *mokṣa* and in their pleading assume that the unliberated individual can make an effort to attain it, and also that making an effort is neither impossible, nor unnecessary. This means that they *assume* that he is free to make this effort. The same stand they take when they insist on his cultivating a moral virtue. That is, they *assume* that he is free to cultivate it and his trying to cultivate it is neither bound always to fail nor is at any time unnecessary. At the same time they also stick to the view that his *prārabddha* determines his character and therefore his virtues which are nothing but some traits of it.

The two positions—(a) that the *prārabddha* of an individual determines his life-style and (b) that he is free to cultivate and practise virtues, as well as to make an effort, to attain and can attain *mokṣa*—are not concordant with each other. But classical Indian thinkers seem to hold both of them. It may be uncharitable to think that they do not notice the discordance between them. But it is also difficult to explain why then they hold both of them. Perhaps they do not want to give up anyone of them because the belief in the overall determinance of the *prārabddha* is a consequence of the *karmic* worldview which is basic to their conception of the world, or the human world, and the belief in man's freedom or ability to lead a moral life and to attain *mokṣa* is basic to their axiology. Therefore, they seem to let the two beliefs lie in peace with each other as basic constituents of their philosophy of man, even though the two are discordant with each other. That their discordance mars the logical symmetry or elegance of their metaphysical as well as ethical theory, cannot be ignored by a moral philosopher who has no ancestral prejudice. But he who has the *ṛṣi* bias and therefore believes that classical philosophers, who are *ṛṣis*, cannot commit a mistake, may not notice the discordance, or try to explain it away in some non-logical manner.

15.7 *PRĀRABDDHA*, POTENCY FOR EFFECTUATION (*APŪRVA*) AND REBIRTH

An action is done by an individual in a certain situation. It is a temporal thing which begins at a certain point of time, continues for some duration and then is over. It involves both mental and physical factors. Being a thing of the natural world it works as a cause of certain occurrences, For example, Yudhiṣṭhira does the act of announcing the untruth that Aśvathāmā has been killed, Aśvathāmā's father Droṇa believes it, lays down his arms, sits quiet in a meditative pose and is killed by Dhṛṣṭadyumna. All this happens within a short span of time. The effect of Yudhiṣṭhira's act of telling the lie thus initiates or leads to, a series of occurrences, finally resulting in Droṇa's death which greatly facilitates Yudhiṣṭhira's winning the war. Every action has some such effects in the natural world. They may be called, therefore, its natural, physical, physico-mental, or factual effects. I shall call such effects naturalistic, though they are also called natural. I avoid calling them natural and choose to call them naturalistic, which is not phonetically a very pleasant word, because the word 'natural', in some uses of it, means the opposite of unnatural, unusual, abnormal, etc.

An action may also be said to produce for its doer some moral merit or demerit on account of which he deserves some pleasure or pain, reward or punishment. Such effects I shall call moral effects. It is this kind of effects which classical thinkers, primarily, have in mind who they characterize the *karmic* theory as maintaining that every desireful action produces some (moral or morally relevant) effect in the form of pleasure or pain which its doer deserves to experience, must experience and actually experiences in his present life or in his next life or lives. A naturalistic effect of an action may occur sometimes soon after the action is done, as it happens in the case of Yudhiṣṭhira's telling the lie. Even a moral effect may also sometimes be produced soon after the action is done, but normally, the tradition says, it is produced after a gap, and sometimes a long gap, of time. Yudhiṣṭhira gets the punishment for telling the lie after a long gap of his telling it. To account for how an action produces its moral effect long after it has been done and come to an end, say, in the doer's next life, classical thinkers say that it first produces a potency to effectuate (*apūrva, karmāsaya, adṛṣṭa*). This potency, they say, continues to exist until it ripens or matures and then produces the moral effect or consequence of the action which is necessarily borne by the doer.

The concept of potency, *apūrva*, is, thus, a theory-generated, and not an empirical, one. As its synonym *adṛṣṭa* literally means, it is something which cannot be seen or observed. It has to be assumed to explain how an action produces its moral result after it has ceased to exist. Classical thinkers have to hypothesize it to explain their claim that actions done in one life may produce their results even in *another* life. Even this claim is not an empirically testable claim; this too is an assumption. It is a component of the other assumption that the doer of the action must experience all of its moral consequences. Therefore, if there is any such consequence which he does not experience in one life, since he has to experience it and he can experience it only when he is alive, he would have to experience it in his next life. Therefore, there must be another life for him to live, or he must have a rebirth after his death, i.e. the end of his present life. The *karmic* theory thus has to have a belief in rebirth. This belief too, like the belief in *apūrva*, is theory-generated, i.e. a belief which the *karmic* theory has to assume or presuppose in order to sustain itself. It has to because of its being a demand of the theory that the agent must experience the moral consequence of every action of his.

The belief in rebirth, by its very nature, cannot be claimed to be empirically grounded, i.e. supported by a set of unquestionable empirical evidences. The *karmic* theory itself cannot be used to prove that the belief in rebirth is true. We cannot say that an individual is reborn because he has to reap the unreaped consequences of his *prārabddha* actions. One of the central theses of the *karmic* theory is that he *necessarily* reaps all the consequences of his actions because those he does not reap in one life he reaps in the next one he is reborn into. This thesis assumes, or depends on, the belief in rebirth. Therefore, using the *karmic* theory as a ground or reason for the truth of the belief in rebirth will be palpably circular. But many writers do that without noticing the circle in their reasoning.

The fact is that we cannot sustain the *karmic* theory's claim that an individual experiences all the consequences of his actions without assuming the truth of the belief in rebirth, and we cannot sustain the truth of the belief in rebirth *without assuming* the truth of the belief that he experiences all the consequences of his actions, i.e. the *karmic* theory. This is so because neither the *karmic* theory, nor the theory of rebirth, is an empirical theory. For none of them do classical thinkers give any conclusive, or convincing, empirical evidence; they do not present any one of them as an inductive theory. They have not, because they cannot. That every individual necessarily experiences all consequences of his actions, being a necessary universal proposition, cannot be empirically, or inductively, proven because empirical generalization or induction can give only a probable one. That an individual, for any reason whatsoever, is reborn after his death obviously cannot be empirically proven because it is not possible to give empirical evidence for it. Both of these theories, the *karmic* theory and the rebirth theory, are, in effect, postulates, or, presuppositions, of Indian philosophy. Since they cannot be rationally proven, they may be called, in a non-pejorative sense, dogmas, as well as, in an honorific sense, basic or foundational, principles of Indian philosophy. However, some justification, or vindication, has been given of the karmic theory involving the belief in rebirth as well. We shall examine that in the last section of this chapter.

Returning to the *karmic* theory, then, the only reason which the *karmic* theory has to assume the possibility of rebirth is the necessity for an individual to reap the unreaped consequences of his actions. But this condition applies only to desireful actions since only they yield such consequences which their doer has to necessarily exhaust by experiencing them. Desireless actions are exempt from this condition; they do not, as we have said earlier, produce any such consequence which he has to experience and therefore they do not require him to be reborn. This notion of a desireless action is not only central to the *karmic* theory but to the entire Indian ethical, or axiological, corpus. Therefore, its role in the Indian philosophy of morals needs to be discussed in some detail befitting the dignified status it has acquired in it. This the section that follows will do.

15.8 REBIRTH, FREEDOM FROM REBIRTH AND DESIRELESS ACTION (*NIṢKĀMA KARMA*)

To explain how an agent is subject to necessarily experiencing all the consequences of his *prārabddha* actions, we have seen, the *karmic* theory has to take recourse to its belief in the rebirth of the agent. But when it is pressed to give a reason for this belief, it has nothing to offer other than saying that he is reborn because he has to experience the consequences he had to experience but did not experience in his previous life. There is a circle in saying both of the things but it seems to me that the *karmic* theory has to live with it. Many writers on Indian ethics happily move in this circle without realizing that by moving from one belief to another and then back to the former they justify neither of them. But even after recognizing it and its weakening influence on the *karmic* worldview, let us not bother about it at this point and proceed to understand the alleged close link between rebirth and desireless action.

Rebirth is considered by all classical Indian thinkers as an evil and therefore worth getting rid of. The reason for this view is that to be reborn is to live in the world and to live in the world is to necessarily have at least some suffering. The remedy suggested, which is relevant here, is that by doing all that one does in a desireless (*niṣkāma*) manner, he can terminate the very liability of his to be reborn. To terminate this liability is to terminate his liability to live in the world as an individual; that is, to cease to be an inhabitant of the world, of course, after his death. Since he has to die at some point of time, ultimately he ceases to be an individual after becoming freed from rebirth and returns to his original status of being the pure self he really is. To return to this state is his final goal, to achieve it the highest value. Therefore, we can say that freeing oneself from rebirth is ultimately to get rid of one's individuality (*jīvatva*). It is definitely to free oneself from the very possibility of experiencing any suffering but also to become totally unrelated to the human world, or the world, and human society and therefore to have gone outside the zone of morality.

To plead for freeing oneself from rebirth, being really to plead for ceasing to be an individual, is definitely to a great degree undervalue, or devalue, the importance, or the role, of the individual and to highly rate, or overrate, that of the self. In fact, the Indian ethos does not shy away from admitting that this is what it really does. In doing it, it is not clear why it does not realize that there are some very important things which only the individual can do. The self cannot do these because it can do nothing. This is so because, as per the Indian conception, it is a non-agent.

It is only the individual who can and who does lead a moral life, who can be kind, benevolent, just, etc. It is he alone who can propound the doctrine of *mokṣa*, or of desireless action, who can highlight the elevated status of the self, who can indulge in intellectual, aesthetic, technological, political, etc., activities, who can give to the world philosophy, science, poetry, painting, music, etc. If everyone does only desireless actions and therefore ceases to be reborn after his death, then, there may come a stage in which there is no individual and therefore there is no philosophy, science, culture, etc. Indian thinkers do not think this possibility would ever become a reality because the number of individuals, according to them, is infinite. But they cannot deny that if a large number of people follow their precept of desireless action, and after their death are not reborn as individuals capable of contributing to such intellectual-cultural-ethical enterprises, the world would get thereby greatly impoverished. As a consequence, there may be a great increase in the amount of suffering which the then reduced group of existing individuals would have to experience.

All this is very likely to happen because *only an individual* can ameliorate the unhappy condition of another individual, or contribute to his moral or general betterment. After freeing himself from the possibility of being reborn, the freed individual attains complete freedom only from all of *his own* sufferings once and for all. He also thereby ceases to be an agent for helping anyone else, i.e. to be a moral agent, because he ceases to be an agent of any sort. On behalf of the philosophies which admit the possibility of being liberated while alive, i.e. freed from rebirth, it may be said that, while alive, the freed person would contribute to the world's moral betterment. But this he would do only as long as he is alive, i.e. for a short period of time, since he too would meet his physical death. The assumption of this possibility too has some conceptual problems to which we shall come a little later. At this point let us note that even after making the above assumption, we cannot deny the fact that the recommendation for doing desireless actions in order to free oneself from rebirth may very well be taken as one to run away from the task of making the world morally, or even intellectually-culturally, better.

On the other hand, if an individual is advised, or he himself aspires, to do such actions which ensure his rebirth again and again but as a person devoted to making the world better and better, the recommendation, or the individual's own aspiration, would not amount to his making any attempt at to run away from his moral obligation to the world. Perhaps it is the realization of some such possibility or possibilities which prompts some Buddhist thinkers to propound the doctrine of *bodhisattva* which legislates that an individual, after becoming fit to attain *nirvāṇa*, or *mokṣa*, i.e. freedom from rebirth, should postpone attaining it until he helps all those who have not yet become fit to attain this sort of freedom. Laying down this condition, as we have said earlier, amounts to recommending that nobody should really attain his own freedom because the number of individuals needing his help is infinite. It is true that the problems mentioned here from the moral point of view, or as pertinent to Indian moral philosophy, are more conceptual than empirical. But they owe their origin to the assumption of the possibility of rebirth and identifying complete freedom from suffering with freedom from rebirth. This belief in rebirth, too, like the belief in the *karmic* law, is non-empirical, or not empirically certifiable, and therefore the concept of rebirth is a non-empirical, non-instantiable, concept. Consequently, the conceptual problems which it raises cannot be brushed aside as irrelevant or of no consequence.

In spite of the above handicap, the belief in rebirth, if adhered to by an individual, gives to him a very good reason, as said earlier, against committing suicide. If he has ever thought of committing it, he has been prompted to do so primarily because of his belief that by ending his life at this time he would forever end his life, and therefore its sufferings, worries, etc. But now his belief in rebirth would belie this hope. It would imply that he would be reborn and might have similar, or more severe, sufferings, etc. The clear fallout of the belief, that the end of this life need not be the end of life, may thus prove a great deterrent to his choosing to end his life. Perhaps this is the reason why we do not come across anyone committing suicide even in any tale, or any discussion of the permissibility of euthanasia in any condition in a classical Indian ethical or even a medical work.

Indian ethical theory, thus, is built on the assumption of this belief in rebirth (and some others) and considers desireless action (*niṣkāma karma*) a necessary condition for attaining freedom from rebirth. Therefore, let us return to the concept of desireless action to ascertain what exactly it denotes, the role it is ascribed to play by Indian ethical theory, and also how far it can play that role.

The term '*niṣkāma*' means desireless, and therefore *niṣkāma karma* means desireless action. A desire is the main, or one of the main, motivating forces of a voluntary action which a moral action is, though every voluntary action need not be moral. Even among desireful, i.e. desire-motivated, actions, only some can be called moral and some others immoral. For example, Duryodhana's arranging that the Pāṇḍava family be lodged in the lac house with the desire or intention to get all members of it burnt to death, is definitely immoral, or morally wrong. Similarly, Vidura's arranging that a man digs out in the house an underground passage, with the intention that they may, through it, get out of the house before being burnt, is definitely a moral, or morally right action. This illustrates the common-sense truth that some intentions or desires are morally commendable and some morally condemnable, implying that all desires must not be gotten rid of. The theory of desireless action, on the other hand, holds that every desireful action, no matter whether its motivating desire is morally commendable or condemnable, leads to rebirth and should therefore be shunned. The reason behind this view is, as has been explained earlier, the belief that any sort of desireful action is rebirth-causing. This reason is obviously not a moral reason. But this point we shall take up a little latter since we are at the moment concerned with explicating the concept of a desireless action and its status in Indian axiology.

That desires, and therefore desireful actions, cause bondage, we have seen, has been very much emphasized by the *Bṛhadāraṇyaka Upaniṣad.*[23] In a desireful action, the real culprit, it says, is not the action, but the desire which motivates the doer to do it. Therefore, if the desire is gotten rid of, i.e. the action is made desireless, the action does not bind. Commenting on IV.iv.9, Śankara says that 'when desire is gone, work, though present, does not lead to the accumulation of merit or demerit. Even if he' (the individual)' 'goes on doing good and bad deeds, these, bereft of the desire, produce no results; therefore, desire is the root of transmigratory existence',[24] which is what bondage means.

The unambiguous lesson which the *Upaniṣad* yields is that an action may be done but without any desire to end the possibility of transmigration or rebirth. Even the *Gītā* seems to hold a similar view, or one quite close to it, at some places in it. For example, it says at one place that 'when one fully renounces all the desires that have entered the mind, and, remains satisfied in the Self alone by the Self, then he is called a man of steady wisdom' (i.e. *sthitaprajña*).[25] The attainment of this state of wisdom is the *Gītā*'s equivalent of that of freedom from rebirth while alive, i.e. *jīvanmukti.*

If we take seriously such remarks about getting rid of all desires and also recollect the Indian emphasis on the pursuit of *puruṣārthas*, we cannot fail to notice a glaring self-inconsistency in the Indian general theory of value and consequently in its theory of ethical value and obligation as well. A *puruṣārtha* means an object of a human desire. Therefore, one who becomes desireless cannot pursue any value, or rather, any object whatever. If he cannot seek anybody's ill-fare, he cannot seek his welfare either. If this line of thinking is pursued further, it will be easily seen that he cannot lead a moral life. Nay, he cannot even seek *mokṣa* which too, being the highest *puruṣārtha,* is a *puruṣārtha.* That the pursuit of *mokṣa* also requires a desire to pursue it is admitted by Indian value theory. It not only avers the existence of such a desire and calls it *mumukṣā,* which means nothing but the desire for *mokṣa,* but recommends that everyone ought to inculcate it. Rather, its inculcation is considered to be a virtue and its non-inculcation a vice or a serious lapse. Therefore, abnegation of all desires does not go well with the theory of *puruṣārthas* and therefore with Indian ethical theory. This point is noticed by Indian ethicists. As we have seen in 10.1, they recognize the importance of desires and do not consider all of them to be evil or undesirable, and clearly admit that they are springs of human action. Giving up all desires is bound to tell on or undermine our activities in every walk of life and therefore to make it poorer.

That without action, i.e. by shunning all actions, we cannot survive even for a moment in the world is too obvious a truth to be denied by any theory. This fact too is not only recognized but emphasized by classical Indian thinkers. The *Gītā* unhesitatingly affirms that 'A person does not attain fulfilment merely through renunciation' (of all actions), 'Because, no one ever remains even for a moment without doing work. For all are made to work under compulsion by the *guṇas* born of Nature.'[26]

We have stated above the *Gītā*'s pleading for the abnegation of all desires, and now we find it asserting that we cannot live if we give up all actions. But since actions spring from, or are motivated by, desires, giving up all desires may amount to giving up all, or a large number of, actions. This means that both, requiring that all desires be given up and admitting all actions cannot be given up, cannot be maintained without making some adjustment or modification in the general theory of action assumed here. The *Gītā* seems to realize the need of doing that and seems to do it by adding that an individual, in order to attain freedom from rebirth, does not have to give up actions but only desire or attachment for any of the results of his actions. That is, he may not give up desires for actions, that his actions may be motivated by some desires, but must not have any desire or attachment for their results. A desireless action would now mean, not one which is not motivated by a desire, but one for any result of which its doer has no desire.[27] It is such actions of the doer in doing which he is completely indifferent to what it leads to which would cause no bondage, i.e. would not require him to be reborn. We have now another notion of a desireless action, according to which an action may itself be done desirefully but there should be no desire for, or interest in, whatever may be its result. Because of the importance given to it in discussions of Indian ethics it needs to be given some special attention. This we shall do in the section that follows.

15.9 DESIRELESSNESS ABOUT THE RESULT OF AN ACTION (*PHALASANYĀSA*)

This notion of a desireless action (*niṣkāma karma*) is commonly taken to be by most writers on Indian ethics as not only the real, or standard, view of classical Indian ethicists but also as a faultless and impeccable one in its own right. But when closely looked into as an ethical principle to be used as a guide in actual life or living practice, it may be said to have one pragmatic advantage in its favour and two disadvantages, one on account of a conceptual deficiency and the other because of a normative or ethical impropriety, both ingrained in it because of its involving a truncated conception of human action. The two disadvantages take away a large part of, or greatly water down, the pragmatic advantage it seems to possess. But this they will do only for him who is logically sensitive and morally serious. However, simply saying these things, without showing them, would cut no ice either with a layman or with a philosopher.

Let us first take up what I have called its two disadvantages, beginning with the conceptual one. We shall take as an example of an action Arjuna's act of killing unarmed Karṇa by hitting hard his neck with his arrow, cutting the neck off the rest of his body and thereby causing his instantaeous death. The result of this action is obviously Karṇa's death. Since Arjuna has been taught the ethics of the *Gītā* by Kṛṣṇa himself and accepts it in toto, it can safely be assumed that he has no attachment for the result of what he does, namely, the death of Karṇa. But the action itself, let us assume, is motivated by a desire of his, since we have taken the concept of a desireless action to denote one which itself may be desireful but is not imbued with any attachment to its result. This concept of action separates the action from its result. But a complete account of an action cannot be given without mentioning its result since it is the result which determines the action's identity. For example, whether it is an act of killing, or of practising archery, can be decided only by knowing what the archer is trying to achieve by it, no matter whether he succeeds or fails in his attempt. And, unless he tries to produce a result, his action would not be a voluntary action that would be entitled to be judged as morally right or wrong. It is the attempted result which directs, or determines, the way of conducting the action. Arjuna chooses to Karṇa him when he is unarmed and hits at his neck which is the surest way to cause his death. He chooses to attack him when he is unarmed because he is not too sure of being able to kill him if he has his bow and arrow in his hands. To do a voluntary action, the kind of action which is morally assessable, is, thus, to do a desireful one. This means that a moral theory cannot recommend to anyone to do only desireless actions. Perhaps this is the reason why the advocates of desirelessness are interpreted as not holding that one should do only desireless actions, since it is not possible to do anything morally relevant without any desire. Rather, they are said to hold the view that he should have no desire to produce any result by whatever he does.

It deserves to be noted that if a morally relevant action itself has to be desireful, then there is bound to be a desire for its result. The desire motivating it is nothing but a desire for attaining a result by doing it. An action is a means for achieving an end, a result, and the desire for doing the action is nothing but the desire for achieving that result. It is the intended or desired result of the action which makes it an intentional or desireful action. This point is very clearly emphasized by Śankara. In his commentary on 3.v.1 of the *Braḥadāraṇyaka* he avers that 'Every desire for means is a desire for results...people adopt different means, actuated by the desire for results.'[28]

After having achieved the result a sobre moral agent may not exult over it, or after having failed to achieve it he may not suffer heartbreak. But in preparing to do the action, or while doing it, if he is completely desireless about, unattached to or detached from, what it may result in, i.e. indifferent to its result, he would not be able to give any definite direction to his action. The pilot of an aircraft cannot fly it in a definite direction if he is indifferent to what the flight results in, whether it safely lands at a particular airport, or it crashes. All this is conceptually true because the concept of the result of an action is a constituent of the very concept of a desireful action, and a voluntary action by definition is a desireful or intentional action.

It is also true that an agent's attachment to the result of his action does not necessarily lower the moral value of the action if the action itself is morally right or commendable. For example, Hanūmāna's attachment, or, interestedness, in locating Sītā in Lanka does not lower the moral value of his action which even Rāma calls an excellent example of sincerity and dutifulness. Gandhi's great attachment to the amelioration of the deplorable condition of the people then considered untouchable does not lower but heightens the morality of steps he takes to achieve his end.

But the Indian ethical tradition greatly admires, and so do almost all of its modern interpreters, the ethical grandeur of detachment, as for example, the complete detachment attained by the king Janaka. As the story goes, the king has attained complete desirelessness and thereby knowledge of ultimate reality. To test his attainment of detachment, the great god Viṣṇu appears on earth in the form of a *brāhmaṇa* human being. He sets the city of Mithilā, the capital of Janaka's kingdom, on fire. But even on seeing the city burning, Janaka remains completely composed and detached. He declares that he has attained the highest wisdom and knowledge of reality and therefore he would lose nothing even if the entire city were to be reduced to ashes. The god is convinced of his being completely detached i.e. of his having become a *jīvanmukta,* is pleased with him and restores the city to its earlier flourishing condition.[29]

Let us reflect, from a non-traditionalist, purely philosophical or moral, point of view, on the example of Janaka as a paradigmatic one of an individual who has attained complete detachment. Let us also not bother about whether it is a merely mythical or a real, historical one. It would be clear then that Janaka's, or any detached person's attainment is purely personal. It may keep his mental peace and sedateness undisturbed come what may. It does not show his moral perfection either as an individual with a great concern for the welfare of others, or as a king morally obligated to look after the welfare of the people of his kingdom.

The second, normative, disadvantage, which the principle of being detached towards, or unconcerned about, the result of any of one's actions has, ensues from the way the law of *karma* is said to function and also from the concept of desert, or of deserving anything. The law is said to function in such a way that an agent necessarily gets what he ought to get or deserves. Therefore, since he is necessarily going to get the result of an action of his because he ought to, there is nothing wrong if he is also eager, keen, or desirous, to get it. In addition, taking into account the very meaning of the concept of 'ought' or of desert, irrespective of the law of *karma*, if as a result of a particular action of his, he ought, or deserves, to get something, then he has a moral right to get it. Therefore, it is morally right for him to feel concerned about getting it and to feel resentment if he does not get it. That is, his claim, or desire, to get it, or his attachment for it, is morally justified, and in no way morally wrong. This means that a desire for, or attachment towards, getting what he ought to get, a getting which is his moral right, is morally justified. A clear implication of it is that an attitude of non-attachment or of detachment towards the result of *every* action cannot be called morally justified.

If may be suggested that if he is not attached to the attainment of the result, then, if perchance he does not get it, he would not feel frustrated or unhappy. Therefore, to avoid the possibility of ever being made unhappy on that account, it is better to have no desire, or no attachment for the result of any action he ever does. Such a man may never be unhappy. Therefore, the cultivation of non-attachment for the results of all of his actions is a sound practical thing for anyone to do. This is so because the world is not under his control which is why it is possible that sometimes, or perhaps often, he may not get even the deserved results of some or most of his actions. There may, thus, be a practical advantage in accepting the principle of desirelessness, or complete detachment. It is this advantage which we have called above the pragmatic advantage that the principle of non-attachment or desirelessness may be claimed to yield.

However, as has been already hinted at, this advantage cannot be had by him who understands the logic of the concept of an intentional action, that is, by him who knows that this concept includes the concept of the result an intentional action aims at producing, and that therefore it is not possible for an agent of it to be unconcerned about or inifferent to the result. If he is, then he cannot do this action. The advantage cannot be had by him as well who understands that the pursuit of a *puruṣārtha* is a purposive action, i.e. one which is motivated by a desire because a *puruṣārtha* is an object of a desire, and therefore its pursuit cannot be desireless and consequently the agent of the pursuit cannot be desireless in, or non-attached to, attaining the object of the pursuit, the *puruṣārtha* concerned. His stand is supported by the fact that classical thinkers consider even the pursuit of *mokṣa* to be the pursuit of the object of a desire, i.e. of *mumukṣā*. The pragmatic advantage can neither be had by him who understands the functioning of the law of *karma* as not only entitling an agent to get what he deserves as the result of an action of his but also as necessitating that he gets it. Nor can it be had by him who, even while standing outside the boundary of Indian ethics, knows what the logic of the concept of 'ought' or 'desert' implies. The upshot of all this is that it can be had by him alone who is naive enough to be oblivious of the above logical implications that the Indian general theory of value and *karmic* worldview have.

It is true, however, that Indian ethicists aver that only desireless or non-attached actions can lead to the termination of their agent's liability to be reborn and thereby to his eternal freedom from suffering, which is his *mokṣa.* But as we have already said, this goal may at the best be called a personal or theological goal, and not a moral one. It is their high regard for this state which prompts them to insist on desirelessness or non-attachment, though even attaining it is also the fulfilment of a desire. As we have already shown, the logic of this desire is not different from that of any other desire, though its rank among desires may be called the highest. But that would be not because it is conceptually different from all other desires but because its object, *mokṣa,* is given the highest rank among the objects of human desires, i.e. the *puruṣārthas.*

It may be said, and is sometimes said, that the *Gītā* offers a way of solving the problem of motivation for doing something even after becoming desireless by pointing out that an agent, even after becoming desireless, can do something being guided, or motivated, by his sense of duty, i.e. he would do it then not because he has a desire to do it but because doing it is his duty. This means that his sense of duty can function as a motive without there being in him a desire for doing it. It would be interesting to discuss as an independent issue whether not such a position can be maintained and modern as well as contemporary moral philosophers in the West have taken stands on both the sides, some maintaining that by itself duty can, and some that it cannot, work as a motive. But entering into their controversy would not be relevant in this work. Here we can discuss only the *Gītā*'s stand referred to above. To anticipate what we are going to say soon, we would say here that though the *Gītā seems* to hold that duty by itself can be a motive, it cannot really do that because it can do that only at the cost of being self-inconsistent as well as being inconsistent with the general trend of Indian ethics.

It is true that at one point in the *Gītā* when Arjuna says that he has no desire to fight the *Mahābhārata* war because of the bloodshed and other evil effects it is going to cause, Kṛṣṇa says that he should not be guided by this desire of his but by his duty as a *kṣatriya.* His duty as a *kṣatriya,* he says, is to fight a righteous war which this war is. That is why, he goes on, he should fight in spite of his disinclination to do that.[30] What is to be noted here is that this is the duty of Arjuna as a *kṣatriya,* i.e. his *varṇadharma,* and therefore a *dharma* and therefore a *puruṣārtha* of his. Being a *puruṣārtha* it must be an object of a *kṣatriya*'s, and consequently of his, desire. As the dialogue proceeds, Kṛṣṇa uses several types of arguments, good or not so good, to arouse in him the desire to fight and ultimately makes him disposed to fight and actually fight. And, from the way he fights, it is fully evident that he fights in the manner in which a combatant desirous of winning a war fights.

There is another problem in cultivating desirelessness. When desires are said to cause bondage, they include each and every desire, even a moral desire, for example, the desire to do benevolent or altruistic actions. Therefore, the precept to become completely desireless may be taken to imply that one should become a recluse and totally inactive. To ward off this wrong implication Kṛṣṇa says that the desireless person should not become inactive but continue doing his duties. By duties he means caste-duties (*varṇadharmas*). His reason for saying this is that he should remain active for the sake of *lokasangraha*. The phrase 'for the sake of, *lokasangraha*', or its Sanskrit equivalent '*lokasangrahārtham*', as Madhusādana Sarasvatī in his commentary on the *Gītā*'s 3.20 rightly says, 'means making people undertake their own duties and preventing them from taking the wrong path...'[31] i.e. from abstaining from doing their own caste-duties. This is its meaning according to Śankara as well. Some other commentators on the *Gītā*, like Rāmānuja and Śrīdhara Svāmī, also interpret it in the same manner.[32]

By using no rule of Sanskrit grammar can the above phrase be interpreted to mean 'for the sake of altruistic or benevolent actions'. That is why no classical commentator on the *Gītā* takes it to mean that. But almost all Indian writers on the *Gītā*, or Indian ethics, do that. For example, Kalidas Bhattacharya unhesitatingly takes the *Gītā* to prescribe that actions which are *niṣkama*, desireless, be done *lokasangrahārtham*, meaning thereby that they are to be done because they are altruistic.[33] It does not occur to him that an altruistic action, i.e. one done with the *desire* to do some good to some other person, cannot be called *niṣkāma* or desireless.

Perhaps these writers (wrongly) interpret '*lokasangrahārtham*' to mean 'for the sake of benevolence' or '*lokakalyāṇārtham*', out of a patriotic motivation. This motivation of theirs seems to be that by giving this interpretation they can save Indian ethic's emphasizing the importance of desirelessness from having the implication of ruling out the cultivation of even a moral desire like that of doing benevolence. They forget that there are other ways, like some of those which have been used in this work, in some of its earlier chapters, to show that Indian ethics gives as much importance to benevolence and other moral desires or virtues as any other ethics does, if not more.

15.10 *KARMIC* RETRIBUTIVISM AND JUSTIFIABILITY OF *KARMIC* WORLDVIEW

From the discussions given in the preceding and earlier sections, it is clear that *karmic* theory, or even the *karmic* worldview, which it adumbrates, is unambiguously retributivist. However, its retributivism is a very strong kind of moralism, completely divested of any element of revengefulness. According to it an individual gets what he *morally deserves*, and not simply what he deserves and only that which he morally deserves, nothing more and nothing less, and he gets it because of the nature of the *karmic* world, i.e. because of the world, as governed by the *karmic* law, being what it is. The dispensation of what he deserves to him is linked with, we have seen, his past, as well as his future, birth or births. Therefore, there is no possibility of there ever occurring an excess or a deficit in the award of what he deserves. In a world smacking of, or permitting, any kind of revengefulness there is always a possibility of one's being given a more severe kind of punishment than he deserves and in one imbued with charitableness that of his being given a greater amount of benefits than is his right to get. Taking all this into account, the *karmic* world may be called retributivist because of its nature or ontological constitution and not because of its human management, thereby guaranteeing a fully moral distribution of benefits and burdens among its inhabitants.

For a worldview of this type, or rather for any worldview, no validation, either deductive or inductive, is possible. For the *karmic* view, therefore, only some sort of indication, on the basis of some indirect evidence, may be given; or, it may be called justified by some on the ground of its being propounded in some works considered to be scriptural, particularly because of its involving a belief in past and future births of individuals, a belief which cannot be empirically tested or verified. Justifying it on scriptural authority may be considered in order in a religious work but not in a philosophical one which the present work is. Historians of Indian philosophy have tried to justify it on the basis of some indirect evidence. Let us see how far this move can succeed.

To offer indirect evidence for a theory is to refer to some empirical facts or problems which are alleged to be explained, or made intelligible, by accepting the theory, or admitting the validity of the claims made by it, even though the theory is not inductively or deductively confirmable. The *karmic* theory is generally accepted by writers on Indian philosophy, or even by Indologists, to be a sound or convincing one about the working of the human world on some such ground or grounds. These grounds, when logically probed into, are quite often found to be a mixture of some empirical, some moral, and some contentual-looking-but-really-tautological, considerations, as will be shown below.

It is an ethical or, more specifically, retributively ethical, tautology that everyone himself, and none else, ought to get what an action of his entitles him to get and nothing more or less. It would be good if it is also empirical that he actually gets it, and would be better if he necessarily gets it. Rather, a world in which an agent and none else necessarily gets what his and only his actions make him deserve would be a very good ethical world in which the 'ought' merges with the 'is'. It is such a world which the *karmic* theory is said to ensure. Further, it is believed by classical proponents of the theory that the world is really of this sort and that it is therefore that they call it a *karmic*, or law-of-*karma*-governed, world. If we find an instance of an individual who seems not to be getting what he seems to deserve in virtue of his present style of life, the theory can be used to justify it either by saying that it is due to his style in his past birth, or that he would get his due in his next birth. Therefore, the argument goes, the theory is justified because it ensures a morally fully fair world. Consequently, it is said to generate in us the hope that leading a morally good life would be rewarding and thereby it strengthens our moral will to lead such a life. This kind of reasoning can be called offering a moral argument for the *karmic* theory, or the *karmic* conception of the world. It is debatable whether or not a worldview can be defended on the basis of its allegedly generating a hope and the unverifiable belief in the theory of rebirth. But we shall mention here another problem which the Indian ontological theory of the distinction between the individual (*jīva*) and the self generates and which seems to imply that he who does an action in one birth is not the same individual as the one who gets its due in the next birth. This implication goes directly counter to the claim made by the *karmic* theory. It can be shown as follows:

The agent of an action is the individual who is an embodied self. He has in him a self but it is also necessary for him to have a body and all that goes with having a body. On the other hand, the self does not need a body at all. The individual, thus, has a self but is not identical with it. It is the individual who is a moral agent, and not the self. The self is a non-doer, a non-agent, and therefore cannot be a moral agent. It is also clear that two individuals, even though they may have identical selves, are ontologically different because of having different bodies. Therefore, if an individual dies and is reborn, then in his next birth, in spite of his having in this birth (or rebirth) the same self which he had in his previous one, he is a different individual. He has to be different because of his having a different body and all that goes with having a body, like agency, propensities, passions, desires, proneness to feel pleasure and pain, motivations, etc. None of these things can any self, as per Indian ontology, have. Since a moral action is done by the individual, it happens that if he does it in his present birth and therefore deserves to receive its due but gets the due in his next birth, in that birth he would have become a different individual as shown above. This means that one individual does an action and another one gets what the former, the real doer, deserves. The identity or sameness of the self in the two individuals does not cause any dent in this argument or to its conclusion because the self is neither the doer of an action nor the enjoyer or sufferer of what the action yields. The argument and its conclusion show the opposite of what the *karmic* theory claims to hold.[34] This is a fallout of the Indian metaphysics of the duality of the self and the individual. It demonstrates that basing ethics, or an ethical theory, on a highly speculative, rarified, metaphysics may prove fatal for it and thereby also for morality.

One of the basic claims of the karmic theory, we have seen, is that an agent necessarily reaps the consequences of his and only his own actions. If an action does not mature enough to fructify in the life in which it is done and thus remains a karmic residue at the time of the agent's death, the agent necessarily reaps its consequences in his next birth (of course, only if by then it becomes ready to yield its results). But the argument given in the preceding paragraph has validly proven that, because of the agent's having become in the next birth a person different from what he, the action's doer, was in the previous birth, the doer of the action and the experiencer of its consequences are two *different* persons. This conclusion is the direct contrary of the karmic theory's claim mentioned at the beginning of this paragraph as well as repugnant to our untutored moral common-sense.

The non-identity of the agent in any two of his births is entailed, as has already been shown, by the fact that he has a different body in the two different births. An orthodox believer in the theory may try to counteract this entailment by using the theory of the subtle body (*liṅga śarīra, sūkṣma śarīra*) to maintain that there is also a common body possessed by him in his two births, though this body is not visible as his two different bodies in the two births are. If this is really the case, then the non-identity of his two different bodies in different births will not be a conclusive reason for his being two different persons in those births. Let us see if it is so by having an objective look at what the theory of the subtle body is and assessing how much of probative force it can supply to the believer's defence of the karmic theory by proving the identity of the agent in two different births, in spite of his having empirically different bodies in all different births.

According to the theory of the subtle body every individual has two bodies, a gross body (*sthūla śarīra*) and a subtle body (*sūkṣma śarīra*). His gross body is the one which we empirically find him having and using in doing whatever he does. It dies and it is its death which is called his death. When he is reborn, he has another gross body the nature of which is determined by the actions done by him in his preceding birth. The subtle body, on the other hand, is not observable or cognizable by any sense organ, external or internal. It is this body in which are stored the karmic residues, the tendencies generated by those actions which have not yielded their consequences. It transmigrates with the self of an individual, after his death, to his next birth. Therefore, it is the same subtle body which is present in any two births of his. The believer in the karmic theory says that it is this body which accounts for his being the same, identical, person in his two, or all, births.

The theory of the subtle body can be used to solve the problem of personal identity provided it is a defensible theory. But no classical work presents a detailed account of it with valid grounds on which its authenticity can be said to rest. Generally, the nature of the subtle body as well as that of its passage from one birth to another is given in mythological terms. This is so because no empirical support or logical reasoning can be given to prove its existence because the concept of a subtle body is allegedly a denoting concept but one which cannot be instantiated or exemplified. We cannot give an example of a subtle body by showing that an individual has a subtle body of such and such a type. It is for the same reason, or even without that, equally obvious that we cannot exemplify how the subtle body of a person A passes into the being of the person ARB (A reborn as B) after the death of A.

The theory of the subtle body is ontological, or metaphysical, and therefore one which makes a factual claim that everyone has a subtle body without being able to prove the validity of the claim. It seems to me that classical Indian thinkers had some awareness of the problem of the identity of a person in two births of his and to solve it they introduced the concept of a subtle body. However, because of its being claimed to be a denoting concept, but handicapped by the impossibility of its being exemplified by any denotatum, they could not do more than mythologise about it and about its passage after an individuals's death to his reborn state. Therefore, a belief in the theory can be taken only to be a mythological one, and, consequently, cannot be used to prove the identity of a person in one birth with what he is in his next birth. This means that it cannot save the karmic theory from entailing that the doer of an action and the experiencer of its consequences are two different persons, and therefore from nullifying its contention that the doer is necessarily the experiencer.

All this happens because the belief in rebirth is itself a mythological one, though it too claims to be a factual one. Conjoining it with the belief in a subtle body, another mythological belief, to solve the problem of personal identity which the belief in rebirth gives rise to, cannot make the belief in rebirth less vulnerable than what it by itself is. A conjunction of two questionable beliefs is in no way less, if not move, questionable than each one of the two conjoined beliefs by itself is. This is very much similar to the logical truth that a conjunction of two unmaintainable or false propositions is in no way less unmaintainable or less false (if the expression 'less false' is permissible) than each one of its conjuncts singly is.

Any discussion, or assertion, about what happens after the death of a person, and therefore about the transmigration of an entity, as well as about the transmigrating entity, like the subtle body, can neither be empirical nor conceptual, i.e. logical. That is why perhaps, the nature of a subtle body and of its transmigration is talked about more in some *purāṇas* than in any classical Indian philosophical work, though all the Indian philosophical schools, except the *Cārvāka*, accept the theory of transmigration. *Purāṇas* are mythological works, though some ethical, philosophical, ideas may be found in them here and there. A *purāṇic* account is not likely to be an empirically, or logically, supported one. For example, the *Brahmavaivarta Purāṇa*, which also calls the subtle body *jīva*, says that it 'has the form of a man, the size of a thumb: this subtle body is taken on (transmigrates) in order to experience (the fruits of karma). That subtle body does not turn to ashes even in the blazing fire in hell; it is not destroyed in water, even after a long time, nor by weapons, or swords, or missiles,...It is not burnt or broken'.[35]

Several purāṇas describe what happens to an individual after his death but what they say is purely mythical. Their account may be of some interest to an orthodox Hindu, as for example, in many families, after the death of a person the *Garuda Purāṇa* is read out by a priest and listened to by the members of the family. This *purāṇa* describes in great detail what, according to it, happens to a dead man. But on that basis, or on the basis of any *purāṇic* account, no maintainable theory of a subtle body can be constructed.[36]

On this topic even philosophical works do not fare any better. For example, Śaṅkara in his commentary on the *Brahmasūtra* simply states that, after the death of the individual 'when acquiring a fresh body' (in the individual's rebirth) 'after leaving the present one' (i.e. after his death) 'it sallies forth enveloped by the subtle parts of the mixed elements which are the seed of the next body'.[37] This is only to aver that the soul or self goes from one body to another with the subtle body. That is, not only the self but the subtle body too transmigrates to the next life, which means the rebirth of the (dead) individual.

Śaṅkara reiterates on the same page the *Bṛhadāranyaka's* statement that 'Just as a leech supported on a straw goes to the end of it, takes hold of another support, and contracts itself, so does the soul throw this body aside, take hold of another support and contracts itself'.[38] This statement too is allegorical and does not give any matter-of-fact, convincing, account of transmigration or of the reality of a subtle body.

Even in his own commentary on the *Bṛhadāranyka's* statement Śaṅkara does not give anything more informative about the nature of the subtle body.[39] Further, in his commentary on the *Brahmasūtra* he avers that other systems like the *Sānkhya, Buddhism, Vaiśeṣika, Jaina,* etc. do not admit anything of the type of a subtle body. According to the Jains, he says, 'the soul alone jumps from one body to another like a parrot from one tree to another...'.[40] There is no reason to think that Śaṅkara's understanding of the other systems' position on this theme is wrong.

We can say therefore that all the systems do not accept the reality of a subtle body and those which do are not able to give an acceptable theory of a subtle body. But all of them accept the karmic theory and hence the theory of rebirth; Therefore, an appeal to the concept of a subtle body cannot be used to solve the problem of the identity of an individual in any two births of his. This means that the theory of a subtle body cannot be used to refute my conclusion that, if the karmic theory is meticulously probed into, it entails that the doer of an action and the experiencer of its consequences are two different persons. This entailment goes against its claim that the two are the same, identical, individual. Moreover, we have seen that when we go through any account of the nature of a subtle body or that of transmigration, it becomes fully obvious that we have reached a zone which is very different from what Indian philosophy, which is a cognitive inquiry, really is.

Another, more earthly, justification for the *karmic* theory is given by pointing to some social-moral anomalies for which we do not have any readily available, common-sensical, empirical explanation. For example, we may come across a man, or a group of men, afflicted with terrible suffering though, to the best of our knowledge, they have done nothing wrong. Such cases may be made intelligible, it is said, by using the *karmic* theory and saying that they suffer because of what they had done in their previous life or lives. Such an explanation can work for him who believes in the theory of birth–death–rebirth. But it may also justify *any kind* of happening, undesirable or desirable, miserable or pleasurable, as it does with Gandhi when he attributes the sufferings caused by the earthquake to its victims' past sins, as already referred to.

What these problems in constructing a justification for the *karmic* theory exhibit is that the theory needs to be rethought in their light as well as in the light of modern advances in ethical theorizing in conceptual as well as applied directions. And this is true not only of this theory of classical Indian moral philosophy, but of any theory of any classical moral philosophy whatsoever. These problems relate to the way or ways in which ontology has been used in Indian moral philosophy. A few of them have been briefly discussed in some of the earlier chapters of this book. A fuller treatment of all of them, however, needs a book-length discussion. This shows the great vitality of classical Indian philosophy for prompting more and more reconstructive explorations into it, and not just for undertaking archaeological excavations into it to discover some intellectual or spiritual artifacts to be stored in a philosophical museum.

NOTES AND REFERENCES

1. Swāmi Gambhīrānanda's translation, (Advaita Ashram, Calcutta), 2.2.8, p. 132.
2. Ibid.
3. Swāmi Gambhīrananda (trans.), *Brahma-Sūtra Bhāṣya of Śankarācārya* (Advaita Ashram, Calcutta), IV.i.15, 19.
4. Ibid., pp. 839–40.
5. Ibid., p. 846.
6. Swāmi Vīreśvarānanda and Swāmi Ādidevānanda (trans.), *Braha-Sūtras with Śrī Bhāṣya of Ramanuja* (Advaita Ashram, Calcutta), pp. 446–49.
7. *Vanaparva*, 207: 56–57.
8. '*Eka bāta ekānta men suna lo, jagadādhāra: Taren mere karma to Prabh ka kyā Upakāra?*' Quoted by B.G. Tilak in his *Gītārahasya* (Poona, 1950), p. 430. 'O, the ultimate basis of the world, listen to one word from me in your seclusion (i.e. attentively). If my own actions are to liberate me then what favour is done to me by you, my Master?' (the present author's translation).
9. G.R. Malkani, 'The Rationale of the Law of Karma' in *Philosophical Quarterly*, 32/4, January 1965, p. 257.
10. Gambhīrānanda's translation, IV.iv.5–6.
11. Swāmi Gambhīrānanda (trans.) The *Brahma-Sūtra Bhāṣya of Śankarācārya*, II.i.34, pp. 362–63.
12. Swāmī Vireśvarānanda and Swāmī Ādidevānanda (trans.), *Brahma-Sutras with Śrī Bhāṣya of Śrī Rāmānuja* (Advaita Ashram, Calcutta), pp. 237–38.
13. G.R. Malkani, 'The Rationale of the law of Karma', p. 258.
14. M. Hiriyanna, *The Essentials of Indian Philosophy* (Allen & Unwin, London), p. 46.
15. S.N. Dasgupta, *A History of Indian Philosophy*, Vol. I (Cambridge), p. 71.
16. D.M. Datta, *Philosophical Perspectives: A Selection of Essays* (Bharati Bhavan, Patna), p. 93.
17. S.C. Chatterjee and D.M. Datta, *Introduction to Indian Philosophy* (Calcutta University, Calcutta), p. 18.
18. M. Hiriyanna, *The Essentials of Indian Philosophy*, p. 48.
19. *Gandhi's Campaign Against Untouchability 1933–34, An Account from the Raj's Secret Official Reports*, ed. by Baren Ray (Gandhi Peace Foundation, New Delhi, 1996), pp. 140–41.
20. *The Collected Works of Mahatma Gandhi*, LVII (January 16–May 17, 1934) (Publications Division, Government of India), p. 603.
21. Kalidas Bhattacharyya, 'Traditional Indian Philosophy as a Modern Indian Thinker Views It' in S.S. Rama Rao Pappu and R. Puligandala (eds.), *Indian Philosophy: Past and Future* (Motilal Banarsidass, Delhi), pp. 201–02.
22. Vidyāraṇya Svāmī, *Jīvanmuktiviveka* (Chaukhamba, Varanasi), pp. 23–25.
23. Swāmī Mādhavānanda's translation, with Śankarācārya's commentary, IV.iv.6, p. 498.
24. Ibid., p. 497.
25. *Gītā*, Trans. Swāmī Gambhīrānanda with Śankarārārya's commentary, 2.55, p. 101.

26. Ibid., 3.4,5, pp. 137, 140.
27. Ibid., 2.47, 48, pp. 93, 94.
28. Swāmi Mādhavananda, op. cit., p. 335.
29. *Mithilāyām Pradiptāyām na me Kinchana dahyate. Mahābhārata, Śāntiparva*, 219.62. Nothing of mine gets burnt even after the entire Mithilā's having been burnt.
30. *Gītā*, 2.31.
31. *Gītā*, 3.20.
32. Swāmī Gambhīrānanda (trans.), *Bhagavad-Gītā* with *Gūdhārtha Dīpikā* of Madhusūdana Sarasvati (Advaita Ashram, Calcutta), p. 236. See Rāmānuja's commentary on the *Gītā* published by Gita Press, pp. 111–12 and Śrīdhara Svāmī's published by Ramakrishna Math, Madras, pp. 99–100.
33. Bhattacharyya, 'Traditional Indian Philosophy as a Modern Indian Thinker Views It' op. cit., p. 209.
34. For an expanded version of this argument and a different but more critical account of the *karmic* theory, see my *Karma, Causation and Retributive Morality* (ICPR), Chapter 13.
35. R.N. Sen (trans.), The *Brahmavaivarta Purāṇa* (two vols), 2.32.27–32. The Sacred Books of the Hindus, Series No. XXIV, Panini Offices, Allahabad, 1920–22.
36. Ernest Wood and S.V. Subramaniam (trans.), The *Garuḍa Purāṇa*. The Sacred Books of the Hindus, Series No. IX, Panini Offices, Allahabad, 1911.
37. Swāmī Gambhirananda (trans.), *The Brahmasūtra Bhāṣya of Śankarācārya* (R.K. Mission, Calcutta, 1977), III.i.II, p. 555.
38. Swāmī Mādhavānanda (trans.), *The Brhadāarayaka Upaniṣad* with the Commentary of Śankārācārya. (Advaita Ashram, Calcutta, 1993), IV.iv.3, p. 493.
39. Ibid., pp. 493–94.
40. Swāmi Gambhīrananda, Ibid., p. 556.

Select Bibliography

Bhagavadgītā: with the commentary of Madhusūdana Sarasvati, trans. by Swāmi Gambhīrananda (Advaita Ashram, Calcutta, 1998).

——— with the commentary of Rāmānujācārya (Hindi) trans. by Goendakā Harikṛṣna Dās (Gita Press, Gorakhpur).

——— with the commentary of Śankarācārya, trans. by Swāmi Gambhīrānanda (Advaita Ashram, Calcutta, 1994).

——— (Hindi) trans. by Goendakā, Harikṛṣna Dās (Gita Press, Gorakhpur, 1988).

——— with the commentary of Śrīnivāsa Swāmī trans. by Swāmī Vireśvarānanda (Ramakrishna Math, Madras, 1948).

Brahma-Sūtras: With *Śrī Bhāṣya* of Śrī Rāmānuja, trans. by Swāmi Ādidevānanda (Advaita Ashram, Calcutta 1995).

——— with *Bhāṣya* of Śankarācārya, trans. by Swāmi Gambhīrānanda (Advaita Ashrama, Calcutta, 1977). (For some other works of Śankara see under 'Śankara').

Bhattacharyya, Haridas.: The *Cultural Heritage of India*, Vol. IV (Ramakrishna Mission, Calcutta, 1993).

Bulke, Kamil: *Rāmakathā* (Hindi Pariśad, Prayag University Allahabad, 2004).

Dasgupta, S.N.: *A History of Indian Philosophy*, 5 volumes (Motilal Banarsidass, Delhi, 1992).

Datta, D.M.: *Philosophical Essays* (Bharati Bhawan, Patna, 1995).

The Dharmasūtra: The Law Codes of Āpaṣṭamba Gautama, Baudhāyana, and Vasiṣṭha, annotated text and translation by Patrick Olivelle (Motilal Banarsidass, Delhi, 2000).

Hiriyanna, M.: *Indian Conception of Values* (Kavyalaya Publishers, Mysore, 1975).

Īśvarakṛṣṇa: *Sānkhyakārikā* (Madras University, Madras, 1973).

Keith, A.B.: *The Religion and Philosophy of the Veda and Upaniṣads*, Parts I & II (Motilal Banarsidass, Delhi, 1998).

The Mahābhārata: text and translation in Hindi, 6 vols. (Gita Press, Gorakhpur).

Manusmṛti: Hindi translation by Hariścandra Vidyālankāra (Arya Samaja, Delhi).

Nāgeśa Bhatta: *Paribhāṣendu śekhara* (Choukhamba, Varanasi).

Nitisāra Anka: *Kalyāṇa* (Gita Press, Gorakhpur, 2002).

Pappu, S.S. Rama Rao and R. Puligandala, (eds.): *Indian Philosophy: Past and Future* (Motilal Banarsidass, Delhi, 1982).

Prasad, Rajendra: *Regularity, Normativity and Rules of Language* (Poona University, Pune, 1989).

——— *Karma, Causation and Retributive Morality* (ICPR, New Delhi, 1989).

——— *Varnadharma, Niskama Karma and Practical Morality: A Critical Essay on Applied Ethics* (D.K. Printworld, New Delhi, 1999).

——— *Dharmakirti's Theory of Inference: Revaluation and Reconstruction* (OUP, New Delhi, 2002).

Ṛgveda Sanhitā: Hindi translation by Ramagovinda Trivedi (Choukhamba, Varanasi, 1992).

Śankara: *Upadeśasāhasrī* (Ramakrishna Math, Madras, 1989).

Śankara Mishra: *Vaiśeṣikasūtrapaskāra* (Choukhamba, Varanasi, 2002).

Śrīharśa: *Kanḍanakhanḍakhādya* (Acyuta Granthamala, Varanasi, 1938).

Tilak, B.G.: *Gītārahasya* (Poona).

Tulsidas: *Rāmacaritmānasa* (Hindi) (Gita Press, Gorakhpur).
Upaniṣads: *Bṛhadāraṇyaka* with the commentary of Śankarācārya, text, translation by Swāmī Mādhavānanda (Advaita Ashram, Calcutta, 1993).
——— *Chāndojñya* with the commentary of Śankāracārya, translated by Swāmi Gambhīranada (Advaita Ashram, Calcutta, 1992).
——— *Isa, Kena, Katha, Taittiriya*, with the commentary of Śankarācārya, text, translated by Swāmi Gambhirānanda in his *Eight Upaniṣads* Vol. I (Advaita Ashram, Calcutta, 1989).
——— *Aitareya, Munḍaka, Māndūkya, Praṣna*, with the commentary of Śankarācārya, text, translated by Swami Gambhīrānanda, in his *Eight Upanisads*, Vol. II (Advaita Ashram, Calcutta, 1990).
——— *Upaniṣad Anka of the Kalyāṇa*, containing all *Upaniṣads*, some in full, some in summary form, along with some essays on them (Gita Press, Gorakhpur).
Vidyāraṇya Svāmi: *Jīvanmuktiviveka*, Hindi translation by Thakur Udayanarayana Sinha (Choukhamba, Varanasi).
——— *Panchadaśī* trans. (Swāmi Svāhānanda (Ramakrishna Math, Madras, 1967).
Visvanātha: *Nyāya Siddhāntamuktāvalī* (Varanasi, 1958).
Viṣṇu Śarmā: *Pancatantra* (Choukhamba, Varanasi, 2002).
Vivekacuḍāmaṇi: (Hindi) translation by Munilal (Gita Press, Gorakhpur, 1988).
Yogavāśiṣṭha Anka, Kalyāna (Gita Press, Gorakhpur, 1961).

Index

*	Part 5	Development of Modern Indian Thought and the Social Sciences	S. Bhattacharya (ed.)
*	Part 6	Aspects of India's International Relations 1700 to 2000: South Asia and the World	Jayanta Kumar Ray (ed.)
*	Part 7	Political Ideas in Modern India: Thematic Explorations	V.R. Mehta & Thomas Pantham (eds.)
VOLUME XI Consciousness, Science, Society, Value and Yoga (CONSSAVY)			
*	Part 1	Philosophical Consciousnes and Scientific Knowledge: Conceptual Linkages and Civilizational Background	D.P. Chattopadhyaya (ed.)
*	Part 2	Self, Society and Science: Theoretical and Historical Perspectives	D.P. Chattopadhyaya (ed.)
*	Part 3	Consciousnes, Indian Psychology and Yoga	Kireet Joshi & Matthijs Cornelissen (eds.)
*	Part 4	The Enworlded Subjectivity: Its Three Worlds and Beyond	R. Balasubramanian (ed.)
VOLUME XII Levels of Reality (CONSSAVY)			
*	Part 1	A Conceptual-Analytic Study of Classical Indian Philosophy of Morals	Rajendra Prasad
➢	Part 2	A Historical-Developmental Study of Classical Indian Philosophy of Morals	Rajendra Prasad (ed.)
*	Part 3	Vedic Vision of Consciousness and Reality	S.P. Singh
➢	Part 4	Modern Atomism in Europe and India	J. Pasupathy (ed.)
➢	Part 5	Materialism and Immaterialism in India and Europe	Partha Ghose (ed.)
➢	Part 6	Life and Organicism	N.S. Rangaswamy (ed.)
VOLUME XIII Theories of Natural and Life Sciences (CONSSAVY)			
➢	Part 1	India in the World of Physics: Then and Now	A.N. Mitra (ed.)
➢	Part 2	From Physiology and Chemistry to Biochemistry	D.P. Burma (ed.)
➢	Part 3	Psychology and Psychoanalysis	Girishwar Mishra (ed.)
➢	Part 4	Cognitive Sciences: Brain, Psychology and Computer	Shobini L. Rao (ed.)
➢	Part 5	Foundations of Sciences	B.V. Sreekantan (ed.)
➢	Part 6	History of Science and Philosophy of Science	P.K. Sengupta (ed.)
➢	Part 7	History of Science and Philosophy of Science	P.K. Sengupta (ed.)
➢	Part 8	Science in India	J.V. Narlikar (ed.)
VOLUME XIV Natural and Cultural Sciences (CONSSAVY)			
➢	Part 1	Relations between Nature and Culture	Roddam Narasimha (ed.)
➢	Part 2	Social Sciences: Communication, Anthropology and Sociology	Yogendra Singh (ed.)
➢	Part 3	Economics and Ethics	Ashok (ed.)
➢	Part 4	Different Types of History	Bharati Ray (ed.)
➢	Part 5	History of India's Polity, Governance and Constitutional Culture	Subhash C. Kashyap (ed.)
VOLUME XV Science, Technology and Philosophy (CONSSAVY)			
*	Part 1	Science, Technology, Imperialism and War	J.B. Dasgupta (ed.)
➢	Part 2	Science and the Public	Ashok Jain (ed.)
➢	Part 3	Science, Literature and Aesthetics	Amiya Dev ((ed.)
➢	Part 4	Science, Colonialism and Nationalism, c. 1820 to c. 1940	Uma Das Gupta (ed.)
➢	Part 5	Old Wisdom and New Horizon	Manoj Kumar Pal
VOLUME XVI Yoga (CONSSAVY)			
➢	Part 1	Cognitive Anomalies, Consciousness and Yoga	K. Ramakrishna Rao (ed.)
➢	Part 2	History of Yoga in India	S.P. Singh (ed.)
➢	Part 3	Varieties of Yogic Experience	Manoj Das (ed.)
➢	Part 4	Synthesis of Yoga	Kireet Joshi (ed.)
•	Part 5	Yoga, Evolution and Mutation of Human Species	(Under Plan)

Monographs

*	1.	Science, Philosophy and Culture in Historical Perspective	D.P. Chattopadhyaya & Ravinder Kumar (eds.)
*	2	Some Aspects of India's Philosophical & Scientific Heritage	D.P. Chattopadhyaya & Ravinder Kumar (eds.)
*	3.	Mathematics, Astronomy and Biology in Indian Tradition: Some Conceptual Preliminaries	D.P. Chattopadhyaya & Ravinder Kumar (eds.)
*	4.	Language, Logic and Science in India: Some Conceptual and Historical Perspectives	D.P. Chattopadhyaya & Ravinder Kumar (eds.)
*	5.	Primal Spirituality of the Vedas: Its Renewal and Renaissance	R. Balasubramanian
*	6.	Interdisciplinary Studies in Science, Technology, Philosophy and Culture	D.P. Chattopadhyaya
*	7.	Ancient Yoga and Modern Science	T.R. Anantharaman
*	8.	Prolegomena to Any Future Historiography of Cultures & Civilizations	Daya Krishna
*	9.	Science and Spirituality: A Quantum Integration	Amit Goswami & Maggie Goswami
*	10.	On Rational Historiography	V. Shekhawat
*	11.	*Kauṭilīya Arthaśāstra* Revisited	Surendra Nath Mital
*	12.	The Ways of Understanding the Human Past	D.P. Chattopadhyaya
*	13.	The Architecture of Knowledge	Subhash Kak
*	14.	Karnataka Music as Aesthetic Form	R. Sathyanarayana
*	15.	Indian Philosophy and Philosophy of Science	Sundar Sarukkai

* Already Published
➢ In the Process of Publication
• Under Plan